WORLDMARK
ENCYCLOPEDIA
of National
Economies

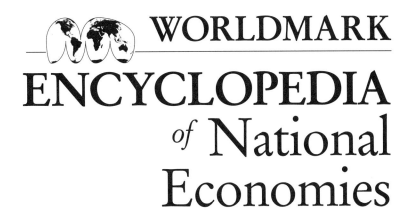

WORLDMARK
ENCYCLOPEDIA
of National
Economies

Volume 2 – Americas

Sara Pendergast and Tom Pendergast, Editors

GALE GROUP
™
THOMSON LEARNING

Detroit • New York • San Diego • San Francisco
Boston • New Haven, Conn. • Waterville, Maine
London • Munich

Jeffrey Lehman and Rebecca Parks, *Editors*
William Harmer, *Contributing Editor*
Brian J. Koski, Jeffrey Wilson, *Associate Editors*
Shelly Dickey, *Managing Editor*

Mary Beth Trimper, *Manager, Composition and Electronic Prepress*
Evi Seoud, *Assistant Manager, Composition Purchasing and Electronic Prepress*

Barbara J. Yarrow, *Manager, Imaging and Multimedia Content*
Randy Bassett, *Imaging Supervisor*
Pamela A. Reed, *Imaging Coordinator*
Leitha Etheridge-Sims, Mary K. Grimes, David G. Oblender, *Image Catalogers*
Robyn V. Young, *Project Manager, Imaging and Multimedia Content*
Robert Duncan, *Senior Imaging Specialist*
Christine O'Bryan, *Graphic Specialist*
Michelle DiMercurio, *Senior Art Director*
Susan Kelsch, *Indexing Manager*
Lynne Maday, *Indexing Specialist*

Library of Congress Control Number: 2001099714

TABLE OF CONTENTS

Countries are listed by most common name. Official country names are listed in the entries.

PREFACE

The *Worldmark Encyclopedia of National Economies* joins the Worldmark family of encyclopedias and attempts to provide comprehensive overviews of the economic structure and current climate of 198 countries and territories. Each signed entry provides key data and analysis on a country's economic conditions, their relationship to social and political trends, and their impact on the lives of the country's inhabitants. The goal of this set is to use plain language to offer intelligent, consistent analysis of every important economy in the world.

It is our sincere hope that this set will open the reader's mind to the fascinating world of international economics. Contained within this collection are a number of fascinating stories: of Eastern European nations struggling to adapt to capitalist economic systems in the wake of the collapse of communism; of Pacific Island nations threatened with annihilation by the slow and steady rise of ocean levels; of Asian nations channeling the vast productivity of their people into diversified economies; of the emerging power of the European Union, which dominates economic life across Europe; of Middle Eastern nations planning for the disappearance of their primary engine of economic growth, oil; and many others. To make all this information both accessible and comparable, each entry presents information in the same format, allowing readers to easily compare, for example, the balance of trade between Singapore and Hong Kong, or the political systems of North and South Korea. Economics has a language of its own, and we have **highlighted** those economic terms that may not be familiar to a general reader and provided definitions in a glossary. Other terms that are specific to a particular country but are not economic in nature are defined within parentheses in the text.

This set contains entries on every sovereign nation in the world, as well as separate entries on large territories of countries, including: French Guiana, Martinique, and Guadeloupe; Macau; Puerto Rico; and Taiwan. The larger dependencies of other countries are highlighted within the mother country's entry. For example, the entry on Denmark includes a discussion of Greenland, the United Kingdom includes information on many of its Crown territories, and the United States entry highlights the economic conditions in some of its larger territories.

ENTRY OBJECTIVES

Each entry has two objectives: one, to offer a clear picture of the economic conditions in a particular country, and two, to provide statistical information that allows for comparison between countries. To offer comparable information, we have used some common sources for the tables and graphs as well as for individual sections. Even the most exhaustive sources do not provide information for every country, however, and thus some entries either have no data available in certain areas or contain data that was obtained from an alternate source. In all entries, we tried to provide the most current data available at the time. Because collection and evaluation methods differ among international data gathering agencies such as the World Bank, United Nations, and International Monetary Fund, as well as between these agencies and the many government data collection agencies located in each country, entries sometimes provide two or more sources of information. Consequently, the text of an entry may contain more recent information from a different source than is provided in a table or graph, though the table or graph provides information that allows the easiest comparison to other entries.

No one source could provide all the information desired for this set, so some sources were substituted when the main source lacked information for specific countries. The main sources used included: the *World Factbook 2000* and *2001,* which provided the common information on the countries' gross domestic product (GDP) at purchasing power parity, the division of labor, balance of trade, chief imports, chief exports, and population, unless otherwise noted in the text; the World Bank's *World Development Indicators,* which was a valued source for information about the infrastructure and consumption patterns of many countries; the *Human Development Report,* from the United Nations, which provided GDP per capita information on many countries; and the International Monetary Fund's *International Financial Statistics Yearbook,* which provided historical records of trade balances for most countries. Each entry also contains a bibliography that lists additional sources that are specific to that entry.

ENTRY ORGANIZATION

All entries are organized under 16 specific headings to make it easy to find needed information quickly and to compare the conditions in several different countries easily. (The sole exception is the entry on the Vatican, whose unique features necessitated the removal of several sections.) The sections are as follows:

COUNTRY OVERVIEW. This section includes information about the size of all land surfaces, describing coastlines and international boundaries. It also highlights significant geographical features in the country and the location of the capital. The size of the country is compared to a U.S. state or, for smaller countries, to Washington, D.C. Also included is information on the total population, as well as other important demographic data concerning ethnicity, religion, age, and urbanization. Where relevant, this section also includes information about internal conflicts, major health problems, or significant population policies.

OVERVIEW OF ECONOMY. This overview is meant to provide an analysis of the country's overall economic conditions, mentioning those elements that are deemed most important to an understanding of the country. It provides context for the reader to understand the more specific information available in the other sections.

POLITICS, GOVERNMENT, AND TAXATION. This section identifies the structure of the government and discusses the role the government, political parties, and taxes play in the economy.

INFRASTRUCTURE, POWER, AND COMMUNICATIONS. This section offers a description of the roads, railways, harbors, and telecommunications available in the country, assesses the modernity of the systems, and provides information about the country's plans for improvements.

ECONOMIC SECTORS. This section serves as an overview for the three more specific sections that follow, providing a general description of the balance between the country's different economic sectors.

AGRICULTURE. This section discusses the agriculture, fishing, and forestry sectors of the country.

INDUSTRY. This section discusses the industrial sector of the country, including specific information on mining, manufacturing, and other major industries, where appropriate.

SERVICES. This section concentrates on major components of the diverse services sector, usually focusing on the tourism and banking or financial sectors and sometimes including descriptions of the retail sector.

INTERNATIONAL TRADE. This section focuses on the country's patterns of trade, including the commodities traded and the historical trading partners.

MONEY. This section offers a brief description of the changes in inflation and the exchange rates in the country, and the impact those may have had on the economy. It also mentions any recent changes in the currency and the nature and impact of the central banking function.

POVERTY AND WEALTH. This section paints a picture of the distribution of wealth within the country, often comparing life in the country with that in other countries in the region. It includes governmental efforts to redistribute wealth or to deal with pressing issues of poverty.

WORKING CONDITIONS. This section describes the workforce, its ability to unionize, and the effectiveness of unions within the country. It also often includes information on wages, significant changes in the workforce over time, and the existence of protections for workers.

COUNTRY HISTORY AND ECONOMIC DEVELOPMENT. This section provides a timeline of events that shaped the country and its economy. The selected events create a more cohesive picture of the nation than could be described in the entries because of their bias toward more current information.

FUTURE TRENDS. To provide readers with a view to the future, the entry ends with an analysis of how the economic conditions in the country are expected to change in the near future. It also highlights any significant challenges the country may face.

DEPENDENCIES. This section discusses any major territories or colonies and their economies.

BIBLIOGRAPHY. The bibliography at the end of the entry lists the sources used to compile the information in the entry and also includes other materials that may be of interest to readers wanting more information about the particular country. Although specific online sources are cited, many such sources are updated annually and should be expected to change.

In addition, a data box at the beginning of each entry offers helpful economic "quick facts" such as the country's capital, monetary unit, chief exports and imports, gross domestic product (GDP), and the balance of trade. The U.S. Central Intelligence Agency's *World Factbook* (2000 and 2001) was the main source of this information unless otherwise noted. Each entry also includes a map that illustrates the location of the country. Since economic conditions are often affected by geography, the map allows readers to see the location of major cities and landmarks. The map also names bordering countries to offer readers a visual aid to understand regional conflicts and trading routes.

ACKNOWLEDGMENTS

We wish to thank all those involved in this project for their efforts. This set could not have been produced without the unfailing support of the publisher and our imaginative advisory board. At the Gale Group, managing editor Shelly Dickey and Peggy Glahn in New Product Development were especially helpful. We would also like to thank Gale editor William Harmer for his work in the early stages of the project, but special thanks must go to editors Rebecca Parks and Jeffrey Lehman who brought the set to publication. Copyeditors Edward Moran, Robyn Karney, Karl Rahder, Jennifer Wallace, and Mary Sugar must also be commended for their work to polish the entries into the form you see here.

COMMENTS

We encourage you to contact us with any comments or suggestions you may have that will benefit future editions of this set. We want this set to be a meaningful addition to your search for information about the world. Please send your comments and suggestions to: The Editors, *Worldmark Encyclopedia of National Economies,* The Gale Group, 27500 Drake Road, Farmington Hills, MI 48331. Or, call toll free at 1-800-877-4253.

—*Sara Pendergast and Tom Pendergast*

NOTES ON CONTRIBUTORS

Abazov, Rafis. Professor, Department of Politics, La-Trobe University, Victoria, Australia. Author, *Formation of the Post-Soviet Foreign Policies in Central Asian Republics* (1999), and annual security and economic reports, *Brassey's Security Yearbook*, and Transitions Online.

Abazova, Alfia. LaTrobe University, Victoria, Australia. Reviewed for *Pacifica Review* and *Europe-Asia Studies.*

Amineh, Parvizi Mehdi, Ph.D. Department of Political Science, University of Amsterdam, the Netherlands. Author, *Towards the Control of Oil Resources in the Caspian Region* (New York: St. Martin's Press, 1999); *Die Globale Kapitalistische Expansion und Iran: Eine Studie der Iranischen Politischen Ökonomie (1500–1980)* (Hamburg-London: Lit Verlag).

Arnade, Charles W. Adviser. Distinguished Professor of International Studies, University of South Florida. Author, *The Emergence of the Republic of Bolivia.*

Audain, Linz, M.D., J.D., Ph.D. Staff physician, Greater Southeast, INOVA Fairfax and Southern Maryland hospitals; former professor of law, economics, and statistics at various universities; editor, *Foreign Trade of the United States* (2nd ed.), *Business Statistics of the United States* (6th ed.).

Benoit, Kenneth, Ph.D. Lecturer, Department of Political Science, Trinity College, University of Dublin, Ireland.

Bouillon, Markus R. Doctoral student in international relations with a regional focus on the Middle East, St. Antony's College, University of Oxford.

Burron, Neil. Graduate student in International Development, The Norman Paterson School of International Affairs, Carleton University, Ottawa.

Campling, Liam. Lecturer in International Politics and History, Seychelles Polytechnic (University of Manchester Twinning Programme). Editor, *Historical Materialism—Special Issue: Focus on Sub-Saharan Africa* (2002). Contributor to *West Africa* and *African Business* magazines.

Carper, Mark Daniel Lynn. Instructor of Geography, Central Missouri State University.

Cavatorta, Francesco. Doctoral candidate in the Department of Political Science, Trinity College, Dublin, Ireland. Author, "The Italian Political System and the Northern League," in *Contemporary Politics,* March 2001.

Chari, Raj. Lecturer, Department of Political Science, Trinity College, Dublin, Ireland. Author, "Spanish Socialists, Privatising the Right Way?" in *West European Politics,* Vol. 21, No. 4, October 1998, and "The March 2000 Spanish Election: A 'Critical Election'?" in *West European Politics,* Vol. 23, No. 3, July 2000.

Chauvin, Lucien O. Freelance journalist, Lima, Peru. President of the Foreign Press Association of Peru.

Childree, David L. Graduate student in Latin American Studies at Tulane University, specializing in politics and development.

Conteh-Morgan, Earl. Professor, Department of Government and International Affairs, University of South Florida, Tampa, Florida. Co-author, *Sierra Leone at the End of the 20th Century* (1999).

Costa, Ecio F., Ph.D. Post-doctoral associate, Center for Agribusiness and Economic Development, Department of Agricultural and Applied Economics, University of Georgia, Athens, Georgia. Author, "Brazil's New Floating Exchange Rate Regime and Competitiveness in the World Poultry Market," in *Journal of Agricultural and Applied Economics.*

Cunha, Stephen, Ph.D. Professor of Geography, Humboldt State University, Arcata, California. Consultant, USAID, World Bank, National Geographic Society.

Davoudi, Salamander. Graduate student in Middle Eastern economics, Georgetown University, Washington, D.C. Former aid at the Royal Jordanian Hashemite Court.

Deletis, Katarina. M.I.A. (Master of International Affairs), Columbia University, New York. International communications officer, Deloitte Touche Tohmatsu, New York.

Divisekera, Sarath. Ph.D., School of Applied Economics, Victoria University, Melbourne, Australia. Author, *Income Distribution, Inequality and Poverty in Sri Lanka* (1988).

Eames, Rory. Honors student, School of Resources, Environment, and Society, The Australian National University, Canberra, Australia.

Easton, Matthew. Independent consultant, Cambridge, Massachusetts. Author, *In the Name of Development: Human Rights and the World Bank in Indonesia* (1995).

Feoli, Ludovico. Graduate student in Latin American Studies, Tulane University, New Orleans, Louisiana. Publications director and academic coordinator, CIAPA, San José, Costa Rica.

Ferguson, James. Writer and researcher specializing in the Caribbean. Author, *A Traveller's History of the Caribbean* (1999).

Florkowski, Wojciech J. Associate professor, Department of Agricultural and Applied Economics, University of Georgia.

Foley, Sean. Ph.D. candidate, History, Georgetown University, Washington, D.C. Author of various articles and a chapter in *Crises and Quandaries in the Contemporary Persian Gulf* (2001).

Foroughi, Payam. Ph.D. student in International Relations, University of Utah. International development consultant, NGOs, USAID, and the United Nations, Central Asia; freelance writer.

Friesen, Wardlow. Senior lecturer, Department of Geography, The University of Auckland, New Zealand. Author, "Tangata Pasifika Aotearoa: Pacific Populations and Identity in New Zealand," in *New Zealand Population Review*, Vol. 26, No. 2, 2000; "Circulation, Urbanisation, and the Youth Boom in Melanesia," in *Espace, Populations, Sociétés*, Vol. 2, 1994; "Melanesian Economy on the Periphery: Migration and Village Economy in Choiseul," in *Pacific Viewpoint*, Vol. 34, No. 2, 1993.

Fry, Gerald W. Adviser. Professor of International/Intercultural Education, and director of Graduate Studies, Department of Educational Policy and Administration, University of Minnesota—Twin Cities; former team leader on major Asian Development Bank funded projects in Southeast Asia.

Gazis, Alexander. Commercial specialist, U.S. Embassy, N'Djamena, Chad. Author, *Country Commercial Guides* for Chad (Fiscal Year 2001 and 2002).

Genc, Emine, M.A. Budget expert, Ministry of Finance, Ankara, Turkey.

Genc, Ismail H., Ph.D. Assistant professor of Economics, University of Idaho, Moscow, Idaho.

Gleason, Gregory. Professor, University of New Mexico. Former director, USAID Rule of Law Program in Central Asia.

Guillen, April J., J.D./M.A. International Relations candidate, University of Southern California, Los Angeles, with an emphasis on International Human Rights Law.

Hadjiyski, Valentin, Ph.D. New York-based freelance author, former United Nations expert.

Hodd, Jack. Queen's College, Cambridge, researching graphical presentations of general equilibrium models.

Hodd, Michael R. V. Adviser. Professor of Economics, University of Westminster, London, and has worked as a consultant for the ILO and UNIDO. Author, *African Economic Handbook,* London, Euromonitor, 1986; *The Economies of Africa,* Aldershot, Dartmouth, 1991; with others, *Fisheries and Development in Tanzania,* London, Macmillan, 1994.

Iltanen, Suvi. Graduate of the European Studies Programme, Trinity College, Dublin, Ireland.

Jensen, Nathan. Ph.D. candidate in political science, Yale University, and visiting scholar at UCLA's International Studies and Overseas Programs. He is currently completing his dissertation titled "The Political Economy of Foreign Direct Investment."

Jugenitz, Heidi. Graduate student in Latin American Studies, Tulane University, New Orleans, Louisiana. Research assistant, Payson Center for International Development and Technology Transfer.

Kiyak, Tunga. Ph.D. candidate in marketing and international business, Michigan State University. Research assistant, Center for International Business Education and Research (MSU-CIBER). Curator, International Business Resources on the WWW.

Kuznetsova, Olga. Senior research fellow, The Manchester Metropolitan University Business School, Manchester, UK. Author, *The CIS Handbook. Regional Handbooks of Economic Development: Prospects onto the 21st Century,* edited by P. Heenan and M. Lamontagne (1999).

Lang-Tigchelaar, Amy. Graduate student in joint MBA/MA in Latin American Studies Program, Tulane University, New Orleans, Louisiana.

Lansford, Tom. Assistant professor, University of Southern Mississippi, Gulf Coast. Author, *Evolution and Devolution: The Dynamics of Sovereignty and Security in Post-Cold War Europe* (2000).

Lynch, Catherine. Doctoral candidate in political science, Dublin City University, Ireland. Areas of interest include the political economy of implementing peace agreements, the politics of peace building, the implementation of policy, and other aspects of comparative political science.

Mahoney, Lynn. M.A., University of Michigan. Associate director of development, director of communications, American University of Beirut New York Office; freelance writer.

Mann, Larisa. Graduate student of economic history, cultural studies, and legal studies, London School of Economics. Presented "Shaky Ground, Thin Air: Intellectual Property Law and the Jamaican Music Industry" at the "Rethinking Caribbean Culture" conference at the University of West Indies, Cave Hill, Barbados.

Mazor, John. Writer and journalist specializing in economic and political issues in Latin America and the Levant. Graduated from Boston University with a degree in literature and studied intelligence and national security policy at the Institute of World Politics in Washington, D.C.

Mobekk, Eirin. MacArthur postdoctoral research associate, Department of War Studies, King's College, London, United Kingdom.

Mowatt, Rosalind. Graduate student in Economics, Wits University, Johannesburg, South Africa. Former economist for National Treasury, working with Southern African Development Community (SADC) countries.

Muhutdinova-Foroughi, Raissa. M.P.A., University of Colorado at Denver. Journalist, Radio Tajikistan; consultant, United Nations, World Bank, and Eurasia Foundation, Commonwealth of Independent Nations; freelance writer.

Mukungu, Allan C. K. Graduate student, University of Westminster, London, and has done consultancy work for the World Bank.

Musakhanova, Oygul. Graduate, University of Westminster; economist, Arthur Anderson, Tashkent, Uzbekistan.

Naidu, Sujatha. LL.M. in Environment Law, University of Utah. Ph.D. student in International Relations, Department of Political Science, University of Utah; freelance writer.

Nicholls, Ana. Journalist. Assistant editor, *Business Central Europe*, The Economist Group. Author of three surveys of Romania.

Nicoleau, Michael. J.D. Cornell Law School, Ithaca, New York. Co-author, "Constitutional Governance in the Democratic Republic of the Congo: An Analysis of the Constitution Proposed by the Government of Laurent Kabila," in *Texas International Law Journal,* Spring 2000.

Nuseibeh, Reem. Graduate student in Comparative Politics/Human Rights, University of Maryland, Maryland. Middle East risk analyst, Kroll Information Services, Vienna, Virginia.

Ó Beacháin, Donnacha. Ph.D. Political Science from National University of Ireland, Dublin. Civic Education Project visiting lecturer at the Departments of International Relations and Conflict Resolution at Tbilisi State University and the Georgian Technical University, respectively, 2000–2002.

Ohaegbulam, F. Ugboaja. Professor, Government and International Affairs, University of South Florida. Author, *A Concise Introduction to American Foreign Policy* (1999), and *Nigeria and the UN Mission to the Democratic Republic of the Congo* (1982).

O'Malley, Eoin. Doctoral candidate in Political Science at Trinity College, Dublin, and visiting researcher at UNED, Madrid, Spain. Author, "Ireland" in Annual Review section of the *European Journal of Political Research* (1999, 2000, 2001).

Ozsoz, Emre. Graduate student in International Political Economy and Development, Fordham University, New York. Editorial assistant for the Middle East, The Economist Intelligence Unit, New York.

Peimani, Hooman, Ph.D. Independent consultant with international organizations in Geneva, Switzerland. Author, *The Caspian Pipeline Dilemma: Political Games and Economic Losses* (2001).

Pretes, Michael. Research scholar, Department of Human Geography, Research School of Pacific and Asian Studies, The Australian National University, Canberra, Australia.

Sabol, Steven. Ph.D., the University of North Carolina at Charlotte. Author, *Awake Kazak! Russian Colonization of Central Asia and the Genesis of Kazak National Consciousness, 1868–1920.*

Samonis, Val, Ph.D., C.P.C. Managed and/or participated in international research and advisory projects/teams sponsored by the Hudson Institute, World Bank, CASE Warsaw, Soros Foundations, the Center for European Integration Studies (ZEI Bonn), the Swedish government, and a number of other clients. Also worked with top reformers such as the Polish Deputy Prime Minister Leszek Balcerowicz, U.S. Treasury Secretary Larry Summers, the World Bank, and OECD Private Sector Advisory Group on Corporate Governance, and with the Stanford Economic Transition Group; advisor to the Czech government (Deputy Prime Minister Pavel Mertlik), the Lithuanian parliament, and several Lithuanian governments, international organizations, and multinational corporations; founding editor, *Journal of East-West Business* (The Haworth Press Inc).

Sezgin, Yuksel. Ph.D. candidate in Political Science, University of Washington. Former assistant Middle East coordinator at the Foreign Economic Relations Board of Turkey.

Schubert, Alexander. Ph.D., Cornell University.

Scott, Cleve Mc D. Ph.D. candidate and graduate assistant, Department of History, University of the West Indies, Cave Hill Campus, Barbados.

Stobwasser, Ralph. Graduate student in Middle Eastern Studies, FU Berlin, Germany. Worked in the Office of the Chief Economist Middle East and North Africa, World Bank, Washington, D.C.

Strnad, Tomas. Ph.D. student, Department of the Middle East and Africa, Charles University, Czech Republic. Chief editor of the *Arab Markets Magazine*; author of "The Kuwaiti Dilemma," "OPEC—Main Sinner or Sheer Scapegoat?," and "Globalization in the Arab and Muslim World" in *International Policy* and other magazines.

Stroschein, Sherrill. Assistant professor of Political Science, Ohio University. Frequent contributor to scholarly journals on East European topics and a former contributor to *Nations in Transit* (1995 and 1997 editions).

Thadathil, George. Associate professor of History, Paul Quinn College, Dallas, Texas. Author, "Myanmar, Agony of a People" in *History Behind Headlines*, 2000. His research interests include South and Southeast Asia, and Asian collective security.

Thapa, Rabi. Editor and environmentalist, France. Environment/development assignments in Nepal, 1998.

Tian, Robert Guang, Ph.D. Associate professor of Business Administration, Erskine College. Author, *Canadian Chinese, Chinese Canadians: Coping and Adapting in North America* (1999).

Ubarra, Maria Cecilia T. Graduate student in Public Policy and Program Administration, University of the Philippines, Quezon City, Philippines. Research fellow, Institute for Strategic and Development Studies; case writer, Asian Institute of Management, Philippines.

Vivas, Leonardo. M.Phil., Development Studies, Sussex University (UK); Ph.D., International Economics and Finance, Nanterre University (France); fellow, Weatherhead Center for International Affairs, Harvard University.

Viviers, Wilma. Program director, International Trade in School of Economics, Potchefstroom University, South Africa.

Zhang, Xingli. Ph.D. student, University of Southern California, Los Angeles. Author, "Brunei" in *East Asian Encyclopedia* (in Chinese).

INTRODUCTION

THE POWER OF ECONOMIC UNDERSTANDING

The economies of the world are becoming increasingly interconnected and interdependent, a fact dramatically illustrated on 2 July 1997 when the Thai government decided to allow its currency to "float" according to market conditions. The result was a significant drop in the value of the currency and the start of the Asian economic crisis, a contagion that spread quickly to other Asian countries such as the Republic of Korea, Indonesia, Malaysia, and the Philippines. Before long the epidemic reached Brazil and Russia.

In this way, a small economic change in one less-developed country sent economic shock waves around the world. Surprisingly, no one predicted this crisis, though economist Paul Krugman in a prominent 1994 *Foreign Affairs* article argued that there was no Asian economic miracle and the kind of growth rates attained in recent years were not sustainable over the long term. In such an interconnected global economy, it is imperative to have an understanding of other economies and economic conditions around the world. Yet that understanding is sorely lacking in the American public.

Various studies have shown that both young people and the public at large have a low level of literacy about other nations. A survey of 655 high school students in southeast Ohio indicated that students were least informed in the area of international economic concerns, and the number of economics majors at the college level is declining. The economic and geographic illiteracy has become such a national concern that the U.S. Senate recently passed a resolution calling for a national education policy that addresses Americans' lack of knowledge of other parts of the world.

The information provided by the media also frequently reflects a distorted understanding of world economies. During the Asian economic crisis, we often heard about the collapse of various Asian countries such as Korea and Thailand. They were indeed suffering a severe crisis, but usually companies, not countries, collapse. The use of the "collapse" language was therefore misleading. In another example, a distinguished journalist writing in a prominent East coast newspaper claimed that Vietnamese women paid more in transportation and food costs than they were earning while working in a factory manufacturing Nike shoes. Such a statement, while well intended in terms of genuine concern for these women workers, makes no economic sense whatsoever, and is actually not accurate. The wages of these women are indeed extremely low by U.S. standards, but such wages must be viewed in the context of another society, where the cost of living may be dramatically lower and where low salaries may be pooled. At other times, a fact—such as the fact that a minority of the Japanese workforce enjoys employment for life—is exaggerated to suggest that the Japanese economy boomed as it did in the 1980s *because* of the Japanese policy of life-long employment. Such generalizing keeps people from understanding the complexities of the Japanese economy.

"THINGS ARE NOT WHAT THEY SEEM." In defense of this lack of economic understanding, it must be said that understanding economics is not easy. Paul A. Samuelson, author of the classic textbook *Economics* (1995), once stated about economics "that things are often not what at first they seem." In Japan, for example, many young women work as office ladies in private companies as an initial job after completing school. These young ladies often stay at home with their parents and have few basic expenses. Over several years they can accumulate considerable savings, which may be used for travel, overseas study, or investing. Thus, as Samuelson noted in his textbook, actual individual economic welfare is not based on wages as such, but on the *difference* between earnings and expenditures. Wages are not the only measure of the value of labor: one must also consider purchasing power and how costs of living vary dramatically from place to place. Without taking into account purchasing power, we overestimate economic well-being in high-cost countries such as Japan and Switzerland and underestimate it in low-cost countries such as India and Cambodia.

Consider the following examples: The cost of taking an air-conditioned luxury bus from the Cambodian capital of Phnom Penh to its major port, Sihanoukville, is less than $2. The same bus trip of equal distance in Japan or the United States would cost $50 or more. Similarly, a (subsidized) lunch at a factory producing Nike shoes in Vietnam may cost the equivalent of 5 U.S. cents in 1998, while lunch at a student union on a U.S. college campus may cost $5. Thus a teaching assistant on a U.S. campus pays 100 times more for lunch than the Vietnamese factory worker. Who is more "poorly paid" in these situations? Add to this the reality that in many developing countries where extended families are common, members of the family often pool their earnings, which individually may be quite low. To look only at individual earnings can thus be rather misleading. Such cultural nuances are important to keep in mind in assessing economic conditions and welfare in other nations.

Various economic puzzles can also create confusion and misunderstanding. For example, currently the United States has the highest trade deficit in world history: it imports far more that it exports. Most countries with huge trade deficits have a weak currency, but the U.S. dollar has remained strong. Why is this the case? Actually, it is quite understandable when one knows that the balance of trade is just one of many factors that determine the value of a nation's currency. In truth, demand for the U.S. dollar has remained high. The United States is an attractive site for foreign investment because of its large and growing economic market and extremely stable politics. Second, the United States has a large tourism sector, drawing people to the country where they exchange their currency for U.S. dollars. Several years ago, for the first time ever, there were more Thais coming to the United States as tourists than those in the United States going to Thailand. Third, the United States is extremely popular among international students seeking overseas education. Economically, a German student who spends three years studying in the United States benefits the economy in the same way as a long-term tourist or conventional exports: that student invests in the U.S. economy. In the academic year 1999-2000, there were 514,723 international students in the United States spending approximately $12.3 billion. Thus, the services provided by U.S. higher education represent an important "invisible export." Fourth, 11 economies are now dollarized, which means that they use the U.S. currency as their national currency. Panama is the most well known of these economies and El Salvador became a dollarized economy on 1 January 2001. Other countries are semi-officially or partially dollarized (Cambodia and Vietnam, for example). As the result of dollarization, it is estimated by the Federal Reserve that 55 to 70 percent of all U.S. dollars are held by foreigners primarily in Latin America and former parts of the U.S.S.R. Future candidates for dollarization are Argentina, Brazil, Ecuador, Indonesia, Mexico, and even Canada. With so many countries using U.S. dollars, demand for the U.S. dollar is increased, adding to its strength. For all these reasons, the U.S. currency and economy remained strong despite the persisting large trade deficits, which in themselves, according to standard economic logic, suggest weakness.

SYSTEMS OF CLASSIFICATION. As in other fields, such as biology and botany, it is important to have a sound system of classification to understand various national economies. Unfortunately, the systems commonly used to describe various national economies are often flawed by cultural and Eurocentric biases and distortion. After the end of World War II and the start of the Cold War, it became common to speak of "developed" and "underdeveloped" countries. There were two problems with this overly simplistic distinction. First, it viewed countries only in terms of material development. Second, it implied that a nation was developed or underdeveloped across all categories. As an example, "underdeveloped" Thailand has consistently been one of the world's leading food exporters and among those countries that import the least amount of food. Similarly, in "developed" Japan there are both homeless people and institutions to house the elderly, while in "underdeveloped" Vietnam there are no homeless and the elderly are cared for by their families. Which country is more "developed"?

Later the term "Third World" became popular. This term was invented by the French demographer Alfred Sauvy and popularized by the scholar Irving Horowitz in his volume, *Three Worlds of Development*. "First World" referred to rich democracies such as the United States and the United Kingdom; "Second World" referred to communist countries such as the former U.S.S.R. and former East Germany. The term "Third World" was used to refer to the poorer nations of Africa, Latin America, and Asia (with the exception of Japan). But this distinction is also problematic, for it implies that the "First World" is superior to the "Third World." Another common term introduced was modern versus less modern nations. The Princeton sociologist Marion J. Levy made this distinction based on a technological definition: more modern nations were those that made greater use of tools and inanimate sources of power. Thus, non-Western Japan is quite modern because of its use of robots and bullet trains. Over time, however, many people criticized the modern/non-modern distinction as being culturally biased and implying that all nations had to follow the same path of progress.

More recently, economists from around the world have recognized the importance of using a variety of factors to understand the development of national economies. Each of these factors should be viewed in terms of a continuum. For example, no country is either completely industrial or completely agricultural. The entries in this volume provide the basic data to assess each national economy on several of these key criteria. One can determine, for example, the extent to which an economy is industrial by simply dividing the percentage of the economy made up by industry by the percentage made up by agriculture. Or one can determine how much energy national economies use to achieve their level of economic output and welfare. This provides an important ecological definition of efficiency, which goes beyond limited material definitions. This measure allows an estimate of how "green" versus "gray" an economy is; greener economies are those using less energy to achieve a given level of economic development. One might like to understand how international an economy is, which can be done by adding a country's exports to its imports and then dividing by GDP. This indicator reveals that economies such as the Netherlands, Malaysia, Singapore, and Hong Kong are highly international while the isolationist Democratic People's Republic of Korea (North Korea) is far less international.

Another interesting measure of an economy, particularly relevant in this age of more information-oriented economies and "the death of distance" (Cairncross 1997), is the extent to which an economy is digitalized. One measure of this factor would be the extent to which the population of a given economy has access to the Internet. Costa Rica, for example, established a national policy that all its citizens should have free access to the Internet. In other economies, such as Bhutan, Laos, and North Korea, access to the Internet is extremely limited. These differences, of course, relate to what has been termed "the digital divide." Another important factor is whether an economy is people-oriented, that is, whether it aims to provide the greatest happiness to the greatest number; economist E.F. Schumacher called this "economics as if people mattered." The King of Bhutan, for example, has candidly stated that his goal for his Buddhist nation is not Gross National Product but instead Gross National Happiness. Such goals indicate that the level of a country's economic development does not necessarily reflect its level of social welfare and quality of life.

Another important category that helps us understand economies is the degree to which they can be considered "transitional." Transitional economies are those that were once communist, state-planned economies but that are becoming or have become free-market economies. This transitional process started in China in the late 1970s when its leader Deng Xiaoping introduced his "four modernizations." Later, Soviet leader Mikhael Gorbachev introduced such reforms, called *perestroika,* in the former Soviet Union. With the dissolving of the U.S.S.R. in 1991, many new transitional economies emerged, including Belarus, Uzbekistan, Kyrgyzstan, and the Ukraine. Other countries undergoing transition were Vietnam, Laos, Cambodia, and Mongolia. These economies can be grouped into two types: full transitional and partial transitional. The full transitional economies are shifting both to free markets and to liberal democracies with free expression, multiple parties, and open elections. The partial

transitional economies are changing in the economic realm, but retaining their original one-party systems. Included in the latter category are the economies of China, Vietnam, Laos, and Cuba. This volume provides valuable current information on the many new transitional economies emerging from the former Soviet world.

KEY THEMES IN THE WORLD ECONOMY. In looking at the economies of countries around the globe, a number of major common themes can be identified. There is increasing economic interdependence and interconnectivity, as stressed by Thomas Friedman in his recent controversial book about globalization titled *The Lexus and the Olive Tree: Understanding Globalization.* For example, the People's Republic of China is now highly dependent on exports to the United States. In turn, U.S. companies are dependent on the Chinese market: Boeing is dependent on China for marketing its jet airliners; the second largest market for Mastercard is now in China; and Nike is highly dependent on China and other Asian economies for manufacturing its sports products. Such deep interdependence augurs well for a peaceful century, for countries are less likely to attack the countries with whom they do a vigorous business, even if their political and social systems are radically different. In fact, new threats to peace as reflected in the tragic terrorist attack of 11 September 2001, primarily relate to long-standing *historical* conflicts and grievances.

Conventional political boundaries and borders often do not well reflect new economic realities and cultural patterns. Economic regions and region states are becoming more important. The still-emerging power of the European Union can be gauged by reading the essays of any of the countries that are currently part of the Union or hoping to become a part of it in the coming years. This volume may help readers better understand which nations are becoming more interconnected and have similar economic conditions.

The tension between equity (fairness) and efficiency is common in nearly all national economies. In some economies there is more stress on efficiency, while in others there is more stress on equity and equality. Thus, as should be expected, countries differ in the nature of the equality of their income and wealth distributions. For each entry in this volume, important data are provided on this important factor. The geographer David M. Smith has documented well both national and international inequalities in his data-rich *Where the Grass is Greener* (1979).

Invisible and informal economies—the interactions of which are outside regulated economic channels—represent a growing segment of economic interactions in some countries. In his controversial but important volume, *The Other Path* (1989), the Peruvian economist Hernando de Soto alerted us to the growing significance of the informal economy. In countries such as Peru, research has shown that in some cases individuals prefer work in the informal to the formal sector because it provides them with more control over their personal lives. The Thai economist Pasuk Phongpaichit and her colleagues have written a fascinating book on Thailand's substantial invisible economy titled *Guns, Girls, Gambling, and Ganja* (1998). Thus, official government and international statistical data reported in this volume often are unable to take into account such data from the hidden part of economies.

In an increasingly internationalized economy in which transnational corporations are highly mobile and able to move manufacturing overseas quite rapidly, it is important to distinguish between real foreign direct investment and portfolio investment. At one point during Thailand's impressive economic boom of the late 1980s and early 1990s, a new Japanese factory was coming on line every three days. This is foreign direct investment, involving actual bricks and mortar, and it creates jobs that extend beyond the actual facility being constructed. In contrast foreign portfolio investment consists of a foreign entity buying stocks, bonds, or other financial instruments in another nation. In our current wired global economy, such funds can be moved in and out of nations almost instantaneously and have little lasting effect on the economic growth of a country. Economies such as Chile and Malaysia have developed policies to try to combat uncertainty and related economic instability caused by the potential of quick withdrawal of portfolio investments.

Some argue that transnational corporations (owned by individuals all over the world), which have no national loyalties, represent the most powerful political force in the world today. Many key transnational corporations have larger revenues than the entire gross national products of many of the nations included in this volume. This means that many national economies, especially smaller ones, lack effective bargaining power in dealing with large international corporations.

Currently, it is estimated by the International Labor Office of the United Nations that one-third of the world's workforce is currently unemployed or underemployed. This means that 500 million new jobs need to be created over the next 10 years. Data on the employment situation in each economy are presented in this volume. The creation of these new jobs represents a major challenge to the world's economies.

The final and most important theme relates to the ultimate potential clash between economy and ecology. To the extent that various national economies and their peoples show a commitment to become greener and more environmentally friendly, ultimate ecological crises and catastrophes can be avoided or minimized. Paul Ray and Sherry Anderson's *The Cultural Creatives: How 50 Million People Are Changing the World* (2000) lends cre-

dence to the view that millions are changing to more environmentally conscious lifestyles.

In trying to understand the global economy, it is critically important to have good trend data. In each of the entries of this volume, there is an emphasis on providing important economic data over several decades to enable the reader to assess such patterns. Some trends will have tremendous importance for the global economy. One phenomenon with extremely important implications for population is the policy of limiting families to only one child in China's urban areas. This deliberate social engineering by the world's most populous country will have a powerful impact on the global economy of the 21st century. The global environmental implications are, of course, extremely positive. Though there is much debate about the economic, political, and socio-cultural implications of this one-child policy, overall it will probably give China a tremendous strategic advantage in terms of the key factors of human resource development and creativity.

THE POWER OF UNDERSTANDING. By enhancing our knowledge and understanding of other economies, we gain the potential for mutual learning and inspiration for continuous improvement. There is so much that we can learn from each other. Denmark, for example, is now getting seven percent of its electrical energy from wind energy. This has obvious relevance to the state of California as it faces a major energy crisis. The Netherlands and China for a long period have utilized bicycles for basic transportation. Some argue that the bicycle is the most efficient "tool" in the world in terms of output and energy inputs. Many new major highways in Vietnam are built with exclusive bike paths separated by concrete walls from the main highway. The Vietnamese have also developed electric bicycles. The efficient bullet trains of Japan and France have relevance to other areas such as coastal China and the coastal United States. Kathmandu in Nepal has experimented with non-polluting electric buses. In the tremendous biodiversity of the tropical forests of Southeast Africa, Latin America, and Africa, there may be cures for many modern diseases.

We hope to dispel the view that economics is the boring "dismal science" often written in complex, difficult language. This four-volume set presents concise, current information on all the economies of the world, including not only large well-known economies such as the United States, Germany, and Japan, but also new nations that have emerged only in recent years, and many microstates of which we tend to be extremely uninformed. With the publication of this volume, we hope to be responsive to the following call by Professor Mark C. Schug: "The goal of economic education is to foster in students the thinking skills and substantial economic knowledge necessary to become effective and participating citizens." It is our hope that this set will enhance both economic and geographic literacy critically needed in an increasingly interconnected world.

—Gerald W. Fry, University of Minnesota

BIBLIOGRAPHY

Brown, Lester R., et al. *State of the World 2000.* New York: W. W. Norton, 2000.

Buchholz, Todd G. *From Here to Economy: A Shortcut to Economic Literacy.* New York: A Dutton Book, 1995.

Cairncross, Frances. *The Death of Distance: How the Communications Revolution Will Change Our Lives.* Boston: Harvard Business School Press, 2001.

Friedman, Thomas F. *The Lexus and the Olive Tree: Understanding Globalization.* New York: Anchor Books, 2000.

Fry, Gerald W., and Galen Martin. *The International Development Dictionary.* Oxford: ABC-Clio Press, 1991.

Hansen, Fay. "Power to the Dollar, Part One of a Series," *Business Finance* (October 1999): 17-20.

Heintz, James, Nancy Folbre, and the Center for Popular Economics. *The Ultimate Field Guide to the U.S. Economy.* New York: The New Press, 2000.

Horowitz, Irving J. *Three Worlds of Development: The Theory and Practice of International Stratification.* New York: Oxford University Press, 1966.

Jacobs, Jane. *The Nature of Economies.* New York: The Modern Library, 2000.

Korten, David C. *When Corporations Rule the World.* West Hartford, CT: Kumarian Press, 1995.

Levy, Marion J. *Modernization and the Structure of Societies.* 2 vols. New Brunswick, NJ: Transaction Publications, 1996.

Lewis, Martin W., and Kären E. Wigen. *A Critique of Metageography.* Berkeley: University of California Press, 1997.

Lohrenz, Edward. *The Essence of Chaos.* Seattle: University of Washington Press, 1993.

Ohmae, Kenichi. *The End of the Nation State: The Rise of Regional Economies.* London: HarperCollins, 1996.

Pasuk Phongpaichit, Sungsidh Priryarangsan, and Nualnoi Treerat. *Guns, Girls, Gambling, and Ganja: Thailand's Illegal Economy and Public Policy.* Chiang Mai: Silkworm Books, 1998.

Pennar, Karen. "Economics Made Too Simple." *Business Week* (20 January 1997): 32.

Ray, Paul H., and Sherry Ruth Anderson. *The Cultural Creatives: How 50 Million People Are Changing the World.* New York: Harmony Books, 2000.

Salk, Jonas, and Jonathan Salk. *World Population and Human Values: A New Reality.* New York: Harper & Row, 1981.

Samuelson, Paul A., William D. Nordhaus, with the assistance of Michael J. Mandal. *Economics.* 15th ed. New York: McGraw-Hill, 1995.

Schug, Mark C. "Introducing Children to Economic Reasoning: Some Beginning Lessons." *Social Studies* (Vol. 87, No. 3, May-June 1996): 114-118.

Schumacher, E.F. *Small is Beautiful: Economics as if People Mattered.* New York: Perennial Library, 1975.

Siegfried, John J., and Bonnie T. Meszaros. "National Voluntary Content Standards for Pre-College Economics Education." *AEA Papers and Proceedings* (Vol. 87, No. 2, May 1997): 247-253.

Smith, David. *Where the Grass Is Greener: Geographical Perspectives on Inequality.* London: Croom Helm, 1979.

Soto, Hernando de; translated by June Abbott. *The Other Path: The Invisible Revolution in the Third World.* New York: Harper & Row, 1989.

Stock, Paul A., and William D. Rader. "Level of Economic Understanding for Senior High School Students in Ohio." *The Journal of Educational Research* (Vol. 91, No. 1, September/October 1997): 60-63.

Sulloway, Frank J. *Born to Rebel: Birth Order, Family Dynamics, and Creative Lives.* New York: Pantheon Books, 1996.

Todaro, Michael P. *Economic Development.* Reading, MA: Addison Wesley, 2000.

Wentland, Daniel. "A Framework for Organizing Economic Education Teaching Methodologies." Mississippi: 2000-00-00, ERIC Document, ED 442702.

Wood, Barbara. *E.F. Schumacher: His Life and Thought.* New York: Harper & Row, 1984.

Wren, Christopher S. "World Needs to Add 500 Million Jobs in 10 Years, Report Says." *The New York Times* (25 January 2001): A13.

ANTIGUA AND BARBUDA

CAPITAL: St. John's.

MONETARY UNIT: East Caribbean dollar (EC$). One Eastern Caribbean dollar (EC$) equals 100 cents. Paper currency comes in denominations of EC$100, 50, 20, 10, and 5. Coins are in denominations of EC$1, and 50, 25, 10, 5, 2, and 1 cents.

CHIEF EXPORTS: Petroleum products, manufactures, food and live animals, machinery and transport equipment.

CHIEF IMPORTS: Food and live animals, machinery and transport equipment, manufactures, chemicals, oil.

GROSS DOMESTIC PRODUCT: US$524 million (purchasing power parity, 1999 est.).

BALANCE OF TRADE: Exports: US$38 million (1998 est.). **Imports:** US$330 million (1998 est.).

COUNTRY OVERVIEW

LOCATION AND SIZE. Antigua and Barbuda is located in the "Heart of the Caribbean" between the Greater and Lesser Antilles, about 402 kilometers (250 miles) east-southeast of Puerto Rico or 60 kilometers (37.5 miles) north of Guadeloupe. This territory consists of several islands, the largest being Antigua (281 square kilometers, or 108 square miles), Barbuda (161 square kilometers, or 62 square miles), and Redonda (1.6 square kilometers, or 0.5 square miles). The smaller islands include Guiana Island, Bird Island, and Long Island. The combined area of this multi-island state is 442 square kilometers (171 square miles) making the territory about 2 and a half times the size of Washington, D.C. Antigua's coastline measures 153 kilometers (95 miles). The country's capital, St. John's, is located on the northwestern coast of Antigua. The main towns include Parham and Liberta on Antigua, and Codrington on Barbuda.

POPULATION. As of July 2000, the population of Antigua was estimated at 66,422, which means that the 1991 population of 63,896 increased by 3.95 percent. In 2000

the birth rate was reported as 19.6 births per 1,000 population while the death rate was 5.99 deaths per 1,000 population. In 2000, it was estimated that the population was growing at a rate of 0.73 percent per annum. The population is expected to reach 82,000 by 2010. Migration has been identified as the main reason for the relatively slow population growth. The net migration rate in 2000 averaged 6.32 migrants per 1,000 population.

The population density is 150 people per square kilometer (389 per square mile). As of 1999 about 37 percent of the population lived in the urban areas. About 91 percent of the population are of African descent. Other races found in relatively small numbers include Amerindian/Carib, East Indian, Chinese, Portuguese, Lebanese, and Syrian.

Close to 67 percent of the country's population are in the age group 15–64. The population is young, with 28 percent of the population aged 0–14 years and only 5 percent aged 65 years and over. In the late 1980s, about one-fifth of all births were to mothers aged under 19 years. Hence, the government, with the aid of the UNFPA Peer Counselling and Youth Health Services Project, has been teaching teens the use of contraceptives, among other birth control techniques, in an effort to reduce teenage pregnancies.

There are about 3,000 residents of Montserrat living in Antigua and Barbuda. These persons are evacuees who fled the island because of the volcanic eruption in 1997.

OVERVIEW OF ECONOMY

Sugar production dominated the economy of Antigua and Barbuda for centuries. Sugar declined in importance after World War II and by the early 1970s it was almost irrelevant to the economy. Thereafter, islanders have dabbled in a variety of agricultural activities, but with limited rainfall there was not much success. Tourism therefore emerged as the major economic activity and, except for the ravages of hurricanes, this sector has experienced steady growth.

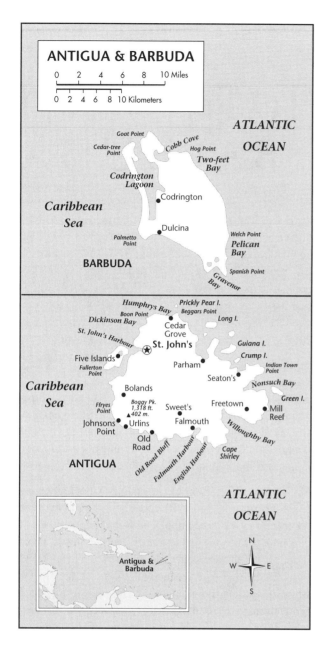

ANTIGUA & BARBUDA

0 2 4 6 8 10 Miles

0 2 4 6 8 10 Kilometers

ATLANTIC OCEAN

Goat Point
Cedar-tree Point
Cobb Cove
Hog Point
Two-feet Bay
Codrington Lagoon
Codrington

Caribbean Sea

Dulcina
Palmetto Point
Welch Point
Pelican Bay

BARBUDA

Spanish Point
Gravenor Bay

Humphrys Bay
Prickly Pear I.
Beggars Point
Boon Point
Dickinson Bay
Long I.
St. John's Harbour
Cedar Grove
St. John's
Guiana I.
Crump I.
Five Islands
Fullerton Point
Parham
Indian Town Point
Seaton's
Nonsuch Bay

Caribbean Sea

Bolands
Boggy Pk. 1,318 ft. ▲402 m.
Ffryes Point
Sweet's
Freetown
Green I.
Johnsons Point
Urlins
Falmouth
Mill Reef
Old Road
Falmouth Harbour
English Harbour
Willoughby Bay
Cape Shirley

ANTIGUA

ATLANTIC OCEAN

Antigua & Barbuda

N
W   E
S

The economy is based on an open and free enterprise system. Since the mid-1980s there has been an upsurge of huge **trade deficits**, however, which have led to **arrears** in payments to foreign investors, which in turn reduced foreign capital inflows. In the first half of the 1990s economic growth slowed sharply (from an average of 8 percent in 1984–89 to 2 percent in 1990–95), mainly because the large public investment in tourism-related projects started in the 1980s could not be sustained.

In the late 1990s the growing offshore financial sector came under scrutiny from some European countries. The sector was affected in 1999 when the United States and United Kingdom applied **sanctions** on the government in an effort to compel more stringent controls on

money laundering. Yet Antigua and Barbuda was not named in 2000 among the so-called "non-co-operative **tax havens** " by the Paris-based Organization for Economic Co-Operation and Development (OECD), a 29-nation grouping of some of the world's wealthiest nations.

As the 21st century opened, tourism continued to be the mainstay of the economy, accounting for over 40 percent of GDP. Recovery in the tourism sector has resulted from rehabilitation efforts and new marketing strategies. There have also been some recent attempts to strengthen the manufacturing sector.

Overall economic growth for 1998 was 3.9 percent, and expanded to about 4.6 percent in 1999. **Inflation** has been moderate, averaging 3 to 4 percent annually, since 1993. It is apparent that economic growth in the medium-term will be tied to income growth in the industrialized regions, particularly the United States and the United Kingdom, where most tourists originate.

Antigua and Barbuda's **external debt** continues to grow, increasing from US$357 million in 1998 to US$433.7 million in 1999. The large debt has had a negative effect on the economy because these loans must be repaid in a short period at very high interest rates. Debt payment accounted for 21.52 percent of the country's 2000 budget. Economic aid averages around US$2 million annually.

While most firms in Antigua and Barbuda are locally owned, overseas companies own most of the hotels. Among the largest companies are Cable and Wireless Antigua Ltd., the state-owned Antigua Public Utilities Authority (APUA), and the Antigua Brewery, which is 80 percent foreign-owned. The state-owned Central Marketing Authority regulates the importation and distribution of basic food items. There are a good number of reputable International Business Companies (IBCs) registered in Antigua, including international banks, trusts, insurance firms, and corporations.

To foster industrial development, the government has adopted a policy of providing local and foreign investors with incentives such as **duty**-free imports, **tax holidays**, and other exemptions. A recent government initiative is the establishment of a "**Free Trade Zone**."

POLITICS, GOVERNMENT, AND TAXATION

Antigua and Barbuda is a constitutional monarchy whose parliament is fashioned on the British Westminster system. The Bird family has governed the country for over 30 years. The Antigua Labour Party (ALP), first led by Vere C. Bird and then by his son Lester B. Bird, has won all but the 1971 elections since universal adult suffrage was granted in 1951. In the most recent general elections held in March 1999 the ALP captured 12 of the 17 seats, thereby increasing its majority by 1 seat. The other political parties in parliament are the United Progressive Party (UPP), led by Baldwin Spencer, with 4 seats, and the Barbuda People's Movement (BPM), led by Hilbourne Frank, with 1 seat. The other parties are the Barbuda National Party (BNP), the Peoples Democratic Movement (PDM), and the Barbuda Independence Movement (BIM). The next general election is due to take place by 2004.

The government appears committed to encouraging **private-sector** growth principally in tourism and the offshore sector. The offshore sector includes IBCs such as banks located in the host country that operate in foreign countries such as the United Kingdom and the United States. IBCs opt to set up in these "tax havens" or "free zones" to benefit from the smaller rate of taxation charged there in comparison to the countries where many of their customers actually live. Moreover, the regulations governing IBCs' operation in the tax havens are often less restrictive than in the larger countries in which they also operate. The government has a policy of selling land for tourist and residential projects while it leases land for agricultural purposes.

Antigua and Barbuda has been rated as the least-taxed country in the Caribbean by a variety of regional and extra-regional financial institutions. Only 17 percent of the country's GNP comes from taxes, while other Caribbean countries get around 27 percent of their GNP from tax revenues on average. In 2000 the government introduced a new 2 percent tax on gross sales of EC$50,000 per year. This tax replaced a 25 percent business tax on profits. Some hotels had threatened to close while the commercial sector ceased importing goods from abroad, except for perishables, to cajole the government into rescinding the tax. However, the government has stood its ground. The International Monetary Fund (IMF) has suggested to the government that it should introduce a **value-added tax** (VAT) as a step towards increasing tax revenues. There is no personal **income tax** in Antigua and Barbuda. While the government was reporting cash-flow problems as recently as January 2001, the prime minister has made it clear that his government will not resort to personal income tax to ease its financial problems.

The Antigua and Barbuda Defence Force (ABDF) assists with surveillance on drug trafficking, and recently signed an agreement with the Canadian armed forces for assistance. The U.S. Air Force has a tracking station on Antigua.

INFRASTRUCTURE, POWER, AND COMMUNICATIONS

Antigua has had an impressive road network since colonial times, mainly because of its relatively flat terrain. There are in excess of 250 kilometers (155 miles) of roads, about 25 percent of which can be classified as highway. Buses usually operate on a limited service, and taxis charge fixed rates. The number of motor cars continues to grow annually as the country has one of the highest per capita incomes in the anglophone (English-speaking) Caribbean. There are 77 kilometers (48 miles) of railroad tracks in the country, used almost exclusively for transporting sugar cane.

The island's lone international airport, V. C. Bird International, is located north-east of St. John's. It is serviced by several international airlines including American Airlines, British Airways, Air Canada, Air France, and BWIA. Antigua also has an excellent seaport which accommodates containerized cargo with state-of-the-art

Communications

Country	Telephones[a]	Telephones, Mobile/Cellular[a]	Radio Stations[b]	Radios[a]	TV Stations[a]	Televisions[a]	Internet Service Providers[c]	Internet Users[c]
Antigua & Barbuda	28,000 (1996)	1,300 (1996)	AM 4; FM 2; shortwave 0	36,000	2	31,000	16	8,000
United States	194 M	69.209 M (1998)	AM 4,762; FM 5,542; shortwave 18	575 M	1,500	219 M	7,800	148 M
Jamaica	353,000 (1996)	54,640 (1996)	AM 10; FM 13; shortwave 0	1.215 M	7	460,000	21	60,000
St. Lucia	37,000	1,600	AM 2; FM 7; shortwave 0	111,000	3	32,000	15	5,000

[a]Data is for 1997 unless otherwise noted.
[b]Data is for 1998 unless otherwise noted.
[c]Data is for 2000 unless otherwise noted.

SOURCE: CIA *World Factbook 2001* [Online].

equipment. Heritage Quay pier in St. John's was constructed solely to accommodate cruise ships.

Electricity is produced by the state-owned Antigua Public Utility Authority (APUA). In 1999 the company produced 90 million kilowatt-hours (kWh). All electricity is produced from oil as the island does not have hydro plants or any other type of generation plants.

Domestic telecommunications services are provided by the APUA while the British-based multi-national Cable and Wireless, through Cable and Wireless Antigua Ltd., provides international telecommunications services. In 1994 it was estimated that the country had about 20,000 telephone lines in use. International traffic is moved via a submarine fibre optic cable as well as an Intelsat earth station. Cable and Wireless, through its Caribsurf subsidiary, is the main Internet service provider with about 6,000 Internet subscribers. In January 2001, Antigua Computer Technology (ACT) was launched as the second Internet service provider with a start-up capacity to connect at least 1,000 subscribers. The country has 2 television broadcast stations and an estimated 31,000 television sets.

ECONOMIC SECTORS

The services sector, in particular tourism and offshore financial services, dominate the economy. Consequently, the economy is heavily dependent on visitor arrivals from the United States and the United Kingdom. In fact, between January and September 2000 the pace of economic activity was much slower compared to the similar period for 1999, principally because of a decline in the number of visitors. However, it is expected that a marketing effort to be funded by the government and pri-

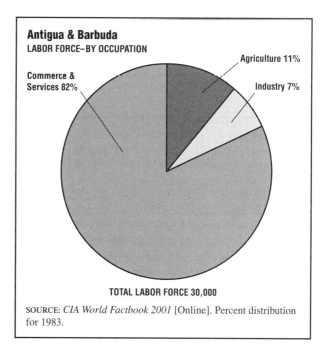

Antigua & Barbuda
LABOR FORCE—BY OCCUPATION

Agriculture 11%

Commerce & Services 82%

Industry 7%

TOTAL LABOR FORCE 30,000

SOURCE: *CIA World Factbook 2001* [Online]. Percent distribution for 1983.

vate sector will lead to an increase in stay-over arrivals from North America and Europe (particularly the United Kingdom) in 2001 and beyond. A major threat to tourism has been hurricane and storm damage from 1994 to 1999.

AGRICULTURE

The collapse of the sugar industry in the 1970s left the government in control of 60 percent of Antigua's 66,000 acres of sugar cane plantations. The main agricultural exports include cotton to Japan and fruit and vegetables to other Caribbean territories. Hot peppers and vegetables are exported to the United Kingdom and Canada. Other agriculture products are bananas, coconuts, cucumbers, mangoes, livestock, and pineapples.

Agriculture accounts for a rather insignificant part of the economy, making up 4 percent in 1996 and falling to 3.6 percent in 1998. According to the *Americas Review 1999*, there were 2,000 persons employed in agriculture in 1999. However, it appears that cultivation is on the rise. In 1998 there were 279.8 acres of land planted with vegetables. In 1999 there were 340.1 acres under cultivation, 73.3 acres of which were planted with onions. In 1999 alone some 319,275 pounds of vegetables were produced. The government has received the assistance of the European Development Fund to develop the livestock subsector.

Problems confronting the agricultural sector include soil depletion and drought. Antigua does not have any rivers and is short on groundwater. Consequently, drinking water is collected from rainfall or imported from neighboring territories. Several hotels have seawater de-

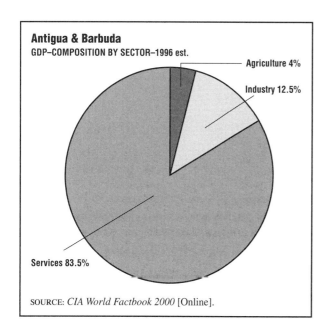

Antigua & Barbuda
GDP—COMPOSITION BY SECTOR—1996 est.

Agriculture 4%

Industry 12.5%

Services 83.5%

SOURCE: *CIA World Factbook 2000* [Online].

salination facilities. The state also supplements its water distribution service with desalinated water.

Some 3 million pounds of fish are caught per year, according to 1997 figures. At that time Barbuda alone was exporting 260,000 pounds of lobster annually. Fish hauls increased in 1998, an indication that this sector has recovered significantly from hurricane damage sustained between 1995 and 1998. The East Caribbean Central Bank reported in 1999 that fish as well as crop production were the main contributors to agriculture in 1999. There are a few shrimp and lobster farms on Antigua. In addition, the Smithsonian Institute runs a project which farms Caribbean king crabs for domestic consumption.

INDUSTRY

MANUFACTURING. Manufacturing is not a major contributor to the economy. However, output from manufacturing rose by 5.5 percent in 1998 and 5 percent in 1999. Between 1996 and 1998, manufacturing contributed an average of just over 2 percent of GDP.

An industrial park located at Coolidge near the V. C. Bird International airport produces exports such as paints, galvanized sheets, furniture, paper products, and the assembly of household appliances, vehicles, and garments. Local manufacturers are provided with incentives such as tax and duty-free concessions.

Manufacturers can export to the United States, European, Canadian, and Caribbean markets as a result of trade agreements such as the Lomé Convention, the Caribbean Basin Initiative (CBI) and Caribbean Common Market (CARICOM).

In 1999 the government signed an agreement with the People's Republic of China to use local cotton in the manufacture of textiles for the export market. A factory is to be constructed to facilitate this project.

CONSTRUCTION. Much of the buoyancy in the economy over the last few years has been due to the steady growth in the construction sector. Private and government investments have facilitated this growth. Construction contributed on average 11 percent of GDP between 1996 and 1998.

SERVICES

TOURISM. Tourism is the mainstay of the economy of Antigua and Barbuda and is the leading sector in terms of providing employment and creating foreign exchange. In 1999 it contributed 60 percent of GDP and more than half of all jobs. According to the *Americas Review 1998*, tourism contributed 15 percent directly and around 40 percent indirectly to the GDP in 1998.

Real growth in this sector has moved from an average of 7 percent for the period 1985–89 to 8.24 percent for the period 1990–95. There was slow growth between 1995 and 1998.

Figures released by the East Caribbean Central Bank (ECCB) in 2000 show that total visitor arrivals increased steadily from 470,975 in 1995 to 613,990 in 1998. In 1999 total visitor arrivals declined by about 4.1 percent to 588,866, yet the number of visitors staying at least 1 night or more increased by 1.9 percent over 1998 to total 207,862. Arrivals via cruise ships in 1999 dropped to 325,195, a fall of 3.4 percent over 1998. The fall-off in cruise passengers was mainly the result of one of the larger cruise ships being out of service for a brief period. Most of the tourists in 1999 came from the United Kingdom and the United States. Visitor expenditures have increased steadily since 1990, with total expenditures of EC$782.9 million.

To combat increasing competition from other Caribbean destinations, the government and the Antigua Hotel and Tourist Association have established a joint fund to market the country's appeal as a tourist destination. The Association has agreed to match the proceeds from a 2 percent hotel guest **levy** introduced by the government.

At the start of March 2001, the Antigua Workers Union (AWU), the trade union which represents close to 7,000 workers in the tourism industry, described tourism as an industry in crisis. The AWU claimed the industry is on the decline because some airlines are pulling out of the country, and government was not spending enough money to promote tourism. While the government has conceded that it was not spending enough on marketing because of cash flow problems, it has rejected the AWU's contention that the industry is in crisis.

FINANCIAL SERVICES. Antigua and Barbuda is advertised as "an attractive offshore jurisdiction." The country was the first to sign the United Nations' anti-money laundering pact. This agreement came out of a conference in 1999 which urged worldwide offshore financial centers to introduce laws to tighten their policing of money laundering activities. The United Kingdom exerted considerable pressure on Antigua and Barbuda to reform laws to combat money laundering, even issuing an advisory in April 1999 to British financial institutions that Antigua and Barbuda's anti-money laundering laws were wanting. Antigua and Barbuda responded to this concern, and a subsequent joint United States and United Kingdom review reported they were satisfied that the country had taken positive steps to check illegal activity in this sector. In September 2000 the government of Antigua and Barbuda announced that it had strengthened its surveillance of money laundering and drug trafficking.

Trade (expressed in billions of US$): Antigua & Barbuda		
	Exports	Imports
1975	.020	.067
1980	.026	.088
1985	.017	.166
1990	.021	.255
1995	.030	.299
1998	N/A	N/A

SOURCE: International Monetary Fund. *International Financial Statistics Yearbook 1999.*

Exchange rates: Antigua & Barbuda	
East Caribbean dollars (EC$) per US$1	
2001	2.7000
2000	2.7000
1999	2.7000
1998	2.7000
1997	2.7000
1996	2.7000

Note: The exchange rate has been fixed since 1976.

SOURCE: CIA *World Factbook 2001* [ONLINE].

RETAIL. The **retail** sector is dominated by the sale of food and beverages, clothing and textiles, and vegetables. The main markets are located in the capital, St. John's. There are many street vendors and duty-free shops. The government has been taking steps to improve this sector. A US$43.5 million vendors' mall and market has been built to provide better facilities for retailers in the capital. In addition, a US$27 million fisheries complex now provides improved facilities for fish processing and retailing. A growing area of computer business on Antigua is Internet casinos.

INTERNATIONAL TRADE

This small multi-island state imports most of its food as well as other goods that it does not manufacture. In 1998 the value of imports was as much as 9 times the value of exports. In 1998 total exports amounted to US$38 million while imports stood at US$330 million.

The Organization of Eastern Caribbean States (OECS) comprised 26 percent of the country's exports, Barbados took in 15 percent, Guyana 4 percent, and Trinidad and Tobago 2 percent. The United States imported only .03 percent. Of imports, some 27 percent came from the United States, 16 percent from the United Kingdom, 4 percent from Canada, and 3 percent from the OECS.

The country is a party to several trade agreements, including the Caribbean Basin Initiative (CBI) with the United States, Caribcan with Canada, the Lomé Convention (a cooperation agreement between the EU and the ACP, the latter consisting of several African, Caribbean, and Pacific countries), and the Caribbean Common Market (CARICOM).

MONEY

The **exchange rate** of the East Caribbean dollar has remained steady since 1976 at 2.70 to the U.S. dollar. This is partly because the agreement establishing the East Caribbean Central Bank, which regulates the currency, requires all countries that use the currency to agree to **devaluation**.

The country does not have its own stock exchange. Instead, it is part of the St. Kitts-based Eastern Caribbean Securities Exchange (ECSE). An associate institution of the Eastern Caribbean Central Bank (ECCB), the ECSE is scheduled to start trading in 2001. The fully automated exchange will be linked via local telecommunications providers and will employ an electronic book-entry system for recording the ownership of securities.

To assist with its development, the ECSE has received US$2 million in grants, counter-part loans, and money from the Multilateral Investment Fund (MIF) of the Inter-American Development Bank (IDB). The funds were channeled through the Barbados-based Caribbean Development Bank (CDB).

POVERTY AND WEALTH

According to *Sub-Regional Common Assessment of Barbados and the OECS*, some 12 percent of the population lived below the poverty line in the 1990s. This is much less than the average in the eastern Caribbean. Research has shown that the level of poverty was 17 percent in Grenada in 1998, 19 percent in St. Lucia in 1995, and 31 percent in St. Vincent and the Grenadines in 1996. About 35 percent of the eastern Caribbean is classified as poor (i.e., people in these countries earn less than

GDP per Capita (US$)					
Country	1975	1980	1985	1990	1998
Antigua & Barbuda	N/A	4,057	5,164	6,980	8,559
United States	19,364	21,529	23,200	25,363	29,683
Jamaica	1,819	1,458	1,353	1,651	1,559
St. Lucia	N/A	2,076	2,150	3,542	3,907

SOURCE: United Nations. *Human Development Report 2000; Trends in human development and per capita income.*

Household Consumption in PPP Terms

Country	All food	Clothing and footwear	Fuel and power[a]	Health care[b]	Education[b]	Transport & Communications	Other
Antigua & Barbuda	36	3	8	3	18	9	23
United States	13	9	9	4	6	8	51
Jamaica	24	7	3	1	9	8	48
St. Lucia	40	5	11	4	17	11	11

Data represent percentage of consumption in PPP terms.
[a]Excludes energy used for transport.
[b]Includes government and private expenditures.
SOURCE: World Bank. *World Development Indicators 2000.*

US$15–25 per day). Indicators point to the possibility of increasing poverty in Antigua unless the slowdown in the economy is reversed and more employment is provided.

The **GDP per capita** in 1998 was US$8,559. The *Human Development Report 2000* gave Antigua and Barbuda a Human Development Index (HDI) ranking of 37th among the United Nations' 174 members. The HDI is computed by the UN and ranks its member nations based on an index which takes into account a country's healthcare system, life expectancy, school enrollment, adult literacy rate, educational attainment, and per capita income to arrive at a score.

Antigua and Barbuda enjoys one of the highest employment rates in the Caribbean, and the second-highest wages and salaries per capita in the region. Life expectancy in 1999 was 75 years, about the same as in the United States.

The population benefits from national insurance and contributory pension schemes. Poor and elderly persons receive public assistance. The Antigua Medical Benefits Scheme (MBS) provides medical benefits to workers who contribute to it. However, at the beginning of 2001, the government was pressured to investigate alleged financial wrong-doing at the MBS. This has weakened confidence in the scheme. Workers are increasingly questioning the ability of the scheme to adequately finance health care in light of the charges of financial wrongdoing.

The government has operated a series of statewide free health clinics since the colonial period and these have expanded in the 1980s and 1990s. Although the government intends to introduce minimum user fees, it has promised to make provisions for the poor. The government also provides education at all levels.

WORKING CONDITIONS

The total active **labor force** in 1998 was about 30,000. Of this figure 8,319 were immigrant workers. In 1998 the government employed 10,984 persons, or about 38.3 percent of the total labor force, a trend that has gone as far back as 1994.

The unemployment rate fell from 9 percent in 1997 to 5 percent in 1998. During the latter part of 2000, the government announced a freeze on employment after cash flow problems made it difficult for it to meet its wage and pension bills, which amount to as much as US$5.1 million monthly.

The lowest age for employment is age 16. Children do not form part of the labor force, but they usually assist on family agricultural plots in the afternoon after school and during school vacations. The government has a youth skills training program which provides on-the-job training.

As much as 45.5 percent of the country's workforce are women. More significantly, close to 60 percent of all **public sector** employees are women. Most women who work are employed in the hotel industry and in teaching.

The leading trade unions in Antigua and Barbuda are the Antigua Workers' Union, the Antigua Trades and Labour Union, the Antigua and Barbuda Public Service Association, the Antigua and Barbuda Union of Teachers, and the Leeward Islands Air Line Pilots' Association. A 1975 labor code governs labor relations in the country. There was some industrial unrest in the airline industry and commercial sector during 1999 and 2000.

In 1997 the government granted public sector workers a 6 percent increase in wages and salaries for the period 1997–2000. In 1998 private sector workers had wage increases averaging around 4 percent. These wage hikes were long overdue and were granted to meet the rise in the cost of living.

COUNTRY HISTORY AND ECONOMIC DEVELOPMENT

1632. English settlers arrive from St. Kitts and colonization begins.

1674. The first large-scale sugar plantation established.

1736. Major slave uprising led by Prince Klaas.

1834. Complete freedom granted to slaves.

1939. The first trade union is formed on advice of British officials.

1943. Vere C. Bird becomes president of the Antigua Trades and Labour Union.

1951. Universal adult suffrage introduced; the Antigua Labour Party (ALP) led by Vere C. Bird comes to power.

1967. Antigua, Barbuda, and Redonda become an associated state with Britain.

1971. ALP voted out of office.

1972. Sugar industry goes into dormancy.

1974. Antigua and Barbuda joins CARICOM.

1976. ALP returned to office.

1981. Antigua and Barbuda obtains its political independence from Britain.

1994. Vere C. Bird hands over ALP to his son, Lester Bird.

1995-99. Series of hurricanes damage the islands' **infrastructure**.

FUTURE TRENDS

The government has pointed to the need for new and varied sources of revenue, especially since the tourism industry is likely to face competition in the not too distant future from Cuba, which has larger hotels, good facilities, and is located closer to the United States. There is also the threat posed by the OECD to the offshore finance sector. This organization has placed enormous pressure on the government to tighten its regulatory control over the sector and such action could result in its stagnation.

The IMF has recommended that the country adopt a comprehensive macro-economic program with medium- to long-term plans for improving government finances. The government fears that an IMF Economic **Structural Adjustment Program** (ESAP), which advocates cutting down the size of the public sector, will lead to unemployment, which in turn can lead to poverty and crime. Thus, the government has declined to participate in the

IMF program and has instead opted to devise its own economic **restructuring** program with the aid of the Eastern Caribbean Central Bank (ECCB).

With its cash flow problems, Antigua and Barbuda may reduce the size of the public sector, which presently employs close to 11,000 persons. It may also take at least some of the IMF's advice and toughen its **fiscal policy**, implement reforms to increase efficiency and governance in the public sector, and work out a suitable repayment plan with its creditors. With revenue being lost through reduced **tariffs**, the administration may be looking to the VAT to fill the gap. However, government officials have hinted that the 2001 national budget, to be presented to Parliament in March of that year, will include reductions in duty-free concessions in an effort to address the cash-flow problem. In 2000 close to US$37 million was granted in such concessions.

DEPENDENCIES

Antigua and Barbuda has no territories or colonies.

BIBLIOGRAPHY

The Americas Review, 17th edition. New Jersey: Hunter, 1998; 18th edition, 1999.

Antigua and Barbuda: Statistical Annex. Washington, D.C.: International Monetary Fund, 1999. <http://www.imf.org/external/pubs/cat/longres.cfm?sk=3344.0>. Accessed August 2001.

Caribbean Development Bank Annual Report 1999. Bridgetown, Barbados: Caribbean Development Bank, 1999.

The Caribbean Handbook 2000. St. John's, Antigua: FT International, 2000.

East Caribbean Central Bank Economic and Financial Review. Vol. 20, No. 3, September 2000.

East Caribbean Central Bank Report. St. Kitts, West Indies: ECCB, 2000.

"Small States, Big Money." *The Economist.* September 23, 2000.

"Sub-Regional Common Assessment of Barbados and the OECS: The UN Development System for the Eastern Caribbean, January 2000." *United Nations Development Programme for Barbados and the OECS.* <http://www.bb.undp.org/pub/pub_text.html>. Accessed August 2001.

United Nations Development Program. *Human Development Report 2000.* New York: Oxford University Press, 2000.

U.S. Central Intelligence Agency. *World Factbook 2000.* <http://www.odci.gov/cia/publications/factbook/index.html>. Accessed August 2001.

—Cleve Mc D. Scott

ARGENTINA

Argentine Republic
República Argentina

CAPITAL: Buenos Aires.

MONETARY UNIT: Peso (P). One peso equals 100 centavos. Coins are in denominations of P5, 2 and 1 and 50, 25, 10, 5 and 1 centavos. Peso paper currency is in denominations of P100, 50, 20, 10, 5 and 2.

CHIEF EXPORTS: Edible oils, fuels and energy, cereals, feed, motor vehicles.

CHIEF IMPORTS: Machinery and equipment, motor vehicles, chemicals, metal manufactures, plastics.

GROSS DOMESTIC PRODUCT: US$367 billion (purchasing power parity, 1999 est.).

BALANCE OF TRADE: Exports: US$23 billion (f.o.b., 1999 est.). **Imports:** US$25 billion (c.i.f., 1999 est.).

COUNTRY OVERVIEW

LOCATION AND SIZE. Argentina is located in the southern region of South America. The nation borders Chile to the west and south; the Atlantic Ocean, Uruguay, and Brazil to the east; and Bolivia and Paraguay to the north. Argentina has a total area of 2,766,890 square kilometers (1,068,296 square miles) and is the second-largest nation in South America (after Brazil). It is about the size of the United States east of the Mississippi River. The nation's coastline is 4,989 kilometers (3,100 miles) long. Argentina's land borders total 9,665 kilometers (6,005 miles). This includes borders of 832 kilometers (517 miles) with Bolivia, 1,224 kilometers (760 miles) with Brazil, 5,150 kilometers (3,200 miles) with Chile, 1,880 kilometers (1,168 miles) with Paraguay, and 579 kilometers (360 miles) with Uruguay. Argentina has 30,200 square kilometers (11,660 square miles) of water within its territory. The country's capital, Buenos Aires, is located on the Rio de la Plata (an estuary of the Paraná and Uruguay rivers) on the Atlantic Coast. Buenos Aires has a population of 3 million, although the larger metropolitan area has 13 million people. The nation's second-

largest city is Cordoba, located in the center of the nation, with a population of 1.2 million.

POPULATION. Argentina's population is 36,955,182, according to a July 2000 estimate. In 2000, the population growth rate was 1.16 percent and the nation's birth rate was 18.59 births per 1,000 people. Its fertility rate is 2.47 children born per woman. This gives Argentina one of the lowest population growth rates in Latin America. The population is relatively young with almost half of all people under the age of 30. However, this trend is expected to slowly reverse itself so that by 2025, the differences in the number of people in each age group will be minimal. By 2050 the largest single group of people will be those aged 35 to 55. By 2010 Argentina's population is expected to exceed 41 million. Argentina's mortality rate is 7.58 deaths per 1,000 people, and its infant mortality rate is 18.31 deaths per 1,000 live births. In 2000, the life expectancy was 71.67 years for males and 78.61 years for females.

The majority of Argentines are of European descent (mainly Spanish and Italian). This group makes up 85 percent of the population. Mestizos (people of mixed European and Native-American descent) comprise 12 percent of Argentineans while Native Americans comprise 3 percent of the population. Spanish is the official language, although English, Italian, German, and French are also spoken in certain areas of the country. Most Argentineans are Roman Catholic (92 percent), but there are small numbers of Protestants (2 percent) and Jews (2 percent). The nation's indigenous population numbers about 700,000 and is concentrated in the northwest and some southern areas of the country. There are large immigrant communities in Argentina. During the 19th and early 20th centuries, there were several waves of **immigration** from Europe which included Germans, English, and Italians. From 1850 through 1940, approximately

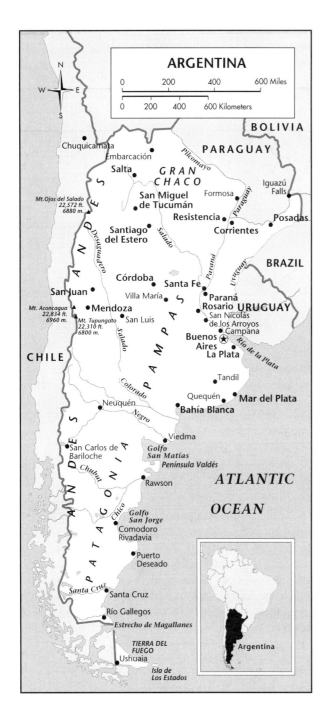

the literacy rate is 96.2 percent. Because of the relative wealth of the society, Argentina has recently experienced new waves of immigration, mainly from other Latin American countries.

The people of Argentina are highly urbanized. About 80 percent of Argentineans live in towns with populations of 2,000 or more. Some 13 million people—or about one-third of the population—live in the greater Buenos Aires metropolitan area. Because of this urban concentration, the nation's population density is quite low. Argentina ranks number 200 in the world in terms of population density with only 13.42 people per square kilometer (34.76 per square mile). In comparison, the population density of the United States is 28.4 per square kilometer (73.56 per square mile).

OVERVIEW OF ECONOMY

Argentina's economy is one of the richest and most diversified in Latin America. The nation has a variety of natural and other resources which have combined to produce an economy that is based on a strong industrial base, an export-oriented agricultural sector, and a growing service sector. The Argentine population is highly educated and skilled, and the country has a variety of natural resources including lead, zinc, copper, iron petroleum, uranium, and rich agricultural areas. However, after repeated periods of military dictatorship, the nation faced a variety of economic problems when the first sustained period of civilian control of the government began in 1983. By 1989, the nation had an enormous **external debt**, and **inflation** had reached a level of 200 percent per month. In response, the government undertook a variety of programs to reform and reinvigorate the economy. In 1991, it initiated a series of programs which provided a **fixed exchange rate** between the peso and the U.S. dollar and ultimately reformed the banking system. This dramatically lowered inflation and helped stabilize the economy. The government in 2001 continued an economic program which raised taxes and cut government spending in an effort to lower the nation's **budget deficit** and overall debt.

Argentina underwent an economic boom period in the early 1990s. By 1997, GDP growth had reached 8 percent per year. Reforms in the economy led to increased competition and output. These reforms also attracted significant new foreign investment. Between 1992 and 1999, exports more than doubled from US$12 billion to US$25 billion. In overall terms, international trade remains only a small part of the Argentine economy. In 1995 Argentina, Brazil, Chile, and Uruguay created a free trade area named MERCOSUR. The trade organization has dramatically lowered **tariffs** between the member nations with reductions in some tariffs of 100 percent. As a result, trade between the member states increased from

6,608,700 Europeans **emigrated** to Argentina. During the late 20th century, new groups of immigrants settled in the country, including those from Syria and Lebanon. Middle Eastern immigrants now number about 500,000. The nation continues to encourage immigration from Europe through a variety of programs.

Argentina's economy has performed well over the past few decades and the nation enjoys one of the highest standards of living in Latin America. In 2000, the **GDP per capita** was US$10,000. About half of the people consider themselves to be middle-class. In addition,

US$4 billion in 1991 to US$23 billion in 1999. Argentina accounts for 27 percent of MERCOSUR's total GDP. Brazil is now Argentina's largest trading partner. Argentina's exports to MERCOSUR countries are expected to continue to increase and to help spur the economy.

In 1998, the nation began a severe **recession** that ended in 2000. In 1999, GDP fell by 3 percent, but by 2000 growth had returned at a 2 percent annual rate. However, unemployment in the nation continues to be problematic. Unemployment peaked in 1995 at 18.4 percent. Although it has fallen, it remained at 15.4 percent as of 2000. Increases in productivity and reforms of the labor market are expected to decrease unemployment as more foreign investors locate or relocate firms and factories in Argentina.

The strongest areas of the Argentine economy are telecommunications, food processing, banking, energy production, and mining. Food processing alone accounted for 23 percent of GDP in industry in 1998 and is one of the few areas in which Argentina has a **trade surplus**. The nation's large agricultural sector produces a variety of products that are used by domestic food industries and then exported. Agriculture provides about 40 percent of Argentine exports. Besides food processing, Argentina's main industries are automobile production, textiles, chemicals and petrochemicals, steel, mining, and consumer durables. After falling by 7 percent in 1999, industrial production recovered slightly in 2000, with a modest growth of 2 percent. Many major international car manufacturers have plants in Argentina, including Ford, Volkswagen, Fiat, General Motors, and Renault. Mining production is expected to double by 2004, with strong growth in gold and copper production. The Argentine telecommunications sector was one of the first in Latin American to be **privatized**. Since 1991, the sector has experienced continued growth as consumers have sought new technologies, including cellular phones, pagers, and cable television. Reforms in 1994 eliminated restrictions on foreign-owned banks, and insurance firms and many multinational financial companies operate in Argentina. Some of the larger firms include the U.S.-owned American Express Bank, Citibank, Chase Manhattan, Bank Boston, the Dutch-owned ABN Amro Bank, and the British-owned Lloyds Bank.

Argentina continues to face yearly deficits—US$4 billion or 2.5 percent of GDP in 1999 alone. In 1999, the country's debt was US$149 billion. However, Argentina is a net recipient of foreign aid. It receives about US$2 billion a year from international organizations such as the European Union (EU) and the World Bank. In 1999, the International Monetary Fund (IMF) established a contingency fund of US$7.4 billion that can be loaned to Argentina in order to maintain the nation's currency and economic stability.

POLITICS, GOVERNMENT, AND TAXATION

Argentina declared independence from Spain in 1816. The nation then underwent a political struggle between groups that favored a strong central government and those that favored a less rigid federal system. In 1853, the 2 factions established a new constitution and a government of national unity, thereby establishing Argentina as a constitutional democracy. The remainder of the 1800s were marked by increasing industrialization and a large amount of foreign investment, especially from Great Britain, in areas such as railways and port facilities.

Conservatives dominated Argentine politics until 1916 when the Radical Civic Union (URC) gained control of the government. The Radicals worked to expand political participation through fair elections and helped strengthen the political power of the middle class. However, in 1930 the military overthrew the legally-elected president. A succession of military governments tried to cope with the economic problems of the 1930s, but continued labor and social unrest led Juan Domingo Peron to power in the 1940s. Peron dramatically expanded union membership and the power of the working class. In 1947, women were given the right to vote. Peron and his wife Eva, popularly known as Evita, enjoyed great support among the working class and the poor. However, the Peron regime was marked by political corruption and repression. Peron also undermined the Argentine economy by **nationalizing** industry and trying to manage the economy through state-controlled economic policies and adherence to a series of 5-year plans. The military overthrew Peron in 1955, and through the 1950s and 1960s, Argentina had a succession of civilian and military governments, none of which could establish long-lasting political stability.

Meanwhile, the nation suffered from economic decline and a rise in both terrorism and formal rebellion by anti-government forces. This instability led voters to return Peron to power in 1973, with his third wife, Maria Estela, as his vice-president. However, both liberal and conservative extremist groups continued campaigns against the government, and the economy continued to decline. Peron died in office in 1974 and his wife, who succeeded him, was overthrown by the military in 1976. From 1976 to 1983, the military ruled Argentina and conducted a brutal campaign to eliminate opposition forces. At least 10,000 people were abducted and killed during this period that is known as the "Dirty War." Argentina also lost a war with Great Britain over possession of the Falkland Islands (called the Malvinas Islands by the Argentines). Popular pressure led to elections in 1983 and the restoration of democracy.

Argentina is once again a constitutional democracy. The 1983 elections installed Raul Alfonsin as president for a 6-year term. Alfonsin worked to establish civilian control over the military and fix the nation's economic problems. However, by 1989 inflation had soared to 4,923 percent and the country's economy was in shambles. Alfonsin was defeated in the elections in 1989 and replaced by Carlos Saul Menem. The inauguration of Menem marked the first peaceful transfer of power in Argentina in more than 60 years. Menem adopted a variety of reform programs which included privatization efforts and a pro-United States foreign policy. Menem also initiated monetary reforms which fixed the Argentine peso to the U.S. dollar.

In 1994, there were major revisions to the Argentine constitution. In the past, the president had been chosen by an electoral college, similar to that of the United States, for a 6-year term. Under the new constitution, the president is directly elected by the people for a 4-year term and can serve only 2 terms in office, but can be re-elected after leaving office for at least 1 term. The president serves as the chief of state, the commander-in-chief of the military, and the head of the government. The Argentine president has more power than his American counterpart, including a line item veto (the ability to reject a single item from a legislative bill, rather than the whole bill). Argentina's legislative branch is a **bicameral** (2-chamber) body known as the National Congress. The upper chamber is the Senate, which has 72 members who are elected for 6-year terms. There are 3 senators for each of the nation's 23 provinces and the Federal District. The lower chamber is the Chamber of Deputies, which has 257 members who are elected for 4-year terms. Half of the deputies are elected on a proportional basis (each political party receives a percentage of the seats in the Congress based on their election totals, so that a party receiving 40 percent of the votes would receive 40 percent of the seats). The 1994 constitution improved the accountability of judges by establishing a Judicial Council which oversees judicial conduct. All judges are appointed by the president, subject to approval by the Senate. The nation's 23 provinces have significant power, not unlike the states in the United States, and each has a constitution that mirrors that of the national government.

There are 2 main political parties in Argentina. The Justicialist Party (JP) or Peronist Party is the party of Juan Peron. The JP is now a centrist party, but its main base of support continues to be with the working class and labor unions. Under Carlos Menem, the JP has embraced free-market, economic **liberalization** as the cornerstone of their economic program. The second major party in Argentina is the Union Civica Radical (Radical Civil Union or UCR), which evolved from the old Radical Party that was founded in 1890. The UCR's main base is among the middle class, and the party is now the more

conservative of the 2 main political factions in Argentina. Under Raul Alfonsin, the UCR attempted wide-ranging economic reforms, but was unable to implement them in the face of popular opposition. Leftist members of the JP split with the party in the 1990s and formed the Front for a Country in Solidarity (FREPASO). In 1997, the UCR and FREPASO joined together in a coalition that is known as the Alliance for Work, Justice and Education, or simply as the Alliance. In 1999, the leader of FREPASO, Fernando de la Rua, was elected president. Despite the leftist leanings of FREPASO, its coalition with the UCR has brought the Alliance to the center politically. President de la Rua continued the economic reforms of Menem. There are also a number of minor and regional parties.

Under de la Rua, the government's policies were based on continuing liberalization of the domestic economy through privatizations and a reduced role for the state in the economy. The government is also working to reduce trade barriers and thereby increase foreign trade through integration in organizations such as MERCOSUR and direct trade agreements with other countries such as the United States. In its ongoing effort to increase trade, Argentina has worked to end a number of minor disputes with other countries, including border disputes with Brazil and Chile. Argentina has also restored relations with Great Britain, which were broken in the wake of the Falkland Islands war. The key component of economic policy that has united all of the main political parties is the continued fixed exchange rate between the peso and the dollar. This has served to practically eliminate inflation and to make Argentina attractive to foreign investors and to international organizations that provide economic assistance.

An ongoing problem for the government is the continuing budget deficit. By 1999, the deficit had climbed to 2.5 percent of GDP or almost US$9 billion. In an effort to reduce the deficit, President de la Rua implemented an economic program that expanded the privatization of government-owned businesses and included both spending cuts and tax increases. Among the most significant privatization programs over the last decade have been the selling-off of the nation's state-owned telephone company and reforms in the banking and insurance sector. The government has also expanded the availability of private pension plans, which has reduced the strain on the nation's social security system. Corporations in Argentina pay a standard 30 percent tax on profits each year. Individuals pay a graduated **income tax** that ranges from 11 to 30 percent, depending on income. There is also a 0.5 percent annual wealth tax on individuals who have a net worth of more than US$100,000.

Approximately 919,000 Argentines work for the government. In 2000, the government's budget was US$28 billion, but its revenues were only US$24 billion leading to a US$4 billion deficit. Repeated deficits have led to a large external debt of US$149 billion. In another effort to increase revenues, the government has been engaged in a long-running effort to improve tax collection and simultaneously decrease corruption in the **public sector**.

After decades in which it enjoyed a high degree of political power and prestige, the Argentine military has shrunk dramatically. The nation's military is now an all-volunteer force. In 1999, Argentina spent only 1.3 percent of GDP or US$4.3 billion on defense (compared with as much as 5 percent in the 1980s). Argentina has developed close military relations with a number of countries, including the United States, Israel, Spain, Germany, France, and Italy. In 1998, Argentina was designated a major ally by the North Atlantic Treaty Organization (NATO). Argentina has recently participated in a number of international humanitarian military operations such as the intervention in Haiti and NATO missions in the former Yugoslavia.

INFRASTRUCTURE, POWER, AND COMMUNICATIONS

Argentina has a good **infrastructure** system in comparison with other Latin American nations, but many areas need significant improvement. The nation has 215,434 kilometers (133,870 miles) of roads, including 734 kilometers (456 miles) of expressways or highways, but only 63,553 kilometers (39,492 miles) of the country's roads are paved. Argentina has been the recipient of a number of aid packages to improve infrastructure. For instance, the United States has provided US$7 million and the World Bank provided US$450 million for highway construction. There is an extensive rail system that transports both freight and passengers around Argentina, with a total of 38,326 kilometers (23,816 miles) of track.

Argentina has 10,950 kilometers (6,804 miles) of navigable waterways. However, most of the country's ma-

jor ports are located on the Atlantic coast, and little freight is transported along the inland waterways. The nation's main ports include Bahia Blanca, Buenos Aires, Comodoro Rivadavia, La Plata, and Mar La Plata (all located on the Atlantic Coast). Inland river ports include Rosario and Santa Fe, while the port of Ushuaia is located in the extreme southern tip of the nation near Cape Horn where the Atlantic and Pacific Oceans meet. Argentina has a small merchant marine of 26 ships with more than 1,000 tons of gross weight. This includes 11 petroleum tankers. In order to provide fuels to inland areas and ship resources to ports for export, there is a broad pipeline system. There are 4,090 kilometers (2,542 miles) of crude oil pipelines, 2,900 kilometers (1,802 miles) for other petroleum products, and 9,918 kilometers (6,163 miles) of natural gas pipelines.

Buenos Aires has an extensive system of public transportation, including subways and buses, but most smaller cities and towns in Argentina have limited transportation resources. Most major cities are connected by passenger railways and there is an extensive commuter rail system in the greater Buenos Aires metropolitan area.

There are 1,359 airports in Argentina, although only 142 have paved runways. Buenos Aires has 2 major airports. The first, Ezeiza International Airport, is the main point of arrival and departure for most international flights. Most domestic or regional flights, including those to Brazil, Uruguay, and Paraguay originate from the second major airport in Buenos Aires, Aeroparque Jorge Newbery. Most major international air carriers offer service to Buenos Aires, including the U.S. carriers United and American Airlines. Argentina's national airline is Aerolineas Argentinas. The government is involved in a program to privatize airports. Thus far, 33 major airports have been turned over to private companies to operate.

Argentina has a telephone density of about 20 private phones per 100 people. There are also some 12,000 public telephones. **Deregulation** of the telecommunications industry is ongoing, and service and infrastructure

Communications

Country	Newspapers	Radios	TV Sets[a]	Cable subscribers[a]	Mobile Phones[a]	Fax Machines[a]	Personal Computers[a]	Internet Hosts[b]	Internet Users[b]
	1996	1997	1998	1998	1998	1998	1998	1999	1999
Argentina	123	681	289	163.1	78	2.0	44.3	27.85	900
United States	215	2,146	847	244.3	256	78.4	458.6	1,508.77	74,100
Brazil	40	444	316	16.3	47	3.1	30.1	18.45	3,500
Chile	98	354	232	44.8	65	2.7	48.2	21.45	700

[a]Data are from International Telecommunication Union, *World Telecommunication Development Report 1999* and are per 1,000 people.
[b]Data are from the Internet Software Consortium (http://www.isc.org) and are per 10,000 people.

SOURCE: World Bank. *World Development Indicators 2000.*

have improved dramatically. Companies such as AT&T, MCI, and Sprint can now provide long-distance service to a limited degree. There are currently 40 earth stations that support the telephone system's microwave relay complex and 3 earth satellite stations. Nonetheless, many areas of the country experience telephone outages, particularly after heavy storms. There are also continuing restrictions on satellite services. The cable television system has also expanded and now includes a number of international channels such as CNN International, CNN Espanol, and MTV, as well as channels from Brazil, France, Germany, and Italy. Initiatives to increase Internet usage have broadened access and in 1999 there were 47 Internet service providers. By 2000, about 10 percent of the adult population used cellular phones (there are about 2.5 million mobile phones in use).

In 1998, total electric production was 75,237 kilowatt-hours (kWh). Fossil fuels provided 42.71 percent of production while hydroelectric sources provided 47.55 percent and nuclear power 9.47 percent. The electric industry in Argentina was deregulated in 1991, and most power distribution sources have now been privatized, although a small number remain under government control. Behind Venezuela, Argentina has the second-largest proven reserves of natural gas in South America with 24 trillion cubic feet. The country also has significant oil reserves (2.8 billion barrels) and produces about 900,000 barrels of crude oil per day.

ECONOMIC SECTORS

Argentina has a mixed economy that has well-developed agricultural, industrial, and service sectors. From the 1930s well into the 1970s, there was a con-

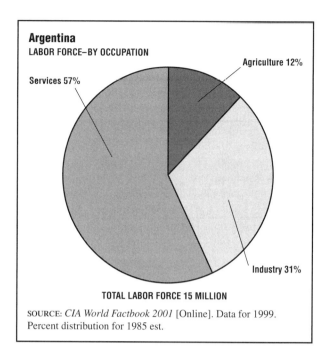

Argentina
LABOR FORCE–BY OCCUPATION

Services 57%
Agriculture 12%
Industry 31%

TOTAL LABOR FORCE 15 MILLION

SOURCE: *CIA World Factbook 2001* [Online]. Data for 1999. Percent distribution for 1985 est.

centrated effort to develop industries and expand industrial capacity. However, the economic problems of the 1970s and 1980s, combined with political instability, led to a period of decreased economic production and the decline of many of the country's major industries.

Agriculture remains a major component of Argentina's economy as crops and livestock provide much of the nation's domestic food needs. These products also provide raw materials for the growing food processing industry. Agriculture directly accounts for 7 percent of the nation's GDP. The agriculture sector is driven by the export of crops and livestock. This makes the sector vulnerable to economic problems with Argentina's main trading partners. In the past, Argentine livestock production suffered from problems with diseases such as hoof-and-mouth disease, as well as restrictions on imports by nations such as the United States. Beginning in the 1980s, agriculture in Argentina began to diversify beyond the traditional products such as beef and sheep. Many food-based oils and specialty crops are now raised. In addition to beef, some of Argentina's main agricultural products include sunflower seeds, lemons, soybeans, grapes, corn, tobacco, peanuts, tea, and wheat. Fishing has declined significantly in recent years as decades of over-fishing have limited stocks of the most popular catches.

Industry in Argentina is diversified and driven by a large and relatively affluent domestic market. Only recently has the nation begun to export significant amounts of manufactured or finished products. Argentina's membership in MERCOSUR has been one of the main factors driving industrial exports as it has expanded access to existing markets and opened new markets. Industry ac-

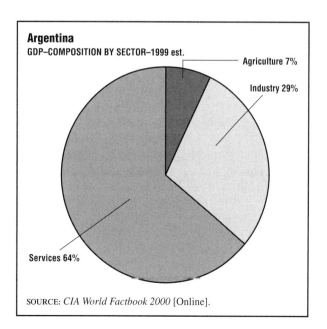

Argentina
GDP–COMPOSITION BY SECTOR–1999 est.

Agriculture 7%
Industry 29%
Services 64%

SOURCE: *CIA World Factbook 2000* [Online].

counts for 29 percent of GDP. As a result of economic problems in Brazil, industrial production growth in Argentina declined by 7 percent in 1999, but rebounded in 2000 by posting a modest level of growth of 2 percent. Among the main industries in Argentina are food processing, automobile production, textiles, energy production, and mining. The nation also has a growing chemical industry.

The service sector is now the leading component of the Argentine economy. In 1999, it accounted for 64 percent of GDP. Much of the growth in the service sector has been the result of the economic liberalizations of the 1980s and 1990s. Several key sectors, including telecommunications and financial services, have seen dramatic expansions as foreign companies have invested in these areas, and there been an increase in domestic consumer demand. While many segments of the service sector have experienced growth, the economic problems of the late 1990s led to declines in other areas. For instance, **retail** and wholesale businesses have seen little or no growth as consumer spending has been constrained by the most recent recession.

AGRICULTURE

Argentine agriculture has experienced a period of transition and diversification over the past decade. Traditional products such as beef and sheep have declined in relative value while newer products such as food oils have grown in popularity with farmers. Argentina is the world's fifth-largest producer of food and beef. It is also the world's largest producer of lemons and lemon juice and the largest producer of olive oil in South America. Finally, the nation is also one of the world's main producers of wheat and flour.

In 1998, the total value of agricultural exports was US$13.25 billion and the total value of imports was US$1.73 billion. In 2000, about 12 percent of the population was employed by agriculture. Agricultural workers earn an average of about US$400 per month, which is twice the national minimum wage. There are 40 million hectares devoted to agriculture in Argentina, of which 20–25 million hectares are used for grains and crops, while the rest is used for livestock grazing. In 2000, there were approximately 420,000 farms in the nation. However, the largest 10 percent of farms accounted for more than 50 percent of total production.

CROPS. Since the early 1990s, agricultural production has increased dramatically, although there was a brief period of decline in 1999 when output fell by 4.7 percent. With that exception, production increased by an average of 10 percent per year during the 1990s. Lower demand for Argentine products by the nation's MERCOSUR partners may continue to constrain exports, but new access

to markets in Europe and the United States has provided outlets for increases in production. The main crops include bananas, barley, potatoes, rice, sugar cane, soy beans and soy bean oil, corn, wheat, lemon juice, and sunflower seed oil. On average, each year Argentina produces about 200,000 tons of cotton, although the domestic market only uses about 80,000 tons. Total crop production in 1999 was 70.68 million metric tons. The largest crop yields were sugar cane at 19.4 million metric tons, soybeans at 18 million metric tons, wheat at 14.5 million metric tons, and corn at 13.18 million metric tons.

LIVESTOCK. The main livestock products include beef and veal, chicken, duck, goose, horse, lamb, pork, and turkey. Argentina's geographic position makes it ideally suited for raising livestock. In most areas of the country, cattle and sheep may graze year round. Livestock accounts for about 85 percent of exports.

Argentine farms have some 53.6 million head of cattle. Each year the nation exports about 460,000 tons of beef. However, much of the beef production is consumed domestically; Argentina has the highest per capita beef consumption in Latin America, with an average annual consumption of 60 kilograms per person. Sheep and pig farming is also extensive. There are 21.6 million sheep in Argentina and 5 million pigs, but most pork production is for domestic consumption. The nation also produces 660,000 tons of poultry products each year.

Argentina is noted for its horses and has an international reputation for producing exceptional racing and show horses. There are some 3.3 million horses in the country. Besides producing thoroughbreds for competition, there is also extensive use of horses on ranches and farms as work animals.

The dairy sector is one of the strongest segments of agriculture. In 2000, dairy products were worth US$4.685 billion. Exports of dairy products totaled US$400 million that same year. Growth in the dairy sector was 4 percent in 2000, and it is expected to increase by at least 2 percent annually. In addition to milk and cheeses, a number of novelty products are produced, including cream cheese, frozen yogurt, ice cream, and specialty cheeses.

FISHING. Argentina is among the world's top 20 fishing nations. Fishing accounts for about US$1.2 billion annually and total yearly catches often exceed 640,000 tons. Since the 1970s, fishing catches have increased by 400 percent. This has led to dramatic over-fishing and international efforts to limit catches on some species, mainly swordfish. Argentina is party to a number of international agreements which are designed to limit fishing and preserve species. However, the richness of the nation's coastal waters has led many fishing vessels, both Argentine and foreign-owned, to illegally over-fish many species, including swordfish and hake. Since the 1970s, the number of Argentines engaged in fishing has decreased by about 30 percent.

Hake is the most common catch and accounts for 60 percent of total harvests. Although Argentina is at the extreme southern range of swordfish, these fish are among the most valuable species caught. At its height, the swordfish industry routinely had annual catches of 500 tons; however, during the 1980s catches fell to 350 tons because of over-fishing. From 1993–1997, catches were down to the point that exports ceased entirely. Current production has risen again to 350 tons (where it has stabilized over the past few years) and exports have resumed.

FORESTRY. Forestry accounts for only a small portion of the Argentine economy. Wood is mainly used as a building material and as a fuel source for rural Argentines. There are 59.5 million hectares (147 million acres) of timberland in the country. The main trees that are commonly harvested are elm, willow, oak, pine, and cypress. Cedar is harvested in small quantities for furniture manufacturing. White quebracho is often harvested for use as fuel wood and red quebracho is widely used to produce tannin for the tanning industry.

INDUSTRY

Industry in Argentina is highly developed and diversified. Argentine workers are skilled and educated, but recently labor costs have exceeded increases in production. As a result, many industries are no longer profitable since foreign manufacturers are able to produce the same items at a much lower cost due to their lower labor costs. Efforts to reform the nation's labor system by reducing the corruption of some unions have been unsuccessful. In addition, high interest rates, currently about 15 percent, make it difficult for domestic companies to get loans in order to **restructure** their operations. Nonetheless, many industries, including the chemical sector and energy production, remain profitable and have experienced growth. Argentina's geographic position allows it easy access to markets in Brazil and surrounding nations, and the country's rich natural resources provide the basis for continued expansions in certain industries. In 2000, 23 percent of Argentines worked in industry. The average wage for industrial workers is US$870 per month or about 4 times the national minimum wage.

FOOD PROCESSING. The food processing industry takes advantage of the country's rich agricultural resources. Processed food products are consumed domestically and exported to Argentina's MERCOSUR partners and to markets in east Asia. In 1999, exports totaled US$89 million. Brazil alone accounts for 48 percent of Argentine processed food exports to MERCOSUR countries, followed by Uruguay at 19 percent, Chile at 17 percent, and Paraguay at 15 percent. Food processing accounts for about one-quarter of the total value of industrial production or about US$25 billion. Among the main segments of the industry are meat-packing, prepared dairy products, prepared fruits and vegetables, and cooking fats and oils.

MANUFACTURING. Many of the main areas of the Argentine manufacturing sector have gone through economic difficulties that began in the late 1990s. The textile industry has been hardest hit. Since the 1980s, it has been undergoing a period of consolidation as smaller companies are bought out by larger firms. Efforts to make the sector more competitive with foreign suppliers have not been successful since the international firms have significantly lower labor costs.

A significant force in Argentine industry is automobile manufacturing. A number of international car companies have plants in Argentina which produce a variety of vehicles that range from passenger cars and light trucks to buses and commercial trucks. Ford, General Motors (GM), Volkswagen, Renault, Fiat, and Peugeot all produce passenger cars, while Ford and Mercedes Benz produce buses and truck chasses. By 1999, total annual production was about 350,000 units. Domestic growth is expected to average 10 percent per year over the next decade. MERCOSUR has helped spur this growth. After the establishment of the organization in 1995, Argentine exports of automobiles increased by 122 percent from 1995 to 1997. About 90 percent of exports went to Brazil. As a result of expected increases in production, several companies are planning major investments in new facilities. For instance, Ford is investing US$1 billion in new plants to manufacture Escorts and Ranger light trucks. Meanwhile, Toyota has begun construction of a US$150 million plant to produce small cars. Total foreign investments from 1995 to 2000 were US$8.53 billion.

MINERALS AND MINING. Argentina has a variety of mineral resources. It has significant reserves of natural gas and oil, and has stocks of valuable minerals such as gold, copper, and iron. Argentina's natural gas sector is now privately owned, after the state **monopoly** Gas del Estado was split into a number of private companies in 1992. The largest pipeline company in Argentina (and all of South America) is TGS, which is 70 percent-owned by the U.S. company Enron. It provides two-thirds of Argentina's natural gas consumption. Many international companies have entered the Argentine oil market. Chevron, BP Amoco, Shell, Unocal, and the French-based company Total all have a presence in the country and seek to expand operations as exploration continues offshore on the country's continental shelf. The Argentine company Repsol-YPF accounts for about 50 percent of the country's total refining capacity, followed by Shell at 17 percent, and Esso at 16 percent. The remaining production is divided among 4 small companies. YPF has

US$6 billion in annual revenues and plans to invest US$15 billion over the next decade in new oil exploration. By 1999, total oil production was 900,000 barrels per day, with exports of 372,000 barrels per day.

In 2000, total mining exports were US$1 billion. Estimates are that this figure will grow to US$2.3 billion by 2004, as total investments in mining are expected to reach US$5 billion by 2005. Major minerals include gold, lead, silver, uranium, iron, and zinc. In 1998, gold production amounted to 19,459 kilograms. Copper production was 170,273 metric tons, lead was 15,004 metric tons, and zinc was 35,560 metric tons. Several major international companies are investing in new operations in Argentina. Major mining companies include Japan's NKK and the Argentine company Minera Alumbrera.

In 1994, the nation's main steel company, Aceros Zapla, was privatized. Since then, steel production has increased at an average annual rate of 4 percent. Crude steel production averages about 4.19 million metric tons. The majority of steel products, almost 90 percent, are used domestically. Argentina also produces a variety of building products that are mainly used in the domestic market. Forest and timber plantations cover some 1 million hectares and produce mainly softwoods that are used to make plywood and other composite building materials. Declines in construction have hurt the building materials industry which has been operating at only 57 percent of capacity since 1997. Although the construction industry has been in decline, industrial production of building materials has increased—mainly as a result of exports. Production of cement in 1999 amounted to 6.9 million metric tons. However, two of Argentina's main cement companies, Loma Negra and Juan Minetti, are set to dramatically increase production. For instance, Juan Minetti is building a US$90 million plant that will allow the manufacturer to increase its production to 1.2 million metric tons of cement per year.

CHEMICALS. The chemical industry in Argentina is one of the main segments of the nation's economy. Chemical production accounts for about 3 percent of GDP, or about US$10.75 billion in annual output. There are 2,300 chemical companies in Argentina. Of these, about 150 are considered to be medium or large in size (employing more than 100 people). In 1999 there were 64,410 people employed by chemical companies. While many other segments of the nation's economy have experienced little or no growth since the late 1990s, the chemical industry has had an average annual growth rate of 3.5 percent and an average growth rate of 3 percent in exports. Consumer demand has outpaced domestic production, however, and imports of chemicals rose 18.5 percent in 2000. Among the main chemical products are plastics and resins, especially those used in the production of manufactured products.

SERVICES

The Argentine service sector includes a variety of different types of businesses and companies. The most prominent segments of the sector include financial services, retail, and tourism. In 2000, 69 percent of Argentines worked in the service sector. On average, workers in the service sector earn US$710 per month, or about 3.5 times the minimum wage. Workers in the financial services sector are the highest paid in Argentina and earn an average monthly wage of US$1,840, while telecommunications workers earn an average of US$990 per month.

FINANCIAL SERVICES. Financial services and insurance now account for 8 percent of GDP. After decades of financial instability, the Argentine banking sector has begun to experience growth and has gained credibility in international financial markets. Government reforms of the sector have dramatically increased its competitiveness. The most significant reform was the 1991 Convertibility Law, which fixed the peso to the dollar and ultimately lowered inflation to around 1 percent. Insolvency among debtors has kept consumer interest rates at a high 15 to 25 percent.

There was a significant period of consolidation in Argentine banking, and the number of banks declined from 206 in 1994 to 132 in 1998. The 20 largest banks in Argentina accounted for 75 percent of the nation's total bank deposits. Total deposits in 1999 exceeded US$80 billion, which marked a dramatic rise from 1995 when deposits hit a record low of US$37 billion. There are 31 major international banks in Argentina with 374 branches. The largest include American Express, Bank of America, Bank Boston, Chase Manhattan, ABN Amro, Deutsche Bank, Lloyds Bank, and Hong Kong and Shanghai Bank (HSBC). Six of the nation's 10 largest banks are American or European. The largest domestic commercial bank is Banco de la Nacion, which is government-owned. Efforts to privatize the bank have met with widespread opposition because of the potential for lay-offs.

Part of the growth in the financial sector has been spurred by government programs which established privatized pension plans. In 1997, total private pension assets amounted to 2 percent of GDP, or about US$6 billion. By 2010, this figure is expected to rise to US$118 billion. Since privatization, the insurance sector has increased by an average of 10 percent per year. From 1998 to 2000, the total value of the Argentine market increased from US$570 million to US$660 million. Foreign companies have increased their presence in Argentina, with U.S. firms providing US$200 million worth of insurance-related services.

RETAIL. The retail sector in Argentina has experienced a period of decline since 1998. The country's economic slowdown has constrained consumer spending. However, some segments—including restaurants and certain retail franchises—have undergone continued growth. Small markets and family-owned retail outlets have gradually been replaced by larger chain stores. By 2000, about 80 percent of the nation's food and beverage sales were through supermarkets and large chain outlets. Argentina now has a number of major international hypermarkets (large stores which sell a variety of products, including food, clothing, hardware, and pharmaceuticals). Examples of these international hypermarkets in Argentina include Wal-Mart, Carrefour, Ahold Casino, and Makro. There are now 54 different chains in the nation. There are 10 Wal-Marts with combined sales in 2000 of US$300 million. The largest hypermarket is the French-owned chain Carrefour, which has 162 stores and sales of US$2.6 billion. In 2000, there were also 1,240 superstores, 12,861 supermarkets, 100,884 grocery stores and 5,230 convenience stores.

One of the strongest segments of the retail market remains computer and computer equipment sales. In 2000, these products had sales of US$1.74 billion. The computer market is expected to increase by 10 percent annually over the next decade. U.S.-brand products account for 67 percent of the market. The leading U.S. firms are Compaq, Hewlett Packard, and IBM. Besides personal computers, the best selling products include printers, laptop computers, CD-ROM drives, hard drives, and memory expansion kits.

There are more than 30,000 restaurants in Argentina, about one-third of which are located in Buenos Aires. Despite the economic slowdown of the late 1990s, restaurant sales have averaged 10 percent growth over the past decade. The largest restaurant chain is Arcos Dorados, which operates McDonald's franchises. There are 160 McDonald's with average annual sales of US$230 million. Burger King is the second-largest chain with 25 stores and US$25 million in sales. Wendy's is number 3 and also has 25 stores and just under US$25 million in annual sales. The most profitable Argentine-owned restaurant chain is the La Caballeriza steak house, which has 4 restaurants and US$10 million in revenues. Almost 6 percent of total family income is spent dining out.

TOURISM. In 2000, the tourist sector provided US$1.57 billion to the Argentine economy. This represented a 4 percent increase from the previous year. In 2000, 5 million foreign tourists visited Argentina. The nation has almost 6,000 hotels, 1,600 of which are located in Buenos Aires. Buenos Aires is the tourist capital of the country and accounts for 73 percent of the tourist trade. Many foreign tourists also visit the Argentine coastline and the southern region of the nation, Patagonia. A variety of international hotel firms have outlets in Argentina. The nation's largest hotelier is Sheraton, which has US$60 million in annual

sales. The second-largest hotelier is Marriott, with annual sales of US$9 million. Despite the nation's recession, tourism grew by 1 percent in 1999. As the economy recovers, tourism is expected to expand by 11 percent per year. In 1999, there were 18 different high-level hotel construction projects underway.

INTERNATIONAL TRADE

Growth in foreign trade, especially trade with MERCOSUR partners, has been one of the main factors driving the Argentine economy. In 1990, 11 percent of the nation's GDP was tied to foreign trade; by 1999 that figure had grown to 17 percent. Exports account for 7 percent of GDP. Lower tariffs and improvements in domestic industries have helped decrease the nation's trade deficit, which fell from US$5 billion in 1998 to US$2.2 billion in 1999. In 1999 exports declined by 12 percent, while imports fell by 19 percent. Argentina has a large trade deficit with the United States. In 1999 it amounted to US$2.4 billion.

In 1999 Argentina's main export partners were Brazil with 24 percent of exports, the EU with 21 percent, and the United States with 11 percent. Its main import partners were the EU with 28 percent of imports, the United States with 22 percent, and Brazil with 21 percent. Increases in exports of beef and oil have helped drive exports. Following a brief period when beef exports were banned by several countries because of the potential for hoof-and-mouth disease, exports of beef and beef products have met or exceeded export quotas.

MERCOSUR serves as the main outlet for Argentine exports. In addition to Argentina, Brazil, Paraguay, and Uruguay, the trade organization now includes Chile and Bolivia as associate members. Brazil is the dominant economic force in MERCOSUR and accounts for 70 percent of the organization's GDP, while Argentina accounts for 27 percent. Intra-MERCOSUR trade rose from US$4 billion in 1991 to US$23 billion in 1998. Much of the in-

Trade (expressed in billions of US$): Argentina		
	Exports	Imports
1975	2.961	3.947
1980	8.021	10.541
1985	8.396	3.814
1990	12.353	4.076
1995	20.967	20.122
1998	25.227	31.402

SOURCE: International Monetary Fund. *International Financial Statistics Yearbook 1999.*

crease in trade has been the result of decreases in tariffs. Almost 90 percent of intra-MERCOSUR trade is now **duty**-free, but there are still substantial tariffs on goods imported from outside MERCOSUR. Approximately 85 percent of imported goods are subject to tariffs.

Argentina has initiated negotiations to enter into trade agreements with the EU, Mexico, and the Andean Pact (an economic organization of South American nations which includes Bolivia, Colombia, Ecuador, Peru, and Venezuela). It has also been supportive of the effort to develop a Free Trade Area of the Americas (FTAA) which would bring all of the nations of the Western Hemisphere together in a free trade organization. In 1994 the United States and Argentina signed a bilateral investment agreement which allows U.S. companies to invest in most sectors of the Argentine economy on the same basis as domestic companies. Argentina has trade treaties with 56 other nations.

Since Argentina fixed its currency to the U.S. dollar, it has become much more attractive for foreign investment. Spain is the largest investor in Argentina. The United States is the number two investor, and by 1999 direct U.S. investment was US$16 billion. U.S. investments are concentrated in manufacturing (at US$3.65 billion), finance, banking, and real estate (at US$3.8 billion) and petroleum (at US$1.565 billion).

Another broad effort to attract international trade has been the establishment of **free trade zones**. There are 3 large zones and a number of minor areas. The largest of these is the La Plata Free Trade Zone, which was established in 1997. The zone is close to Buenos Aires and has 500 meters of dock, 400,000 square meters of warehouse space, and 5,000 square meters of office space. La Plata has 1,942 different commercial users. The largest companies in the zone include Sharp, Pioneer, Daewoo, Ford, General Motors, Nike, Nissan, Mazda, and Zenith.

MONEY

Throughout much of the latter half of the twentieth century, Argentina was plagued by a weak currency and high inflation. In 1985, in an effort to fight inflation, which had reached 2,000 percent, the government replaced the nation's traditional currency (the peso) with a new currency called the austral. One austral equaled 1,000 pesos. However, inflation continued to rise. In 1989, inflation reached 5,000 percent, making the nation's currency almost worthless. In response, the government again changed the currency in 1992, replacing the austral with the nuevo peso Argentino (new Argentine peso). One nuevo peso was equal to 10,000 australs. Inflation was finally brought under control when the government fixed the nuevo peso to the dollar at a one-for-

Exchange rates: Argentina	
Argentine peso per US$1	
2001	1.000
2000	1.000
1999	1.000
1998	1.000
1997	1.000
1996	1.000

Note: The exchange rate is pegged to the US dollar.

SOURCE: CIA *World Factbook 2001* [ONLINE].

one **exchange rate**. While this almost completely wiped out inflation, it also meant that the government has little control over the value of its currency. After the currency was pegged to the dollar, it once again became simply known as the "peso."

The Argentine peso is fixed at one-for-one exchange rate with the U.S. dollar. While the dollar fluctuates freely on world markets, it has brought a significant degree of monetary stability to the Argentine currency and economy.

The nation's currency and banking system are overseen by the Argentine Central Bank, which was established in 1935. The Central Bank maintains currency reserves of US$25 billion, which would cover 9 months of imports. The bank has also arranged a US$7 billion emergency fund that is financed by international organizations and international banks. This fund may be used to protect the nation's financial stability. High interest rates continue to constrain the economy. On average, banks charge 10 percent interest to preferred business customers while consumers pay interest rates of between 15 to 25 percent.

The Buenos Aires Stock Exchange (BASE) was established in 1854. It is the oldest in Latin America. By 1996, BASE had a total **market capitalization** of US$45 billion and had 147 companies listed. The exchange is dominated by 3 companies—YPF, Telefonica, and Telecom—which together account for 50 percent of the total market.

POVERTY AND WEALTH

There are deep disparities in income and wealth in Argentina. In 2000, the richest 10 percent of the population earned 36 percent of the country's income, while the poorest 10 percent earned 1.5 percent of income. About 36 percent of the population lives below the poverty line. The nation's poverty level is US$490 per month for a family of 4. The average wage in the nation is US$676 per month, which is more than 3 times the national minimum wage. About 60 percent of workers earn less than

GDP per Capita (US$)

Country	1975	1980	1985	1990	1998
Argentina	7,317	7,793	6,354	5,782	8,475
United States	19,364	21,529	23,200	25,363	29,683
Brazil	3,464	4,253	4,039	4,078	4,509
Chile	1,842	2,425	2,345	2,987	4,784

SOURCE: United Nations. *Human Development Report 2000; Trends in human development and per capita income.*

US$450 per month. About 20 percent of the population only lives on US$2 per day. As many as 8 million Argentineans work in the **informal sector**, or **black market**. In some areas of the country, the black market accounts for 60 percent of economic activity. These types of economic activities include personal service jobs (people who work as plumbers, electricians, domestic servants, and so forth). People who work in this informal sector also run small, unregulated shops and restaurants. Since these jobs are unregulated by the government, people do not pay taxes on their income and are therefore able to earn higher pay.

Government estimates are that 11 percent of the population cannot meet their basic food needs. Poverty rates are about 20 percent higher in the rural areas than they are in the urban areas. In the greater Buenos Aires metropolitan area the poverty rate is 29.8 percent, while in the subtropical jungle areas of the Northeast, the rate is 60 percent. The second-poorest area of the country is the mountainous region of the Northwest where the poverty rate is 53.6 percent.

Women make up a larger share of the poor. They comprise a large percentage (60 percent) of those employed in part-time or low-skill (and therefore low-paying) jobs. In overall terms, their poverty rates are twice as high as males. Children also have higher rates of poverty than the national average. About 50 percent of children under the age of 14 live in poverty.

WORKING CONDITIONS

The Argentine workforce numbers approximately 15 million (this includes those working or actively seeking employment). About 60 percent of the workforce is male. In 2000, the unemployment rate was 15.4 percent. The unemployment rate was highest in urban areas, and in Buenos Aires it was close to 18 percent. In addition to the high unemployment level, Argentina has a significant **underemployment** rate.

The nation's constitution guarantees workers the right to form unions, although union membership has steadily declined in Argentina. During the 1950s, about 50 percent of the workforce was unionized. However, by 2000, only about 35 percent of the workforce belonged to unions. For much of their modern history, unions were associated with Peron and during the early 1970s, Peronists accounted for 70 percent of union leadership. During the military regime that began in the late 1970s, the unions were purged of Peronists. Unions remain very active and in 2000 2 general, nationwide strikes virtually shut down most government and many private businesses. These strikes were in response to government labor reform laws. Foreign companies have found Argentina's labor market to be inflexible and expensive. Companies have to pay employees a month's salary for each year the employee has worked in cases of lay-offs, and labor agreements often forbid the transfer of employees from location to location or from job to job. Corruption in labor and government has often resulted in foreign firms being forced to pay large bribes in order to do business. One of the most celebrated cases occurred in 1994 when IBM officials were forced to pay millions in bribes in exchange for a US$249 million contract to provide computers for the Banco de la Nacion.

The national minimum wage is US$200 per month, but most workers earn more. All Argentinean workers are entitled to an annual bonus that is equal to 1 month's pay. This bonus is paid in 2 installments in June and December. The maximum work week is 48 hours and the max-

Household Consumption in PPP Terms

Country	All food	Clothing and footwear	Fuel and power[a]	Health care[b]	Education[b]	Transport & Communications	Other
Argentina	30	9	17	15	15	5	9
United States	13	9	9	4	6	8	51
Brazil	22	13	18	15	34	4	−6
Chile	17	10	24	20	15	6	9

Data represent percentage of consumption in PPP terms.
[a]Excludes energy used for transport.
[b]Includes government and private expenditures.

SOURCE: World Bank. *World Development Indicators 2000.*

imum workday is 8 hours. Work done beyond these limitations must be paid an overtime rate of 1.5 times salary. All workers receive annual vacation time which ranges between 14 and 35 days per year. Since 1995, average wages for Argentine workers have increased by 5 percent. Employers must contribute payments to workers' pension and health-care plans that equal 33 percent of the worker's salary. Individual workers make payments that equal 17 percent of their salary for these social guarantees. The retirement age is 60 for women and 65 for men. Upon retirement, workers receive a social security payment known as the "basic universal benefit." In order to qualify, employees must have worked a minimum of 30 years. Many workers have chosen to invest in the nation's private pension plans that pay an average of 20 percent per year more than the basic universal benefit.

Children under the age of 15 are not allowed to work, except in rare circumstances, usually on family farms. Government permits must be granted for these exceptions. Children between the ages of 15 and 18 may work up to 6 hours per day and a maximum of 35 hours per week. Studies have revealed that about 5 percent of children under the age of 15 are illegally employed. Women face discrimination in hiring and wages. On average, women earn about 70 percent of what their male counterparts earn in similar occupations. Only 12 percent of the executives of the nation's largest companies are female.

COUNTRY HISTORY AND ECONOMIC DEVELOPMENT

1580. The Spanish establish a permanent colony in what is now Buenos Aires.

1776. Buenos Aires, a flourishing port, is made the seat of the newly established Vice Royalty of Rio de la Plata. The population of the Vice Royalty reaches 20,000.

1816. Jose de San Martin leads the struggle for independence in Argentina, Chile, and Peru. Argentina gains full independence and is initially called the United Provinces of the Rio de la Plata.

1819–20. Civil war between those Argentines who favor a strong central government and those who advocate a federal system with the provinces retaining significant political power.

1829. General Juan Manuel de Rosas is elected president. He institutes a federal system and the country's name is changed to the Argentine Confederation.

1853. Rosas is overthrown and a new constitution is promulgated. The nation changes its name to the Argentine Republic.

1879–80. The War of the Desert between Argentine troops and settlers and Native Americans ends with an Argentine victory. The suppression of the Native American tribes opens up the interior regions of the country for settlement by Europeans and greatly expands the area under agricultural cultivation.

1916. The period of conservative control of Argentina is ended following the election of a Radical Civic Union (URC) candidate as president.

1930. President Hipolito Yrigoyen of the URC party is overthrown by a military coup.

1943. A coup brings Juan Peron to power as part of a military government.

1946. Juan Peron is elected president.

1947. Peron announces the first of his 5-year economic plans. Women gain the right to vote.

1949. A new constitution is promulgated.

1952. Peron is reelected in an election marred by corruption and irregularities. Evita Peron dies from cancer.

1953. The government implements the second 5-year economic plan. Under this plan a number of commercial trade treaties are signed, including accords with Great Britain, Chile, and the Soviet Union. These agreements lead to a favorable balance of trade, but inflation rises to 200 percent and prompts widespread economic problems.

1955. The military ousts Peron from power in a civil war in which at least 4,000 people are killed.

1956. The constitution of 1949 is rescinded and the nation reverts to the 1853 constitution.

1959. The nation begins receiving substantial foreign loans and economic aid. By the following year, Argentina has received US$1 billion from the United States alone. These loans help maintain economic stability and high wages in spite of growing inflation.

1960–1980. Argentina is a member of the Latin American Free Trade Association (LAFTA). During this period, Argentine trade with other nations in Latin America expands significantly.

1973. Argentina has general elections which return Peron to power with his third wife as vice-president.

1974. Peron dies in office and is succeeded by his wife, Maria Estela.

1975. There is increasing instability in the nation as terrorist activities by both left-wing and right-wing extremist groups claim the lives of some 700 people in a one-year span. After inflation reaches 335 percent, there are widespread strikes and unrest as workers seek higher wages.

1976. The military again takes power and the constitution is once again rescinded. From 1976 to 1983 10,000 people "disappear" (the majority are secretly taken prisoner by the government and tortured and killed).

1980. The Latin American Integration Association (LAIA) replaces LAFTA. LAIA initiates a number of agreements which reduce tariffs between Latin American nations.

1982. Argentina is defeated by the United Kingdom in the Falkland Islands war after Argentine forces invade and conquer the territory known to the Argentines as the Malvinas Islands.

1983. The nation has democratic elections after popular pressure forces the military to cede power. Raul Alfonsin of the URC is elected president and the constitution is reinstated.

1989. Carlos Menem of the Peronist Party is elected president.

1990. A dramatic period of decline in the fisheries sector begins and, by 1993, exports of swordfish cease entirely and are not resumed until 1998.

1991. Reforms are initiated that ultimately fix the peso to the U.S. dollar. Laws are enacted to liberalize the telecommunications industry.

1992. Diplomatic and trade relations, which had been severed as a result of the Falkland Islands War, are reestablished with Great Britain.

1993. A new law liberalizes the mining sector and leads to dramatic growth in the industry.

1994. The constitution is amended. The U.S. and Argentina sign a bilateral investment treaty. All restrictions on foreign ownership of banks are rescinded.

1995. Menem is reelected president. Argentina, Brazil, Chile, Uruguay, and Paraguay join together in a free trade agreement known as MERCOSUR.

1997. The United States allows imports of Argentine beef for the first time in 60 years. The government initiates a program to establish a number of free trade zones in order to increase trade.

1999. Fernando de la Rua of the Alliance is elected president. Argentina assumes the chairmanship of the Free Trade Area of the Americas (FTAA) Negotiating

Committee. The nation undergoes a recession in which GDP drops 3 percent and exports by 25 percent.

2000. Argentina and Brazil negotiate new agreements that strengthen MERCOSUR by further lowering trade barriers.

2001. The recession continues. Unemployment rises to approximately 20 percent. In mid-December, 2 days of rioting sweep the nation and lead to President de la Rua's resignation. Predictions are made that the Argentine government soon will default on debts totaling almost US$100 billion.

FUTURE TRENDS

Argentina has undergone a dramatic economic transformation since the early 1980s. Throughout most of the second half of the 1900s, Argentina suffered from high inflation and economic instability. Although the population was generally well paid and GDP per capita was among the highest in Latin America, inflation eroded the value of employees' wages. Corruption and inefficiency also plagued Argentine companies. Inflation reached a crisis level in the 1980s, and forced the nation to acquire a large **foreign debt** in order to maintain living standards. When Argentina fixed its currency to the U.S. dollar, it began a period of economic recovery, which continues. Government efforts to reduce expenditures and privatize many state-owned businesses also helped spur economic growth. The nation's economy is now well-placed to compete with other countries and to expand Argentina's share of international trade.

While the most significant economic reforms have already been implemented, there remains the need for a number of other structural readjustments. In overall terms, Argentine workers are not as productive as their counterparts in countries such as Brazil or Chile. The nation's workers are high-paid, however, and this means that labor costs in Argentina are high when compared to other nations in MERCOSUR. In addition, a number of state-owned companies, including the country's largest bank, still need to be privatized. Long-term economic growth is also dependent on the elimination of the government's annual deficit and reductions in the **national debt**.

Membership in MERCOSUR and other economic organizations will continue to expand Argentine foreign trade. International support and aid for Argentina, including loans from the World Bank and the International Monetary Fund, have alleviated some of the pressure of the large national debt, but further assistance is necessary to ensure continued economic growth. The reform and partial privatization of the nation's pension system has increased the capital available to companies to invest in new equipment and new products. In addition, the establishment of free trade zones has lured a significant amount of foreign investment and a number of foreign companies to Argentina. These factors should allow the nation to continue its economic recovery in the wake of the recession of the late 1990s.

DEPENDENCIES

Argentina has no territories or colonies.

BIBLIOGRAPHY

Coffey, Peter, editor. *Latin America: MERCOSUR.* Boston: Kluwer Academic Publishers, 1998.

Economist Intelligence Unit. *Country Profile: Argentina.* London: Economist Intelligence Unit, 2001.

Embajada Argentina en Washington D.C./Argentine Embassy in Washington D.C. <http://www.embajadaargentina-usa.org>. Accessed August 2001.

U.S. Central Intelligence Agency. *World Factbook 2000.* <http://www.odci.gov/cia/publications/factbook/index.html>. Accessed July 2001.

U.S. Department of State. *Argentina: Country Reports on Human Rights Practices, 1999.* <http://www.state.gov/g/drl/rls/hrrpt/1999/index.cfm?docid=372>. Accessed February 2001.

———*Background Notes: Argentina.* <http://www.state.gov/r/pa/bgn/index.cfm?docid=2904>. Accessed February 2001.

———*FY 2001 Country Commercial Guide: Argentina.* <http://www.state.gov/www/about_state/business/com_guides/2001/wha/index.html>. Accessed February 2001.

Whittle, Janet, et al. *Argentina Business: The Portable Encyclopedia for Doing Business With Argentina,* 2nd edition. San Rafael, CA: World Trade Press, 1998.

—Tom Lansford

THE BAHAMAS

Commonwealth of the Bahamas

CAPITAL: Nassau.

MONETARY UNIT: Bahamian dollar (B$). One Bahamian dollar equals 100 cents. The Bahamas issues bank notes of B$0.50, 1, 3, 5, 10, 20, 50, and 100. There are coins of 1, 5, 10, 15, 25, and 50 cents.

CHIEF EXPORTS: Pharmaceuticals, cement, rum, crawfish, refined petroleum products.

CHIEF IMPORTS: Foodstuffs, manufactured goods, crude oil, vehicles, electronics.

GROSS DOMESTIC PRODUCT: US$4.5 billion (purchasing power parity, 2000 est.).

BALANCE OF TRADE: Exports: US$376.8 million (2000 est.). **Imports:** US$1.73 billion (2000 est.).

combined facts give the nation an overall growth rate of 1.01 percent. By 2015, the islands are expected to have a population of 330,000.

Bahamians are primarily of African descent (85 percent). People of European ancestry make up 12 percent of the population and the remaining 3 percent is of Asian or Hispanic origin. English is the official language, and

COUNTRY OVERVIEW

LOCATION AND SIZE. The Bahamas is a chain of 700 islands and about 2,000 cays (low islands or reefs of sand or coral). However, only 29 of the islands are inhabited. The Bahamas is in the North Atlantic Ocean on the eastern edge of the Caribbean, just 72 kilometers (45 miles) southeast of Florida. It has an area of 13,939 square kilometers (5,382 square miles) and is a bit smaller than Connecticut. The islands have a total coastline of 3,542 square kilometers (1,368 square miles). The largest city in the nation is Nassau, the capital, and the second largest is Freeport.

POPULATION. The population of the Bahamas was estimated to be 294,982 in July 2000. The nation has a high birth rate with 19.54 births per 1,000 people compared with 6.81 deaths per 1,000. The fertility rate is 2.33 children born per woman. Because of the increase in AIDS, the infant mortality rate is high, with 16.99 deaths per 1,000 inhabitants. The population is young, with 30 percent under the age of 15 and only 6 percent over 65. Life expectancy is 68.25 years for men and 73.94 years for women. The rate of people moving out of the country is high at 2.67 per 1,000 people. These

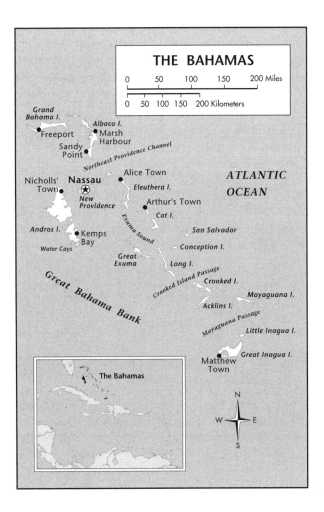

religious worship is largely Christian. The Baptist church has the biggest following (32 percent), with the Anglican, Roman Catholic, and Protestant churches well represented. The literacy rate is high, almost 100 percent.

Most Bahamians reside in urban areas, with two-thirds of the population living on New Providence Island where Nassau is located. Many others live in or near Freeport on Grand Bahama Island. There are small settlements throughout the outer islands, called the "Family Islands".

OVERVIEW OF ECONOMY

Tourism and financial services dominate the economy of the Bahamas. Tourism is the main economic sector, accounting for 60 percent of the **gross domestic product** (GDP) and employing almost half of the population. The government has undertaken extensive marketing to attract visitors and bring foreign investment to the tourist vacation industry. The importance of tourism to the Bahamas makes the nation reliant on the economic fortunes of vacation-oriented nations, particularly the United States from where most of its visitors come.

The country has benefited from its status as a **tax haven** and international banking center. To exploit this advantage, the Bahamian government has passed laws aimed at encouraging foreign companies to incorporate themselves there, and has created free trade areas where goods can be trans-shipped without being taxed. Many shipping firms use the Bahamas to register their vessels.

The mild climate of the islands and their proximity to the United States make the Bahamas an ideal tourist destination for Americans. It is also ideally situated for American companies to relocate to avoid U.S. corporate taxes. The nation is also aided by its history of political stability and the sound **infrastructure** of the main islands. However, the geographical position of the archipelago makes it vulnerable to natural disasters such as hurricanes and tropical storms.

A negative effect of the Bahamas' proximity to the United States is that international criminals often use the country as a base for their activities. The main criminal activities involve smuggling of illicit drugs, illegal immigrants, and **money laundering**. The government cooperates closely with the United States, which provides substantial aid in anti-narcotic initiatives, in attempting to counter these problems.

The nation has a small fisheries industry and exports limited quantities of lobster and other fish. The main manufacturing company is PFC Bahamas, which makes pharmaceutical products. BORCO maintains an oil refinery in the islands and several breweries in the islands produce rum and assorted beers for export to the United

States and Western Europe. Freeport has repair facilities for cruise ships.

The Bahamian government has tied its currency to the U.S. dollar, which has helped maintain economic stability. The country has been the recipient of generous foreign aid that includes bilateral assistance from nations such as the United States and the United Kingdom, and multilateral aid from organizations such as the European Union (EU).

POLITICS, GOVERNMENT, AND TAXATION

A British colony from 1717, the Bahamas was granted self-government by the British in 1964 and full independence in 1973. A parliamentary democracy and a member of the British Commonwealth of Nations, the country's traditions and its legal system closely resemble those of Great Britain. The British monarch is the chief of state and is represented in the islands by an appointed governor general. The head of the government is an elected prime minister, who presides over a **bicameral** (2-chamber) legislature consisting of the House of Assembly and the Senate. The House has 40 elected members who serve 5-year terms and the Senate consists of 16 members, also serving for 5 years, appointed by the governor general after consultation with the prime minister and the leader of the opposition.

There are 2 main political parties in the Bahamas: the Free National Movement (FNM) and the Progressive Liberal Party (PLP). The FNM has controlled the government since 1992. Its main priority has been economic development and the diversification of the economy. A related priority has been job creation, including worker retraining. As part of this effort, the government has engaged in **privatization** initiatives since 1992, which included the selling of all but one of the formerly state-owned hotels. The government-owned telecommunications company, Batelco, is being privatized and there are proposals for the sale of its national airline, Bahamasair, as well as the Bahamas Electric Company. Nonetheless, with a total workforce of 22,000, the state remains the largest employer in the islands.

As part of efforts to diversify the economy are programs to develop the fishing industry in particular, the government has opened 2 shrimp hatcheries. Government infrastructure programs also contribute to the economies of the Family Islands by providing jobs. In 1990, the government enacted the International Business Companies Act to reduce the cost to foreign companies of incorporating in the Bahamas. This is a clear success: on top of the presence of 415 banks, by 2000 84,000 companies had incorporated themselves in the Bahamas.

The Bahamas has one of the lowest levels of taxation in the world. Bahamians do not pay income or sales taxes, and there are no corporate taxes. Government revenue comes from import **duties**, business license fees, stamp duties, and departure tax. The government's budget for 2001 was US$998 million, with most funds earmarked for social services, including US$178.64 million for education and US$142.36 million for health care. US$103.86 million was given to law enforcement, most of it to be spent on measures to combat the drug trade.

The government supports efforts to reduce trade barriers in the hemisphere. It has entered into negotiations for a Free Trade Area of the Americas. However, since the majority of state revenue comes from trade **tariffs**, the government needs to develop new sources of revenue and taxation. Nonetheless, it adamantly refuses to consider any form of **income tax**.

The judiciary is independent and the legal system is based on British common law. Since independence, the Bahamian government has adopted business legislation from American models of commercial law. The legal system is fair and impartial, though many foreign companies have charged that the system is slow and often favors Bahamian companies over their competitors. Partly in response to these complaints, the government began reforms in 1993 to overhaul the system. Much of the reform effort has been funded by aid from the United States.

INFRASTRUCTURE, POWER, AND COMMUNICATIONS

The Bahamas has a good infrastructure for a developing nation and the government is engaged in a long-term program to improve roads and communications. Major road construction has been completed in Nassau and on the Family Islands, which have also benefited from improvements in their electricity systems and airports. Traffic congestion has been alleviated in Nassau and a second bridge built between Nassau and Paradise Island. The islands have 2,693 kilometers (1,673 miles) of roads, of which 1,546 kilometers (960 miles) are paved. The water systems in Nassau and the Family Islands have been upgraded.

The islands have 62 airports, but only 33 are paved and only 2 have more than 3,047 meters (9,998 feet) of paved runways, and there is 1 heliport. The 3 main seaports are in Freeport, Matthew Town, and Nassau. Regular air and sea service is available between the inhabited islands, and between the United States and the Bahamas. Since the government allows foreign ships to register themselves under the Bahamian flag, there is a large merchant marine of 1,075 ships, which includes vessels from 49 separate nations. The largest number of ships belong to Norway (177), Greece (141), and the United Kingdom (113). Turmoil in Liberia, where many companies had their vessels registered, has caused several to switch registration to the Bahamas (21 in 2000).

Telecommunication service is widely available but installation and maintenance of equipment is slow by North American standards. There are 4 Internet providers in Nassau and the Cable Bahamas company has been granted a license to establish a center to provide web hosting sites for foreign companies. The company has also announced plans to build a US$15 million fiber-optic system to create a high-speed communication system between the Bahamas and the United States.

The country is self-sufficient in electricity, which is supplied by fossil fuel. Electricity production amounted to 1.34 billion kilowatt-hours (kWh) in 1998, while consumption was 1.246 billion kWh.

Communications

Country	Telephones[a]	Telephones, Mobile/Cellular[a]	Radio Stations[b]	Radios[a]	TV Stations[a]	Televisions[a]	Internet Service Providers[c]	Internet Users[c]
Bahamas	96,000	6,152	AM 3;FM 4; shortwave 0	215,000	1	67,000	19	15,000
United States	194 M	69.209 M (1998)	AM 4,762; FM 5,542; shortwave 18	575 M	1,500	219 M	7,800	148 M
Jamaica	353,000 (1996)	54,640 (1996)	AM 10; FM 13; shortwave 0	1.215 M	7	460,000	21	60,000
St. Lucia	37,000	1,600	AM 2; FM 7; shortwave 0	111,000	3	32,000	15	5,000

[a]Data is for 1997 unless otherwise noted.
[b]Data is for 1998 unless otherwise noted.
[c]Data is for 2000 unless otherwise noted.

SOURCE: CIA *World Factbook 2001* [Online].

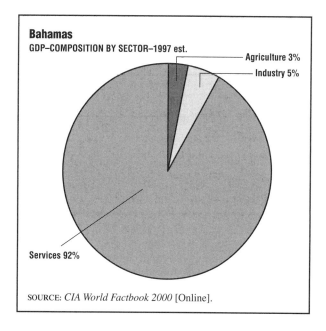

Bahamas
GDP–COMPOSITION BY SECTOR–1997 est.

Agriculture 3%

Industry 5%

Services 92%

SOURCE: *CIA World Factbook 2000* [Online].

ECONOMIC SECTORS

Most of the Bahamas' GDP comes from tourism and financial services, and there is little industry. There is, however, some production of minerals, consisting of cement, salt, sand, and gravel. One of the main labor-intensive industries is construction, which continues to expand because of the building of new housing, even as commercial construction has declined over the past few years.

Tourism is the economic backbone of the Bahamas. It provides the biggest percentage of the nation's GDP and employs more people than any other economic sec-

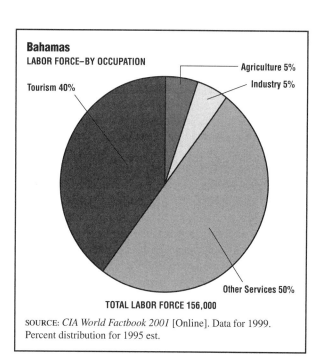

Bahamas
LABOR FORCE–BY OCCUPATION

Agriculture 5%

Industry 5%

Tourism 40%

Other Services 50%

TOTAL LABOR FORCE 156,000

SOURCE: *CIA World Factbook 2001* [Online]. Data for 1999. Percent distribution for 1995 est.

tor. Financial services form the second chief component of the economy, encompassing banking, insurance, stocks and bonds, and mutual funds.

There is about 1 percent of arable land throughout the islands but plenty of fresh water. With 32 percent of the land comprised of forest, timber is a plentiful natural resource. Most agricultural production is on Grand Bahama Island and the outer islands. While the cultivation of several crops, notably ornamental plants and citrus fruits, has expanded, the farming of poultry and livestock has declined. The government has aggressively looked for foreign investment to improve crop quality and output, while its support for fisheries has improved output and profits.

AGRICULTURE

The Bahamas is a net importer of foodstuffs, buying 80 percent of its consumables. Agriculture and fisheries make up about 5 percent of GDP and about 5 percent of employment. Also, temporary jobs become available during the harvest season and during specific fishing seasons, such as the lobster harvest. Companies have requested that they be allowed to use foreign workers during harvests but the government usually refuses such requests.

The islands' primary crops are bananas, corn, and, by far the most important, sugar cane. In 1998 sugar cane provided 45,000 metric tons of the total crop production of 46,200 metric tons. In addition, beef and veal, chicken, and pork are raised. There are 240,000 acres of land used for agriculture, mostly on the outer islands. Most farms are small and most products are for domestic consumption. Because of the 1999 hurricane season, crop output fell 16.5 percent or US$8.8 million, and poultry and meat production declined by US$6.4 million. However, the output of ornamental plants increased by 11.2 percent. Citrus production has also increased in the past few years.

There have been continued increases in fish output. Total harvests in 1999 were 6.3 million pounds with a value of US$74.1 million (a 4.3 percent increase from the previous year). Lobster or crawfish make up 88 percent of total output and rose by 23 percent in 2000. Fish production will continue to expand and diversify as the government establishes new fish farms and funds efforts to broaden harvests to new species.

INDUSTRY

In 1999, the small industrial sector of the Bahamas only made up about 5 percent of the nation's GDP and 5 percent of employment. Government infrastructure projects and private construction provide the main industrial activity. The 1 shipyard in the Bahamas is at Freeport and it specializes in the repair of passenger or cruise ships. There is limited production of minerals. Sand is dredged off the Bahamas Bank and used for limestone and the production of commercial sand, which supply the local construction industry. There is also limited production of salt for export to the United States.

The pharmaceutical company, PFC Bahamas, produces a small quantity of products for export and the oil company, BORCO, has a refinery in the islands, but these are individual enterprises and do not represent any large industrial presence. There is a substantial brewing industry. Companies such as Bacardi, Inc., distill rum and other spirits in the islands, while other international breweries such as Commonwealth Brewery, produce different beers including the Heineken, Guinness, and Kalik brands.

The construction industry seemed to peak in 1998 with the completion of several new resorts. By 1999, new construction projects had fallen by 15.9 percent, with 817 continuing commercial projects valued at US$123 million. However, private housing completions were up by 18.3 percent with a value of US$112.1 million. This reflects an increasing demand for more upscale housing in the nation.

SERVICES

Tourism dominates the Bahamian economy. In 1999, 3.65 million people visited the islands, with 2.2 million of them arriving by cruise ship. Revenue from tourism made up 60 percent of the nation's GDP. The average tourist spent US$958 while vacationing in the Bahamas, and tourist spending overall amounted to US$1.5 billion. In 2000, there were about 81,700 people employed in the tourist industry. Most visitors are from the United States (83 percent in 1999). However, in recent years the number of European tourists has increased by 9 percent.

The largest resort in the island is the 2,340 room mega-resort Atlantis, which is owned by Sun International. It employs 5,500 people and is the second largest employer in the nation after the government. Other major resorts in the islands include Club Med (popular with the French), Sandals (attracting the British), and Holiday Inn. The Grand Bahama Development Company plans to spend US$50 million upgrading airport and cruise ship facilities to accommodate an additional 555,000 visitors per year.

Although the majority of the tourist industry in the Bahamas has been driven by private enterprise, the Bahamian government did own 20 percent of the hotel accommodations in 1992. Privatization programs since that time have reduced the government holdings to 5 percent.

All major cruise lines operate services to the Bahamas. To extend the stay of passengers, the government has enacted legislation that allows ships to open their casinos and stores only if they remain in port for more than 18 hours.

Thanks to the tourist trade, **retail** companies prosper in the Bahamas. There is a strong preference for rec-

ognizable name-brand products, and major American brands do well in the islands. However, the government requires that retail and wholesale businesses be Bahamian-owned.

In 1995, the government changed laws to allow betting on sporting events. Gambling is permitted on events both in the Bahamas and elsewhere in the world. The same law also lowered the taxes on winnings in casinos that are smaller than 10,000 square feet, which has resulted in the proliferation of sports bars and small casinos.

The financial services sector is the second chief component of the Bahamian economy. In 1998, this sector added US$300 million to the economy and employed 4,000 people, accounting for some 15 percent of the GDP. Government legislation has also encouraged the formation of international companies known as shell corporations, which are established to hide or protect their assets from national taxes at home by incorporating themselves in a foreign nation. As a result there are over 100,000 such corporations. Although many of these firms employ Bahamians, they add little to the nation's economy since they essentially act as conduits for transferring money.

INTERNATIONAL TRADE

The Bahamian economy is dependent on trade with the United States. Most of the tourists that visit the nation are from the United States, and there are 110 American-owned businesses in the islands. In addition, 55 percent of Bahamian imports come from the United States, and American distributors also handle many of the nation's other imports. Other than the United States, which supplies 27.3 percent of Bahamians imports, the Bahamas' other main import partners are Italy with 26.5 percent, Japan with 10 percent, and Denmark with 4.2 percent. The country's main export partners are the United States at 22.3 percent, Switzerland at 15.6 percent, the United Kingdom at 15 percent, and Denmark at 7.4 percent. In 1998, the Bahamas had exports of US$300 million and imports of US$1.87 billion.

Trade (expressed in billions of US$): Bahamas		
	Exports	Imports
1975	2.508	2.697
1980	5.009	7.546
1985	2.707	3.078
1990	.241	1.112
1995	.176	1.243
1998	.300	1.872

SOURCE: International Monetary Fund. *International Financial Statistics Yearbook 1999.*

Exchange rates: Bahamas

Bahamian dollar (B$) per US$1

2001	1.000
2000	1.000
1999	1.000
1998	1.000
1997	1.000
1996	1.000

Note: Fixed rate pegged to the US dollar.

SOURCE: CIA *World Factbook 2001* [ONLINE].

GDP per Capita (US$)

Country	1975	1980	1985	1990	1998
Bahamas	8,030	12,727	13,835	13,919	N/A
United States	19,364	21,529	23,200	25,363	29,683
Jamaica	1,819	1,458	1,353	1,651	1,559
St. Lucia	N/A	2,076	2,150	3,542	3,907

SOURCE: United Nations. *Human Development Report 2000; Trends in human development and per capita income.*

The government supports efforts to set up a free trade area that would end tariffs and other taxes on goods imported from or exported to members of the agreement in the Caribbean region. However, since most of the Bahamas' revenue comes from tariffs and duties on imported goods, the government would have to dramatically change its tax system.

MONEY

The Bahamian dollar is fixed to the U.S. dollar on a one-to-one exchange ratio. As such, the Bahamian currency is dependent on the strength or weakness of the U.S. dollar.

There are over 400 banks in the Bahamas, but only 9 are regular, full-service commercial institutions. The others specialize in international banking and investment. In 1998, the government established the Bahamas Financial Services Board to promote the nation as a major financial center and to coordinate financial services. In 2000 the Bahamas International Securities Exchange was launched as the nation's first stock market.

POVERTY AND WEALTH

Although the Bahamas suffers from extremes of wealth and poverty, the standard of living is high and the average per capita income in 1998 was US$14,492. On many outer islands, where the people exist as **subsistence farmers** and fishermen, modern amenities, including sanitation, are badly lacking. Meanwhile, the standard of living in Nassau and Freeport is the same as many highly developed nations. The poverty rate in the Bahamas has declined from about 9 percent in 1993 to about 5 percent, which is low by international standards and points to an improved economy.

The United Nations *Human Development Report 2000* ranks the Bahamas high in human development, placing it at number 33 in the world. This ranking is based on a combination of per capita income, standard of living, and access to health care, education, and so forth.

WORKING CONDITIONS

In 1999, the **labor force** was estimated at 156,000. The unemployment rate was 9 percent by 1998 estimates. Except for members of the police, military, and fire departments, under the constitution of the Bahamas all workers have the right to join unions. About 25 percent of the workforce are unionized, but for workers in the hotel industry the rate is closer to 50 percent. Children under the age of 14 are not allowed to work during school hours or in industrial jobs, and those under the age of 16 may not work at night. There is no national minimum wage, but government employees earn a minimum of

Household Consumption in PPP Terms

Country	All food	Clothing and footwear	Fuel and power[a]	Health care[b]	Education[b]	Transport & Communications	Other
Bahamas	32	4	5	3	8	9	41
United States	13	9	9	4	6	8	51
Jamaica	24	7	3	1	9	8	48
St. Lucia	40	5	11	4	17	11	11

Data represent percentage of consumption in PPP terms.
[a]Excludes energy used for transport.
[b]Includes government and private expenditures.

SOURCE: World Bank. *World Development Indicators 2000.*

US$4.12 per hour. The working week is limited to 48 hours and there is mandatory overtime pay for hours that exceed this limit.

COUNTRY HISTORY AND ECONOMIC DEVELOPMENT

1492. Spanish explorer Christopher Columbus lands in the Bahamas.

1500s. The Spanish conduct raids in the islands and enslave the Lucian Indians, who are sent to work the gold and silver mines in Central and South America. Over a 25-year period, the native tribes of the Bahamas are wiped out.

1647. British religious refugees settle on Eleuthera Island.

1717. The Bahamas becomes a British Crown Colony.

1718. Woodes Rogers, the first governor of the colony, drives out pirates who were based in the islands.

1700s. Sugar cane production becomes the main source of revenue in the colony.

1861–65. The Bahamas becomes a center for Confederate blockade raiders during the American Civil War.

1917–33. The Bahamas again becomes a center for American smugglers, this time for those transporting illegal alcohol into the United States during the Prohibition period.

1939–45. The Allies use the Bahamas as a base for air and naval operations during World War II.

1964. The nation is granted self-government.

1973. The Bahamas gains full independence.

1992. After 25 years of rule, the United Bahamian Party loses power to the FNM.

FUTURE TRENDS

The economy of the Bahamas remains dependent on tourists, especially from the United States, and is therefore vulnerable to downturns in the prosperity of Americans. The government has started efforts to diversify the economy and the success of these initiatives will determine how badly the islands may suffer from future problems with the U.S. economy. The nation's dependency on tourism makes it vulnerable to competition from other destinations. The development and expansion of the tourist trade elsewhere in the Caribbean stands to have a negative effect on tourism in the Bahamas. The islands are also subject to disruption from hurricanes and other weather-related disasters.

Efforts to develop a free trade area in the region will require a dramatic **restructuring** of the Bahamian economy since most of the government's revenue come from tariffs and duties on imported goods. Yet, the establishment of a free trade area could well attract more foreign businesses to the islands, since they would be able to use the Bahamas as a strategic base for economic interaction with the United States. The Bahamas would also be able to expand its international financial services sector as other islands in the Caribbean have done.

DEPENDENCIES

The Bahamas has no territories or colonies.

BIBLIOGRAPHY

Eneas, William J. Godfrey. *Agriculture in the Bahamas: Historical Development, 1492–1992.* New York: Media Publishing, 1998.

Sealey, Neal E. *The Bahamas Today: An Introduction to the Human and Economic Geography of the Bahamas.* London: Macmillan Caribbean, 1993.

U.S. Central Intelligence Agency. *World Factbook 2000.* <http://www.odci.gov/cia/publications/factbook/index.html>. Accessed August 2001.

U.S. Central Intelligence Agency. *World Factbook 2001.* <http://www.odci.gov/cia/publications/factbook/index.html>. Accessed September 2001.

U.S. Department of State. *Background Notes: The Bahamas.* 1999. <http://www.state.gov/r/pa/bgn/index/cfm?docid=1857>. Accessed August 2001.

———. *1999 Country Reports on Human Rights Practices: The Bahamas.* 2000. <http://www.state.gov/g/drl/rls/hrrpt/1999/index.cfm?docid=373>. Accessed August 2001.

———. *FY 2001 Country Commercial Guide: The Bahamas.* <http://www.state.gov/>. Accessed August 2001.

—Tom Lansford

BARBADOS

CAPITAL: Bridgetown.

MONETARY UNIT: Barbados dollar (BDS$). One dollar equals 100 cents. There are coins of 1, 5, 10, 25 and 50 cents and 1 dollar, and notes of 1, 2, 5, 10, 20, 50, and 100 dollars. The Barbados dollar is pegged to the U.S. dollar at the rate of BDS$1:US$0.49771, or US$1:BDS$2.011.

CHIEF EXPORTS: Sugar and molasses; rum; other food and beverages; chemicals; electrical components; and clothing.

CHIEF IMPORTS: Consumer goods, machinery, foodstuffs, construction materials, chemicals, fuel, and electrical components.

GROSS DOMESTIC PRODUCT: US$4 billion (purchasing power parity, 2000 est.).

BALANCE OF TRADE: Exports: US$260 million (2000 est.). **Imports:** US$800.3 million (2000 est.).

COUNTRY OVERVIEW

LOCATION AND SIZE. Barbados is an island situated between the Caribbean Sea and the Atlantic Ocean, northeast of Venezuela and east of the Windward Island chain. It covers an area of 430 square kilometers (166 square miles), roughly 2.5 times the size of Washington, DC. Its coastline is 97 kilometers (60 miles) in length and its capital, Bridgetown, is situated at a natural harbor on the southwest coast of the island.

POPULATION. The population of Barbados was estimated at 274,540 in mid-2000, representing a growth rate of 0.55 percent over the preceding year. The average annual rate of population increase from 1995 stands at 0.3 percent. At current rates, the island's population will reach approximately 288,000 by 2010. The government wants to restrict population growth because Barbados is one of the most densely populated countries in the world (estimated at 619 people per square kilometer in 1997, or 1,603 people per square mile). There is a well-organized family planning program in the island and the birth rate,

at 14.45 per 1,000 population in 2000, is one of the lowest in the region. The migration rate was extremely high until the 1970s but, at 0.32 migrants per 1,000 population, is now low by regional standards.

The age structure of Barbadians reflects government planning policy and high living standards, with only 22

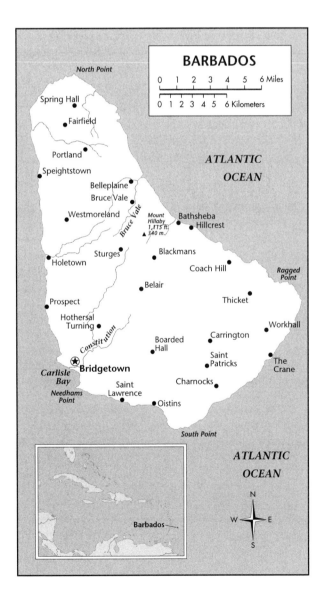

percent of citizens aged 0–14 years, 69 percent between ages 15 and 64, and 9 percent over 65. The infant mortality rate is 12.37 per 1000. Approximately 80 percent of people are of African descent, while a small but economically powerful white minority accounts for about 4 percent of the population. The rest are of mixed ethnic background. English is both the official and the spoken language, and the religion is Christian, represented by Protestant, Anglican, Roman Catholic, and other conventional churches.

OVERVIEW OF ECONOMY

Despite its high population density and limited natural resources, Barbados has one of the more diversified and successful economies in the Caribbean. Since gaining independence from the United Kingdom (UK) in 1966, the island has enjoyed political stability, a factor that has encouraged the growth of tourism and other service industries. As a result, the country has dramatically reduced its dependence on sugar exports (although sugar remains the most important agricultural activity) and has developed not only its service sector but also some areas of manufacturing.

Strong growth in the 1970s came to an end with a **recession** in the late 1980s, as **gross domestic product** (GDP) contracted by 12.9 percent between 1989 and 1992. This drop was caused, in part, by difficulties in the sugar industry and by a downturn in tourism, due largely to a recession in North America. The International Monetary Fund (IMF) offered financial aid in return for a **structural adjustment program** that included pay cuts for **public-sector** workers and other austerity measures. The Barbados dollar was not devalued, however, as the government realized that the island's dependence on imported goods, including food, from the United States would create unacceptable hardship in the event of **devaluation**. By 1993 the worst of the recession was over. In the late 1990s gross domestic product (GDP) growth was steady as tourism and export markets recovered. Growth between 1996 and 1998 was estimated at 4 percent annually, falling to 3.2 percent in 1999 and 2.8 percent in 2000.

The economic problems of the 1980s revealed underlying weaknesses in the Barbadian economy, which still exist today. The country runs a huge **trade deficit**, with imports 4 to 5 times the value of exports due to high demand for imported goods and food combined with poor export performance. The large public sector strains government resources in terms of salaries and other recurrent expenditures, resulting in regular fiscal deficits. The external debt stood at an estimated US$550 million in 1998. Tourism remains crucial to the economy, but Barbados faces serious competition from other Caribbean destinations, while its offshore manufacturing sector has been largely eroded by competition from lower-wage countries such as Mexico and the Dominican Republic.

More positively, the island has a diversified range of industries, producing **consumer goods** for the national and local markets. It also has a small but significant petroleum industry, producing enough fuel to meet about one-half of local needs, as well as significant reserves of natural gas.

POLITICS, GOVERNMENT, AND TAXATION

The political stability of democratic Barbados has been the envy of the Caribbean since independence in 1966. As a former British colony, the country parallels the British electoral and parliamentary systems, which has ensured regular and fair elections and the orderly transfer of power between political parties. The country is a member of the British Commonwealth, with the British monarch the constitutional head of state, represented by a governor general appointed by the Crown. The head of government is the prime minister, who presides over a cabinet appointed by the governor general on his advice. The bi-cameral, or 2-chamber, parliament consists of a 21-member Senate appointed by the governor general and a 28-member House of Assembly, elected by popular vote every 5 years.

Despite lively exchanges of views in parliament, Barbados's political system is based more on consensus than confrontation. Modern Barbadian politics has been dominated by 2 main parties, the Barbados Labour Party (BLP) and the Democratic Labour Party (DLP). Both are broadly social-democratic in outlook, favoring a mixed economy with a strong **private sector** and a measure of government intervention. The DLP is rather more left of center than its rival, while the BLP was for many years identified with the small, economically dominant, white elite. The BLP won elections in 1994 and again in 1999, capturing 26 out of 28 parliamentary seats with an unprecedented 64.8 percent of the vote. The National Democratic Party (NDP) has not held office.

Government has a strong and direct impact on the economy through its management of the large public sector, its tax policy, and its encouragement of foreign investment in key sectors. During the recession of the late 1980s, for instance, the DLP government was forced to introduce an 8 percent pay cut for public-sector workers in a bid to reduce state expenditure. In 1999, the BLP government finally agreed to restore this pay cut in 3 stages over a given period. The government regularly meets with representatives from the private sector and the trade unions, and a series of tripartite protocols covering wages, prices, and working conditions has revealed an unusually strong degree of consensus.

Taxation has been an important economic factor in recent years as governments have tried to balance the need for increased revenue with goals of social equality. In 1997 a radical change took place with the introduction of **value-added tax** (VAT) to replace 11 different **indirect taxes**. The immediate result was greatly improved tax revenue, which reduced the government's fiscal shortfall from the equivalent of 2.5 percent of GDP in 1996 to 0.3 percent in 1997. However, in the same year, the VAT forced prices up and led to **inflation** of 7.7 percent. The government responded by removing the VAT from 50 essential food items, with the result that consumer prices fell by 1.3 percent in 1998, benefiting the basic household expenditure of poorer families. The basic **income tax** is payable on earnings greater than BDS$625 per month, with higher rates for larger incomes.

The Barbadian government is active in encouraging foreign investment in tourism, manufacturing, and the informatics (data processing) sector. It offers a range of financial incentives to prospective investors, including tax concessions, and has made considerable efforts to attract offshore financial businesses, such as foreign banks and insurance companies, by introducing the legal and fiscal regulation required. So far, moves to **privatize** state assets such as the Barbados National Bank, the Caribbean Broadcasting Company, and the Barbados National Oil Company have been planned but not implemented.

INFRASTRUCTURE, POWER, AND COMMUNICATIONS

Barbados has a network of roads totaling 1,578 kilometers (980 miles), with only a few miles remaining unpaved. There are no railways. The main commercial port is at Bridgetown, but there is also an important marina development at Port St. Charles, north of Speightstown. There is 1 international airport, which receives many daily flights from Europe, North America, and other Caribbean countries. The road **infrastructure** is generally good and has received substantial government investment over recent years, as have port and airport facilities and a modernized sewerage system on the south coast.

The island's energy needs are partly met by an onshore field in St. Philip parish, which produced 850,000 barrels of crude petroleum in 1999, equivalent to half of annual local consumption. Energy production in 1998 was estimated at 672 million kilowatt-hours (kWh), in excess of consumption of 625 million kWh. Natural gas production has also increased, and most urban and suburban residents have access to a piped gas supply. A United States-owned company, Conoco, is engaged in offshore exploration for oil and gas reserves.

Communications in Barbados are generally good and the government is committed to **liberalizing** the telecommunications sector, currently dominated by the Cable & Wireless company, by the end of 2002. In 1997 it was estimated that there were 97,000 telephone lines in use, and cellular and Internet access are growing steadily. The government is also attempting to boost the data-processing and telemarketing sector by promoting Barbados as a regional communications center offering a sophisticated technological infrastructure as well as a highly literate workforce.

ECONOMIC SECTORS

The structure of the economy in Barbados today is unrecognizable from that of 50 years ago. Agriculture in 1946 accounted for 37.8 percent of GDP and 55 percent

Communications

Country	Telephonesa	Telephones, Mobile/Cellulara	Radio Stationsb	Radiosa	TV Stationsa	Televisionsa	Internet Service Providersc	Internet Usersc
Barbados	108,000	8,013	AM 2; FM 3; shortwave 0	237,000	1	76,000	19	6,000
United States	194 M	69.209 M (1998)	AM 4,762; FM 5,542; shortwave 18	575 M	1,500	219 M	7,800	148 M
Jamaica	353,000 (1996)	54,640 (1996)	AM 10; FM 13; shortwave 0	1.215M	7	460,000	21	60,000
St. Lucia	37,000	1,600	AM 2; FM 7; shortwave 0	111,000	3	32,000	15	5,000

aData is for 1997 unless otherwise noted.
bData is for 1998 unless otherwise noted.
cData is for 2000 unless otherwise noted.

SOURCE: CIA *World Factbook 2001* [Online].

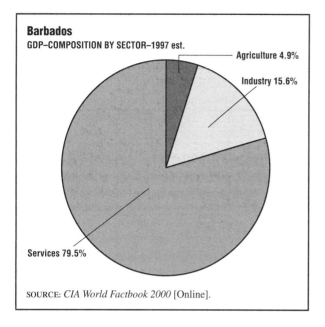

Barbados
GDP–COMPOSITION BY SECTOR–1997 est.

Agriculture 4.9%

Industry 15.6%

Services 79.5%

SOURCE: *CIA World Factbook 2000* [Online].

1998, total manufactured exports, excluding the traditional products of refined sugar and rum, earned US$139 million.

The major contributor to the Barbadian economy is the service sector, which represented 80 percent of GDP in 1998. The sector includes government services, the tourism industry, and the 2 recently developed areas of financial services and informatics. Of these, tourism is the principal foreign exchange earner, and the Caribbean Development Bank (CBD) estimates that tourist expenditures in the island reached US$703 million in 1998.

The growth of services is counterbalanced by stagnation in manufacturing and the limited contribution made by agriculture. High costs probably account for problems in manufacturing. Both wages in the sector and necessary inputs are higher in Barbados than in other Caribbean countries, but the island's reputation for stability and high-quality service explain the growth in the newer sectors of the economy.

of foreign exchange earnings, while in 1998 it represented only 4 percent of GDP and only 2.9 percent of foreign exchange earnings. Sugar is still the island's main agricultural commodity, earning approximately US$34 million annually.

Industry has grown significantly over the same period, reaching 16 percent of GDP in 1998, although parts of this sector have declined since the recession of the late 1980s. The island's industry is divided between manufacturing for local consumption and export-oriented assembly work aimed at the North American market. In

AGRICULTURE

In colonial times, the country's largely flat, fertile land, its large slave workforce, and a handful of large-scale, sometimes absentee, landowners, made Barbados the plantation economy par excellence. The sugar industry survived into the 20th century (and has continued into the 21st century), but it began to decline from the 1960s onwards as long-haul flights fueled the development of the tourism industry. By the recession of the late 1980s, the sugar sector was in serious trouble, and in 1992 the state sugar company in debt by some US$100 million. The IMF insisted on its dismantling as part of the structural adjustment program and a full **restructuring**, under the aegis of the British Booker-Tate company, took place. Despite plans for increased production of 75,000 tons annually, Barbados has since struggled to produce the 54,700 tons which the European Union (EU) agrees to import at preferential prices each year. In 1999, sugar production increased 10.8 percent on the previous year but was still only 53,200. Were it not for the EU quota and a smaller U.S. quota of 5,000 tons, the industry would probably collapse. As it is, high labor and input costs, droughts, and outdated technology have made its future uncertain, with production costs often higher than the price paid by the EU. Today the rum industry is forced to import half of its annual requirement of molasses. As the workforce in the sugar industry grows older and landowners increasingly look to capitalize on tourism or new housing developments, sugar is under threat.

Inadequate rainfall and lack of irrigation has prevented the development of other agricultural activity, although some vegetable farming takes place on a com-

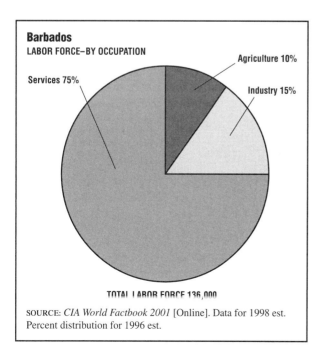

Barbados
LABOR FORCE–BY OCCUPATION

Services 75%

Agriculture 10%

Industry 15%

TOTAL LABOR FORCE 136,000

SOURCE: *CIA World Factbook 2001* [Online]. Data for 1998 est. Percent distribution for 1996 est.

mercial scale. Apart from self-sufficiency in milk and poultry, the limited agricultural sector means that Barbados imports large amounts of basic foods, including wheat and meat. There is some fishing, aimed mostly at the tourist and local market. In all, some 5,000 people are employed in agriculture.

INDUSTRY

The manufacturing sector in Barbados has yet to recover from the recession of the late 1980s when bankruptcies occurred and almost one-third of the workforce lost their jobs. Today, approximately 10,000 Barbadians work in manufacturing. The electronics sector in particular was badly hit when the U.S. semi-conductor company, Intel, closed its factory in 1986. Leaving aside traditional manufacturing, such as sugar refining and rum distilling, Barbados's industrial activity is partly aimed at the local market which produces goods such as tinned food, drinks, and cigarettes. The export markets have been severely damaged by competition from cheaper Caribbean and Latin American competitors. But domestic manufacturing also faces serious potential problems, as trade liberalization means that the government can no longer protect national industries by imposing high **tariffs** on imported goods. Thus, Barbadian manufacturers must compete with those from other regional economies, whose wage costs and other overheads are usually much lower.

A construction boom, linked to tourism and residential development, has assisted the recovery of a large cement plant in the north of the island that was closed for some years and reopened in 1997. The other significant industrial employer is the petroleum sector, although the island's small oil refinery was closed in 1998 and refining moved to Trinidad and Tobago, where labor and other costs are cheaper.

SERVICES

Tourism is Barbados's crucial economic activity and has been since the 1960s. At least 10 percent of the working population (some 13,000 people) are employed in this sector, which offers a range of tourist accommodations from luxury hotels to modest self-catering establishments. After the recession years, tourism picked up again in the mid-1990s, only to face another slowdown in 1999. This drop was in part due to increasing competition from other Caribbean countries such as the Dominican Republic, and in part to a reduction in visits from cruise ships as they shifted to non-Caribbean routes or shorter routes such as the Bahamas. Cruise ship visitors totaled 445,821 in 1999, a reduction from 517,888 in 1997, but stay-over visitors rose to 517,869 in 1999, setting a new record. Overall, the country witnessed over US$700 million in tourism receipts in 1999.

The real problem for Barbados is that tourist facilities are too densely concentrated on the south coast, which is highly urbanized, while the Atlantic coast, with its rugged shoreline and large waves, is not suitable for beach tourism. There are few large brand-name hotels (the Barbados Hilton was closed for refurbishment in 2000) which makes marketing the island in the United States difficult. On the other hand, the absence of conglomerates and package tours results in a far greater **trickle-down** of tourist spending among the general population.

Informatics employed almost 1,700 workers in 1999, about the same number as the sugar industry. The island has been involved in data processing since the 1980s and now specializes in operations such as database management and insurance claims processing. Costs in Barbados are higher than elsewhere in the Caribbean (although still only half of costs in the United States), but the island offers strong advantages such as a literate English-speaking workforce and location in the same time zone as the eastern United States. Despite these factors, employment has fallen in recent years, reflecting increasing mobility on the part of foreign companies, which frequently relocate to lower-cost areas.

The financial services sector has also faced problems as licenses issued to new financial companies have slowed down since 1998. There are an estimated 47 **offshore banks**, as well as hundreds of other insurance and investment companies, all catering to overseas clients. Figures are hard to track, but it is estimated that these financial activities earned BDS$150 million in foreign earnings in 1995. In 1998, approximately 7,500 people were employed in the banking and insurance sector. The financial sector is also under threat of **sanctions** from the EU and the Organization for Economic Cooperation and Development (OECD), both of which have expressed concerns about **money laundering**, tax evasion, and other financial improprieties in Caribbean offshore centers.

Retailing is an important economic activity, especially in Bridgetown where there are large department stores and supermarkets. In the countryside, most stores are small and family-run. Some 18,000 people work in the **retail** sector.

INTERNATIONAL TRADE

Barbados generally imports nearly 4 times more than it exports (US$800.3 million in imports as opposed to US$260 million in exports in 2000), creating a huge trade imbalance that is only partly offset by tourism revenues and other service sector income. According to the CDB,

Trade (expressed in billions of US$): Barbados		
	Exports	Imports
1975	.107	.217
1980	.228	.527
1985	.354	.611
1990	.211	.704
1995	.236	.764
1998	.251	1.009

SOURCE: International Monetary Fund. *International Financial Statistics Yearbook 1999.*

Exchange rates: Barbados	
Barbadian dollars (BDS$) per US$1	
2001	2.000
2000	2.000
1999	2.000
1998	2.000
1997	2.000
1996	2.000

Note: Fixed rate pegged to the US dollar.

SOURCE: CIA *World Factbook 2001* [ONLINE].

the **balance of payments** was in deficit by BDS$76 million in 1999. This situation is sustainable only so long as tourism receipts remain stable, but the island faces real problems of dependency on imported foodstuffs and other basic items.

The main source of imports, according to CDB statistics in 1999, is the United States, which provided 40 percent of the total, followed by regional economies such as Trinidad & Tobago, and the United Kingdom. In terms of exports, Caribbean markets, particularly Jamaica and Venezuela, were the biggest, accounting for approximately 40 percent of the island's export trade. The United Kingdom is an important market for Barbadian sugar and rum.

MONEY

Regular economic growth and low inflation marked most of the 1990s for Barbados, but by the end of the decade there were anxieties over another possible recession. Consumption of imported goods was too high in relation to export earnings, and credit was too easily available to consumers; therefore, in 1999, the government raised interest rates in an attempt to restrain spending. The Barbadian dollar, which has long been pegged to the U.S. dollar at a rate of BDS$2.000:US$1, is probably overvalued, but it would be extremely difficult for any government to devalue the currency, as so many basic items are imported from the United States.

There is a small local securities exchange, the Securities Exchange of Barbados, founded in 1991, which had a **market capitalization** of US$2 billion at the end of 1999. Most larger local companies are listed for share trading, together with several companies from Trinidad & Tobago and Jamaica.

POVERTY AND WEALTH

In terms of poverty eradication, Barbados is a success story, with high per capita GDP, a good level of so-

cial service provision, and positive health indicators. The United Nations Human Development Index places it third among all non-Organization for Economic Cooperation and Development (OECD) countries for its development statistics, ahead of Singapore and other economic successes. Although many Barbadians continue to live in small wooden houses, access to clean water, electricity, and medical facilities is universal. Public education is of a good standard, as are health services. The political culture of consensus has ensured that all Barbadian governments have aimed to eradicate poverty and bring about a degree of wealth redistribution.

As a result of these policies, Barbados has a large, literate, and financially comfortable middle class, many of whom are employed in the public sector. No recent statistics are available regarding percentage share of household income, but it is certain that Barbados does not suffer the same extremes of social division as other Caribbean countries.

However, there remains a wealthy minority, part of which is directly descended from the white plantation owners of the colonial period. Known still as the "plantocracy," these families have extensive interests in retailing, tourism, and the financial sector. Since the country's independence this small elite has retained its economic influence, although its political power has waned, and it remains distanced from the majority black population.

GDP per Capita (US$)					
Country	1975	1980	1985	1990	1998
Barbados	5,497	6,764	6,373	7,340	7,894
United States	19,364	21,529	23,200	25,363	29,683
Jamaica	1,819	1,458	1,353	1,651	1,559
St. Lucia	N/A	2,076	2,150	3,542	3,907

SOURCE: United Nations. *Human Development Report 2000; Trends in human development and per capita income.*

WORKING CONDITIONS

Working conditions in Barbados are generally good for a workforce estimated at 136,300 in 1998, and there is a strong tradition of consultation between employers and trade unions. Even the small remaining rural workforce is well organized and is capable of negotiating acceptable improvements in wages and conditions. The public sector is particularly well represented and governments are obliged to hold regular consultations with the unions that represent teachers and other civil servants. Pay and working conditions in the service industries are also above average for the region. High levels of literacy are the norm. Legislation is in place against unlawful dismissal and other employer malpractice in Barbados and is mostly observed. All Barbadian workers are part of a National Insurance system that provides sick pay and small retirement pensions.

There is little or no child labor in Barbados, and women are generally offered equal employment opportunities at all levels. A small **informal sector** exists, mostly catering to tourists, and some women are employed as informal sector beach vendors. The island's remaining problem in social terms is unemployment, which in 1999 affected almost 10 percent of the workforce, a fall from 12.3 percent the previous year.

With relatively high wage levels and regulated employment conditions, Barbadians enjoy a higher standard of living and quality of life than many other Caribbean people. However, in a globalized economy, these advantages are also a disincentive to foreign investors in search of the cheapest possible labor costs.

COUNTRY HISTORY AND ECONOMIC DEVELOPMENT

1627. The first English colonial settlement is established, and Barbados remains a British colony until 1966.

1639. First meeting of the Barbados House of Assembly. This body is the third oldest legislative body in the Western Hemisphere.

1650s. The sugar industry enjoys its most productive and profitable period.

1834. Slavery is abolished in the British empire.

1930s. Widespread unrest and rioting erupts in protest against poor working conditions and inadequate pay and prompts social reforms.

1938. The Barbados Labor Party is founded by Sir Grantley Adams.

1951. The British government grants Barbados full internal autonomy under the British Crown and the Barbados Labor Party is elected to government, with Sir Grantley Adams as prime minister.

1966. On November 20, Barbados becomes a fully independent state within the British Commonwealth.

1989–1992. Recession forces the government to adopt an IMF-approved austerity program.

1999. The Barbados Labor Party wins a second consecutive term in office by a large majority.

FUTURE TRENDS

The continuing success story of Barbados, based on social fairness and democratic consultation, will largely depend on its ability to fend off competition in the tourism and service sectors. Agriculture will almost certainly continue to decline, while sugar production will survive only as long as the EU continues to subsidize it with preferential quotas and prices. Manufacturing, while strong in terms of local markets, cannot compete as a low-wage offshore activity. As a result, tourism and the new informatics industries will play an increasingly crucial role in generating foreign currency. But as recent experience has shown, both are highly competitive in a regional and global context, and Barbados will face difficulties in increasing its market share without considerable investment in advertising and training.

The greatest cause for concern is the island's huge trade deficit and continuing reliance on imports for everyday food items. Should another recession occur, Barbados would be extremely vulnerable to balance of payments problems and increased indebtedness, factors that might jeopardize the considerable strides made in the country's development since the 1970s.

DEPENDENCIES

Barbados has no territories or colonies.

BIBLIOGRAPHY

Caribbean Development Bank. *Annual Report 1999*. Barbados, 2000.

Economist Intelligence Unit. *Country Profile: Bermuda, Bahamas, Barbados, Netherlands Antilles, Aruba, Turks & Caicos Islands, Cayman Islands, British Virgin Islands*. London: Economist Intelligence Unit, 2001.

Government of Barbados Information Network (GOBINET). <http://barbados.gov.bb>. Accessed September 2001.

International Monetary Fund. <http://www.imf.org/external/np>.

U.S. Central Intelligence Agency. *World Factbook 2001.* <http://www.odci.gov/cia/publications/factbook/index.html>. Accessed August 2001.

U.S. Department of State. *Background Notes: Barbados, August 2000.* <http://www.state.gov/www/background_notes/barbados_0008_bgn.html>. Accessed September 2001.

U.S. Department of State. *FY 2001 Country Commercial Guide: Barbados.* <http://www.state.gov/www/about_state/business/com_guides/2001/wha/index.html>. Accessed September 2001.

—James Ferguson

BELIZE

CAPITAL: Belmopan.

MONETARY UNIT: The Belize dollar, which is pegged to the U.S. dollar at a rate of 2:1. One Belize dollar (Bz$) is equal to 100 cents. Belizean currency comes in 100-, 50-, 20-, 10-, 5-, and 2-dollar bills with the occasional 1-dollar bill. Coins come in 1-dollar, 50, 25, 10, 5, and 1 Belizean cent units. The 25-cent piece is called a shilling.

CHIEF EXPORTS: Sugar, bananas, citrus fruits, clothing, fish products.

CHIEF IMPORTS: Food, consumer goods, building materials, vehicles, machinery, petroleum products.

GROSS DOMESTIC PRODUCT: US$740 million (purchasing power parity, 1999 est.).

BALANCE OF TRADE: Exports: US$150 million (1998 est.). **Imports:** US$320 million (1998 est.).

COUNTRY OVERVIEW

LOCATION AND SIZE. Formerly known as British Honduras, Belize is a Central American nation roughly the size of Massachusetts. Belize shares borders with Guatemala and Mexico, to the west and the northwest, respectively. To the east it borders the Caribbean Sea, with a coastline of 240 miles. It has an area of 22,966 square kilometers (8,867 square miles). The capital, Belmopan, is located in the center of the country.

POPULATION. Belize, with an estimated 249,183 people in 2000, is the most sparsely populated nation in Central America. The population has been growing at about 2.86 percent a year since 1995, when the population stood at 216,500.

The Belizean population is ethnically diverse, with the majority of the inhabitants being of multiracial descent. Approximately 46 percent of the people are mestizo (of mixed Mayan and European descent), 30 percent are African and Afro-European (Creole), 10 percent are Mayan, and 6 percent are Afro-Amerindian (Garifuna).

The remainder are European, Chinese, East Indian, Middle Eastern, and North American.

The Belizean population is young, with 43 percent below the age of 15 in 2000. Life expectancy is 71 years. In 2000, only 3 percent of the population was over 64. The birth rate in 2000 was 32.29 per 1,000, while the death rate was 4.81 per 1,000.

Over half of Belizeans live in rural areas. About 25 percent live in Belize City, the former capital which is also the principal port and commercial center.

OVERVIEW OF ECONOMY

In 1999, Belize's GDP grew at a quick pace, reaching to US$740 million. The per capita income (at PPP) was approximately US$3,100 a year (1999 est.). Economic figures for 2000 were expected to drop due to damage stemming from Hurricane Keith, which caused massive damage to the primary agricultural sector. In addition, the country had US$244 million in **foreign debt**.

Well into the 1900s, Belize depended on forestry to sustain its economy. When timber supplies began to dwindle, cane sugar emerged as the main source of foreign exchange. Although a majority of the arable land in Belize had still not been cultivated in 1999, agriculture was one of the most vibrant sectors of the economy, contributing 13.4 percent of GDP. Sugar was the leading export earner, bringing in approximately 50 percent of all domestic export revenues and accounting for half of all farmland in Belize.

While sugar production remained a staple in the last half of the 1990s, agricultural performance was accentuated by the production of citrus fruits (primarily oranges and grapefruits), which nearly doubled between 1995 and 1999. Bananas, the second most important crop, accounted for 16 percent of total exports in 1999.

The performance of agricultural products was enhanced by preferential access to U.S. and European markets. Under the Caribbean Basin Initiative (CBI), which was launched in August of 1990, products derived from citrus fruits, such as frozen concentrated juices, enjoyed

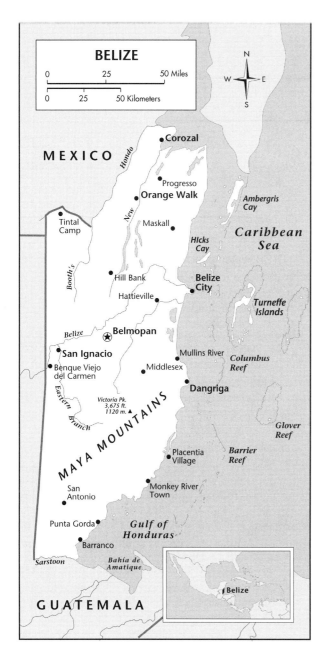

growth in the sector. An Export Processing Zone (EPZ) allowing for the duty-free import of equipment and machinery was established near the international airport at Belize City, and a commercial **free zone** providing similar tax exemptions was set up at Corozal, along the Mexican border. The government in Belize took significant steps to shore up the country's **infrastructure**, promoting tourism and attracting foreign investment. In 1999, some 185 U.S. companies had operations in Belize. Tourism has risen steadily, and was the fastest growing sector of the Belizean economy in 2000.

POLITICS, GOVERNMENT, AND TAXATION

The first settlement in Belize was established by a shipwrecked British seaman in 1638. The British government began administering the territory in 1786 and made it a crown colony in 1871. Self government in Belize was first granted by the British in 1964, when the country was still known as British Honduras. In 1973 the country's name was changed to Belize, and by 1974 a 2-party political system had emerged. This system continued after Belize gained independence from Britain on 21 September 1981. At the time of independence, Guatemala claimed a portion of territory on the western border of Belize. This border continues to be a point of contention between the countries, even after Guatemala formally recognized Belize's independence in 1991.

Under the independence constitution of 1981, the executive branch of the government is made up of the prime minister and the cabinet. Cabinet ministers are members of the majority political party in the Parliament, or National Assembly, which is made up of 2 houses: a 29-member House of Representatives, and a Senate of 8 appointed members.

A parliamentary democracy, Belize is a member of the British Commonwealth. The head of state is Queen Elizabeth II. She is represented in Belize by a governor-general, whose role is largely ceremonial. In 2000, Sir Colville Young held the post. Chief administrative duties fall to the prime minister, a position held by Said Musa, elected in August 1998.

The country's 2 main political parties are the People's United Party (PUP), established in 1950, and the United Democratic Party (UDP), which was established in 1974. The UDP is considered the more conservative of the 2 parties. It has a strong following in the urban Creole population. The PUP grew out of the trade union movement and has traditionally drawn support from the mestizo population. Both parties have curbed government spending to lower the deficit and they have financed this deficit with foreign aid. Both parties have sought to ex-

duty-free access to American markets. Sugar and banana producers also relied on favorable quotas to maintain high export levels to the European Union. This preferential access was called into question in 1995 when the World Trade Organization (WTO) ruled that the European Union (EU) went against free trade legislation by giving preference to Caribbean banana exports. In preparation for the potential loss of this particular market, Belize began to diversify its exports, increasing the farming of nontraditional crops such as chili peppers, papayas, and vegetables.

The manufacturing base in Belize is fairly limited, accounting for only 9 percent of the employed **labor force**; however, initiatives have been taken to stimulate pand the manufacturing base, and have tried to diversify trade. The 2 parties differ on tax policy.

The UDP, after winning elections in 1993 for only the second time in history, levied a 15 percent **value-added tax** (VAT) on goods and services. This VAT was instituted to offset revenue losses stemming from Belize's entry into the Caribbean Community (CARICOM) in 1974, which had lowered import and export **tariffs**. The move was strongly criticized by the PUP, and during the run up to the 1998 election, the PUP vowed to repeal the tax. The PUP won the 1998 election, taking 26 of the 29 seats in the House of Representatives, and Said Musa became the country's prime minister.

Musa's administration made good on election promises. The VAT was abolished and replaced by an 8 percent sales tax. Taxes on the purchase of petroleum products, alcohol, and tobacco increased. Foods and medicines, as well as basic utilities such as water and electricity, were exempted from the tax, as were small businesses. The personal **income tax** was reduced to a maximum level of 25 percent. PUP officials hoped the tax policy would stimulate business activity and raise consumer spending so that government revenues would increase despite lower tax rates. The PUP also promised to decentralize government power, build 10,000 new houses, and create 15,000 new jobs.

INFRASTRUCTURE, POWER, AND COMMUNICATIONS

There are 1,594 miles of roads in Belize, 303 of which are paved. Of the 4 main highways in Belize, 2 provide border crossings into Mexico and Guatemala. All the main towns and villages are linked to the capital, Belmopan, and to Belize City. Some roads, including major sections of highway, are vulnerable to damage or closure

during the rainy season. The road network in Belize was improved in the 1980s, but not enough to support a significant growth in travel, tourism, and manufacturing. A US$14.7 million renovation of the Southern Highway began in 1998. Another US$8.5 million was allocated for the construction of a bypass road and 2 bridges in northern Belize. Funds from the United States Agency for International Development (USAID) were used to improve rural access roads. There is regular bus service to and from all main towns.

Belize has 10 ports of entry, the largest of which is at Belize City. Nine major shipping lines run cargo services in and out of Belize City. The main southern ports are at Punta Gorda and Big Creek. The Philip Goldson International Airport, 9 miles from Belize City, handles a majority of the country's commercial air traffic. The airport is served by 3 international carriers: American Airlines, Continental Airlines, and Grupo Taca. From Belize, direct flights are available to Miami, Houston, Dallas, and San Salvador.

The communications network in Belize is extensive. Belize Telecommunications, which was **privatized** between 1988 and 1992, operates the network and provides modern service to the entire country. The number of subscribers grew from over 3,300 in 1995 to over 30,000 in 1999. Cell phone and Internet use are on the rise. There are no daily papers published in Belize, but there are 2 main weeklies: the *Belize Times,* which is sympathetic to the PUP, and the *Guardian,* which favors the UDP. The Broadcasting Corporation of Belize ran only 2 radio stations before it was privatized in 1998. As of 2000 there were 15 radio stations. Television viewers have access to a number of local television stations as well as cable television, which provides up to 50 international channels.

Communications								
Country	Telephones[a]	Telephones, Mobile/Cellular[a]	Radio Stations[b]	Radios[a]	TV Stations[a]	Televisions[a]	Internet Service Providers[c]	Internet Users[c]
Belize	31,000	3,023	AM 1; FM 12; shortwave 0	133,000	2	41,000	2	12,000
United States	194 M	69.209 M (1998)	AM 4,762; FM 5,542; shortwave 18	575 M	1,500	219 M	7,800	148 M
Mexico	9.6 M (1998)	2.02 M (1998)	AM 865; FM about 500; shortwave 13 (1999)	31 M	236	25.6 M	51	2.5 M
Guatemala	665,061 (2000)	663,296 (2000)	AM 130; FM 487; shortwave 15 (2000)	835,000	26	1.323 M	5	65,000

[a]Data is for 1997 unless otherwise noted.
[b]Data is for 1998 unless otherwise noted.
[c]Data is for 2000 unless otherwise noted.

SOURCE: CIA *World Factbook 2001* [Online].

Residents in Belize receive their energy from Belize Electricity (BEL), which, after power sector reforms in 1992, emerged as the single producer and distributor of electric power. In 1999 the government gave up majority control of the company, selling a portion of its shares to the public and the rest to Fortis of Canada, boosting Fortis's ownership to 62.96 percent. The majority of Belize's fuel needs are met through the import of oil from the United States.

ECONOMIC SECTORS

While efforts to diversify the Belizean economy are underway, the leading economic sector is still agriculture, leaving the country's economic performance vulnerable to fluctuations in international demand and shifts in commodity prices. To bolster economic stability and increase foreign investment, the Belizean government targeted tourism as its primary growth sector. An intensive marketing campaign was launched on U.S. television in the late 1990s to attract visitors, and loans were secured for the restoration of archeological sites. Manufacturing is another sector that has been targeted for growth. Manufacturing proceeds made a solid contribution to the GDP, but in 1998 industry employed only 32 percent of the labor force, less than the 38 percent employed in the agricultural sector. Mining is limited because of a lack of extensive resources. Construction activity increased in 2000 due to reconstruction from Hurricane Keith, but contracts for major projects are often awarded to overseas firms who generally have more building experience and wider access to skilled labor.

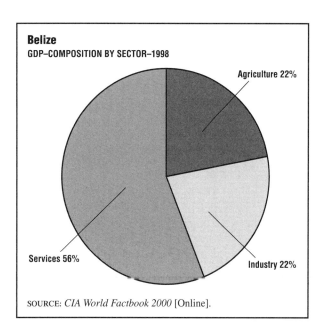

Belize
GDP–COMPOSITION BY SECTOR–1998

Agriculture 22%
Industry 22%
Services 56%

SOURCE: *CIA World Factbook 2000* [Online].

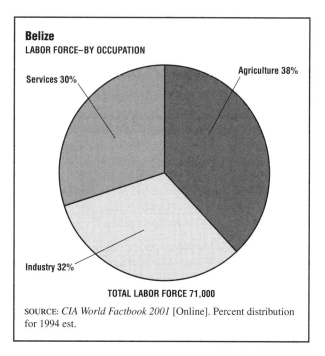

Belize
LABOR FORCE–BY OCCUPATION

Services 30%
Agriculture 38%
Industry 32%

TOTAL LABOR FORCE 71,000

SOURCE: *CIA World Factbook 2001* [Online]. Percent distribution for 1994 est.

AGRICULTURE

Agriculture, which employs over one-third of Belize's labor force, is vital to the country's economy, accounting for nearly 22 percent of the GDP in 1999 and about 68 percent of export earnings.

Sugar is produced in the north of the country and is the nation's largest agricultural export, accounting for 50 percent of domestic export revenues and half of all arable land use. Preferential quotas and tax rates on sugar exports granted by the United States and the European Union have kept sugar revenues high. The United States bought 16,772 tons and the European Union bought 39,400 tons of sugar from Belize in 1999.

Fruits, such as bananas, oranges, and grapefruits, are the country's second largest agricultural export. Fruit production, which occurs in the Stann Creek Valley, is affected by weather and international market conditions. For example, Hurricane Keith caused great setbacks in the agricultural sector in 2000. Also, export revenues rose to record levels in 1995–96, but as international prices fell, earnings slumped. Citrus concentrate and bananas enter the United States duty free under the Caribbean Basin Initiative (CBI). Recent developments in the industry could make the citrus sector more competitive against the banana market. In 1998–99, 2 citrus companies were purchased by the Commonwealth Development Corporation (CDC). The company wants to increase citrus production by making factories more efficient and by rehabilitating existing groves.

Banana production is significant, accounting for 16 percent of total exports in 1999. Production was controlled by the state-run Banana Control Board until 1991. It was then taken over by a growers' association which, through efficient management, raised banana production to record levels by the mid-1990s. Other export crops include assorted vegetables and tropical fruits, chili peppers, papayas, and organic cocoa.

Increased rearing of livestock has helped Belize become self-sufficient for fresh meat and poultry products. Belizean slaughter houses produced 3.3 million pounds of beef in 1999, along with 1.9 million pounds of pork. Some of this output was exported to Honduras and Guatemala. Despite increased production, processed meats were still imported from the United States. Fishing is an important component of the economy, providing food for domestic consumption as well as an important source of foreign exchange. Belize exported over 5,200 tons of marine products in 1999, most of it lobster and shrimp.

The timber industry, which once dominated the economy, has continued to struggle, contracting 6.9 percent in 1999. While 79 percent of Belize is covered by forest and woodlands, only 15 percent is suitable for timber production. Sawnwood exports earned only US$2.1 million in 1999, approximately 1.3 percent of total export revenue.

Most farms in Belize are small, less than 20 hectares. Government financing has generally favored large export-producing farms, making it difficult for small farmers to obtain capital for improvements. To help remedy the situation, the government (in November of 1998) created the Small Farmers and Business Bank to meet small farmers' needs.

INDUSTRY

MINING. While gold, bauxite, barytes, and cassiterite do exist in Belize, they are not found in sufficient quantities to render them commercially viable. Dolomite limestone, which is used as road ballast and agricultural fertilizer, was the only mineral exploited in 2000. Agricultural-grade dolomite is sold on the domestic market to banana and citrus producers. It is also exported to the Windward Islands and Jamaica. Belize Minerals, the main local producer of dolomite, has sought new export markets in Central and South America, and has tried to produce a different grade of dolomite for use in the steel industry.

MANUFACTURING. The manufacturing sector in Belize was targeted for growth, but in 1999 was still fairly small. Most manufacturing is done for domestic consumption. Export production generally involves the processing of agricultural products or the assembly of garments from imported fabric for **re-export** to the United States under the CBI. The assembly sector in Belize has had trouble competing with low-cost producers, especially those in Mexico. Between 1993 and 1995 earnings in the sector dropped 50 percent.

CONSTRUCTION. The government pledge to build 10,000 new houses, along with commitments to improve the infrastructure, stimulated increased activity in the construction sector, but contracts were primarily awarded to foreign firms that had more highly skilled workers and more building experience. Reconstruction after Hurricane Keith in 2000 was expected to produce a leap in construction activity.

SERVICES

TOURISM. Belize has all the ingredients of an attractive holiday destination. It has a mild climate, calm blue waters, and a large barrier reef that is ideal for scuba diving. It is also home to jungle ecosystems and ancient ruins. The government, wishing to capitalize on these attractions, targeted the tourist industry for expansion.

In 1996, Belize ratified the Munda Maya agreement with Honduras, Guatemala, El Salvador, and Mexico, pledging cooperation in the management of Mayan archeological sites. In 1997 Belize launched a marketing campaign to attract visitors, producing commercials for American television and putting ads in U.S. magazines. And in 1999, the country obtained a US$11.4 million loan from the Inter-American Development Bank (IDB) to further advance the sector's development. That same year, the government was planning to build a tourist village in Belize City which would cater primarily to cruise ship passengers who come to shore for brief periods of time.

In 1995, 121,270 people visited Belize. By 1999, that number had increased to 167,096, a majority of which were Americans. Cruise ship arrivals, which numbered 7,953 in 1995, had risen to 34,130 by 1999. By the end of the decade, tourists were contributing over US$100 million a year to Belize's economy. In 1999, 1,365 jobs (over 30 percent of the jobs created that year) were added in the services sector.

FINANCIAL SERVICES. There are 4 commercial banks in Belize. Belize Bank is owned by Carlisle Holdings. The other 3 banks are subsidiaries of larger foreign banks: Barclays Bank (UK), the Bank of Nova Scotia (Canada), and the Atlantic Bank (Honduras).

There are 2 development banks: the Small Farmers and Business Bank, which was established to help meet the needs of small farmers and businessmen, and the Development Finance Corporation (DFC), which caters to the needs of large-scale producers. The DFC typically directs institutional funds from other agencies such as the Caribbean Development Bank (CDB) to meet the government's development priorities.

Trade (expressed in billions of US$): Belize

	Exports	Imports
1975	.067	.088
1980	.111	.150
1985	.090	.128
1990	.108	.211
1995	.143	.257
1998	.154	.325

SOURCE: International Monetary Fund. *International Financial Statistics Yearbook 1999.*

Exchange rates: Belize

Belizean dollars (Bz$) per US$1

2001	2.000
2000	2.000
1999	2.000
1998	2.000
1997	2.000
1996	2.000

Note: Fixed rate pegged to the US dollar.

SOURCE: CIA *World Factbook 2001* [ONLINE].

Small enterprise owners who are in need of credit or technical assistance can also receive help from the National Development Foundation of Belize, a lending institution that was established from grant funds from the U.S. Agency for International Development (USAID).

INTERNATIONAL TRADE

Belize is highly dependent on the United States and Great Britain for trade. These 2 countries alone bought 80 percent of Belize's exports in 1999. That same year, the United States supplied Belize with over half its imported goods.

Due to its limited export base and high degree of dependence on imported goods for much of its domestic consumption, Belize has run persistent **trade deficits**. In 1999, export receipts amounted to US$182.7 million. This was less than half the import bill of US$374.4 million, resulting in a trade deficit of about US$192 million.

Trade with the United States has been stimulated by Belize's participation in the Caribbean Basin Initiative (CBI), a U.S.-sponsored program to increase investment in Caribbean nations. The initiative allows member countries duty-free access to American markets. Other major trading partners include the European Union, Canada, Mexico, and CARICOM member states.

MONEY

The Central Bank of Belize regulates the primary financial mechanisms of the country, setting **liquidity** and cash reserve requirements and determining the interest rate structure. The Central Bank also regulates most forms of foreign exchange in the country. At the end of September 1996, after receiving a US$20 million loan from Taiwan and issuing a US$10 million regional bond, international reserves in Belize reached an all-time high of US$79 million. Budget controls and high reserves in the early 1990s gave way to increased spending and

widening government deficits in 1997–98, putting pressure on Belize's **fixed exchange rate** with the United States. Reserves fell sharply, dwindling to US$43 million by 1998. The declines were reversed in 1999 due to increased borrowing and larger inflows of foreign exchange stemming mainly from the sale of home mortgages to the Royal Merchant Bank of Trinidad. By the end of 1999 monetary reserves had rebounded to US$70.2 million.

POVERTY AND WEALTH

According to a census carried out in 1991, 38,000 people, or about 23 percent of the population, fell below the World Bank Poverty Threshold (meaning they made less than US$740 a year). The same census showed that 7 percent of the population was extremely poor (lacking the sufficient food and rudimentary services to ensure good health). Belize City has traditionally received a disproportionate share of government revenues because of the population representation system. Money is channeled directly into the Belizean Central Bank, and the resulting distorted spending has accelerated population growth in the port city, exacerbating poverty and social problems. The rural populations, particularly in the poorer districts of Toledo, Cayo, and Stann Creek have limited access to basic education, health care, safe drinking water, and sanitation. In 2001, 7 percent of the population was illiterate and 17 percent of the population did

GDP per Capita (US$)

Country	1975	1980	1985	1990	1998
Belize	1,624	2,036	1,822	2,543	2,725
United States	19,364	21,529	23,200	25,363	29,683
Mexico	3,380	4,167	4,106	4,046	4,459
Guatemala	1,371	1,598	1,330	1,358	1,533

SOURCE: United Nations. *Human Development Report 2000; Trends in human development and per capita income.*

Household Consumption in PPP Terms

Country	All food	Clothing and footwear	Fuel and power[a]	Health care[b]	Education[b]	Transport & Communications	Other
Belize	27	10	5	3	13	5	38
United States	13	9	9	4	6	8	51
Mexico	30	6	4	2	7	5	46
Guatemala	N/A	N/A	N/A	N/A	N/A	N/A	N/A

Data represent percentage of consumption in PPP terms.
[a]Excludes energy used for transport.
[b]Includes government and private expenditures.

SOURCE: World Bank. *World Development Indicators 2000.*

not have access to safe drinking water. Life expectancy for both men and women was 71 years and the infant mortality rate was high, at 28 deaths per 1,000 live births.

WORKING CONDITIONS

Unemployment was estimated at 14.3 percent in 1998, among a total workforce of 71,000. Workers in Belize have the right to organize unions, and the law bars discrimination against employees on the basis of union affiliation. However, it is not uncommon for union sympathizers to be fired on grounds purportedly unrelated to their union activities. Effective redress for workers in this situation is difficult. They can file complaints with the Labor Department, but their cases are often difficult to prove. There were 11 unions in Belize in 2000 whose members comprised about 11 percent of the workforce. While officially the unions are independent of the political parties, most hold strong sympathies for either the UDP or the PUP.

Forced labor in Belize is forbidden by law, as is child labor. Children under the age of 14 are not permitted to enter the workforce, and those under 17 are not allowed to operate dangerous machinery. Children between 5 and 14 years old are required to attend school, although truancy and dropout rates are significant.

There is a minimum wage in Belize which applies to all full-time workers. The wage is generally set at US$1.10 per hour but fluctuates depending on the field of work. Those in the export industries receive at least US$1.00 per hour. Domestic workers in private homes and shop assistants are paid an hourly minimum rate of US$0.87. The minimum wage, as a sole source of income, is not enough to provide a decent standard of living. Most workers are paid more than the minimum. The standard workweek is 45 hours over 6 days. Anything more is considered overtime. Over the course of a year workers are given 13 public holidays and 2 weeks vacation.

Working conditions for documented workers are fairly good. For undocumented workers, especially the Hispanic laborers who make their livings on the banana farms, things can be more difficult. Worker housing on banana farms often lacks running water and electricity. Many times this housing is placed close to the fields, where exposure to pesticides is high. There are health and safety regulations in Belize covering numerous industries. However, enforcement and inspection are generally limited to urban areas or accessible rural areas where violations have been reported.

COUNTRY HISTORY AND ECONOMIC DEVELOPMENT

1502. Christopher Columbus sails along the coast of what is now Belize.

1638. The first recorded settlement is established by a shipwrecked English seaman.

1871. Belize becomes a Crown Colony of the British Empire. The territory is known as British Honduras.

1950. The PUP is founded.

1954. Universal suffrage is introduced.

1961. A ministerial system is established.

1964. The British grant the colony self government.

1973. British Honduras becomes Belize.

1974. The UDP is founded. Belize joins CARICOM.

1981. Belize gains independence and drafts a new constitution. Guatemala claims part of Belizean territory.

1984. The UDP wins elections.

1989. The PUP wins elections.

1991. Belize is admitted to the Organization of American States (OAS). Guatemala recognizes independence.

1992. Belize joins the Inter-American Development Bank (IDB).

1993. The UDP takes over once again, instituting a 15 percent VAT.

1994. Britain withdraws its garrison of 1,200 army and 300 air force personnel.

1998. The PUP comes to power; the 15 percent VAT is abolished and replaced with an 8 percent sales tax.

FUTURE TRENDS

Belizean development was set back by Hurricane Keith, which swept through the country in October 2000. The damage, concentrated primarily in the north, amounted to US$280 million according to the U.N. Economic Commission for Latin America. Promoting recovery in the agricultural sector, the infrastructure, and livestock will require a sustained, massive investment. Increased activity in construction resulting from damages caused by the hurricane was expected to boost the economy by 7 percent in 2001, but **inflation** was also expected to rise due to lowered agricultural production and a rise in the cost of food. The tourism sector will probably suffer until reconstruction is completed, but tourism has been touted as the most optimistic sector of the Belizean economy.

DEPENDENCIES

Belize has no territories or colonies.

BIBLIOGRAPHY

Economist Intelligence Unit. *Country Profile: Belize*. London: Economist Intelligence Unit, 2000.

U.S. Central Intelligence Agency. *CIA World Factbook*. <http://www.odci.gov/cia/publications/factbook/geos/bh.html>. Accessed July 2001.

U.S. Department of State: Bureau of Democracy, Human Rights, and Labor. *1999 Country Reports on Human Rights Practices: Belize*. <http://www.state,gov/global/human_rights/1999_hrp_report/beli ze.html>. Accessed July 2001.

U.S. Department of State: Bureau of Western Hemisphere Affairs. *Background Notes: Belize*. <http//www.tradeport.org/ts/countries/belize/bnotes.html>. Accessed July 2001.

U.S. Department of State. *FY 2001 Country Commercial Guide: Belize*. <http://www.state.gov/www/about_state/business/com_guides/2001/wha/index.html>. Accessed July 2001.

World Bank. <http://www.worldbank.org/bz>. Accessed July 2001.

—John Mazor

BOLIVIA

Republic of Bolivia
República de Bolivia

CAPITAL: **Constitutional capital:** Sucre. **Actual capital:** La Paz. (The Supreme Court of Bolivia is permanently located in Sucre.)

MONETARY UNIT: Boliviano (Bs). One boliviano equals 100 cents. There are coins of 10, 20, and 50 cents and Bs1 and 2. (A Bs5 coin is scheduled to be put into circulation sometime in 2001.) Paper bills are for Bs5, 10, 20, 100 and 200.

CHIEF EXPORTS: Tin, antimony, lead, zinc, gold, petroleum, natural gas, soybeans, sugar, coffee, quinoa, rice, vegetable oils, timber, native jewelry, alpaca wool.

CHIEF IMPORTS: Consumer goods, foodstuffs, and agricultural, industrial, and transportation equipment.

GROSS DOMESTIC PRODUCT: US$8.5 billion (1998; Bs47.2 billion, according to the Bolivia report from the IMF). [The CIA *World Factbook 2001* indicates a GDP of US$20.9 billion in 2000, determined at purchasing power parity. The CIA figures are disputed in Bolivia.]

BALANCE OF TRADE: **Exports:** US$1.104 billion (1998); US$1.018 billion (1999 estimated); US$1.459 billion (2000) (according to the National Institute of Statistics of Bolivia). **Imports:** US$1.766 billion (1998); US$1.436 billion (1999 estimated); US$1.976 billion (2000) (according to the National Institute of Statistics of Bolivia). [The CIA *World Factbook 2001* indicates exports of US$1.26 billion (f.o.b, 2000) and imports of US$1.86 billion (f.o.b., 2000). The CIA figures are disputed in Bolivia.]

COUNTRY OVERVIEW

LOCATION AND SIZE. Bolivia is a central South American country. It shares borders with Brazil in the northeast and east; Paraguay in the east and southeast; Argentina in the south; Chile in the west; and Peru in the west and northwest. Bolivia has an area of 1,098,580 square kilometers (424,162 square miles), of which 14,190 square kilometers (5,479 square miles) are water. Bolivia is just slightly less than 3 times the size of the U.S. state of Montana. Bolivia is divided into 3 distinct geographical areas: (1) the high mountains (*cordillera*) with its high plateau (*altiplano*), (2) the intermediate valleys (between the mountains and the lowlands), and (3) the eastern plains of the Amazon and Plate river system.

POPULATION. The population of Bolivia was estimated to be 8,280,000 in 2000. In 1950, it was 2.7 million. The annual population growth rate is 2.2 percent. One of the greatest changes has been the shift from rural to urban areas. It is estimated that currently 65 percent of the population reside in urban locations, and in some urban areas the growth rate has been close to 5 percent. The growth rate of the rural population between 1950 and 2000 has remained at about 1 percent, and in some areas there has been a steady population loss. The cities of La Paz-El Alto (twin cities) have over a million inhabitants: La Paz with 792,000 and El Alto with 405,000. The city of Santa Cruz has a population of 1,300,000, and Cochabamba has 408,000.

There has been a notable exodus of the high plateau (*altiplano*) and mountain (*cordillera*) population to the eastern lowlands. This movement was due mainly to the decline of the mining industry, the harsh climatic conditions, and the availability of land in the east. It is estimated that between 1975 and 1985 about 5,000 families migrated per year, totaling around 300,000 people. The integration of the newcomers of different ethnicity and language (Aymara and Quechua) has been relatively smooth and peaceful. The first generations of these migrants, who moved from an environment of frigid temperatures to a subtropical climate, have maintained their culture to a great extent. About 55 percent of the Bolivian population is composed of people of indigenous lifestyle

(Quechua, 30 percent; Aymaras, 25 percent); there is a small number in the southeast who are Guaranís with their own language. (Guaraní is an official language in neighboring Paraguay.) Those of mixed race (Indian and European origin) comprise 30 percent of Bolivians. Those of European origin (mainly Spanish), plus some from the Near East who arrived between 1890 and 1920 and from the Far East (mainly Japan), make up another 15 percent. Percentages are inexact as people are identified by their ethnic lifestyle, dress, and primary language. There are several main Indian languages of which Quechua is the dominant, Aymara a close second, and Guaraní a distant third. Official languages are Spanish, along with Quechua,

Aymara, and Guaraní in the regions where they are spoken. In 1992, 87 percent of all Bolivians could speak Spanish as compared to 78 percent in 1976. About 12 percent can speak only the indigenous languages, compared to 20 percent in 1976. There have been attempts to introduce bilingual education, especially in the rural areas. Financial constraints and the lack of qualified teachers are impediments to full implementation.

OVERVIEW OF ECONOMY

Since the early Spanish period and until recently, Bolivia was a mineral producing country. The silver extracted from the rich mountain of Potosí was a mainstay of Spain and her colonial empire. There is a saying that, if it were possible, a wide bridge made of pure silver could be constructed from Potosí to Madrid with all the silver that was mined from this fabulous *Cerro Rico*. Currently small quantities are still mined at Potosí. The famous mint, *Casa de Moneda,* in Potosí is a heritage site visited by many tourists. For most of the 20th century Bolivia was one of the largest world producers of tin and tungsten (known in Bolivia as wolfram).

During World War II, the allied nations depended on Bolivian tin since Malaya (today Malaysia), the other leading tin producer, was occupied by Japanese forces. In fact, Bolivia was, until recently, considered a country with a mono-economy (an economy based on a single activity), and it depended on the price fluctuations in the world market of the minerals that it produced. As of 2001, Bolivia has a more diversified economy. Exports of oil and natural gas are important components of Bolivia's exports. Agriculture has also emerged as a large sector and produces many exports, including agro-industrial products which are the fastest growing segment, especially soybeans. Growing conditions on the eastern plains are exceptionally good for soybeans. In 2000 Bolivia's exports rose by 20 percent because of greater production of soybeans and natural gas.

Tourism has consistently increased. Statistics from the *Financial Times* indicate that the country averaged about 250,000 tourists per year in the early 1990s, though Bolivian sources claim a much higher number. Production for 500,000 tourists to visit Bolivia every year which is quite realistic. The country has multiple attractions: traditional societies, fine handicrafts, a great variety of climates with majestic landscapes, preserved colonial sites, a wide diversity of animals and plants, many years of political and economic stability with a rather low crime rate, and reasonable prices. Bolivia has many attractions for **eco-tourism**. However, lack of a good **infrastructure** including poor ground transportation, the presence of illegal coca leaf cultivation (Bolivia often is falsely portrayed as a leading cocaine-producing country), and the high altitudes of western Bolivia (historically and culturally the most interesting part of the country) have impeded more rapid growth in tourism.

A slow but constant growth of the **gross national product** (GNP) and annual per capita income is encouraging. Yet unemployment in early 2001 was 8 percent, and involuntary **underemployment** was around 40 percent. Bolivia is one of the 22 countries that has been classified as a highly indebted poor country (HIPC) by the World Bank and the International Monetary Fund (IMF).

Bolivia tries to cope with its illegal coca leaf production and the needs of its growing population. Coca leaf production has declined a great deal due to the pre-

sent government's determined policy to eradicate all illegal plants. But in early 2000, there were still 2,300 hectares in production. While Bolivia is still relatively sparsely inhabited, the annual population growth remains 2.2 percent. This rate is among the highest of the South American countries and needs more attention. Improvement in basic education, reduction in poverty, underemployment, and the level of corruption are also priorities which concern the people and government of Bolivia. Vibrant and free media bring Bolivia's weaknesses and strengths to local, national, and international attention.

COCA. The coca leaf is the basic ingredient for producing cocaine. Several decades ago Bolivia was the largest producer of the coca plant, from which the leaves are harvested. In the 1970s when cocaine became a valuable product in the international drug culture, the coca leaf assumed an importance that it never had before. Bolivia became an important country for the illegal production of cocaine because it grew the basic ingredient—the leaf. Coca plants suddenly became an important element in the Bolivian economy and politics.

Historically, coca leaves were cultivated as early as the pre-Inca epochs. They were used with frequency, mainly by the Indian population, to help alleviate hunger and the effects of the frigid temperatures and the altitude. The leaves are legal, and in modern times are used to make coca tea which is thought to help altitude sickness and stomach ailments. But also in modern times the leaves can be converted into coca paste which is then made into cocaine. In general, Bolivia is not a cocaine-producing nation. The leaves are harvested and illegally sold to those who convert it into paste and then into cocaine outside of Bolivia (although some paste is now made in Bolivia). Since the demand for coca leaves increased rapidly in the 1980s and 1990s, growing and selling more than was needed for traditional internal consumption became illegal. So coca leaf production was classified as "legal" (for the traditional use) and "in excess," avoiding the locally unpopular term, "illegal."

The cultivation and sale of the illegal crop became an undetermined but appreciable part of the Bolivian economy and exports. It is often claimed that in the 1980s coca leaf (and some paste) exports equaled or surpassed all legal exports, coming to at least 15 percent of Bolivia's real revenues. The Bolivian government estimates that coca-leaf production expanded from 1.63 million kilograms from 4,100 hectares in 1977 to 45 million kilograms from 48,000 hectares in 1987. The number of growers rose from 7,600 to about 40,000. Most of this took place in the central sub-tropical region of Chapare (the transitional area from the mountainous valleys to the eastern lowlands), which is well-suited for producing leaves of high acidity—a characteristic that is desirable for making cocaine.

In 1988, a new law allocated 12,000 hectares in the Yungas region east of La Paz for the legal growth and harvesting of coca leaves for traditional use in Bolivia. Coca grown in the Yungas region lacks acidity—a characteristic that is preferred for traditional uses. Incentives were provided with U.S. aid to convert the illegal farming, mainly in the Chapare, into productive crops such as bananas, pineapples, and hearts of palm. In 2000, Bolivia and the United States claimed that about 40,000 hectares of coca had been eradicated and the land converted into new crops since 1998 in the Chapare. The goal is to eliminate all illegal coca by 2002. In February 2001, the Bolivian government claimed that all "in excess" coca production had been eradicated, but the responsible Bolivian media claimed that 2,300 hectares of illegal coca plants still were in production in early 2001. The government also stipulated that the legal coca harvest in the Yungas can be bought only by 700 registered retailers. Currently, Bolivia has had commendable success in a noticeable reduction of illegal coca plants. However, protests by the growers of "in excess" coca, most of them modest farmers, continues.

POLITICS, GOVERNMENT, AND TAXATION

Bolivia gained independence from Spain in 1825. It has had 61 presidents, 1 of them a woman, Lydia Gueiler Tejada (1979–80). Some held the office more than once, consequently making 79 governments. The shortest were a few days long, the longest 10 years. Only 37 presidents came to power by legal means; the others gained the presidency by revolution. Most of the revolutions were simple bloodless palace revolutions (coups d'etat). A few presidents who achieved power by revolution were later elected legally, including President Hugo Banzer, who was elected in 1997 for a 5-year term. He had been a military dictator from 1971 to 1978. Bolivia has had 18 constitutions; the last one from 1967 was extensively amended in 1994.

The significant revolution of 1952 which introduced great economic, political, and social reforms was engineered by the Movement of the National Revolution (MNR) Party. The MNR is still one of the dominant parties although it has splintered. One splinter is the Movement of the Revolutionary Left (MIR), which is far more moderate than its name implies. It held the presidency between 1989 and 1993, and then the MNR returned to power. In 1997, ex-dictator Hugo Banzer won the presidency as a candidate of the Democratic National Action (ADN) Party, which is considered right of center, forming a coalition with the left of center MIR and several smaller parties. In the forthcoming election of 2002 the MNR, MIR, and ADN are expected to present candidates, as will some other parties which have little hope of winning. These others can be defined as 6 leftist parties, 3 populist parties, 1 evangelical party, and 3 indigenous parties. The indigenous parties have been quite visible with colorful public demonstrations and displays but have little broad support.

Candidate, leader of the MNR party, and president (1993–97), Gonzalo Sánchez de Lozada was educated and lived in the United States. The MNR shifted its leftist and nationalist tendencies to a more centrist position that was devoted to **privatization** and globalism (generally identified as neo-liberalism). This charge produced lively debates and intense political activities which have continued into the Banzer presidency. Banzer's coalition government has only fine-tuned the policies of his predecessor, with much emphasis on the eradication of illegal ("in excess") coca plants and the substitution of other crops that are useful for export. Former president Sánchez de Lozada is a leading candidate for the presidency in 2002. Another leading candidate is the MIR leader Jaime Paz Zamora who was president from 1989 to 1993.

The main source of government revenue is taxation. According to the IMF Bolivia report of 2000, the total revenues of Bolivia in 1998 represented 24.8 percent of its GDP, with tax revenues at 19.5 percent of the GDP. In 1998, **indirect taxes** constituted 47.4 percent of tax revenues, including the **value-added tax** (VAT) with 29 percent, **excise taxes** with 6.7 percent, and transaction taxes with 8.4 percent. Transaction taxes are often known as stamp taxes. Taxes from hydrocarbons provided 23.8 percent of total taxes, mining royalties only 0.04 percent, and customs **duties** 7 percent. Personal income and property taxes constituted 6.9 percent, and corporate income and property taxes were 0.1 percent.

Personal **income tax** is a flat 13 percent, but for everyone there is a basic deduction of 2 minimum salaries. (As of January 1998 the minimum salary was Bs300 per month.) The VAT tax paid for personal consumption is deductible from the income tax with proper receipts. There is a social security system which was reformed and partially privatized in 1997. Employees must contribute 12.5 percent of their salaries with a ceiling of 60 minimum salaries (computed as US$415 a month). There are no local income taxes and no joint filing for husband and wife.

INFRASTRUCTURE, POWER, AND COMMUNICATIONS

Bolivia has a changing infrastructure. Communication has rapidly adapted to new technology, as exemplified by the continued rapid growth of cellular phone use. At the same time some of the traditional and still useed infrastructure has deteriorated, especially the fine railway system in western and central Bolivia whose construc-

Communications

Country	Newspapers	Radios	TV Sets[a]	Cable subscribers[a]	Mobile Phones[a]	Fax Machines[a]	Personal Computers[a]	Internet Hosts[b]	Internet Users[b]
	1996	1997	1998	1998	1998	1998	1998	1999	1999
Bolivia	55	675	116	N/A	27	N/A	7.5	0.47	78
United States	215	2,146	847	244.3	256	78.4	458.6	1,508.77	74,100
Brazil	40	444	316	16.3	47	3.1	30.1	18.45	3,500
Peru	84	273	144	14.1	30	N/A	18.1	3.09	400

[a]Data are from International Telecommunication Union, *World Telecommunication Development Report 1999* and are per 1,000 people.
[b]Data are from the Internet Software Consortium (http://www.isc.org) and are per 10,000 people.

SOURCE: World Bank. *World Development Indicators 2000.*

tion started in 1877. In 1976 diesel engines replaced steam locomotives.

The 3,685-kilometer (2,290-mile) single track railroad, most of it narrow gauge, has 2 unconnected systems. The Western Network, built much earlier, connects La Paz with Cochabamba and the Chilean ports of Arica and Antofagasta. It also connects with Argentina. In bygone days a railroad journey from La Paz to Buenos Aires was popular and comfortable. The Eastern Network connects the city of Santa Cruz to Sao Paulo, Brazil. Another line goes from Santa Cruz to Argentina. Many attempts to connect the 2 systems with a link from Cochabamba to Santa Cruz have never succeeded. The same is true of the so-called "inter-oceanic corridor" that would go from the Brazilian Atlantic coast to the Chilean Pacific coast, passing through Bolivia. Currently most Bolivian railroads are in disrepair. In 1964 there were 103 locomotives, but only 34 in 1995. The Bolivian railway system was a state corporation known as ENFE. In 1991, a Japanese study estimated that upgrading the railway system would require US$46 billion over 30 years. Hopes to privatize and capitalize the system were only partially accomplished when in 1995 the Chilean consortium, Cruz Blanca, acquired 50 percent of ENFE. By 1999, Bolivia again had 55 operating locomotives with around 2,000 railway cars. The passenger load was 750,000 in 1992 and is still below 1 million per year. Freight also has declined sharply.

Currently most Bolivians travel by inter-city buses, called *flotas*. There are many private bus companies, large and small. Those who can afford it go between the principal cities by air, and if going on to a nearby small town use the *flota*. Until 1992, there was a single national airline owned by the state, Lloyd Aereo Boliviano (LAB), established in 1925 and one of the oldest airlines in the Americas. As with the railroads it was capitalized and privatized when 50 percent was acquired by the Brazilian airline company, VASP. The completely private company, Aerosur, competes with LAB for internal flights.

The Bolivian armed forces operate Transportes Aereos Militares (TAM) which carries paying passengers. In 1999, LAB still had 65 percent of the customers. LAB also flies to the United States (Miami) and neighboring South American countries. About a dozen foreign airlines fly to the 3 Bolivian international airports, La Paz/El Alto, Cochabamba, and Santa Cruz which have runways over 3,050 meters long. An Argentine airline flies to Tarija which is close to Argentina and Paraguay. The *World Factbook* claims that Bolivia has 1,382 airports, of which 1,016 have paved runways of under 915 meters. Many of these are little used.

Bolivia is an inland country but has free port privileges in Argentina, Brazil, Peru, and Chile, and river ports in Paraguay. There is some shipping on the large inland lake, Titicaca, which also carries many tourists between Bolivia and Peru. Navigation on the many large rivers that are part of the Amazon and Plate river systems is unorganized, underdeveloped, and uncounted but offers much potential with small, primitive river ports currently available. Navigation is possible on about 19,000 kilometers (11,806 miles) of the rivers.

Bolivia has about 43,000 kilometers (26,720 miles) of highways of which only 2,000 kilometers (1,242 miles) are paved. In recent years, Bolivia has made highway construction and maintenance a priority. Bolivia's electric power generating capacity is rated at 787 megawatts. Electricity consumption in 1998 was 2,412 billion kilowatthours. The state electric agency, ENDE, was also capitalized and privatized by 3 U.S. consortia in 1997. The state-owned long distance telephone company, ENTEL, was purchased in 1995 by an Italian firm. ENTEL has a **monopoly** until 2001. It is an active cellular phone provider, with service among the cheapest in Latin America. In 1998, there were 27 cellular phones per 1,000 inhabitants (in 1996, 18 per 1,000), and use is growing at an ever increasing rate. Local traditional phone calls are managed by local owner cooperatives but are state regulated. In the largest cities (La Paz, Cochabamba, and Santa

Cruz) 3 of these are responsible for 85 percent of all local calls. In 1987, Bolivia had 145,000 telephones, which grew to 370,000 in 1996. The use of computers is also accelerating. In 1998, there were 7.5 per 1,000 inhabitants. Televisions are 116 per 1,000 (about one-quarter are black and white) and radios 675 per 1,000. Bolivia has 18 significant newspapers. Currently it is reported that there are approximately 190 radio stations and 60 TV stations.

The privatization of the state-owned LAB, ENFE, ENDE, and ENTFL has created much controversy and is an important issue in present-day Bolivian politics.

ECONOMIC SECTORS

Bolivia is a country known for its great contrasts, and that reputation also applies to the country's economy. An often cited remark attributed to an early traveler is that Bolivia is a "beggar sitting on a golden throne." There is a core of truth to this comment. Its fabulous riches have often served Bolivia badly. Since independence in 1825, Bolivia has lost close to 50 percent of its national territory, including its Pacific coast, to its neighbors who coveted the riches. But Bolivia is still rich in resources. In March 2001, the excellent newspaper *La Razón* of La Paz stated that Bolivia has recently been identified as the country with the largest petroleum deposits in South America. It reported that Bolivia has a possible 70 trillion cubic feet of reserves, surpassing those of Venezuela. Yet Bolivia is among the 2 dozen countries in the world that has been classified as a highly indebted poor country (HIPC) by the World Bank. Bolivia is one of 8 countries that is now receiving full HIPC

assistance since it has fulfilled all the World Bank requirements for debt reduction aid.

Traditionally Bolivia's main economic sector was mining, and a decline in mining brought severe hardships aggravated by political instability, nationalist rhetoric, and a rapid increase in the cultivation of coca to serve as a basis for cocaine. In recent years, however, the economy has been diversified, led by increased agricultural production, especially in the fast developing eastern lowlands, with much of the output destined for export. Nearly all of the illegal coca production has been curtailed. Natural gas and oil are developing. For example, according to *La Razón,* exports of natural gas to Brazil increased by 170 percent from early 1999 to early 2001.

Reducing the high level of poverty is a priority of all economic and political sectors and is supported by ample foreign aid from many countries who welcomed Bolivia's economic prudence in the 1990s.

AGRICULTURE

Agriculture remains an important sector of the total. In the 1990s, it represented about 16 percent of the Bolivian economy. Estimates showed a 3.5 percent decline in 1998 because of adverse weather conditions, but a 2.6 percent growth was predicted for 1999. Bad weather in 2000 and 2001, especially the worst rains in many decades, will have a serious impact. Agro-industrial products have the fastest growth of Bolivia's exports. The eastern Amazon plains are rich in nutrients that yield above average harvests, such as 2.5 to 3 metric tons per hectare for soybeans, compared to the usual 1.5 metric tons elsewhere. At the same time, the climate allows 2 harvests per year. Much of the soybean crop is processed into oil, flour, and animal feed. The annually increasing soybean and soy products output and their export represent a most promising element in the Bolivian economy.

Modern agro-industrial activity in the east stands in contrast to traditional small-scale and **subsistence farming** in the mountainous west, especially on the cold and windy high plateau (*altiplano*). There farming has been in crisis for decades. One positive element is the great increase of quinoa production. This traditional, nutritious grain is grown only at high altitudes and has been used for thousands of years by the local inhabitants. Production has grown an average 20 percent per annum in recent years, as quinoa has become popular as a health food in the United States, Canada, and Europe. In 1992, over 2 million kilograms were exported. There also has been a much greater demand, stimulated by exports of sweaters and textiles, for alpaca wool. (The alpaca is a type of llama indigenous to the *altiplano*.) In 1994, exports of alpaca wool came to US$4 million, and they have been rising. Bolivia, Peru, and Ecuador are the countries in

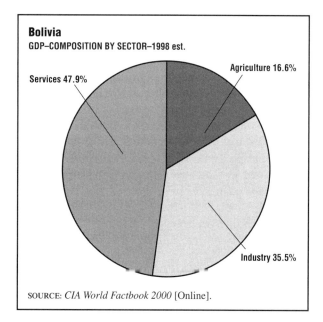

Bolivia
GDP–COMPOSITION BY SECTOR–1998 est.

Services 47.9%

Agriculture 16.6%

Industry 35.5%

SOURCE: *CIA World Factbook 2000* [Online].

which the potato originated and from which it was taken by the Spanish to Europe. With over 100 varieties, potatoes represent the most traditional crop of the subsistence farming in the western high mountains and the *altiplano*. Other agricultural products of Bolivia are coffee, cocoa, corn, sugarcane, rice, tropical fruits, temperate climate fruits from the transitional central valleys, especially Cochabamba, and a variety of timber. Legal coca must also be included. Coca leaves are used in coca tea (legal) which is used for medical purposes mainly against effects of the altitude and against diarrhea.

INDUSTRY

MINING. Until recently mining has been the mainstay of the Bolivian economy. In the 1940s, minerals constituted over 70 percent of Bolivia's exports, mainly tin and tungsten. During World War II, the Allied Powers depended on Bolivian tin.

In the past, Bolivia was considered a mono-economy, but minerals currently constitute a smaller part of Bolivia's exports, declining to below 40 percent and to less than one-third of Bolivia's foreign exchange. But recently mining regained a larger share because of increased extraction of gold and especially zinc. Zinc production in 1997 was 154,230 metric tons. Still, in 1997 mining represented only 5.5 percent of the GDP; that production consisted of zinc, gold, lead, tin, antimony, tungsten, silver, copper, cement, and ulexite (a white crystalline mineral). There are expectations of developing Bolivia's large iron reserves. El Mutun, a 40,000 metric ton deposit located close to the Brazilian border, is considered one of the largest in the world. About 80,000 Bolivians still depend on mining for their livelihood.

The 1952 Bolivian Revolution **nationalized** most of the mines, then owned mainly by 3 men usually identified as the Tin Magnates. A state mining agency, Corporacion Minera Boliviana (COMIBOL), was established and in the 1980s was responsible for two-thirds of Bolivia's mining output. In the late 1980s, Bolivia slowly began to capitalize on and privatize mining, and by the mid-1990s COMIBOL's share of mineral production had fallen to less than 30 percent. COMIBOL's bloated workforce, which had reached about 30,000 in 1984, was reduced to under 3,000. At the same time **joint ventures** between COMIBOL and private concerns came into existence. In 1997, COMIBOL produced 30.6 percent of the declining tin production and only 4.3 percent of the increasing zinc production; all other mineral production was by private enterprise.

Petroleum and natural gas are now important in the Bolivian economy, making up 5.6 percent of the GDP. The State Petroleum Corporation (YPFB) is no longer the largest producer, though, since the 1996 Hydrocabon Law permitted capitalization and privatization of YPFB as well as concessions to foreign companies, most of which are from the United States, Brazil, and Argentina. In 1998, petroleum production was 12,628,000 barrels of which the YPFB share was 7,110,000. Natural gas production in 1998 was 109,673 million cubic feet of which 99 percent was from private enterprise. Starting in 1999, the US$450 million, 488-kilometer (303-mile) gas pipeline permitted exports to Brazil. Bolivia's hydrocarbon production satisfies national demand, with roughly one-third available for export, mainly to Brazil and Argentina. According to official sources in Bolivia, the country hopes to become the natural gas distributor for the Southern Cone (southern nations of South America).

MANUFACTURING. The principal manufactures have hardly changed in several decades. Growth is related to population growth, and from 1990 to 1996 the annual increase in manufacturing averaged 4.6 percent per year. Traditional woolens, weavings, leather goods, and jewelry generally grew more because of their greater popularity outside Bolivia and with tourists whose numbers to Bolivia also increased.

The manufacturing industry represents 16.8 percent of the GDP. In 1997, according to the Bolivian Statistical Institute, there were 1,725 manufacturing enterprises with at least 5 workers, altogether employing 52,000 people. This number represents 15 percent of the Bolivian **labor force**. The 330 manufacturers that had over 50 employees accounted for 36,000 workers. In 1997, total industrial output was valued at US$1.03 billion. Manufacturing sectors include food and beverages and tobacco; textiles, clothing, leather and footwear; wood products and furniture; printing and publishing; industrial chemicals and pharmaceuticals; and plastic, glass, and rubber products. Most of the manufacturing industries are located in the cities, especially in La Paz/El Alto, Cochabamba, and Santa Cruz. Except for traditional jewelry, leather, and woolen goods, the manufactured goods are mostly for internal consumption.

SERVICES

TOURISM. Bolivia is a popular destination for tourists who are motivated and somewhat hardy. Tourism is a growth industry because of the country's many attractions. There are traditional cultures; antiquity sites; preserved colonial villages, towns and cities; diverse climates with majestic scenery; a variety of flora and fauna with good fishing in the rivers and lakes; availability of exquisite textiles and jewelry; sports like trekking, mountain climbing to over 6,000-meter peaks, skiing, and rafting; and camping in rather undeveloped but unforgettable national parks. Bolivia is ideal for eco-tourism. The country has, at 6,000 meters, the highest ski slope (Chacaltaya) in the world near La Paz. Among the popular tourist spots are the pre-Inca ruins of Tihuanaco, Lake Titicaca, the still preserved colonial cities of Potosí and Sucre, and the colonial Jesuit missions in the eastern lowlands. Then there is La Paz, the highest capital city of the world; Cochabamba, often called the "city of eternal spring"; and dynamic Santa Cruz, the large urban center of the eastern lowlands. Numerous local fiestas draw many visitors, the best known being La Diablada in Oruro during carnival week. New attractions for some tourists are the locations where the celebrated 20th-century **Marxist** leader Che Guevarra was captured and mortally wounded, and the stark village of San Vicente on the windy *altiplano* where in 1908 the romanticized U.S. outlaws, Butch Cassidy and the Sundance Kid, were ambushed and killed.

In 1997, 375,000 tourists visited Bolivia. Of these 60 percent came from the Americas, 35 percent from Europe, 4 percent from Asia, and 1 percent from Africa. Income from tourism in 1997 was US$180 million. Bolivia would like to boost this to US$1 billion by 2005. The government is actively promoting tourism and encouraging tourists to stay longer and also make it a prime destination. Most tourists spend only a few days in the country, combining their visit with longer stays in the neighboring countries.

FINANCIAL SERVICES. By mid-1995, Bolivia's Superintendency of Banks reported 58 financial institutions. In 1995, banking assets totaled US$4 billion, representing a growth of 11 percent from the previous year. In 2000, the assets came close to US$5 billion. The Superintendency had licensed 17 banks and 13 savings and loan institutions. Later 2 banks, Banco Sur and Banco Cochabamba, went into receivership, and 2 banks, Multibanco and Banco La Paz, were absorbed by Citibank and Banco de Crato, respectively.

These events highlighted the importance of the Superintendency of Banks, a government agency created in 1993. The Superintendency is in charge of the licensed SBEF (Bolivian Banking and Financial Institutions) which includes licensed banks, savings and loan institutions, credit unions, and small financial service institutions. Of the licensed banks 6 are responsible for 71 percent of all transactions (Banco de Santa Cruz, Banco Industrial, Banco Hipotecario Nacional, Banco Nacional de Bolivia, Banco Mercantil, and Banco Boliviano Americano). The director of the Superintendency is appointed by the president of the Republic from nominees presented by the National Senate, who must choose them with at least a two-thirds vote. The person selected by the president must then have the approval of the lower house of the Congress. The director is appointed for 6 years. A new director was selected and appointed in March 2001. The Banco Central, the national bank, is in charge of is-

suing and controlling the Bolivian national currency and is not under the control of the Superintendency of Banks.

RETAIL. Bolivia, like most nonindustrial nations, has not developed the **retail** sector. Its larger cities have many retail stores, most of them family owned. There are hardly any chain or international franchise stores. Small towns have basic stores that are privately owned. Bolivia is a country of small traders and street vendors. The town markets are most important and draw numerous vendors, traders, and **hawkers**. These shopping areas are well regulated by the municipalities. Nearly all of them have stalls selling prepared food, which are popular with moderate and low income inhabitants. Probably the largest market is *La Cancha* in Cochabamba, with a few thousand independent traders and all kinds of wares. It has become a popular place for tourists. While it remains impossible to calculate the total business transactions of these individual entrepreneurs, they are an important and dynamic part of the Bolivian economy.

INTERNATIONAL TRADE

In 1998, Bolivia's exports were valued at US$1.103 billion and imports totaled US$1.983 billion. (The CIA *World Factbook* indicates 2000 trade figures of US$1.26 billion in exports and US$1.86 billion in imports.) Chief trading partners for exports were the European Union (16 percent), the United States (12 percent), Peru (11 percent), Argentina (10 percent), and Colombia (7 percent). Imports were from the United States (32 percent), Japan (24 percent), Brazil (15 percent), Argentina (11 percent), Peru (4 percent), and Germany (3 percent). The Central Bank of Bolivia reports that the United States is the largest trading partner when both exports and imports are considered.

Bolivia is a member of the Andean Community (along with Colombia, Venezuela, Ecuador, and Peru) that is supposedly free of trade barriers. Since 1994, Bolivia has had a free trade agreement with Mexico. The EU, Japan, and the United States all permit Bolivian exports to enter their market free or at reduced rates. Bo-

Trade (expressed in billions of US$): Bolivia

	Exports	Imports
1975	.444	.558
1980	.942	.665
1985	.623	.691
1990	.926	.687
1995	1.101	1.424
1998	1.103	1.983

SOURCE: International Monetary Fund. *International Financial Statistics Yearbook 1999.*

livia ratified membership in GATT in 1990 and in 1995 in the World Trade Organization (WTO). Bolivia is an associate member of MERCOSUR, which gives it trade benefits with the 11 members of the Latin American Integration Association (ALADI). By 2007, 95 percent of the trade with MERCOSUR will be **tariff** free. Bolivia is also a signatory to the Amazonic Cooperation River Basin Treaty. Bolivia has 9 **Free Trade Zones** (FTZ) fully operating. The most important are El Alto (serving La Paz), Cochabamba, Santa Cruz, Desaguadero on the border with Peru, and the dynamic Puerto Aguiffe on the Brazilian border.

MONEY

The Bolivian currency has had severe fluctuations as a consequence of the Chaco War (1932–35); the 1952 revolution with its drastic economic, political, and social reforms; and the collapse of much of the mining industry, especially tin extraction and export. In 1975, the boliviano was devalued by 66 percent (US$1=Bs20.40). In 1979, there was a further 25 percent **devaluation**. By 1982, the Bolivian currency had totally collapsed, and until 1985 Bolivia suffered hyperinflation, one of the worst cases in recent world history. **Inflation** reached 23,000 percent with US$1 traded at Bs1,055,000. In 1985, strong economic measures were undertaken to reconstruct the Bolivian economy and its currency. Currently it is one of the most stable currencies in Latin America, with a free **floating exchange rate** and pegged to the U.S. dollar. Inflation has declined from 13 percent to 3 percent in 1999. In March 2001, US$1=Bs6.48. (In 1995, it was Bs4.86.) The U.S. dollar circulates freely and is generally accepted as payment, mainly in urban areas.

Bolivia has about 18 private banks, some with links to foreign banks such as Citibank. The Banco Central (Central Bank), established in 1929 but with roots going back to 1871, is a semi-independent government agency. Its mandate is to implement the Bolivian government's fiscal and **monetary policies**, including issuing the currency. Its governing board is nominated by the president of the Republic, and it needs the approval of two-thirds of the elected representatives of the lower chamber. Terms are staggered, and the term of the president of bank cannot coincide with the term of the president of the Republic. The Banco Central and some private banks have recently received praise from international agencies for their stability and fiscal soundness.

There is a small Bolivian Stock Exchange which was started in 1989, but there is no published index of stock prices. In 1989, the exchange's transactions came to Bs4.3 billion but only to Bs3.9 billion in 1999. The exchange deals mostly with fixed-income securities. It is expected that the stock exchange will grow and become more important and visible.

POVERTY AND WEALTH

Bolivia is considered a poor country with the lowest **GDP per capita** among the Latin countries of South America (Guyana, Suriname, and French Guiana are lower). At the same time, Bolivia's exact ranking depends on the varied use and interpretations of the statistical information by different organizations and media. While the excellent *Financial Times* survey of Bolivia of 1994 places it as the second poorest country in the hemisphere (after Haiti), the U.S. Agency for International Development (USAID) ranks Bolivia in 2000 as the fifth poorest. Yet there has been improvement. In 1993, the per capita income was given as US$856 and is currently cited as just over US$1,000. Bolivia is one of the 22 countries that have qualified for **debt relief** by the World Bank in its HIPC (highly indebted poor countries) program. At the same time, the *Human Development Report 2000* has Bolivia in the category of Medium Human Development (as are Ecuador, Peru, and Paraguay—the last 2 share a border with Bolivia) and not in the Low category such as Haiti and many African nations. Bolivia's neighbors, Brazil, Chile, and Argentina, are in the High rank.

In 1998, Bolivia signed a 3-year ESAF (enhanced structural adjustment funding), now called poverty reduction growth facility (PRGF), agreement with the International Monetary Fund. Bolivia was able to comply with

---

Exchange rates: Bolivia

bolivianos per US$1

Jan 2001	6.4071
2000	6.1835
1999	5.8124
1998	5.5101
1997	5.2543
1996	5.0746

SOURCE: CIA *World Factbook 2001* [ONLINE].

GDP per Capita (US$)

Country	1975	1980	1985	1990	1998
Bolivia	1,010	1,016	835	836	964
United States	19,364	21,529	23,200	25,363	29,683
Brazil	3,464	4,253	4,039	4,078	4,509
Peru	2,835	2,777	2,452	2,012	2,611

SOURCE: United Nations. *Human Development Report 2000; Trends in human development and per capita income.*

Distribution of Income or Consumption by Percentage Share: Bolivia

Lowest 10%	2.3
Lowest 20%	5.6
Second 20%	9.7
Third 20%	14.5
Fourth 20%	22.0
Highest 20%	48.2
Highest 10%	31.7

Survey year: 1990
Note: This information refers to income shares by percentiles of the population and is ranked by per capita income.

SOURCE: *2000 World Development Indicators* [CD-ROM].

the World Bank criteria and those of PRGF, which made it eligible for "enhanced" HIPC aid. The Bolivian media reported in February 2001 that Bolivia and 8 other countries of the 41 countries classified as poor with a high indebtedness reached all the required steps for the enhanced program. Bolivia's debt will be reduced by 45 percent.

Bolivia's Ministry of Finance shows evidence of improvement with a decrease in the poverty rate from 85.5 percent in 1976 to 70.2 percent in 1992. The World Bank reported for 1999 that Bolivia had a 67 percent overall rate of poverty, which was 81 percent in the rural areas. In 2000, USAID reported that 94 percent of Bolivians who live in rural areas live below the poverty level, and of these 88 percent are considered indigenous people. Poverty remains a leading cause for the high infant (67 per 1,000) and maternal (3.9 per 1,000) mortality rates. Poverty in the rural areas, with 65 percent involuntary underemployment, is the single main cause for migration to the urban areas.

Bolivia can appear to the visitor as a rather prosperous country compared to many other poor countries, mostly because it has enjoyed a stable economy and political system since the mid-1980s, a tolerable crime rate,

and an expanding middle class. In 1991, 20 percent of the workforce received 54 percent of all income, and 50 percent received only 17 percent. To this must be added that Bolivia still has low population density of 7.9 persons per square kilometer (20 per square mile) of land suited for agriculture.

Bolivia is favored with much foreign aid because of its qualification for enhanced HIPC, its coca plant eradication and crop substitution policies, and its economic and political stability. In 1997, U.S. aid funding came to US$163 million, Japan US$65 million, Netherlands US$60 million, Germany US$47.5 million, and Sweden US$20 million. Multilateral donations came to US$264.2 million. The IMF reported that in 1998 total foreign aid was Bs598 billion. The Paris Consultative Group of 26 donor countries pledged a 44 percent increase in 1998 to support Bolivia's socio-economic reforms and investment programs. Therefore, Bolivia has, and will in the future, depend heavily on foreign aid if it continues a policy that encompasses globalization (identified by those opposed as neo-liberalism).

WORKING CONDITIONS

The Bolivian labor force is variously estimated at 2.5 million to 3.4 million. Reliable, exact data are not available, mainly because agricultural workers are uncounted. In addition, increasing numbers of the workforce rely on self-employment. Labor participation in 1997 from the available workforce was 82.3 percent male and 59.8 percent female, giving an overall 70.7 percent. Unemployment runs close to 40 percent. At the same time, hunger and homelessness are hardly present. Extended family ties and intra-family support are strong and traditional. Out-migration of unskilled workers to neighboring countries, especially Argentina, is estimated at 30,000 per year. There is a minimum wage (often not complied with) of about US$45 per month as of March 2001.

Household Consumption in PPP Terms

Country	All food	Clothing and footwear	Fuel and power[a]	Health care[b]	Education[b]	Transport & Communications	Other
Bolivia	37	6	11	9	14	5	20
United States	13	9	9	4	6	8	51
Brazil	22	13	18	15	34	4	−6
Peru	26	7	17	13	5	7	25

Data represent percentage of consumption in PPP terms.
[a]Excludes energy used for transport.
[b]Includes government and private expenditures.

SOURCE: World Bank. *World Development Indicators 2000*.

Labor unions in Bolivia are a significant political and economic force. But the number of members, past and present, is in dispute. There are 2 unions, the Confederation of Bolivian Workers (COB), which has a monopoly of the urban workers, and the Confederation of the United Workers of Bolivian Peasants (CSUTCB), which represents all rural workers. Both COB and CSUTCB have their roots in the social and political struggle of the 1940s which culminated in the revolution of 1952. For decades, both of these unions were an integral part of the government and claimed co-responsibility for the 1952 revolution that introduced radical political, economic, and social changes. However, in the 1980s, the unions became less influential and their membership declined. A reliable source estimated that COB membership in 1992 was between 150,000 and 200,000. COB and CSUTCB are ideologically oriented—anti-free market and strongly opposed to privatization and capitalization, to the World Bank and IMF and their programs and loans to Bolivia, and to foreign ownership or co-ownership of means of production. COB still can mount frequent strikes, stoppages, and demonstrations as leverage.

CSUTCB's roots also go back to the 1940s with the struggle for indigenous rights which included universal voting rights, significant agrarian reform including the breakup of the large private farms, and the abolition of peonage (a system which forces debtors into the service of their creditors), all of which were achieved in 1952. In the 1980s, CSUTCB too lost government affiliation and support which has never been regained. The exodus of many rural highlanders to the eastern lowlands weakened the group's power base in the western highlands and central valleys. In the late 1980s and the 1990s, the CSUTCB regained strength because of the policies of the government, pressured by the United States, to destroy the illegal coca farms with crop substitution, which nearly all of the growers (with mostly small farms and plots) strongly opposed. One union leader was elected by the coca growers to the Bolivian legislature. Like the COB, the CSUTCB opposes privatization which is often with foreign funding, presence, and pressures (identified as neo-liberal policies of the government).

A power struggle between various leaders of the supposedly united rural federation has lately been intense, primarily because regional differences undermine a unified front. For example, the coca issue is predominant in the central valleys, especially in the Chapare (Department of Cochabamba), where the farmers of coca have gained some modest economic affluence. Yet, the coca problem is not too meaningful to the rural inhabitants of the mountains and highlands (*altiplano* and *cordillera*) of western Bolivia, where poverty is the main issue. This region has also experienced a resurgence in ethnic pride and identity, including a nostalgic look back to the pre-colonial

days of the great Inca Empire. There are current claims that the great gains of the 1952 revolution were too little or are being reversed by the "neo-liberal" policies of the IMF, World Bank, the United States, and the EU. These rural leaders, even more than the COB, have often been disruptive by organizing marches, blockades, demonstrations, sit-ins, and hunger strikes, but so far they have failed to change the government policies.

The COB and CSUTCB and their leaders use modern technologies such as cellular phones and web sites to present their case to the Bolivian people and the international community. All indications are that they will actively participate in the 2002 general elections. As working conditions have improved slowly over the years the unions have failed to gain more support. Average personal income in 2000 reached US$1,300 a year, up from somewhat less than US$1,000 in the 1980s.

COUNTRY HISTORY AND ECONOMIC DEVELOPMENT

PRE–15TH CENTURY. The country now known as Bolivia is inhabited by the Tihuanaco, Aymara, and Kolla civilizations (rich in archaeological remains).

MID-15TH CENTURY. Most of modern Bolivia becomes part of the Inca Empire, mainly during the rule of Inca Pachacuti (1438–71), who imposes the Inca economic system and the Quechua language. Administratively this southern region of the Inca Empire is called Kollasuyo.

1538. The Spanish establish the city of Chuquisaca (now called Sucre). This part of the Spanish Empire is known as Charcas or Upper Peru.

1545. The rich silver deposits of the hill of Potosí are located and the great age of silver begins. The royal city of Potosí becomes one of the largest and richest in the Spanish Empire.

1809. The War of Independence in Spanish America starts in the city of Chuquisaca.

1825. The independence of Upper Peru/Charcas is declared on August 6. The new nation is called Bolivia in honor of Simon Bolivar.

1828–48. Attempts to unify Peru and Bolivia fail.

1847–64. The age of quinoa, a nutritious grain indigenous to high altitudes, provides a large income to the Bolivian treasury.

1864–80. The discovery of rich deposits on the Bolivian Pacific coast (in the Atacama Desert) produces the age of guano and saltpeter.

1867. Bolivia is forced to sign an unfavorable treaty with Brazil, ceding 300,000 square kilometers (115,830 square miles) that had provided easy access to the Amazon and Plate river systems.

1879–80. In the War of the Pacific Bolivia, allied with Peru, Bolivia defends its ownership of the guano and saltpeter deposits. Chile captures the entire Bolivian coast and converts Bolivia into a landlocked nation.

1889. Rubber extraction begins in the tropical northeast of Bolivia, bringing Bolivia again into conflict with Brazil.

1898. A short civil war is fought mainly over the issue of moving the capital to the more dynamic and rapidly growing city of La Paz. The opposition party that supported La Paz is victorious but the constitution is not changed to make La Paz the constitutional capital.

1899. La Paz becomes the seat of the government although the Supreme Court remains in Sucre.

1903. Bolivia is forced to cede the rubber-rich Acre region to Brazil.

1932–35. The large-scale Chaco War with Paraguay erupts over disputed ownership of the Chaco region of southeast Bolivia, with its rich oil deposits. Paraguay gains most of the Chaco but the greatest oil reserves remain with Bolivia. By 1935, Bolivia has lost 49 percent of its 1825 territory to its bordering neighbors through war or forced treaties.

1942–45. During World War II, Bolivia becomes one of the main suppliers of needed minerals, such as tin, to the allied nations.

1952. The Movement of the National Revolution (MNR) gains power by a revolution and undertakes drastic reforms: universal suffrage, nationalization of the tin mines, significant agrarian reform, abolition of peonage, and creation of a new Bolivian military.

1969. The Andean Pact which includes Bolivia, Peru, Ecuador, Colombia, and Venezuela is established.

1981. Bolivia starts its longest period of peaceful democratic elections and government.

1996. Bolivia becomes an associate member of the regional Southern South American Economic Zone called MERCOSUR.

1997. The Andean Pact becomes operative with a permanent Andean Community secretariat in Lima, Peru.

2001. President Hugo Banzer resigns for health reasons. Vice President Jorge Quiroga becomes Bolivia's 63rd president.

FUTURE TRENDS

Since the mid-1980s, Bolivia has had political and economic stability, with fiscal prudence beyond most South American countries. Annual economic growth during the 1990s averaged about 4 percent and is expected to continue. Still, from 1999 to 2000 the economy slowed for various reasons, including a decline in international prices for some of Bolivia's exports. International financial organizations also believe that exports will grow to nearly US$1.5 billion in the next few years, which would be a 20 percent increase. This prediction is based on expected greater exports of natural gas to Brazil and increased cultivation of soybeans.

Bolivia is strongly committed to reducing the high poverty level, which requires more funding for basic education, especially in the rural areas. The goal is to reduce poverty by 40 percent by 2015. Secondary and university educations must be more attuned to modern technologies. The unmeasured migration of skilled professionals to industrial countries, such as the United States, Canada, and EU members, needs to be reduced by providing more opportunities and better salaries. For the general election in 2002, few anticipate any meaningful disturbances and most predict a smooth transition. The energetic freedom of the media is expected to continue. Opposition from labor and certain business sections to the fiscal reforms necessary for HIPC debt relief as well as other structural changes will continue. The restlessness of the illegal coca leaf growers and their opposition to the destruction of their crop and to crop substitution is not expected to end and will likely produce limited, sporadic violence. The same can be said of the indigenous groups, especially in the highlands, in their demands for more cultural rights and awareness. The significant radical changes of the 1952 revolution as well as the more conservative economic reforms since the 1980s all have borne fruit. Currently, Bolivia is far more peaceful and stable at the present than the 2 other Andean nations, Peru and Ecuador, which also have a considerable indigenous population.

DEPENDENCIES

Bolivia has no territories or colonies.

BIBLIOGRAPHY

Arnade, Charles. *Bolivian History.* Cochabamba: Los Amigos del Libro, 1984.

"Bolivia: Inequality and Poverty: A Macrovision." *Social Watch.* <http://www.chasque.apc.org:8081/socwatch/>. Accessed March 2001.

"Bolivia: Interim Poverty Report Reduction Strategy Paper, January 13, 2000." *International Monetary Fund.* <http://

www.imf.org/external/NP/prsp/2000/bol/01/index.htm>. Accessed February 2001.

"Country Assistance Strategy: Bolivia, 1998." *World Bank Group.* <http://www.worldbank.org>. Accessed March 2001.

Crabtree, John, and Laurence Whitehead, editors. *Towards Democratic Viability: The Bolivian Experience.* Palgrave Press in association with St. Antony's College: Oxford, 2001.

"Financial Times Survey: Bolivia." *Financial Times.* 9 November 1994.

Guzman, Augusto. *Historia de Bolivia.* 8th edition. Cochabamba: Los Amigos del Libro, 1998.

IMF. *Bolivia: Statistical Annex. IMF Staff Country Report No. 00138.* Washington DC: International Monetary Fund, March 2000.

IMF. *Debt Relief under the Heavily Indebted Poor Countries (HIPC) Initiative: A Factsheet.* <http://www.imf.org/external/ np/hipc/hipc.htm>. Accessed March 2001.

La Razón. <http://www.la-razon.com>. Accessed February 2001.

"Latin America and Caribbean: Bolivia, 1999." *World Bank Group.* <http://www.worldbank.org>. Accessed March 2001.

Lehman, Kenneth D. *Bolivia and the United States.* Athens: University of Georgia Press, 1999.

MacLean Stearman, Allyn. *Camba and Kolla: Migration and Development in Santa Cruz, Bolivia.* Gainesville: University of Florida Presses, 1985.

Morales, Waltraud. *Bolivia, Land of Struggle.* Boulder: Westview Press, 1992.

Muller, Karin. *Along the Inca Road.* Washington D.C.: National Geographic Society, Adventure Press, 2000.

Osborn, Harold. *Bolivia: A Land Divided.* 3rd edition. London: Oxford University Press, 1964.

Republica de Bolivia: INE (National Institute of Statistics). <http://www.ine.gov.bo>. Accessed March 2001.

Statesman's Yearbook. London: Palgrave, annual.

U.S. Agency for International Development (USAID). *Bolivia.* <http://www.usaid.gov/pubs>. Accessed March 2001.

U.S. Central Intelligence Agency. *The World Factbook 2001.* <http://www.odci.gov/cia/publications/factbook>. Accessed October 2001.

U.S. Department of State. "International Narcotics Control Strategy Report, 1998: Bolivia." <http://www.state.gov/www/ global/narcotics_law/1998_narc_report/samer98.html>. Accessed March 2001.

—Charles W. Arnade

BRAZIL

Federative Republic of Brazil
República Federativa do Brasil

CAPITAL: Brasília.

MONETARY UNIT: Brazil's currency, the real (R$), was introduced on 1 July 1994. One real equals 100 centavos. There are coins of 1, 5, 10, 25, 50 centavos, and 1 real, and notes of 5, 10, 20, 50, and 100 reals.

CHIEF EXPORTS: Manufactures, iron ore, soybeans, footwear, coffee.

CHIEF IMPORTS: Machinery and equipment, chemical products, oil, electricity.

GROSS DOMESTIC PRODUCT: US$1.057 trillion (purchasing power parity, 1999 est.).

BALANCE OF TRADE: Exports: US$46.9 billion (f.o.b., 1999 est.). Imports: US$48.7 billion (f.o.b., 1999 est.).

COUNTRY OVERVIEW

LOCATION AND SIZE. Located in South America, Brazil is the fifth largest country in the world, after Russia, Canada, China, and the United States. Brazil has an area of 8,511,965 square kilometers (3,286,482 square miles), extending 4,320 kilometers (2,684 miles) from north to south and 4,328 kilometers (2,689 miles) from east to west, and a total coastline of 7,491 kilometers (4,655 miles). Brazil borders all the countries of South America except Chile and Ecuador. Brazil's capital city, Brasília, is located in the country's midwest; its largest cities, São Paulo and Rio de Janeiro, are located in the southeast.

POPULATION. The population of Brazil was approximately 172.86 million in July 2000, which was an increase of 17.7 percent from the 1991 population of 146.83 million. In 2000 the birth rate was estimated at 18.84 births per 1,000, and the death rate at 9.37 deaths per 1,000. The population growth rate declined by an average of 1.9 percent annually between 1980–1990, to 0.94 percent in 2000, reflecting the effect of birth control programs developed by the Brazilian government during the 1990s. It was forecasted that the population would reach approximately 190 million by the year 2010.

Brazil is the most populous country in Latin America and the fifth most populous country in the world. The highest concentration of Brazilians live in the Atlantic coastal region. Of the total population, the states of Minas Gerais, Rio de Janeiro, and São Paulo contain approximately 41 percent; the states of Rio Grande do Sul, Bahia, Pernambuco, and Ceará contain about 23 percent; and the remaining states hold about 36 percent. The population is extremely urbanized with 78 percent of the population living in cities. Approximately 29 percent of the population is between 0–14 years old, 66 percent is between 15–64 years old, and only 5 percent is over 65 years old.

About 55 percent of the Brazilian population is comprised of whites, the descendants of Portuguese, German, Italian, Spanish, and Polish immigrants; 38 percent are mixed white and black; 6 percent are blacks of African descent; and others comprise 1 percent. **Immigration** was a major determinant of the population structure in Brazil. During colonial times, Portuguese and Africans immigrated to the northeastern region of Brazil. During the period between 1821–1945, approximately 5.2 million Europeans immigrated to Brazil, settling in the southern agricultural regions. After World War I, the Japanese community in Brazil grew to become the largest expatriate Japanese group of the world, with more than 1 million immigrants.

OVERVIEW OF ECONOMY

Before World War II Brazil was the leading world producer of many agricultural goods. Sugar, rubber, and coffee were important exports. However, price variations in the world market for these commodities left the Brazilian economy vulnerable. After the war, the government

succeeded in rapidly industrializing the economy in order to diversify and decrease its dependency on imported goods. Brazil became one of the only industrialized nations of South America and an important exporter of manufactured goods. Industry and agriculture are today the country's major economic sectors. However, the country's growing prosperity was offset by the **inflation** caused by **budget deficits**.

Brazil is unable to produce enough oil to meet domestic demand, and needs to import most heavy indus-

trial machinery and equipment. The government provides incentives for domestic petroleum production, and gives legal and fiscal incentives promoting foreign investment in heavy industry. **Multinationals** dominate Brazilian industry, followed by government-owned companies. The biggest government-owned company is Petróleo Brasileiro, or Petrobras, an oil drilling and processing company. Brazil has oil reserves located on the coast and in the Amazon Basin. The geography and topography are also extremely beneficial to agriculture. Most of the country has either a tropical or subtropical climate. Extensive water reserves provide for the growth of grains, which are extensive enough to meet domestic consumption and allow for substantial exports.

Government **external debt** more than doubled during the 1980s and 1990s. Total outstanding and disbursed debt grew from US$61.3 billion in 1979, to US$114.5 billion in 1989, and to US$221.8 billion in 1999. The increase in government debt was due mainly to increased interest paid to its lenders and the borrowing of new money to implement economic and social plans in the country. However, because the new loans were used ineffectively, the **debt service** increased significantly. By making bigger payments to offset the debt, the government was left with few resources to carry on its own economic and social development plans. Total debt service (the interest paid on loans) increased from US$11.3 billion in 1979, to US$14.1 billion in 1989, and to US$73.7 billion in 1999.

The Brazilian government follows International Monetary Fund (IMF) economic, fiscal, and social objectives in order to receive funds. Brazil started a **structural adjustment program** at the request of the IMF, receiving a US$41.5 billion financing package in November 1998. The **privatization** policy adopted by President Fernando Henrique Cardoso decreased government participation in industry, and brought in much-needed foreign investment. In 1999, Brazil's debt-to-GDP ratio of 48 percent beat the IMF target. After the currency was **devaluated** by more than 60 percent in 1999, Brazil negotiated with the IMF on adjustments to the 1999–2001 economic program. Lowered economic targets were agreed upon in January 1999, when the debt-to-GDP ratio was set to fall below 46.5 percent by the end of 2001.

POLITICS, GOVERNMENT, AND TAXATION

The Brazilian Constitution, created in 1988, supports a democratic government with universal suffrage by direct and secret ballot. Voting is compulsory for literate persons between 18 and 69 years of age and is optional for persons who are illiterate, over 70 years of age, or 16 and 17 years of age. There are 3 branches of government: the executive, legislative, and judicial. The president exercises executive power, and is elected by direct ballot to a 4-year term. Legislative power is exercised by the **bicameral** (2-chambered) National Congress comprised of: the Federal Senate, or upper house, whose 81 members are elected by a system of **proportional representation** for 4 years; and the Chamber of Deputies, or lower house, whose 513 members are elected for 8 years by direct ballot, and whose districts are proportional to the size of the population. Each state has a directly elected governor and

an elected legislature. The municipalities are governed by directly elected mayors and an elected legislature.

Judicial power is exercised by the Supreme Federal Tribunal, whose judges are appointed for life and who are elected by their own tribunal members. Brazil's judicial system plays an important role in the Brazilian economy. It is responsible for compliance to laws regarding the economy, which are determined by the constitution. Any government decision affecting the rights of the individual is contested and supported by an independent judicial system. Therefore, radical changes in legislature regarding the economy are almost impossible if the judicial system disapproves.

Brazil went through decades of military dictatorship. The military overthrew the left-wing regime of President João Goulart in 1964 and ruled Brazil until 1985. The Brazilian military exerted complete control over the economy, politics, and popular media. All mass communication, art, and popular opinion were censored by military intelligence. Many leftist politicians were arrested and exiled to other countries during these dark years. However, in 1985, popular pressures and a **recession** led to peaceful democratic elections and indirect elections for the presidency. The legislative election of 1985 resulted in the formation of the democratic regimes of the 1980s and 1990s, and the military lost its power and influence in the economy. Since then there have been military, navy, and aviation ministries in the Brazilian government, but their influence has not been felt in the most important economic and political decisions.

A coalition of the Party of Brazilian Social Democracy (PSDB), the Liberal Front Party (PFL), and the Party of the Brazilian Democratic Movement (PMDB) has held power since Brazil became a democracy. This coalition is opposed by the coalition of the Worker's Party (PT) and other smaller parties. The PSDB and the PT were the strongest political forces during the 1990s, directly opposing each other in the national congress and throughout the states.

The Democratic Workers' Party (PDT), led by Leonel Brizola, criticized the military dictatorship of the 1970s. The Brazilian Democratic Movement (MDB), which later turned into the PMDB, also opposed the military regime. The PFL represents the conservative front of Brazil with alliances to the winner of the 1989 presidential elections. The **Communist** Party of Brazil (PC) represents extreme opposition to the government and has alliances with the organizers of the Landless Movement.

Brazil had its first democratic presidential elections in 1989 after decades of military dictatorship. Luís Inácio da Silva, also known as Lula, represented a coalition of worker union parties (including the PT), but lost to Fernando Collor de Mello who represented a liberal, pro-business party. In the democratic elections of 1994 (the second since 1960), Lula fell again to Fernando Henrique Cardoso. Cardoso developed a strong economic policy, cutting inflation, and decreasing government spending in order to meet IMF targets and receive loans. The Brazilian real was then tied to the U.S. dollar and forced to maintain a constant **exchange rate**. Inflation stabilized, but the cuts in government expenditure generated a recession in the country. In 1997 Brazil's congress approved a constitutional amendment enabling Fernando Henrique Cardoso to run for reelection in 1998. He was reelected for a second term, beating Lula again and continuing his economic policies.

Brazil's government plays a large role in the economy, controlling many sectors of the economy that are considered strategic, including power generation, oil extraction, mining of natural resources, water supply, and telecommunications. Fernando Henrique Cardoso began to adopt policies to end these **monopolies**. The policies include privatization of state-run companies, and **deregulation** of the energy and mining sectors.

Nearly 61 percent of government revenue comes from tax payments. Personal **income tax** rates are progressive, with a maximum rate of 25 percent. The income tax rate on corporations and other legal entities are also progressive, with a maximum of 30 percent. Profits are taxed at up to 50.5 percent and capital gains at 25 percent. A **value-added tax** that ranges from 10 percent to 15 percent is payable on sales and transfers of goods in accordance with the nature of the production. Apart from personal income taxes, government taxes are applied on corporation income, **turnover**, sales, financial operations, minerals, fuels, electric power, real estate, municipal service, and urban real estate. Tax evasion is rampant in Brazil, but this crime came under attack during 2000. The Central Bank of Brazil and the Ministério da Receita (Ministry of Income) compared their records in order to determine which Brazilians had not filed income taxes.

INFRASTRUCTURE, POWER, AND COMMUNICATIONS

Roads are the primary method of transportation in Brazil of both passengers and freight. With an estimated 21.31 million passenger cars and 5.5 million commercial vehicles in 1998, the highway system is inadequate and poorly maintained. There are approximately 1.98 million kilometers (1.23 million miles) of highways in Brazil, but only 184,140 kilometers (114,425 miles) of these roads were paved in 1996. A study by the World Bank shows that in the early 1990s 28 percent of the country's highways were in poor condition. Furthermore, the lack of proper maintenance increased transportation costs in Brazil by nearly 15 percent over the same period. The government implemented road construction plans in order to integrate the industrialized south with the less developed northeastern and northern areas. This integration enabled agricultural producers to move goods to ports located in the coastal areas for exportation. The railway system in Brazil is very limited. There are only 27,882 kilometers (17,326 miles) of tracks in Brazil (excluding urban commuter lines) and this number is in decline as track falls out of service.

In contrast, Brazil's air transportation is well developed with 48 main airports, 21 of which are international. In 1998 about 31 million passengers used Brazilian airlines, traveling a total of 27.39 million kilometers (17.02 million miles). The total weight of airline freight was equal to 602.74 million metric tons and Brazilian airlines carried freight over 2.2 billion kilometers (1.36 billion miles). Guarulhos International Airport at São Paulo and Galeão International Airport at Rio de Janeiro are the most important and active international airports of Brazil.

Hydroelectric plants generate most of Brazil's electrical power, responsible for 91 percent of the total production. Secondary sources include fossil fuels and nuclear energy. Only state companies are allowed to supply electrical power to the population, producing a total of 316.927 billion kilowatt-hours (kWh) of electricity in

Communications

Country	Newspapers	Radios	TV Sets[a]	Cable subscribers[a]	Mobile Phones[a]	Fax Machines[a]	Personal Computers[a]	Internet Hosts[b]	Internet Users[b]
	1996	1997	1998	1998	1998	1998	1998	1999	1999
Brazil	40	444	316	16.3	47	3.1	30.1	18.45	3,500
United States	215	2,146	847	244.3	256	78.4	458.6	1,508.77	74,100
Argentina	123	681	289	163.1	78	2.0	44.3	27.85	900
Colombia	46	581	217	16.7	49	4.8	27.9	7.51	664

[a]Data are from International Telecommunication Union, *World Telecommunication Development Report 1999* and are per 1,000 people.
[b]Data are from the Internet Software Consortium (http://www.isc.org) and are per 10,000 people.

SOURCE: World Bank. *World Development Indicators 2000.*

1998. Domestic production falls 20 billion kWh short of domestic need, causing Brazil to import electricity from neighboring countries such as Paraguay. Power supply is reliable most of the time, and shortages and blackouts are infrequent in urban areas.

Telecommunications services are well developed. Privatized in 1999, telephone service is provided by a number of privately held foreign capital companies. The country has approximately 19 million main lines in use (1997 est.) and 8 million mobile cellular phones in use (1998 est.). There are 138 television broadcast stations (1997) that are sent to 316 television sets per 1,000 people (1998). Computer access is still limited, evidenced by the number of personal computers (30.1) and Internet hosts (1.84) per 1,000 people recorded in 1998.

ECONOMIC SECTORS

Brazil's major economic sectors are all well developed. The agricultural sector of Brazil represented a larger percentage of the **gross domestic product** than industry until 1945. At that time, the government supported industrialization and direct investment in industry, with **subsidies** and trade protection for Brazilian industrial products. Industry was almost 3 times more valuable than agriculture as a percentage of gross domestic product by 1999. In the agriculture sector, Brazil is one of the world's largest producers of soybeans and coffee. International competitors watch Brazil's weather to determine the success of the soybean and coffee season, setting international prices based on Brazil's harvest. The agriculture sector represented 8.4 percent of the gross domestic product in 1999 and employed 31 percent of the workforce.

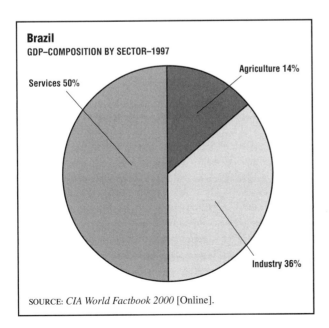

Brazil
GDP–COMPOSITION BY SECTOR–1997

Services 50%

Agriculture 14%

Industry 36%

SOURCE: *CIA World Factbook 2000* [Online].

The government uses import taxes to protect many Brazilian industries against international competition. These industries include textiles, shoes, chemicals, cement, lumber, iron ore, tin, steel, aircraft, motor vehicles and parts, and other machinery and equipment. The footwear industry is the most important finished good exported from Brazil. Government-owned Petrobras and Brazilian Aeronautics Enterprise are important companies headquartered in Brazil that produce oil and aircraft, respectively. The industrial sector represented 31.7 percent of the gross domestic product in 1999. Twenty-seven percent of the employed workforce was in the industrial sector.

The third most important developed sector of the Brazilian economy is the services sector. It represented 59.9 percent of the gross domestic product in 1999. Tourism has increased rapidly with an estimated 4.82 million foreign tourist arrivals and receipts of US$3.68 billion from foreign tourists in 1998. This represented an increase from 2.67 million foreign tourist arrivals and receipts of US$2.47 billion in 1996. Forty-two percent of the employed working force was in the service sector.

AGRICULTURE

Brazil has been the world's second largest exporter of agricultural goods since 1977. With the exception of imported wheat, Brazil is self-sufficient in food. In 1993, 48.9 million hectares (121 million acres) of land was available for agriculture in Brazil, the fifth largest agricultural area in the world. In 1999 agriculture accounted for 8.4 percent of the total GDP, a decrease from 11 percent in 1979. Average annual growth of agriculture as a percentage of the total gross domestic product was 3.4 percent in the 1979–1989 period, and 2.9 percent in the 1989–1999 period. Annual growth of agriculture as a percentage of gross domestic product leapt to 9.5 percent in 1999, due to the expansion of the export sector. This expansion occurred because the Brazilian government devalued its currency by nearly 60 percent in 1999, making Brazilian agricultural exports extremely cheap. Brazil is the largest producer of coffee, oranges, and sugar in the world; and is a primary exporter of coffee, cocoa, soybeans, orange juice, and sugar. The country imports rice, wheat, and barley.

Livestock, dairy, and poultry production play an important role in Brazilian agriculture. Since the 1940s, cattle have become one of the country's major sources of income. The area devoted to open pasture in 1994 was equal to 185.5 million hectares (458.38 million acres). This area occupied more than one-fifth of the total country. The government provided incentives to stimulate production, food conservation, and a more effective distribution of meat and dairy products.

COFFEE. Brazil's coffee production increased from 1 million metric tons in 1995–96 to 2.14 million metric tons by 1998–99, more than doubling in 4 years. However, production decreased slightly to 1.85 million metric tons in 1999–2000. The decline in production for 1999–2000 was linked to an agreement of the Association of Coffee Producing Countries (ACPC). ACPC developed a program to reduce the world supply of coffee in order to increase its price. The volume of coffee held back by each country is set at 20 percent of exports. However, Brazil still remains the largest producer and exporter of coffee in the world.

SOYBEANS. Soybean production in Brazil increased considerably for the 1999–2000 harvest. The average production of soybeans for 1994–99 was 28.23 million metric tons and for 1999–2000 alone was 32.5 million metric tons. The increase in soybean production for the 1999–2000 harvest was equivalent to 15 percent over the 1994–99 average. This increase was due to favorable weather in the southeast area of Brazil, where most of the farms are located. Another positive effect was that the world market increased imports from Brazil after the currency devaluation. The increase in soybean exports was equal to 24 percent, from 8.93 million metric tons for 1998–99 to 11.16 million metric tons for 1999–2000. Brazil is the second largest soybean producer and exporter (after the United States) in the world. The total area used for soybean production is equal to 13.4 million hectares (33.16 million acres).

ORANGES. Brazil is the largest producer and exporter of oranges and orange juice in the world. Brazil's total production was equal to 1.1 million metric tons in 1999–2000, or 47 percent of the world total. Orange juice consumption in Brazil is very small, only 18,000 metric tons for 1999–2000. The remainder is exported, at 1.16 million metric tons for 1999–2000 (including tangerine juice). Brazil's orange production and export volume declined from 1998–99 levels by 19 and 11 percent, respectively, in 1999–2000.

SUGAR. Since the time of Portuguese colonization, Brazil has been the largest producer and exporter of sugar in the world. Sugarcane production is concentrated in the northeastern area. Brazilian companies process sugarcane into sugar and alcohol. Sugar is mostly exported to the rest of the world while alcohol is mostly used as fuel for passenger vehicles. Passenger vehicles in Brazil are powered by either a combination of oil and alcohol, or solely alcohol. The Brazilian government developed research and financial incentives for utilization of alcohol in passenger vehicles after the world oil crisis in 1973–74. Brazil's sugar production in 1999–2000 was equal to 20.1 million metric tons. Sugar exports for 1999–2000 were equal to 11.3 million metric tons.

TOBACCO. Tobacco is another major agricultural product. Brazil is the third largest producer (after China and India) and largest exporter of tobacco in the world. During the 2000 calendar year, 493,100 metric tons were produced and 350,000 metric tons of tobacco were exported from Brazil. Tobacco production in Brazil increased from 365,000 metric tons in 1996 to 493,100 in 2000, an increase of 35 percent. Tobacco exports in Brazil increased from 282,500 metric tons in 1996 to 350,000 in 2000, an increase of 24 percent.

COCOA. Cocoa production in Brazil has suffered the effects of mixed weather patterns and infection by the witches-broom fungus since 1989. Despite these problems, Brazil is the third largest cocoa producer and exporter in the world (after Côte D'Ivoire and Ghana). Cocoa production for 2000 was the lowest in 30 years, decreasing by 21 percent, from 159,119 metric tons in 1999 to 125,290 metric tons in 2000. Exports, however, increased by 3 percent, from 93,295 metric tons in 1999 to 96,100 metric tons in 2000. Brazil's chocolate consumption rose 89 percent from 1988–89 to 1995–96, from 62,700 metric tons to 118,500 metric tons. Cocoa imports in 2000 increased by 67 percent, setting an all-time high, from 50,350 metric tons in 1999 to 84,100 metric tons in 2000. The government tried to develop new cocoa strains resistant to the fungus, and to use pest management systems, but without success.

CORN. Brazil is the third largest producer of corn in the world (after China and the European Union). Corn production for 1999–2000 yielded 31.6 million metric tons, a decrease of 2 percent from the 1998–99 production of 32.35 million metric tons. Consumption after 1996–97 was higher than production, generating a need for imports. Corn imports were small, amounting to only 1.79 million metric tons in 1999–2000. It is expected corn production will surpass consumption in the future due to government production incentives.

BEEF. Brazil is the world's second largest producer (after the United States) and third largest exporter of beef (after Australia and the United States). Beef production for 2000 was 6.3 million metric tons, an increase of 4 percent from the 1999 production of 6.05 million metric tons. Beef exports for 2000 were equal to 650,000 metric tons, an increase of 18 percent from the 1999 export of 550,000 metric tons. In 2000 the mad cow disease in Europe helped boost beef exports from Brazil. In 1999 the European Union was the market for nearly 70 percent of Brazilian beef exports. However, Brazilian exporters expanded to other existing markets (such as the United States) and to new markets (mainly in Asia). Even though exports to the United States rose 50 percent in 1999 to 50,376 metric tons, the United States joined Canada (its NAFTA partner) in temporarily banning all imports of beef in 2001.

DAIRY. Brazil's dairy production is the sixth largest in the world (after the United States, India, Russia, Germany, and France), but all of its production is consumed domestically. Total production of fresh cow's milk was equal to 22.8 million metric tons in 2000.

POULTRY. Brazil's poultry production ranks third in the world (after the United States and China). Broiler meat exports from Brazil also rank third in the world (after the United States and Hong Kong). Broiler production has increased significantly throughout the last 5 years. Broiler meat production increased from 4.05 million metric tons in 1995 to 5.45 million metric tons in 2000, an increase of 35 percent. Broiler meat exports went from 424,000 metric tons in 1995 to 850,000 metric tons in 2000, an increase of 100 percent in only 5 years. Most of the increase in exports happened in the years of 1999 and 2000, when the devalued real boosted broiler meat exports. In 2000 the mad cow disease in Europe helped to increase broiler meat exports. Poultry exports increased 26 percent in 1999, and 20 percent in 2000. The European Union increased its imports of Brazilian poultry by 50 percent in 2000.

OTHER. Brazil's pork production was equal to 1.95 million metric tons in 2000, mostly for domestic consumption. Fishing is limited, and lamb and sheep are not raised in Brazil due to the tropical weather.

INDUSTRY

Peak industrial growth was achieved in 1973, when the manufacturing sector grew by 15.8 percent. In 1999 the industrial sector accounted for 31.7 percent of the total gross domestic product, decreasing from 40.6 percent in 1979. The average annual industrial growth rate was 2.3 percent during 1979–1989, and 2.1 percent during 1989–1999. Industrial growth decreased 1.3 and 1.7 percent in 1998 and 1999, respectively; however, industry grew by 6.5 percent by the end of 2000. The industries that developed most in the year 2000 were the automobile (18.9 percent), parts and machinery (18 percent), mining (11.9 percent), electrical and communications (11.9 percent), and metal processing (7.6 percent) industries. Industry in Brazil employed 27 percent of the workforce. Industrial products included iron and steel, automobiles, petroleum, chemicals, and cement.

MANUFACTURING. The manufacturing sector contributed 22.7 percent of the gross domestic product in 1999, engaging 11.8 percent of the workforce in 1998. The manufacturing sector decreased as a percentage of gross domestic product from 31 percent in 1979 to 29.5 percent in 1989, and 22.7 percent in 1998 and 1999. This was caused in part by a lack of foreign investment and inflationary problems during the 1980s and 1990s. The instability generated by inflation and uncertain government policies caused tremendous fluctuations in manufacturing growth rates. Major products in the manufac-

turing sector are televisions, VCRs, telephones, and computer chips. There are a few national companies that are domestically oriented, such as Consul and Brastemp. There are also companies that are primarily export oriented, such as Nokia, Intel, and Compaq.

State participation in manufacturing occurs in the production of textiles and clothing, footwear, food, and beverages. These industries comprise a large proportion of the manufacturing sector, but there are also new industries that have been developed in the last few decades with government aid. Machinery and transport equipment, construction materials, sugar cane and wood derivatives, and chemicals are important manufacturing industries. Direct government participation is noticed in the oil processing industry and passenger jet aircraft industry through partial ownership of such companies. Indirect government participation is noticed in the textile industry and machinery industry through export subsidies and low interest loans.

TRANSPORT VEHICLES. Automobiles are the most important manufactured items in Brazil. Brazil's passenger automotive production was approximately 1.25 million passenger car units, 350,000 commercial vehicles, and 17,000 tractors in 1998. Machinery and transport equipment were the biggest exports from Brazil, accounting for US$12.6 billion in 1998, or 25 percent of total exports. Brazil has manufacturing plants for General Motors, Volkswagen, Ford, Fiat, Honda, and Toyota. Workers are highly unionized, receiving the highest salaries among the manufacturing industries. In 1998, 292,290 people were employed in the industry.

STEEL. Crude steel production in 1998 was 25.76 million metric tons. Vast reserves of ore and high domestic demand for steel products have helped the industry. Brazil exported US$3.67 million in steel and ore in 1998.

TEXTILES. The national textile industry is responsible for 3 percent of world production. Total sales average US$19 billion per year; exports were US$2.9 billion in 1998. Brazil has the largest textile operating facilities in Latin America. The textile industry is also labor intensive, employing 1.43 million people in 1998. Fibers and leather are used to produce clothing, shoes, and luggage. Brazilian shoes are exported mainly to Europe, where they are famous for their quality. The Brazilian textile industry was comprised of 44,478 mostly small producers in 1998.

PAPER. The Brazilian paper and pulp industry was responsible for the production of 273,000 metric tons of newsprint in 1998. The industry consisted of approximately 200 companies, employing approximately 80,000 people directly in their processing operations and 60,000 people in forestry operations. Pulp and waste paper exports were US$1 billion for 1998.

MINING. The mining sector was protected by the 1988 constitution against foreign majority participation of direct mining companies. This was a setback for the development of the mining sector because domestic investors lacked the capital for extensive mineral exploration. Private Brazilian investors and Brazilian corporations own the majority of the mineral industry. The participation of foreign capital is very limited due to Brazilian mining laws. However, in 1995 the Congress approved an amendment to the constitution allowing private companies (including foreigners) to participate in the mining industry through **joint ventures**, deregulating investments, and the privatization of state-owned mining plants. Shortly afterwards, the state-owned Companhia Vale do Rio Doce was privatized.

In 1999 mining contributed 0.6 percent of the gross domestic product of Brazil. The country is the world's largest producer of bauxite, gemstones, columbium, gold, iron ore, kaolin, manganese, tantalum, and tin. Major exports are iron ore, tin, and aluminum. The states of Minas Gerais, Bahia, and Goiás, located in the midwest of Brazil, have deposits of diamonds and other precious and semiprecious stones. In 1991 production of diamonds accounted for 1,500 carats, sixth in the world. Reserves of petroleum in Brazil were estimated in 1997 to be at 657 million metric tons.

Brazil's iron ore reserves are estimated at 20 billion metric tons. Mining operations started in 1942, extracting iron ore from the state of Minas Gerais, located on the country's Midwest. With the help of foreign investments, iron ore production increased to 59.4 million metric tons in 1974, and by 1985 output was 186 million metric tons. In 1981 Brazil became the world's leading exporter of iron ore, exporting 131 million metric tons in 1985, mostly to Japan and Germany.

SERVICES

The services sector accounted for 59.9 percent of the gross domestic product in 1999. Government participation in this sector was extremely high, with interests in land, air, and water transportation; postal, telecommunications, and financial services; and research and development. Approximately 42 percent of the workforce was employed in the services sector. The service sector's contribution to gross domestic product was 48.3 percent in 1979, 48.8 percent in 1989, and 59.9 percent in 1999. Average annual growth was 1.9 percent for the 1979–89 period and 2.7 percent for 1989–99.

TOURISM. The number of tourists that visit Brazil increased considerably during the 1990s. In 1994, 1.8 million foreign tourists visited Brazil, generating receipts of US$1.9 billion. In 1999, 5.1 million foreign tourists arrived, spending over US$4 billion. Argentina ranked first with 1.5 million visitors in 1999, American tourists ranked second with 0.6 million visitors, and Germans ranked third with 0.3 million visitors. The average annual income of visitors in 1999 was US$37,000 and they spent an average of US$79 per day, excluding expenses of international airfare. Brazil has over 10,000 hotels and other forms of accommodation. Approximately 63 percent of the existing hotel rooms were occupied in 1998. Hotels generate over 1 million jobs and pay over US$400 million in taxes.

Tourists are attracted to Rio de Janeiro for its notable sights: the Pão de Açúcar (Sugar Loaf Mountain), with its cable car; the Corcovado, with its statue of Jesus Christ the Redeemer; and Copacabana Beach, with its beautiful people and mosaic sidewalks. The historic city of Ouro Preto in Minas Gerais, and the churches of Bahia also attract many tourists. **Ecotourism** is developed in the Amazon Valley cities such as Belém and Manaus, the Iguaçu Falls in the south, and in the flooded areas of the Pantanal located in the western central region. Brazil is most famous for its Carnival, that usually takes place in February. Rio de Janeiro's Desfile das Escolas de Samba (Samba Schools Parade) attracts millions of tourists every year.

Foreign and government investments in tourism are important to the economy. The Inter-American Development Bank (IDB) and the Brazilian government invested 1.2 billion in the northeast region, starting in 1994. Investments in that region were responsible for renovating airports, improving public sanitation, preserving natural ecosystems, and restoring cultural practices. These investments rapidly boosted the tourist economy in the northeast, and foreign investment helped with the construction of multimillion dollar resorts in the coastal areas of the northeast. Such investments helped attract an increasing number of tourists to the northeast region. Other investments funded by the IDB and Brazilian government are planned for the Amazon and Pantanal regions, and in the south of Brazil.

FINANCIAL SERVICES. The government owns most of the financial sector, the largest component of the services industry. The 3 largest banks of Brazil—the Bank of Brazil, Federal Economic Register, and National Bank of Economic and Social Development (BNDES)—accounted for US$181.5 billion in total assets in 2000. The assets of the 3 major banks represented approximately 23 percent of the gross domestic product in 1999. The government holds the majority of the stocks of 3 national banks and a variety of state banks, with the exception of the privatized State Bank of São Paulo (BANESPA), the seventh largest bank in Brazil, and the State Bank of Rio de Janeiro (BANERJ).

The Bank of Brazil is the largest bank in Brazil and the largest financial institution in Latin America. It has

12.9 million customers and agencies in 30 different countries, employing 90,378 people. The total assets of the Bank of Brazil were worth roughly US$71 billion in 2000. The second largest bank, the Federal Economic Register, had assets worth approximately US$63 billion, employing 102,614 people in 2000. BNDES's assets were worth approximately US$48 billion, employing 1,246 people.

The Brazilian Discount Bank (BRADESCO) and Itaú have the largest assets in the **private sector**. BRADESCO has 3.6 million customers and more than 26 million checking accounts. Total assets for 2000 accounted for US$40 billion and US$27 billion for BRADESCO and Itaú, respectively.

The total assets of the 50 largest banks in Brazil were worth US$436 billion in 2000. This represented more than 50 percent of the total gross domestic product of that year. This part of the financial services sector employed 492,230 people in 2000.

RETAIL. This sector is responsible for the highest number of employed people in all sectors of the services industry. The number of companies that employ 500 or more workers is low; there were 75 companies which hired 500 or more workers in 1997 in the **retail** section, and 31 companies with 500 or more workers in the wholesale section. The bulk of employed people in this sector come from companies that employ less than 500 employees. Combined retail and wholesale sectors were made up of 708,635 retail and wholesale outlets. Total sales in the sector amounted to approximately US$300 billion in 1998. There are few retail chains in the economy. Most of them are located in the capitals of each state but are not part of the retail context in the less developed economies in rural areas. Food, grocery, and other retail chains are located in the coastal areas whereas small family-owned businesses compose the retail sector in smaller cities. The smaller retail businesses are responsible for employing a large number of people.

INTERNATIONAL TRADE

Brazil's overall trade flow (the sum of imports and exports) increased from US$63.8 billion in 1993 to US$97.2 billion in 1999, a 52 percent rise. Most of the increase in trade flow is due to the 94 percent increase in imports, from US$25.3 billion to US$49.2 billion. Exports increased by 24 percent during the same period, from US$38.6 billion to US$48 billion.

From 1981 until 1994, Brazil exported more than it imported. Beginning in 1995, however, Brazil began to run a **trade deficit**, due to the stabilization policies adopted by President Fernando Henrique Cardoso. Since then, the imbalance has grown considerably. Brazil's

Trade (expressed in billions of US$): Brazil		
	Exports	Imports
1975	8.670	13.592
1980	20.132	24.961
1985	25.639	14.332
1990	31.414	22.524
1995	46.506	53.783
1998	51.120	N/A

SOURCE: International Monetary Fund. *International Financial Statistics Yearbook 1999.*

trade deficit increased to record numbers in 1997, to US$6.8 billion. This continued in 1998 at US$6.6 billion, but in 1999, the trade deficit decreased to US$1.2 billion. Forecasts for the year 2000 are that exports will exceed imports. The decrease in the deficit can be attributed to the devaluation of the real in 1999.

The primary trading partners of Brazil are the United States and Argentina. The United States is the major importing country of Brazilian goods. Exports to the United States reached US$9.7 billion, representing 19 percent of all exports (this percentage has been the same since 1996). Major exports were manufactured goods, iron ore, soybeans, footwear, and coffee. Argentina was Brazil's second largest exporting destination with US$6.7 billion, or 13 percent; followed by Germany with US$3 billion, or 6 percent; the Netherlands with US$2.7 billion, or 5 percent; and Japan with US$2.2 billion, or 4 percent.

Major imports come from the United States. In 1998 Brazil imported goods valued at US$13.5 billion, representing 23 percent of all imports. Major imports were machinery and equipment, chemical products, oil, and electricity. The second largest imports come from Argentina with US$8 billion, or 14 percent of the total imports to Brazil; followed by Germany with US$5.2 billion, or 9 percent; Japan with US$3.3 billion, or 6 percent; and Italy with US$3.2 billion, or 6 percent.

Brazil is a member of the General Agreement on Tariffs and Trade (GATT) and the Law of the Sea treaties. Brazil is also member of MERCOSUR, a South American free trade agreement that includes Argentina, Paraguay, and Uruguay. Bolivia, Chile, and Venezuela were being considered for membership to the MERCOSUR free trade area.

MONEY

From the 1970s onwards, government spending and service of the public debt were the reasons for high inflation, and the subsequent rise in prices. Inflation was Brazil's greatest monetary problem until President

Exchange rates: Brazil	
reals (R$) per US$1	
Jan 2001	1.954
2000	1.830
1999	1.815
1998	1.161
1997	1.078
1996	1.005

Note: From October 1994 through January 14, 1999, the official rate was determined by a managed float; since January 15, 1999, the official rate floats independently with respect to the US dollar.

SOURCE: CIA *World Factbook 2001* [ONLINE].

GDP per Capita (US$)					
Country	1975	1980	1985	1990	1998
Brazil	3,464	4,253	4,039	4,078	4,509
United States	19,364	21,529	23,200	25,363	29,683
Argentina	7,317	7,793	6,354	5,782	8,475
Colombia	1,612	1,868	1,875	2,119	2,392

SOURCE: United Nations. *Human Development Report 2000; Trends in human development and per capita income.*

Fernando Henrique Cardoso in the mid-1990s adopted measures to slow down government spending and renegotiate public debt in order to contend with inflationary pressures. Brazil's currency was constantly devalued against the U.S. dollar. Currency devaluations generated incentives for the export market, decreasing the trade imbalance caused by debt payments and excess imports of manufactured goods. Devaluation helped the export market, which expanded its production when exports were given a price advantage provided by cheaper products in the world markets, but also represented a burden for domestic consumers who faced higher prices on imported goods. In the period from 1995 to 2000, the real devalued by approximately 100 percent. In 1995, 1 U.S. dollar was equal to 0.9176 reals. In 2000, 1 U.S. dollar was equal to 1.8302 reals. The devaluation was largely felt in early 1999, when the central bank of Brazil adopted a **floating exchange rate** system. The real then fell by 56 percent from 1998 to 1999.

In the past, Brazil had as many as 9 regional stock exchanges. However, with consolidations of the stock markets in the early 1990s and the advent of electronic trading, all securities transactions in Brazil are carried out in São Paulo, at the São Paulo Stock Exchange (BOVESPA). There are approximately 1,100 companies listed on the São Paulo exchange. The total market valuation of all listed companies on the São Paulo Exchange was US$228.6 billion in February 2001. Daily transactions are published in the leading newspapers and are available on the Internet. BOVESPA is part of the leading technology exchanges, offering electronic and after-hours trading options. The Rio de Janeiro Stock Exchange is the oldest financial institution in the country, founded in 1845. The Rio de Janeiro exchange is responsible for all the transactions in government bonds. Futures transactions are carried out at the Mercantile Futures Exchange (BM&F). Located in São Paulo, the BM&F has been operating since 1986 and is used mainly by coffee, beef, and cattle producers and buyers.

POVERTY AND WEALTH

Brazil has a few wealthy people and a large number of very poor people. The gap between the highest and the lowest social levels is high, even if it decreased during the late 1990s. Stabilization of the economy, through lower inflation levels, has given more purchasing power to the poor. Social indicators show that since 1994, when Fernando Henrique Cardoso became president, the percentage of people living below the poverty line decreased from 19 percent of the total population in 1993 to 14.51 percent in 1999, the lowest level in decades.

The income received by the top 10 percent of the Brazilian people represented 47.75 percent of the total income received in 1999. Meanwhile, the income received by the bottom 50 percent of the Brazilian people represented only 12.55 percent of the total income received in 1999. The top 1 percent of Brazilian people received 13.31 percent of the total income in 1999, more than the income for the bottom 50 percent combined.

Health services are free for all Brazilians, but the service is questionable. Medical doctors are well educated, but the demand in urban areas is much higher than what is available. Health and sanitary conditions vary from region to region. The south and southeast have better health services and sanitary conditions than the north and northeast.

Distribution of Income or Consumption by Percentage Share: Brazil	
Lowest 10%	0.9
Lowest 20%	2.5
Second 20%	5.5
Third 20%	10.0
Fourth 20%	18.3
Highest 20%	63.8
Highest 10%	47.6

Survey year: 1996

Note: This information refers to income shares by percentiles of the population and is ranked by per capita income.

SOURCE: *2000 World Development Indicators* [CD-ROM].

Household Consumption in PPP Terms

Country	All food	Clothing and footwear	Fuel and power[a]	Health care[b]	Education[b]	Transport & Communications	Other
Brazil	22	13	18	15	34	4	−6
United States	13	9	9	4	6	8	51
Argentina	30	9	17	15	15	5	9
Colombia	N/A	N/A	N/A	N/A	N/A	N/A	N/A

Data represent percentage of consumption in PPP terms.
[a]Excludes energy used for transport.
[b]Includes government and private expenditures.
SOURCE: World Bank. *World Development Indicators 2000.*

Despite a government program against illiteracy, developed in 1971, 15 percent of the population aged 15 and higher were still illiterate in 1999. This number is higher than the percentage in Latin America and the Caribbean Islands as a whole. The percentage of illiteracy among the upper-middle class is 10 percent. Education is free at the school and university levels. Secondary school is the responsibility of the municipalities, and universities are the responsibility of the federal and state governments.

The biggest social challenge facing the Brazilian government and society is the lack of education, housing, health care, and nutrition for the homeless children of Brazil. Thousands of children live in the streets, abandoned by their parents who cannot afford to raise them. Confronting starvation and living in deplorable conditions, these children abuse drugs, commit crimes, and resort to prostitution in order to survive. The government has developed programs through the Ministry of Social Assistance to combat the poverty and starvation of homeless children.

WORKING CONDITIONS

Brazil employed approximately 24.49 million people in 1998: 66 percent between 18 and 39 years of age, 31 percent between 40 and 64 years of age, 2 percent under 17 years of age, and 1 percent 65 years of age or older. The rate of unemployment for 2000 was 7.1 percent, a decline from the 1999 rate of 7.6 percent. This rate was calculated by the Instituto Brasileiro de Geografia e Estatística, (IBGE, Brazilian Institute of Geography and Statistics) in the 6 largest metropolitan areas of the country (Recife, Salvador, Belo Horizonte, Rio de Janeiro, São Paulo, and Porto Alegre). Unemployment rates for the 1998–2000 period were the highest in the decade, and at least as high as in 1984, the last year that the military held power.

Unions represent all major segments of industry. The National Confederation of Industrial Workers, the Na-tional Confederation of Commercial Workers, the National Confederation of Bank Workers, and the National Confederation of Ground Transport Workers are examples of the major labor unions in Brazil. Unions are legal, and financed by compulsory payments deducted from workers' paychecks and by membership dues. Approximately 7 million workers are unionized, accounting for 20–30 percent of the employed **labor force**. Brazilian workers have had the right to strike since 1984. In 1992 the economy was hit by an organized strike of port workers, airport workers, teachers, drivers, fare collectors, and government employees. In the late 1990s strikes were still common in Brazil.

The minimum wage was established in 1940. After correcting for inflation, the initial minimum wage was approximately US$100 per month in 1940; it rose to its maximum in 1960 at US$170 per month, and was equal to US$75 per month in December 2000.

Even though children under 14 years of age are prohibited from working, it is estimated that 14 percent of all children between 10 and 13 work. Maternity benefits include a 90-day leave for mothers and a one-week leave for fathers. Racial discrimination is illegal, but still practiced by many businesses in Brazil. Non-white workers and women are often underpaid. The role of women in the workforce has changed considerably in the 1980s and 1990s. According to the constitution, there must be equal pay for equal work regardless of sex. The government also provides special protection for women. While the more industrialized areas in Brazil, mostly the southeast region, employ women and treat them equally to male workers, the less industrialized regions, mostly the northern regions, still underpay women and discriminate against them.

COUNTRY HISTORY AND ECONOMIC DEVELOPMENT

1500. Portuguese Admiral Pedro Álvares Cabral discovers Brazil.

1549. Governor-general Tomé de Souza establishes the first government in Brazil.

1773. Pedro I proclaims Brazil's independence from Portugal on 7 September and is crowned emperor.

1883. Revolution establishes the Federal Republic of the United States of Brazil.

1888. Slavery is abolished in Brazil.

1891. First constitution under the Republic.

1930. Getúlio Vargas is named president, brought to power by the military with some civilian support.

1946. Eurico Dutra is elected president.

1950. Vargas returns, creating the National Development Bank and the state petroleum company.

1964. Military dictatorship. Congress appoints Humberto de Alencar Castelo Branco to the presidency.

1967. Arthur da Costa e Silva becomes president under a new constitution.

1973. Oil crisis results in a significant setback for Brazil's economy.

1979. General João Baptista de Oliveira Figueiredo becomes president and allows democratic elections.

1982. First democratic elections since 1964.

1985. Tancredo Neves, a senator from Minas Gerais from the opposition party, becomes president.

1988. The constitution is ratified, reestablishing direct elections for the presidency.

1989. Fernando Collor de Mello is elected president, and implements a **liberalization** plan.

1992. Itamar Franco takes over the presidency and tries to control inflation, which he does in 1994 with his "Real Plan."

1994. Fernando Henrique Cardoso is elected president on the strength of his economic plan.

1998. Fernando Henrique Cardoso is reelected.

FUTURE TRENDS

The continued success of economic measures adopted by Fernando Henrique Cardoso upon his re-election in 1998 depends upon the ability of the government to maintain a tight **monetary policy** and maintain fiscal restraint facing both national and international economic pressures. In the long run, the government needs to implement structural reforms, such as reforms of the tax and social security systems, decentralization of governmental spending to state and municipal governments, and privatization of major enterprises. Most of these measures require additional constitutional amendments or legislation.

The presidential election on October 2002 will have a strong influence on the political, fiscal, and economic programs adopted by President Cardoso. The triumph of the leftist parties shown in the 2000 municipal elections suggest that there is a disapproval of the harsh measures taken by Cardoso to restore stability. Since there is no popular candidate from the governing coalition for the 2002 presidential elections, there might be difficulties passing unpopular laws if the opposition comes into power. Contentious legislation such as tax reform and social security payments from retired civil servants may not be considered until after Cardoso's presidency ends. The passage of such laws would greatly improve the quality of the fiscal situation.

DEPENDENCIES

Brazil has no territories or colonies.

BIBLIOGRAPHY

Baaklini, Abdo I. *The Brazilian Legislature and Political System.* Westport, CT: Greenwood Press, 1992.

Bacha, Edmar L., and Herbert S. Bacha, editors. *Social Change in Brazil, 1945–1985: The Incomplete Transition.* Albuquerque: University of New Mexico Press, 1989.

Bak, Joan L. "Political Centralization and the Building of the Interventionist State in Brazil." *Luso-Brazilian Review.* Vol. 22, No. 1, Summer 1985.

Banco Central do Brasil. <http://www.bcb.gov.br>. Accessed February 2001.

Becker, Bertha K. *Brazil: A New Regional Power in the World-Economy.* New York: Cambridge University Press, 1992.

Brazilian Embassy in Washington. <http://www.brasilemb.org/>. Accessed in January 2001.

Burns, E. Bradford. *A History of Brazil,* 3rd ed. New York: Columbia University Press, 1993.

Economist Intelligence Unit. *Country Profile: Brazil.* London: Economist Intelligence Unit, 2001.

Fausto, Boris. *A Concise History of Brazil.* Cambridge, U.K.: Cambridge University Press, 1999.

Instituto Brasileiro de Geografia e Estatística (IBGE). <http://www.ibge.gov.br>. Accessed February 2001.

Instituto de Pesquisa Econômica Aplicada (IPEA). <http://www.ipea.gov.br./>. Accessed February 2001.

International Cocoa Organization (ICCO). *1997/98 Annual Report.* <http://www.icco.org/anrep.htm>. Accessed February 2001.

Latin American Network Information Center (LANIC). *Brazil.* <http://www.lanic.utexas.edu/la/brazil/>. Accessed February 2001.

Levine, Robert M. *The History of Brazil.* Westport, CT: Greenwood Press, 1999.

Ministério do Esporte e Turismo. *EMBRATUR: Empresa Brasileira de Turismo.* <http://200.236.105.128/estatisticas/estatisticas.htm>. Accessed August 2001.

Parkin, Vincent. *Chronic Inflation in an Industrialising Economy: The Brazilian Experience.* New York: Cambridge University Press, 1991.

Payne, Leigh A. *Brazilian Industrialists and Democratic Change.* Baltimore: Johns Hopkins University Press, 1994.

Schneider, Ronald M. *Brazil: Culture and Politics in a New Industrial Powerhouse.* Boulder, CO: Westview Press, 1996.

U.S. Central Intelligence Agency. *World Factbook 2000.* <http://www.odci.gov/cia/publications/factbook/index.html>. Accessed August 2001.

U.S. Department of State. *FY 2001 Country Commercial Guide: Brazil.* <http://www.state.gov/www/about_state/business/com_guides/2001/wha/index.html>. Accessed February 2001.

The World Bank Group. *Countries: Brazil.* <http://www.worldbank.org/html/extdr/offrep/lac/br.htm>. Accessed February 2001.

—*Ecio F. Costa*

CANADA

CAPITAL: Ottawa.

MONETARY UNIT: Canadian dollar (Can$). One Canadian dollar equals 100 cents. There are coins of 1, 5, 10, and 25 cents as well as 1 and 2 dollar coins. Paper currency comes in denominations of Can$1, 2, 5, 10, 20, 50, and 100.

CHIEF EXPORTS: Motor vehicles and parts, newsprint, wood pulp, timber, crude petroleum, machinery, natural gas, aluminum, telecommunications equipment, electricity.

CHIEF IMPORTS: Machinery and equipment, crude oil, chemicals, motor vehicles and parts, durable consumer goods, electricity.

GROSS DOMESTIC PRODUCT: US$722.3 billion (purchasing power parity, 1999 est.).

BALANCE OF TRADE: Exports: US$277 billion (f.o.b., 1999 est.). **Imports:** US$259.3 billion (f.o.b., 1999 est.).

COUNTRY OVERVIEW

LOCATION AND SIZE. Canada is located in the northern-most region of North America. Its southern territories run along the northern border of the continental United States. Canada is one of the largest countries in the world, second only to Russia in territorial size. It has a total area of 9.9 million square kilometers (3.8 million square miles). This includes 755,170 square kilometers (291,571 square miles) of water. The country touches 3 oceans—the Atlantic, the Arctic, and the Pacific—and its coastline is 243,791 kilometers (151,473 miles) long. Canada's border with the United States is 8,893 kilometers (5,526 miles) in length and includes a 2,477-kilometer (1,539-mile) border with Alaska. Toronto is the largest city in Canada with a population of 4.3 million. Other major cities include Montreal (3.3 million people), Vancouver (1.8 million people), and Ottawa (1 million people). Located in the southeast corner of the nation, Ottawa is the nation's capital. The climate and geography of Canada vary greatly from temperate in the south to arctic in the north and from islands and plains in the east to mountains in the west.

POPULATION. For its size, Canada has a small population. Although physically it is the second-largest country in the world, its population was only 31,281,092, according to a July 2000 estimate, or just under one-tenth the size of that of the United States. The nation has a low birth rate of 1.64 children born to each woman, or 11.41 births per 1,000 people. The mortality rate is 7.39 deaths per 1,000. However, the infant mortality rate is low with 5.08 deaths per 1,000 live births. Average life expectancy for males is 76.02 years and 83 for females. The population growth rate is moderate at 1.02 percent, although the positive growth rate is chiefly due to **immigration**. Each year there is an average of 6.2 immigrants for every 1,000 people. Canada has a liberal immigration policy and it goes to great lengths to accept refugees and asylum seekers from around the world. In 2000, Canada allowed 41,800 asylum seekers to settle in the country.

Despite the vastness of the nation, 90 percent of the Canadian population is located within 160 kilometers (100 miles) of the U.S. border. With the exception of some notable groups, most of the nation's people live in urban areas. By 2000, 75 percent of Canadians lived in cities or towns. The nation is ethnically diverse. People of British ancestry make up 28 percent of the population, while the French comprise 23 percent. Other Europeans, mainly Eastern Europeans, make up 15 percent. There is a small but visible Native American population (2 percent). About 6 percent of the population is divided between people of Asian, Arab, African, and Hispanic descent, while the remaining 26 percent of Canadians are of mixed ancestry. Canada is almost evenly divided between Protestants and Roman Catholics. There are deep divisions between the English-speaking Canadians and the French-speakers who are concentrated in the province of Quebec. The people of Quebec have a distinct culture and the government accepts and even encourages efforts to maintain Quebec's identity. Because of these divisions, the nation has 2 main official languages, English and French. The government also recognizes several Native American languages. However, tensions between the English and French have led to repeated efforts by na-

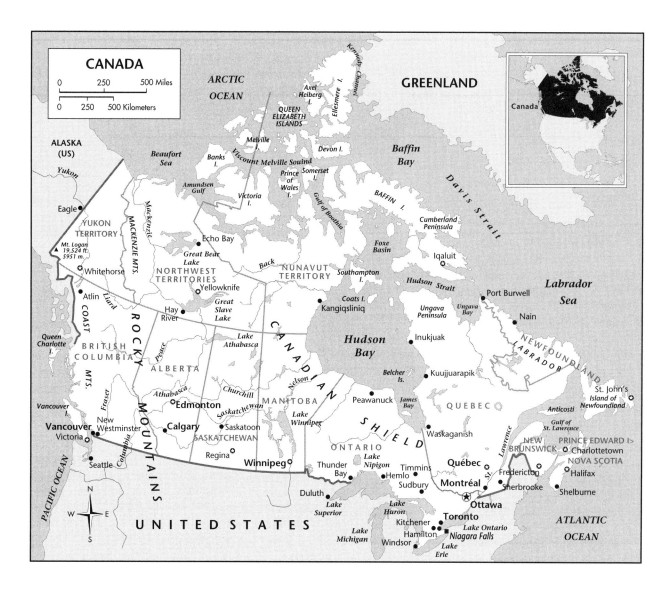

tionalists in Quebec to break away and form their own nation. The debate over independence for Quebec is Canada's most serious political issue and there is yet to be a permanent settlement of the question.

There are other regional differences in Canada that are similar to the differences in the United States. People in the maritime provinces of Nova Scotia, New Brunswick, and Prince Edward Island have a similar culture to those in the New England region of the United States, while the western regions of both nations are also closely related with numerous ranches and farms. Also like the United States, the population of Canada is aging. The fastest growing segment of the population is over age 65, which now makes up 13 percent of the population. Meanwhile, 19 percent of the population is under the age of 15.

OVERVIEW OF ECONOMY

Canada has the seventh-largest economy in the world. Most of the businesses are privately-owned, al-

though the government does play a major role in the health-care system and operates many services including transportation and utility companies. The Canadian economy is diverse and highly developed. It is very similar to the American economy, although smaller in size. In the aftermath of World War II, the nation was transformed from a rural economy, based on agriculture, to one based on industry and mining. The nation's economy has been further transformed since the 1970s and services now provide the main economic output.

The foundation of the Canadian economy is foreign trade and the United States is by far the nation's largest trade partner. Foreign trade is responsible for about 45 percent of the nation's **gross domestic product** (GDP). Free trade agreements between the 2 nations have increased trade by eliminating **tariffs**. Each day approximately US$1 billion worth of goods crosses the U.S.-Canadian border. To understand the scale of U.S.-Canadian trade, it is important to point out that the United States sends more products to Canada than it does to all of Latin America.

Despite the small size of its population, the Canadian economy is one of the most prosperous in the world. For instance, its **GDP per capita** was US$23,300 in 1999, reflecting Canadian workers' high wages compared to many other countries. Prospects for continued positive economic performance are good. Canada has a highly skilled and productive workforce. In 1999, there were 15.9 million people in Canada's workforce, and the nation had an unemployment rate of 7.6 percent, which was almost twice the American rate.

Like Americans, Canadians tend to have high levels of **disposable income**. This disposable income drives the Canadian economy as consumers spend their excess wages on a variety of products and services. This creates demand for increased production and the development of new products, which also means more and better-paying jobs. Also like the United States, advertising has a major impact on Canadian consumer spending. Television is the number-one form of advertising in Canada.

The nation's **infrastructure** is excellent and most of its factories and manufacturing plants are modern. In fact, Canada's transportation network is ranked as the best in the world by the World Economic Forum's *Global Competitiveness Report*. Canada has a variety of natural resources, including petroleum and natural gas, and a variety of metals and minerals. Over the past decade, Canada has also emerged as one of the leading nations in the high-tech and computer industry. Most of this growth has occurred in central Canada, mainly Ontario and Quebec, and is responsible for the increased migration of people to these areas. Much of the economic growth in Canada today is fueled by small- to medium-sized companies. Because Canada has abundant energy resources, the global oil crisis which began in 1999 has helped its energy companies increase their outputs and profits. The nation has abundant natural resources that include iron ore, nickel, copper, zinc, gold, lead, silver, timber, fish, coal, petroleum, natural gas, and hydropower.

Regionally, the Canadian economy varies greatly. In the Eastern provinces, marine industries—including fishing, telecommunications, and energy production—are the main components of the economy. In the French-speaking region of Quebec, the city of Montreal has become one of the nation's centers for high-technology firms. This includes a large number of computer software companies. There is also a large industrial base which includes companies that produce pharmaceuticals, aerospace products, and telecommunications equipment. Ontario is the nation's main industrial center. About half of all Canadian manufactured goods are produced in Ontario. The province is second only to Michigan as the largest producer of automobiles and car parts in North America. Ottawa, the nation's capital, is located in On-

tario. Other industries include chemicals, aerospace, steel, and food processing. The plains (or prairie) provinces of Alberta, Manitoba, and Saskatchewan are the home to four-fifths of Canada's agricultural lands. They are also the home to the majority of mining and fuel production. Alberta itself provides 90 percent of the nation's energy exports and is the home of Canada's oil and natural gas industry. British Columbia is in the Pacific Northwest. Forestry and tourism were traditionally the main elements of the region's economy, but financial services, including banking and insurance, have grown dramatically over the past decade. There is also a growing high-tech sector that is bolstered by the province's proximity to American firms such as Microsoft in the state of Washington. The Northern territories of the nation comprise one-third of its total size, but are home to only 100,000 people. These areas are home to Canada's Native American population, many of whom continue to follow traditional lifestyles based on hunting and fishing. Mining is the principal industry and there has been steady growth in diamond mining and finishing. Tourism also provides a substantial part of the region's economy.

Each of the nation's main economic sectors is highly developed. Although the agricultural sector is small, it takes advantage of the nation's generous natural resources. Increasingly, agriculture and fishing are concentrated in certain geographic regions of the country, mainly the west and southeast. The United States is the main market for all Canadian agricultural exports. In addition, the United States is the main destination for most of Canada's timber exports. Canada is also a major supplier of energy resources, including electricity and petroleum, to the United States. While industry has declined since the 1970s, it remains an important component of the country's economy. Automobile products provide one of Canada's principal exports, but the nation also produces a variety of consumer products and machinery. Nonetheless, large companies such as Ford and General Motors provide a significant percentage of the nation's industrial output. Services have seen the most dramatic growth in the Canadian economy over the past 2 decades. In addition to consumer-based businesses such as **retail** and tourism, financial services and telecommunications firms have grown dramatically. The government has offered significant support to these new technologies. For instance, the government has supported the development and installation of the only fiber-optic network in the world which carries only Internet traffic. The system, CA*Net3, will have 16 times the capacity of the largest U.S. system.

Budget surpluses over the past 3 years have allowed the government to begin paying down Canada's **national debt**. The debt has been reduced by Can$19 billion, and in 2000 it stood at Can$565 billion. The surpluses have also allowed the government to spend more on federal programs and to reduce some taxes. The nation is a net donor of foreign aid. In 1997, it provided US$2.1 billion in international aid.

There are several potential problems facing the Canadian economy. The most significant is the continuing question over the status of Quebec. Should Quebec become independent, it would significantly disrupt the Canadian economy, and the nation would lose a sizable proportion of its GDP. The second most pressing problem for Canada has been the migration of some of its best educated and trained workers to the United States. This "brain drain" is the result of lower taxes and higher wages in the United States. Finally, Canada's dependence on trade makes it vulnerable to slow downs in the economies of its major trade partners. This is especially true of the United States. In the 20th century, when the United States experienced economic **recessions** or depressions, Canada soon after suffered similar economic problems.

POLITICS, GOVERNMENT, AND TAXATION

Canada was formerly a British colony that gained independence in 1867. The nation is a parliamentary democracy and a confederation (a system in which the regional governments have a high degree of power). Canada is divided into 10 provinces and 3 territories. Each of the provinces has a substantial degree of political independence and power, more so than an American state.

The head of state is the British monarch, currently Queen Elizabeth II. She is represented in Canada by a governor-general whom she appoints on the advice of the prime minister for a 5-year term. The actual head of the government is the prime minister, who is the leader of the majority party in Parliament. Parliament itself is **bicameral** (2-chamber). The upper house is the Senate, whose 104 members are appointed for life by the governor-general upon the advice of the prime minister. Most of the real political power in Canada is in the lower chamber, the House of Commons. It consists of 301 members who are directly elected by the people to serve 5-year terms. Each province has an elected premier and a **unicameral** (single chamber) assembly. There is also a lieutenant-governor who is appointed by the governor-general.

Unlike the United States, which has only 2 main political parties, Canada has a number of different parties. The Bloc Québécois represents those who wish independence for Quebec. The Liberal Party is moderate and similar to the American Democratic Party, while the Progressive Conservative Party and the Canadian Alliance are similar to the American Republican Party. There are also a number of other minor parties, including the New Democratic Party. All of the major political parties support private enterprise to varying degrees, although the New Democratic Party favors more government oversight of the economy. There are also disagreements among the parties over free trade.

While the majority of businesses in Canada are privately owned, the government does play a major role in the economy. This is true of both the national and provincial governments. When the 2 levels of government are combined, they account for 21 percent of the nation's GDP. At times the provincial and national governments have disputes over economic policy. For instance, there is an ongoing disagreement between the national government and the maritime provinces over control of fishing rights and mineral resources in the Atlantic. Western provinces want more control over their own mineral and energy deposits while the central region of the nation seeks increased government spending to support economic development.

Often economic differences focus on environmental issues and worker concerns. The national government tends to favor more environmental regulation, even if it is economically disadvantageous. The same is true of issues such as worker safety and pay. However, since 1984 the national government has been engaged in a broad effort to return control over social and economic policies to the provinces. The main reason for devolution is economic; the national government has not had the financial resources to enforce many of its programs and regulations, so it has divested itself of them. In 1999, the national and provincial governments reached a sweeping agreement that called for combined authority over new social spending. Furthermore, the national government has given control of job training and worker retraining back to the provinces, but it has strengthened its role in regulating trade between the provinces and attempted to develop national regulations on stock trading and other financial services.

In 1998, the Canadian national government had revenues of US$121.8 billion and expenditures of US$115.1 billion. Compared with the United States, Canada's taxes are high, about 30 percent higher for the average person. In Canada, people with low incomes pay 16 percent of their income in taxes; the tax rates rise to 22 percent, then to 26 percent for those with incomes between Can$61,000 and Can$100,000, and finally to 29 percent for those with incomes over Can$100,000 per year. In 1998, taxes accounted for 38 percent of the nation's GDP. Significantly, taxes accounted for 60 percent of the growth in the Canadian economy from 1990–96. The country has a national 7 percent sales tax known as the Goods and Services Tax (GST). The GST is particularly unpopular among the Canadian people. Because of these high taxes, it is estimated that the **underground economy** is responsible for as much as 20 percent of economic activity. In 1999, the Canadian government estimated that it lost US$9 billion in tax revenues because of the underground economy.

On the other hand, these high taxes allow all Canadians to have full access to health care. The Canadian system is known as "Medicare" and it allows people to go to private doctors and a network of 950 hospitals and have their costs paid for by the government. The individual provinces and territories direct health-care planning and financing. The nation's taxes help keep the cost of prescription drugs low for individuals. However, limits on care and lengthy delays in care have led more and more people to pay for private care out of their own pockets. Some 30 percent of all new health-care spending is made in the **private sector**. In addition, education costs are low. Canada spends more per person on education than any of the other industrialized countries and the cost of college is very low compared with the United States. Nonetheless, the high tax rate has contributed to the brain drain from Canada and has caused some foreign companies to invest in the United States rather than Canada.

Although Canada is dependent on foreign investment to fuel its continuing economic expansion, it restricts investment in several key areas of its service sector. There is only 1 special trade zone in Canada and no **free trade zones**. Instead, Canada pursues free trade through multinational forums such as the World Trade Organization (WTO). It also works to deepen trade with partner countries such as the United States.

The United States and Canada cooperate on environmental issues and border disputes. The main mechanism to facilitate this cooperation is the International Joint Commission (ICJ). The 2 major environmental accords are the Great Lakes Water Quality Agreement of 1972, which controls water pollution in the Great Lakes, and the Air Quality Agreement of 1991, which helps coordinate policies on problems such as acid rain.

Canada spends only a small percentage of its GDP on defense. In 1998, it spent 1.2 percent of GDP or US$7.4 billion, compared with an average of around 2.5 percent of GDP for most developed nations. The long border with the United States does not need to be militarily defended, but Canada is a frequent contributor of troops for United Nations peacekeeping forces. It is also a member of the North Atlantic Treaty Organization (NATO, a military alliance consisting of Canada, the United States, and many European countries). As a NATO member, Canadian military forces have participated in the peacekeeping mission to Bosnia and in the military action against Serbia as a result of the atrocities in Kosovo in 1999.

INFRASTRUCTURE, POWER, AND COMMUNICATIONS

Canada has one of the best-developed infrastructures in the world. It meets the requirements for high-tech business and international trade. The telephone system is state-of-the-art and supported by a satellite system and 300 earth-based relay centers. There are also 5 international underwater cables (4 across the Atlantic and one across the Pacific). In addition, there are 750 Internet providers. All major cities have high-speed Internet capabilities. The nation's new CA*Net3 Internet system is scheduled to be completed in 2001. Canada has the lowest Internet access costs of the developed world. In 1997, there were an estimated 7–8 million Internet users, or about 1 in 4 Canadians.

Canada is an energy exporter. Its main exports are natural gas and oil. However, in 1998 the majority of electricity in Canada was produced by hydroelectric plants (59.77 percent). Fossil fuels provided the second-largest share of electricity with 27.18 percent of the total. Atomic power provided 12.25 percent. Total electric power production was 550.85 billion kilowatt hours (kWh). The nation consumed 484.51 billion kWh of electricity. It exported 39.5 billion kWh of power and imported 11.72 billion kWh of power.

Communications

Country	Newspapers	Radios	TV Sets[a]	Cable subscribers[a]	Mobile Phones[a]	Fax Machines[a]	Personal Computers[a]	Internet Hosts[b]	Internet Users[b]
	1996	1997	1998	1998	1998	1998	1998	1999	1999
Canada	159	1,077	715	263.8	176	33.3	330.0	422.97	11,000
United States	215	2,146	847	244.3	256	78.4	458.6	1,508.77	74,100
Mexico	97	325	261	15.7	35	3.0	47.0	23.02	1,822
Brazil	40	444	316	16.3	47	3.1	30.1	18.45	3,500

[a]Data are from International Telecommunication Union, *World Telecommunication Development Report 1999* and are per 1,000 people.
[b]Data are from the Internet Software Consortium (http://www.isc.org) and are per 10,000 people.

SOURCE: World Bank. *World Development Indicators 2000.*

The transport system is a blend of private and government-owned firms. Canada has 36,114 kilometers (22,441 miles) of railways, including 2 transcontinental systems. In 1995, the government **privatized** the freight carrier Canadian National. Passenger service is provided by the government-owned company VIA. There are 901,902 kilometers (560,442 miles) of roadways in the country, of which 318,371 kilometers (197,390 miles) are paved, including 16,571 kilometers (10,298 miles) of expressways. The nation's main east-west route is the 4,500-kilometer (2,796-mile) Trans-Canada Highway. All major cities have well-developed and inexpensive public transportation systems that are subsidized by provincial and local governments. The nation's trucking and rail systems are well-integrated with American distribution networks and vice versa. Each year some 400 million tons of goods are transported across Canadian highways. Trucks carry 70 percent of the goods that Canada annually exports to the United States. Canada has 1,411 airports, but only 515 have paved runways. Of these, 10 are international airports. There are also 15 heliports. U.S. and Canadian air carriers have unrestricted access to each other's airspace. Air Canada is the nation's major airline, but there are 25 U.S. and 47 other international airlines that fly into Canada. Air Canada controls 80 percent of the domestic market and this has led to higher than average air fares.

There are 3,000 kilometers (1,864 miles) of navigable waterways, including the massive Saint Lawrence Seaway which allows ocean-going vessels to sail from the Atlantic to ports such as Chicago and Thunder Bay, Ontario. There are 20 major ports, including Halifax, Montreal, Quebec, Saint John, Thunder Bay, Toronto, Vancouver, and Windsor. The busiest port is Vancouver, on the west coast. The nation's merchant marine consists of 114 ships, not including smaller vessels that travel only on the Great Lakes. Canada has an extensive network of pipelines to support its large energy industry. There are 23,564 kilometers (14,642 miles) of crude or refined oil pipelines and 74,980 kilometers (46,593 miles) of natural gas pipelines. Many of these pipelines deliver energy across the U.S.-Canada border.

ECONOMIC SECTORS

Since the 1970s the Canadian economy has been transformed from one based on industry and mining to one dominated by the service sector. Concurrently, the nation's agricultural sector has declined significantly. All sectors of the economy have incorporated increasing levels of technology. As a result, the economy has become less labor-intensive and more high-tech. In the past, as much as 60 percent of the nation's exports were based on minerals or other resources. However, by 2000, resource-based exports only accounted for 35 percent of

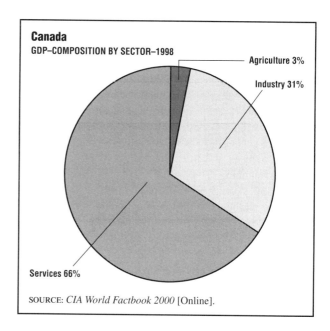

Canada
GDP—COMPOSITION BY SECTOR—1998

- Agriculture 3%
- Industry 31%
- Services 66%

SOURCE: *CIA World Factbook 2000* [Online].

Canada's exports. The world oil shortage continues to fuel Canada's energy exports and Canada remains the world's fifth-largest energy producer when oil, natural gas, hydropower, and atomic power are combined. Major energy companies include Shell Canada, Petro-Canada, BP-Amoco, and Burlington Resources.

The majority of exports are now based on sophisticated technologies. These types of exports include telecommunications equipment, computer software, various environmental technologies, and aerospace products. Canada's Nortel Networks is one of the largest and most respected telecommunications and networking compa-

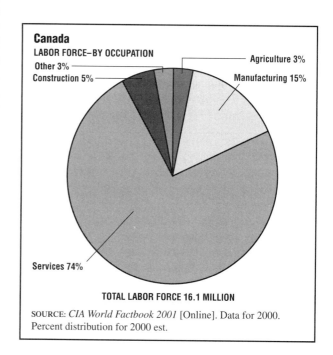

Canada
LABOR FORCE—BY OCCUPATION

- Other 3%
- Construction 5%
- Agriculture 3%
- Manufacturing 15%
- Services 74%

TOTAL LABOR FORCE 16.1 MILLION

SOURCE: *CIA World Factbook 2001* [Online]. Data for 2000. Percent distribution for 2000 est.

nies in the world. But like many companies, Nortel was hit hard by the downturn in this market niche in 2001, when it announced it was laying off thousands of employees and would take a loss of over US$19 billion in the second quarter of that year. Automobiles and car parts remain the leading cash export, followed by machinery and equipment. Exports of service-based items increased by 11.3 percent in 1999. Since 1992, the Canadian economy has experienced continued growth. Much of this is the result of trade with the United States, which enjoyed a sustained period of economic progress through the end of the 20th century. The strength of the nation's economy has led to increased levels of foreign investment. In 1999, foreign investment in Canada increased by 10 percent to reach a total of $240 billion. This accounted for 25 percent of the nation's GDP. Financial services, including insurance, accounted for the largest percentage of foreign investment.

The agricultural sector in Canada is undergoing increasing consolidation. Smaller family farms are being consolidated by large agricultural businesses. Since 1991, the number of farms whose output exceeded US$100,000 per year has increased by 10 percent. These large farms were concentrated in Quebec and Ontario, but there was substantial growth in the west. For instance, the province of Saskatchewan has experienced a 30 percent growth in large farms since 1991. There is also an overall decline in the total area of land being used for agriculture. Nonetheless, agriculture remains highly diverse. Crops range from wheat and barley to tobacco and vegetables. There is also significant timber production. Livestock production includes beef and veal, swine, poultry, duck, turkey, and goose. Furthermore, the nation is one of the world's largest fish harvesters. Agriculture accounts for 3 percent of the nation's GDP and 3 percent of its workforce. In 1999, 12 percent of the rural population lived on farms.

Canadian industry has become more efficient and productive by adopting ever-increasing levels of technology in manufacturing. Industrial productivity has increased by an average of 3 percent per year over the past decade. The principal industrial growth sectors include the automotive industry, electronics, computers and computer equipment, aircraft parts and equipment, and building supplies. The automotive sector is Canada's largest industrial employer and is dominated by companies such as Ford and General Motors. The implementation of the North American Free Trade Agreement (NAFTA), a trade agreement between the United States, Mexico, and Canada which eliminates taxes on goods traded between the 3 nations, has expanded industrial opportunities by opening new markets for Canadian exports in the United States and Mexico. However, NAFTA is a double-edged sword in that inefficient industries face increased competition from companies in Canada's NAFTA partners.

As a percentage of the overall economy, industry continues to decline although there is sustained growth in specific areas. In 1999, industry accounted for 31 percent of the nation's GDP and 16 percent of employment.

The service sector is the fastest growing segment of the Canadian economy. The nation's highly developed infrastructure has helped support the expansion of services by providing state-of-the-art telecommunications, transportation, and utilities. Services account for 66 percent of the nation's economy and employ 74 percent of the country's workforce. Of Canada's skilled workers, 80 percent are employed by the service sector. The strength of the service sector varies from region to region. Tourism and retail dominate areas of the southeast and west, while financial services are key components of the economy of central Canada. The banking sector is strong and composed of both domestic and foreign banking firms. In an effort to protect domestic businesses, Canada has a number of restrictions in place that limit foreign ownership of companies in the service sector that do business in the country.

AGRICULTURE

Agriculture in Canada is among the most sophisticated and technologically advanced in the world. Farmers use scientific crop and soil analysis as well as state-of-the-art equipment. By 1996, more than one-quarter of all Canadian farmers used a computer in the management of their crops and livestock. In 2000, there were 7,100 square kilometers (2,741 square miles) of irrigated land. While it produces substantial quantities of food for domestic consumers and for export, Canada also imports a significant amount of agricultural products. Total agricultural imports in 1999 amounted to US$10.8 billion. The United States supplies Canada with roughly two-thirds of its total agricultural imports. Conversely, the United States is Canada's main market for agricultural goods. In 1999, the United States was the destination for one-third of Canada's exports of crops, livestock, and fish.

While the overall number of Canadian farms continues to decline, the decline has slowed in recent years and several provinces are in fact adding or gaining new farms. The decline in farms has slowed to under 1 percent per year, the lowest level of decline since 1941. Since 1991, British Columbia has increased its number of farms by 12.6 percent, Alberta by 3 percent, Nova Scotia by 1 percent, and Newfoundland by 0.8 percent. Ontario continues to have the largest overall number of farms—over 68,000—followed by Alberta with 58,000, and Saskatchewan with 56,000. The total number of farms in Canada is approximately 275,000. The average size of a Canadian farm is 608 acres. Contrary to the trends in the rest of the country, British Columbia has experienced dramatic growth in the number of its small farms. About half of all new farms in the province have gross profits of US$10,000 or less. The number of new small farms in British Columbia has increased by 14.7 percent since 1991.

The nation's main crops are wheat, barley, corn, potatoes, soybeans, rice, and sugar beets. The dominant crop is wheat. In 1998 Canada produced 24,076,300 tons of wheat. However, there is less wheat under cultivation in Canada than at any time in the 20th century. This is the result of increased diversification and low worldwide wheat prices. The number-two crop was barley and the country harvested some 12,708,700 tons of it. Total crop output in 1998 was 53,701,500 tons. The primary livestock products are beef, chicken, duck, turkey, goose, and pork. Beef production is concentrated in the western areas of the nation while poultry production is concentrated in the east. About two-thirds of all poultry farms were in eastern Canada. Most livestock is consumed domestically. For instance, in 2000 beef production was valued at US$1.5 billion. Of this, US$70 million worth of beef was exported while the rest was consumed in Canada. The country also imported US$140 million of beef, almost all of it supplied by the United States. One out of every 4 farms in Canada raised beef.

One of the fastest growing segments of Canadian agriculture is organic products (food grown naturally and without pesticides, and sold without preservatives or additives). The organic food industry has been growing at a rate of 20 percent per year. There are now about 1,500 registered organic food producers in Canada. Organic production is strongest in the western areas of the country. There are also a growing number of specialty farms. For instance, there are now 1,593 farms whose main output is Christmas trees. In addition, the number of bison raised on farms for buffalo meat has tripled since the early 1990s, and the total number of head are around 45,000. There are also a number of exotic species, including llama and elk, being raised for sale in specialty markets. For instance, elk and deer antlers are sold to Asian nations for use in food products and tea. Specialized crop products include various herbs and spices such as garlic, ginseng, and coriander, cut flowers such as roses or lilies, and tobacco.

While fishing remains a prominent part of the economy of some provinces, depletion of fish stocks caused by over-fishing have led to significant declines in fish production. Fishing now accounts for only about 0.1 percent of the nation's GDP or US$3.2 billion per year. Since the early 1990s, fishing's share of the nation's GDP has declined at an average of 2 percent per year.

Environmental problems have created concerns for Canadian agriculture. One of the major problems is that of animal waste and fertilizer runoff contaminating waterways. In 1996, there were 61 million acres that were treated with some form of chemical fertilizer and 57 million acres treated with herbicides. This represents a 15 percent increase in fertilizer use since 1991, and a 7 percent increase in herbicide use. A second major problem is that of soil erosion caused by overproduction.

INDUSTRY

Although the automotive industry is the dominant industrial force in Canada, the nation's industrial base is highly diversified. In addition to the manufacture of cars and car parts, major Canadian industries include electronics, processed and unprocessed minerals, food products, wood and paper products, chemicals, and petroleum and natural gas. Manufacturing accounts for about 18 percent of total industrial output. The most significant growth areas in industry are electronics, which grew by 15 percent in 2000, communications with 7.5 percent growth, furniture and fixtures with 7.4 percent growth, and crude oil and natural gas, which grew by 4.5 percent. Meanwhile transportation equipment declined by 5 percent while textiles were off by 3 percent.

MINERALS AND RESOURCES. Mining and fuel extraction and production accounted for 4.5 percent of Canada's GDP or some US$36.1 billion. Fuel exploration and production dominate this sector, but the processing of other types of mineral resources has grown significantly. In 1996, the top non-fuel minerals were gold with production of US$2.05 billion, copper US$1.47 billion, nickel US$1.45 billion, and zinc US$1.25 billion. There was also significant production of lead and iron. There are about 50 major gold mines in Canada and the country leads the world in technologies which extract gold from rock and soil. The nation is the world's largest producer of zinc and the fifth largest producer of lead. Among the provinces, Ontario is the top producer of non-fuel mineral resources, followed by Quebec, British Columbia, Saskatchewan, and Newfoundland. Each year Canadian companies spend over US$600 million to find or develop new mines and fuel supplies. However, environmental concerns and increased regulation have led many Canadian mining companies to shift exploration elsewhere. Latin America is becoming a favorite choice for Canadian mining companies.

While overall mineral production is dispersed throughout Canada, fuel production is concentrated in the west, with a few major exceptions. Canada is a major exporter of energy and fuels. In 1998, natural gas was the main export with 34.2 percent of total, petroleum was next at 28.6 percent, hydroelectricity at 20.7 percent, coal at 11.4 percent, and atomic energy at 5.1 percent. The United States has traditionally been Canada's largest market for energy exports, purchasing 90 percent of the nation's fuel and energy exports. Energy production accounts for 8 percent of the nation's economy. Approximately 65 percent of energy production is in Alberta, which is also the home of the nation's oil industry. The number-two producer was British Columbia at 13 percent, followed by Saskatchewan at 8 percent, and Quebec at 5 percent. The atomic industry is centered in Quebec.

MANUFACTURING. The manufacturing sector is dominated by the auto industry. Including imports, Canadians purchased 1.4 million new vehicles in 1999. That same year, there were 2.8 million new cars and light trucks produced in Canada, or 4.5 percent of the world's total output. About 90 percent of Canadian-built cars are exported to the United States. In 1999, exports to the United States alone equaled US$64.7 billion. Exports to the EU ranked second and amounted to US$299 million. Canada is the world's ninth-largest market for the purchase of new automobiles. In 1999, the auto parts market in Canada was worth US$33.8 billion. Of this total, US$22.7 billion worth of parts were produced in Canada. Canadian companies exported US$18 billion of the parts produced. The United States is both the main market for Canadian auto exports and the main supplier of the nation's imports. The strength of the auto sector is founded on the U.S.-Canada Auto Pact of 1965 which provided for free trade in cars and car parts. The pact also served as the model for later trade agreements between the 2 countries.

Electronics and electronic components constitute the main growth industry in Canada. These products include telecommunications equipment, computer software, home electronics equipment, and industrial and automotive electronics. Most electronics producers are located in Ontario and Quebec, although a growing number of firms are building plants in the south of British Columbia. Total production of electronics exceeded US$5.2 billion in 2000 and Canada had US$3.3 billion in exports. This does not include computers and computer hardware equipment, which accounted for an additional US$6.7 billion in production and US$6.4 billion in exports. One of the fastest growing electronics markets in Canada is that of personal communications, including mobile phones and pagers. Since 1995, this market has expanded 150 percent. In 1999, there were 3 million mobile phones in use.

There is a variety of other manufacturers in Canada. Aircraft and aircraft parts provide US$7.9 billion to the nation's GDP and some US$7.3 billion in exports. This makes Canada the world's fifth-largest producer of aerospace products and estimates are that the nation will take over the number-three spot by 2004 as the industry continues to expand. The main products are airframes, which form the main body of jet aircraft, and engines. Some of the major Canadian aerospace firms include Lockheed

Martin Canada, Canadian Marconi Company (CMC), and Sextant. Canada's Bombardier company, with over US$10 billion in revenues in 2001, is a major producer of business jets, and is the world's third-largest civil aircraft producer, behind Boeing and Airbus. Canada also has a major building products industry which in 2000 produced goods worth US$29 billion. It produces goods such as lumber, plywood, and shingles. About three-quarters of these materials are used in the domestic construction market. The other quarter is exported. Canada also imports a large amount of construction and building materials. The majority of these imports come from the United States (75 percent) and the remainder from Asian nations. Furniture and furniture accessories account for US$6 billion worth of products annually, including US$3.4 billion in exports. A staggering 97 percent of Canada's furniture exports go to the United States. The plastics industry manufactured some US$4.8 billion in products in 2000 while environmental concerns have created a thriving pollution control industry with goods worth US$4.3 billion that same year. Other major industrial sectors include medical equipment and pharmaceuticals, pulp and paper products, and sporting goods and recreational equipment. Canadian sporting goods manufacturers have strong brand identification for a number of products, including ice hockey equipment, snowboards, and swim goggles.

SERVICES

Services employ the greatest number of Canadians and account for the largest share of the nation's GDP. Some 10.4 million Canadians are employed in the sector, which also accounts for two-thirds of small businesses and the self-employed. Since 1976, employment in services has increased by 46.5 percent. With 1.7 million employees, retail is the number-one employer in the service sector. Retail is followed by business services at 1.3 million, personal services at 1 million, transportation and communications at 980,000, and financial services with 789,000. Financial services is the highest paying employment category in the sector. Workers in this field earn an average of Can$700 per week while retail workers only average Can$350 per week. The average overall wage in the services sector is Can$580 per week.

The wholesale, retail, and food service sectors are very similar to their counterparts in the American economy. In fact, American retail stores and restaurants are common throughout most of Canada. The banking and financial services sector is also very comparable to that of the United States. Finally, Canada is the number-one foreign destination for American tourists. These close ties between the service sectors of the 2 nations mean that Canadian companies watch the development of new services, products, and techniques in the United States very closely.

BANKING AND FINANCIAL SERVICES. The banking sector in Canada is highly developed and, following reforms in the 1990s, it is open to foreign investment and the establishment of foreign-based banks in the country. However, it was not until 1999 that foreign banks were allowed to open branches in Canada without first establishing a subsidiary company (a local or domestic branch of a foreign firm that is incorporated in the country in which it operates, not in the country of the parent company). In January of 2000, Canada had about 8,200 bank branches and close to 15,500 automated teller machines (ATMs). This includes 11 domestic and 42 foreign-owned banks. However, Canada's banking system is dominated by 6 domestic banks which together control about 90 percent of the nation's total assets. Even though foreign banks are now allowed to enter Canada's banking market, most choose to concentrate on peripheral services, including credit cards or commercial lending, because of the domination of the 6 banks which prevent any real market openings in retail banking.

Banking and financial services represent 5 percent of the country's GDP, and provide over Can$22 billion a year in payroll. Each year they also provide Can$50 billion in exports. Access to foreign markets has become a critical component in the success of this sector. For instance, 5 of the country's largest banks each have approximately 30 percent of their assets overseas. In addition, the 2 largest Canadian insurance companies make more profits abroad than they do in Canada. The nation's 4 largest insurance companies are Mutual Life Assurance of Canada, Manufacturers Life Insurance Company, Sun Life Assurance Company of Canada, and the Canadian Life Assurance Company.

RETAIL. Retail sales in Canada in 1999 were Can$260 billion (including automotive sales). Excluding car sales, food was the number-one product sold in retail outlets (mainly supermarkets). Food sales totaled Can$59 billion in 1999 with Can$55 billion of that sold in supermarkets and grocery stores. Clothing was number-two with Can$14.3 billion in sales, followed closely by drug and medicine sales with Can$13.3 billion. Supermarkets had the highest sales volume, followed by general merchandise stores and department stores.

Unlike the United States, Canada's retail sector is not dominated by large chain stores. Independent stores make up 61 percent of the market, chain stores comprise 32 percent, and department stores 7 percent. Stores with 1–4 employees make up 53 percent of the sector, shops with 5–9 employees comprise 23 percent, and those with more than 50 employees only account for 3 percent. There are regional differences in the retail trade. Ontario leads the nation in retail sales with Can$7.9 billion in

sales. Quebec is number-two with sales of Can$3.3 billion. In Newfoundland, there are 2 grocery stores per every 1,000 people, but in Ontario there are only 0.5 per 1,000. One potential problem for retail is the increasing number of part-time workers employed in the sector. In 1999, 32 percent of retail workers were part-time. Because they work part-time, these workers usually do not have benefits and therefore must rely on government social services for health care and retirement.

TOURISM. Canada ranks number-nine in the world in terms of tourist revenues, and has 2.2 percent of the world's total tourism market. In 1998, there were 93.3 million tourists who had overnight stays in Canada. This included 18.8 million foreign visitors and 74.4 million domestic tourists. The majority of domestic tourists traveled to overnight destinations within their home province (70.8 million) while only a small number of Canadians stayed overnight in a different province (3.4 million). In 2000, tourism employed 524,300 people. In 1999, tourism receipts amounted to Can$50.1 billion or 6.2 percent of GDP.

INTERNATIONAL TRADE

Canada's economy is dependent on international trade. Roughly 59 percent of its economy is based on trade. In 1999 Canada exported US$277 billion worth of goods and services and imported US$259.3 billion. While the overwhelming majority of the country's trade is with the United States, the Canadian government supports the expansion of foreign trade through international treaties and agreements. In 1989, Canada and the United States signed the Free Trade Agreement (FTA) which eliminated many tariffs and taxes on goods that were traded between the 2 nations. As a result, trade increased by 50 percent before NAFTA superceded the FTA in 1994. In 1999, trade between the 2 nations equaled US$365 billion. When investments and services are included, the total rises to US$450 billion. Canada now has a **trade surplus** with the United States that in 1999 was US$32.1 billion. With NAFTA, trade between Canada and Mex-

Trade (expressed in billions of US$): Canada		
	Exports	Imports
1975	34.074	36.106
1980	67.734	62.544
1985	90.950	80.640
1990	127.629	123.244
1995	192.197	168.426
1998	214.327	206.233

SOURCE: International Monetary Fund. *International Financial Statistics Yearbook 1999.*

ico also increased substantially. Canada's major export partners are the United States, Japan, the United Kingdom, Germany, South Korea, the Netherlands, and China. The majority of the country's imports come from the United States, Japan, the United Kingdom, Germany, France, Mexico, Taiwan, and South Korea.

Because of the success of the FTA and NAFTA, Canada has sought to enter into similar agreements with other nations. It has started negotiations with nations including Costa Rica, Israel, and Singapore. In 1997, it initiated a version of the FTA with Chile. This agreement is designed to prepare Chile for entry into NAFTA. Canada is a member of a number of international economic organizations including the WTO, the Free Trade Area of the Americas, and the Asia-Pacific Economic Cooperation (APEC) forum.

While the United States and Canada generally cooperate on trade issues, there are a number of areas where the 2 countries have disagreements. When disputes arise between the 2 nations, they are usually submitted to international bodies for resolution. The WTO and NAFTA are the most common forums to arbitrate controversies. The main areas of dispute most commonly involve agriculture and cultural industries. A major fisheries dispute that centered around the Gulf of Maine was settled by the International Court of Justice in 1984. In 1990 the United States and Canada signed the Fisheries Enforcement Agreement that was designed to discourage illegal fishing. This was followed by the 1999 Pacific Salmon Agreement that settled disagreements over salmon fishing.

One of the main areas of contention between the United States and Canada is over trade with Cuba. Since the 1960s, the United States has maintained a trade **embargo** on Cuba. However, Canada conducts trade with Cuba. In fact, Americans who want to travel to Cuba often go to Canada and then depart from there, since direct travel between the United States and Cuba is prohibited by the U.S. government.

The most significant barriers Canada has to free trade are restrictions on the ownership of companies that are headquartered in the country. Foreign individuals and companies are limited to 25 percent ownership in Canadian airlines and 20 percent ownership of telecommunications companies. They are also restricted to 49 percent stakes in commercial fishing ventures. Furthermore, Prince Edward Island, Nova Scotia, and Saskatchewan limit real estate sales to people or companies from outside of the province.

Because of the potential influence of American culture, Canada has taken steps to try to preserve its culture from being overwhelmed by the United States. For instance, the Canadian government exempted cultural industries such as movies, music, or literature from the provisions of NAFTA. In addition, Quebec requires that all products marketed in the province be labeled in French, and throughout Canada both French and English are used in packaging and labels.

While 90 percent of all goods enter Canada without any form of tax or tariff, certain products face tariffs that range from 0.9 percent to 13 percent. The highest level of tariff is applied to goods such as vegetables, cut flowers, sugar, wine, textiles, clothing, footwear, and boats. These tariffs apply to 35 different countries. In addition, Canada uses 300 percent tariffs to protect the dairy and poultry industry from competition, although in 1999 the WTO agreed with the United States and New Zealand that such tariffs were in violation of WTO regulations.

MONEY

In August 2001, 1.51 Canadian dollars equaled 1 U.S. dollar. The value of the Canadian dollar has remained fairly constant in relation to the U.S. dollar since hitting an all-time low in 1985. In 1995, 1 U.S. dollar equaled 1.3724 Canadian dollars. Recent weaknesses in the Canadian dollar have helped the nation's economy by making its exports cheaper for countries like the United States, a development that has helped spur the increase in Canadian exports.

The Bank of Canada is the nation's central bank. Its main purpose is to regulate **monetary policy**. The Bank of Canada prints paper currency and mints coins and is responsible for setting interest rates. The Bank is a private institution that is independent of the government. However, the members of the board of directors that oversee the Bank are appointed by the federal government's Finance Minister for 3-year terms. It is not a regular commercial bank and it loans money only to other banks or government bodies. The Bank is also in charge of administering the national debt and making payments on the debt. In an effort to combat the drug trade and counterfeiting, the Bank has undertaken a variety of measures in recent years, including adding new security features to

Exchange rates: Canada	
Canadian dollars (Can$) per US$1	
Jan 2001	1.5032
2000	1.4851
1999	1.4857
1998	1.4835
1997	1.3846
1996	1.3635
SOURCE: CIA *World Factbook 2001* [ONLINE].	

currency and eliminating the Can$1,000 bill (since it was rarely used by legitimate businesses, but commonly used in the drug trade).

The Toronto Stock Exchange (TSE), founded in 1852, is one of the largest in North America. Its "TSE 300" index, which lists the 300 largest companies on the exchange, is usually used as the major Canadian stock index. Other major Canadian stock exchanges include the Alberta, Montreal, Vancouver, and Winnipeg stock exchanges. The total value of these exchanges in 1998 was US$543.4 billion. There were 1,384 domestic companies listed in these exchanges in addition to a host of international companies.

POVERTY AND WEALTH

Canada is a prosperous and affluent country. It has a highly developed **social welfare system** that includes a progressive health-care system. The nation aggressively pursues policies which emphasize human rights. In terms of the welfare of its citizens, Canada is one of the world's most progressive nations. The combination of a thriving economy and generous social benefits gives Canada one of the highest standards of living in the world. In the *Human Development Report 2000,* published by the United Nations, Canada ranks number-one in the world in human development. Furthermore, over the past 25 years Canada has consistently ranked number-one or two in the report. The GDP per capita in 1999 was US$23,300. Education is mandatory through age 15 and the literacy rate exceeds 97 percent.

The highest 10 percent of the population accounts for 23.8 percent of all income. At the same time, the lowest 10 percent makes only 2.8 percent of all income. The majority of Canadians fall into what is considered to be the middle class. While most people in Canadian society share in the nation's prosperity, there are several groups that are generally excluded from the affluence of the country. Among these groups are the native people of Canada and recent immigrants. Women and the disabled

also face inequities in employment and wages. While women have the same property rights and are guaranteed equal employment under the law, many women are paid less than male workers in similar jobs. Women head over 85 percent of single-parent households and these households have a higher level of poverty than their traditional 2-parent family counterparts.

Native Americans in Canada generally do not share in the nation's prosperity. They have higher rates of unemployment, alcoholism, suicide, and poverty than the national averages. Increasingly, the tribes have sought greater autonomy and political control over themselves and their land. In response, the government has allocated US$400 million for programs designed to alleviate the worst problems of the tribes since 1996. The federal government is also currently in negotiations with over 350 different tribes over issues of self-government.

The Canadian health-care system is often described as a model for other nations. The system is a combination of public financing and private delivery of medical care. In other words, private doctors and health-care providers treat people, but the costs are paid for by the government. The federal government sets standards and provides funds for the provincial governments. Each province is responsible for specific planning, public health, and the financing of the health-care system. Over 95 percent of Canadian hospitals are private non-profit ventures that are run by community boards and munici-

GDP per Capita (US$)					
Country	1975	1980	1985	1990	1998
Canada	14,535	16,423	17,850	19,160	20,458
United States	19,364	21,529	23,200	25,363	29,683
Mexico	3,380	4,167	4,106	4,046	4,459
Brazil	3,464	4,253	4,039	4,078	4,509

SOURCE: United Nations. *Human Development Report 2000; Trends in human development and per capita income.*

Household Consumption in PPP Terms							
Country	All food	Clothing and footwear	Fuel and power[a]	Health care[b]	Education[b]	Transport & Communications	Other
Canada	14	5	10	4	21	9	38
United States	13	9	9	4	6	8	51
Mexico	30	6	4	2	7	8	46
Brazil	22	13	18	15	34	4	−6

Data represent percentage of consumption in PPP terms.
[a]Excludes energy used for transport.
[b]Includes government and private expenditures.

SOURCE: World Bank. *World Development Indicators 2000.*

Distribution of Income or Consumption by Percentage Share: Canada

Lowest 10%	2.8
Lowest 20%	7.5
Second 20%	12.9
Third 20%	17.2
Fourth 20%	23.0
Highest 20%	39.3
Highest 10%	23.8

Survey year: 1994
Note: This information refers to income shares by percentiles of the population and is ranked by per capita income.

SOURCE: *2000 World Development Indicators* [CD-ROM].

palities. For-profit hospitals exist mainly to provide long-term care. In 1998, total health-care expenditures were Can$82.5 billion or Can$2,694 per person. Each year, health care usually accounts for about 10 percent of GDP, and about one-third of total spending by the provincial governments. The main complaint about the system is the length of time that patients often have to wait before they receive certain treatments. In 1999, the average time between referral by a primary care doctor and treatment by a medical specialist was 14 weeks.

WORKING CONDITIONS

Total employment in Canada in 1999 was 15.9 million. That same year, the unemployment rate was 7.6 percent. Unemployment in Canada has remained fairly constant at this rate during the 1990s, despite the strong economy. However, there were real declines in unemployment compared with the 1980s, when unemployment hovered near 10 percent.

With the exception of members of the armed forces, all workers in Canada have the right to form unions. Unions may organize strikes, but employees of the government who provide essential services, including law enforcement and medical care, are forbidden to strike. In 2000, there were a number of notable strikes, including one in British Columbia that closed the province's seaports for 10 days. The province also saw an illegal nurses strike in 2001, as well as a crippling public transit strike in Vancouver which shut down the bus and light rail system for 4 months. Specific laws that oversee the formation and conduct of unions vary from province to province. Unions are independent of the government and often form coalitions with other trade organizations or international bodies. Outside of the government, union membership is 29.5 percent nationwide. The government vigorously enforces union protections, and there are provincial and federal agencies that monitor and investigate working conditions and worker safety.

The standard work week varies from province to province. It ranges from 40 to 48 hours per week, but all provinces mandate at least one 24-hour rest period during the week. The minimum wage rates are set by each province and also vary widely. The lowest minimum wage is Can$5.25 per hour in Newfoundland and the highest is Can$7.60 in British Columbia. In addition, Alberta and Ontario have lower minimum wages for workers under the age of 18. The minimum wage is not sufficient for a single worker to support a family and, in fact, those families with only a single wage earner making minimum wage are classified as being below the national poverty line. There are prohibitions on child labor, and children under the age of either 15 or 16—depending on the province—are not allowed to work without parental consent. Some provinces also have restrictions on youths working at night or in hazardous jobs.

Several groups are under-represented in the workforce and are often paid less than their counterparts in similar occupations. Native American peoples are particularly subject to discrimination and their proportion of the workforce is far lower than their proportion of the population. The same is true of people with disabilities. People with disabilities who are capable of work represent 6.5 percent of the total population, but only 2.7 percent of current employees. Women are employed in all sectors of the economy and laws guarantee equality in all areas of employment except the military. Under the terms of a 1998 court decision, the federal government has been paying back wages to women who were paid less than their male counterparts in the same occupation. However, disparities in income still exist between men and women with similar jobs.

Although the nation is officially bilingual, cultural pressure and regulations force many English-speakers in Quebec and French-speakers elsewhere in the country to use the language of the majority of that particular province. For instance, the provincial government of Quebec limits access to English-language schools and places restrictions on the use of English for commercial purposes and in advertising.

COUNTRY HISTORY AND ECONOMIC DEVELOPMENT

1600. King Henry IV of France grants a fur trading **monopoly** in the Gulf of St. Lawrence to a French company.

1608. Samuel de Champlain founds Quebec, the fist permanent European settlement in Canada.

1644. Wheat is planted and harvested for the first time in Canada.

1670. The Hudson's Bay company is formed by British merchants to trade in the Hudson Bay area.

1731–43. French fur trappers go into the territory beyond Lake Winnipeg and begin to send furs back to the east, establishing a lucrative trade.

1756–63. French and Indian War or Seven Years War results in British control of Canada, including Quebec.

1775–83. American Revolutionary War. British and Canadian forces defeat several American invasion attempts. Thousands of Americans loyal to England **emigrate** to Canada during the war.

1791. Many British loyalists settle in western Quebec, leading to the division of Quebec into Upper Canada (Ontario) and Lower Canada (Quebec). A year later George Vancouver begins his explorations of the Pacific Coast.

1807. Slavery is abolished in Canada.

1812–14. The War of 1812 is fought between the United States and Great Britain. The Americans burn York (Toronto), the capital of Ontario, but British forces retaliate by burning Washington, D.C.

1821. The 2 major economic forces in Canada, the Hudson's Bay Company and the Northwest Company, merge. This creates widespread unemployment.

1838. Rebellions by Native Americans and French-speaking Canadians break out across the colonies.

1841. The Act of Union unites Upper and Lower Canada into the single colony of Canada.

1857. Ottawa becomes the capital of Canada.

1867. Great Britain's North American colonies are united in a confederation to form the Dominion of Canada and are given semi-independent status, including self-government.

1870s. The northern bison herds are decimated. This leads to the collapse of the west's economy.

1880–84. A transcontinental railway is built, mainly by immigrant Chinese laborers.

1897. Gold is discovered in the Klondike. This leads to a widespread gold rush that attracts thousands, including many Americans.

1917. The **income tax** is adopted during World War I, but never repealed.

1922. The Canadian Northern and Canadian Transcontinental Railways merge to create Canadian National Railways. Four Canadian scientists share the Nobel Prize for their discovery of insulin.

1923. Anti-immigration sentiment leads the government to virtually halt Chinese immigration.

1931. The Statute of Westminister grants Canada full control over internal and external affairs. The governor-general becomes the representative of the British monarch.

1932. The Ottawa Agreements establish preferential trade between Canada and the other British Commonwealth nations.

1935. The Bank of Canada is established as the nation's central bank.

1937. Trans Canada Air Lines establishes regular flights.

1945. Canada joins the United Nations. The nation's first atomic reactor is built in Ontario.

1959. St. Lawrence Seaway opens.

1962. The Trans-Canada Highway opens. Canada becomes the third nation in space with the launch of a satellite.

1965. Canada and the United States sign the Auto Pact. The Maple Leaf flag is adopted.

1980. In a referendum in Quebec, voters reject independence from Canada.

1982. Canada gains a new constitution. The most severe economic recession since the Great Depression begins.

1984. The Gulf of Maine dispute between Canada and the United States is settled by the International Court of Justice.

1987. The Meech Lake Accords fail to solve the question of the status of Quebec.

1989. U.S.-Canada Free Trade Agreement goes into effect.

1990. The Goods and Services Tax (GST), a 7 percent national sales tax, is enacted. Canada and the United States sign the Fisheries Enforcement Agreement.

1992. Canada is the first nation to sign the bio-diversity treaty following the United Nations Earth Summit in Brazil.

1994. Trade restrictions between the provinces are eased and cigarette taxes are lowered following widespread smuggling from the United States. Canada joins the North American Free Trade Agreement (NAFTA).

1995. Voters in Quebec narrowly reject independence.

1996. Substantial cuts in government spending are announced.

1997. Canada initiates a free trade agreement with Chile.

1999. Canadian forces participate in the NATO-led military operation against Serbia in Kosovo. Canada and the United States sign the Pacific Salmon Agreement.

FUTURE TRENDS

The most pressing problem for the future of Canada is the question of Quebec's independence. A significant percentage of the Canadian economy is centered in Quebec. Independence for Quebec would raise a variety of problems since it would require a division of the assets of the federal government and require Quebec to assume part of the federal debt. Since the 1980s, there have been repeated efforts to reach some sort of permanent solution to the problem. However, the Bloc Québécois continues to push for independence. In 1998, the nation's Supreme Court ruled that a unilateral declaration of independence by Quebec would be illegal, but if a majority of the residents of Quebec vote for separation, then the federal government has to negotiate eventual independence. The English-speaking residents of Quebec and the province's native peoples both oppose independence and have expressed their wish to remain part of Canada if Quebec gains its independence.

Another problem facing the Canadian economy is the high level of taxation. On the positive side, these taxes provide the basis for the nation's very generous social benefits, including health care and education. On the negative side, taxes increase the cost of living for average Canadians and increase the costs of business for companies. In addition, even with the high level of taxation, the government has been forced to deficit spend in order to pay for services. As a result, the nation's debt increased substantially during the 1990s and only recently has the government begun to pay down the debt. The most pressing problem related to the high level of taxation is the aforementioned brain drain. Many younger Canadians who are highly skilled and/or educated are moving to the United States where they can earn much higher wages while paying lower taxes. Canada's tax burden is also blamed for the continuing unemployment levels of around 7 percent (while the American unemployment has been around 4 percent for several years).

Canada's pursuit of free and open trade has led it to join a number of international organizations. Membership in these organizations has allowed the country to take advantage of international trade so that it now contributes a significant portion of the Canadian economy. Much of the country's future growth is dependent on trade. Because of this dependence, Canada is particularly sensitive to downturns in the economies of its major trade partners, especially the United States.

DEPENDENCIES

Canada has no territories or colonies.

BIBLIOGRAPHY

Bretton, John N.H., editor. *Canada and the Global Economy: The Geography of Structural and Technological Change.* Buffalo, NY: McGill-Queen's University Press, 1996.

Burke, Mike, Colin Moers, and John Shields, editors. *Restructuring and Resistance: Canadian Public Policy in the Age of Global Capitalism.* Halifax, Canada: Fernwood, 2000.

Department of Foreign Affairs and International Trade. *Investing and Doing Business with Canada,* 2nd edition. Ottawa: Dept. of Foreign Affairs and International Trade, 1997.

"Dog Watch: Nortel Networks." *Forbes.com.* <http://www.forbes.com/2001/06/15/0615dog.html>. Accessed August 2001.

Economist Intelligence Unit. *Country Profile: Canada.* London: Economist Intelligence Unit, 2001.

Green, Randy. "U.S. Wins Panel Decision On Canadian Dairy Practices." *Agriculturelaw.com.* <http://www.agriculturelaw.com/links/seattle/dairy.htm>. Accessed August 2001.

U.S. Central Intelligence Agency. *World Factbook 2000.* <http://www.odci.gov/cia/publications/factbook/index.html>. Accessed August 2001.

U.S. Department of State. *Background Notes: Canada.* <http://www.state.gov/r/pa/bgn/index.cfm?docid=2089>. Accessed February 2001.

U.S. Department of State. *Country Reports on Human Rights Practices, 1999: Canada.* <http://www.state.gov/g/drl/rls/hrrpt/1999/index.cfm?docid=378>. Accessed December 2000.

U.S. Department of State. *FY 2001 Country Commercial Guide: Canada.* <http://www.state.gov/www/about_state/business/com_guides/2001/wha/index.html>. Accessed February 2001.

Watson, William. *Globalization and the Meaning of Canadian Life.* Toronto: University of Toronto Press, 1998.

—Tom Lansford

CHILE

Republic of Chile
República de Chile

CAPITAL: Santiago.

MONETARY UNIT: Chilean peso (P). One Chilean peso equals 100 centavos. There are coins of 1, 5, 10, 50, 100, and 500 pesos and notes of 500, 1,000, 5,000 and 10,000 pesos.

CHIEF EXPORTS: Copper, fish, fruits, paper and pulp, chemicals.

CHIEF IMPORTS: Consumer goods, chemicals, motor vehicles, fuels, electrical machinery, heavy industrial machinery, food.

GROSS DOMESTIC PRODUCT: US$185.1 billion (purchasing power parity, 1999 est.).

BALANCE OF TRADE: Exports: US$15.6 billion (f.o.b., 1999 est.). **Imports:** US$13.9 billion (c.i.f., 1999 est.).

COUNTRY OVERVIEW

LOCATION AND SIZE. A coastal country located in the southwest region of South America, Chile has an area of 756,950 square kilometers (292,258 square miles) and a total coastline of 6,435 kilometers (3,998 miles). Chile shares its northern border with Peru and its eastern border with Bolivia and Argentina. Comparatively, the area occupied by Chile is nearly twice the size of California. Chile's capital city, Santiago, is located at the country's latitudinal mid-point. By bus, Santiago is approximately 1.5 hours inland from the Pacific Ocean and 1.5 hours west of the Andes Mountains foothills. From its northern border to its southernmost tip, Chile covers a diverse geographic array. In the north is the Atacama Desert, one of the driest places on earth, while the southern tip points towards the polar ice of Antarctica.

POPULATION. The population of Chile was estimated at 15,153,797 in July of 2000 with an annual growth rate of 1.7 percent, an increase of 7.9 percent from the 1994 population of 13,950,557. In 2000 the birth rate stood at 17.19 per 1,000 while the death rate stood at 5.52 per 1,000. According to the Population Reference Bureau,

with a projected annual population growth rate of 1.29 percent, the population is expected to reach 19.55 million by the year 2025 and 22.21 million by 2050.

A majority of the Chilean population is *mestizo* (of mixed European and American Indian descent). In 1848 the Law of Colonization was passed by Spanish colonists interested in attracting foreign immigrants. Consequently, a large German population relocated to Southern Chile and mixed with the Mapuche Indians who inhabited the region. Miscegenation (intermarriage between different races) was prevalent throughout the country between Mapuches and other Europeans. **Immigration** also produced significant populations of Palestinians, Jews, Italians, Asians, Yugoslavs, and Greeks. Because of this great racial diversity, most Chileans feel that there is little racial prejudice in their country. However, prejudice based on class status is very prevalent in the urban centers.

The population of Chile is highly stratified with the middle class being the largest social sector. The importance of surnames, private schools, and living in the right neighborhood reveals a society that places much emphasis on class. The upper class in Chile consists of aristocrats, big business executives, and highly trained professionals making US$6,000 or more per month and constituting approximately 10 percent of the population. The middle class consists of small-business people, lower-rank professionals, public employees, and teachers. This group averages between US$600-$5,000 per month and constitutes 60 percent of the population. The lower class includes indigenous groups, retirees, students, small farmers, and servants. These people make between US$75-$500 per month and make up 30 percent of the population.

The population of Chile is highly urbanized, with 86 percent of the population residing in urban areas. The

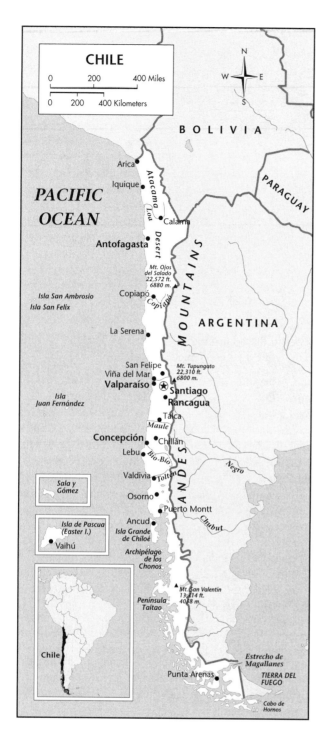

Patricio Aylwin's democratic government (1990–93), Chile's reputation grew as the role model for economic reform in Latin America. **Gross domestic product** (GDP) growth averaged 8 percent during the 1991–97 period but fell to about 4 percent in 1998 because of tight **monetary policies** implemented by the government; such policies were an attempt to keep the current account deficit in check. In 1999 a severe drought exacerbated the **recession** by reducing crop yields and causing hydroelectric shortfalls and rationing. For the first time in 15 years, Chile experienced negative economic growth. However, Chile managed to maintain its reputation for strong financial institutions and sound economic policies. By the end of 1999 exports and economic activity had begun to recover, and a return to strong growth was predicted. The March 2000 inauguration of President Ricardo Lagos (2000-present)—President Eduardo Frei's (1994–99) successor—left the presidency in the hands of the center-left Concertacion coalition that has held office since the return to civilian rule in 1990.

Chile arrived at its present strong economic state after years of political and economic turmoil. Civilian governments replaced the repressive military dictatorship in March 1990 and continued to reduce the government's role in the economy, pushing for the development of a free-market economy. **Inflation** has been on a downward trend and hit a 60-year low in 1998. Chile's currency and **foreign exchange reserves** are also strong, due in large part to sustained foreign capital inflows of direct investment. Still, the Chilean economy remains largely dependent on a few sectors—namely copper mining, fishing, and forestry. Sustained economic growth is largely dependent on world prices for these commodities, continued foreign investor confidence, and the government's ability to maintain an orthodox **fiscal policy**.

Chile's credit rating remains the best in Latin America, and in order to finance investment, Chilean firms have raised money abroad through loans, selling bonds, and issuing stock. Additionally, Chile has a high rate of foreign investment with private U.S. corporations conducting a significant amount of independent and **joint ventures** in the country. Total private and public investment in Chile accounted for 33 percent the GDP in 1997. The government is aware that increasing investment is necessary to ensure worker productivity. Chile is very fortunate not to be plagued by international debt, in part due to foreign aid it receives. Although it still has a significant **foreign debt** it is not enough to constitute major structural problems. As such, Chile is better off than many of the lesser-developed Latin American countries that struggle to maintain economic policies designed to generate enough revenue to pay back their foreign debts. Minimal foreign debt pressures and strong economic growth help Chile remain one of the most economically successful countries in Latin America.

country is also young, with 28 percent of the population under the age of 15. Additionally, the population is predominantly Roman Catholic (estimated at 89 percent), with the remaining 11 percent affiliated with other religions.

OVERVIEW OF ECONOMY

Chile's market-oriented economy is characterized by a high level of foreign trade that has been solidified over the years through economic reforms. Under President

POLITICS, GOVERNMENT, AND TAXATION

Chile is divided into 13 administrative regions, each headed by an administrator (*intentente*) appointed by the central government. Each region is divided into 40 provinces, each being administered by a governor (*gobernador*) also appointed by the central government. The provinces are further divided into municipalities headed by appointed mayors (*alcaldes*).

Chile's system of government, with its separation of powers, was patterned after that of the United States. There are 3 branches to the government: executive, judicial, and legislative. It is a multiparty republic with a presidential system based on the 1980 constitution.

The Chilean Constitution of 1980 sets the format for the National Congress, composed of a Senate and a Chamber of Deputies. The Senate has 47 members (38 elected and 9 appointed) who serve 8-year terms. The Chamber of Deputies has 120 members who are directly elected for 4 years. The president is elected for a 6-year term without possibility for re-election. The constitution requires the president to be at least 45 years of age, meet the constitutional requirements for citizenship, and have been born on Chilean territory. The president is elected by an absolute majority of the valid votes cast.

The executive branch in Chile is composed of 16 ministries and 4 cabinet-level agencies: the Central Bank, the Production Development Corporation (Corfo), the National Women's Service, and the National Energy Commission. Each minister is appointed exclusively at the president's discretion.

During the brutal dictatorship of General Augusto Pinochet, which lasted from 1973 to 1990, political parties were severely repressed. After the return to a civilian democratic government, political parties began re-emerging and eventually consolidated into 2 major blocs, the center-right and the center-left. Historically, Chilean politics have been split 3 ways: the right, center, and left. The center-left is currently the governing coalition and includes the centrist Christian Democratic Party (PDC), the Radical parties, the moderate leftist Party for Democracy (PPD), and the Socialist Party (PS). The opposition center-right includes the National Renewal Party (RN) and the Independent Democratic Union Party (UDI). In addition to these parties, Chile has several small-scale leftist parties, including the **Communist** Party. While these parties are not represented in the Executive Branch or Congress, they do have elected representatives in some local governments.

The 2000 presidential election was a close race between Ricardo Lagos, representing the center-left, and Joaquin Lavin Infante, representing the center-right. Lavin's party platform, as a member of UDI, focused on promises of higher wages, larger pensions, and better eco-nomic and social performance. These promises were made in the wake of the largest recession Chile has experienced in years. Lagos's platform, as a member of the PPD, advocated stability, continuation of reform processes tied to economic **liberalization**, high levels of economic growth, and reduced unemployment.

The Coalition of Parties for Democracy (Concertacion) is an umbrella coalition that encompasses all political parties, from the powerful PDC to Lagos's PPD. One of the fundamental tenants of this bloc was to unite in support of a single presidential candidate. For the 2000 election, the Concertacion elected Lagos, making him the first avowedly leftist president since Salvador Allende, the socialist president who died during the coup (an internal takeover of a government) that put General Pinochet in power. Many older Chileans were concerned about Lagos's candidacy because they still remembered the very severe economic conditions that plagued the country under Allende. As the newly elected president, Lagos promised to maintain the same **liberal-economic** reform policies that have been adhered to since the overthrow of the Allende government. Although both the center-left and center-right support free-market liberal economies, the center-right tends to identify more with Pinochet and his neoliberal policies. The center-left understands and supports free-market policies but expresses ties to **socialist** ideology. In Chile, political identification remains closely tied to a person's socio-economic class.

The government's biggest impact on the economy is maintaining neoliberal economic policies that favor foreign investment and international trade. Regulation of the Chilean economy by the government is limited. The most heavily regulated areas of the economy are utilities, the banking sector, securities markets, and pension funds. The government is increasing the amount of foreign investment in the country by introducing rules that permit **privatization** of Chilean state-owned ports, water-treatment facilities, and private investment in the construction and operation of domestic **infrastructure** projects.

Chilean Decree Laws attempt to establish favorable investment climates for foreign investors by treating them nearly the same as Chilean investors. There are minimal administrative issues that need to be dealt with in order to pursue investment opportunities in Chile, and the highly stable democratic government helps boost investor confidence. With a well-developed legal system and government support of foreign investment, the economy thrives on the inflow of foreign capital. The government also promotes exports by offering non-market incentives to exporters. For example, paperwork requirements are made simpler for nontraditional exporters.

An 18 percent VAT is applied to all sales transactions and accounts, generating over 40 percent of total tax revenues. There is a **tariff** on almost all imports originating in countries that have not entered into a free trade agreement with Chile. In 1998 the tariff was 11 percent; it dropped to 9 percent in 2000 and will fall by 1 percent through the year 2003, at which time it will stabilize at 6 percent. Personal **income taxes** are applied only to individuals making more than US$6,000 per year. People earning over about US$75,000 are taxed at the highest rate of 45 percent. Businesses are taxed 15 percent on the profits they keep as earnings and 35 percent for those that they distribute. Businesses are given tax breaks for their donations to educational institutions. In 1999, 73 percent of total government revenues were derived from taxes. Tax evasion is not a serious problem in Chile.

Chile's economy is extremely open to free trade and the government rarely intervenes with protectionist measures. Chile's Foreign Investment Law and its tax structure are indicative of a country that is interested in attracting foreign investment. Chile has negotiated free trade agreements with various countries, including the United States, Canada, Mexico, Brazil, Paraguay, Uruguay, and Argentina.

The military played a significant role in the economy during the Pinochet dictatorship by enforcing a drastic 180 degree turn in the economy. They changed the Chilean economy from one that was heavily **nationalized**, domestically protected, and industrializing through **import-substitution** to one that favored free-market neoliberal policies. While the military no longer plays a direct role in the country's economic planning, the economic structure that was implemented under its rule is still followed currently and policymakers of the military government are still on the boards of the largest firms in the country.

INFRASTRUCTURE, POWER, AND COMMUNICATIONS

Chile's internal transportation network is relatively well-developed, although it is in need of some improve-

ment. Historically, Chile had heavy government regulation of the transportation sector—including railroads, air transport, marine shipping, and buses. These laws served as a tremendous barrier to international competitiveness due to inefficiency. As a result, reforms, begun in the late 1970s, aimed at establishing a competitive environment and increasing participation by the **private sector**.

RAILWAYS. The nation's rail system consists of 6,782 kilometers (4,214 miles) of railroads. Four international railways run to northwestern Argentina, Bolivia, and Peru. Two of these lines run from Chile to Bolivia (from Arica to La Paz) and from Antofogasta to La Paz via the Calama Desert. Except for these 2 international routes, passenger service to areas north of Santiago is not permitted. The Chilean State Railways (Empresa de Ferrocarriles del Estado) operates under the auspices of the Ministry of Transport and Telecommunications. Congress approved privatization of EFE's train services. However, the infrastructure remains under state control.

ROADWAYS. Although Chile's railroad system is the fourth-largest network in Latin America, it is a comparatively slow and inefficient method of transportation. Roads are the principal means of moving people and freight given that the Pan-American Highway is in excellent condition and runs the length of the country. In 1960 the first paved road was completed, linking the extreme north with Puerto Montt, located at the far southern tip of the Central Valley (Valle Central). Transversal roads run east and west from the north-south highways. Chile's network of roads totals approximately 79,025 kilometers (49,103 miles). Of this total network 9,913 kilometers (6,160 miles) are paved, 33,140 kilometers (20,592 miles) are gravel roads, and 35,972 kilometers (22,352 miles) are improved and unimproved earth roads. The Santiago and Central Valley regions are the areas most frequently traveled. There are about 1.1 million motorized vehicles of all kinds in Chile, including approximately 700,000 automobiles and 300,000 trucks and buses. Chile's national bus service and San-

Communications									
Country	Newspapers	Radios	TV Sets[a]	Cable subscribers[a]	Mobile Phones[a]	Fax Machines[a]	Personal Computers[a]	Internet Hosts[b]	Internet Users[b]
	1996	1997	1998	1998	1998	1998	1998	1999	1999
Chile	98	354	232	44.8	65	2.7	48.2	21.45	700
United States	215	2,146	847	244.3	256	78.4	458.6	1,508.77	74,100
Brazil	40	444	316	16.3	47	3.1	30.1	18.45	3,500
Argentina	123	681	289	163.1	78	2.0	44.3	27.85	900

[a]Data are from International Telecommunication Union, *World Telecommunication Development Report 1999* and are per 1,000 people.
[b]Data are from the Internet Software Consortium (http://www.isc.org) and are per 10,000 people.

SOURCE: World Bank. *World Development Indicators 2000.*

tiago's metro system run on time and are considered excellent.

Chile supports an extensive tourist infrastructure through the use of bus transportation from the extreme north of the country to the southern Lake District. A bus trip from the capital city of Santiago to Puerto Montt takes about 17 hours. Although it is a significant amount of time to spend on a bus, the views are extraordinary, Chileans make great conversation, and once you reach the south you get to see one of the most beautiful places on earth. It is almost untouched by capitalist industrialization and the people are comfortingly and inspiringly simple. A portable CD player is a totally foreign object to them.

WATER. Chile has 4 major state-owned water utilities that are in desperate need of substantial investment to improve efficiency. Starting in 1998 the government began considering the possibility of selling approximately 35 percent of the utilities to private firms. Partially privatizing this sector would allow private companies to invest capital in the **restructuring** of the utilities. Such contributions would improve drinking water services, sewers, and sewage treatment. These changes require substantial investment in order to be realized. According to the Communication and Culture Secretariat of Chile, a planned investment of US$1.56 billion by the year 2000 was expected to substantially improve the water sector in Chile. This significantly exceeds the US$235 million that was spent in 1998.

PORTS. Chile's extensive coastline has very few naturally protected bays. In general the sea is rough and the topography is abrupt. A total of 95 percent of Chilean exports and 87 percent of international trade is done through port facilities. As of 1999, Chile had 36 operational ports: 10 were state-owned and offered public service; the other 26 were privately-owned ports, of which only 15 offered public service. These ports tend to focus on trade and shipping.

Port infrastructure, equipment, technology, and services have been clearly inadequate to efficiently serve the growing demands of globalization and international trade. As a result, the Chilean Congress approved a Port Law in December of 1997. This legislation was intended to foster competition and improve the capacity, efficiency, and competitiveness of the state-owned ports. The law mandated the conversion of 10 state-owned ports, previously managed by Emporchi (Chilean Port Authority), into 10 independent companies. These new companies are now fully responsible for port management, development, financial administration, and assets. However, the ports are still owned by the state. Chile has limited inland waterways, navigable for only about 725 kilometers (450 miles), and located mainly in the southern Lake District.

AIR TRANSPORT. Air transport has become an important way of moving people and freight through Chile, given its territorial extremes. Chile has 351 usable airports but only 48 of them have paved runways. The international airport is located in the capital, Santiago. Eighteen international airlines serve through Santiago. Chile has 2 national airlines. The first is Línea Aérea Nacional de Chile (LAN Chile), which was privatized in 1989 and merged with Southeast Pacific in 1992. LAN Chile serves major cities in Chile and also carries passengers to international destinations. The second, Linde Aérea del Cobre (Ladeco), is owned by the country's copper company and handles the majority of domestic travel.

ELECTRICITY. Power shortages occurred frequently in 1999 and to some degree in 1998. Shortages are typically a result of drought conditions since most of the country depends heavily on hydroelectricity. Power rationing had to be instigated in Santiago and some other regions for a while. In April 1999, blackouts would occur for up to 3 hours a day. The government did not intervene in the situation because private corporations own the electric companies, and the government did not want to scare investors away. However, the blackouts continued to be severe enough that the government fined 10 power companies for not meeting the terms of their contracts. New power plant construction, started in 1996, will continue through at least 2008. According to the most recent projections of the Comision Nacional de Energia (National Energy Commission [CNE]), electricity demand will grow over 8 percent yearly into the next century. Thus, the electricity sector has grown much faster than the overall Chilean economy.

TELECOMMUNICATIONS. Chile has an excellent telecommunications infrastructure supporting the use of cable, fax machines, telephones, and the Internet (in 1999 there were 26 Internet service providers). The phone system is completely digital and there are 8 international long distance carriers and 3 cellular telephone networks.

The telecommunications sector in Chile changed dramatically once it became privatized in 1989. As a result, private companies were forced to compete on the open market. Competition caused these businesses to provide their services in the most efficient and effective manner possible in order to ensure customer satisfaction. Since privatization, the number of phone lines increased from 800,000 in 1990 to 3.1 million in 1999. Cellular phones were introduced in 1990, and by the end of 1999 there were more than 2 million being used nationwide. Long distance calls made within the country increased from 500 million minutes in 1990 to almost 3 billion minutes in 1999. Long distance calls made to other countries increased from 50 million minutes in 1990 to almost 250 million minutes in 1999.

The Internet has become efficient in Chile due to heavy U.S. investment, but penetration is still limited given that only about 24 percent of homes have a computer. However, computer use is expected to grow 6 percent in the year 2001, as consumer confidence resumes after the Y2K scare. Chilean imports of computer equipment were estimated at approximately US$400 million for 1999. Imports have been gradually increasing over the past few years. The Internet is used mainly for education and entertainment purposes with only about 7 percent of Internet users shopping on-line. Furthermore, local access charges on Internet usage make logging on expensive. Nevertheless, Chile has the most developed telecommunications infrastructure in Latin America and is attempting to further develop its Internet infrastructure through private investment in order to become the preferred country for Internet investments.

RADIO. The radio is Chile's principal way of reaching the mass population. An estimated 93 percent of the nation's population listens to the radio; the percentage is higher in the metropolitan Santiago area, estimated at 97 percent. Radio broadcasts are the prime source for current news for a majority of the population. New stations have a large budget used to maintain professional news staff to meet the news demands of the country. There are an estimated 17 million radio sets in Chile, far surpassing the estimated population of the country.

ECONOMIC SECTORS

The key economic sectors making up the Chilean economy are agriculture, industry and manufacturing, and services. Agriculture has increased slightly over the years but still makes up only a small percent of annual GDP. In 1979 agriculture constituted 7.4 percent of the GDP, rising to 8.7 in 1989, and 8.4 in 1998. Industry constituted

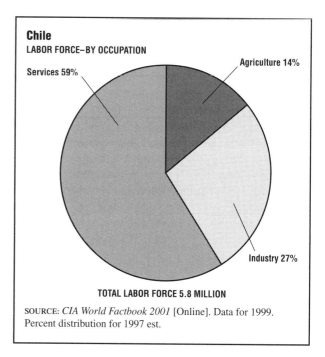

Chile
LABOR FORCE–BY OCCUPATION

Services 59%
Agriculture 14%
Industry 27%

TOTAL LABOR FORCE 5.8 MILLION

SOURCE: *CIA World Factbook 2001* [Online]. Data for 1999. Percent distribution for 1997 est.

37.9 percent of GDP in 1979, with 21.6 of that coming from manufacturing. In 1989 those figures were 41.8 and 18.9 percent, respectively. By 1998, industry declined to 34.2 percent and manufacturing sank further, to 16.4 percent. The service sector in Chile accounted for approximately 61 percent of the GDP in 1999. Services in Chile include tourism, banking, and finance and **retail**.

AGRICULTURE

In 1970 Chile was exporting US$33 million in agriculture, forestry, and fishing products. By 1991 exports had increased substantially to US$1.2 billion. Currently, exports of agricultural products constitute approximately 6 percent of the total GDP. However, this sector of the economy is extremely susceptible to fluctuations in world demand.

FRUIT. Chile is the region's leading fruit exporter, with the agricultural sector employing about 14 percent of the workforce in 1997 and contributing around 6 percent to the GDP in 1999. The fruit industry is the most developed and high-profile agricultural industry. Chile is said to be the world's largest exporter of table grapes, not counting the ones used in the well-developed wine industry. Both of these industries benefit from the favorable conditions of the country's fertile and well-drained soil, cheap labor, and in recent years, government policies. About 25 percent of grapes eaten in the United States are imported from Chile, as well as 35 percent of kiwi fruit and 10 percent of nectarines. Other major crops include apples, apricots, pears, and avocados. About 50 percent of Chile's fruit production is exported, mainly to

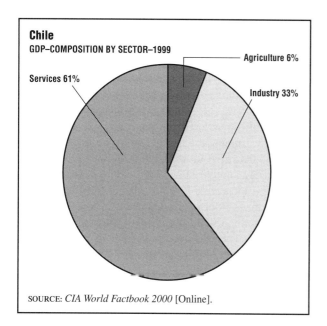

Chile
GDP–COMPOSITION BY SECTOR–1999

Services 61%
Agriculture 6%
Industry 33%

SOURCE: *CIA World Factbook 2000* [Online].

the United States and Europe. One of the greatest advantages of this sector is that it coincides with the northern hemisphere's winter season. Between 1989–91, exports of fresh fruits reached significant importance. Grape exports to the northern hemisphere during the winter season were a virtual Chilean **monopoly** until Argentina began to compete. The fruit packing industry also expanded, providing seasonal employment to thousands of workers.

WINE. Chilean wines have earned a prestigious position among international wine connoisseurs. The quality of these wines have earned Chile a spot as one of the world's leading wine producers, behind Italy and France. Chilean wine exports increased significantly between 1987 and 1998 (from 14 million liters to 229 million liters). In 1993–98, wine exports increased from US$129 million to US$500 million. Favorable climate and soil conditions make growing premium grapes an asset for this sector of the Chilean economy. Chile's microclimates (climates of a very small area) provide outstanding soil, sunlight, temperature, and moisture conditions for wine production.

Additionally, the industry has introduced new technologies and attained a highly skilled **labor force**. Industry upgrades in technology and production processes have been facilitated through foreign investment in local operations. France, the United States, Australia, and the United Kingdom have had successful Chilean operations since 1979.

FISHING. Chile's extensive coastline makes it one of the world's greatest fishing nations. The natural conditions—including favorable currents, tides, rainfall, and inland water—provide for a large harvest of fish products. Chile has developed an advanced technology for use in fishing and aquaculture. Most Chilean fish products are now shipped frozen and pre-packaged. In 1994 Chile was the largest producer of finfish and shellfish with a 7 million ton catch, approximately 6 percent of the world's total. Fishing accounts for 2 percent of Chile's GDP and 11 percent of its global exports. In 1985 the sale of frozen and pre-packaged products stood at 1,120 tons. By 1998 this figure had significantly increased to 294,062 tons.

The Chilean fishing industry produces high quality fish meal, fish oil, salmonids, sea bass, Antarctic whiting, kingclip, swordfish, sea urchin, oysters, scallops, and king crab. Finfish and shellfish exports in 1998 were worth US$1.6 billion, an increase of 31 percent over 1997 exports. About 52.7 percent of 1998 exports were harvested at sea with 47.3 percent being produced through inland aquaculture.

Chile is one of the top 15 aquaculture nations in the world. Since the 1980s Chilean aquaculturalists have worked hard to become the second largest producers of salmon and trout. They raise Coho, Atlantic, and Chinook salmon, as well as rainbow trout. The industry is made up of 90 firms operating 185 farms in over 47,000 hectares of inland waters. Importers of refrigerated and frozen Chilean salmon include Japan (60 percent), the United States, Brazil, and the European Union. In 1998 salmon sales provided approximately 42 percent of industry revenue and accounted for greater than 4 percent of global country exports.

FORESTRY. Chilean forestry is extremely successful due to its natural resource endowments. Chile's competitive advantage is due to an abundance of water, diversified climates throughout the country, and fertile soil. For example, the locally grown Radiata Pine reaches maturity in 15 to 30 years, much faster than in its own native homeland of Monterey, California. Moreover, the industry growth can be attributed to extensive research and species introduction coordinated through the efforts of public and private universities, government agencies, and private institutions.

In 1998 forest exports reached an impressive US$1.66 billion, although this was down 9.3 percent from 1997. These export levels are achieved by 100,000 workers in approximately 800 small, medium-sized, and large firms that make up the industry. In 1998 Chile sold forest products to 95 countries, with Asia leading at 34.8 percent, followed by North America with 24 percent, and Europe at 23 percent. The United States was the single largest buyer with imports totaling US$358 million.

The success of the forestry industry has attracted much foreign investment and has contributed to the globalization that is characteristic of the Chilean economy. In 1998 a U.S.-based company, Boise Cascade, undertook a joint venture with the Chilean company Maderas Condor. Both companies invested US$150 million to build a new plant in Valdivia, the lake region of Chile. Additionally, the Canadian firm ForAction International, together with the Chilean company Moreno Vial Ltda., started building a wood production and export plan in the town of Curanilahue, which involves a US$30 million investment.

INDUSTRY

Chile's industry sector is based primarily on local mineral resources, agricultural raw materials, and forestry. Current industries include copper refining, nitrate products, iron smelting and steel production, oil refining, cement, chemicals, timber and pulp, furniture, and various wood products. There is also a large textile, clothing, and leather industry concentrated mainly in the urban centers, with Santiago being the largest, employing 20 percent of the local labor force.

MINING. Chile is the world's largest producer of copper, constituting 28 percent of the world's reserves. It has the world's most productive mine, located in the northern region in the city of Chuquicamanta. The Chilean economy is also very dependent on copper, and this industry employs about 6 percent of the Chilean workforce. According to the International Monetary Fund (IMF), in 1997 copper accounted for 42 percent of exports and 8 percent of the country's GDP. Major external investment in Chilean copper mining and the many industries across the world that require copper indicate that this sector will continue to play an important role in Chile's economy. North America and Western Europe are the biggest users of copper, constituting a combined world demand of 59 percent.

Corporacion Nacional del Cobre de Chile (CODELCO) is the largest company in Chile engaged in extracting and selling copper from state-owned mines. CODELCO is owned by the Chilean government and received annual profits of around US$1 billion per year during the 1990s. It is responsible for producing 10 percent of the world's copper.

Before the 1970s most copper mines were owned by American **multinational corporations**; in 1971 these mines were nationalized by the Chilean government. CODELCO was created in 1976 by the military government to run the nationalized copper mines. Thus, the Chilean government had a monopoly over the large mines, accounting for 85 percent of copper production.

Beginning in 1980 the military government began to loosen its grip on the copper mines, permitting foreign investment in the new large mines. As a result, **foreign direct investment** in the mining sector grew from approximately US$90 million between the years 1974–89 to US$803 million in 1990. Between the years 1989–95 more than half of the foreign direct investment in Chile went directly to the mining sector. This pattern reflects a strong international demand for copper, a metal that is used in the construction industry, in air conditioning, and in manufacturing electronic equipment. Copper is also used in the automotive industry for electrical equipment and in telecommunications to build copper cables.

Chilean mining companies are also beginning to explore opportunities in other parts of Latin America, specifically Argentina, Bolivia, and Peru. International demand affects the price of copper. In 1998–99 the Asian financial crisis reduced that region's demand for copper, causing the price to significantly decrease. The Asian economies rebounded and the price of copper increased with a positive short-term outlook for the industry.

Northern Chile also has significant amounts of rich, high-grade iron-ore deposits located mainly in Coquimbo. Most of this ore is exported, with the surplus being used by the local iron and steel industry. Chile is also the leading nitrate supplier in the world, with large deposits of the mineral in the Atacama Desert. Nitrate is used for fertilizers and in the production of explosives. The mining and export of this mineral flourished during the last part of the 19th century and the beginning of the twentieth century. Chile produces gold, silver, molybdenum, manganese, zing, lead, bauxite, sulfur, potash, uranium, cobalt, antimony, and tungsten.

TEXTILES. Chile's textile and garment industry faces strong international competition from Asian manufactures such as China, India, and Indonesia. In order to remain competitive, Chile has broadened its export market and sought new trading partners. In 1998 the top exports were denim cloth, polyester viscose, and combed wool. The leading purchasers of these exports were Argentina, Bolivia, and Brazil. Despite international competition, this sector of the Chilean economy has been able to remain efficient and has even expanded production and sales. Between the years 1993 to 1997, garment exports rose from US$148.2 million to US$208.6 million.

The textile sector has been growing due to Chile's new international trade agreements. MERCOSUR (a free trade agreement between Argentina, Brazil, Uruguay, Paraguay, and Chile) has been the greatest benefit to this industry, accounting for 37 percent of all foreign sales in 1998. The leading buyers of Chilean-made garments in 1998 were Argentina (purchasing US$33.1 million worth of men's and women's suits, ensembles, and hosiery), followed by Bolivia (US$27.8 million), and Mexico (US$21.9 million).

Chile has approximately 2,000 textile and garment companies, with around 30 of them having foreign sales of greater than US$1 million. Some of the top exporters of 1998 include Machasa—Chile's largest producer of denim fabrics—with US$23.1 million in sales, wool fabric manufacturers Bellavista Oveja Tome with US$16.3 million, and Textiles Pollak Hermanos with US$12.3 million.

As of 2000, the textile sector of Chile was the most labor-intensive of industries, with around 160,000 workers. The Textile Institute of Chile, a trade organization, estimated that 9 to 10 new jobs are created with every US$10,000 invested in this industry.

METAL MANUFACTURING. There has been strong growth in this sector over the past few years, encouraging foreign investment in plants and capital. This industry has over 2,000 firms and provides 100,000 jobs. Metal manufacturing is central to Chilean development efforts, constituting 6 percent of the GDP. Leading export items in 1998 included copper wire (US$75.4 million), automotive vehicles (US$63.9 million), automotive gearboxes (US$39.7 million), and machine parts (US$38 million).

In 1998 this industry earned US$883.2 million from exports, increasing from US$722.4 million in 1996 and US$456.9 million in 1993. Metal manufacturing consists of 2,000 companies, based mostly in central and southern Chile, and about 20 percent of the total industry workforce. There is a general consensus that Chile has remained competitive in this sector as a result of technological innovation, easily accessible raw material sources, and skilled local engineers. Some of these companies are also partly foreign-owned, keeping in tune with Chile's desire to attract foreign direct investment. For example, Brazil contributed US$80 million in 1997 to build a new hot-rolled steel plant in the town of Colina.

CONSTRUCTION. The construction sector in Chile is predominantly import-driven. Foreign manufacturers supply over 95 percent of the Chilean market for construction equipment. In 1998 construction accounted for 3 percent of the country's GDP. In 1999, due to a regional recession, the Chilean construction sector was one of the worst performers of the year. Housing construction has an average demand of 140,000 units and 110 million square feet of lumber per year. Over the last decade, new housing construction has averaged 11 percent annual growth while construction as a whole averaged 9 percent growth. During 1998–1999 construction growth declined dramatically, but current signals indicate that by 2001 it should be back on its old growth path. Construction of retail and wholesale space (including warehousing) has also experienced remarkable expansion. As of 2000, new malls (in cities where none existed), large "hypermarkets," and new industrial development projects are regaining their once frantic activity around major cities. Currently, the Chilean government is also promoting the construction of a storm-sewer system for Santiago and other large cities. These projects will require large private investments. Private investors have also announced new large investments in high-rise office buildings. Such projects are expected to be worth close to US$1.5 billion. Future urban developments are expected to contribute US$500 million in private investment over the next 10 years.

GAS AND OIL. Chile is not a major oil or gas producer, having only occasionally derived more than 50 percent of its consumption from its own reserves. Local oil production in 1992 contributed only 11 percent of total oil consumption and continues declining, while consumption and imports increase. Chile has oil and natural gas fields near the Straits of Magellan and Tierra del Fuego, on the country's southern coast. However, reserves in these sites are quickly being depleted. The National Petroleum Enterprise (Empresa Nacional de Petrole [ENAP]) was created as a Chilean government enterprise in 1950. The objective of its creation was to develop activities related to exploration, importation, and distribution of crude oil products. ENAP has continually sought new ways to meet domestic demand for petroleum by engaging in production contracts with Argentine, Brazilian, Colombian, and Ecuadorian companies. In 1982 domestic production was at 2.48 million cubic meters. In 1986 4.358 million cu-

bic meters of gas were produced. By 1990 production had declined to 1.38 million cubic meters. ENAP estimates for production in 1998 were not expected to reach more than half a million cubic meters. Thus, for that year 90 percent of Chile's consumption was to be imported by ENAP. Since Chile has been experiencing solid economic growth over the last couple of decades, its oil demands have consistently been met through imports from other countries. Petroleum exploration efforts undergone in Chile have proven to be unsuccessful. In 1999 ENAP's general manager issued a statement indicating that exhaustive exploration had failed to find new oil fields and that currently exploited deposits would be depleted within 6 years. Thus, Chile will continue to depend on imports for its gas and oil needs

SERVICES

TOURISM. Chile is a popular spot for tourism with its extensive natural attractions and exceptional services, with the summer months of January and February being the most popular. Tourists can choose from an array of natural climates including deserts, temperate regions, lake districts, beaches, glaciers, and native forests. Natural wonders and excellent hotel and transportation infrastructures supported 1.8 million tourist visits in 1998. About 45 percent of the tourists come from Argentina. During the summer months Argentineans come to Chile to enjoy the vast array of beaches, Vina del Mar being one of the most popular. Chilean revenues from tourism were estimated at US$1.2 billion in 1998, up 7 percent from 1997. Spain, Germany, and France constitute the majority of European visitors. Two-thirds of all visitors come to Chile for vacations. Due to increased political stability and economic growth in the 1990s, there has been a significant increase in business travelers and convention attendees, accounting for 23 percent of total visitors. The average visitor stays 11 days and spends US$55 per day.

Accommodations in Chile are exceptional with some 1,700 hotels providing over 200,000 jobs. Tourism has been particularly strong in and around metropolitan Santiago. It has 15 five-star hotels—12 in Santiago and 3 in the nearby Valle Nevado ski resort. Chile has 15 ski resorts, making up the most comprehensive skiing infrastructure in Latin America. Another popular spot is the San Rafael Lagoon. Tours take visitors on cruise ships through channels and archipelagos of Aysen, entering into an inlet of the Pacific Ocean to the final attraction, the striking 30,000-year-old San Rafael Glacier. Torres del Paine National Park is located in southernmost Chile and offers striking views of glaciers and challenging climbs.

The Chilean government actively promotes expansion of the tourism industry. The National Forestry

Corporation (CONAF) is inviting private foreign operators to provide a wide range of services within Chile's Wildlife Preserve System. Many foreign investors have also started building upscale hotels in Santiago and northern Chile. For example, Marriott International—a U.S. corporation—is building a US$96 million, 42-story, 250-room hotel in Santiago's upscale east end.

BANKING AND FINANCE. Chile's banking system has changed significantly over the past decade. In the beginning it was relatively exclusive, offering credit only to wealthy Chileans. The rest of the population had to rely on department stores for credit. In the early 1990s the banking sector expanded quickly and began accommodating new account holders and even offering credit cards to average Chileans. Middle-class Chileans are now able to access credit through banks and are offered online "home banking." In 2001, nearly 1 out of every 5 Chileans had a credit card.

The Chilean banking sector is now one of the most developed and promising of the region. But competition from foreign banks is rising as a favorable investment climate has induced many foreign banks to open up shop in Chile. Large numbers of bank mergers have also occurred, raising government concerns over potential monopolies. As of 2001, Spain's Banco Santander Central Hispano (BSCH) controlled both Banco Santiago and Santander Chile, 2 of the largest Chilean banks. BSCH had a market share of nearly 30 percent. Financial authorities have asked it to reduce its share to 20 percent.

During Allende's presidency the financial system of Chile was near collapse. However, under the new dictatorship the financial sector experienced a remarkable boom, improving significantly between 1975–1990, with the implementation of an orthodox economic policy. By 1992 the financial sector had become modern and dynamic. But it was not until 1997 that banking law reform broadened the scope of permissible foreign activity for Chilean banks. Domestically, Chileans have recently begun to enjoy the benefits of new financial tools such as home **equity** loans, leasing, and debit cards. Increases in the use of traditional instruments, such as loans and credit cards, have also benefitted the Chilean population. Moreover, Chile has a private pension system with estimated assets of over US$30 billion at the end of 1997. Such assets have provided an important source of investment capital for the stock market. There has also been a significant increase in the number of firms with shares traded on the stock market as it continues to grow.

RETAIL. Chile's retail sector is in a state of transition. Small neighborhood stores still hold a substantial market share, yet very large retail outlets such as hypermarkets are carving out an expanding share of sales. The number of large retail outlets has increased substantially in the past decade, and expansion is most apparent in the capital city. Well-designed shopping malls have proven successful in Santiago and other larger cities throughout Chile. Products most commonly displayed in Chile's malls include textiles and apparel, electronic appliances and devices, sporting goods, cosmetics, office supplies, and kitchen utensils.

Chile's retail sector constituted approximately 8.8 percent of the GDP during the 1990s. Sales in this sector rose 4-fold from the mid-1980s through the 1990s, to US$21.50 billion. The retail hotel and restaurant sector of the economy constitutes about 17 percent of the overall GDP. The retail sector is the second highest employer, comprising 18 percent of the workforce, or just under 1 million persons. About half of these workers are in the capital region of Santiago. The remainder are located in the more populated provinces, such as Vina del Mar and La Florida, where malls have been a growth industry since the 1990s.

INTERNATIONAL TRADE

Chile's economy is heavily reliant on international trade to sustain its economy. In 1997, exports reached US$17 billion and imports US$18.9 billion. Chile's main trading partners are the United States, Japan, Germany, and Brazil. However, Chile's export markets are geographically diverse, spanning Asia, the European Union, the United States, and Latin America. Latin America has been the fastest growing export market for Chile. Since 1991, Chile has signed free-trade agreements with Canada, Mexico, Venezuela, Colombia, and Ecuador. An associate agreement with MERCOSUR went into effect in October 1996.

Chilean exports have traditionally been dependant on copper and have been consumed mostly by industrialized countries. However, non-mineral exports have grown faster than those of copper and other minerals in recent years. In 1975, non-mineral exports were about 30 percent of total exports; by 1997 they accounted for 52 percent of export earnings. The most important of these non-mineral exports are forestry and wood products, fresh and processed fruit, fishmeal and seafood, and other manufactured products.

Trade (expressed in billions of US$): Chile

	Exports	Imports
1975	1.552	1.525
1980	4.705	5.797
1985	3.804	3.072
1990	8.373	7.742
1995	16.024	15.914
1998	14.895	18.828

SOURCE: International Monetary Fund. *International Financial Statistics Yearbook 1999.*

According to the latest statistics, Chile has 4 main markets of destination for its exports. First, Asia accounts for about one-third of total exports. Chile's principal Asian partner is Japan, although trade with the People's Republic of China, the Philippines, and Hong Kong is increasing. Trade with the European Union accounts for a quarter of overall trade, with the United Kingdom (5.8 percent) and Germany (4.8 percent) as the leading partners. With respect to Latin America, there has been a marked increase in exports to Brazil and Argentina. Their share in overall exports in 1997 was 6.1 percent and 4.6 percent respectively. The United States remained Chile's most important partner. In 1997 it accounted for 16.7 percent of Chile's total world exports.

Chile's imports originate mainly in the North American Free Trade Agreement (NAFTA) countries—the United States, Mexico, and Canada. Together, imports from these countries constituted 30.5 percent of all imports for 1997. In the same year, Latin America accounted for 26.5 percent, the European Union was at 19.8 percent, and Asia comprised 15.5 percent of imports. More specifically, by country, in 1997, Chile imported 23.1 percent from the United States, 9.2 percent from Argentina, and 6 percent from Brazil.

Chile is a party to bilateral trade agreements with Bolivia, Colombia, Canada, Cuba, Ecuador, Mexico, Peru, and Venezuela. Chile is also a member of the Asian Pacific Economic Cooperation (APEC). Currently, Chile is negotiating trade agreements with Central America (Costa Rica, El Salvador, Guatemala, Honduras, and Nicaragua) and plans to initiate negotiations with the European Union, New Zealand, Japan, and other countries. The current trade agreements have had a positive impact on international trade for Chile and are predicted to do so in the future. Past negotiations to obtain a free trade agreement between Chile and the North American Free Trade Association were unsuccessful. However, the current Summit of the Americas negotiations are intended to create a **free trade zone** from North America to Argentina.

MONEY

Historically, Chile has witnessed periods of inflation, stagnant growth, and recession when international events triggered a lowered demand for Chilean exports. Since Chile's economy has traditionally been heavily reliant on the export of natural resources, declines in demand have adverse effects on Chile because the amount of imports it needs to sustain its economy is not balanced against its exports.

Inflation in Chile has declined every year since 1990 when it stood at 27 percent. In 1996 inflation was 8.2 percent, and it fell to 6.1 percent in 1997. By 1999 inflation had dropped to 2.3 percent. Chile's overall eco-

Exchange rates: Chile	
Chilean pesos per US$1	
Jan 2001	571.12
2000	535.47
1999	508.78
1998	460.29
1997	419.30
1996	412.27
SOURCE: CIA *World Factbook 2001* [ONLINE].	

nomic performance during 1990–97 was very strong. During this period, financial authorities at the Central Bank focused on further reducing the **inflation rate**, adjusting short-term interest rates to achieve this objective, and maintaining strong **public sector** finances.

The independent Central Bank of Chile was granted autonomy by constitutional law in 1990. Its primary goal was to raise interest rates, when necessary, in order to bring down inflation. Although Chile suffered a slight recession in the 1998–99 period, blamed in part on the East Asian economic crisis, consumer demand started to grow and the economy began recovering in early 2000. Inflation had been on a gradual downturn prior to the recession. The recession further reduced it to about 2.6 percent at the end of 1999. However, although inflation might be low, recession stunts domestic economic growth and has adverse effects on unemployment and GDP.

The Central Bank manages the foreign **exchange rate** through incremental changes to account for periods of extreme capital inflows. In September 1999, the Central Bank moved to a freely **floating exchange rate** system that is determined largely by market forces. It had initially held an exchange-rate band along which incremental changes were made in response to economic indicators. After the change in exchange rate systems the Chilean peso devalued by 5 percent within 6 weeks before stabilizing and slightly recovering. The value of the peso versus the U.S. dollar fell about 18 percent in 1999 (473 pesos to the dollar in December 1998 to 547 in December 1999). With the Central Bank intervening minimally to stabilize the economy, the exchange rate should return to normal standards by the year 2001.

POVERTY AND WEALTH

Currently more than 40 percent of the country's wealth is concentrated in the hands of just 10 percent of the population. In Latin America, only Brazil and Guatemala have less equitable income distribution. This huge disparity has created a large social divide in which a relatively small middle class is caught between a huge

GDP per Capita (US$)

Country	1975	1980	1985	1990	1998
Chile	1,842	2,425	2,345	2,987	4,784
United States	19,364	21,529	23,200	25,363	29,683
Brazil	3,464	4,253	4,039	4,078	4,509
Argentina	7,317	7,793	6,354	5,782	8,475

SOURCE: United Nations. *Human Development Report 2000; Trends in human development and per capita income.*

mass of urban and rural poor and a small and extremely powerful elite. Fundamental to the shifts in economic policy over the years is the importance attached to income distribution by the changing administrations.

Wages have risen faster than inflation each year since 1990, a reflection of greater productivity in the country. Increased wages have produced public benefits of increased living standards and an expansion in the labor force. The number of Chileans with incomes below the poverty line (roughly US$4,000 per year for a family of 4) fell from 46 percent of the population in 1987 to 23 percent in 1997. Unemployment has varied with the business cycle in recent years, with annual rates between 4.5 to 6 percent.

The administration led by President Lagos has emphasized a commitment to better social conditions. They have addressed 4 priority areas: health, public safety, unemployment, and labor reforms. Finance Minister Nicolas Eyzaguirre has committed himself to fiscal discipline so that additional government resources can be used for social development. The secretary general to the presidency, Alvaro Garcia, has declared labor reforms and the creation of an unemployment benefit mechanism a priority. Analysts believe that even if unemployment rates are brought down through an expanding economy, Chile will still need to tackle fundamental problems of poverty and social disaffection if it is to avoid civil and labor unrest.

The Chilean constitution states that the government has an obligation to "promote, protect, restore health and rehabilitate the health status of individuals." Government administrations have made an effort to meet this goal. Chile currently spends about 7 percent of its GDP on health care. As of 1997 the public health system covered 67 percent of the Chilean population while private health insurance covered 27 percent. Public health care is somewhat inefficient, and the government is moving toward privatization of this sector.

THE RICH AND THE POOR. A wealthy Chilean family has a nice house located in one of Santiago's more affluent neighborhoods. The family generally owns fancy cars and their children attend the private Catholic University. A nanny is usually hired to help the mother raise the children and clean the house. Nannies are typically lower-class Chileans or immigrants from Peru or Bolivia. The children of these families normally go on exchange programs to the United States or Europe and are able to speak English well. Wealthy families often travel internationally to places like New York and Florida and domestically to the Chilean beaches and the southern Lake District.

A poor Chilean family generally lives in a shanty neighborhood, and their children do not attend a university. The parents work long hours in either the **informal sector** or a place of business. Their children usually get jobs at a young age to help support the family. These families do not take extravagant vacations or buy expensive imported products. They live a very hard life.

WORKING CONDITIONS

In 1998 the Chilean workforce amounted to 5.8 million individuals. Unemployment has been rising in Chile, from 6.2 percent in 1993 to 7.5 percent in 1997. In 1998, Chile faced its first recession in 20 years. Unemployment increased in certain cities such as Valparaiso, where the local unemployment rate was 13 percent, and Santiago, where it was estimated at 14.4 percent. However, the

Household Consumption in PPP Terms

Country	All food	Clothing and footwear	Fuel and power[a]	Health care[b]	Education[b]	Transport & Communications	Other
Chile	17	10	24	20	15	6	9
United States	13	9	9	4	6	8	51
Brazil	22	13	18	15	34	4	−6
Argentina	30	9	17	15	15	5	9

Data represent percentage of consumption in PPP terms.
[a]Excludes energy used for transport.
[b]Includes government and private expenditures.

SOURCE: World Bank. *World Development Indicators 2000.*

economy was expected to recover in the upcoming years leading to a decline in unemployment rates.

Chile is relatively developed in its labor laws compared to other Latin American countries. Workers are not required to request authorization to join or form a union. Approximately 12 percent of the workforce belongs to a union. Legislation passed in 1995 gave government employees many of the same rights as union members, with the exception that they may not legally strike. Reforms made to the labor code in 1990 helped to facilitate workers' right to strike.

Under the Pinochet dictatorship, labor unions were severely limited to the point of futility. Immediately after the coup that brought Pinochet to power in 1973, labor institutions were dismantled. The structural reforms the new regime wanted to implement had severe negative ramifications for the working class. In order for the government to continue with its economic changes, working conditions such as wages were once again regulated, and the ability to strike had to be allowed.

Forced labor is prohibited under the constitution and the labor code, and is not prevalent in the country. Child labor laws are codified, setting the minimum age to work at 14, with the permission of the child's parents or guardians. However, child labor is restricted to certain types of labor and is most prevalent in the informal economy, since this area is more difficult to regulate. The Chilean government estimates that approximately 50,000 children between the ages of 6 and 14 work. Such labor is concentrated in the countryside or with the children's parents.

According to the U.S. Department of State, minimum wages, hours of work, and occupational safety and health standards are regulated by law, with the legal work week set at 48 hours. The minimum wage is currently around US$190 per month and is set by the government, management, and unions. If representatives from these groups cannot come to an agreement, the government decides. Family **subsidies** are provided for workers in the lower income category. Overall, wages have risen steadily over the last several years. Moreover, poverty rates have declined in recent years from 46 percent of the population in 1987 to 21.7 percent in 1998. Currently, 11 percent of salaried workers earn the minimum wage.

COUNTRY HISTORY AND ECONOMIC DEVELOPMENT

1540. Spanish explorer Pedro de Valdivia conquers Indians in Chile and makes Chile a colony of Spain.

17TH CENTURY. Ranching becomes Chile's primary export trade, with large estates employing bonded peasants as European diseases reduce the native population.

18TH CENTURY. Around 20,000 Spaniards **emigrate** to the new Chilean colony.

1750. Chile is permitted by Spain to mint its own coins.

1791. Governor Ambrosio O'Higgins y Ballenary, a Spanish officer of Irish origin who became the governor of Chile, outlaws forced labor.

1810. Criollo (people of Spanish heritage born in Latin America during the times of conquest) leaders of Santiago declare independence from Spain.

1814. Spanish troops from Peru reconquer Chile at the Battle of Rancagua. Chile is once again a colony of Spain.

1817. Troops led by Bernardo O'Higgins Riquelme (the first Chilean head of state) and General Jose de San Martin (an officer of the Spanish Army and one of the principal leaders of the independence movement) defeat the Spanish in the Battle of Chacabuco. O'Higgins becomes supreme director of Chile and is eventually dubbed the "father of Chile."

1818. Chile wins formal independence from Spain after San Martin defeats the last large Spanish force in the Battle of Maipu. The first provisional constitution is approved in plebiscite.

1823. Slavery is abolished.

1839. The first bank notes of Chilean currency go into circulation.

1884. Bolivia loses access to the South Pacific Ocean upon losing a border war with Chile.

1927. Economic and political crises in Chile bring army officer Carlos Ibanez to power. He creates a powerful state system and establishes the national airline LAN Chile.

1970. The left wing coalition Popular United, led by Salvador Allende, wins the presidency, beginning Chile's first socialist government. Allende nationalizes the copper mines and begins to expropriate lands for government use and distribution. He enacts sweeping program reforms on the banking, commerce, insurance and industry sectors.

1973. Allende's government is overthrown in a military coup led by General Augusto Pinochet. President Allende is said to have denied an offer by the military to move him and his family out of the country. Allende then dies in circumstances that remain a matter of controversy.

1980. A new constitution is put in place by the military regime stipulating a referendum on a continued dictatorship in 1988.

1988. Fifty-four percent of voters reject Pinochet's regime in a national referendum. The country has grown tired of his harsh military rule resulting in thousands of murdered and tortured Chilean citizens.

1989. Patricio Aylwin from the Christian Democratic Party is elected president. The country returns to democracy and continues with the market-oriented reforms of the military regime.

1991. Chile begins an aggressive campaign to negotiate free trade agreements with other Latin American countries.

1994. Chile signs free trade agreements with various nations. The United States officially invites Chile to join the North American Free Trade Agreement during the closing ceremony of the Summit of the Americas in Miami.

1996. Chile becomes an associate member of MERCOSUR (a trade group which includes Argentina, Brazil, Paraguay, Uruguay).

1998. The Chilean economy begins to feel the effects of the East Asian crisis, and demand for Chilean exports declines. Pinochet retires as commander in chief of the armed forces and visits Britain. While he is in London, Spain requests the general's extradition for human rights abuses against Spanish citizens, and he is held under house arrest pending a legal decision.

1999. The Chilean economy begins to recover from a recession that began in 1998 as a result of the East Asian crisis. Pinochet is released by the British Home Secretary on grounds of ill health and returns to Chile where he remains under house arrest.

2000. The Chilean economy recovers well from the East Asian crisis and continues along a path of growth, increased globalization, and free trade.

FUTURE TRENDS

Although Chile's economy has been expanding over the past 15 years, it began to experience a slowdown in 1998 that lasted throughout most of 1999. Positive GDP growth in the beginning of 2000 marked the official end of the recession with growth projections being estimated at 6 percent. Since Chilean growth is heavily reliant on exports, concentrated mainly in primary products and processed natural resources, the country is extremely vulnerable to a decreased demand by other countries, which invariably lowers the prices of these commodities and slows the country's growth. However, continued foreign investment and government policies, designed to stimulate the economy, are expected to lead to a sustainable recovery.

In general, the international community is not concerned about the slight recession of the Chilean economy. Nevertheless, the Chilean government is watching the market carefully to ensure that the economy remains strong and continues to grow. As such, Chile is likely to continue with its free trade negotiations, having launched exploratory trade talks in early 2000 with the European Union. It has also expressed strong interest in becoming a full member of MERCOSUR. The political and economic situation in Chile looks promising and is likely to carry the country to increased growth and success for years to come.

DEPENDENCIES

Chile has no territories or colonies.

BIBLIOGRAPHY

Caistor, Nick. *Chile: A Guide to the People, Politics, and Culture.* Brooklyn, NY: Interlink Publishing, 1998.

"Chile and the IMF." *International Monetary Fund.* <http://www.imf.org/external/country/CHL/index.htm>. Accessed August 2001.

Economist Intelligence Unit. *Country Profile: Chile.* London: Economist Intelligence Unit, 2001.

Embassy of Chile. <http://www.embassyofchile.org>. Accessed August 2001.

Insight Guide: Chile. London: APA Publications, 2000.

Marcel, Mario, and Andres Solimano. "The Distribution of Income and Economic Adjustment." In Barry P. Bosworth et al, editors, *The Chilean Economy: Policy Lessons and Challenges.* Washington, D.C.: The Brookings Institution, 1994.

U.S. Central Intelligence Agency. *World Factbook 2000.* <http://www.odci.gov/cia/publications/factbook/index.html>. Accessed August 2001.

U.S. Department of State. "Background Notes: Chile." <http://www.state.gov/r/pa/bgn/index.cfm?docid=1981>. Accessed January 2001.

U.S. Department of State. *FY 2001 Country Commercial Guide: Chile.* <http://www.state.gov.www.about_state/business/com_guides/index.html>. Accessed January 2001.

U.S. Library of Congress. *Chile: A Country Study.* <http://lcweb2.loc.gov/frd/cs/cltoc.html>. Accessed December 2000.

—*April J. Guillen*

COLOMBIA

Republic of Colombia
República de Colombia

CAPITAL: Bogotá (Santa Fe de Bogotá).

MONETARY UNIT: Colombian peso. One peso equals 100 centavos. There are coins of 10, 20, and 50 centavos and 1, 2, 5, 10, 20, and 50 pesos, and notes of 100, 200, 500, 1,000, 2,000, 5,000, and 10,000 pesos.

CHIEF EXPORTS: Petroleum, coffee, coal, bananas, chemicals, gold, cut flowers.

CHIEF IMPORTS: Industrial equipment, transportation equipment, consumer goods, chemicals, paper products, fuels, electricity.

GROSS DOMESTIC PRODUCT: US$245.1 billion (purchasing power parity, 1999 est.).

BALANCE OF TRADE: Exports: US$11.5 billion (f.o.b., 1999 est.). **Imports:** US$10 billion (f.o.b., 1999 est.).

COUNTRY OVERVIEW

LOCATION AND SIZE. Shaped like an odd-looking pear with a thin top, Colombia is located in the northwestern corner of South America, alongside the Caribbean Sea between Panama and Venezuela, and bordering the Pacific Ocean between Panama and Ecuador. Colombia has an area of 1,138,903 square kilometers (439,733 square miles) and a total coastline of 3,207 kilometers (1,993 miles) distributed between the Caribbean Sea and North Pacific Ocean. It shares borders with Venezuela to the east, Brazil to the southeast, Peru and Ecuador to the south-southwest, and Panama to the northwest. With the fifth-largest area in Latin America in terms of size, Colombia is one-ninth the size of the United States, and is approximately the same size as the United Kingdom, France, and Germany combined. The capital city, Bogotá, is located in the center of the country in a mountainous setting.

Topographically, Colombia is divided into 4 regions: the central highlands, the Caribbean lowlands, the Pacific lowlands, and Eastern Colombia (east of the Andes mountains). In this diverse geography one important feature is the 3 chains of high mountains (cordilleras) that cut the country from south to northeast.

POPULATION. In Latin America, Colombia ranks fourth in overall population and tenth in population density. Its population was estimated at 39.68 million in July of 2000, up from 25.4 million in 1975. In 2000 the birth rate stood at 22.85 per 1,000 while the death rate was 5.73 per 1,000. With a projected annual growth rate of 1.6 percent between 2000 and 2015, the population is expected to reach 53.2 million by the year 2015.

At the end of World War II, Colombia's population growth accelerated dramatically, peaking at about 3.2 percent per year by the 1960s. In 1951 Colombia's population was 11.5 million, and by 1973 it had doubled to 22.9 million. Beginning in the late 1960s the annual population growth rate dropped dramatically, such that between 1973 and 1985 it stood at only 2 percent. This drop was partly the result of a control policy initiated during the Lleras Restrepo administration (1966–70). Colombia was one of the few Latin American countries to adopt family planning as an official policy and to integrate it into development plans.

Population distribution is highly uneven. Roughly 94.5 percent of the population is concentrated in 42 percent of the territory, mostly in the plateaus and basins scattered among the Andes cordilleras and the valleys of the Magdalena and Cauca rivers, which run south to north in the western half of the country. Some 58 percent of the territory, mostly the 9 eastern departments (administrative units, much like provinces), accounts for a scant 5.5 percent of the population. Three-fourths of the population live in the Central Highlands in the temperate and cool zones and the remainder in the Caribbean lowlands.

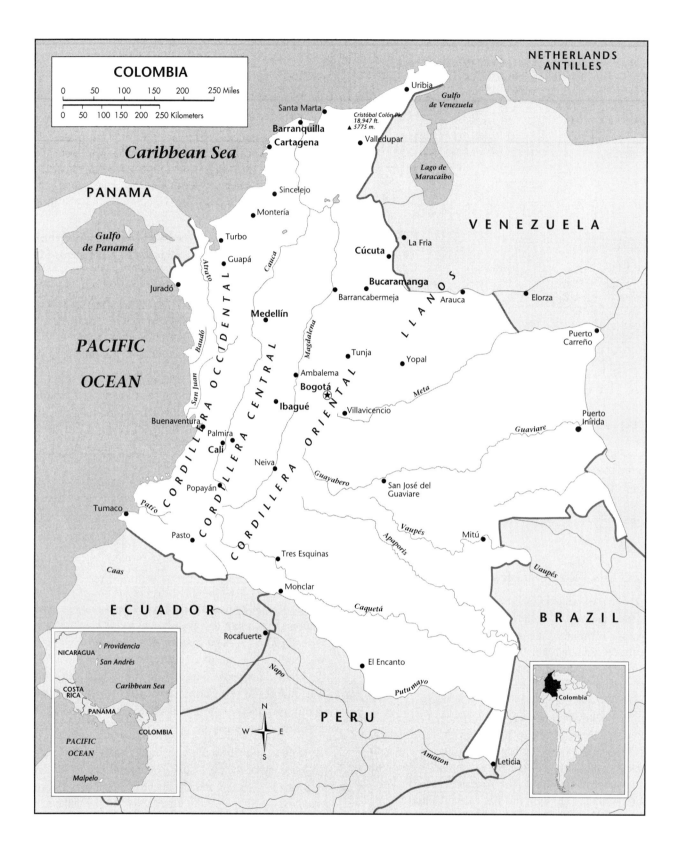

Visitors travelling to Colombia during the 1950s and 1960s were struck by the social and economic changes in the country. The population explosion was accompanied by significant migrations from the countryside to intermediate and big cities, which led to rapid urbaniza-

tion. According to the 1938 census, 30.9 percent of the population lived in urban municipal towns. By 1951 this had increased to 38.7 percent and continued to increase sharply so that by 1985 it had reached 67.2 percent. By the mid-1980s urban growth had consolidated the change from a predominantly rural to an urban economy. According to the 1993 census, Bogotá, the capital city, had a population of 5,399,000. Other major cities are Medellín (2,556,000 people) in the western province of Antioquia; Cali (2,064,000), southwest of Bogotá; and Barranquilla (1,329,000), on the Caribbean.

Colombia is one of the most Spanish of all South American nations, although persons of pure Spanish descent constitute only 20 percent of the population. The mestizos (people who are a mixture of white and indigenous Amerindians) comprise 58 percent. The mulattos (a mixture of African and white ethnicities) make up 14 percent, and those of African descent are only 4 percent of the population. The zambos (those of mixed African and Amerindian origins) comprise 3 percent of Colombia's people.

Colombia is a country composed primarily of young people, with 63 percent aged between 15 and 64 years, 32 percent below the age of 14, and 5 percent of the population older than 65.

An important feature of the latter half of the twentieth century has been a strong tendency for Colombians to **emigrate**. The 2 main destinations of emigrants are the United States and Venezuela. Up until the end of the 1980s, most of the emigrants to the United States were professionals, which represented a considerable brain drain (when talented professionals leave their home country due to better pay and living conditions abroad). However, in the 1990s the composition of emigrants also included less qualified professionals. Emigration to Venezuela has also been a major demographic phenomenon. The number of Colombians living illegally in Venezuela has been variously estimated at between half and three-quarters of a million. If legal migrants are considered, there may be as many as a million Colombian migrants in that neighboring country. The illegal migration is virtually impossible to control because the border is long and open, and Colombians are indistinguishable from Venezuelans. During the 1990s the trend has diminished due to Venezuela's economic problems. Overall, Colombia's emigration problem has been the result of not only better economic opportunities elsewhere, but rampant insecurity in the country.

OVERVIEW OF ECONOMY

Colombia is a market economy with major commercial and investment links to the United States, and more recently to its neighbor countries in the Andean region. For close to a century the country was known as a "coffee economy." As the twentieth century came to close, Colombia remained a major coffee producer, though coffee was second to oil as a generator of foreign exchange earnings. By the end of the century, even

chemicals had surpassed coffee in export earnings. In the last 25 years the country has also gained an unfortunate reputation as a haven for illegal drug cultivation and manufacture.

Colombia has attained greater diversification both in terms of production and exports, allowing the country to cushion the external shocks typically felt by less developed countries which are dependent on shifting world prices for their major exports. Apart from oil production, recent examples of success range from the export of fresh-cut flowers to the chemical industry, a leading exporter to other Latin American countries.

The net result has been an economy growing steadily—though moderately—over the last 50 to 60 years, with an important positive impact upon the welfare of the population measured by almost any indicator. Life expectancy, nutrition, and access to health and education have all improved. Major services such as electricity, urban sewage, roads, and telecommunications have increased substantially. Furthermore, **GDP per capita** has risen, although it is still unevenly distributed.

To continue this process, Colombia has required many technology inputs, both in terms of equipment, chemical products, and raw materials for production, as well as consumer products to match the needs of a sophisticated urban society. Colombia's growth has been close to the average of developing countries, but this growth has not been steady. Annual GDP growth in the 45 years after World War II was about 4.8 percent, but it varied from a high of 6.08 percent between 1967 and 1972 to a more modest 2 percent between 1990 and 1997. In 1999 GDP diminished by about 5 percent, the only negative result in close to 70 years as investment activity and demand plummeted.

Topographical conditions have made internal communications very difficult, isolating most regions from one another. For close to a century such difficulties prevented the consolidation of an integrated national market. Today, modern transportation **infrastructure** is still lacking, both for the internal market and for exports.

Unlike most other Latin American countries, Colombia was never very cut off from the world in economic terms. During the second half of the twentieth century, the country managed a mixture of relatively open and moderate economic strategies combined with industrial and export promotion policies. One good example is currency management. Up to 1967 the currency had several values through multiple **exchange rates**. The government then chose to have one rate, with its value fluctuating over time using a **crawling peg** mechanism. In addition, several other mechanisms were designed to promote exports. Following such changes, exports expanded, bring in new sources of foreign exchange.

Such policies—unusual in the region—allowed Colombia to avoid the hardship of the 1980s, known throughout the area as the "lost decade." One major difference was the **national debt**. During the 1980s Colombia managed to avoid the "debt trap" with a debt of roughly 7 percent of GDP, although in the last 7 years it increased to 30 percent. The country's total **external debt** by 1998 was US$35 billion. So when the times were ripe for major changes, Colombia was able to launch economic reforms without the strains suffered by other countries. The first 5 years of **liberalization** in the late 1980s and early 1990s were characterized by higher economic growth than the previous decade (between 4 to 5 percent annually). Subsequently, the GDP growth rate fell to 0.6 percent in 1998, and close to -5.0 percent in 1999 during the **recession** which affected all of Latin America.

Despite its comparative advantages, Colombia has suffered from the introduction and expansion of a powerful illegal drug industry that today stands as a major threat to the consolidation of the country as a democratic society and operates as a major fuel to social and political violence. Originating in the early 1970s, the narcotics business managed to profit from weak social and legal controls, political corruption, and the collusion of some authorities. With their headquarters established in the regions of Antioquia and Cauca, the Medellín and Cali cartels set up a vast international network of coca, marijuana, and poppy cultivation, the manufacture of cocaine and heroine, distribution channels, and **money laundering** .

POLITICS, GOVERNMENT, AND TAXATION

Colombia was one of the first South American nations to gain independence from Spain in 1824. A part of the Gran Colombia (comprising also Venezuela, Ecuador, and Panama) until 1830, from the 1840s the country started on its own route, oriented toward a mild form of economic and social liberalism. From those early years onwards the country has been characterized by 3 major political features: first, a dominance of 2 major parties, the Liberals and Conservatives. From around the mid-19th century, traditional political parties have dominated the political scene, adapting to major social, economic, and international conditions. Second, the pervasive presence of political violence. The greatest bloodshed came in the War of the Thousand Days (1899–1902) in which 100,000 people died, and the "Violencia" (1948–66) during which between 100,000 and 200,000 lost their lives. Currently Colombia is plagued by violence from several leftist guerrilla groups and high levels of violence involving both street criminals and drug lords.

Paradoxically, the third feature has been a relatively long stability of democratically elected governments from 1910 onwards, with the exception of the period from 1949 to 1958. Apart from that brief period, Colombia's military forces have been known for their support of civilian-elected governments. In response to the mid-twentieth-century violence, the 2 traditional parties formed the National Front coalition under which Liberals and Conservatives alternated the presidency and shared power in Congress and the government bureaucracy from 1958 to 1974.

The political regime is presidential, with presidents elected directly every 4 years with no opportunity for re-election. The current president is Andrés Pastrana, elected in 1998. Every now and then there have been pressures toward more provincial autonomy, but the regime remained quite centralized from the enactment of the 1886 Constitution until a new one was drafted and approved in 1991. Regarding the judiciary system, the top of its hierarchy is selected by Congress. There is a **bicameral** (2-chamber) Congress; governors, mayors, and local councilors are also elected every 4 years, though on different dates. Although political confrontation has been bitter and even violent occasionally, the 2 parties have shared power most of the time, either through implicit agreements or under constitutional provisions, such as those forming the National Front.

The National Front era contributed to diminishing differences over policy, especially in economic matters, and served as a positive factor for stability and growth. At the same time, however, it was a means to exclude other players in the legal arena, which created incentives for armed struggle. During the National Front period—as well as other periods when compromise governments formed—it was virtually impossible to create a political organization outside the Liberal or Conservative parties.

For more than half a century Colombia has suffered from the action of left-wing guerrillas. From the late 1940s, growing discontent over poverty and social inequities in rural areas led to the formation of guerilla groups, which evolved into 2 major organizations, the Fuerzas Armadas Revolucionarias de Colombia (FARC, **communist** oriented), and the Ejercito de Liberacion Nacional (ELN, which supported Cuban leader Fidel Castro). During the 1970s and 1980s, the guerrillas turned their attention to the cities, and several attempts toward peace ended in bloodshed. Today the 2 former guerrilla groups have turned to the narcotics business in their search for financial support. In their pursuit of total power, the guerrillas have failed to topple the government but have caused major disruptions. That is also the case of the growing power of the drug cartels and paramilitary groups.

In 1991 a new constitution was drafted by a Constituent Assembly and later approved by a majority of

Colombians. It cleared the way for new entrants to the political scene, instituted direct elections of provincial governors and mayors, and strengthened the office of the Attorney General, Constitutional Council, and the Electoral Authority. Other constitutional provisions regarding the political system, such as banning re-election and a 4-year presidential period, were maintained.

The strategy of the Pastrana administration has been to reinitiate peace negotiations with the 2 major groups (FARC and ELN) while at the same time obtaining important financial support from the U.S. government. This program—called Plan Colombia—is designed to combat the illegal drug plantations, laboratories, and the commercial drug network, thus depriving the guerrillas of financial support.

The size and influence of government over the economy has been rather mild. According to the World Bank, the central government revenues in 1998 were only 12 percent of GDP. Though the level of state involvement increased from the 1940s to the 1970s, Colombia never concentrated major portions of wealth creation in the hands of the state. Coffee production, with its wide participation of private growers and commercial **retail** networks, has been an important factor both in terms of tax collection and the presence of private capital.

For many years financial policy was shared between the executive branch and congress, with participation of the **private sector**, but from the mid-1960s, most of the responsibility has rested with the former, with **monetary policy** in the hands of the Banco de la Republica (central bank). Traditionally, the government has regulated the prices of electricity, water, sewage, telephone services, public transportation, rents, education tuition, and pharmaceuticals. During the 1960s the government also established a set of public financing institutions and in the 1980s, amid a financial crisis, it **nationalized** a number of private banks.

In general terms, Liberals and Conservatives have agreed on major policy issues like monetary stability, the avoidance of high **inflation**, export promotion, and the cautious development of oil. During the 1980s and 1990s, most differences between the parties were over the pace of economic reforms. The Liberal party advocates milder and slower reforms while Conservatives tend to support more open market policies. In 1990, the administration of President Cesar Gaviria (1990–94) initiated economic liberalization, or apertura, and it has continued since then, though at a slower pace. It consists of **tariff** reductions, financial **deregulation**, **privatization** of state-owned enterprises, and the adoption of a more flexible foreign exchange system. After a period of lack of interest in liberalization during the Samper administration (1994–98), the Pastrana administration has regained the pace of economic reforms.

According to the *World Development Indicators 1999* more than one-quarter of Colombia's current revenues come from **indirect taxes**, primarily from domestic taxes on goods and services, and another quarter from **direct taxes** on income, profit, and capital gains. An unfavorable aspect of the tax situation in Colombia has been a recurrent tendency of several administrations to pardon unpaid taxes accumulated by firms and individuals over the years.

INFRASTRUCTURE, POWER, AND COMMUNICATIONS

For many decades Colombia suffered from a weak and even non-existent infrastructure that made national market integration difficult. The 3 mountain chains that cut through the most populated areas rendered road and railroad construction very costly. After the 1930s important programs of public investment in infrastructure began, and in recent decades the situation has somewhat improved, though infrastructure still does not meet general needs. Colombia has 115,543 kilometers (71,811 miles) of roads, of which only 13,866 kilometers (8,618 miles) are paved. The rail system is small and outdated, with only about 3,379 kilometers (2,100 miles) in the whole country.

Communications

Country	Newspapers	Radios	TV Sets[a]	Cable subscribers[a]	Mobile Phones[a]	Fax Machines[a]	Personal Computers[a]	Internet Hosts[b]	Internet Users[b]
	1996	1997	1998	1998	1998	1998	1998	1999	1999
Colombia	46	581	217	16.7	49	4.8	27.9	7.51	664
United States	215	2,146	847	244.3	256	78.4	458.6	1,508.77	74,100
Brazil	40	444	316	16.3	47	3.1	30.1	18.45	3,500
Ecuador	70	419	293	11.7	25	N/A	18.5	1.42	35

[a]Data are from International Telecommunication Union, *World Telecommunication Development Report 1999* and are per 1,000 people.

[b]Data are from the Internet Software Consortium (http://www.isc.org) and are per 10,000 people.

SOURCE: World Bank. *World Development Indicators 2000.*

Colombia has a network of 1,101 airports, of which only 90 have paved runways. There are 10 international airports, with heavy traffic in Bogotá, Cali, Barranquilla, Medellín, and Cartagena. The most important airport is "El Dorado," located in the capital city. The difficulties in land communication and transport have made aviation profitable, so for many years Colombia was far ahead of its neighbors in this area. The airports are served by 9 large and medium airlines and also a group of small airlines. In addition, Colombia has 18,136 kilometers (11,272 miles) of waterways navigable by river boats and a number of important ports and harbors, mostly related to tourism.

Electrical power capacity in Colombia falls short of current and projected needs. Electricity production was 45.02 billion kilowatt hours (kWh) in 1998, with 69 percent of production coming from hydroelectric sources, 30.11 percent from fossil fuel, and the rest from other sources. According to World Bank sources, electricity use decreased from 904 kWh per capita in 1996 to 885 kWh per person in 1998. It is also very decentralized, with 37 companies providing power. Among these firms are Interconexion Electrica ISA, Generadora Union, Codensa, Transelca, Genercauca, Centrales Electricos del Norte de Santander, Electrocost, Electromag, Conelca, and EEPP.

Electricity became a lagging sector during the 1990s. Programmed cuts during the mid-1990s ran for several hours a day in the main cities for as long as 2 years. As a result, by 1999 imports of electricity jumped to 94 million kWh. These shortcomings, however, have not affected exploitation of new natural resources such as oil and coal, since investment in those areas usually involve their own infrastructure requirements, like pipelines, integrated camps, and airfields.

Colombia has a relatively modern telephone system represented by a nation-wide relay system, a domestic satellite system with 41 earth stations, and a fiber optic network linking 50 cities. The telecommunications business in Colombia is experiencing a major boom: there were 75 telephone lines per 1,000 people in 1990, doubling in 1998 to 173 lines per 1,000 persons. Cellular subscribers have also increased substantially. In 1990 cell phones were nonexistent, while in 1998 there were 49 subscribers per 1,000 people. Among the many telecommunications companies are Globalnet Telecom, Energia Integral Andina, Skytel, Intelsa, Americatel, Metrotel, Andicel, Cetell ISP, and Colomsat.

According to the *CIA World Factbook 2000*, Colombia had 5,433,565 telephones main lines in use by 1997 and 1,800,229 cellular telephones in 1998. By 1999 Colombia had 13 Internet service providers. Thus Colombia is moving towards greater connectivity, higher den-

sity in mass media, and dynamism in the telecommunications sector.

ECONOMIC SECTORS

Colombia is the world's second-largest coffee grower and coffee exporter (after Brazil), accounting for 31.2 percent of the world's production. Coffee production and exports were a major engine of growth during most of the twentieth century. However, by the end of the century, the country had achieved greater diversification. By 1999, agriculture accounted for 19.7 percent of GDP, while manufacturing attained 18.9 percent, and the banking and insurance sector accounted for 15.8 percent. Of less significance were commerce, restaurants and similar activities with 8.8 percent, mining at 4.2 percent, government services with 8.9 percent, construction at 3.4 percent, and electricity, gas, and water with only 1.1 percent. An overview of the productive landscape shows agriculture diminishing over time, with a considerable increase in services, a mining sector (mostly oil and coal) growing in terms of output and exports though diminishing in terms of employment, and a stagnating manufacturing sector. Although these sweeping changes led to the diminishment of agriculture, some agricultural products have seen higher levels of revenue over the last forty years, either through modernization in the production of established crops (cotton, sugar cane, bananas, and cocoa) or through introduction of new ones, like cut flowers.

Changes in population growth have been accompanied by a major shift in the distribution of the economically active population. In 1960, 50.1 percent of the **labor force** was engaged in agriculture, 19.5 percent in industry, and 30.4 percent in services. By 1980 the fig-

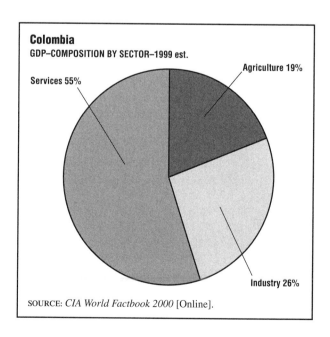

Colombia
GDP–COMPOSITION BY SECTOR–1999 est.

Services 55%
Agriculture 19%
Industry 26%

SOURCE: *CIA World Factbook 2000* [Online].

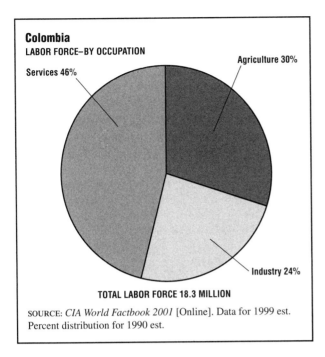

Colombia
LABOR FORCE–BY OCCUPATION

Agriculture 30%

Services 46%

Industry 24%

TOTAL LABOR FORCE 18.3 MILLION

SOURCE: *CIA World Factbook 2001* [Online]. Data for 1999 est. Percent distribution for 1990 est.

ures were 34.3, 23.5, and 42.2 percent, respectively, and by 1999 they stood at 30 percent, 24 percent, and 46 percent, respectively. These shifts reflect a different composition of economic output and have altered many economic relations in the country.

AGRICULTURE

For a long time agriculture was the main source of living for many Colombians. By the year 2000, however, it accounted for roughly 19 percent of GDP, though still employing 30 percent of the population and accounting for 17.4 percent of exports, with coffee the major export. Coffee employs one-fourth of the agricultural labor force, accounts for 20 percent of the cultivated area, and contributes nearly 9 percent to GDP. Production by 1998 was estimated by Colombia's Departamento Administrativo Nacional de Colombia (DANE) at 2,445,224 metric tons.

Colombia has a diversity of other agriculture products, including bananas for export (2,061,992 metric tons), rice (1,818,726 metric tons), potatoes (1,476,869 metric tons), sugarcane (1,061,272 metric tons), cassava (970,951 metric tons), oilseed (378,481 metric tons), and other products like cotton, cocoa beans, and tobacco. There are an estimated 167,000 cattle ranches in the country, of which 40 percent are in the departments of Atlantico, Bolivar, Cordoba, and Magdalena, and 15 percent in Boyaca, Meta, and Arauca.

Of the total land area of Colombia (113,891,400 hectares), an estimated 27 percent is agricultural land, most of it in elevated regions of the temperate zone. Mechanization trends have stagnated in the last twenty

years. By 1980 the number of hectares of arable land per tractor was 183, and by 1997 the number rose only slightly to 211 hectares per tractor. Under the traditional system of slash-and-burn agriculture, fields are usually cleared at the beginning of the dry season and the brush from the cleared land is burned. This practice results in soil exhaustion and erosion. Yields are generally low and variable because of the inadequacy of flood control systems and irrigation. Although the country receives adequate rainfall, droughts are common. The U.S. government is working with the Pastrana administration to modernize the agricultural sector and provide incentives for farmers to switch from coca production to other crops.

Colombia ranks high in terms of land concentration and disparities in land ownership. Of the total farmland, 68 percent is owned by 4.3 percent of landowners, and half of Colombia's farms account for less than 2.3 percent of the farmland. Although 69 percent of the farms and 75 percent of the farmland are owned by individual farmers, 62 percent of these farms are too small to provide a living. The number of landless workers is estimated at 1 million, representing close to a third of the population engaged in agriculture. Traditional rural labor markets have virtually disappeared. Migration from traditional agricultural areas to the cities has contributed to more modern hiring and land tenancy systems.

The economic reforms of the 1990s ended most special protective measures for particular sectors, which led to a weakening in the production of some traditional crops like corn, cotton, and cassava. As a member of the Andean Community (formerly Andean Pact), a common trade agreement established during the 1960s and revamped in the 1990s, Colombia still enjoys special protection for many agricultural products. To do this, the "Andean price band system" is employed, which imposes tariffs on certain commodities that vary according to a pre-determined range. Fourteen basic agricultural commodities including wheat, sorghum, corn, rice, barley, milk, and chicken parts are subject to tariffs under the price-band system employed as part of this agreement.

Colombia is also an illicit producer of the drugs coca, opium poppies, and cannabis. According to recent information disclosed by Colombia's Ministry of Defense, the country is the world's leading coca cultivator (coca is used in the production of cocaine). The country was responsible for 67 percent of world supply by 2000, and total land area devoted to coca was approximately 122,500 hectares by the end of 1999, more than a 35 percent increase from 1997, with a refining potential of 710 tons of pure cocaine per year. Cultivation of opium in 1998 remained steady at 6,600 hectares a year.

As of 1999, most small farmers were involved in coca cultivation, largely because of the steady demand from markets in the United States and elsewhere. Coca is harvested from 3 to 6 times a year. Payment is in cash, and this helps farmers maintain a steady source of income. Nevertheless, the U.S. Department of State reports that small coca farmers "barely manage to survive, partially due to the 'protection' fees charged by the guerrilla and paramilitary forces." Small farm plots may account for roughly one-quarter to one-third of coca cultivation, or 30,000 to 40,000 hectares.

INDUSTRY

MINING. One significant part of the transformation of the Colombian economy from the 1970s has been the expansion of the mining sector, mostly comprised of oil production and coal, though it also includes gold and valuable gems such as emeralds. Oil production in Colombia has been declining as of late, with 700,600 barrels a day (bbl/d) in 2000, down 125,000 bbl/d from the previous year. The country's reserves are estimated at about 2.6 billion barrels, but the potential reserves are much higher. Colombia's main oil export market is the United States, with 332,000 bbl/d in 2000. Production is located mainly in the Cusiana and Cupiagua fields in the Andes foothills and in the Cano Limón field near the Venezuelan border. British Petroleum has major operations at Cusiana and Cupiagua, while the Cano Limón field is operated by U.S.-based Occidental.

All foreign investment in petroleum exploration and development in Colombia must be carried out under a profit-sharing association contract between the investor and the state petroleum company, Ecopetrol. In the face of U.S. oil companies' interest in increasing exploration and production if contract and tax requirements are smoothed, the Pastrana administration has responded by liberalizing contracting terms.

Colombia produces more than 90 percent of the world's emeralds; it is the second-largest South American producer of gold and the most important coal producer in Latin America. Coal reserves have been estimated between 12 billion and 60 billion tons, approximately 40 percent of all Latin American reserves. Important levels of production began in 1984, attaining 4,000 metric tons, which jumped to close to 13,000 metric tons by 1993 and 28,500 metric tons in 1997. Excluding oil production, there was a relative decline in mining from 1992 to 1996, accompanied by a decline in the number of persons employed to almost 20,000.

MANUFACTURING. The economic landscape of Colombia has changed dramatically in the last 40 years, and one clear example is the changes in the manufacturing industry by the late twentieth century. Industrial manufacturing is quite varied. According to DANE, by the year 2000 the most important products included basic chemicals (5.3 billion pesos), beverages (3.5 billion pesos),

milling and cereal processing (3 billion pesos), oil refining (2.9 billion pesos), and pulp, paper and derived products (2.1 billion pesos). Though an important proportion of production is for the domestic market, the relative level of sophistication in some of these products can be measured by the extent to which they are exported. In 2000 manufactured products accounted for nearly 40 percent of all exports, with chemicals and textiles ranking near the top.

Manufacturing is located mostly in the provinces of Antioquia, Cauca, in the capital district, and to a lesser extent in Barranquilla, on the Atlantic coast. The number of people employed by this sector is 588,681—approximately 20 percent of the economically active population.

The lowering of many trade barriers in the 1990s served to streamline Colombian industry, and most sectors have managed to remain competitive with other Latin American competitors, leading to an increase in exports to those countries.

The construction industry, one of the largest employment sectors in Colombia, has been very dynamic over the last 2 decades, totaling close to 7,000 companies. In the years from 1998 to 2001, however, it was hit hard by the recession and tight credit conditions.

SERVICES

FINANCIAL SERVICES. Colombia has an extensive banking sector. According to DANE, it accounted in 1995 for close to 16 percent of GDP, clearly the most important service activity. It is headed by the Bank of the Republic, which functions as the central bank. There are approximately 1,700 companies devoted to financial services, of which 37 are established banks, 30 are investment companies, nearly 70 stock and bond brokers, and a small number of leasing and real estate leasing. There are 17 long-term and development financial institutions, including the government-owned Industrial Development Institute. The government has played an important role in the financial sector since the 1970s because of the unwillingness of banks to make long-term loan commitments to riskier projects such as coal development, and because of the necessity for periodic public intervention to stabilize financial markets.

The 6 largest of these corporations hold 86 percent of all assets in this sector. In the mid-1980s there was a crunch in the banking system that forced the government to nationalize a number of troubled domestic banks. It also created the Financial Institutions Guarantee Fund (Fondo de Garantías de Instituciones Financieras) as the authority to intervene or recapitalize those financial institutions in great need of support. By the end of the 1980s the government set out plans for privatization, the second phase of which took place by the end of the 1990s.

TOURISM. Tourism is a relatively minor activity in the country. In 1997 inbound tourists to Colombia numbered 1,193,000 people, contributing US$955 million in foreign exchange, representing 6 percent of exports. In 1980 the corresponding figures were US$357 million and 6.7 percent of exports, so in twenty years there was a slight decline in tourism's contribution to the economy. If hotels and travel agencies are included, the number of people involved in tourism by 1997 was only 23,700. Most tourist activities are concentrated in the Atlantic coast, in the cities of Cartagena, Santa Marta, and Barranquilla. Tourists are mainly attracted to a mixture of beaches and historic sites. As part of the viceroyalty of Nueva Granada during colonial times, the coastal cities retain a good part of this heritage. With Colombia suffering from violence for 2 decades and targeted as a high-risk country, it is quite understandable that there are not more tourists.

RETAIL. The commercial sector is very important in most urban areas, and it has modernized substantially over the years, though suffering from the recession from 1998 to 2000. According to the most recent DANE survey, by 1997 personnel employed in supermarkets, "hypermarkets," and malls was nearly 84,000, with sales of 2.87 billion pesos. These figures declined to 74,000 persons employed and 2.02 billion pesos worth of sales in 2000. Main lines of sales are food, clothing, and pharmaceuticals, though automobiles have increased their share over the last 5 years. Although most retail is regionally based, there are 3 main chain stores—Almacenes Exito, Vivero, and Carulla—which have remained strong despite the downturn of the economy by the end of the 1990s. Also important national and regional companies—including the 3 just mentioned—have forged alliances or have opened participation to foreign owners, mostly in the coastal area, while new foreign firms have established retail operations of their own.

TRANSPORTATION. Despite geographical and political difficulties, transportation has become over the years an activity of increasing importance, attaining 8.8 percent of GDP by 1997. According to the Asociación Nacional de Instituciones Financieras (ANIF), the transport of cargo and passengers by land represents 76 percent of revenues in the sector, while air transportation accounts for 10 percent, and maritime only 3.3 percent. Passenger transportation accounted for 75 percent of revenues, with the rest going to cargo. According to ANIF, rail transportation's importance diminished by 1997 to a third of the value in 1987.

Colombia's domestic air-transport market was deregulated in 1990, a move that led to domestic passenger traffic doubling to just over 6 million people by 1996. International traffic more than doubled to 1.7 million passengers by the same year. Colombia also concluded an agreement with Venezuela, which led to flights between Venezuela and Bogotá increasing dramatically.

INTERNATIONAL TRADE

One of the most striking aspects of Colombia's economic performance over the years has been the change in the export mix. Once predominantly a coffee economy, by the year 2000 coffee accounted for only 8.43 percent of foreign exchange earnings, while oil and related products jumped to 35.34 percent and manufacturing products accounted for 39.54 percent of exports. However, Colombia still exports oil and coffee to the developed world (the United States, Japan, Germany, and Belgium), while most of its exports to countries such as Venezuela, Mexico, and Ecuador are manufactured products.

At the same time, the relative importance of Colombia's partners has also changed. The United States remains the main trading partner, receiving 37.2 percent of Colombia's exports and providing 32 percent of Colombia's imports in 1998. However, the role of Venezuela as a trading partner has increased substantially. In 1996 the United States was the destination of US$5,991 million of exports, while Venezuela had climbed to US$1,178 million. Ecuador accounted for US$413 million, Germany US$353 million, Peru US$338 million, and Japan US$216 million. This trend diminished after 1997, mostly due to the recession on both sides of the Venezuela-Colombia border. The year 2000 has shown a relative recovery between both partners.

More than 70 percent of Colombian exports to the United States are primary products such as food (mainly coffee, bananas, cut flowers, tuna, shrimp, and sugar), and fuel (petroleum and coal). The United States also holds the largest share of **foreign direct investment**, with US$4.3 billion, or 28.1 percent of the estimated total direct foreign investment of US$15.4 billion.

Imports to Colombia also grew extensively during the 1990s, creating a **trade deficit** until 1998. Through

Trade (expressed in billions of US$): Colombia		
	Exports	Imports
1975	1.465	1.495
1980	3.924	4.739
1985	3.552	4.141
1990	6.766	5.590
1995	10.126	13.853
1998	N/A	N/A

SOURCE: International Monetary Fund. *International Financial Statistics Yearbook 1999.*

September 1999, Colombia's overall trade balance has swung from a US$2.7 billion deficit to a US$1.1 billion surplus, while the U.S.-Colombia trade balance swung from a US$292 million U.S. surplus to a US$1.8 billion deficit. The type of imports also show the overall changes in the Colombian economy. While during most of the twentieth century imports were mainly **consumer goods**, and later **capital goods**, the trend has changed. According to DANE, in the year 2000 21.9 percent of imports were capital goods, 51.99 percent were raw materials, 8.57 percent were transportation equipment, and 18.72 percent consisted of consumer goods.

MONEY

The value of the Colombian peso per US$1 was 2,179.3 in December 2000. This reflects a loss of over half its value against the dollar since 1995, when it traded at 912.83 pesos to the dollar.

Colombia's monetary policies are formulated by the Junta Monetaria (Monetary Board), and banking operations are regulated and supervised by the Superintendencia Bancaria. The Central Bank conducts monetary policy based on behavior of the financial sector, and determines the amount of money in the system and makes other decisions in line with indicators such as inflation and growth of the economy at large.

The Colombian peso has floated freely against the dollar and other currencies since 25 September 1999, when the Central Bank abandoned the crawling band exchange regime, which acts like a crawling peg. Under that system, the Bank intervened in the market by buying or selling dollars to keep the dollar's price in pesos within the band. Soon after abolition of the band—by December 1999—the peso had depreciated 20 percent from the beginning of the year, increasing the competitiveness of Colombian exports to the United States.

Inflation has always been moderate in Colombia, with peaks in the mid-twenty percent range. By the end of 1999 inflation was 9.2 percent, more than 5 percentage points below the previous year, mainly as a consequence of the recession. The figure for 2000 was 10 per-

cent as consumption reversed the downward trend and the government restrained wage hikes. Despite economic recovery and a slight weakening of the peso, officials were not able to relax monetary policy later in year 2000. Average interest rates were 19.5 percent in 1999 and about 15.3 percent in 2000.

In August 1989 the government authorized plans to return to private ownership 65 percent of the assets of all financial institutions nationalized after the financial crisis of 1987.

POVERTY AND WEALTH

Colombia is neither a poor nor a rich country. Income per person was by year 1999 roughly equal to the world average. According to the Andean Community, GDP per capita was US$1,487 in 1993, and rose to US$2,090 by 1995. The CIA's *World Factbook* estimates income per capita for 1999 at US$6,200. More interesting, however, are changes over time. By 1980 income per capita was about 108 percent higher than in 1950, with most of the growth having occurred between 1969–1979 when it increased by 50 percent. During the 1980s economic growth declined significantly, but income per capita managed a modest percent increase given a population growth slowdown.

Income distribution has also shown important changes during the last fifty years. Total income inequality peaked in the 1960s. Later on, when education levels improved drastically and the relative income of agricultural workers improved somewhat, inequalities in income levels became less extreme. Among the poorest workers, the picture is also positive. In *Political Economy and Illegal Drugs in Colombia,* Francisco Thoumi sums up the trends this way: "Based on a constant poverty line, the incidence of poverty has declined continuously during the fifty-year period. A head-count index shows that three-fourths of the population was poor in 1938, half in the mid-1960s, and one-fourth in the late 1980s. The poor declined from 70.5 percent of the country's population in 1973 to 45.6 percent in 1985, while the extreme poor declined from 44.9 to 22.8 percent." All the changes notwithstanding, according to the ANIF, Colombia's in-

Exchange rates: Colombia	
Colombian pesos (Col$) per US$1	
Jan 2001	2,241.43
2000	2,087.90
1999	1,756.23
1998	1,426.04
1997	1,140.96
1996	1,036.69
SOURCE: CIA *World Factbook 2001* [ONLINE].	

GDP per Capita (US$)					
Country	1975	1980	1985	1990	1998
Colombia	1,612	1,868	1,875	2,119	2,392
United States	19,364	21,529	23,200	25,363	29,683
Brazil	3,464	4,253	4,039	4,078	4,509
Ecuador	1,301	1,547	1,504	1,475	1,562

SOURCE: United Nations. *Human Development Report 2000; Trends in human development and per capita income.*

Distribution of Income or Consumption by Percentage Share: Colombia

Lowest 10%	1.1
Lowest 20%	3.0
Second 20%	6.6
Third 20%	11.1
Fourth 20%	18.4
Highest 20%	60.9
Highest 10%	46.1

Survey year: 1996
Note: This information refers to income shares by percentiles of the population and is ranked by per capita income.

SOURCE: *2000 World Development Indicators* [CD-ROM].

come inequality is still one of the highest in Latin America, and deteriorated greatly between 1997 and 2000, particularly in the urban areas. Rural GDP is only 50 percent of that of urban areas.

Education has also improved substantially in the last forty years. According to Thoumi, in 1951 "44 percent of the population was illiterate [and] in 1955 it was estimated that only 57 percent of 7 to 12-year-olds were enrolled in elementary schools. Under state control, elementary school enrollment ... reached nearly 100 percent by 1970. Increases in high school and college enrollments have also been substantial. In 1960 high school enrollment was only 11.9 percent, while college enrollment was only 1.8 percent. By 1980 these rates had increased to 44 and 10.6 percent respectively, the latter achieving 28 percent by 1997."

In health care, Colombia also shows continuous improvement. First of all, the control of tropical diseases like malaria in the countryside and improvement in sewage systems in the cities strongly contributed to a diminishing trend in infant mortality rates (from 123.3 for each 1,000 new births in the early 1950s to 48.6 by the end of the 1980s, and 23 by the year 2000). Life expectancy has risen in Colombia; by the end of the 1980s the figure stood at 68 years, and reached 70 years in 2000. This is a far cry from the early 1950s, when the average was barely 50 years. A contributing trend has been the construction of a health care network for the growing urban population. A pension system created in 1993 allows access to both public and privately-funded health care for all employees. This program has both taken the pressure off of the public health system and has supplemented it, leading to a net improvement in the quality of health facilities in the country.

The quality of housing has also improved. According to data quoted by Thoumi from the 1951 census, "52.7 percent of the housing units had earth floors and 90.3 percent had walls made of 'precarious' materials. By the

1985 census these percentages had dropped to 17.1 and 24.4 respectively. Similarly, in 1951 only 28.8 percent of the units had running water, 25.8 percent had electricity, and 32.4 percent had sewage or septic tanks. By 1985 these figures had increased to 69.7, 78.2, and 77 percent respectively. In urban areas ... these percentages were much higher: 89.8, 95, and 93.6 respectively."

While the physical standard of living has improved, the country has actually become less livable. Colombians today enjoy better housing, health services, and education; they own cars, telephones, and have greater access to information about their country and the world. They are more broadly traveled and they have more material goods than in the past. But many fundamental aspects of the quality of life, such as physical security and property protection, have deteriorated sharply due to the increase in political and criminal violence associated with both guerrilla terrorism and the narcotics war. According to ANIF, life expectancy among male Colombians dropped 3 to 4 years between 1994 and 1997 largely due to the rise in violence, both political and criminal.

WORKING CONDITIONS

The workers' movement emerged by the end of World War I. From that time, the labor movement was greatly influenced by episodes of violent confrontation. The most critical of these occurred during the first massive industrial action, aimed at the United Fruit Santa Marta complex in 1928 when railroad, banana, and field workers went on strike to force changes in wages, hours, and non-wage compensation. The human toll was 1,000 dead. The aftermath of this tragedy diminished the dominance of the Conservative Party and contributed to the Liberal Party winning the presidency. The incoming government had a more open and pragmatic stance toward labor activities and pressed for important labor reforms, which helped in union expansion nation-wide. During this period, there was a greater participation of labor in national politics, mainly through the Liberal Party. The Confederation of Colombian Workers (Confederacion de Trabajadores Colombianos, CTC) was created in 1935, and represented the first successful attempt at uniting smaller unions from various professions into a collective organization. Later, Cold War ideological confrontation led to fears by more conservative elements that the CTC was too left-wing; thus in 1946 the Catholic Church established the Union of Colombian Workers (Union de Trabajadores Colombianos, UTC), which gained important support from the more moderate unions.

A second labor confrontation occurred in 1947 during a strike by port workers on the Magdalena River, which also ended in the loss of lives. During the "Violencia" (1948–66), organized labor became increasingly demoralized and weakened. After 1960, however, 2 more labor federations emerged: the Trade Union Confederation of Colombian Workers (Confederacion Sindical de Trabajadores Colombianos, or CSTC) and the General Confederation of Workers (Confederacion General de Trabajadores, or CGT). The former was aligned with the communists and the latter with the tiny Social Christian party. However, although the percentage of workers enrolled in unions more than doubled from 1959 to 1965, union membership was still a very low 13.4 percent.

Later on, in September 1986, an important group of independent unions and those affiliated with the CSTC joined forces to create the United Workers Central Organization (Central Unitaria de Trabajadores, or CUT). The CUT represented 70 to 75 percent of the organized workforce, and emerged as a major voice against organized violence. This organization proved to be less timid in terms of industrial action, and by the late 1980s the labor movement appeared to play a greater role in representing workers' social and political rights. Working conditions and wages are governed by the Labor Code of 1950 and some additional laws. The work week is 48 hours, except in agriculture. Fringe benefits include annual vacations and sick benefits. Employees are eligible for a retirement pension after 20 years of service. Social security is compulsory with the employer paying half the cost and the employee and the government paying a quarter each.

The total workforce of Colombia reached 18 million by 1999, with a record 20 percent unemployment level due to the recession, which has affected living standards and poverty levels, especially in the countryside.

COUNTRY HISTORY AND ECONOMIC DEVELOPMENT

1821. Gaining independence from the Spanish empire, Colombia emerges from colonial rule as part of Gran Colombia, together with Venezuela, Ecuador, and Panama.

1859. Emergence of the Liberal Party. Tobacco accounts for 28 percent of exports while gold's share is down to 33 percent.

1860S-70s. Liberal constitution establishes **liberal economic** principles and quasi-federal autonomy to provinces. The 1870s marks efforts in railroad building. The Conservative Party is founded. By late 1870s coffee production, carried by rail and financed by banks, becomes even more important.

1886. A conservative constitution is promulgated, marking a major swing toward a more centralized state.

1898. Coffee reaches 50 percent of exports.

1899. Colombia's greatest civil war ruins the country. Coffee-producing areas are greatly affected, and chaos shakes the economy.

1903. Panama is separated as a consequence of the war, supported by U.S. intervention. After the war, Congress reforms monetary system, budget, customs, tariff legislation, and some **protectionist policies**.

1904-09. Rule of dictator Rafael Reyes. His conservative administration starts reconstruction under economic orthodoxy.

1910-30. Bipartisan consensus emerges with constitutional reform. Paper money is banned, and minority party representation established. Coffee production takes place on larger farms, and has a greater impact on the domestic economy.

1920s. A strong coffee export trend (11.3 percent of world production by 1930) allows for the tripling of public spending, mostly in infrastructure.

1930-46. Known as the Liberal Republic, this is a period of social reform, slower economic development, and growing tension between the parties. The collapse of coffee prices is partially compensated for by greater exports and the strengthening of domestic industry. Liberal dissident Jorge Eliecer Gaitan rises to prominence.

1946. Split in Liberal party ends the period of liberal rule. Gaitan dominates the Liberal party.

1948. Assassination of Gaitan leads to a virtual civil war known as "The Violence" (1948–66).

1950. Extreme Conservative Laureano Gomez comes to power, unleashing terror against liberal insurgencies in the countryside. Exports start a diminishing trend.

1953. A military coup supported by both traditional parties brings in General Rojas Pinilla. Political calm is affected by a downturn in coffee prices and a weak economic performance.

1958. Beginning of the National Front, under which Liberals and Conservatives alternate the presidency and share government posts at all levels.

1960s. After economic difficulties and currency instability, the largest post-war economic expansion period comes after 1964.

1969. Colombia joins the Andean Pact, a trading agreement among several South American countries.

1974-84. A period of economic instability and political stability. An increase in coffee prices reduces foreign exchange constraints, allowing an upward trend in income, lower unemployment, and an increase in international reserves. After 1980, a collapse in coffee prices produces slow growth, an industrial setback, rising unemployment, and an increase in deficits.

1987–89. Political violence starts again; prominent politicians are kidnapped or assassinated by drug dealers trying to overthrow the government.

1990–94. The Cesar Gaviria administration opens up the economy and leads the approval of a new constitution.

1994–98. The Ernesto Samper administration begins under accusations of campaign financing by drug dealers. The pace of economic reforms slow down, while the narcotics business and the guerrilla activities grow.

1998–2000. Peace negotiations with the guerrillas begin under President Andrés Pastrana. Plan Colombia against illicit drug production and trafficking is launched.

FUTURE TRENDS

Most of Colombia's dilemmas at the beginning of the 21st century are political rather than economic. The confrontation between guerrilla groups allied to the narcotics industry has become highly delicate, and is likely to remain so throughout the rest of the Pastrana presidential period, which will end in 2002. This situation will also affect the modernization of the political system and any economic recovery. Despite a better structural situation than other countries in the region, the continuous violence not only stops major advances, due to the uneasiness of foreign investors, but also creates major incentives for the emigration of the elite and professional groups. Putting all his eggs in the basket of the peace process has led to frustration over the failure of Pastrana's efforts. The weak economic performance has additionally undermined the popularity of the president. His administration has enjoyed strong support from the U.S. government, which in 2000 agreed to an aid package of US$1.7 billion (Plan Colombia) to combat illegal drugs in the south, southeast, and northern areas.

According to most sources, peace talks with the guerrillas that started in 1999 continue against a background of violence. Although some progress has been made, the conflict has escalated and the guerrillas' commitment to ending the hostilities is questionable. Negotiations with the largest guerrilla group, the Fuerzas Armadas Revolucionarias de Colombia (FARC), have followed a stop-and-go trend, stagnating for half a year and then resuming after continuous confrontations. So far the clashes have not ended. Pastrana and his successor are likely to come under increasing pressure to abandon talks and opt for a purely military solution if progress continues to prove elusive. Despite the eventual promise of military support from the United States, it is unlikely that such an option will be followed, mostly because of the risks involved in an open civil war against well-armed and widely dispersed guerrilla forces. Also, the peace talks still enjoy the support of important civil sectors, including the Church and non-government organizations (NGOs). While Bogotá continues to try to negotiate a settlement, neighboring countries worry about the violence spilling over their borders.

Colombia's leading exports, oil and coffee, face an uncertain future. New exploration is badly needed to offset a pending decline in oil production, and the coffee harvest has dropped because of aging plantations and natural disasters. The lack of public security is a key concern for investors, making progress in the government's peace negotiations with insurgent groups an important driver of economic recovery. Net foreign direct investment fell to about US$675 million in 1999 from US$2.5 billion in 1998, reflecting poor business confidence. The tide changed again in 2000, more than doubling the previous figure amid lower interest rates, greater oil investment, and privatization. Officials are also offering better contract terms to encourage greater foreign investment in the oil industry. In spite of pipeline bombings and kidnappings, current oil prices remain a powerful incentive for further oil investments, especially since Colombia's untapped oil reserves are estimated to be huge. According to the International Energy Agency, oil production is expected to top 1.2 million barrels a day within the next 5 years and show little decline through 2020.

Despite the end of the recession, investor sentiment and economic recovery will remain vulnerable to further troubles in the beleaguered financial sector and the delicate peace process.

DEPENDENCIES

Colombia has no territories or colonies.

BIBLIOGRAPHY

Asociación Nacional de Instituciones Financieras. <http://www.anif.org>. Accessed February 2001.

Bergquist, Charles, Ricardo Peñaranda, and Gonzalo Sánchez, editors. *Violence in Colombia: The Contemporary Crisis in Historical Perspective.* Wilmington, Delaware: Scholarly Resources Books, 1992.

Bushnell, David. *The Making of Modern Colombia.* Berkeley: University of California Press, 1993.

"Colombia." *Energy Information Administration.* <http://www.eia.doe.gov/emeu/cabs/colombia.html>. Accessed August 2001.

DANE: Departamento Administrativo Nacional de Colombia. <http://www.dane.gov.co>. Accessed February 2001.

Economist Intelligence Unit. *Country Profile: Colombia.* London: Economist Intelligence Unit, 2001.

Kurian, George Thomas, editor. *Encyclopedia of the Third World.* New York: Facts on File, 1987.

Ocampo, José Antonio, editor. *Historia Económica de Colombia.* Bogotá: Presidencia de la República, Imprenta nacional, 1997.

Thoumi, Francisco E. *Political Economy and Illegal Drugs in Colombia.* Boulder, Colorado: Lynne Rienner Publishers, 1995.

U.S. Central Intelligence Agency. *World Factbook 2000.* <http://www.odci.gov/cia/publications/factbook/index.html>. Accessed August 2001.

—Leonardo Vivas

COSTA RICA

Republic of Costa Rica
República de Costa Rica

CAPITAL: San José.

MONETARY UNIT: Colón (C). One colón is composed of 100 céntimos, but céntimos are no longer used. The smallest unit of money in circulation is the 5 colón coin, followed by the 10, 25, 50, and 100 colón coin. Bills circulate in denominations starting at 1,000 colones, and are available in 2,000, 5,000, and 10,000 colones.

CHIEF EXPORTS: Coffee, bananas, sugar, textiles, electronic components, electricity.

CHIEF IMPORTS: Raw materials, consumer goods, capital equipment, petroleum, electricity.

GROSS DOMESTIC PRODUCT: US$26 billion (purchasing power parity, 1999 est.).

BALANCE OF TRADE: Exports: US$6.6 billion (1999 est.). **Imports:** US$5.9 billion (1999 est.).

COUNTRY OVERVIEW

LOCATION AND SIZE. Costa Rica is a central American nation, located between Nicaragua and Panama. Its borders span 309 kilometers (192 miles) with Nicaragua and 330 kilometers (205 miles) with Panama. Costa Rica also borders the Pacific Ocean and the Caribbean Sea, its coastline reaching across 1,290 kilometers (802 miles). The country has 51,100 square kilometers (19,730 square miles) of land, which is slightly less than the size of West Virginia, including the Isla del Coco (a small island in the Pacific Ocean).

San José, the capital, is located in a highland valley in central Costa Rica called the Meseta Central. Most of the country's population is located in this area formed by 2 basins separated by low, volcanic hills ranging from 900 to 1,500 meters above sea level. Other important cities are Cartago (the old colonial capital), Alajuela, and Heredia. The main port cities are Limón on the Caribbean Sea and Puntarenas on the Pacific.

POPULATION. The country's population was estimated at 3.5 million in July of 2000. It is growing at a rate of 1.69 percent, which means that the population should reach approximately 4.1 million by 2010 and should double to over 7 million by the year 2035. Over 60 percent of the population is between the ages of 15 and 64, and only 5 percent of citizens are over 65 years old. The population is young, posing a challenge for the government to provide adequate schooling and training for youngsters. About 95 percent of the population can read and write. The larger, younger generation will also require greater health and retirement services as it begins to age.

Birth rates are at 20.69 per 1,000 people and death rates are at 4.31 per 1,000 people. There are approximately 2.52 children born per woman. Infant mortality rates are 11.49 deaths per 1,000 live births. There are approximately 1.02 males for every female in Costa Rica. The average life expectancy is 75.82 years: 73.3 years for males, and 78.5 years for females.

Adding to the high birth rate, the Costa Rican population also increases due to **immigration**—particularly from Nicaragua and other Central American countries. Immigrants come to Costa Rica in search of work opportunities, which they usually find in the agricultural sector. They are attracted by the relatively higher standards of living that are enjoyed in the country. The immigration rate for 2000 was estimated at 0.54 immigrants per 1,000 citizens.

The population of Costa Rica is mainly white (94 percent, including mixed European and Amerindian mestizos) and Roman Catholic (85 percent). There is a small proportion of black (3 percent), Amerindian (1 percent), and Chinese (1 percent) residents, and the second most important religious group is Evangelical Protestant (14 percent).

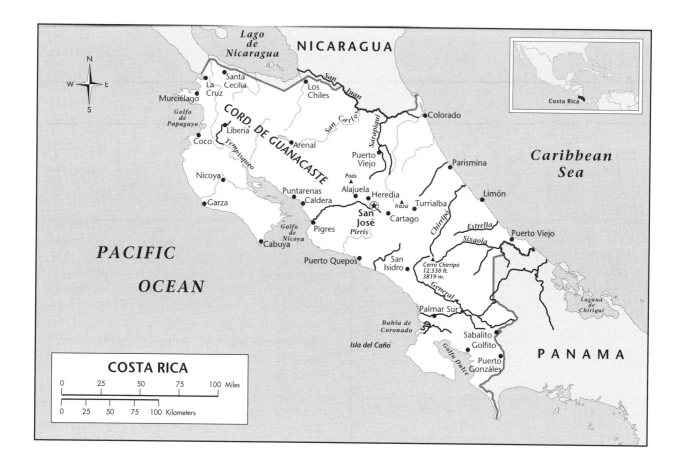

OVERVIEW OF ECONOMY

Costa Rica has a mixed economy in which both public and private companies play an important role. The government has supported **socialist** policies for decades. The emphasis in the economy has been placed on the governmental promotion of human development and welfare, while still allowing private companies to operate in some industries. These efforts were intensified in the 1950s, when political and social forces supported a method of economic development (planned growth) that was heavily dependent upon the state.

The biggest indication of the government's socialist ideology was its purchasing of goods and companies that were in trouble. When the state bought an interest in key industries such as banking, electricity, telecommunications, insurance, medicine, and education during the second half of the 1900s, the economy underwent **nationalization**. Under government control, Costa Rica achieved a relatively high standard of living.

However, this strategy relied on deficit spending, which meant that the Costa Rican government was spending money that it did not have. Even worse, the government also financially supported **import substitution** industrialization (ISI) policies during the 1960s and 1970s. Such policies were supposed to make the country more self-sufficient in industrial production, but ISI policies put Costa Rica deeper in debt.

The worldwide **recession** of the 1980s helped cause a Latin American debt crisis. Facing a devalued currency and an **inflation rate** of over 100 percent, Costa Rica experienced the most severe recession since the 1930s. The country was forced to make economic reforms and to **liberalize** the economy. This process began with a currency stabilization program (to stop **inflation**), and led to a **structural adjustment program** (SAP) that tried to reduce government intervention in the economy.

The government sold many companies in which it had invested, but state control of the main industries persisted, with the exception of the banking industry. The people of Costa Rica preferred a state-run economy, and chose to finance their debt through the attraction of **foreign direct investment**. Public funds continued to be directed towards the manufacture and export of industrial goods. In spite of an increase in taxes, deficit spending continued, and the public debt grew. Interest payments on this debt absorbed a third of public accounts annually, making the economy unstable. Foreign direct investment helped the growth of local supply networks and supported export growth. The Intel Corporation opened a microprocessing plant in Costa Rica in 1998. The country has also been successful at promoting tourism, which has become an important source of foreign investment, has increased employment, and has generated substantial exchange revenue.

High levels of **gross domestic product** (GDP) growth achieved during 1998 and 1999—around 8 percent—proved unsustainable in 2000 when the demand for microprocessors plummeted. GDP growth during 2000 fell to a mere 1.5 percent. Economic policy focused on controlling inflation (at a historically low 10 percent), but the fiscal deficit remained above 4 percent, limiting economic growth.

POLITICS, GOVERNMENT, AND TAXATION

Costa Rica differed from other Spanish colonies in that it never developed a system of large land holdings. Agricultural production was limited to the size of families, and the distribution of land and other resources was relatively equal. Independence from Spain came without violence in 1821. After joining the Mexican Empire briefly in 1822, the Central American colonies—Guatemala, Honduras, El Salvador, Nicaragua, and Costa Rica—created a federated republic in 1823, which collapsed in 1829. Costa Rica is a democratic republic organized under the 1949 constitution. The president, 2 vice-presidents, and single-chamber congress (the Legislative Assembly) are directly elected for 4-year terms. The Supreme Court justices are elected by the Legislative Assembly for 8-year terms.

Liberal political reforms in the late 1800s facilitated the expansion of democratic institutions and processes. The middle class of Costa Rica flourished along with the development of commerce, services, and manufacturing. As economic conditions worsened through the Great Depression of the 1930s, the role of the state increased, and the citizens of Costa Rica demanded economic reform. Much of the country's character was defined in the 1950s through the abolition of the army, the nationalization of the main industries, and the construction of a **social welfare system**.

The main political forces in the country since the introduction of the social welfare system have been the Social Democrats (Liberación Nacional) and the Christian Democrats (Unidad Social Cristiana). Both Social and Christian Democrats have pursued an active involvement of the state in economic affairs. As a result, Costa Rica is a country in which the **public sector** plays a major role. The wave of **privatization** that has shaken most Latin American countries has not been significant in Costa Rica. The state continues to control key industries such as electricity, telecommunications, banking, insurance, health, oil refinery, and alcohol distillation. This situation has resulted more from public opposition to privatization than from government policy. As a result, the state has focused on administrative reforms that attempt to improve the efficiency of public companies.

Although there has been an increase in the level of participation of the **private sector**, the state is still in control. Banking is no longer a state **monopoly**, but the 3 largest banks are state owned. Medicine is also practiced privately, but the largest and most modern hospitals are owned and operated by the government's social security system. A law passed in 2000 allows the handling of old-age pensions by private companies, but the majority of pensions are still under state control.

The central government has a significant impact on the economy with its expenditures totaling over 30 percent of GDP in 1998. This is much higher than the level of expenditures in Canada (24.7 percent of GDP), the United States (21 percent) or the East Asian countries (10.4 percent), but is lower than the level in France (46.6 percent), Italy (44.6 percent), the U.K. (37.9 percent), Spain (36.1 percent), or Germany (32.9 percent). According to Central Bank figures (1999), the main sources of government revenue were import **duties** (42 percent), **income taxes** (22 percent), sales taxes (16 percent), and consumption taxes (5 percent).

Since tax revenues are lower than 23 percent of GDP, the government finances its expenditures through debt. This creates a deficit that in 1996 amounted to 4 percent of GDP and, although it was lowered to levels closer to 3 percent during 1998, has resurged during the past 2 years. Public debt has risen as a result, to a point where it represents more than the total of goods and services produced by the country, and thus represents a major source of economic instability. Interest payments on the debt absorb up to a third of the national budget, restricting the amount of funds that can be devoted to building schools, roads, and hospitals. The country's Central Bank has a limited ability to control the money supply and to fight inflation.

In spite of these negative trends, the government devotes over 5 percent of GDP to education and almost 7 percent of GDP to health. This compares well to the Latin American averages of expenditure in education and health, at 4.5 percent and 3.1 percent, respectively, and is comparable to international levels. The result of this policy has been an educated, skilled workforce.

INFRASTRUCTURE, POWER, AND COMMUNICATIONS

One of the greatest challenges facing the country is the maintenance of its **infrastructure**. Investments in this area have not kept pace with economic growth. There is more traffic than the old roads and ports can safely

Communications

Country	Newspapers	Radios	TV Sets[a]	Cable subscribers[a]	Mobile Phones[a]	Fax Machines[a]	Personal Computers[a]	Internet Hosts[b]	Internet Users[b]
	1996	1997	1998	1998	1998	1998	1998	1999	1999
Costa Rica	94	271	387	13.8	28	2.3	39.1	10.41	150
United States	215	2,146	847	244.3	256	78.4	458.6	1,508.77	74,100
Mexico	97	325	261	15.7	35	3.0	47.0	23.02	1,822
Nicaragua	30	285	190	40.2	4	N/A	7.8	2.21	20

[a]Data are from International Telecommunication Union, *World Telecommunication Development Report 1999* and are per 1,000 people.
[b]Data are from the Internet Software Consortium (http://www.isc.org) and are per 10,000 people.

SOURCE: World Bank. *World Development Indicators 2000.*

handle, and the communication and power networks are not strong enough for the country's demands. A law was passed in 1998 to allow the development and administration of the infrastructure through private contracts, but by 2000 not one contract had been granted.

Costa Rica's communication infrastructure is less advanced than other Latin American countries. For example, in 1998 telephone lines per 1,000 inhabitants were at 172, better than the Latin American average of 118. But cellular phones per 1,000 inhabitants were at 28, compared with 43 for all of Latin America, while Internet hosts were at 0.85 per 1,000 inhabitants compared to 4.85 for Latin America. Television sets were at a level of 387 per 1,000 inhabitants, compared to 255 per 1,000 for Latin America, but cable subscribers were at 13.8 per 1,000, compared to 28.3 per 1,000 for Latin America.

The country has over 35,705 kilometers (22,187 miles) of roads, of which 20 percent corresponds to national highways and 80 percent to local roads. About 56 percent of the national roads and 12 percent of the local roads are paved. Two major projects were underway by the end of 2000 to improve the carrying capacity of the main roads connecting the capital to the Pacific Coast.

Electric power generation and telecommunications are handled by a state monopoly, the Instituto Costarricense de Electricidad (ICE). Efforts to open these sectors to competition and privatization sparked riots and public protests in early 2000. The government claimed that it needed help from the private sector in order to service demand. Rioters were afraid that privatization would result in higher rates and the neglect of rural locations. The country's power source is mostly hydroelectric, although geothermal and wind sources are also used. The Costa Rican Congress was discussing a **restructuring** of the ICE in 2000–01 that would allow the establishment of **joint ventures** for the development of energy and telecommunication projects. It would, however, fall short of allowing competition by private participants in these sectors.

An index compiled by the Instituto Centroamericano de Administración de Empresas (INCAE), the Harvard Institute for International Development, and the Central American Bank for Economic Integration shows Costa Rican infrastructure lagging behind that of other Central American and East Asian countries. Values assessed ranged from 1 to 7 with higher values representing better infrastructure conditions. Costa Rica obtained a value of 2.29 compared to 3.46 for Guatemala, 3.56 for Nicaragua, 4.55 for South East Asia, and 4.64 for the United States, Japan, Ireland, Sweden, and China. This means that Costa Rican business faces greater challenges to compete against other nations.

ECONOMIC SECTORS

The Costa Rican economy is concentrated in the service sector, with 60.5 percent of its 1998 GDP represented in this category. The main service activity in the

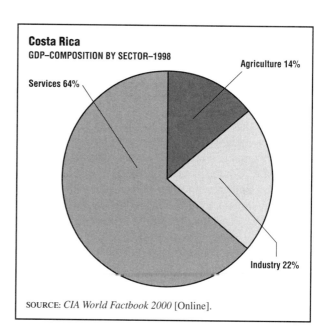

Costa Rica
GDP–COMPOSITION BY SECTOR–1998

Services 64%
Agriculture 14%
Industry 22%

SOURCE: *CIA World Factbook 2000* [Online].

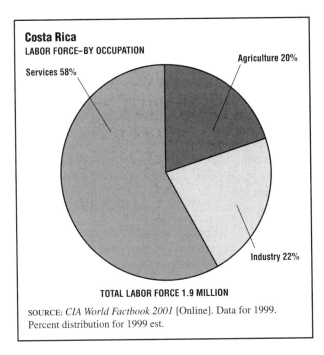

Costa Rica
LABOR FORCE–BY OCCUPATION

Services 58%

Agriculture 20%

Industry 22%

TOTAL LABOR FORCE 1.9 MILLION

SOURCE: *CIA World Factbook 2001* [Online]. Data for 1999.
Percent distribution for 1999 est.

country is tourism, with over 1 million visitors in 1999. Industry is the second most important sector, representing 24 percent of GDP in 1998, followed by agriculture, which represents 15.2 percent of GDP.

The amount that industry contributes to GDP in Costa Rica is average for Latin America but is low when compared to that of East Asia (44 percent of GDP), the Arab nations (40 percent of GDP), and Eastern Europe (35 percent). However, it has become an area of aggressive growth through government stimulus. Efforts to build a high technology park through foreign direct investment have attracted firms like Intel Corporation, Baxter Medical, Microsoft, Abbot Laboratories, Conair, and Alcoa.

Government policies have attempted to reduce dependence on agriculture as a source of employment, production, and foreign exchange revenue. This has reduced the relevance of agriculture from close to 40 percent of GDP in the 1950s to its current 15.2 percent level. However, it still employs about 20 percent of the **labor force**.

AGRICULTURE

Costa Rica's temperate (warm) climate and fertile soils are suitable to agricultural production. There is an abundance of water—yearly rainfall averages 4 meters—and irrigation has been successfully applied to develop more arid (dry) regions. The government supports growers through research, training, and technical assistance.

The agricultural sector in Costa Rica has been declining in importance since the 1950s, but in 1998 still

accounted for 15 percent of GDP and employed one-fifth of the labor force. Almost 10 percent of the country's land is used for agriculture. Agriculture is still an important contributor to foreign trade. Excluding **free zone** companies, agricultural exports represent approximately 60 percent of export flows. Traditional crops, like coffee and bananas, have been the staples of agricultural production since the 18th century. However, a wide range of nontraditional products has appeared since the 1980s that have begun a revival in agricultural exports.

Coffee is the country's oldest agricultural product and has been exported since the 1790s. In the 1820s the Costa Rican government stimulated its production by distributing free coffee plants and offering tax exemptions to interested families. This approach resulted in a group of small producers that, in spite of the existence of large-scale growers, has managed to remain in existence. Costa Rican coffee has been characterized by its high quality and efficient production, boasting some of the highest area yields in the world. In 1999 the country produced 147,000 metric tons of coffee. Although for many years coffee was the country's main source of foreign exchange, low international prices eroded its importance. Production for 1994–99 averaged 2.9 million bags (133,000 metric tons) with revenues of US$370 million annually. While such revenue represented about 11 percent of total export earnings in 1994, it only amounted to 4 percent of total export earnings in 2000.

Banana production surpassed coffee as the main agricultural product in 1992. Local farmers have cultivated it for over a century on the country's coasts, although primarily **multinational corporations** handle its export and sale. Production grew constantly during the 1990s, and prices remained steady. Exports for 1994–99 averaged 2,045,000 metric tons with revenues of US$624 million. This represented almost twice the revenue generated by coffee. Costa Rica devotes 50,000 hectares to growing bananas, almost 1 percent of its territory. It is the second largest producer in the world with an annual crop of approximately 115 million boxes sold in the United States and Europe. Growers estimate that their industry generates over 40,000 direct jobs and 100,000 indirect jobs. Workers in banana production enjoy the highest salaries and benefits in the Costa Rican agricultural sector.

Costa Rica is also an important producer of sugar. Yearly export volumes average 130,000 metric tons per year, with revenues of US$39 million. However, unlike coffee or bananas, sugar production is largely for local consumption, which exceeds 2.6 million metric tons. Over 48,000 hectares of land are dedicated to the production of sugar.

Nontraditional agricultural goods have been rising in importance over recent years. Most of them are export oriented and linked to various forms of agroindustry.

Examples are African palm used for the extraction of vegetable cooking oil, and oranges processed for their juice and exported as fluid or concentrate. Although African palm has been cultivated since the 1970s, its period of strong growth began in the 1990s. By 1996 over 27,000 hectares were in production generating a volume of 422,000 metric tons. Orange production began in earnest as recently as 1990, spurred by the construction of 2 processing plants. Production areas doubled in 6 years, reaching 23,500 hectares and 165,000 metric tons. Other important nontraditional agricultural products are hearts of palm, ornamental plants, and macadamia nuts.

INDUSTRY

Costa Rican industry expanded in the 1960s and 1970s through government investment and protection. Sizable industrial investments were undertaken by the state through its development agency, CODESA. The investments aimed at reducing foreign dependence. However, the halt of foreign competition through trade protection resulted in inefficiency and products of poor quality. The strategy was abandoned in the mid-1980s as the government initiated a process of trade liberalization.

Industrialization policies since then have supported nontraditional exports. They have relied on direct **subsidies** such as the CAT (Certificado de Abono Tributario—a tax refund certificate) program; and indirect subsidies such as income tax exemptions, preferential import duties, and streamlined import-export facilities.

The result has been a sustained increase in the flow of industrial exports that has more than doubled their dollar value in less than 10 years, from US$518 million in 1991 to US$1.1 billion in 1999. Since 1996, industrial exports have contributed over 40 percent of all exports, excluding those from the free zone. About 15 percent of the workforce is employed in manufacturing activities.

Industry has also been promoted through the attraction of foreign investment. The country's industrial policy has been successful in attracting high technology companies, the most noteworthy being Intel Corporation, which invested over US$200 million in the construction of microprocessor production facilities in 1998. Total export volumes nearly doubled as a result of these investments, from US$3.5 billion in 1995 to US$6.6 billion in 1999. The export volume of the free zone sector was greater than the combined revenues of the normal export sector.

Because small industry is rarely eligible for free zone benefits but is subject to all forms of regulation and taxes—including payroll taxes that can reach up to 50 percent of workers' salaries—a growing number of establishments have been appearing in the **informal sec-**

tor. The Costa Rican Chamber of Industry estimates that 84 percent of all the industrial firms established in the 1990–98 period belonged to the informal sector.

MINING. Gold is mined on the southern Pacific Coast and northwestern regions of the country. Some controversy exists as to the ecological impact of the methods employed in these extractions. Silver is also mined—though not extensively—in the western part of the country. Deposits of manganese, nickel, mercury, and sulfur exist but remain unexplored. Petroleum deposits have been identified in the southeastern region, but their exploitation has been deemed uneconomical. Salt is produced from seawater.

MANUFACTURING. Until recently, most of the country's industry consisted of small-scale light manufacturing enterprises. Intel Corporation's arrival in 1998 marked the first large-scale manufacturing venture. Coffee-drying plants, sugar mills, cheese factories, sawmills, woodworking factories, breweries, and distilleries characterize the manufacturing sector. There is a single petroleum refinery that is state owned, and several hydroelectric plants with capacity to produce close to 6 billion kilowatt hours of electricity. Factories produce petroleum products, furniture, paper, textiles, chemicals, pharmaceuticals, plastics, footwear, cigars, cigarettes, jewelry, and clothing.

About half of the 4,856 industrial firms are located in the capital, San José. Next in importance are Alajuela (20 percent), Heredia (11 percent), and Cartago (10 percent). Of these firms, 2,411 (49.6 percent) are microenterprises employing between 1 and 4 workers. There are 1,547 (31.9 percent) small industries with 5 to 19 employees, 624 (12.9 percent) medium industries, with 20 to 29 employees, and 274 large industries (5.6 percent) with 100 or more employees.

According to the Ministry of Commerce and Industry, 24 percent of all industrial establishments process foods, drinks, and tobacco; 21 percent are metal and mechanic shops; 15 percent process wood, furniture, or other wooden products; 14 percent produce textile or leather products; 9 percent are in paper and printing; and 8 percent are in chemicals, rubber, and plastics.

SERVICES

Over 50 percent of the Costa Rican workforce is employed in the service sector, producing over 60 percent of the country's GDP.

TOURISM. The most dynamic portion of the service sector is tourism. Costa Rica pioneered **ecotourism** (the practice of touring natural habitats in a manner that minimizes ecological impact). Because of its great biodiversity the country enjoys a natural advantage in this sort of activity. The number of tourists visiting Costa Rica has increased steadily during the 1990s, at an average rate of 15 percent per year. During 1999 over 1 million people visited the country, and the Costa Rican tourist board estimates that number increased by over 10 percent in 2000. Since 1986 a flow of investment exceeding US$800 million has been devoted to developing the sector. In 2001 there were over 13,400 rooms available for tourists. In 1998 US$883 million was generated by the tourist industry. This amount was over twice the revenue generated by coffee and 1.3 times that of banana exports. The government promotes the development of tourism through the Instituto Costarricense de Turismo (ICT), or tourist board, which prepares a yearly development plan. ICT runs specialized educational facilities to train workers in hotel management and other tourism-related activities.

RETAIL. Retailers currently employ about 20 percent of the active workforce. Most **retail** firms are small to medium companies, although large discount retailers and hypermarkets have established themselves in the market during the past 2 years. There are 4 main supermarket chains—Automercados, MasxMenos, Super2000, and Perifericos—as well as a number of one-location markets of considerable size. Coverage of retail stores is limited to the Central Valley, although some have made inroads into the provinces during recent years. The oldest and largest department stores are La Gloria, with significant coverage in the Central Valley, and Llobet, located mainly in Alajuela.

FINANCIAL SERVICES. About 5 percent of the workforce is employed in financial services. The sector generates about 3.6 percent of GDP. Banking was a state monopoly until 1987, when private institutions were allowed to coexist legally with the state banks, although they were limited to offering time deposits and were not allowed to offer checking or savings deposits. Reforms in the 1990s allowed private banks to offer the entire range of financial services, virtually eliminating the previous state monopoly. The only difference that persists between private and public banks is that the latter enjoy unlimited deposit guarantee from the state whereas private deposits are unsecured. There are 3 public banks—Banco Nacional, Banco de Costa Rica, and Banco Crédito Agrícola de Cartago—which represent 41 percent of total credit, and 20 private banks which represent 35 percent of total credit (2000). Other financial institutions include a workers' bank known as the Banco Popular y de Desarrollo Comunal which is capitalized through mandatory payroll contributions from workers and employers, a public funding agency for mortgage financing known as the Banco Hipotecario de la Vivienda, savings and loan cooperatives, mutual fund companies, and finance companies. The social security fund also engages in long-term mortgage financing. Insurance is presently a state monopoly; all insurance business is handled by the Instituto Nacional de Seguros.

There is a private stock exchange, the Bolsa Nacional de Valores (BNV), which is the oldest and largest in Central America. Its current annual volume is approximately US$28 billion, but over 80 percent of the volume traded is in public instruments. Only a small fraction of this volume (under 1 percent) is in **equities**. Some international transactions are also handled through the exchange. There are 27 brokerage companies currently participating at the exchange.

There are 3 regulatory entities in the financial sector: the Superintendencia de Entidades Financieras (Financial Superintendence), regulating banks, credit cooperatives, and other financial institutions; the Superintendencia de Pensiones (Pension Superintendence), regulating pension administrators; and the Superintendencia de Valores (Securities Superintendence), regulating securities and exchanges. All 3 entities are governed by a national board or commission, the Consejo Nacional de Supervisión Financiera.

COMPUTER SOFTWARE. A burgeoning sector in Costa Rican services is the production of computer software. The National Chamber of Software Producers estimates the country currently boasts the highest number of per capita software producers in the world. About 85 percent of these firms, all nationally owned, export their products with yearly revenues of over US$50 million. The sector is estimated to have generated over 1,500 jobs in 1998. The high level of education and technical expertise available in the population favors the development of this industry, which is expected to continue growing.

INTERNATIONAL TRADE

Following a period of protectionism during the 1960s and 1970s, Costa Rica has slowly opened to greater foreign investment. The result has been an increase in import and export activity. Whereas imports and exports each barely amounted to US$200 million in 1969, in 1998 they had reached levels of US$6.2 and US$5.5 billion, respectively. The bulk of this growth occurred during the

Trade (expressed in billions of US$): Costa Rica

	Exports	Imports
1975	.493	.694
1980	1.002	1.540
1985	.976	1.098
1990	1.448	1.990
1995	3.453	4.036
1998	5.511	6.230

SOURCE: International Monetary Fund. *International Financial Statistics Yearbook 1999.*

1990s. In the case of imports it took the country from 1977 to 1990 to double its import volume from US$1 to US$2 billion, but only 8 years (1990–98) to triple that level to US$6.2 billion. The main sources of these imports in 1998 were the United States (41 percent), Japan (8.1 percent), Mexico (7.3 percent), and Venezuela (4 percent). In the case of exports it took from 1980 to 1992 (12 years) to double its export volume around the US$2 billion level, but only 6 years (1992–98) to more than double again and reach US$5.5 billion. The country's main export destinations in 1999 were the United States (49 percent), the European Union (22 percent), and other Central American nations (10 percent).

This growth has been accompanied by an important shift in the composition of trade. The importance of agricultural exports has diminished in favor of industrial exports. From 1991 to 1999, industrial goods went from 49 percent to 77 percent of total exports, whereas agricultural goods fell from 51 percent to 23 percent, respectively. This shift was largely the result of policies conducted to promote direct foreign investment and stimulate exports. These investments were carried out in free zone areas and their contribution to exports grew from 22 percent in 1991 to 60 percent in 1999. During the same period, local industry reduced its contribution to exports from 27 percent to 17 percent.

This growth of exports was driven by the arrival of foreign manufacturers—most importantly, the Intel Corporation. With its arrival in 1997, free zone exports shot up by a factor of 4, from US$891 million to US$3.6 billion. The relevance of Intel's exports can be gauged by their impact on the total volume of country exports, which rose from US$4.2 billion in 1997 to US$6.6 billion in 1999.

Since Costa Rica relies heavily on imports of raw materials and **capital goods**, industrial export growth has been accompanied by a substantial growth in imports. The country has carried a deficit in its **balance of trade** for every year since 1995, except 1999. However, the deficit has shrunk from over 33 percent of total exports in 1995 to just over 7 percent of total exports in 2000. This trade deficit has been financed by foreign capital flows, which have totaled US$2.4 billion in the past 5 years. Income from the service sector, particularly from tourism, has also helped finance the trade deficit.

The country's dependence on foreign capital flows to sustain imports is one of its recognized weaknesses. Although so far it has managed to attract sufficient levels of investment through its aggressive promotion policies, its stable social and political circumstances, and its highly educated workforce, the inability to generate sufficient foreign exchange through exports alone makes the country vulnerable to changes in international circumstances. Investment attraction policies have also been

Exchange rates: Costa Rica	
Costa Rican colones (C) per US$1	
2001	318.95
2000	308.19
1999	285.68
1998	257.23
1997	232.60
1996	207.69
SOURCE: CIA *World Factbook 2001* [ONLINE].	

criticized as expensive and fiscally unsustainable since they require substantial subsidies and tax exemptions.

MONEY

Costa Rica has suffered from chronic inflation during the last 25 years. Inflation rates exceeded 100 percent at the height of the debt crisis in the early 1980s, but monetary authorities have successfully managed to bring the inflation rate under control. Inflation rates at the end of the 1990s varied from 10 percent to 15 percent annually.

The country's high level of social spending generated fiscal deficits that were financed through the Central Bank. An administrative structure that provided for government control of the Central Bank allowed its easy manipulation. Although subsequent reforms granted the Central Bank more freedom from the government, it still carries the burden of high debt. Since interest payments on the public debt represent as much as 30 percent of the spending budget, total debt is increasing, requiring ever larger amounts of public funds and limiting the ability of the government to spend in other areas such as health and education. The government's inability to balance the fiscal budget has led to inflationary pressures.

The persistence of inflation has led to periodic currency **devaluation** in order to protect the competitiveness of Costa Rican exports. The government's policy aims at maintaining a neutral currency value by comparing domestic inflation to an index of international inflation rates. The goal is to maintain the local currency at its 1992 level, adjusting for inflation so that its purchasing power is neither greater nor lower than what it was at that date. Devaluation rates typically follow inflation rates, and are currently at a 10 percent to 12 percent annual level. The **exchange rate** for January 2001 was approximately 320 colones to the dollar.

Although the legal currency is the colón, dollar-denominated transactions are legal and widespread. This practice developed in the 1980s as people tried to protect themselves against inflation and devaluation. Legal-ization took place in the early 1990s. Convertibility of the colón to the dollar is unrestricted and can be done at every bank and financial institution. Loans and invest-ments can be contracted in dollars, and rent contracts are typically denominated in dollars.

POVERTY AND WEALTH

Costa Rica has a large, professional middle class, and a relatively equal distribution of wealth. For the years between 1987 and 1998, the poorest 20 percent of the population held 4 percent of total income, whereas the richest 20 percent held 52 percent of total income. Approximately 9.6 percent of the population was re-ported under the World Bank poverty line (PPP US$1 a day) in 1998, compared to an average of 15.6 percent for Latin America and the Caribbean. The country had a per capita income (at **purchasing power parity**) of US$7,100 in 1999.

The GINI coefficient is an index of inequality that measures the distance between a perfectly equitable dis-tribution of income and the actual distribution across the population. A coefficient of 0 entails perfect equality, and a coefficient of 1 entails perfect inequality. Costa Rica's GINI coefficient for 1996, as reported by the World Bank, was 0.4607. This compared favorably with the distribution of income for its neighboring countries: El Salvador (0.052), Guatemala (0.0596), Honduras (0.537), Nicaragua (0.503), and Panama (0.485). The United States had a GINI coefficient of 0.408.

The Economic Commission for Latin America and the Caribbean classifies countries according to the inci-dence of inequality as measured by 5 risk factors: urban income inequality, urban poverty, urban unemployment, percentage of youngsters between 13 and 17 that are out of school, and the percentage of children that have not completed 6 years of schooling by age 15. Costa Rica is classified as having a low incidence of income inequal-ity, measured as a ratio no greater than 8 between the richest 10 percent and the poorest 40 percent. It is also considered to have low incidence of poverty, measured

Distribution of Income or Consumption by Percentage Share: Costa Rica	
Lowest 10%	1.3
Lowest 20%	4.0
Second 20%	8.8
Third 20%	13.7
Fourth 20%	21.7
Highest 20%	51.8
Highest 10%	34.7

Survey year: 1996
Note: This information refers to income shares by percentiles of the population and is ranked by per capita income.

SOURCE: *2000 World Development Indicators* [CD-ROM].

as a maximum of 20 percent of urban households classi-fied as poor. In the other 3 categories Costa Rica is clas-sified as having a median incidence of inequality: urban unemployment between 6 percent and 10 percent, be-tween 8 percent and 15 percent of youngsters from 13 to 17 out of school, and between 10 percent and 20 percent of children under 15 that have not completed 6 years of schooling.

Costa Rica has also been classified by the **United Nations Development Program** as a country with medium human development in the 2000 report. The Human Development Index (HDI) is a composite index that measures different aspects of development, such as life expectancy at birth, education, and income. Costa Rica was ranked 47th in the world according to the HDI report 2000.

The Costa Rican government provides a compre-hensive safety net through its social security system. Al-though coverage is far from universal and the system is plagued by high rates of evasion, payroll taxes insure a majority of the working population and their families. There is no unemployment insurance, but the law requires employers to pay up to 8 months of severance to dis-missed employees. A legal reform passed in 2000 re-quires employers to pay monthly contributions into pen-sion and severance funds that will be at the disposal of employees when required. Education is mandatory and free at the primary and secondary levels, and public uni-versities provide high quality, low cost education at the undergraduate and graduate level. High quality medical attention is available and open to all citizens in the na-tional hospitals.

Despite these achievements certain tendencies have started to erode the benefits of social services, creating a growing gap between the higher and lower sectors of the population. The quality of private education, for exam-ple, has surpassed that of public education. Service at

GDP per Capita (US$)					
Country	1975	1980	1985	1990	1998
Costa Rica	2,231	2,482	2,176	2,403	2,800
United States	19,364	21,529	23,200	25,363	29,683
Mexico	3,380	4,167	4,106	4,046	4,459
Nicaragua	999	690	611	460	452

SOURCE: United Nations. *Human Development Report 2000; Trends in human development and per capita income.*

public clinics and hospitals is poor, and there are long waits for medical appointments and procedures that tend to exclude those most in need. Public pensions are low and lag behind inflation. Reform efforts are underway that will attack these situations, but until they are passed, governmental authorities will continue to be challenged by these problems. Although government spending in these areas has not been reduced, critics believe that even higher amounts are required. The reforms partly hinge on this matter, but also aim at increasing the efficiency and effectiveness of administrators.

WORKING CONDITIONS

The labor force was estimated to be 1.377 million in 1998, with 5.6 percent unemployment and 7.5 percent **underemployment** (employment that does not require all the skills held by the employee). Working conditions are regulated in Costa Rica by a Labor Code (Código de Trabajo), and by administrative directives issued through the Ministry of Labor. Among the basic stipulations in effect are a minimum salary, a maximum workday with overtime stipulations, minimum safety and health requirements at the workplace, paid vacations and resting days, severance pay, a mandatory Christmas bonus, and maternity leave. Wage statistics published by the Interamerican Development Bank show that, although real minimum wages in Costa Rica fell by 1.4 percent between 1990 and 1992, they rose by 15 percent between 1992 and 1998.

Enforcement of the laws and regulation is conducted by Labor Ministry inspectors and through the labor courts. All employers are required to insure their workers against job-related injuries. Coverage is provided exclusively through the National Insurance Company (INS), and covers medical expenses, lost wages, and compensation in case of disability. Costa Rica has ratified, to date, 48 of the International Labor Organization (ILO) Conventions.

Labor unions have existed legally in Costa Rica for a long time and there are at least 4 national labor organizations or confederations: Confederación de Trabajadores Rerum Novarum (CTRN), Central del Movimiento de Trabajadores Costarricenses (CMTC), Confederación de Trabajadores de Costa Rica (CTCR), and Confederación Unitaria de Trabajadores (CUT). The influence of labor is greatest in the public sector.

During the 1990s, fiscal constraints led the government to curtail some of the privileges of public sector employees. These privileges were considered excessive and disproportionate to the benefits of workers in the private sector. Among the privileges that were discontinued were shortened workweeks, extended vacation periods, wage premiums linked to seniority and not productivity,

and severance bonuses. This resulted in strikes held by public sector employees. Inability to solve the disputes led unions to process claims of labor rights violations at the International Labor Organization. During the 1990s, the ILO reports that strikes and lockouts averaged 18.5 per year, with the worst year being 1990. About 70 percent of these occurred in the public sector.

COUNTRY HISTORY AND ECONOMIC DEVELOPMENT

1502. Columbus lands on Costa Rica.

1522. Spanish colonizing expedition led by Gil Gonzalez Davila names the area Costa Rica, or "Rich Coast" because of the large amounts of gold given to them by the natives.

1562. Establishment of first permanent settlement, Cartago, by Juan Vázquez de Coronado "the true conqueror of Costa Rica," who acts as governor.

1821. Costa Rica gains independence from Spain, and votes to join the Mexican empire.

1823. Costa Rica joins the United Provinces of Central America, with Guatemala City as the capital.

1824. Juan Mora Fernández elected to be the first head of state. He presides over 9 years of stable progress.

1838. Costa Rica withdraws from Central American federation and declares complete independence.

1840s. Great wealth comes to several coffee growers, called "coffee barons."

1870–82. Investment in railroads and public works during the military rule of Tomás Guardia.

1871. Minor Copper Keith, the eventual founder of the United Fruit Company, comes to Costa Rica to manage production of the railway.

1873. Keith begins growing bananas to feed railway workers.

1889. Democracy established in Costa Rica.

1920–30s. Economic depression. Public calls for government reform culminate with **communist**-led strike against United Fruit Company.

1940–44. Rafael Angel Calderón Guardia continues the reformist movement as president by creating the social security system and introducing a labor code. He also founds the University of Costa Rica.

1948. A 40-day civil war kills 2,000 people; José Mariá Figueres Ferrer becomes head of the government, founds the Partido de Liberacion Nacional

(PLN), and nationalizes the banks and insurance companies. (He dies a national hero in 1990.)

1950–60s. Period of expansion in government intervention in the economy and creation of a **welfare state** and public school system.

1980. Economic crisis due to inflation, currency devaluation, high oil prices, low prices for coffee, bananas, and sugar, high costs of the welfare state, and the disruption caused by the war in Nicaragua. Costa Rica has the world's highest per capita debt.

1981–84. The United States and IMF pour US$3 billion in aid into the Costa Rican economy.

1987. Costa Rican president Oscar Arias Sanchez wins Nobel Peace Prize for his efforts to establish peace in Central America.

1990. Rafael Angel Calderón Fournier, son of Calderón Guardia and opposition leader, is elected president. He promotes reform of the tax codes.

1994. José María Figueres Olsen, son of Figueres Ferrer and Liberación Nacional leader, is elected president. He initiates policies to attract direct foreign investment in high technology.

1998. Conservative economist and opposition leader Miguel A. Rodríquez is elected president. His narrow victory at the polls leads to an experiment with "Concertación" (an effort to consult civil society on national problems), especially on the issue of privatization.

FUTURE TRENDS

Economic policy in Costa Rica will hinge upon institutional reforms that will alter the balance between the state and the private sector. Although popular sentiment is antagonistic to privatization of public companies, there is a growing awareness of the need for these companies to achieve greater efficiency and effectiveness. At the same time, the budgetary constraints faced by the country in the year 2000 are restricting its ability to invest in infrastructure, health, and education. Since future competitiveness relies on these investments, a reassessment of public finances will be inevitable.

Recent revisions of the methodology employed by the Central Bank to calculate GDP revealed that national production figures reported in past years have been understated. This has led critics to point out that the tax burden—measured by tax revenues as a percentage of GDP—in the country is inordinately low. A reform of the tax code could ameliorate the fiscal constraints of the government. Reform is also required to adjust accounting for the effects of inflation, which reduces the effective tax rates. However, these effects will probably not

materialize in the short term because of the political challenges they pose.

DEPENDENCIES

Costa Rica has no territories or colonies.

BIBLIOGRAPHY

"Balance preliminar de las economías de América Latina y el Caribe, 2000." Comisión Económica Para América Latina y el Caribe, 2000.

Banco Central de Costa Rica. "Indicadores Económicos." <http://websiec.bccr.fi.cr>. Accessed January 2001.

Bolsa Nacional de Valores de Costa Rica. "Estadísticas." <http://www.bnv.co.cr/estadist/>. Accessed January 2001.

Cámara de Industrias de Costa Rica. "Crecimiento de las empresas industriales formales e informales." <http://www.cicr.com/indicadores>. Accessed 15 January 2001.

Corporación Bananera Nacional. "Realidad bananera en Costa Rica." <http://www.corbana.co.cr/realidad.htm>. Accessed January 2001.

Costa Rica Tourist Board. <http://www.tourism-costarica.com>. Accessed January 2001.

Diamond, Larry, Jonathan Hartlyn, Juan J. Linz, and Seymour Martin Lipset, editors. *Democracy in Developing Countries,* second edition. Boulder, Colorado: Lynne Rienner Publishers Inc., 1999.

"El 2000: un mal año." *La Nación.* 19 December 2000.

"Equidad, desarrollo y ciudadanía." Comisión Económica Para América Latina y el Caribe, 2000.

"Estabilidad resiste: Golpes del 2000." *La Nación.* 20 December 2000.

Instituto Costarricense de Turismo (ICT). "Area Estadísticas."

International Coffee Organization. "Coffee Export Statistics." <http://www.ico.org/>. Accessed 10 January 2001.

International Labor Organization. "International Labor Statistics." <http://database.iadb.org/>. Accessed 14 February 2001.

International Monetary Fund. *International Financial Statistics Yearbook 2000.* Washington, D.C.: International Monetary Fund, 2000.

Ministerio de Agricultura y Ganadería, Costa Rica. "Estadísticas Agropecuarias." <http://www.infoagro.go.cr/estadisticas>. Accessed 10 January 2001.

Ministerio de Planificación Nacional y Política Económica (MIDEPLAN). "Sistema de Indicadores sobre Desarrollo Sostenible (SIDES)." <http://www.mideplan.go.cr/sides>. Accessed January 2001.

La Nación Digital/Revista Viva. "Programas de software a la tica." <http://www.nacion.co.cr/viva/1997/julio/14/compu1.html>. Accessed 15 January 2001.

La Nación Digital/TecnoAvances #1. "Software con calidad de Exportación." <http://www.nacion.co.cr>. Accessed 15 January 2001.

Naranjo, Fernando. "Economía en picada." *La Nación.* 17 December 2000.

Organización Internacional del Trabajo. "ILOLEX: Las Normas Internacionales del trabajo." <http://ilolex.ilo.ch:1567/public/50normes/ilolex>. Accessed 14 February 2001.

"Programa de las Naciones Unidas para el Desarrollo." Informe Sobre Desarrollo Humano, 2000.

United Nations. *Human Development Report 2000.* New York and Oxford: Oxford University Press, 2000.

U.S. Central Intelligence Agency. *World Factbook 2000.* <http://www.odci.gov/cia/publications/factbook/index.html>. Accessed April 2001.

World Bank. *2000 World Development Indicators.* Washington, D.C.: World Bank, 2000.

—Ludovico Feoli

CUBA

CAPITAL: Havana (La Habana).

MONETARY UNIT: Cuban peso (C$). One peso equals 100 centavos. Coin denominations include 1, 2, 3, 5, 10, 20, 40, and 100 centavos. Paper-bill denominations include 1, 3, 5, 10, 20, 50, and 100 pesos. The U.S. dollar is an important monetary unit in Cuba, owing to the Pesos Convertibles (convertible pesos) that are also in circulation in denominations of 1, 5, 10, 20, 50, and 100 dollars. The dollar and the Peso Convertible are used for most transactions. Cuban pesos, often called Moneda Nacional, have fallen into disuse, except for a few government-subsidized businesses, like bodegas (small grocery stores) selling rationed foods, public transportation, movie theaters, and peso taxis.

CHIEF EXPORTS: Sugar, nickel, tobacco, shellfish, medical products, citrus fruits, coffee.

CHIEF IMPORTS: Petroleum, food, machinery, chemicals.

GROSS DOMESTIC PRODUCT: US$18.6 billion (purchasing power parity, 1999 est.).

BALANCE OF TRADE: Exports: US$1.4 billion (f.o.b., 1999 est.). **Imports:** US$3.2 billion (c.i.f., 1999 est.).

COUNTRY OVERVIEW

LOCATION AND SIZE. An island located 208 kilometers (129 miles) south of Florida, Cuba is washed by the Caribbean Sea on the south, the Gulf of Mexico on the northwest, and the Atlantic Ocean on the northeast. Its westernmost point is separated from Mexico by the Straits of Yucatan. With 110,860 square kilometers (42,803 square miles) of total surface area, Cuba, the largest island in the Antilles archipelago, is about the size of Pennsylvania. It is 1,199 kilometers (745 miles) long, but averages only 97 kilometers (60 miles) in width. Its coastline is 3,764 kilometers (2,339 miles) long with several excellent harbors. The capital city, Havana, is located

in the northwest of Cuba, almost directly south of Key West across the Straits of Florida. The second largest city in Cuba is Santiago de Cuba. Located in the eastern end of the island, Santiago was the island's first colonial-era capital (1522–89).

POPULATION. The population of Cuba was 11,131,000 in 2000, and is projected to grow to 11,481,000 by 2010. Although the population has doubled since 1950, the growth rate has slowed down considerably, and is now the lowest in Latin America. Population density is 101 people per square kilometer. Cuba is ethnically diverse; about 51 percent of the people are mulatto, 37 percent are white, 11 percent are black, and 1 percent are Chinese. The evidence of miscegenation (mating across racial lines) is prevalent, and it is easy to identify the mixing of white, black, and Chinese features. The population has increasingly darkened due to the exodus of large numbers of whites following the Cuban Revolution in 1959, which installed a **socialist** government led by Fidel Castro. Even though Cuba is a poor country, the literacy rate is high (estimated at 95.7 percent in 1995 compared to 76 percent before the revolution) thanks to the government's strong emphasis on education.

Migration to the United States has had a great effect on Cuba since 1959. Beginning immediately after the revolution, large numbers of middle-class Cubans left the island, settling largely in Miami, Florida, and other U.S. cities. As the Cuban economy worsened in the 1980s, people fled the country any way they could, many in small boats or makeshift rafts. In an incident known as the Mariel Boatlift, President Fidel Castro allowed 125,000 people to leave the island for the United States, thereby reducing the population of Cuba by 1 percent in a single day.

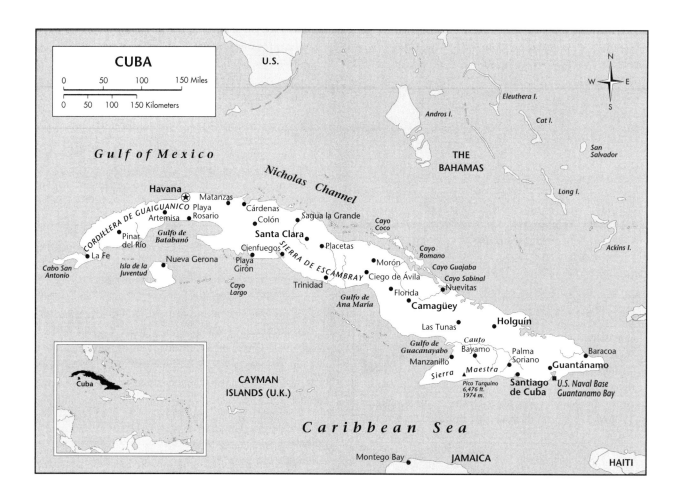

OVERVIEW OF ECONOMY

The Cuban economy has endured a number of up-heavals over the past century. In the early 1900s approximately two-thirds of the businesses in Cuba were owned by U.S. citizens, and around 80 percent of the country's trade was with the United States. In 1959, when Fidel Castro seized the country through revolution, the reforms enacted by the socialist government confiscated most of the privately-held property in Cuba. Relations with the United States became strained, and eventually ended in 1962 when the United States placed an **embargo** (prohibition) on trade with Cuba, which continues to this day. Cuba turned to the former Soviet Union for help, and soon introduced long-range socialist state-managed planning that followed Soviet models. The Soviet Union effectively subsidized the Cuban economy by repeatedly postponing debt payment schedules, creating new credit lines, paying high prices for Cuban exports, and offering military assistance. As a result, many Cuban economic problems did not manifest themselves until the fall of the Soviet Union in 1989.

With the fall of the Soviet Union in 1989, Cuba lost more than 85 percent of its trade and once again had to search for other markets to replace this loss. The 1990s were marked by a period of economic hardship; from 1990 to 1993, Cuba's economy declined by 35 percent, causing the nation to fall into what Castro called "The Special Period in a Time of Peace." The living situation of the Cuban people became very difficult. Because the Soviets had been a source of much of the country's fuel supplies, Cuban homes and businesses suffered daily power blackouts, and the public transportation system all but stopped. Bicycles and horse-drawn carts and tractors had to substitute for motorized transport. Food became scarce, and many Cubans found themselves standing in long lines to procure rationed items or buy them from **black-market** (illegal) sources.

The inability of the state-controlled system to provide scarce **consumer goods** enabled the black market to assume a prominent role in the Cuban economy. During the 1990s, workers commonly stole goods from the state-run factories they worked in to use in their homes or to sell on the streets. As a result, the government was forced to make some drastic changes in policy. Many small in-home restaurants, bed-and-breakfasts, repair shops, etc. that had previously been considered "black market" were legalized. State control was somewhat reduced. The government divided many large state-run farms into smaller cooperatives called Basic Units of Production Cooperatives (UBPC). While the farmers who worked for them still had to sell a certain amount of their produce to the government at set prices, they were now permitted to sell their surplus goods on the free market via *agropecuarios* (farmers' markets). The government also began to require state-run enterprises to be more efficient; any enterprise not showing a profit would be eliminated. The government also began to allow more foreign investment, creating **joint ventures** with foreign companies and eventually allowing a foreign firm to own 100 percent of an enterprise. The U.S. dollar was legalized and, by 2000, became the most commonly used currency. In 1994 Cuba reported economic growth again for the first time since 1989, a situation that has continued into the new century. It is estimated that the continuation of these reforms should contribute to a growth of 4–5 percent in the year 2001. Still, the economy is in a difficult situation, and life for the average Cuban is not easy.

An important contribution to the improvement of the Cuban economy has been the tourist industry, which was the sector reporting the greatest growth in the 1990s. In the years immediately following the revolution in the late 1950s, the Cuban government discouraged tourism, which was viewed as a source of corruption of the Cuban people and a return to what it considered the decadent years of U.S. control (1898–1958). Beginning with some changes in the mid-1980s, the tourist industry is now viewed as an important way for Cuba to support itself while maintaining many of the reforms that had been instituted under the socialist system.

Besides tourism, important export sectors of the Cuban economy are agriculture, especially sugar, coffee, and tobacco crops, and nickel mining. Because of its long-term reliance on a single crop—sugar—the economy has often suffered when world sugar prices have been low. Petroleum is Cuba's most important import. In the 1980s, Cuba received most of its oil from the Soviet Union, a supply that dropped by 50 percent between 1990 and 1992, causing widespread energy problems that severely stunted Cuba's agricultural and industrial production. Cuba responded by reducing its energy use, as by cutting back on gasoline-powered vehicles and by imposing daily blackouts throughout the island. Cuba continued to get much of its reduced oil supplies from Russia, but was required to pay market prices instead of the lower prices that the USSR had traditionally charged Cuba as a gesture of solidarity. By 2000, Cuba was buying its oil at market prices from Venezuela, Russia, and Mexico.

Cuba had an enormous burden of unpaid **external debt** totaling more than US$10 billion by 1999. Cuba has repeatedly refinanced these debts but was forced to suspend interest payments in 1990 due to extreme economic conditions. Because of its poor credit, Cuba has been unable to obtain international loans that would enable it to buy many of the imports it needs. As the Cuban economy improved into the late 1990s, the country did receive more foreign aid. Although Cuba has not yet been approved to receive funds from either the International Monetary Fund or the World Bank, it has received money from various United Nations organizations, but the amounts have been low in comparison to those received by other Latin American countries: US$44 million ($4 per person) in 1993, and US$80 million ($7 per person) in 1998.

POLITICS, GOVERNMENT, AND TAXATION

According to the Cuban constitution, Cuba is an independent socialist republic that is controlled by 1 party: the Cuban Communist Party (PCC), of which Fidel Castro is the head, with his brother, Raul Castro as vice-president. The Communist Party is led by a group of 25 individuals chosen by its head. Molded by this elite group of communists are organizations that encompass every facet of society, including youth, women, workers, and small farmers, among others. Around 80 percent of the population has membership in at least one of these organizations. This network ensures that the agenda of the Communist Party is disseminated (communicated) to the masses.

Fidel Castro, the commander-in-chief of the Cuban Republic, heads both executive bodies of the nation's government, the Council of Ministers, and a Council of State. His brother, Raul Castro, serves as first vice-president of these 2 bodies. The members of the Council of Ministers are proposed by the president of the Council of State and ratified by the National Assembly. The members of the Council of State and its president and vice-president are elected by the National Assembly. At the last election in 1998, Fidel Castro and Raul Castro were elected unanimously. The next elections have not been scheduled.

The National Assembly is the legislative body of the Cuban government. The Assembly is composed of 601 members whose terms last 5 years. For these positions, the Council of State nominates candidates, who are then subject to a direct vote by the Cuban people. The National Assembly also elects the Judicial Branch. On the local level, members of Municipal Assemblies are chosen by direct local election. Local government is closely overseen by the Communist Party. As is evidenced by Fidel Castro's almost complete control over decision-making, most policies are the direct result of his personal desires.

The Cuban governmental structure is heavily bureaucratic (organized into many agencies). Until 1993, the Central Planning Board (JUCEPLAN, or Junta de Planificación Central), was responsible for economic planning. After 1993, in a move to create greater efficiency and to decentralize, different sectors of the economy became the responsibility of various ministerial bodies, including the Ministry of Tourism, the Ministry of Science, Technology, and the Environment, the Ministry of Industry, the Ministry of Sugar Planning, and the Ministry of Foreign Investment and Economic Cooperation, among others.

The economy is largely state-controlled, with 75 percent of the **labor force** employed by the government. Therefore decisions that are made within each of these state-run ministries have a great impact on the economy and on the individual. The Cuban people have very little influence over government policies, most of which are directly handed down from the upper echelons of government. Over the years, Fidel Castro has proved himself somewhat whimsical in his approach to long-term economic planning. Many economic policies are the direct result of his attempts to maintain his tight control on the Cuban population through economic means.

Interestingly, the military has been on the cutting edge of the **restructuring** of Cuba's economy. Since the 1980s, the government has been unable to support the armed forces, forcing the Ministry of the Armed Forces (MINFAR) to become almost completely self-supporting. MINFAR started a tourist company, a construction company, and an agricultural project to grow its own food. The CIA estimated that military expenditures constituted only 4 percent of the **gross domestic product** (GDP) by 1995.

Taxes do not constitute a large part of the government's revenues. Taxes were first introduced in 1994 as a method of controlling earnings from the burgeoning small-business sector. It was based on a flat-tax system with rates fixed at different levels for different businesses. By 2001, a more formalized system of **income taxation**

was in the planning stages, one that might provide a large share of federal revenues in the future.

INFRASTRUCTURE, POWER, AND COMMUNICATIONS

Cuba's **infrastructure**, power system, and communications are all in need of improvement. In 1959 Cuba was one of the most advanced countries in Latin America, but much of the infrastructure has not been updated since the revolution. For example, many of the 29,800 kilometers (18,476 miles) of roads that were listed as paved in 1996 were done so before 1959, and have not been maintained. The original pre-Revolutionary water and sewerage systems were installed using U.S.-made equipment, for which replacement parts are unavailable due to the U.S. trade embargo. Of the 170 airports in Cuba, only 77 had paved runways.

As an island Cuba's ports and harbors are especially important. Cuba's 7 main ports and harbors included Cienfuegos, Havana, Manzanillo, Mariel, Matanzas, Nuevitas, and Santiago de Cuba. The country's merchant marine fleet comprised 15 ships: 1 bulk, 7 cargo, 1 liquefied gas, 1 petroleum tanker, and 5 refrigerated cargo.

Communications systems have seen little change. In 2000 Cuba had about the same number of phone lines as in 1959. There were 353,000 main lines in use and 1,939 cellular phone contracts in 1995. At the same time, Cuba had only slightly more electrical lines, and fewer automobiles on the road (24 cars per 1,000 inhabitants in 1959 as opposed to 23 per 1,000 in 1988) than it did before the revolution. Many of the cars on the road in 2000 dated back to the 1950s. Public transportation was inefficient and overcrowded, and private transportation was difficult because of the lack of available spare parts and the general lack of fuel. Vehicle owners regularly used their cars as a taxi service, commonly charging a small fee to people who need rides. Very few people had access to computers. There were some in government of-

Communications

Country	Newspapers	Radios	TV Sets[a]	Cable subscribers[a]	Mobile Phones[a]	Fax Machines[a]	Personal Computers[a]	Internet Hosts[b]	Internet Users[b]
	1996	1997	1998	1998	1998	1998	1998	1999	1999
Cuba	118	353	239	0.0	0	N/A	N/A	0.06	35
United States	215	2,146	847	244.3	256	78.4	458.6	1,508.77	74,100
Mexico	97	325	261	15.7	35	3.0	47.0	23.02	1,822
Jamaica	62	480	182	73.1	22	N/A	39.4	1.04	60

[a]Data are from International Telecommunication Union, *World Telecommunication Development Report 1999* and are per 1,000 people.
[b]Data are from the Internet Software Consortium (http://www.isc.org) and are per 10,000 people.

SOURCE: World Bank. *World Development Indicators 2000.*

fices and few in the universities. By 1999 Cuba had 1 Internet service provider.

Cuba produced 15 billion kWh of electricity in 1998 and consumed 14 billion kWh. Cuba did not use nuclear plants to generate any of its power, but was working toward that goal, and is predicted to have the ability in 2005, according to the Energy Information Administration of the United States.

ECONOMIC SECTORS

Cuba's important economic sectors are related to its tropical climate, island location, and fertile soils. The sectors that annually contribute the most to the Cuban GDP are tourism (30 percent, US$5.6 billion), construction (20 percent, US$3.7 billion), agriculture, hunting, and fishing (17 percent, US$3.16 billion), and industry (37 percent, US$6.9 billion), according to *Cuba: Informe Económico* in 1996. All of these sectors experienced considerable growth in the latter part of the 1990s as a result of a restructuring of the economy, foreign investment, and new trading partners. Tourism is slated for the most growth in the coming years because it is one of the most attractive sectors for foreign investment.

Compared to worldwide production, Cuba's output of its most important products is relatively small. World production of sugar is 130 million metric tons, and Cuba produces only 3 to 5 million metric tons, still a considerable amount for the size of the island. Cuba experienced a 50 percent drop in sugar production between 1993 and 1994 due to the inability to procure the necessary fuel, fertilizers, and other agricultural products, and bad weather. Again in 1997 and 1998, lack of capital and

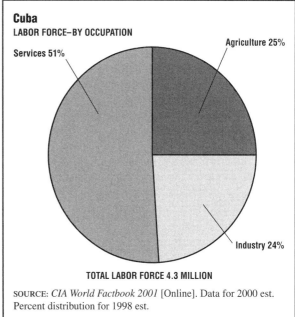

Cuba
LABOR FORCE–BY OCCUPATION

Services 51%

Agriculture 25%

Industry 24%

TOTAL LABOR FORCE 4.3 MILLION

SOURCE: *CIA World Factbook 2001* [Online]. Data for 2000 est. Percent distribution for 1998 est.

inefficiencies caused the harvest to suffer, which barely reached the 50-year low of 3.3 million tons. Other countries that produce more sugar are the United States, Brazil, Mexico, India, and Australia.

AGRICULTURE

Agriculture has always played a very important role in Cuba's economy. The country's fertile plains and tropical climate are excellent for citrus, tobacco, and sugar production. Cuba also has fertile, mountainous zones where coffee is produced. Some 2,600,000 people, or 23 percent of the labor force, are employed in agriculture. The most important crops have always been sugar and tobacco, but Cuba also produces coffee, potatoes, tomatoes, rice, beans, onions, and citrus fruits, though not in exportable quantities. Still, Cuba imports more than 60 percent of its agricultural food products.

SUGAR. Sugar is Cuba's most important agricultural product. Cuba's economy has always been linked to the world price of sugar. After the Revolution of 1959, the Castro government unsuccessfully tried to change Cuba's monoculture (dependence on a single crop). When the United States revoked its annual sugar quota, the Soviet Union assumed the shortfall and the makeup of Cuba's exports did not change. In 1959, 75 percent of Cuba's export dollars came from sugar, a proportion that had increased to 80 percent by 1989. Production rose from an average of 5 million tons per year in the 1970s to an average of 7.5 million tons per year in the 1980s. After the collapse of the Soviet Union, the Cuban sugar harvest fell to a 50-year low of 3.3 million tons as a result of a loss

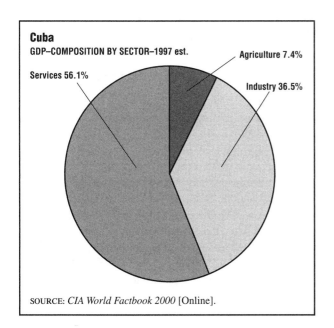

Cuba
GDP–COMPOSITION BY SECTOR–1997 est.

Agriculture 7.4%

Services 56.1%

Industry 36.5%

SOURCE: *CIA World Factbook 2000* [Online].

of fuel, fertilizer, herbicide, and machinery imports. In 1993, the Cuban government began to reorganize the industry. Traditional agricultural methods were encouraged, large farms were broken up into smaller cooperatives, and foreign investment was courted. Difficulty obtaining needed resources caused sugar production to remain low at the end of the century.

TOBACCO. Tobacco is an important Cuban product, and Cuban cigars have long been highly esteemed around the world for their excellence. With the exception of Greece, Cuba dedicates more land to tobacco production than any other country in the world. Cuba also has the lowest yield per hectare than any other country because of its inefficient agricultural sector. Despite this, Cuba's tobacco production is growing. In 1 year alone (from 1994 to 1995), production grew by 52 percent, a trend that continues as a result of foreign investment from Spain, the distribution of lands to small farmers, and increased international marketing.

INDUSTRY

In total, industrial production accounted for almost 37 percent of the Cuban GDP, or US$6.9 billion, and employs 24 percent of the population, or 2,671,440 people, in 1996. Cuban industry encompasses sugar, petroleum, and food processing; the manufacturing of textiles, chemicals, wood, paper and tobacco products, cement, fertilizers, and agricultural machinery; and the extraction of metals. Only in mining and sugar processing does Cuba contribute a noteworthy portion of the world's production.

SUGAR PROCESSING. Although productive and profitable until the early 1990s, the sugar milling and refining industry faced difficult times after the decline of the Soviet Union. By 1999, 50 of the 156 sugar mills in Cuba were closed due to their inability to obtain needed cane to process or because they could not repair their aging machines.

MINING. Cuba has 25 percent of the world's high-quality nickel deposits located on its northeastern coast, the highest concentration in the world. Cuban nickel is inexpensive to extract because there are few environmental controls and wages are low. In 1997 nickel and cobalt brought US$350 million into the Cuban economy. Nickel production grew from 25,787 metric tons in 1994 to 65,300 metric tons in 1998. The increase has been substantial as a result of joint ventures between Cuba and foreign governments. Mining has played an important part in the recovery of the Cuban economy in the second half of the 1990s, although the world price of nickel has dropped.

MANUFACTURING. Cuba manufactures a variety of industrial goods including televisions, refrigerators, pharmaceuticals, and cell phones. This does not contribute a large portion of the GDP, and Cuba is forced to import most of its manufactured products.

BIOTECHNOLOGY. Cuba has prioritized biotechnology over the past 40 years and, due to a highly educated population, has been able to focus on research in a relatively inexpensive manner. This industry has produced approximately 200 pharmaceuticals, including a drug used to treat AIDS and the hepatitis B vaccine. In 1996, the value of Cuban pharmaceutical production was US$4.25 million, and the value of pharmaceutical exports was US$2.5 million. In the late 1990s this sector accounted for only 5 percent of Cuba's earnings, but the Cuban government hoped to further penetrate the world market.

SERVICES

TOURISM. Tourism has recently become Cuba's biggest growth industry. Having produced US$5.6 billion in 1996, it topped sugar as the country's greatest **hard-currency** earner. The tourist industry employs 1,109,000 people, or 10 percent of the population. Cuba's pristine, white-sand beaches and tropical climate make it a vacation paradise. Cuban tourism officials estimate the number of available rooms in Cuba reached 50,000 in 2000, bringing the island's annual capacity for tourists to 2.5 million. Since Cuba has only prioritized the tourist industry for the last fifteen years, it is lacking in the efficiency and comforts that many tourists expect, but is working to improve its services.

RETAIL. Cuba has a very poorly developed **retail** sector. There are no large shopping centers and the commercial districts that existed before the revolution are largely shut down. Those that remain carry few and poorly made products that are priced in dollars and are too expensive for the average Cuban to purchase. The majority of the stores are small dollar stores, bodegas, agro-mercados (farmers' markets), and street stands.

INTERNATIONAL TRADE

Before 1959, the United States was Cuba's most important trading partner, a natural development due to its geographic proximity. That relationship ended in 1960 with the U.S. trade embargo. Cuba then courted the Soviet Union and its Eastern European allies to become its primary trading partners. Due to the strict economic organization of the Communist system, only 50 Cuban companies were allowed to participate in foreign trade until 1987. After the fall of the Soviet Union in 1989, Cuba was soon trading with a number of countries, including Spain, France, Italy, Mexico, Canada, Russia, the Netherlands, and Venezuela. About 40 percent of Cuba's trade is within the Americas and 50 percent is with Europe. Main imports include fuel, food, semi-finished goods, wheat, vegetables, machinery, feed, and corn. Main exports are sugar, fish, nickel, medicinal products, and fruit. Cuba has consistently faced an unfavorable **balance of trade**; in 1999 imports were valued at US$3.2 billion and exports at US$1.4 billion. This situation places Cuba in a dependent position, unable to earn hard currency and reliant on other countries for vital goods.

MONEY

As the Cuban state has experienced a growth in demand for wages, social security, and **subsidies**, there has been a severe shortage of imported products, food, and other goods. Cubans often had to stand in long lines to procure a limited supply of food products. Many necessary items could not be obtained with pesos and were available only on the black market with U.S. dollars. **Inflation** resulted because the government kept printing more pesos though there were few goods available. In order to restore the value of the peso, a program was initiated to reduce the excessive amount of money in circulation. As part of this program, the government increased the prices of many consumer goods and services, enacted a new tax law, and ended subsidies to businesses that were not viable (economically successful). While these measures increased the difficulty of daily living for the average Cuban, they have gradually restored the value of the peso. Though the official **exchange rate** of the Cuban peso to the U.S. dollar is 1:1, the real exchange rate within the country has dropped from 120 pesos to the dollar in 1994 to 20 to the dollar in 1998.

Before 1993, the U.S. dollar, although illegal, was used widely on the black market. In 1993, the dollar was legalized and Casas de Cambio, (houses of exchange) were established to exchange pesos and dollars. Cuba has created a dual system—a dollar economy and a peso economy—that has certain places where pesos can be used and others where dollars only are accepted.

Since 1993, foreign banks had been allowed to do business in Cuba to supply such financial services as insurance, foreign commercial investments, and savings accounts. In 1997, a new central bank, the Banco Central de Cuba, was created to supervise and regulate Cuba's growing banking sector. The old bank, Banco Nacional de Cuba, had performed both the roles of central bank and state-owned commercial bank, but would now operate only as a commercial bank. Nevertheless, a very narrow sector of the Cuban population requires banking services. Very few people earn enough money to be able to invest or save. Those who do are able to earn dollars or receive money from family members in other countries. Cuba has no stock exchange.

POVERTY AND WEALTH

By some measures, Cuba is the most socially egalitarian of the world's nations. Apart from some governmental and military officials, the highest salaries in the country are only 4 times the amount of the lowest salaries. This situation is changing rapidly toward greater inequality; although definitive statistics are not available, there is a great discrepancy between the earning capacity of those in contact with dollars and those without. When Fidel Castro's socialist government came into power, it inherited a social situation similar to most other Latin American countries. There was a small but very wealthy class of landowners and government officials, and large numbers of impoverished peasants in the countryside and poorly-paid urban workers. Havana, on the western end of the island was a wealthy, developed urban center while most of the island was undeveloped, rural, and poor. Most Cubans were uneducated (3 out of 4 were illiterate), and modern health care was not available to them. Castro focused his policies on destroying the middle and upper classes and eliminating the abject poverty of the lowest classes. In some ways he was successful. He confiscated the large landholdings and companies of the very wealthy, causing much of the upper class to flee the country. In **nationalizing** most of the

---

Exchange rates: Cuba

Cuban pesos per US$1

Jan 2001	1.0000
2000	N/A
1999	N/A
1998	N/A
1997	N/A
1996	N/A

Note: Nonconvertible, official rate, for international transactions, pegged to the US dollar; convertible peso sold for domestic use at a rate of 1.00 US dollar per 22 pesos by the Government of Cuba (January 2001).

SOURCE: CIA *World Factbook 2001* [ONLINE].

GDP per Capita (US$)

Country	1996	1997	1998	1999	2000
Cuba	1,480	1,540	1,560	1,700	1,700
United States	28,600	30,200	31,500	33,900	36,200
Mexico	8,100	7,700	8,300	8,500	9,100
Jamaica	3,260	N/A	3,300	3,350	3,700

Note: Data are estimates.

SOURCE: *Handbook of the Nations*, 17th, 18th, 19th and 20th editions for 1996, 1997, 1998 and 1999 data; CIA *World Factbook 2001* [Online] for 2000 data.

---

businesses in Cuba he placed the state in control of the economy, thus allowing it to control wages for all positions. A wage scale was established that had only 4 levels from top to bottom. In 1960, rent prices were established at 10 percent of one's salary. State funds were diverted away from Havana and funneled into the countryside. The state provided or subsidized food, medical care, funerals, transportation, vacations, and other consumer goods.

During the period from 1959 to 1989, the state was also relying heavily on assistance from the Soviet Union (see Overview of Economy). When the Soviet Union was no longer able to help, the **recession** of the early 1990s forced Cuba to change its policies. It loosened control of the markets, allowed people to own their own businesses, allowed foreign ownership within Cuba, encouraged tourism, created a tax system, and legalized U.S. currency. Income inequality has resulted; those who are on a fixed income from the Cuban state are earning far less than those who have contact with U.S. dollars. For example, a doctor might earn 40 dollars a month, while a taxi driver might receive 40 dollars a week in tips.

The Cuban state still provides free education from primary school through the university level, an ironic situation given the difficulties of finding employment after graduation. If a job is available, it will pay less than a job as a waiter or taxi driver. Medical care is also free, and Cuban hospitals do remarkable work considering the available resources; however, people often die from curable diseases simply because the medicines required are unavailable.

While traditionally the rural poor have struggled more than the urban poor, it was easier for the rural poor to maintain a healthy diet during the economic difficulties of the 1990s because of their proximity to farms and their ability to plant small plots of land with fruits and vegetables.

Housing has been a particularly difficult situation in Havana under the Castro government. In the 1990s, the housing deficit grew by 20 percent per year. Out of 2.6 million units of housing in Havana, almost 1 million are in a substandard condition. Most buildings in the city have not been properly maintained since 1959, and little new construction has taken place.

WORKING CONDITIONS

In the early 1900s Cuba experienced a great deal of labor unrest, with strikes and labor slowdowns being commonplace. When Fidel Castro's revolutionary government came into power in 1959 there was great pressure for change from Cuban workers, some 2 million in number, most of whom were living in difficult conditions

due to low wages that made it impossible for them to afford expensive consumer goods and high rents. Workers also lacked health care, access to education, retirement benefits, and vacations. The government complied with the workers' demands; labor contracts were renegotiated, wages were raised, rents were lowered, and the unemployed were given jobs. Many of the most marginalized (poorest) people saw immediate and real benefits giving them a sense of security, gratitude toward the revolution, and hope for the future.

These changes were short-lived, however. Many of the laws that were enacted in 1959 to benefit workers were repealed as early as 1961. Since that year, the revolutionary government fixed wages at a low level, which today are the lowest in the Western Hemisphere, averaging 100–400 pesos (US$5-$20) a month. The worker has been constantly asked to sacrifice for the survival of the revolution. Cuba has a workweek of 48 hours, and workers have been asked to give volunteer time to building projects, education, and harvesting. The only legal workers' union in Cuba, the CTC, is an arm of the Communist Party. It is not legal to strike, and there is no collective bargaining. As a result, the International Labor Organization has condemned Cuba for violations of human rights.

Some Cubans depend on the security net of health care, free education, and social security as motivation to work hard in government-run enterprises, but large numbers of Cubans are unhappy with the difficult conditions. Due to the fact that Cuban workers have had no legal recourse to address the work conditions, many have reacted by decreasing their productivity, sabotaging production, or by stealing products to sell on the black market.

Since the beginning of the revolution, the stated goal of the Cuban socialist state has been **full employment**. It has been relatively successful only on a superficial level. Because the Cuban state has owned almost every enterprise on the island, it has been nearly the sole employer. Even foreign companies that operate in Cuba are required to pay Cuban workers' salaries in dollars to a state organization called CUBALSE (Cubans at the Service of Foreigners). The Cuban state then pays its workers in pesos, at a rate that shortchanges the employee.

In order to keep low unemployment rates, in the past, the Cuban state did not require businesses to earn a profit. Many employees were kept on the payroll even though they were unnecessary to the business. Because of this, a high percentage of the companies in Cuba were continually losing money. The state continued to subsidize those businesses, keeping them functioning at a loss. In the economic crisis of the early 1990s, the Cuban leadership was forced to rethink these practices. Downsizing of these bloated enterprises was one of the first policies enacted to restructure the Cuban economy. Employees who were unnecessary were dismissed, and companies were required to earn a profit. Unemployment increased, but the levels are uncertain because there are no reliable unemployment statistics available for Cuba. However, due to the legalization of the dollar combined with the growth of tourism, and the fact that it is difficult to live on the official government salaries, many people are choosing to work in the **informal economy** or start their own small enterprises. Positions that bring an individual in contact with tourists can often yield far greater monetary rewards.

COUNTRY HISTORY AND ECONOMIC DEVELOPMENT

1492. Christopher Columbus claims Cuba as a Spanish possession.

1538–60. Cuba is constantly under attack by French and English smugglers and pirates. The Spanish authorities create the flota system; a group of armed ships that made each voyage to and from Spain in order to protect their imports and exports.

1717. Spain establishes a tobacco **monopoly** called a Factoría, which incites rebellions of tobacco farmers against the Crown.

1740. Spain establishes the Real Compañía de Comercio in order to control and monopolize Cuban trade and commerce.

1762–63. The English occupy Havana for 10 months and change the laws in order to allow Cuba to enter the international market instead of being controlled by the Spanish Crown's monopoly.

1776. As a result of the American Revolution, trade increases between the United States and Cuba.

1778. A free-trade decree by the Spanish Crown gives Cuba open access to trade with Spain and Spanish colonies.

1789. A Spanish royal decree authorizes a free trade in slaves.

1791. Due to a slave revolt in the French colony of St. Domingue, many coffee and sugar planters move to Cuba and greatly expand Cuba's production in these areas.

1817. Spain and England agree to end the legal slave trade in Spanish colonies by 1820.

1837. A railroad is built in Cuba, which reduces the cost of transporting sugar.

1868–78. The Ten Years' War, with the goal of freeing Cuba from Spain, breaks out in the eastern part of Cuba. The revolt fails when the rebels are unable to seize power in the western portion of the island.

1895–97. The Cuban War for Independence succeeds when Spain grants the island autonomy in October of 1897.

1898. After the U.S. intervention in the Spanish-American War, the Treaty of Paris is signed, which transfers sovereignty over Cuba to the United States. The United States occupies Cuba militarily until 1902, at which point Cuba is granted autonomy and becomes the Republic of Cuba. This begins a period of heavy commerce between Cuba and the United States.

1920. The price of sugar jumps to 22.5 cents per pound, and then collapses to 3.7 cents. The Cuban economy enters a period of depression and chaos.

1953–59. Fidel Castro leads a revolution that ousts the Cuban dictator Fulgencio Batista, who flees Cuba for Miami with considerable wealth. Upon his departure, Castro installs a socialist government.

1960. Cuba and the Soviet Union re-establish relations. Cuba begins to nationalize U.S. properties. In retaliation, the United States cuts the amount of sugar it will buy from Cuba. In October, the United States imposes a trade embargo on Cuba that remains in force as of 2001.

1961. The United States and Cuba terminate diplomatic relations. The United States is embarrassed over its failure to offer effective support to Cuban exiles attempting to overthrow Castro in the Bay of Pigs invasion.

1962. Tensions rise as the United States confronts the Soviet Union over its installation of missile sites in Cuba.

1990–91. With the fall of the Soviet Union, which had accounted for 85 percent of its trade, Cuba enters the "Special Period in a Time of Peace," a period of economic restructuring marked by food and fuel shortages and energy blackouts.

1992. The U.S. Congress passes the so-called Torricelli Bill, which encourages people-to-people exchange between Cuba and the United States. The United States hopes to encourage dissent by putting the Cuban populace into contact with democratic ideas.

1993. Cuba legalizes the U.S. dollar as a medium of exchange, and permits Cubans to engage in some forms of self-employment.

1994. Cuba adopts a new system of taxation and opens all sectors of its economy to foreign investment except public health, education, and national security.

1995. The Cuban National Assembly allows foreign investors to wholly own businesses in Cuba.

1996. The U.S. Congress passes the Helms-Burton law, strengthening its embargo by allowing prosecution of foreign businesses for doing business with Cuban businesses that were previously owned by the United States.

FUTURE TRENDS

The future of the Cuban economy is not easy to predict. The government of Cuba has no clear-cut long-term plan. While the reforms and restructurings of the 1990s have been thought to indicate a desire to slowly restore **capitalism**, the Cuban government insists that these changes are only survival techniques and that they have not given up on the socialist project begun more than 40 years ago. Questions remain whether Cuban leaders will resign themselves to becoming a capitalist economy or, if not, what new forms its economy might take. If present trends continue, the Cuban economy will continue to grow steadily.

For the Cuban people, the dream of total socialism can no longer be sustained. It is apparent that most Cubans do not want a society that has a completely market economy. The majority of Cubans would like to keep alive the social goals of the revolution: free or inexpensive health care for everyone, education, and social security, while allowing market forces to have a greater role in the economy, allow more private property, encourage self-employment, and change the Cuban system to allow it to interact more easily within the international marketplace.

In terms of the future of political leadership, it is likely that Fidel Castro will be succeeded by someone from the upper echelon of leadership closest to him. It is therefore unlikely that Cuban policies will change in the near future, and it is likely that relations with the United States will remain hostile through the transition of power to a new generation of leaders.

DEPENDENCIES

Cuba has no territories or colonies.

BIBLIOGRAPHY

Azicri, Max. *Cuba Today and Tomorrow: Reinventing Socialism.* Gainesville: University Press of Florida, 2000.

Córdova, Efren, and Eduardo García Moure. *Modern Slavery: Labor Conditions in Cuba.* Miami: Institute for Cuban and Cuban-American Studies Occasional Paper Series, 2000.

Del Aguila, Juan M. *Cuba: Dilemmas of a Revolution.* Boulder, San Francisco, and Oxford: Westview Press, 1994.

Economist Intelligence Unit. *Country Profile: Cuba.* London: Economist Intelligence Unit, 2000.

"International Development Options. USA." *Global Development Studies.* Winter-Spring 1999.

Journal of Commerce. "JOC Trade News." <http://www.joc.com>. Accessed January 2001.

Naciones Unidas, CEPAL. *Anuario Estadístico de América Latina y el Caribe.* United Nations, 1999.

Pérez, Louis A. *Cuba: Between Reform and Revolution.* New York and Oxford: Oxford University Press, 1995.

Water and Earth Science Associates, Ltd. "Clean Technologies in Cuba's Sugar Industry 1999." <http://strategis.ic.gc.ca/SSG/ea01833e.html?he=y>. Accessed April 2001.

Wilkie, James W. *Statistical Abstract of Latin America, Volume 36.* Los Angeles: UCLA Press, 2000.

World Development Indicators. International Bank for Reconstruction and Development, 2000.

—Amy Lang-Tigchelaar

DOMINICA

Commonwealth of Dominica

CAPITAL: Roseau.

MONETARY UNIT: Dominica's currency is the Eastern Caribbean dollar (EC$). One EC dollar equals 100 cents. There are coins of 10, 20, and 50 cents. Paper money comes in bills of 1, 5, 10, and 20 dollars.

CHIEF EXPORTS: Bananas, soap, bay oil, vegetables, grapefruit, oranges.

CHIEF IMPORTS: Manufactured goods, machinery and equipment, food, chemicals.

GROSS DOMESTIC PRODUCT: US$225 million (1998 est.).

BALANCE OF TRADE: Exports: US$60.8 million (1998). **Imports:** US$120.4 million (1998).

COUNTRY OVERVIEW

LOCATION AND SIZE. Dominica is an island located between the Atlantic Ocean and the Caribbean. Its total area is 754 square kilometers (291 square miles), making it the largest of the English-speaking Windward Islands, and it is slightly more than 4 times the size of Washington, D.C. Its coastline measures 148 kilometers (92 miles), and its capital and main urban center, Roseau, is located on the southwest coast.

POPULATION. Dominica's population was estimated at 71,540 in mid-2000, marking a decline of 1.14 percent from the preceding year and a fall from the official mid-1998 estimate of 73,000. The decline in population, despite relatively high life expectancy and a birth rate of 18.27 per 1,000 population, is mostly due to a high degree of migration, estimated at 22.39 migrants per 1,000 population in 2000. Migration is largely caused by lack of work opportunities, and Dominicans are to be found working in other Caribbean islands (notably the French overseas departments), the United States, and, to a lesser degree, the United Kingdom. At current rates of population decrease, Dominica could have only 65,000 inhabitants by 2010. The death rate is Dominica is 7.3 per 1,000.

The island's mountainous landscape means that its population is mostly clustered along the coast. About 30 percent of Dominicans live in the parish of St. George, in or around Roseau, while the volcanic interior is very sparsely inhabited. Generally, Dominica is not densely populated, and its population is by regional standards evenly distributed between age groups. Islanders aged 14 and under make up 29 percent of the population, while 63 percent are between 15 and 64 years old. The remaining 8 percent includes those 65 and older. Approximately 90 percent of Dominicans are of African descent, and the island is also home to some 2,000 descendants of the indigenous Carib population. A small minority of these Caribs are the last surviving descendants of the Caribbean islands' pre-Columbian peoples and live in a 3,700-acre reservation in the northeast part of the island.

English is the official language of Dominica, and the literacy rate is 94 percent. Nearly 80 percent of the citizens are Roman Catholic, with Protestants making up 15 percent, and the remainder spread among several other Christian and non-Christian faiths.

OVERVIEW OF ECONOMY

Dominica is the poorest and least developed of the Windward Islands. Its economy is mainly dependent on agricultural exports, especially bananas. The island's exceptionally mountainous landscape prohibits much cultivation. The island is also vulnerable to hurricanes. Even so, agriculture is the main source of employment and income revenue, and remains much more important to Dominica than to other Caribbean islands. As a result, the threatened removal of preferential access for Dominican banana exports into the European market is potentially disastrous for the island's economy.

Tourism has been slower to develop in Dominica than elsewhere, largely because the island has few white

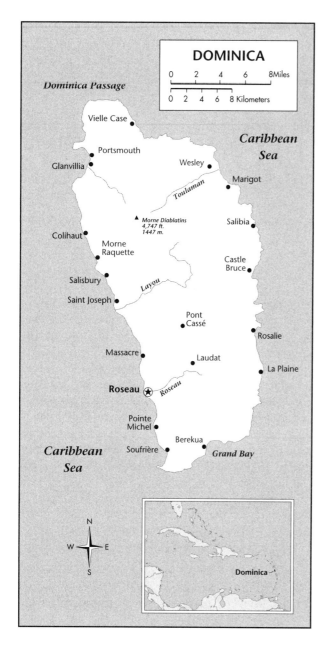

Palmolive corporation, which exports soap manufactured from local coconuts. This, together with other agricultural-processing activities, faces stiff competition from other Caribbean manufacturers. There is relatively little manufacturing aimed at the U.S. export market, as Dominica's limited **infrastructure** is unsuitable for large volumes of exports.

In an attempt to reduce dependency on banana exports, Dominica's government has tried to establish the island as an offshore financial center, offering tax-exempt status to banks, insurance companies, and other International Business Companies (IBCs). So far, a small number of IBCs have established themselves on the island. Of concern to critics of the system is the availability of "economic citizenship" to investors, which enables foreign residents to acquire a Dominican passport in return for a minimum investment in the island. The U.S. State Department has expressed concerns about **money laundering** and other illegal activity in connection with this initiative.

Despite attempts to broaden its economic base, Dominica remains critically dependent on agricultural exports and especially on the threatened banana trade. The resulting uncertainty from this trade has fueled migration since the mid-1990s and led to a decline in production and exports. Rural poverty is a large problem, and economic growth has faltered in recent years due to the banana crisis and natural disasters.

POLITICS, GOVERNMENT, AND TAXATION

Upon gaining independence in 1978, Dominica established a single-chamber parliament under its constitution. The House of Assembly has 21 elected and 9 appointed members. The parliament elects a president, who acts as head of state and elects the prime minister and the cabinet. The country is split into 10 administrative districts, called parishes. Each is named after a Roman Catholic saint.

In the immediate aftermath of independence from the United Kingdom in 1978 Dominica witnessed considerable political turbulence. Stability took hold between 1980 and 1995, when the Dominica Freedom Party (DFP), led by Eugenia Charles, won 3 consecutive terms in office. After a victory by the United Workers Party (UWP) in 1995, the Dominica Labour Party (DLP) and DFP formed a coalition government in early 2000. The sudden death of DLP leader and prime minister Rosie Douglas in October that year led to former minister of communications and works, Pierre Charles, taking over the position of prime minister.

sand beaches (the most popular type of beach) and has no international airport. Since the 1990s, however, it has developed a reputation as an **"eco-tourism"** destination, capitalizing on its spectacular natural beauty and wealth of plants and wildlife. The government has also sought to increase the numbers of cruise-ship visitors, and this sector of the tourism industry has grown substantially since the mid-1990s. The problem remains of balancing the need for increased tourism with protection of the island's unique and vulnerable eco-system.

Manufacturing is not developed in Dominica, but it is able to take advantage of locally generated hydro-electricity. The most successful venture is a large soap production facility, controlled by the U.S. Colgate-

The DLP has been traditionally more left-wing in outlook than the conservative DFP, which has favored strong links with the United States and a robust, pro-business approach to government. The coalition government of 2000 was hence a pragmatic response to the popularity of the UWP, which draws much of its support from the island's banana farmers. In reality, there are few major policy differences between the 3 main parties, with all supporting the beleaguered banana industry and encouraging diversification and direct foreign investment. The main political difference between the DLP-DFP coalition government and its UWP predecessor has been the decision to abandon plans for a new airport and hotel development in the northeast on the grounds of cost and environmental impact.

The government has a direct impact on Dominica's economy as a large employer and because it establishes the legal and regulatory framework for foreign investment. It raises revenues through a mixture of **income tax**, **indirect taxes**, and fees levied on offshore companies. In July 2000, the government announced that it would replace most existing indirect taxes levied on consumption and imported goods with a single **value-added tax** (VAT).

INFRASTRUCTURE, POWER, AND COMMUNICATIONS

Because of its mountainous landscape and rugged shoreline, Dominica's infrastructure is extremely limited. Its roads, mostly confined to the coast, total 780 kilometers (485 miles), of which 393 kilometers (244 miles) are paved. Most of the island is totally inaccessible by car, and many rural roads are little more than impassable dirt tracks. There are no railways, while the 2 main commercial ports are to be found at Woodridge Bay, near Roseau, and the northwest coast town of Portsmouth.

There are also cruise ship facilities at Roseau and at Prince Rupert Bay, near Portsmouth. The island has 2 airports, Melville Hall, in the northeast, and Canefield, north of Roseau. While both have paved runways, neither is able to receive large aircraft. Connections from Europe and North America must be made in Puerto Rico, Antigua, or other larger regional airports.

Telecommunications are also underdeveloped, although cellular phone usage and Internet access are growing, due in part to the development of the offshore financial sector. In 2000, the government announced its intention to **liberalize** the telecommunications sector by inviting foreign companies to compete in providing services.

ECONOMIC SECTORS

According to estimates in 1999, agriculture still accounts for 21 percent of Dominica's **gross domestic product** (GDP), and employs 40 percent of the island's workforce. Bananas are the main agricultural product and export, earning US$17 million in 1998. But production and exports have fallen since 1994, due to uncertainty over the industry's long-term future and adverse weather conditions.

Industry accounted for 16 percent of GDP in 1999 and is dominated by a handful of **agribusinesses**, specializing in soap, dental cream, and beverages. Attempts to build up an export-oriented assembly sector have not led to sustained success.

Services, led by tourism, contributed 63 percent to GDP in 1999. This sector, together with a recently launched financial services sector, is of growing importance to Dominica's economy.

Communications

Country	Telephones[a]	Telephones, Mobile/Cellular[a]	Radio Stations[b]	Radios[a]	TV Stations[a]	Televisions[a]	Internet Service Providers[c]	Internet Users[c]
Dominica	19,000 (1996)	461 (1996)	AM 3; FM 10; shortwave 0	46,000	0	6,000	16	2,000
United States	194 M	69.209 M (1998)	AM 4,762; FM 5,542; shortwave 18	575 M	1,500	219 M	7,800	148 M
Jamaica	353,000 (1996)	54,640 (1996)	AM 10; FM 13; shortwave 0	1.215 M	7	460,000	21	60,000
St. Lucia	37,000	1,600	AM 2; FM 7; shortwave 0	111,000	3	32,000	15	5,000

[a]Data is for 1997 unless otherwise noted.
[b]Data is for 1998 unless otherwise noted.
[c]Data is for 2000 unless otherwise noted.

SOURCE: CIA *World Factbook 2001* [Online].

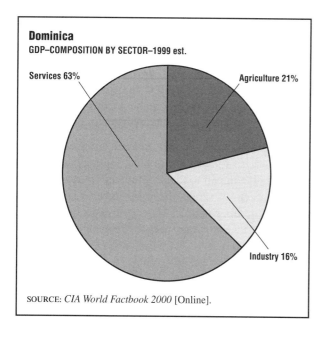

Dominica
GDP–COMPOSITION BY SECTOR–1999 est.

Services 63%

Agriculture 21%

Industry 16%

SOURCE: *CIA World Factbook 2000* [Online].

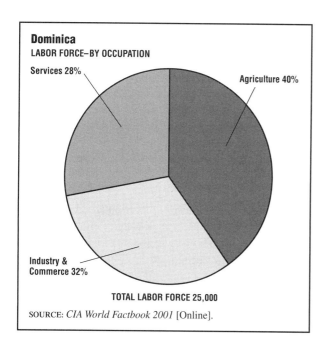

Dominica
LABOR FORCE–BY OCCUPATION

Services 28%

Agriculture 40%

Industry & Commerce 32%

TOTAL LABOR FORCE 25,000

SOURCE: *CIA World Factbook 2001* [Online].

AGRICULTURE

Unlike many other Caribbean island nations, Dominica was never a suitable site for sugarcane cultivation, as rocky and mountainous terrain made plantation production impossible. Only about one-quarter of the island is cultivatable. Climate, fertility, and topography are favorable for tree crops, however, and Dominica has been a producer of coffee, cocoa, and citrus fruits in its history. Citrus crops are still important, being grown for export to other Caribbean islands, but the biggest share of agricultural production since the 1950s has belonged to bananas. Like St. Lucia, St. Vincent and the Grenadines, and

Grenada, Dominica experienced a "banana boom" in the 1980s when it was assured access into the U.K. market. Stable prices brought modest prosperity to many banana-growing communities. During the 1970s and 1980s, banana exports from Dominica tripled in volume, peaking at 70 percent of export earnings. The dangers of this one-crop dependency became evident in 1979 and 1980 when Hurricanes David and Allen destroyed much of the banana crop. Widespread damage due to hurricanes and tropical storms has been experienced again in 1989 (Hurricane Hugo) and 1995, when Hurricane Luis destroyed an estimated 95 percent of banana plants. Then in November 1999, Hurricane Lenny caused considerable damage to banana and other agricultural production. Fortunately, bananas are quick to produce fruit after planting and are hence a suitable crop in hurricane-prone areas.

A much greater threat to Dominica's banana industry, however, is the threatened removal of preferential market access into Europe for the island's exports. In 1995, the United States and several Latin American banana-exporting countries complained that the European Union (EU) was breaching international free-trade legislation by offering protected quotas to banana exports from former colonies in Africa, the Caribbean, and the Pacific. This has brought the future of the EU banana regime into question. If the EU is forced by international pressure to dismantle its existing arrangement with exporters such as Dominica, the island will be forced to compete directly for the European market with large producers from Latin America. Experts agree that Dominica, with its small, family-run banana farms, cannot compete with the large, labor-intensive plantations in countries such as Ecuador or Honduras and will be forced to abandon bananas altogether. As a result, the number of banana farmers has already fallen from 4,366 in 1995 to 2,534 in 1999. One small possibility is that Dominica, together with other Windward island producers, may be able to supply a growing organic and "fair trade" market in Europe.

Given Dominica's topography (layout of land), there are few obvious alternatives to banana cultivation, although some moves to diversify agriculture have already taken place. At the same time, the Dominica Banana Marketing Corporation introduced a recovery plan in 1999 in an attempt to restore confidence among growers and to improve the quality of banana exports. With financial assistance from STABEX grants (money paid by the EU to support agricultural exporters in certain developing countries), the corporation encouraged farmers to replant bananas and to invest in fertilizer and other inputs. As a result, banana production in 1999 increased slightly from the previous year, earning US$11.5 million in the first 9 months of 1999 before the arrival of Hurricane Lenny.

Apart from bananas, Dominica produces a wide range of agricultural produce, both for local consumption (it is self-sufficient in fruit and vegetables) and for export. Some exports are directed to the French overseas territories of Martinique and Guadeloupe, and there is a thriving network of small traders and inter-island commerce. Coconuts, citrus fruit, and essential oils are the main regional exports.

There is a relatively large fishing industry in Dominica, but it is not modernized and almost exclusively serves the domestic market. A successful experiment in fresh-water prawn farming, supported by Taiwanese aid, has produced substantial amounts of prawns for the domestic and local markets. Japan has provided support for a fish landing and processing plant in Roseau.

INDUSTRY

Dominica's small manufacturing sector is almost entirely dependent on agriculture, and the island has built up a handful of successful industries specializing in soaps and other agricultural byproducts. The largest manufacturer is Dominica Coconut Products, controlled by Colgate-Palmolive, which produces soap from coconuts. The factory has an agreement to sell an estimated 3 million bars of soap each year to Royal Caribbean Cruise Lines. Dominican soap is also exported throughout the region, but has recently encountered intensified competition from other regional producers, especially in the important export markets of Jamaica and Trinidad and Tobago.

Other manufacturing is largely restricted to cardboard boxes and beverages, while there is a small export-oriented sector producing clothing. Dominica has not yet been able to attract significant numbers of foreign manufacturers, partly because its wage rates are relatively high and partly because its infrastructure is not suited to high-volume manufacturing. Like other islands, it seeks to attract investors with tax concessions and other financial inducements, but several offshore manufacturing plants have closed after their **duty**-free concessions expired, normally a 10-year span.

There is some mining potential in Dominica, especially in the island's northeast where there are believed to be deposits of copper.

SERVICES

Dominica's tourist industry is in its infancy compared to other Caribbean islands. For many years its rugged terrain, lack of beaches, and underdeveloped infrastructure prevented large-scale tourist development. In recent years, Dominica has successfully marketed itself as the "nature island of the Caribbean," seeking to attract "eco-tourists" interested in landscapes and wildlife. The government realizes that intensive tourism is incompatible with preserving the island's eco-system and in 1997 signed an agreement with Green Globe, the environmental division of the World Travel and Tourism Council, to develop the island as a "model ecotourism destination." The 3-year program provided technical expertise on environmental management as well as helping to market Dominica through specialist travel companies.

At the same time, the government has encouraged a steady increase in Dominica's tourism capacity, with several new hotels being built and considerable investment in cruise ship facilities. The new cruise ship jetty at Prince Rupert Bay, near Portsmouth, has dramatically increased the number of ships calling annually and brought significant tourism-related opportunities to the formerly depressed community of Portsmouth. Annual tourist arrivals are estimated at approximately 200,000, of whom about 75,000 are stay-over visitors. The great majority are cruise ship visitors who spend limited time and money on the island. Tourism receipts in 1998 were estimated at US$15.5 million.

Dominica's tourism industry is mostly small in scale and locally owned, with extensive links to other areas of the economy. Unlike other Caribbean islands, visitors are fed with locally produced food, and Dominica does not unduly extend its import bill by importing foodstuffs for the tourist sector. There is also considerable "**trickle down**" of tourism revenues, with retailers, restaurateurs, and tourist guides benefiting directly from the industry. On the other hand, critics point out that even restricted tourism can have a damaging impact on the environment, especially at the selected sites of natural beauty visited by large numbers of cruise ship tourists.

If the tourism industry has caused some controversy by threatening to spoil Dominica's fragile ecosystem, some initiatives taken by the government since the 1990s have been even more open to criticism. Like other small Caribbean economies, Dominica has tried to broaden its economic base by building up an offshore financial services sector. So far, a relatively small number of **offshore banks** and other international business companies (IBCs) have registered in Dominica, but the government is trying to attract more by making registration economical and easy. A Dominica-based IBC can, for instance, be formed over the Internet, and the government has also granted operating licenses to several Internet gambling companies. The ease with which such companies can be formed and the secrecy surrounding their operations have led some critics to allege that Dominica may be facilitating money-laundering and tax evasion.

Even more controversial has been the issuing of "economic citizenship" to foreign nationals. This means that Dominican passports are provided in return for an

Trade (expressed in billions of US$): Dominica		
	Exports	Imports
1975	.011	.021
1980	.010	.048
1985	.028	.055
1990	.055	.118
1995	.045	.117
1998	N/A	.136

SOURCE: International Monetary Fund. *International Financial Statistics Yearbook 1999.*

Exchange rates: Dominica	
East Caribbean dollars (EC$) per US$1	
Jan 2001	2.7000
2000	2.7000
1999	2.7000
1998	2.7000
1997	2.7000
1996	2.7000

Note: Dominican currency has been at a fixed rate since 1976.

SOURCE: CIA *World Factbook 2001* [ONLINE].

agreed minimum investment, which is supposedly used to develop the national economy. The first economic citizens were mostly Taiwanese, but in 1999 it was reported that 300 Russians had bought Dominican passports for US$50,000 each. This has encouraged allegations that the island may be involved in Mafia-style economic activity.

INTERNATIONAL TRADE

Dominica, although largely self-sufficient in food production, imports approximately twice as much in value as it exports, with imports of US$120.4 million dwarfing exports of US$60.8 million in 1998. Its main export markets are other Caribbean countries, which buy its vegetables, fruit, and soap, and the EU, which imports its bananas. Caribbean Community (CARICOM) countries accounted for about 47 percent of Dominica's exports throughout the 1990s, and Europe for 36 percent. The United States imports little from Dominica, but is the main source of the island's imports (an average of 41 percent in the 1990s), notably machinery and manufactured goods. Dominica's other main suppliers are the CARICOM countries and Britain.

MONEY

After steady growth in the 1980s and early 1990s, Dominica's economy slowed in the late 1990s because of the banana crisis, hurricane damage, and a decline in manufacturing output. GDP growth from 1996 averaged 2.8 percent annually, a lower rate than neighboring countries, and in 1999 there was no growth at all, due largely to damage from Hurricane Lenny. As a result, **inflation** has been low since the mid-1990s.

Dominica's currency, the Eastern Caribbean dollar (EC$), shared with the 7 other members of the Eastern Caribbean Central Bank (ECCB), is stable and has been pegged at a rate of EC$2.7 to US$1 for many years. This means that Dominica is not particularly vulnerable to fluctuating **exchange rates**, although transactions with

Europe have been affected by the low value of the euro. There are plans for ECCB member countries to participate in a regional stock exchange, further integrating the economies of the small islands.

POVERTY AND WEALTH

Dominica is one of the poorer countries of the Eastern Caribbean, but there are not enormous disparities in income. Traditionally a country of small peasant farmers, the island has a small urban middle class, made of professionals and civil servants, and a small urban working class. There are very few extremely wealthy Dominicans, although this may change with the advent of the "economic citizenship" program and the expected influx of rich foreigners. The wealthy few are, for the most part, descended from the plantation-owning elite of colonial times, although Dominica was never the source of enormous wealth and so, unlike Barbados for example, there is no "plantocracy." Although there are luxury homes around the capital, there is little ostentatious wealth, and Roseau does not have the facilities to cater to a millionaire lifestyle.

The poorest Dominicans live in remote rural districts, particularly in the north. Unemployment is officially estimated at around 20 percent of the population and, with the decline in the banana industry, is likely to increase. The poorest social stratum includes the descendants of

GDP per Capita (US$)					
Country	1975	1980	1985	1990	1998
Dominica	N/A	1,679	2,142	2,862	3,310
United States	19,364	21,529	23,200	25,363	29,683
Jamaica	1,819	1,458	1,353	1,651	1,559
St. Lucia	N/A	2,076	2,150	3,542	3,907

SOURCE: United Nations. *Human Development Report 2000; Trends in human development and per capita income.*

Household Consumption in PPP Terms

Country	All food	Clothing and footwear	Fuel and power[a]	Health care[b]	Education[b]	Transport & Communications	Other
Dominica	33	6	11	3	6	8	33
United States	13	9	9	4	6	8	51
Jamaica	24	7	3	1	9	8	48
St. Lucia	40	5	11	4	17	11	11

Data represent percentage of consumption in PPP terms.
[a]Excludes energy used for transport.
[b]Includes government and private expenditures.
SOURCE: World Bank. *World Development Indicators 2000.*

the Caribs, who eke out a unstable living from **subsistence farming**, handicrafts, and boat-building. Social facilities in the countryside are highly limited, and Dominicans have to travel to Roseau for most medical attention. Primary schools are distributed throughout the island, but most higher education takes place in and around the capital. According to UNESCO, there were a total of 152 schools in 1995, with 12,627 pupils attending 64 primary schools. Primary school education is free and compulsory, but families normally have to pay for schoolbooks and uniforms. Basic health care is widely available, but there are fees for doctors, for medicines, and for some hospital treatment. There is little state-organized social security, but church groups and other voluntary agencies are active in supporting homes and nurseries for the elderly.

WORKING CONDITIONS

Working conditions in Dominica are average for the region, although many Dominicans work on small family-run farms without regulation or trade union representation. There are only 2 trade unions of any size or influence, one representing civil servants and the others port and dockside workers. Wages in the small industrial sector are average for the Caribbean, standing at between US$100 and US$250 monthly, while wages in agriculture, where most workers are self-employed small farmers, are lower. Educational attainment can facilitate a career in the financial or associated informatics sector, and it is here that the highest wages, other than those earned by traditional professionals such as lawyers and doctors, can be earned. Physical working conditions in agriculture are arduous, and there is the risk of exposure to insecticides and other chemical inputs. Conditions in the few factories are generally satisfactory.

There is some **informal sector** activity in Dominica, with some related child labor, especially in agriculture and handicraft manufacturing. Women are well-represented in every area of employment.

COUNTRY HISTORY AND ECONOMIC DEVELOPMENT

1494. Dominica sighted by Columbus.

1763. British take possession of island after a century of conflict with France.

1903. Establishment of Carib Territory in northeast of island.

1950s. First banana exports to Britain.

1978. Independence from the United Kingdom.

1979. Hurricane David devastates Dominica; 37 killed, 60,000 left homeless.

1980. Eugenia Charles wins elections, staying in power until 1995.

1983. Prime Minister Charles supports U.S. invasion of Grenada.

2000. Coalition government formed between Dominica Labour Party and Dominica Freedom Party; premature death of Prime Minister Rosie Douglas.

FUTURE TRENDS

Dominica's immediate economic future depends to a large degree on the outcome of the dispute between the World Trade Organization and the EU over the question of banana exports into Europe. If the EU is forced to abandon its preferential treatment of suppliers such as Dominica, the island will face a dramatic and possibly traumatic period of economic hardship. Even if a reprieve occurs, it will have to accelerate its efforts to create a more diversified economy with less dependency on agriculture in general and bananas in particular. There will undoubtedly be some international aid available for facilitating the diversification process, but few alternative crops will be able to offer the security and regularity of income offered by bananas.

Dominica is hampered by its topography and lack of infrastructure in terms of developing its tourist industry. But a massive influx of tourists would, in any case, damage its eco-tourism credentials and lessen the island's appeal as an exclusive nature destination. In the coming years, Dominica will have to balance the need for tourism revenue against the necessity of restricting visitor numbers in the interest of the environment. It remains to be seen whether Dominica's bid to join the Caribbean's offshore financial centers will be successful, but initial signs are not entirely promising.

The island remains unusually vulnerable, not just to devastating hurricanes, but also to economic decisions and developments beyond its control. Even its small manufacturing sector will have to face increased competition from other regional producers as the Caribbean's trade becomes more and more liberalized. Given these uncertainties, it is unlikely that the island will be able to make major steps in reducing poverty, unemployment, or high levels of migration in the near future.

DEPENDENCIES

Dominica has no territories or colonies.

BIBLIOGRAPHY

Honychurch, Lennox. *The Dominica Story*. London: Macmillan, 1995.

Caribbean Development Bank, *Annual Report 1999*. Barbados, 2000.

Dominica: South America, Central America and the Caribbean 2001. London: Europa Publications, 2001.

Economist Intelligence Unit, *Country Profile: OECS*. London: Economist Intelligence Unit, 2000.

International Monetary Fund. <http:// www.imf.org/external/np>. Accessed June 2001.

Welcome to a Virtual Dominica. <http://www.delphis.dm>. Accessed February 2001.

—*James Ferguson*

DOMINICAN REPUBLIC

CAPITAL: Santo Domingo.

MONETARY UNIT: Dominican peso (DOP). The peso is divided into 100 centavos. There are coins of 25 and 50 centavos and 1 and 5 pesos, and notes of 10, 20, 50, 100, 500 and 1,000 pesos.

CHIEF EXPORTS: Ferronickel, sugar, gold, silver, coffee, cocoa, tobacco.

CHIEF IMPORTS: Foodstuffs, petroleum, cotton and fabrics, chemicals, pharmaceuticals.

GROSS DOMESTIC PRODUCT: US$48.3 billion (purchasing power parity, 2000 est.).

BALANCE OF TRADE: Exports: US$5.8 billion (f.o.b, 2000). **Imports:** US$9.6 billion (f.o.b., 2000).

COUNTRY OVERVIEW

LOCATION AND SIZE. A country occupying the eastern two-thirds of the island of Hispaniola (Haiti occupies the western third) between the Caribbean Sea and the Atlantic Ocean, the Dominican Republic has an area of 48,730 square kilometers (18,815 square miles), more than twice the size of New Hampshire. It has a total coastline of 1,288 kilometers (800 miles), and a border with Haiti of 275 kilometers (171 miles). The capital city, Santo Domingo, is located on the country's southern coast.

POPULATION. The population of the Dominican Republic was estimated at 8,442,533 in July 2000, an increase of 15 percent from the 1993 census figure of 7,293,390. In 2000, the birth rate was estimated at 25.15 per 1,000, while the death rate stood at 4.72 per 1,000. At a current growth rate of 1.64 percent annually, the country's population should reach 9,500,000 by 2010.

The Dominican population is mostly of mixed African and European descent, with 73 percent of people describing themselves as mixed-race or mulatto. Some 16 percent define themselves as white, mostly descended from Spanish and other European migrants, while 11 percent are classified as black. The population is generally young, with 34 percent of Dominicans un-

der the age of 14, as opposed to 5 percent over the age of 65. Most people live in urban areas, especially in the Santo Domingo area, which has a population of more than 2.5 million. The average population density of 169.1 per square kilometer (1997) is unevenly distributed, with population concentrations around the coastal towns and Santo Domingo in particular.

The Dominican Republic's population growth rate is offset by a high level of outmigration, estimated at 4 persons per 1,000 in the year 2000. Most migrants aim to settle in the United States, where there are greater economic opportunities. There are no official figures, since a considerable amount of Dominican migration is undocumented, but estimates put the Dominican population in the United States—particularly in the New York area—at more than 1 million. Conversely, the Dominican Republic receives thousands of Haitian migrants each year, many of whom come to cut sugarcane and perform other low-paid jobs.

OVERVIEW OF ECONOMY

Since the 1960s the Dominican Republic's economy has shifted significantly from reliance on sugar and other agricultural commodities to an emphasis on tourism, mining, and manufacturing. Initially the country had a sparse population and was the neglected outpost of the Spanish Empire. Then the territory's ranching economy was replaced by labor-intensive sugar plantations in the wake of the U.S. occupation (1916–24). Sugar remained the dominant economic factor for another half century until large losses incurred by the state-controlled sugar corporation and low international prices spurred a search for diversification.

Commodities, notably ferronickel, gold, and silver, remain important to the Dominican Republic, and sugar is still exported to the United States, but the main areas

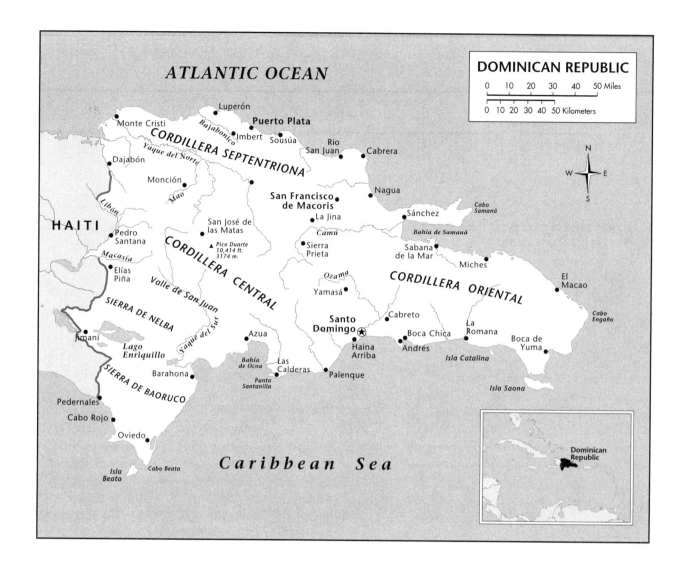

of growth in the last few decades of the 20th century have been tourism and export-oriented manufacturing. The Dominican Republic is now one of the Caribbean's most popular tourist destinations, specializing in all-inclusive resorts. Tourist arrivals averaged more than 1.5 million annually during the 1990s. Annual spending by tourists averaged about US$2 billion. The tourism industry has encouraged a construction boom, with new hotels and other **infrastructure** accounting for a rapid increase in construction share of the GDP.

Successive governments have also attempted to build up the country's manufacturing sector by creating so-called "industrial **free zones**" to which foreign companies are attracted by low wages and a series of tax concessions. Some 500 corporations are based in 50 free zones, mostly involved in assembling clothing and electrical components for the U.S. market. However, the future of such zones has been under question since the creation of the North American Free Trade Area (NAFTA) in 1994, through which Mexico can compete effectively

with the Dominican Republic and other developing countries on low-wage manufacturing and easy access to the U.S. market.

The Dominican Republic has had to come to terms with the economic legacy of the dictator Rafael Leónidas Trujillo, who ruled the country from 1930 to 1961. Trujillo controlled much of the Dominican economy, including sugar plantations and areas of manufacturing, and when he was assassinated, the state inherited these assets. Government attempts to divest itself of large parts of the national economy have been problematic, as many state-owned businesses are heavily indebted and unprofitable. Recently, however, governments have managed to **privatize** the electricity sector and even parts of the sugar industry. Foreign companies have invested in these areas as well as in tourism and manufacturing. The Dominican Republic had an estimated **external debt** of US$4.7 billion in 2000 and remained highly dependent on importing many basic goods. Tourism receipts helped to offset negative trade balances, but tourism remained highly vulnerable to competition, natural disasters, and **recession** in the developed world.

Although the Dominican Republic has undergone considerable modernization and free-market reform, poverty stubbornly remains, with an estimated 25 percent of Dominicans living under the poverty line. Many more are unable to afford anything other than basic items for survival. Rural poverty is particularly prevalent, causing many to move to cities or to attempt **emigrating** to the United States. The **remittances** sent home by Dominicans living overseas are estimated at around US$1.5 billion annually and provide vital income for many poor families.

POLITICS, GOVERNMENT, AND TAXATION

The Dominican Republic is a multi-party democracy, with the president, 149-seat Chamber of Deputies, 30-seat Senate, and local officials elected by popular vote. The Supreme Court judges are elected by a council made up of executive and legislative representatives.

Since the death of Trujillo in 1961, 3 main political parties have dominated Dominican politics. The Dominican Revolutionary Party (PRD), a moderate social-democratic organization, won elections in May 2000, with Hipolito Mejia assuming the presidency. The PRD replaced the Party of Dominican Liberation (PLD), whose president, Leonel Fernández Reyna, had introduced important free-market reforms from 1996. The third party is the Social Christian Reformist Party (PRSC), which presented the 94-year-old Joaquín Balaguer, 7 times president since the 1950s, as its candidate in 2000.

Little separates the main parties in terms of economic policy, although Balaguer's PRSC has proved to be more hostile than the others to privatization. All are in favor of moving towards a free-market economy and encouraging foreign investment in the country. Differences between Dominican parties tend to be more personal than ideological, although the PRSC is generally regarded as more conservative and less committed to redistributing wealth than its competitors. Balaguer's autocratic style of government also concentrated economic decision-making and resources in the hands of the president, allowing him to control a large proportion of the national budget.

Government economic policy since the 1960s has been more or less consistent, but some administrations have been forced to adopt unpopular austerity programs due to recession and a deteriorating economic situation. After the recession of the 1980s, successive Dominican governments have attempted to maintain strong economic growth while keeping **inflation** under control. Priorities have included not only the sale of state-owned enterprises and an end to **subsidies** to these bodies but also considerable investment in roads and other infrastructural development related to tourism and manufacturing. The damage caused by Hurricane Georges in September 1998, estimated at US$2 billion, also required exceptional government investment, but part of this money was provided by grants and loans from multilateral institutions such as the World Bank. The PRD administration elected in 2000 intends to follow free-market reforms, continuing to privatize state assets, attract foreign investment, and promote the country as a tourism destination and stable offshore manufacturing location.

Government tax revenue relies more on sales and business taxes than **income tax**. Low levels of income-tax collection, due in large part to tax evasion and bureaucratic incompetence, have forced successive governments to increase taxes on **consumer goods** and services. Pressure to dismantle **tariff** barriers in keeping with trade agreements with the United States and other countries have reduced revenues on imported goods, with a resulting rise in sales taxes on many basic items. In 2001 the Mejia administration raised a number of **indirect taxes** but was forced to introduce subsidies and relief programs to offset the impact on the poor.

Communications

Country	Newspapers	Radios	TV Sets[a]	Cable subscribers[a]	Mobile Phones[a]	Fax Machines[a]	Personal Computers[a]	Internet Hosts[b]	Internet Users[b]
	1996	1997	1998	1998	1998	1998	1998	1999	1999
Dominican Republic	52	178	95	15.5	31	0.3	N/A	7.63	25
United States	215	2,146	847	244.3	256	78.4	458.6	1,508.77	74,100
Jamaica	62	480	182	73.1	22	N/A	39.4	1.04	60
Haiti	3	55	5	N/A	0	N/A	N/A	0.00	6

[a]Data are from International Telecommunication Union, *World Telecommunication Development Report 1999* and are per 1,000 people.
[b]Data are from the Internet Software Consortium (http://www.isc.org) and are per 10,000 people.
SOURCE: World Bank. *World Development Indicators 2000.*

INFRASTRUCTURE, POWER, AND COMMUNICATIONS

Until the 1960s the Dominican Republic had a backward and crumbling infrastructure, ruined by decades of neglect and under-investment on the part of the Trujillo dictatorship. Since the advent of tourism as a major economic sector, however, Dominican governments, especially those from 1986 onwards, have invested heavily in roads, airports, and docks and other forms of tourism-based construction. These improvements do not, however, benefit the country as a whole. Many of the more remote rural areas still have often impassable roads, made worse by natural disasters such as frequent tropical storms. Small farmers often struggle to bring their produce to market or to other buyers, while coastal resorts enjoy modern highways.

Of the 12,600 kilometers (7,830 miles) of roads existing in 2000, about half were paved, while the others were of variable quality, depending on remoteness and weather conditions. Well-maintained roads connect Santo Domingo with the north coast via Santiago de los Caballeros and run from the capital to the Haitian border and eastward to the modern tourist resorts. Elsewhere, rutted tracks and potholes are commonplace. There are occasional stretches of railway line, but these are owned by sugar plantations and are used for transporting sugarcane rather than passengers.

The Dominican Republic has 13 airports, 5 of them classified as "international." The government's aim is to spread tourist arrivals throughout the country, thereby reducing congestion at the main airport in Santo Domingo. In keeping with its privatization agenda, the government sold control of the airport's management to various foreign consortia (business groups) in 1999. Tourists also disembark from cruise ships at modern port terminals in Santo Domingo and Puerto Plata, while other ports handle merchant shipping.

Perhaps the biggest obstacle to the country's industrial development since the 1960s has been its unreliable electrical service. After years of near bankruptcy and frequent power cuts, the state-run Dominican Electricity Corporation (CDE) was dismantled, and in 1999 the first 50 percent of shares were sold to foreign investors.

Telecommunications are more efficient, although traditional main lines, operated by Codetel or Tricom, are losing ground rapidly to cellular phones. Codetel is also an Internet service provider, but there are frequent complaints about its standard of service. In early 2001, Codetel announced that only 14 percent of Dominicans had a domestic phone connection, 7 percent used mobile phones, and 1 percent had personal access to the Internet.

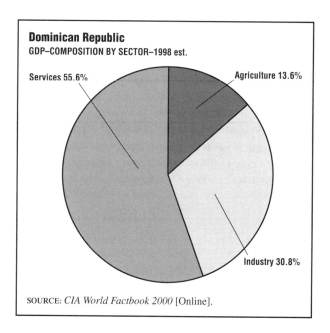

Dominican Republic
GDP–COMPOSITION BY SECTOR–1998 est.

Services 55.6%
Agriculture 13.6%
Industry 30.8%

SOURCE: *CIA World Factbook 2000* [Online].

ECONOMIC SECTORS

Since the 1960s, agriculture's share of GDP has declined in the Dominican Republic, while the share contributed by industry and services has grown. The CIA *World Factbook* estimated that in 1999, agriculture contributed 11.3 percent to the country's GDP, while industry contributed 32.2 percent, and services, mostly tourism, contributed 56.5 percent. Governments have sought to encourage some areas of agriculture by cutting **duties** on imported products and offering cheap loans to farmers, but they have also been willing to sell off the

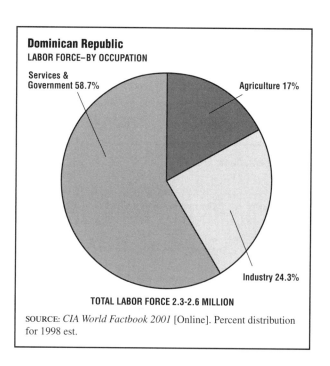

Dominican Republic
LABOR FORCE–BY OCCUPATION

Services & Government 58.7%
Agriculture 17%
Industry 24.3%

TOTAL LABOR FORCE 2.3-2.6 MILLION

SOURCE: *CIA World Factbook 2001* [Online]. Percent distribution for 1998 est.

profitable parts of the state-owned sugar industry and abandon those that are unprofitable.

The economy remains extremely vulnerable to economic developments beyond its control. Competition among Caribbean countries for the North American tourism market, for instance, is extremely fierce, and tourism revenues can be adversely affected by natural disasters, bad publicity, or recession in the United States. Likewise, the Dominican Republic has to compete with Mexico and other developing countries as a supplier of low-cost apparel and electronic components for the North American market. Key sectors of the national economy are also dominated by foreign companies: Canadian in the case of ferronickel, German and Spanish in the case of tourism, and American in the case of offshore manufacturing.

AGRICULTURE

Although it has declined dramatically since the 1960s, agriculture remains an important factor in the economy of the Dominican Republic, accounting for an estimated 11.3 percent of the GDP in 1999. In 1998, about 17 percent of Dominicans were employed in agricultural work, either as small farmers or plantation workers. Sugar continues to occupy first place in the country's agricultural production and exports, but output has fallen considerably since the 1980s, and there are many other crops grown, including food for local consumption and non-traditional exports such as pineapples and exotic fruits destined for the United States. The Dominican Republic is an importer of certain foodstuffs, notably wheat, but it is overall a net exporter of agricultural products, with sugar, coffee, cocoa, tobacco, and meat among its principal exports. Dominican cigars now outsell Cuban ones which are **embargoed** by the United States. In the late 1990s tobacco exports averaged US$100 million annually. Significant growth has also been recorded in non-traditional exports such as cut flowers, ornamental plants, and exotic fruits, which together earned nearly US$200 million in 1997. The Dominican Republic is also a major producer of bananas, and although most are consumed locally, some producers have begun exporting organic bananas to a growing market in Europe and the United States.

Much Dominican farming is aimed at local markets, especially the production of rice. Other crops include maize, plantains, and tomatoes. All agricultural activity is extremely vulnerable to hurricanes, droughts, and other natural hazards.

Although fishing takes place around the country's extensive coastline, there is no export industry, and most fish is destined for hotels and restaurants. Some fish, mostly salted or frozen, is imported.

INDUSTRY

The industrial sector contributed an estimated 32.2 percent to the country's GDP in 1999, led by mining (ferronickel, gold, and silver) and the manufacture of goods for export to the United States. To a lesser extent, there is the manufacture of food products, consumer non-durables, and building materials for the local market and for neighboring Haiti. The sector employed an estimated 24.3 percent of the workforce in 1998.

MINING. It has been estimated that the Dominican Republic contains about 10 percent of the world's ferronickel deposits, but mining is a highly unpredictable part of the industrial sector, vulnerable to fluctuating world prices and unsustainable production techniques. In 1998, for instance, ferronickel exports earned the Dominican Republic US$372 million, but in 1993 declining world prices, due to oversupply, forced the country's export earnings down to US$128.2 million. Since then, prices and export income have stabilized. Gold and silver have been of importance to the Dominican economy since the 1970s, but export earnings have again been irregular. Some gold and silver is exported as basic commodities, while the Dominican Republic also exports semi-finished metals and jewelry.

MANUFACTURING. About 500 companies in the Dominican Republic manufacture goods primarily for the North American market. Situated in 50 industrial free zones around the country, these mostly foreign-owned corporations take advantage of generous tax and other financial inducements offered by the government to businesses that operate within the zones. Approximately 200,000 people, or about 8 percent of the workforce, are employed in this sector. The principal attractions for the foreign companies, which are based in the United States, Canada, Korea, and Taiwan, are a large pool of cheap labor and proximity to the North American market. They mostly produce clothing, electronic components, footwear, and leather goods, which are assembled rather than manufactured by a mainly female workforce. The raw materials or semi-manufactured goods are usually imported duty-free from other developing countries (electronic parts are imported from industrialized Puerto Rico) and put together in the free zones. They are then exported under the terms of the Caribbean Basin Initiative, which gives duty-free entry into the United States to goods produced in the Dominican Republic. The value of exports amounted to US$1.9 billion in 1996, but the contribution to the trade balance was only US$520 million because many of the basic materials for the free zones had to be imported and paid for.

Other, more traditional manufacturing is based on sugar refining, cement, iron and steel production, and food processing. Rum is a significant export commodity, and beer and cigarettes are manufactured for local consumption. Most industry of this sort is located around the working-class perimeter of Santo Domingo and other large towns.

SERVICES

TOURISM. Services were estimated to contribute 56.5 percent of the GDP in 1999 and to employ an estimated 58.7 percent of the workforce, making this the most important sector of the Dominican economy. Tourism is the single biggest revenue earner, with receipts increasing more than tenfold from US$173 million in 1980 to more than US$2 billion by 2000. Successive governments have invested heavily in tourism development, creating upgraded airports and other infrastructure. Foreign investment has also been important, with several large Spanish, German, and French companies building or managing some of the larger hotels. Some 2.1 million tourists arrived in the country in 1999, not including visiting Dominicans. Most come from Europe, with about 25 percent originating from the United States or Canada. The country now has almost 50,000 hotel rooms, more than any other Caribbean country. About 50,000 Dominicans are directly employed in this sector, mostly working in hotels, and another 110,000 are indirectly employed as taxi drivers, tour guides, or tourist-shop staff. Most tourists visit the Dominican Republic on account of its beaches, but there is an expanding **eco-tourism** and outdoor activity sector, focused on the country's mountains and wildlife.

RETAIL. **Retail** activity in the Dominican Republic takes many forms, from U.S.-style supermarkets and shopping malls in Santo Domingo to rural markets and tiny family-run corner stores in villages. A small but affluent middle class can afford to shop at the former, while the large impoverished rural community resorts to buying small amounts of daily essentials from colmados (small stores that often double as bars). Much of this small-scale retail activity occurs within the so-called **informal sector**, and reliable statistics are unavailable. In an attempt to regulate the retail sector, the government has recently reformed taxation laws, so that small shops pay taxes on a regular monthly basis. Many transactions, however, go unrecorded.

FINANCIAL SERVICES. The Dominican Republic does not as yet have a financial services sector aimed at foreign investors, but a securities exchange was opened in 1992 as the first step towards a stock exchange.

INTERNATIONAL TRADE

Since its independence in 1844, the Dominican Republic's main trading partner has been the United States. Initially this trade overwhelmingly consisted of sugar ex-

Trade (expressed in billions of US$): Dominican Republic

	Exports	Imports
1975	.894	.889
1980	.962	1.640
1985	.735	1.487
1990	.735	2.062
1995	.767	3.639
1998	.795	N/A

SOURCE: International Monetary Fund. *International Financial Statistics Yearbook 1999.*

ports, but currently trade is more diversified, with the Dominican Republic still exporting sugar but also other commodities such as clothing, footwear, and electronic components. The United States exports a large range of goods to the Dominican Republic, including automobiles, machinery, chemicals, and some foodstuffs. In 1999, the United States accounted for 66.1 percent of Dominican exports and 56 percent of its imports. Belgium is also an important export market, while Venezuela, the Dominican Republic's main supplier of petroleum, accounts for 23 percent of the import bill. Trade with neighboring Haiti is much less, largely because much of the flourishing informal-sector trade that takes place across the border is not regulated or recorded and hence does not appear in national accounts.

The Dominican Republic has for many years spent much more on imports than it earns from exports. The CIA *World Factbook* estimated that in 2000, for instance, its import bill totaled US$9.6 billion, while exports brought in only US$5.8 billion. This huge **trade deficit** is offset by earnings from tourism (approximately US$2 billion annually) and by the money sent back to the country by Dominicans living overseas (estimated at US$1.5 billion each year). Even so, the Dominican government often records a deficit in its **balance of payments**. While deficits are not necessarily damaging, they generally mean that there is a shortage of foreign reserves in the country's banking system and that the government may need to borrow from abroad to finance its spending.

In 1998 the Fernandez administration signed free-trade agreements with the Central American Common Market (CACM) and the Caribbean Community and Common Market (CARICOM). The Dominican Republic has also made it clear to the United States that it would like to be part of an enlarged NAFTA or similar regional free trade bloc. The country also has preferential access for certain goods into the European Union (EU) and access to EU financial aid.

Exchange rates: Dominican Republic

Dominican pesos per US$1

Jan 2001	16.888
2000	16.415
1999	16.033
1998	15.267
1997	14.265
1996	13.775

SOURCE: CIA *World Factbook 2001* [ONLINE].

Distribution of Income or Consumption by Percentage Share: Dominican Republic

Lowest 10%	1.7
Lowest 20%	4.3
Second 20%	8.3
Third 20%	13.1
Fourth 20%	20.6
Highest 20%	53.7
Highest 10%	37.8

Survey year: 1996
Note: This information refers to income shares by percentiles of the population and is ranked by per capita income.

SOURCE: *2000 World Development Indicators* [CD-ROM].

MONEY

For many years the Dominican peso stood at par with the U.S. dollar, but in 1985 it was devalued as part of an IMF-approved program to pull the country out of recession. Subsequently it was allowed to float against the dollar and has gradually lost much of its value. In 1990, US$1 was worth 11.20 pesos, but in early 2000, the dollar was worth 16.20 pesos. This rate means that imported goods from the United States have steadily become more expensive, including many staple items on which poor Dominicans depend. On the other hand, a cheap peso makes the Dominican Republic attractive both to foreign investors, who can pay even lower wages and to tourists whose dollars stretch further than elsewhere.

The country is currently experiencing relatively low levels of inflation, averaging less than 10 percent annually since the mid-1990s. This rate compares favorably with very high **inflation rates** in the early 1990s, which reached 54 percent in 1991 alone.

POVERTY AND WEALTH

Steady economic growth has brought considerable wealth to some Dominicans, but a considerable sector still lives in extreme hardship, without access to social services or proper educational opportunity. Recent figures are not available, but in 1989 it was estimated that the richest 10 percent of Dominicans accounted for almost 40 percent of national income, while the poorest 10 percent received only 1.6 percent.

While free primary school education is available, many children fail to complete their early education, often because they are required as workers to supplement family income. There is no national system of health care or old-age pensions. The state occasionally attempts to lessen the impact of price rises by subsidizing basic foods such as milk powder or rice and by job-creation schemes in the poorest neighborhoods.

Dominican society is highly stratified, with a very small and very wealthy upper class, a medium-sized middle class, and a very large working class or poor peasant class, many of whom live in absolute poverty. The middle class encompasses professionals such as teachers or hospital workers or those involved in retail, while the poor include agricultural and factory laborers, those working in the informal sector, and the unemployed. There is little upward social mobility, with the exception of musicians or baseball stars who may escape a life of poverty and become millionaires.

The poorest areas of the country are to be found both in Santo Domingo, where shantytowns sprawl around the edges of the city, and in remote rural areas. Perhaps the most impoverished district is in the southwest, near the border with Haiti, where thousands of Haitian migrants and poor Dominican families inhabit rudimentary shacks.

WORKING CONDITIONS

Few Dominicans enjoy pleasant or healthy working conditions. In rural areas, small farmers and agricultural laborers endure back-breaking work, the worst of which is often performed by imported Haitian cane-cutters who do the plantation work that most Dominicans refuse to touch. Conditions in most industries are different, but

GDP per Capita (US$)

Country	1975	1980	1985	1990	1998
Dominican Republic	1,179	1,325	1,325	1,366	1,799
United States	19,364	21,529	23,200	25,363	29,683
Jamaica	1,819	1,458	1,353	1,651	1,559
Haiti	500	607	527	481	370

SOURCE: United Nations. *Human Development Report 2000; Trends in human development and per capita income.*

little better, with workers exposed to a dirty and dangerous environment in return for low wages. Only in tourism, within the more modern resort hotels, are conditions more acceptable, though wages are low.

According to the International Labor Organization, the active Dominican workforce in 1997 numbered 3,464,000, with some 500,000 people unemployed, over 14 percent. Of these a large percentage were defined as working in personal services, meaning in many cases domestic service. The second largest category was trade, restaurants, and hotels, with manufacturing coming third. There is also an enormous unregulated informal sector that offers work to women and children who would not find opportunities within formal employment and which is even more exploitative and low-paid than its formal equivalent.

Approximately 200,000 people, or about 8 percent of the workforce, are employed in the free-zone sector. Wages in the free zones are low, averaging no more than US$120 monthly, with supervisors earning perhaps US$350. Trade unions are in theory legal and entitled to operate in workplaces, but many employers routinely fire union activists as "troublemakers." The industrial free zones, in particular, are notoriously hostile to union activity. The union movement is further weakened and fragmented by inter-party competition. The largest union, the National Confederation of Dominican Workers (CNTD), claims fewer than 200,000 members nationally. **Public-sector** workers such as teachers, doctors, and hospital workers have been especially successful in organizing strikes in recent years.

Supporters of the free zones argue that they bring employment to areas where there are few other opportunities and that women are the main beneficiaries of this work. Women are estimated to comprise about one-third of the formal workforce, but many more are employed informally in private homes, in street vending, and in small-scale sweatshops. The same applies to hundreds of thousands of children, who begin work from ages as low as ten. Women are also particularly in demand in the industrial free zones, where rights are strictly curtailed. There have been allegations that companies hire workers as low-paid apprentices and fire them after their apprenticeship period has ended.

COUNTRY HISTORY AND ECONOMIC DEVELOPMENT

1492. Christopher Columbus arrives on island of Hispaniola; Spanish colonization begins.

1697. Western part of Hispaniola is ceded to France under terms of the Treaty of Ryswick. The French de-velop the colony of Saint-Domingue, while Santo Domingo remains Spanish.

1791. Slave insurrection breaks out in Saint-Domingue, leading to 13-year period of war.

1822–44. Haitian forces occupy Spanish colony of Santo Domingo.

1844. Dominican Republic declares independence.

1861. Spanish sovereignty is re-established at the request of the Dominican government.

1865. Second independence is declared.

1916–24. First U.S. occupation occurs after a period of political chaos. Influx of U.S. capital leads to development of sugar industry.

1930–61. Rafael Leónidas Trujillo is dictator. National assets are centralized under personal control of the Trujillo family.

1939. Dominican Revolutionary Party (PRD) is founded in Havana.

1961. Trujillo is assassinated.

1965. Second U.S. occupation takes place after fighting between supporters of ousted PRD President Juan Bosch and military forces threatens civil war.

1966. Joaquín Balaguer wins election and begins 30-year domination of Dominican politics.

1996. Leonel Fernandez is elected on modernizing program in first free and fair elections.

2000. Hipolito Mejia is elected president.

FUTURE TRENDS

The Dominican Republic enters the 21st century having made considerable strides in modernizing its economy and ridding itself of dependency on sugar. Its economy is now relatively diversified between agriculture, manufacturing and services. It also has considerable potential for expanding its tourism industry, for developing export markets for non-traditional agricultural commodities, and for maintaining a steady level of income from mining. The movement towards privatization is likely to continue, as governments try to divest themselves of loss-making assets. The country is well positioned in terms of international trade to take advantage of preferential treatment both from the United States and from the European Union. After decades of regional isolation, it is now also looking to increase its commercial cooperation with other Caribbean and Latin American countries.

However, severe problems remain. Tourism and manufacturing, as well as mining, are still vulnerable to external economic shocks. Too little manufacturing is aimed at the domestic market, with the result that the country spends too much on imported goods. Stubborn trade deficits and dependency on foreign capital appear likely to continue as obstacles to sustained economic health. Privatization will likely have a negative impact on the poor through reduced employment and rising prices. No Dominican government has yet succeeded in radically altering the imbalance of wealth and opportunity in the country, and it will take unusual political courage to do so.

DEPENDENCIES

Dominican Republic has no territories or colonies.

BIBLIOGRAPHY

The Dominican Republic, South America, Central America and the Caribbean, 2001. London: Europa Publications, 2001.

Economist Intelligence Unit. *Country Profile: Dominican Republic, Haiti and Puerto Rico.* London: Economist Intelligence Unit, 2000.

Embassy of the Dominican Republic in Washington, D.C. <http://www.domrep.org>. Accessed October 2001.

Howard, David. *Dominican Republic in Focus.* London: Latin America Bureau, 1999.

U.S. Central Intelligence Agency. *World Factbook 2001.* <http://www.cia.gov/cia/publications/factbook>. Accessed October 2001.

U.S. Department of State. *Background Notes: Dominican Republic, October 2000.* <http://www.state.gov/www/background_notes/domrep_0010_bgn.html>. Accessed October 2001.

—*James Ferguson*

ECUADOR

Republic of Ecuador
República del Ecuador

CAPITAL: Quito.

MONETARY UNIT: U.S. dollar replaced the Ecuadorian sucres as the official monetary unit in September 2000.

CHIEF EXPORTS: Petroleum, bananas, shrimp, coffee, cocoa, cut flowers, fish.

CHIEF IMPORTS: Machinery and equipment, raw materials, fuels, consumer goods.

GROSS DOMESTIC PRODUCT: US$54.5 billion (1999 est.). [CIA *World Factbook* estimated the GDP at purchasing power parity to be US$37.2 billion in 2000.]

BALANCE OF TRADE: Exports: US$4.141 billion (1998). **Imports:** US$5.503 billion (1998). [CIA *World Factbook* estimated exports to be US$5.6 billion f.o.b. and imports to be US$3.4 billion f.o.b. in 2000.]

COUNTRY OVERVIEW

LOCATION AND SIZE. Located between Colombia and Peru on the west coast of South America, Ecuador has an area of 283,560 square kilometers (176,204 square miles) and a coastline of 2,237 kilometers (1,390 miles). The Galapagos Islands, which rest 960 kilometers (600 miles) to the west of mainland Ecuador in the Pacific Ocean are part of the Republic of Ecuador. Ecuador is slightly smaller than the state of Nevada. Ecuador's capital city, Quito, is located in the Andes mountain range on the equator, while Guayaquil, the country's most populous city, is positioned on the southern coastline about 210 kilometers (130 miles) from Quito.

POPULATION. An estimate in July 2000 put the population of Ecuador at 12,920,092, representing an increase of almost 26 percent over the nation's 1990 population of 10,260,000 and making the country the most densely populated in South America with 187 people per square kilometer (484 people per square mile). The birth rate in Ecuador for the year 2000 was 26.51 per 1,000 inhabi-

tants, while the death rate the same year was 5.52 per 1,000 inhabitants. Population growth is expected to slow slightly to an annual rate of 1.6 percent between 2000 and 2010, bringing the population to 14.9 million by 2010. The percentage of people residing in urban areas has grown steadily since the 1960s and was estimated to

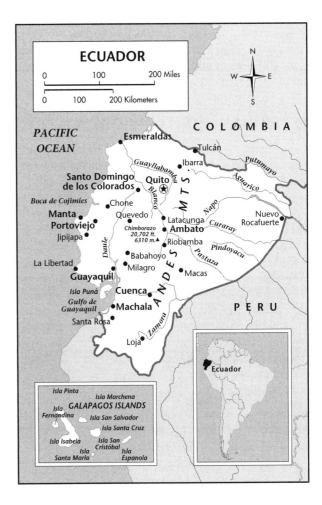

bc 62.7 percent in 2000. Guayaquil, Quito, and Cuenca are the 3 largest cities in the country.

The Ecuadorian people are one of the more diverse groups in Latin America. The Ameridians, descendants of the groups who inhabited the area before Spanish colonization of the Americas, make up 30 percent of the population. The other ethnic groups include the mestizo (mixed Spanish and indigenous descent), Spanish, and black and account for 60 percent, 7 percent, and 3 percent of the population. Indigenous presence in Ecuador is the second highest in South America after Bolivia. The population of Ecuador is also young, with 70 percent of the country's inhabitants under the age of 35. Over the next 10 years, if population growth rate in Ecuador slows and life expectancy improves as anticipated, age distribution should even out slightly.

Sustaining the population is one of the Ecuadorian government's primary national concerns. Article 39 of the Ecuadorian Constitution addresses the issue of population, guaranteeing individuals the right to determine how many children they will have, while noting the accountability of the state to inform and educate individuals about the responsibilities that accompany this right. Because of Ecuador's strong Catholic influence with its emphasis on family, population control is a sensitive topic, and the government is reluctant to make strong statements on the issue. To ameliorate poor crop production and slow rural to urban migration, the government offers small grants to individuals to subsidize their farming practices.

OVERVIEW OF ECONOMY

Because of its rich natural resources and mild climate, Ecuador's economy first developed around the harvesting of agricultural products such as coffee and cocoa. As different regions of the country were settled, other resources were exploited and production diversified to include lumber and oil from the Amazon, shrimp and fish from the coast, and fruits, grains, and other food commodities from the sierra (mountain country) and coastal regions. The economy of Ecuador is still rooted strongly in extractive products and **primary commodities**, particularly in exports. Oil, shrimp, and bananas are the nation's top 3 exports, while the manufacturing sector (including basic manufactured goods, machines, and transport equipment) accounts for less than 7 percent of all exports.

Ecuador faces many economic problems experienced by developing nations. Political instability in the country has affected the national economy, discouraging international and domestic investment in Ecuador's market and sparking higher interest rates. In 1979, Ecuador led the way in Latin America by developing a democratic government. Since then, the country has endured political corruption, inefficiency, and erratic transfers of political power that thwart the pursuit of economic progress. Ecuador's inability to post consistent growth in production has had serious social ramifications, causing half of the population to fall below the poverty line in 2000 and pushing unemployment to 15 percent.

Despite **restructuring** the nation's debt is more than $15 billion, making the country a high-risk area for investors. Ecuador also faces a deteriorating **balance of trade** because of its heavy reliance on primary commodities for export. Without support from foreign investors, there is little hope that the country will be able to develop more profitable industries. In addition, tax evasion and the ineffectiveness of the administration to collect taxes cause great problems to the domestic economy.

Because of the lack of well-paid jobs in Ecuador, almost 60 percent of economically active Ecuadorians turn to the **informal economy** for employment. Informal workers, instead of working for the state or state-recognized private employers, support themselves by working for micro-enterprises or selling items illegally (without permits or income reports to the state) in metropolitan areas or market towns. One of the most visible concentrations of informal employment is in the cities of Quito and Guayaquil, where vendors set up kiosks in the city centers and sell items to passers-by. The scarcity of money has led to child labor. It is common to find young children shining shoes or selling candy on the streets to augment their parents' income. Many international funding organizations (the Inter-American Development Bank, the World Bank, and USAID) sponsor development projects in Ecuador to improve the socio-economic situation, but the scope of these projects has been local and have not made significant contributions to economic stability or growth.

In 1999 unstable export prices and the natural disaster of El Niño combined with internal stresses to induce a severe economic crisis. The crisis spurred the government to adapt a new economic program in 2000, which included the **privatization** of many state-owned enterprises, more flexible labor laws, and reductions in public expenditure. These measures, commonly referred to as structural adjustments and actively endorsed by organizations like the International Monetary Fund (IMF), are expected to bring a strong sense of discipline to the economy and provide the foundation for future growth.

POLITICS, GOVERNMENT, AND TAXATION

Ecuador is a unitary republic that consists of 3 governmental branches: the executive, legislative, and judiciary. Presidents and congressional representatives are elected by popular but compulsory vote, while members of the independent judiciary branch are appointed. Still in the early stages of democracy, Ecuador has not seen the consolidation of political parties. Instead, there is a multitude of parties whose popularity wavers from election to election, sometimes based on the performance of individual politicians. The leading parties to have emerged from the 2000 congressional election are the Social Christian Party (SCP, center-right), the Popular Democratic Party (PDP, center-left), the Democratic Left (DL, center-left) and the newly founded Pachakutik-New Country Party (P-NC, populist-left). All parties support government-funded social programs, but they have dissenting opinions about privatization and the economic role of the state. The SCP supports economic **liberalization** and the privatization of state-owned entities such as water, electricity, and the postal service. The PDP and DL support a broader economic role for the state and, therefore, advocate price **subsidies** and continued state ownership of most utilities. The P-NC is the most liberal of the 4 parties, favoring tax, welfare, and social policies that would benefit the most Ecuadorians rather than the elite.

Ecuador's economic reforms of 2000 established the U.S. dollar (US$) as the official monetary unit and diminished the role of the Ecuadorian government in the economy. Before reform, the state had played an important role in economic affairs, holding a large payroll, providing price subsidies on gasoline, and cooking gas, maintaining ownership of telecommunications, and the production and distribution of electricity. The reform agenda cleared the way for structural adjustments to reduce the number of state employees, auction off utility companies to private enterprise, and adjust the price of gas and other commodities to international levels. The role of the Ecuadorian government in the economy will be much smaller if these reform measures are carried out.

There are several different types of taxes in Ecuador, including **value-added tax**, personal **income tax**, a consumption tax on domestic fuel, and a financial transactions tax. These taxes were adjusted when the liberalization program was adopted, shifting the bulk of taxpayer responsibility to individual Ecuadorians through higher personal income tax. These measures were taken to lower the financial transactions tax and encourage foreign and domestic investment. Tax policies, like most other economic policies in Ecuador, are designed by the executive branch of government and carried out by the legislature.

INFRASTRUCTURE, POWER, AND COMMUNICATIONS

Ecuador is well-served by an accessible transport system and profits from an extensive **infrastructure** of roads and an uncommonly efficient bus system that make travel to almost any region possible. The country has 43,197 kilometers (26,843 miles) of highways, of which 8,165 kilometers (5,074 miles) are paved. Three national airlines—Saeta, Tame, and Ecuatoriana—provide flight services within Ecuador and from the international airports in Quito and Guayaquil to select locations outside the country. Because the vast changes in altitude and terrain in Ecuador can make road travel slow and difficult, tourists and Ecuadorians alike frequently utilize in-country flights. Taxis and buses provide nonstop city transport for very reasonable fares, and a newly constructed trolley line in Quito delivers passengers to the center of the city. The trans-Ecuadorian railway, which extends for 812 kilometers (505 miles), needs renovation and is used for freight purposes.

Telecommunication and electrical services in Ecuador are state-owned and operated. They are available to Ecuadorians at subsidized rates but perform at less-than-desirable levels. The domestic telephone service is inadequate and unreliable because of its dismal 40 percent completion rate. Despite the limited portion of the population that can afford modern communication devices, the communications industry is growing rapidly. Ecuador has 15 television stations, 419 radio broadcast systems, and 8

Communications									
Country	Newspapers	Radios	TV Sets[a]	Cable subscribers[a]	Mobile Phones[a]	Fax Machines[a]	Personal Computers[a]	Internet Hosts[b]	Internet Users[b]
	1996	1997	1998	1998	1998	1998	1998	1999	1999
Ecuador	70	419	293	11.7	25	N/A	18.5	1.42	35
United States	215	2,146	847	244.3	256	78.4	458.6	1,508.77	74,100
Brazil	40	444	316	16.3	47	3.1	30.1	18.45	3,500
Colombia	46	581	217	16.7	49	4.8	27.9	7.51	664

[a]Data are from International Telecommunication Union, *World Telecommunication Development Report 1999* and are per 1,000 people.
[b]Data are from the Internet Software Consortium (http://www.isc.org) and are per 10,000 people.

SOURCE: World Bank. *World Development Indicators 2000.*

Internet service providers, but many individuals cannot afford televisions, radios, or personal computers.

Besides excellent transport for commuters and travelers, its seaports equip Ecuador for international commerce. The largest is at Guayaquil, the main port for oil exports is at Esmereldas, and there are other major ports at Manta and Machala. While the extensive road infrastructure and port system contribute to productive domestic and international trade practices, productivity is hindered by aging vehicles and oil pipelines.

ECONOMIC SECTORS

Although Ecuador originated as an agrarian society, over the past 30 years the global market has shaped the country's economic focus toward industry and services. Part of this shift has occurred because of more advanced production practices. Despite new methods of technology and production, the country experienced severe stagnation in its production of goods and services at the end of the 20th century. In 1999 **gross domestic product** (GDP) shrunk 7 percent from its 1998 level, and imports fell drastically because of the lack of financial capital in the country. The CIA *World Factbook* estimated that agriculture accounted for 14 percent of the GDP, industry for 36 percent, and services for 50 percent in 1999.

Political instability and inefficiency prevented the implementation of economic reforms during the 1980s and 1990s. Loose **fiscal policies**, a burgeoning **external debt**, and rampant **inflation** culminated in a financial crisis in 1999. The crisis caused drastic economic reforms in 2000, including dollarization, privatization of state-owned entities, and liberalization of trade and labor. These policies, advocated by the IMF and the United States government, are expected to bring new growth to the agricultural, industrial, and service sectors of the economy.

Ecuador
GDP–COMPOSITION BY SECTOR–1999 est.

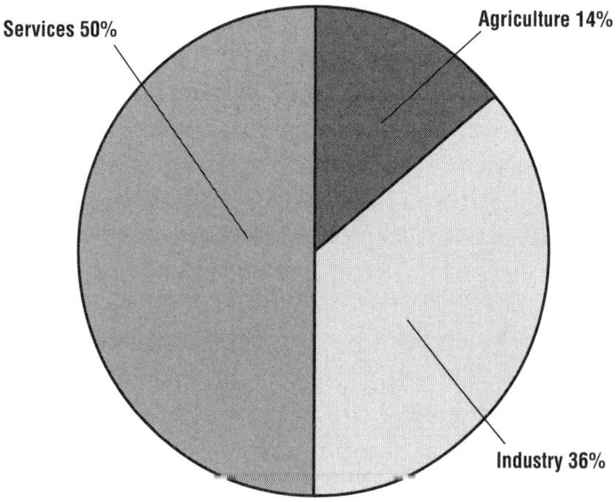

SOURCE: *CIA World Factbook 2000* [Online].

Ecuador
LABOR FORCE–BY OCCUPATION

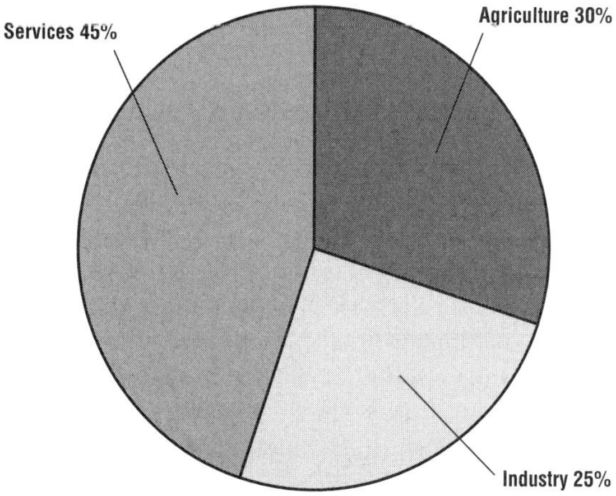

TOTAL LABOR FORCE 4.2 MILLION

SOURCE: *CIA World Factbook 2001* [Online]. Percent distribution for 1999 est.

Remittance pay, the money sent to Ecuadorian residents by family members or friends living and working abroad, is an important factor in Ecuador economy that does not fall into conventional economic sectors. Because of poverty and the lack of well-paid jobs in Ecuador, many Ecuadorians **emigrate** to countries such as the United States and Spain, where jobs are easier to find. These individuals send parts of their paychecks back to Ecuador to support their families or supplement the family income. With increasing rates of poverty and consequent emigration, remittance pay has become an enormous force in the Ecuadorian economy and, valued at US$1.185 billion in year 2000, was the second largest source of national income after petroleum exports.

AGRICULTURE

BANANAS. The agricultural sector, which accounts for about 14 percent of the GDP and 30 percent of the **labor force** (1.25 million workers), is sustained by its largest export, bananas. Owing substantially to the cheap price of unskilled, unorganized labor (Ecuadorian banana workers are not unionized and earn roughly US$2–3 per day), Ecuador provides an attractive base of operation for fruit companies. The banana industry faced temporary difficulties with production in 1998 when El Niño destroyed much of the crop, but it has since recovered its position as the world's top exporter. A more stubborn problem facing the industry is the low price for bananas on the international market. Despite Ecuador's domination of the world banana trade, profits from the industry are declining and thus contributing to the nation's deteriorating trade.

COFFEE AND COCOA. Since 1970, the role of coffee in Ecuador's agricultural sector has diminished. Coffee was once the foundation of Ecuador's export economy, but it has been damaged by the global coffee **recession**, which has seen the production of coffee beans taper off over the past 30 years. From 1995 to 1999, production dropped from 150,000 metric tons to 57,000 metric tons. Nevertheless, coffee is considered a staple of Ecuadorian agriculture and is one of the country's largest exports after bananas. The production of cocoa beans, another of Ecuador's oldest cultivated crops, has remained stable throughout the last decade, probably because cocoa beans are cultivated for domestic consumption.

SUGAR CANE. Ecuador produces more metric tons of sugar cane per year (7 million in 1999) than any other crop. Because of the immense demand for sugar and sugar-based foods, production barely guarantees the country's status as a net exporter of sugar cane. Much of the sugar crop is exported to neighboring countries, but almost as much is imported by Ecuador from surrounding Andean nations. This cross-border exchange usually occurs because of the changing demand for raw and refined forms of sugar in a country at any given time. Ecuador is striving to secure its position as an exporter of sugar by producing more than is needed for domestic consumption.

SMALL-SCALE CROPS. While agro-industries grow crops for export, many Ecuadorians live as **subsistence farmers**, selling or trading the food they produce to support themselves. Because of the multitude of fruits, vegetables, and grains that grow in Ecuador's climate, these small-scale farmers can trade to acquire any food they want. Commonly grown crops include rice, maize, potatoes, manioc, and soybeans. Indigenous Ecuadorians, whose heritage is deeply connected to the land for survival, make up most of the subsistence farmers. Their crops are sold at local markets and do not usually leave the country.

INDUSTRY

First introduced to Ecuador in the 1950s, industry makes up about 36 percent of the GDP and absorbs 25 percent of the total labor force (1 million workers). The chief industrial exports are petroleum and farmed shrimp, but mining of metals is emerging as a lucrative industry. Industry is a volatile component of the economy because Ecuador's industrial sector is oriented toward primary commodities. These command erratic prices on the international market when compared to the more stable demand for manufactured and **value-added** goods. The precarious structure of Ecuador's industrial sector was revealed in 1998 when oil prices dropped and South American shrimp were struck by the deadly Mancha Blanca virus. This double stroke of bad luck, afflicting Ecuador's 2 most important industrial products, led to a shrinking economy in 1999 that aggravated Ecuador's economic woes.

PETROLEUM. Oil is Ecuador's top export, its revenue makes up 10 percent of the GDP. A member of OPEC (Oil and Petroleum Exporting Countries) since the 1970s, Ecuador exports 60 percent of the oil it produces, most of which originates in the Amazon basin. Until recently, the government granted large price subsidies on domestic oil, driving down the price of gasoline for individuals and facilitating inexpensive fares on public transport. In 2000 as part of the nation's new economic reforms, these subsidies were gradually removed, and oil prices were set to international levels, making gasoline unaffordable for many Ecuadorians. Untapped oil reserves belong to the government by authority of the constitution, which decrees all subsurface resources to be the property of the state.

SHRIMP. Ecuador is the world's second largest exporter of shrimp, which makes up 2 percent of the nation's overall GDP. The tools and production of the shrimp industry have changed over the past 2 decades in response to the forces of technology and international demand. The industry used to take its shrimp from the Pacific Ocean, but now shrimp farms are the prevailing method of production for export. Shrimp farms have a negative environmental effect on the mangroves and marine life in the ocean and have caused a serious decline in the wild shrimp population. This phenomenon, combined with the yellow head and white spot viruses that attacked Ecuador's shrimp in the late 1990s, threatens to destroy the shrimp industry if changes are not made to the system.

MINING. With abundant deposits of gold, silver, lead and zinc, Ecuador has great mining potential, but the country does not currently possess the financial resources needed to develop this industry. Mining accounts for only 0.5 percent of Ecuador's GDP, and much of this revenue is earned from **black market** sales. Nevertheless, mining is an **emerging market** in Ecuador and may become an economically vital factor with help from foreign investors.

SERVICES

The service sector, responsible for half of Ecuador's GDP and 45 percent of its labor force (1.9 million workers), embraces tourism, transportation, utilities, communications, parcel delivery, and financial services. Because of its beautiful geography, the diversity of its flora and fauna, and its cultural attractions, Ecuador is a popular destination for travelers and earns good profits from tourism. The other major economic force in the service industry is the informal work sector, which gives many people a means of income when formal employment is in short supply.

TOURISM. Ecuador collected US$281 million in foreign capital from tourist receipts in 1996. The Galapagos Islands, famed for their unparalleled biological diversity and as the site of evolutionist Charles Darwin's studies, are Ecuador's leading tourist attraction. Other main points of interest include Quito, which is stationed almost directly on the equator in the Andean highlands; Cotopaxi, the world's tallest active volcano; and the Amazon rainforest. Tourism is still a budding industry in Ecuador, and the low prices attract many new visitors each year. But political instability and rising crime in 2000 discouraged many visitors and affected tourism revenues.

INFORMAL SECTOR. A huge, unofficial role in Ecuador's service sector is the informal economy, which supports a fluctuating percentage of Ecuadorians according to the availability of official employment opportunities. Products sold in the informal sector include clothing, small appliances, food, artisan crafts, stolen goods, and any item in demand. Vendors set up booths in commercial areas, while others navigate the streets of large cities during rush hour and make sales to motorists. Because of its underground nature, it is hard to estimate the national income that the informal sector generates, but it is playing an increasingly important role in the economy as urbanization and access to common markets escalate.

INTERNATIONAL TRADE

Ecuador's balance of trade fluctuates from year to year according to international demand and economic conditions in the country. In 1998 Ecuador ran a trade deficit, exporting $4.1 billion worth of goods and importing $5.5 billion. In 2000, exports were US$3.4 billion while imports reached US$5.6 billion. Ecuador's main trade partners are the United States, Japan, and Germany, followed by the other nations involved in the Andean Pact trade agreement (Colombia, Venezuela, Peru, and Bolivia). These trade associations have remained stable since the 1970s, and the quantity of goods traded has increased. A border dispute between Peru and Ecuador that flared up in 1994 caused a temporary damper on trade. During its war against Peru (which lasted until 1998), Ecuador imported greater quantities from the non-warring Andean nations to compensate for lost Peruvian goods.

Ecuador's main exports are oil, bananas, shrimp, and other agricultural goods. The United States, which provides a market for 35 percent of the country's exports, imported a total of US$1.2 billion worth of goods from Ecuador in 1998, most consisting of fish, petroleum,

Trade (expressed in billions of US$): Ecuador

	Exports	Imports
1975	.974	.987
1980	2.481	2.253
1985	2.905	1.767
1990	2.714	1.865
1995	4.307	4.153
1998	4.141	5.503

SOURCE: International Monetary Fund. *International Financial Statistics Yearbook 1999.*

fruits, and vegetables. Ecuador sends exports of a similar nature to Europe and Japan, where there is demand for primary products and non-native foods.

MONEY

Until recently, Ecuador struggled with the persistent **devaluation** of its currency (the sucre) on the world market, making it harder for Ecuadorians to afford goods produced in other countries. After a decade of steady depreciation, the value of the sucre plummeted in 1999, prompting then-President Jamil Mahuad to announce the national policy of dollarization in January 2000. In September 2000, the country completed its dollarization process, stopping the printing of sucres and introducing the U.S. dollar as the official monetary unit for all banking and government transactions. Ecuador's problem with currency devaluation has since ceased, but inflation has continued to plague the economy, making basic goods unaffordable for many Ecuadorians.

Dollarization brought many changes to the banking sector. Although the Central Bank of Ecuador used to be

Exchange rates: Ecuador

sucres (S/) per US$1

Jan 2001	25,000
2000	24,988.4
1999	11,786.8
1998	5,446.6
1997	3,988.3
1996	3,189.5

Note: On January 7, 2000, the government passed a decree "dollarizing" the economy; on March 13, 2000, the National Congress approved a new exchange system whereby the US dollar is adopted as the main legal tender in Ecuador for all purposes; on March 20, 2000, the Central Bank of Ecuador started to exchange sucres for US dollars at a fixed rate of 25,000 sucres per US dollar; since April 30, 2000, all transactions are denominated in US dollars.

SOURCE: CIA *World Factbook 2001* [ONLINE].

responsible for setting domestic interest rates and printing money, those responsibilities now rest with the United States Federal Reserve, which sells dollars to Ecuador and decides whether to raise or lower interest rates. Many banks in Ecuador went bankrupt because of the 1999 financial crisis. The government is working to revitalize its banks and pay back investors who lost money because of bank closures. Since adopting the dollar, Ecuador's banks have grown stronger attracting more investors. Interest rates are much lower than they were before dollarization, marking an improvement in investors' perception of the Ecuadorian economy. The GDP grew 2 percent in 2000, a modest but important sign of progress after a decline of 7 percent in 1999. It is too early to deliver a final verdict on the merits of dollarization, but these figures indicate that Ecuador's adoption of the U.S. dollar might well have paved the way for more sustainable economic development.

POVERTY AND WEALTH

Ecuador's population was burdened by an unequal distribution of wealth in the 1990s. In 1996 the wealthiest 20 percent of Ecuadorians earned half of the nation's total income, while the poorest 20 percent collected only 5 percent. The gap between rich and poor grew noticeably during the 1999 economic crisis, when much of the middle-class fell below the poverty line because of rampant currency devaluation and inflation. Figures released by international organizations in 2000 show that half of all Ecuadorians were living in poverty, a dramatic increase from just a few years earlier, when the poverty rate was estimated at 35 percent. Poverty is more pervasive in rural areas of Ecuador, affecting almost 70 percent of non-urban dwellers (2000).

Because of the contraction of Ecuador's middle class, the division between the upper and lower classes has widened, allowing for little upward mobility among the nation's poor. Members of the elite are well established within their specialist fields as doctors, lawyers, politicians, or leading business entrepreneurs. The middle class embraces a wide range of professional and blue-collar workers, including teachers, bus and taxi drivers, service and **retail** employees, oil industry employees, small-business owners, and small-scale farmers. The largest segment of Ecuador's population includes peasants and subsistence farmers, informal sector vendors, **agribusiness** employees, temporary workers, and the unemployed. Most of these Ecuadorians are denied the education and connections to gain access to the small professional sector and are thus confined to low-paid jobs.

Ecuador's constitution, revised in 1998, places strong emphasis on social programs and assistance to the poor, promising free health care and government subsidies to the nation's most needy citizens. However, public welfare expenditure, limited by the government's cumbersome debt and lack of funds, has had little impact on poverty. A cash transfer to the country's poorest families, called a *bono solidario* (solidarity bond), is the most consistent element of Ecuador's poverty relief program, but it reaches only some of the poor. Public health care is officially free, but the quality of medical services is inadequate. A report on Ecuador's health care system released in 1996 by USAID, observed that "The supply and quality of care in Ministry of Public Health facilities is generally agreed to be inefficient and poor." The wealthy can afford private health care of a higher quality, but private care is increasingly beyond the reach of middle- and lower-class Ecuadorians.

The design of Ecuador's education system causes similar problems for economically disadvantaged citizens because the government subsidizes university education at the expense of elementary and secondary schools. Wealthy families can afford to send their children to the best private schools, while poorer families must settle for the variable quality of public education and disruption caused by frequent teacher strikes. Access to education is also divided along rural/urban lines, with public expenditure favoring urban schools and neglecting vocational and manual skills training.

Distribution of Income or Consumption by Percentage Share: Ecuador	
Lowest 10%	2.2
Lowest 20%	5.4
Second 20%	9.4
Third 20%	14.2
Fourth 20%	21.3
Highest 20%	49.7
Highest 10%	33.8

Survey year: 1995
Note: This information refers to expenditure shares by percentiles of the population and is ranked by per capita expenditure.

SOURCE: *2000 World Development Indicators* [CD-ROM].

GDP per Capita (US$)					
Country	1975	1980	1985	1990	1998
Ecuador	1,301	1,547	1,504	1,475	1,562
United States	19,364	21,529	23,200	25,363	29,683
Brazil	3,464	4,253	4,039	4,078	4,509
Columbia	1,612	1,868	1,875	2,119	2,392

SOURCE: United Nations. *Human Development Report 2000; Trends in human development and per capita income.*

Household Consumption in PPP Terms

Country	All food	Clothing and footwear	Fuel and power[a]	Health care[b]	Education[b]	Transport & Communications	Other
Ecuador	26	9	15	13	10	3	24
United States	13	9	9	4	6	8	51
Brazil	22	13	18	15	34	4	−6
Colombia	N/A	N/A	N/A	N/A	N/A	N/A	N/A

Data represent percentage of consumption in PPP terms.
[a]Excludes energy used for transport.
[b]Includes government and private expenditures.
SOURCE: World Bank. *World Development Indicators 2000.*

WORKING CONDITIONS

Employment conditions vary greatly in Ecuador according to type of work, individual management styles, and susceptibility to government inspection. Inefficient government enforcement of labor codes and the pervasiveness of informal employment have created an insecure working environment where labor laws are flagrantly violated. Also, child labor is common, despite legislation that prohibits children under 14 from working.

About 12 percent of Ecuador's 4.2 million workers are unionized. The umbrella group Frente Unida de Trabajadores (United Front of Workers, FUT), the most visible labor advocacy organization in the country, is active in protesting against policies such as outdated minimum wage laws and the elimination of government subsidies on gas, which have a negative impact on Ecuadorian workers. Many formal sector workers, such as teachers, are also organized into independent unions to enable collective negotiation with management. However, the lobbying power of independent unions is weak and does little to improve the pay and benefits of employees. Unions are non-existent in the agricultural and informal sectors, where most Ecuadorians are employed and conditions are often worst. One poignant example of this phenomenon is the plight of Ecuadorian banana workers, who are unorganized and receive derisory wages of $2–3 per day. By contrast, unionized banana workers in Guatemala and other countries receive $10 per day plus benefits.

The Ecuadorian labor code, modified between 1991 and 1996, includes more than 600 articles regulating formal sector labor and the role of the government in arbitrating labor disputes. One of the most important policies outlined in the labor code is the official minimum wage, which was set at US$117.64 per month in 2001, a US$21 per month increase over the minimum wage in 2000. Minimum wage laws change frequently in Ecuador to compensate for rapid inflation. Employers in the formal sector are prohibited from firing workers without the permission of Labor Ministry inspectors. Other labor laws guarantee the right of large-firm workers to form trade unions but limit the length of solidarity strikes to 3 days, permit the hiring of temporary workers in export processing zones, and promise 15-day vacations, social security, and job training. Although these regulations are spelled out thoroughly in Ecuadorian law, they are enforced only in the formal sector and, therefore, do not benefit the majority of workers.

Unemployment lingered at 12 percent in early 2001, down slightly from 2000 but still well over the average rate for the 1990s. One of the most stubborn labor problems for the economy is the lack of skilled workers. The public school system focuses on academic and intellectual education and neglects vocational training, although there are few academic-oriented employment opportunities in Ecuador. The dilemma of vocational education is different for women, who are often pigeonholed into traditionally female work in the service sector, where they receive less pay than men do. While the **GDP per capita** was $4,940 in 1997, the GDP per capita for women was only $1,925.

COUNTRY HISTORY AND ECONOMIC DEVELOPMENT

1450s. Incas conquer indigenous tribes in and around Quito.

1531. Spanish conquistador Francisco Pizarro lands on the Ecuadorian coast.

1534. Spain conquers Ecuador and claims the city of Quito. Ecuador becomes part of the Spanish Viceroyalty of Peru.

LATE 1500s. The Spanish establish large agrarian estates, or *haciendas,* which feature indigenous *peons* working for European owners.

1739. Ecuador becomes part of the Spanish Royalty of Nueva Granada, which also comprises Colombia and Venezuela.

1822. Antonio José de Sucre, one of revolutionary leader Simon Bolivar's field marshals, defeats Spanish Royalists at the battle of Pichincha, near Quito. Ecuador becomes part of Gran Colombia, the independent territory comprised of Colombia, Ecuador, Panama and Venezuela.

1830. Ecuador leaves Gran Colombia to become a fully independent state.

1845–60. A period of political and military instability is caused by minor wars with Peru and Colombia and increasing tension between the conservative center Quito and the liberal metropolis Guayaquil.

1860–75. Autocratic conservative Gabriel Garcia Moreno holds power and establishes education and public works programs.

1895–1912. Radical liberal General Eloy Alfaro rules and reduces the power of the Catholic Church.

1925–48. Ecuador undergoes a period of great instability.

1941. Ecuador loses a border war with Peru and gives up land in the Amazon.

1970s. Ecuador becomes a major producer and exporter of oil.

1979. Ecuador adopts a new democratic constitution and gains official recognition as a democratic nation.

1981. Border conflict with Peru surfaces again.

1988. Rodrigo Borja Cevallos wins the presidency and introduces austerity measures designed to discipline the economy.

1992. Ecuador withdraws from OPEC to avoid export limitations.

1994. President Sixto Duran Ballen's neo-liberal program encounters strong opposition.

1995. War between Ecuador and Peru flares up again.

1997. President Abdala Bucarám flees Ecuador on charges of corruption. Fabian Alarcón becomes interim president.

1998. Jamil Mahuad becomes president and negotiates an end to the 157-year border dispute with Peru.

1999. Economic crisis hits, sparking rampant currency depreciation, high inflation, and severe unemployment.

2000. Mahuad is ousted in a non-violent coup after announcing plans to dollarize the economy. Vice President Gustavo Noboa is installed as president.

2000. Dollarization reaches completion.

FUTURE TRENDS

There are several issues facing Ecuador that will influence its future economic performance. Dollarization and the economic reforms of 2000 will provide the economy with stability and credibility if they are carried out as designed, free of partisan battles. Yet, these reforms will not succeed without cost to the social wellbeing of the nation, since welfare and other social programs will be cut, government jobs will be eliminated, and further inflation will occur connected to the change of currency. The success or failure of reform will depend heavily on the reactions of the Ecuadorian people to these social strains. An uprising like the coup that occurred in January 2000 could upset the entire program and inhibit further progress; conversely, an expression of faith in Ecuador's government could help to consolidate democracy and attract investment from abroad.

Another immediate concern for Ecuador is the turmoil over Plan Colombia, the United States' US$1.3 billion anti-drug offensive in Colombia. A massive influx of people from southern Colombia into northern Ecuador is anticipated, and an overflow of violence into Ecuadorian territory. Ecuador has given the United States military access to its base in Manta, an agreement that created tension between Colombian guerillas and the Ecuadorian government. The severity of Colombia's internal conflict will have major implications for the Ecuadorian economy because the Ecuadorian government does not have money to set up a major operation on the Colombian-Ecuadorian border.

The long-term outlook for Ecuador's economic and social well-being is as precarious as in the short term. While the land is rich in natural resources, the country has not been successful in using this advantage to develop sources of consistent income and growth. Price instability for major exports on the international market makes for further difficulties. Ecuador's oil production will receive a boost from the completion of a new refinery and pipeline, expected within 2 years, but this will not be enough to sustain the national economy. The best hope for future growth in Ecuador is the diversification of its exports and substantial investment in value-added industries that can produce higher-value goods. Such diversification, combined with the consolidation of democracy and a disciplined approach to government expenditure, offers the best solutions for Ecuador's future economic and social advancement.

DEPENDENCIES

Ecuador has no territories or colonies.

BIBLIOGRAPHY

"Access of the Poor to Health Care in Ecuador: Experiences with User Fee Schemes." *BASICS/USAID.* <http://www.basics.org/Publications/Ecuador/contents.htm>. Accessed January 2001.

Economist Intelligence Unit. *Country Profile: Ecuador.* London: Economist Intelligence Unit, 2001.

"Ecuador: Economy." *Country Watch.* <http://www.countrywatch.com/files/054/cw_topic.asp?vCOUNTRY=054&TP=ECO>. Accessed January 2001.

Ecuador: Embassy of Ecuador, Washington, D.C. <http://www.ecuador.org>. Accessed October 2001.

"Ecuador: Foreign Labor Trends." *U.S. Department of Commerce.* <http://www.tradeport.org/ts/countries/ecuador/flt.html>. Accessed December 2000.

"Información Económica y Financiera." *Banco Central del Ecuador.* <http://www.bce.fin.ec/z_inf_ec.html>. Accessed January 2001.

USAID Bureau for Latin America and the Caribbean. *Latin America and the Caribbean: Selected Economic and Social Data.* Washington, D.C.: USAID, 1999.

U.S. Central Intelligence Agency. *World Factbook 2000.* <http://www.odci.gov/cia/publications/factbook/index.html>. Accessed August 2001.

—Heidi Jugenitz

EL SALVADOR

Republic of El Salvador
República de El Salvador

CAPITAL: San Salvador.

MONETARY UNIT: Colón (¢, often called "Peso"). One colón equals 100 centavos. Coins are in denominations of ¢1, and 1, 5, 10, 25, and 50 centavos. Paper currency is in denominations of 5, 10, 25, 50, and 100. U.S. dollars have also been accepted as a dual currency since January 2001.

CHIEF EXPORTS: Coffee, sugar, shrimp, textiles, chemicals, electricity.

CHIEF IMPORTS: Raw materials, consumer goods, capital goods, fuels, foodstuffs, petroleum, electricity.

GROSS DOMESTIC PRODUCT: US$24 billion (purchasing power parity, 2000 est.).

BALANCE OF TRADE: Exports: US$2.8 billion (f.o.b., 2000 est.). **Imports:** US$4.6 billion (f.o.b., 2000 est.).

COUNTRY OVERVIEW

LOCATION AND SIZE. El Salvador, a Central American country slightly smaller than Massachusetts, borders the North Pacific Ocean between Guatemala and Honduras. It has a land area of 20,720 square kilometers (8,000 square miles) and a coastline of 308 kilometers (191 miles). Land boundaries in El Salvador total 545 kilometers (339 miles). It shares a 327-kilometer (203-mile) border with Guatemala in the northwest, and a 341-kilometer (212-mile) border with Honduras in the southeast.

POPULATION. In 2000, the population of El Salvador was about 6.2 million and was growing by approximately 2.1 percent a year. At this rate, the population is expected to climb to nearly 8 million by 2015. The birth rate in 2000 was estimated to be 29.02 per 1000, and the death rate, 6.27 per 1000.

About 90 percent of the Salvadoran population is *mestizo* (of mixed Spanish and Amerindian ancestry). Native Amerindians make up about 1 percent of the population, and whites account for the rest. A significant portion of the population, nearly 40 percent, is under the age of 15. Those 65 and older account for only 5 percent of the population. The percentage of Salvadorans living in rural areas declined in the last half century from 64 percent in 1950 to about 40 percent in 2000.

Over the past 20 years the Salvadoran population has been subject to highly stressful conditions. A number of military coups (domestic takeovers of governments) in the 1970s and sham elections rigged in the army's favor diminished civilian confidence in the political system and spawned a violent guerilla movement (guerilla wars are fought by units with non-conventional military and political tactics). The 1980s were marked by a series of bloody conflicts between leftist rebels and right-wing paramilitary death squads who, with tacit support of the army, violently suppressed opposition. Over the course of the decade, 70,000 people were killed. Thousands fled the country, many coming to the United States. There are currently about 1 million Salvadorans living in the United States, many illegally or with uncertain legal status.

OVERVIEW OF ECONOMY

El Salvador's civil war, which lasted from 1979 until 1990, had a devastating impact on the country's economy. Rebel guerillas during the fight engaged in widespread sabotage, damaging the nation's **infrastructure** and undermining production and distribution. Export levels dropped during the war and earnings declined. Revenue losses during this period amounted to $2.2 billion.

Since the signing of the peace accord between the government and rebel factions in 1992, the economy has improved. Alfredo Cristiani, who as head of the Arena party became president in 1989, launched free market initiatives and tightened fiscal control. Competition was

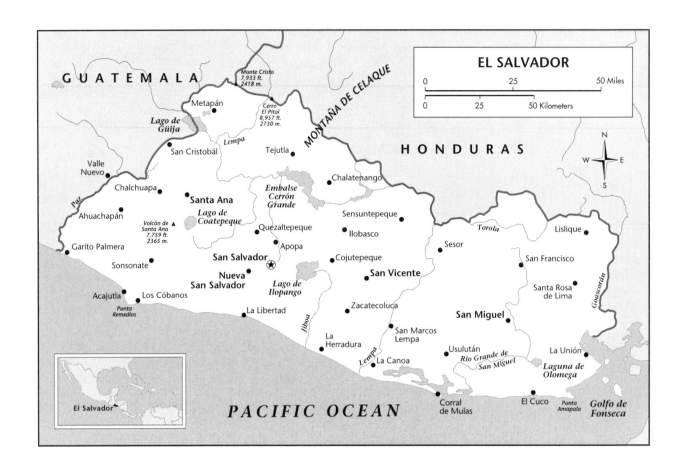

increased in a number of sectors; banks were **privatized**, import **duties** were lowered, and **price controls** on consumer products were virtually eliminated. Successive administrations have continued market **liberalization**. **Tariffs** were further reduced under Armando Calderon Sol, who was elected president in 1994. The Calderon administration also sought to strengthen intellectual property rights, and in 1998 the government privatized the country's main power plants and telecommunications firms, marking the most extensive efforts thus far to liberalize the economy.

Improvements in economic performance in the first half of the 1990s boosted investor confidence and led to a significant rise in the inflow of foreign capital. However, by 1995 the post-war boom was over, and the economy began to cool. Agriculture, once one of the country's primary export producers, registered little growth in the latter part of the 1990s, diminishing its role in the economy. The manufacturing industry, on the hand, grew rapidly during the 1990s, although by the end of the decade its performance, too, had begun to decline. In the late 1990s, no sectors registered significant gains. Overall, GDP growth rates fell: 4.0 percent in 1997, 2.6 percent in 1999, and to 2.5 in 2000.

Commercial and financial services are fast replacing industry and agriculture as the mainstays of the country's economy. As the once rural-based economy gives way to urban dominance, peasants are abandoning farm labor and moving toward the cities in search of higher paying jobs, leading to the development of shantytowns around many urban areas.

The growth in industry, primarily in the *maquila* sector (offshore assembly for **re-export**), added new jobs to the economy in the 1990s. However, a majority of those were taken by women. Unemployment among young males is still high, which some associate with El Salvador's high crime rates.

With no discovered reserves of oil or coal, the country is dependent on imports for fuel and energy. **Trade deficits** in El Salvador, while historically broad, widened in the 1990s. **Remittances** from Salvadorans working overseas, which in 1999 totaled US$1.6 billion, help to offset trade imbalances. However, at least a portion of the trade deficit is generally financed through borrowing, which adds to the country's debt.

Remittances from expatriates are the country's largest source of foreign currency, bringing in more money than all the traditional exports combined. Some of the cash inflows likely come from smuggling and drug-running operations. **Money laundering** is becoming prevalent as well. If El Salvador is unable or unwilling to crack down on these illicit operations, establishing favorable trade deals with the United States will become difficult.

Taxes also provide a significant source of revenue. The **value-added tax** (VAT), which was established in September 1992 at 10 percent, was raised to 12 percent in 1995 to offset losses from tariff reductions. The VAT accounts for more than half of all current government revenue. While tax collection is more efficient than it used to be, the system is still hampered by inefficiency and corruption.

POLITICS, GOVERNMENT, AND TAXATION

The political climate in El Salvador fundamentally changed in 1972 when the military overturned a national election that had been won by the Partido Democrata Cristiano (PDC). Groups of students, peasants, and members of the labor movement abandoned the electoral process, forming guerilla groups in opposition to military rule. Throughout the 1980s, rebels and government forces clashed. Attempts to suppress the rebellion by the army and paramilitary death squads were brutal but ultimately unsuccessful. In November 1989, the guerillas—under the party banner Frente Farabundo Marti para la Liberacion Nacional (FMLN)—launched an attack on the capital, San Salvador. The 2-week siege was effective, convincing government and business elites in El Salvador to seek an end to the war. Negotiations brokered by the UN resulted in the signing of a peace accord that went into effect on 16 January 1992. Members of the FMLN agreed to lay down their arms in return for political and military reforms, including a reduction in the size and role of the military. By the time the war had ended, 70,000 people had been killed.

In March of 1989, the right-wing party Alianza Republicana Nacionalista (Arena) won control of the presidency with its candidate, Alfredo Cristiani. Arena has held the executive branch ever since.

The Salvadoran constitution, enacted 23 December 1983, stipulates that the country be headed by a president and vice president who are elected to 5-year terms. The legislature is made up of an 84-member body elected every 3 years, which is responsible for taxes and the ratification of treaties signed by the executive. Members of the Supreme Court, El Salvador's highest judicial authority, are selected for fixed terms by members of the legislative assembly. El Salvador considers itself a representative democracy.

The Arena party, while controlling the executive branch, has been struggling to maintain its power in the legislature. The FMLN, since laying down its arms, has

become a force in mainstream politics. It captured 31 seats in the legislative assembly in 2000, making it the largest party in the **unicameral** (one chamber) congress. It has also gained control of the municipalities in most major cities, including San Salvador, giving it governing authority over about half the country at the local level. The FMLN's rise to power has forced Arena to abandon some of its far-right positions in an effort to gain legislative support for its policies.

The 1980s in El Salvador were marked by chronic trade deficits and fiscal imbalances. Expenditures outpaced revenues, destabilizing the currency and raising the rate of **inflation**. When Alfredo Cristiani came to office in 1989, he introduced fiscal austerity, liberalization, and privatization as a means to induce economic stability. He also passed a series of tax reforms to lure foreign investment, including the abolition of export tariffs on coffee and sugar. To offset losses from the cut, a 10 percent VAT was implemented in September of 1992. The VAT was increased to 12 percent in 1995 in order to fund cuts in the asset tax, which was revoked in 1994, and capital gains taxes, which were removed in 1996.

The VAT in 1999 accounted for over half of the government's revenue. Still, **public sector** revenues have suffered as tax collection has been persistently corrupt and inefficient.

Armando Calderon Sol, elected in 1994, expanded on the policies of the Cristiani administration, seeking higher investment by reducing import tariffs, accelerating the privatization of state assets, and introducing a **fixed exchange rate**. The Calderon administration privatized 75 percent of the country's 4 regional power plants and split up the national phone company, which was sold to consortia made up of private investors and local partners. The shift from a state-run to a liberal, market economy has continued under the current president, Francisco Flores, but economic growth has been slow.

INFRASTRUCTURE, POWER, AND COMMUNICATIONS

War, corruption, and general neglect have taken a toll on El Salvador's infrastructure, as have a string of earthquakes that hit the country at the beginning of 2001. Improvements are badly needed. There are 10,029 kilometers (6,232 miles) of roads in the country. Less than 1,999 kilometers (1,242 miles) of them are paved. The country's rural and secondary roads often become flooded during the 6-month rainy season. In the cities, population growth and a rise in vehicle ownership have increased traffic congestion.

There are 2 main highways in El Salvador, both of which cross the Lempa River. The bridges servicing the

Communications

Country	Newspapers	Radios	TV Sets[a]	Cable subscribers[a]	Mobile Phones[a]	Fax Machines[a]	Personal Computers[a]	Internet Hosts[b]	Internet Users[b]
	1996	1997	1998	1998	1998	1998	1998	1999	1999
El Salvador	48	464	675	N/A	18	N/A	N/A	1.17	40
United States	215	2,146	847	244.3	256	78.4	458.6	1,508.77	74,100
Mexico	97	325	261	15.7	35	3.0	47.0	23.02	1,822
Guatemala	33	79	126	28.5	10	N/A	8.3	1.26	65

[a]Data are from International Telecommunication Union, *World Telecommunication Development Report 1999* and are per 1,000 people.
[b]Data are from the Internet Software Consortium (http://www.isc.org) and are per 10,000 people.

SOURCE: World Bank. *World Development Indicators 2000.*

highways were destroyed by rebels during the war. Temporary spans were established to accommodate traffic, and in the late 1990s, efforts were underway to rebuild the bridges and repair smaller crossings along the 2 main routes. However, in 1998 the temporary bridges and the repair work were swept away in floods caused by Hurricane Mitch. The reconstruction project, financed by a US$90 million loan from Japan, is expected to be completed in 2001.

While road construction measures have been considered in order to facilitate travel and alleviate urban congestion, there is currently no specified transportation policy. In the 1990s, increased transportation spending resulted in few real improvements. Due to high levels of corruption in the administration of road contracts, several highway projects that got underway were never completed. The government has had a difficult time forcing contractors to meet deadlines and maintain adequate quality standards. In 1999 new legislation was being considered that would regulate bidding and require completion bonds for contracts.

Efforts were renewed to improve the road network in 1999. A construction project was initiated to build overpasses and new interchanges in the capital city to mitigate traffic problems. Other improvements were being considered as well, including the construction of 2 ring roads around the capital area and the creation of a special road fund which would finance highway improvements throughout the country. The fund, however, would likely depend on the creation of a new gasoline tax. As of March 2000, the time of mid-term elections, politicians in El Salvador had refused to acknowledge the need for such a tax, leaving the fund's creation in doubt. A string of earthquakes that struck El Salvador in January and February 2001 will also delay the implementation of road construction programs, as money and foreign aid will be diverted to more urgent reconstruction projects.

El Salvadorans are dependent on 3 main sources for their energy: hydroelectricity, geothermal power (including oil), and firewood. No deposits of oil or coal have been found. Thermal energy was widely utilized until the 1970s when rising world oil prices led to a higher dependence on hydroelectricity. About one-third of the country's energy consumption is still derived from oil imports.

The generation of electricity and the development of energy resources generally falls under the purview of the Comicion Ejecutiva Hidroelectrica del Rio Lempa (CEL), a state-run agency which recently privatized 4 of its regional distribution companies. CEL is also targeting 3 of its thermal generating plants for privatization. It is hoped that opening the market to competition will increase investment in the sector. Customers will likely reap long-term benefits as well, as electricity tariffs are reduced.

ECONOMIC SECTORS

El Salvador relies primarily on financial services and manufacturing for the generation of export revenue. Agriculture, once the country's dominant economic sector, has declined in importance but still plays a strong role in the economy. The economic **restructuring** which occurred over the 1980s and 1990s was undertaken to reduce volatility. Agricultural production was vulnerable to price declines and poor weather, prompting the government to reposition the economy in favor of more stable sources of revenue. The service and manufacturing industries were targeted for development.

Growth in the manufacturing sector was substantial in the 1990s, primarily due to the expansion of the *maquila* (offshore assembly for re-export) industry which has become the country's single largest category in terms of export revenue. Revenues generated by industry exports more than doubled in the last half of the decade. The CIA *World Factbook* estimated that by 1999 agriculture accounted for 12 percent of the GDP, industry 28 percent, and services 60 percent.

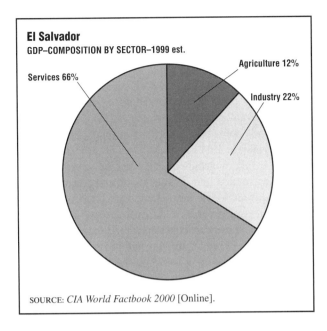

El Salvador
GDP–COMPOSITION BY SECTOR–1999 est.

Services 66%

Agriculture 12%

Industry 22%

SOURCE: *CIA World Factbook 2000* [Online].

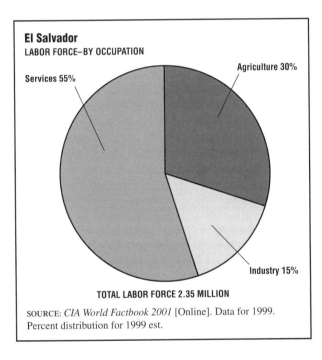

El Salvador
LABOR FORCE–BY OCCUPATION

Services 55%

Agriculture 30%

Industry 15%

TOTAL LABOR FORCE 2.35 MILLION

SOURCE: *CIA World Factbook 2001* [Online]. Data for 1999.
Percent distribution for 1999 est.

AGRICULTURE

Agriculture, while showing negligible growth towards the end of the 1990s, has continued to play a key role in the Salvadoran economy, employing nearly 25 percent of the country's **labor force**, providing a third of its export earnings, and meeting about 70 percent of domestic food needs. In 1996, agriculture accounted for 14 percent of the GDP. By 1999, agriculture accounted for 12 percent of the GDP, but employed nearly 30 percent of the labor force.

Prior to the 1980s most of the land in El Salvador was owned by a minority of wealthy elites. Roughly 70 percent of the farmers who worked the land were **share-croppers** or laborers on large plantations. This situation began to change in 1979, when a military-civilian junta came to power and issued sweeping land and agrarian reforms. The government carried out policies of property redistribution to address the grievances of the rural poor and make up for past injustices. Land was transferred to small farmers in an effort to create a rural middle class. By 1990, when the reforms came to an end, 22 percent of El Salvador's land had been transferred to farmers who had previously worked the land but did not own it. Over 500,000 farmers benefitted from the reforms.

El Salvador's mild climate and fertile soil have proven ideal for the production of the country's main export crops—coffee and sugar. Coffee production, which began on a mass scale in the 1850s, dominated the country's economy for over a century and is still the largest agricultural export, accounting for US$244 million in revenues in 1999, about 10 percent of all export earnings. Sugar, the next largest export, was responsible for about 2 percent of export revenues in 1999, bringing in approximately US$46 million. Fisheries have grown more important to the economy as well, mainly through shrimp production, which is third in agricultural export earnings behind coffee and sugar, generating US$25 million in revenues in 1999, a little over 1 percent of the total.

The earnings from agricultural exports as a percentage of the country's total export revenues diminished in the 1990s. Coffee revenues, especially, began to fall during this time. A surge in coffee prices in 1997 led to a brief revitalization in the sector, but poor harvests and falling prices in 1998 sent revenues plummeting. Between 1997 and 1999, coffee earnings dropped by over 50 percent. Improved harvests may raise coffee-generated revenues in the near future, but coffee will not likely regain the position it once held as a mainstay of the economy. Maize, beans, rice, and sorghum are food crops produced primarily for domestic consumption.

Cattle production plays a role, albeit a slight one, in the economy. Widespread cattle rustling and extortion have made ranching difficult, although milk production has increased.

INDUSTRY

The industrial sector of El Salvador accounted for 28 percent of the GDP and employed 15 percent of the labor force in 1999.

MINING. Mining currently plays a negligible role in the Salvadoran economy, accounting for just 0.3 percent of the GDP in 1997, with mineral production limited primarily to gypsum, sea salt, and construction materials such as limestone. While mineral deposits are thought to exist, there has been little attempt in the past 20 years to exploit them. The country had 2 gold mines in operation until the early 1980s: San Cristobal in Morazan province and El Dorado in Cabanas province. Both fell into disuse during the country's civil war. There has been some renewed interest in mineral exploration at the El Dorado mine. A joint mining venture between Mirage Resources, Bethlehem Resources, and Dejour Mines was launched in July 1993. Although San Cristobal is estimated to contain 200,000 tons of ore, including deposits of gold and silver, efforts have not been made to reestablish large-scale operations there.

MANUFACTURING. El Salvador's manufacturing base was established in the 1950s. As regional markets began to open in the 1960s as a result of the Mercado Comun Centroamericano (Central American Common Market, CACM), the industry began to expand. There was significant growth in the output of **capital goods** and chemicals in the 1970s, but manufacturing contracted in the 1980s as a result of the war and **recession**. The CACM began to collapse, there were shortages of foreign exchange, and the manufacturing base declined. The industry rebounded strongly in the 1990s primarily as a result of growth in the *maquila* sector. However, this growth steadied somewhat towards the end of the last decade as the industry matured. Expansion was also slowed by competition, especially from Mexico, which, as a party to NAFTA, receives trade benefits from the United States. Almost a dozen manufacturing plants in El Salvador closed in 1998. As of 1999, no new ones had opened.

Over the last 10 years, the *maquila* industry has emerged as the largest producer of export revenue in El Salvador, boosting manufacturing to 22 percent of the GDP. Production and export revenues from *maquila* doubled between 1994 and 1998, going from US$650 million to US$1.3 billion. Offshore production has become more important than local manufacturing, employing around 50,000 people, 85 percent of whom are women.

New opportunities have arisen since the 1990s from the revival of regional trade, yet Salvadoran manufacturers have been hard pressed to develop competitive advantages. Failure on the part of manufacturers to modernize operations, which some have blamed on the high cost of investment, have left local manufacturers vulnerable to increased competition. Compounding this liability was the failure to achieve a NAFTA parity agreement with the United States. (NAFTA is the North American Free Trade Agreement.) By enjoying a "parity agreement" under NAFTA, El Salvador would have had the same free trade benefits as NAFTA signatories Mexico and Canada.

CONSTRUCTION. After the peace accord was signed in 1992, construction levels in El Salvador rose, with the building industry growing at an average rate of 6.7 percent a year between 1992 and 1997. Growth peaked in 1994 at 11.5 percent. Due to such rapid expansion, supplies of new property began outpacing demands. Construction began on 6000 new homes in 1997 alone. Many housing and commercial units built during this period have yet to be sold. In 1998, growth slowed to 3.7 percent, and in 1999 it further declined to 2.2 percent amidst allegations of corruption and charges that the sector was being used as a front for money laundering. The Camara Salvadorena de la Industria de la Construccion (Casalco, the construction industry association) is marketing newly-built homes to Salvadoran expatriates in the United States. The earthquakes that hit El Salvador at the beginning of 2001 will also stimulate activity in the construction sector.

SERVICES

El Salvador's service sector was the most dominant sector in the late 1990s. It accounted for 60 percent of the GDP and employed 55 percent of the labor force in 1999.

TOURISM. Although El Salvador has a coastline of over 308 kilometers (191 miles) and is home to ancient ruins, tourism in the country is limited. As of 2000, there had been no major initiatives launched to spur growth in the sector.

FINANCIAL SERVICES. A primary component of the Salvadoran economy is the financial services sector, which has grown rapidly in recent years as the dependence on agricultural exports has declined. The sector registered an annual growth rate of 9.6 percent between 1995 and 1999.

In November 1998, the central bank in El Salvador increased bank reserve requirements by 3 percent. The increase was phased in over 5 months to reduce the available money supply and slow inflation. As a result, the average **reserve ratio** rose from 21 percent to 24 percent. Banks raised interest rates to make up for lost **liquidity**, and the economy slowed. In 1999, requirement rates were restored to their previous levels. A drop in interest rates could help quicken the rate of economic growth.

The rise in bank reserve ratios may also have been implemented to keep banks from overextending themselves. Bank failures in the 1990s lowered client confidence and small banks have suffered as a result, with many depositors transferring funds to the country's 3 or 4 largest institutions.

INTERNATIONAL TRADE

War and civil unrest in El Salvador during the 1980s disrupted production, undermined the export sector, and raised the demand for imported goods. As import levels

Trade (expressed in billions of US$): El Salvador

	Exports	Imports
1975	.531	.614
1980	.967	.966
1985	.679	.961
1990	.582	1.263
1995	.998	2.853
1998	1.263	3.112

SOURCE: International Monetary Fund. *International Financial Statistics Yearbook 1999.*

ment was signed. Mexican industries have become increasingly interested in Central American markets, primarily for the distribution of household appliances, processed foods, clothing, and footwear. Under the terms of NAFTA, trade agreements between Mexico and her neighbors must gain U.S. approval.

El Salvador, at least in the near term, will probably not succeed in its bid to gain NAFTA parity for its exports. NAFTA parity would benefit El Salvador by making merchandise shipped to the United States more competitive. Rising levels of drug trafficking and organized crime in El Salvador could complicate future bids for export parity.

MONEY

Stabilizing El Salvador's currency and keeping inflation down are key components in the government's plan to attract foreign investment. In 1994, the colon was fixed at ¢8.755 = US$1. Strong reserves allowed the Central Bank to maintain the fixed exchange rate. Bank reserves in 1999 were US$1.97 billion, nearly 4 times what they were in 1992, when reserves stood at US$501 million. The end of the civil war, privatization of state assets, and strong family remittances have fueled the growth in reserves, which rose US$204 million in 1999 alone.

On 1 January 2001, the government in El Salvador gave up control of its **monetary policy**. It abandoned the fixed exchange rate and "dollarized" the economy. Thus, U.S. currency can be used in El Salvador as legal tender. El Salvadoran monetary policy is now effectively in the hands of the U.S. Federal Reserve Bank.

Proponents of dollarization say it will keep the currency stable and help drive interest rates down. Critics argue that the export sector could be hurt by the move. They point out that exporters are having trouble maintaining market share in the global economy. Converting to the dollar, they argue, might lock in this competitive disadvantage.

began to surge in the early 1990s, the trade deficit grew, reaching US$1.7 billion in 1995, about 15.4 percent of the GDP. By 1999, the deficit had narrowed slightly to US$1.6 billion, accounting for 13.3 percent of the GDP.

Total exports in 1999 amounted to around US$2.5 billion, and imports were about US$4.1 billion. These amounts rose to US$2.8 billion for exports and US$4.6 billion for imports by 2000, according to the *World Factbook*. Over the years, El Salvador's trade imbalance has been partially offset by family remittances. However, continuing deficits have forced the country to rely on foreign aid to pay for consumption.

El Salvador is dependent on the United States for a majority of its trade. Exports to the United States grew steadily over the latter part of the 1990s, climbing from US$844 million in 1995 to US$1.5 billion in 1999. By the end of the decade exports to the United States accounted for 63 percent of the total. Imports of U.S. goods grew as well during this period, though not as dramatically, rising from US$1.7 billion in 1995 to about US$2.1 billion in 1999. As of 1999, about 52 percent of Salvadoran imports came from the United States.

El Salvador's largest trading partner behind the United States is Guatemala, which accounts for about 11 percent of its exports and 9 percent of its imports. The remaining trade is conducted primarily with Germany, Japan, Costa Rica, Honduras, the Netherlands, Mexico, and Panama. El Salvador's main exports include coffee, sugar, and shrimp, as well as textiles and products derived from offshore assembly.

The Triangulo del Norto (Northern Triangle, or NT, consisting of El Salvador, Guatemala, and Honduras) has negotiated a free trade agreement with Mexico pending approval from the United States. Talks with Mexico stalled in 1998 when NT countries demanded they be given up to 15 years of preferential access to Mexican markets to allow local industries time to retool and to mitigate near-term trade imbalances which might arise from an influx of Mexican goods. Disputes blocking the deal were resolved in the latter part of 2000, and an agree-

Exchange rates: El Salvador

Salvadoran colones per US$1

Jan 2001	8.755
2000	8.755
1999	8.755
1998	8.755
1997	8.755
1996	8.755

Note: Salvadoran currency has been at a fixed rate since 1993.

SOURCE: CIA *World Factbook 2001* [ONLINE].

POVERTY AND WEALTH

The wealth in El Salvador is held by a small minority of the population who made their money from coffee and sugar and have now diversified into finance and commerce. Land reforms and property redistribution in the 1980s improved the situation for many small farmers and peasants, but there is still a substantial divide between the rich and the poor. According to a report from the U.S. Agency for International Development (USAID), El Salvador's per capita income is the fifth lowest in the Western Hemisphere (when adjusted to reflect the cost of living).

The health-care system in El Salvador is in a state of disarray. Medical unions are resisting government moves toward privatization, and as a result strikes by hospital personnel have become common. Supplies of basic drugs and medical equipment are often inadequate. Hospital budgets are used up to pay salaries, with little left over for other costs. Still, general health trends have managed to improve over the last 30 years. The infant mortality rate, though still high, has fallen by over 70 percent in the last 3 decades, from 105 per 1,000 live births in 1970 to 31 per 1,000 in 1997. During the same period, life expectancy increased from 57.4 to 69.1 years. The death rate for children under 5 remains high at 81 per 1,000.

The education system in El Salvador is weak. According to the USAID report published in 1998, less than 50 percent of Salvadorans graduate from the sixth grade, only 1 out of 3 complete the ninth grade, and only 1 out of 5 complete high school. The Ministry of Education has worked to improve the quality of schooling in El Salvador, and some of its efforts have met with success. The Economist Intelligence Unit (EIU) reported in 2000 that programs designed to increase community participation in education at rural schools has increased student enrollment. The school day has been extended as well. Also, in 1995 a program was introduced integrating health care and public works agencies with education initiatives to ensure students had clean water, regular medical examinations, and nutritional monitoring.

Distribution of Income or Consumption by Percentage Share: El Salvador

Lowest 10%	1.2
Lowest 20%	3.4
Second 20%	7.5
Third 20%	12.5
Fourth 20%	20.2
Highest 20%	56.5
Highest 10%	40.5

Survey year: 1996
Note: This information refers to income shares by percentiles of the population and is ranked by per capita income.

SOURCE: *2000 World Development Indicators* [CD-ROM].

El Salvador is highly polluted and suffers from severe environmental degradation. By some estimates, only 59 percent of the population has access to safe drinking water. That figure is likely optimistic. Recent studies have shown that the Lempa river, the country's main potable water source, is contaminated with dangerously high levels of mercury and other heavy metals.

The earthquakes that struck El Salvador in January and February 2001 have made matters worse for the poor. Many were left homeless. Social services have been cut or delayed. The Flores administration has its work cut out for it. Its leadership, or lack thereof, during this crisis will likely determine the future political landscape in El Salvador.

WORKING CONDITIONS

A number of labor laws exist in El Salvador to protect the rights of workers. Some of these laws are enforced more than others. The Ministry of Labor, responsible for upholding labor-related statutes, has limited resources and, as a government agency, has at times been accused of bias when dealing with government-union conflicts.

According to the constitution, workers are guaranteed the right to unionize without the threat of harassment or discrimination. However, this right has not always been recognized. When the government telecommunications firm, CTE, was put up for sale in the 1990s, 72 labor leaders were fired to keep the company union-free for potential purchasers. When the workers appealed, the Ministry of Labor sided with the government on dubious grounds.

Because of its limited resources, the Ministry of Labor cannot conduct thorough labor inspections throughout the country, especially outside the manufacturing districts, and worker complaints of mistreatment, though not altogether common, frequently go uninvestigated.

GDP per Capita (US$)

Country	1975	1980	1985	1990	1998
El Salvador	1,779	1,596	1,333	1,378	1,716
United States	19,364	21,529	23,200	25,363	29,683
Mexico	3,380	4,167	4,106	4,046	4,459
Guatemala	1,371	1,598	1,330	1,358	1,533

SOURCE: United Nations. *Human Development Report 2000; Trends in human development and per capita income.*

Forced labor is generally prohibited by law, although in cases of calamity or national emergency the government can make exceptions. Child labor is prohibited. Children below the age 14 are not allowed to enter the workforce. Minors between the ages of 14 and 18 may work with permission from the Ministry of Labor if their employment is indispensable to either themselves or their family. Many children under 14 work despite the laws, either as street vendors or doing general labor for small businesses in the **informal sector**.

The minimum wage in El Salvador varies depending on the industry. Set by a tripartite commission (consisting of members of government, labor, and business), the minimum wage per day as of 1 May 1998 was US$4.81 for commercial, industrial, and service employees. Coffee plantation workers received US$3.66 plus a food allowance, and sugar and cotton plantation workers were paid US$2.61 plus a food allowance. All other agro-industrial workers were paid a minimum of US$2.47 per day. The minimum wage does not provide a decent standard of living for either individuals or their families.

Workers are on the job 6 days a week, for 8 hours a day. They get paid, however, for 7 days (56 hours) of work each week. Minors between age 14 and 18 are required to work no more than 6 hours a day. Employers are required to provide 1 month's wage per year as a bonus to workers, who are also supposed to be given 2 weeks of paid vacation a year.

COUNTRY HISTORY AND ECONOMIC DEVELOPMENT

1524. The Spanish first attempt to subjugate the territory of what is now El Salvador.

1821. El Salvador gains independence.

1822. El Salvador refuses to join union with Mexico, insists on maintaining its independence.

1823. The country joins the Central American Federation under General Manuel Jose Arce.

1838. The Central American Federation collapses. El Salvador becomes an independent republic.

1850s. El Salvador begins large-scale production of coffee after the discovery of synthetic dyes renders indigo production unprofitable.

1972. Jose Napoleon Duarte, leader of the Christian Democratic Party, wins the presidential election. The election is overturned by the military. Guerilla groups are formed in opposition to military rule.

1977. Right-wing government of General Carlos Humberto Romero comes to power.

1979. Leftist guerilla warfare breaks out in the cities and in the countryside and results in a 12-year civil war. Reform-minded military officers and civilian leaders unite and oust Romero, forming a revolutionary junta.

1980. Duarte, who has returned after being tortured and exiled in 1972, joins the junta.

1982. Salvadorans elect a new constituent assembly.

1983. The assembly drafts a new constitution strengthening individual rights.

1984. Duarte, head of the Nationalist Republican Alliance (Arena), becomes the first freely-elected president in over 50 years.

1989. Arena's Alfredo Cristiani wins the presidency. Talks are initiated in September between government and the Farabundo Marti National Liberation Front (FMLN). Talks break down in November when FMLN guerillas launch a nationwide offensive.

1990. The UN steps in to mediate the conflict. El Salvador allows its **exchange rate** to float.

1991. The New York accord is signed by both sides, setting up a framework for peace. The banking system is re-privatized.

1992. A final peace agreement is signed. The FMLN lays down its arms, transforming itself into a mainstream political party. A value-added tax is instituted at 10 percent.

1994. Armando Calderon Sol of the Arena party takes over the presidency. He introduces reforms aimed at liberalizing the economy, including the privatization of state assets. He also institutes monetary stability.

1995. A plan to dollarize the economy fails. The VAT is increased to 13 percent. The economy starts to slow.

1996. Laws to facilitate privatization of state assets are passed.

1998. State sells 4 of its regional electricity distributors. The state telecoms are broken up. Social security privatization begins.

1999. Francisco Flores of the Arena party becomes president.

2001. Earthquakes hit, damaging homes and infrastructure, killing many people. The government dollarizes the economy.

FUTURE TRENDS

El Salvador's future is uncertain. It is a country besieged by poverty and corruption. Crime rates are high, the standard of living is low, services are scarce, and health care is inadequate. A series of natural disasters have worsened already poor conditions. Hurricane Mitch in 1998 and earthquakes in January and February of 2001 damaged the country's infrastructure, slowed the economy, and destroyed thousands of homes, leaving many in El Salvador, especially the poor, in dire straits. Road and infrastructure improvements will now have to be delayed as funds are diverted to general reconstruction projects. The administration under President Francisco Flores will be tested by the current situation. Flores has already been accused of allocating economic aid along partisan political lines, and his ability to effectively steer the country out of the current crisis will affect his chances for reelection in 2004.

El Salvador has signed a trade agreement with Mexico which will grant Salvadoran exports preferential access to Mexican markets. Trade agreements with the Dominican Republic and Chile should be ratified in 2001–02, which could help boost the economy. What is certain is that solid economic performance will depend on continued growth in the manufacturing and services sectors, whose expansion after the cease-fire helped fuel the postwar boom. Where El Salvador is most vulnerable is in its dependence on U.S. markets, which account for nearly 60 percent of its exports. A high performing U.S. economy will guarantee El Salvador good export earnings. A downturn in the U.S. economy, however, will lower the demand for imports, diminishing one of El Salvador's main sources of foreign exchange.

El Salvador will continue to battle unemployment among young males, which, according to some analysts, has contributed to high crime rates. Smuggling, drug trafficking, and money laundering, if left unchecked, will likely complicate relations with the United States and preclude future trade arrangements.

DEPENDENCIES

El Salvador has no territories or colonies.

BIBLIOGRAPHY

Economist Intelligence Unit. *Country Profile: El Salvador, 2000.* London: Economist Intelligence Unit, 2000.

Embassy of El Salvador, Washington, D.C. <http://www .elsalvador.org/english/index.htm>. Accessed October 2001.

U.S. Agency for International Development. *The USAID FY 1998 Congressional Presentation: El Salvador.* <http://www .usaid.gov/pubs/cp98/lac/countries/sv.htm>. Accessed February 2001.

U.S. Central Intelligence Agency. *World Factbook 2001: El Salvador.* <http:www.odci.gov/cia/publications/factbook/geos/ es.html>. Accessed October 2001.

U.S. Department of State, Bureau of Western Hemisphere Affairs. *Background Notes: El Salvador.* <http://www.state .gov/www/background_notes/elsal_0008_bgn.html>. Accessed February 2001.

U.S. Department of State. *Country Reports on Human Rights Practices, 1999: El Salvador.* <http://www.state.gov/g/drl/rls/ hrrpt/1999/index.cfm?docid=386>. Accessed February 2001.

—*John Mazor*

FRENCH ANTILLES
AND FRENCH GUIANA

French Guiana
Martinique
Guadeloupe

CAPITAL: French Guiana: Cayenne; **Martinique:** Fort-de-France; **Guadeloupe:** Basse-Terre.

MONETARY UNIT: French franc (F). 1 franc equals 100 centimes. Notes are available in denominations of 20, 50, 100, 200, and 500 francs. Coins are in denominations of 5, 10, 20, and 50 centimes, and 1, 2, 5, 10, and 20 francs.

CHIEF EXPORTS: French Guiana: Shrimp, timber, gold, rum, rosewood essence; **Martinique:** Refined petroleum products, bananas, rum; **Guadeloupe:** Bananas, sugar, and rum.

CHIEF IMPORTS: French Guiana: Food (grains, processed meat), machinery and transport equipment, fuels, chemicals; **Martinique:** Petroleum products, crude oil, foodstuffs, construction materials, vehicles, clothing, other consumer goods; **Guadeloupe:** Foodstuffs, fuels, vehicles, clothing and other consumer goods, construction material.

GROSS DOMESTIC PRODUCT: French Guiana: US$1 billion; **Martinique:** US$4.39 billion; **Guadeloupe:** US$3.7 billion (all in purchasing power parity, 1997 est.).

BALANCE OF TRADE: Exports: *French Guiana,* US$155 million; *Martinique,* US$250 million; *Guadeloupe,* US$140 million (all f.o.b., 1997). **Imports:** *French Guiana,* US$625 million; *Martinique,* US$2 billion; *Guadeloupe,* US$1.7 billion (all c.i.f., 1997).

COUNTRY OVERVIEW

LOCATION AND SIZE. French Guiana, Martinique, and Guadeloupe are each separate overseas departments of France. Martinique and Guadeloupe are collectively referred to as the French Antilles, while the 3 countries together comprise the 3 Caribbean Departments of France. Located in northern South America, French Guiana is bordered by Brazil to the south and the east, the Atlantic Ocean to the north, and Suriname to the west. The total area of French Guiana is 91,000 square kilometers (35,135 square miles), rendering it slightly smaller than Indiana, while the coastline spans 378 kilometers (235 miles). Cayenne, the capital of the country, is situated slightly east of the center point along the coastline.

Martinique, a small island that lies between Dominica and St. Lucia in the eastern Caribbean sea, has a total area of 1,103 square kilometers (426 square miles). The capital of Martinique, Fort-de-France, is situated on the northern tip of the island. Martinique is about 6 times the size of Washington D.C.

Guadeloupe, which actually consists of an archipelago of 9 inhabited islands, is also located in the east Caribbean sea, to the north of Martinique, south of the British island Montserrat. The islands of Guadeloupe, including the French part of the island of Saint Martin that is divided with the Netherlands (whose southern portion is named Sint Maarten and is part of the Netherlands Antilles), have a total area of 1,780 square kilometers (687 square miles). The capital of Guadeloupe, the town of Basse-Terre, is located on one of the 9 islands with the same name. Comparatively, Guadeloupe is about 10 times the size of Washington, D.C.

POPULATION. The total population of French Guiana was estimated at 172,605 in 2000, a 4.0 percent increase from the population of 115,930 in 1990. In 2000, the total birth rate was 22.4 births per 1,000 people, while the death rate was reported at 4.76 deaths per 1,000 people. In the same year, life expectancy was estimated at 76.1 years for the total population. With a net migration rate estimated at 11.59 migrants per 1,000 people in 2000, a significant number of French Guianese leave the country in search of opportunities abroad as a result of high levels of unemployment. Still, population growth is quite high and the government has taken measures to increase

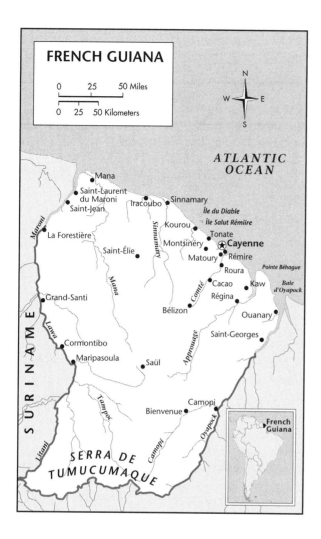

FRENCH GUIANA

0   25   50 Miles

0   25   50 Kilometers

N
W   E
S

ATLANTIC
OCEAN

Mana
Saint-Laurent
du Maroni   Sinnamary
Saint-Jean   Iracoubo
Île du Diable
Île Salut Rémire
Kourou
La Forestière   Tonate
Montsinéry   Cayenne
Saint-Élie   Matoury   Rémire
Roura   Pointe Béhague
Cacao   Kaw   Baie
Régina   d'Oyapock
Grand-Santi   Bélizon
Ouanary
Cormontibo   Saint-Georges
Maripasoula   Saül
SURINAME
Maroni
Lawa
Sinnamary
Mana
Comté
Approuague
Camopi
Bienvenue
SERRA DE
TUMUCUMAQUE
Tampoc
Litani
Camopi
Oyapock

French
Guiana

knowledge and availability of birth control in all the Caribbean Departments of France (CDF). Population growth rates are expected to decline considerably in the near future, reaching 2.1 percent between 2000–10 and 1.3 percent between 2010 and 2020, at which time the population is expected to equal 244,440. The age structure of the population is generally young, with 31 percent of the population between the ages of 0–14 years, 64 percent between the ages of 15–64 years, and only 5 percent over 65 years (2000 est.).

The total population of Guadeloupe was reported at 426,493 in 2000, a 1.2 percent increase from the population of 377,678 in 1990. Similarly, the total population of Martinique was reported at 414,516 in 2000, an increase of 1.0 percent from the population of 373,565 in 1990. Also in 2000, the birth rate in the French Antilles was estimated at 17.25 births per 1,000 people, while the death rate was 6.01 deaths per 1,000 people. Life expectancy for the average person from the French Antilles was 76.99 years. About 25 percent of all persons from the French Antilles are under 14 years of age, 66 percent are between the ages of 15–64 years, and only 9 percent are 65 years and over (2000). For the French Antilles and

French Guiana, young populations have confronted the government with the major task of creating employment to accommodate young workers entering the market. Unemployment rates are exceptionally high (above 20 percent for all 3 departments). With a net migration ratio of -0.15 migrant(s) per 1,000 people in 2000, migration levels are low, despite the high levels of unemployment. As in French Guiana, the population growth is expected to decline considerably over the next 20 years in the French Antilles, from 0.9 percent between 2000 to 2010 and 0.7 percent between 2010 and 2020 in Guadeloupe; and 0.8 percent and 0.5 percent between the same periods in Martinique. The population of Guadeloupe is expected to reach 499,215 in 2020, while the population of Martinique is expected to reach 469,724.

The vast majority of the inhabitants of Martinique and Guadeloupe are of African or mixed African/European ancestry (90 percent). Persons of European ancestry form about 5 percent of the populations of both departments, while the remaining population consists mostly of persons of East Indian, Lebanese, and Chinese descent. Comprising 66 percent of the population in French Guiana, persons of African or mixed ancestry constitute a smaller majority of the population than their compatriots in the French Antilles. Other ethnic groups in French Guiana include persons of European descent (12 percent), Amerindians (12 percent), and persons of East Indian and Chinese descent. Almost all the inhabitants of the 3 separate departments speak French, though many communicate primarily in the French dialect (patois) known as Creole. Approximately 95 percent of the populations of French Guiana and the French Antilles are Roman Catholic.

OVERVIEW OF ECONOMY

The territories that now comprise the 3 Caribbean Departments of France (CDF) were for the most part settled by French settlers throughout the 17th century. The original Carib inhabitants of the islands in the French Antilles were mostly wiped out by the settlers, who subsequently established an economic system based on large sugar plantations and imported African slave labor. Slavery based on African bondage formed the basis of the economy in French Guiana as well, though a significant number of indigenous peoples survived the French onslaught. France abolished slavery in 1848, after which time thousands of Indian and Chinese migrants came to the French Caribbean territories to supplement the newly freed **labor force** on the plantations. The French Caribbean territories continued under colonial rule until 1946, when they became official French departments.

Throughout the post-war period, the economies of the CDF have benefitted from high **subsidies** from the

French government (the French mainland is referred to as the metropolis). According to the Canadian Department of Foreign Affairs (DFAIT) *A Guide for Canadian Exporters* (1997), for instance, French government transfers in the form of salaries, grants, and social welfare equaled approximately 55 percent of the combined GDP of the CDF in 1996. As such, many areas of activity in the economies of the CDF are controlled by the government, although there is certainly much free-market activity. In this sense, the CDF are similar to the larger French economy, which is characterized by a mixed economic system that consists of both public and private economic activity. Indeed, of the 4 largest industrialized economies in the world, France has the highest rate of public economic activity.

Economic policies of the 3 departments have generally been export-oriented, with the vast majority of exports being directed towards France, each other, and other EU members. Exports from the CDF consist mainly of agricultural products. Imports of the CDF consist mostly of higher **value-added** goods, such as machinery, construction equipment, and vehicles, which are more expensive than agricultural commodities. Moreover, since none of the CDF are sufficient in terms of food production, they must import large quantities of foodstuffs. As a result of these factors, the CDF run large **balance of payments** deficits which have led to the accumulation of massive debts. Fortunately, France has helped alleviate debt through annual transfers of aid, thereby preventing the CDF from falling into the **structural adjustment program** (SAP) trap that has negatively affected most of the developing world. SAPs are packages of conditions that developing countries must implement in return for **debt-servicing** funds from the World Bank and the International Monetary Fund (IMF). SAP conditions intended to increase revenue to pay back loans—such as cuts to social spending—have been severely detrimental to the populations of developing countries.

Despite the generous French subsidies designed to encourage development, industrial growth has been slow in the CDF, while unemployment rates remain exceedingly high. The majority of the inhabitants in the CDF are engaged in the service sector, which is also the largest contributor to GDP. In terms of employment and contribution to GDP, industry is the second leading sector, though agriculture remains highly important.

In 1986, the French government adopted a legislative program designed to stimulate the productive sectors of the CDF. The program, which included tax incentives and subsidies for new construction and business investment, has helped stimulate the CDF economies, though they remain subsidy-dependent and agriculturally export-oriented. Further pro-business reforms implemented in the 1990s led to the creation of numerous industrial and commercial zones across the CDF, characterized by tax and import **duty** exemptions.

POLITICS, GOVERNMENT, AND TAXATION

As overseas departments of France, the French Antilles and French Guiana are incorporated into the French political system. As such, the executive branch of the CDF is currently headed by the French president Jacques Chirac, who is represented by a prefect in each respective department. The French legal system and the French constitution are applicable in the CDF, and the Court of Appeals, located in Martinique, has jurisdiction over all the CDF as the highest local court. As semi-autonomous departments, however, the CDF each have a **unicameral** General Council and a unicameral Regional Council, the presidents of which constitute the heads of government. Both councils are elected by popular vote, generally for a 6-year term. Each department also sends representatives to the French National Assembly and to the Senate.

Mainstream leftist parties in the French tradition have dominated politics in the CDF throughout the postwar era. In French Guiana, the Guianese Socialist Party controls both councils, while the General Council and the Regional Council in Martinique are ruled by the leftist parties, the Progressive Martinique Party and the Martinique Communist Party. In Guadeloupe, the General Council is headed by the left-wing Progressive Democratic Party, while the presidency of the Regional Council is headed by the gaullist (right-wing) Rally for the Republic. The presidency of a rightist candidate represents a discontinuity in Guadeloupian politics, though it can be explained by the inability of 2 **socialist** groupings in the council to co-operate effectively. Recent elections for all the councils in all the CDF took place at various points in the late 1990s. Major themes in the politics of the CDF revolve around the economy and the high levels of unemployment. A wide variety of rightist and centrist parties are represented in the councils. There are also a number of small separatist political parties in each CDF, though most parties acknowledge economic dependency on France and are content with seeking further autonomy without independence.

There are 6 tax brackets in the CDF, with taxation rates progressively increasing according to income. Most people are taxed in the bottom tax bracket, however. In Martinique, for example, 118,989 individuals were taxed at the lowest bracket of income, which encompasses those who earn between 0 to 7,624 euros, while 17,341 were taxed at the next lowest bracket and only 6,462 were taxed at the highest (2000 est.). In terms of duties on imports, **tariffs** in the CDF are generally set at the same level as tariffs in metropolitan France. As such, tariff rates fall into 2 categories: **liberalized** imports and non-liberalized imports. Tariffs for the former are generally low, while tariffs on the latter can be as high as 73 percent, in the case of cigarettes, and up to 40 percent in the case of alcohol.

INFRASTRUCTURE, POWER, AND COMMUNICATIONS

Infrastructure in the CDF varies according to the type and the specific department. Railways are entirely absent from both Martinique and French Guiana, though Guadeloupe has some private railway lines, all of which are small-gauge and used for commercial purposes. In terms of paved roads, the islands of the French Antilles collectively have about 3,000 kilometers of paved road network (est. 1997), while French Guiana only has 727 kilometers (est. 1995). The lack of roads and railway in the latter are largely explained by the density of the rainforest, which covers 90 percent of all land. Guadeloupe has a total of 8 airports with permanent surface runways (est. 1997), while French Guiana has 4 airports with paved runways (est. 1999), and Martinique only has 2 (est. 1997). Airlines that operate services to and from the French Antilles include Air France, Air Martinique, Air Caraibes, Air Guadeloupe, and Air Canada.

The French Antilles have ports at Fort-de-France on Martinique, and Basse-Terre and Point-a-Pitre on Guadeloupe. The containerization port on Basse-Terre has a quay length of 250 meters (820 feet) with a depth of water alongside of 10 meters (32.8 feet), while the containerization port on Pointe-a-Pitre, the largest in Guadeloupe, has a considerable capacity of 16 berths and wharves with a total berthing space of 2,000 meters (6,562 feet). French Guiana has ports on Cayenne, Degrad des Cannes, and Saint-Laurent du Maroni (est. 1997).

According to the DFAIT *A Guide for Canadian Exporters,* telecommunications in the French Antilles are generally inadequate. It can take up to a week, for example, to obtain usage of a fax or telephone in certain places. In Guadeloupe, there were only 159,000 telephones in 1995, while there were 68,900 telephones in Martinique in the same year. With a total of 159,000 main telephone lines in use in 1995 and a population of 172,605 in 2000, the telecommunications system in French Guiana is considerably more developed than in the French Antilles.

Producing all of their electricity domestically through fossil fuels, none of the CDF import electricity from abroad. Total electricity consumption in Guadeloupe was 1.135 billion kilowatt hours (kWh) in 1998, 588 million kWh in Martinique in 1992, and 430 million kWh in French Guiana in 1998. All of French Guiana's electricity is generated from a single dam at Petit Saut. Both the telecommunications sector and the electricity sector are **monopolized** by the French government through **parastatal** control.

ECONOMIC SECTORS

Throughout the colonial period, the economies of the CDF were dominated by sugar production on large plantations. Currently, agriculture has been largely replaced in importance by the service and industry sectors, though the latter remains considerably underdeveloped. Key industries in the CDF include food processing activities in the French Antilles, construction in Guadeloupe, and gold mining in French Guiana. Service-oriented activities are by far the largest contributors to GDP and employment in the CDF, with significant percentages of the labor forces of all 3 departments working in the government bureaucracy. Tourism and **retail** are also important activities in the service sector.

Communications

Country	Telephones[a]	Telephones, Mobile/Cellular[a]	Radio Stations[b]	Radios[a]	TV Stations[a]	Televisions[a]	Internet Service Providers[c]	Internet Users[c]
French Guiana and French Antilles	47,000	N/A	AM 2; FM 14; shortwave 6	104,000	3	30,000	2	2,000
United States	194 M	69.209 M (1998)	AM 4,762; FM 5,542; shortwave 18	575 M	1,500	219 M	7,800	148 M
Brazil	17.039 M	4.4 M	AM 1,365; FM 296; shortwave 161 (1999)	71 M	138	36.5 M	50	8.65 M
Suriname	64,000	4,090	AM 4; FM 13; shortwave 1	300,000	3 (2000)	63,000	2	10,000

[a]Data is for 1997 unless otherwise noted.
[b]Data is for 1998 unless otherwise noted.
[c]Data is for 2000 unless otherwise noted.

SOURCE: CIA *World Factbook 2001* [Online].

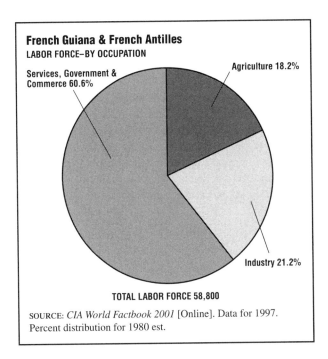

French Guiana & French Antilles
LABOR FORCE–BY OCCUPATION

Services, Government & Commerce 60.6%

Agriculture 18.2%

Industry 21.2%

TOTAL LABOR FORCE 58,800

SOURCE: *CIA World Factbook 2001* [Online]. Data for 1997. Percent distribution for 1980 est.

The CIA *World Factbook* estimated the percentage of each sector's contribution to GDP. In Martinique, the agriculture sector accounted for 6 percent, the industry sector 11 percent, and the service sector 83 percent in 1997. In Guadeloupe, the agriculture sector accounted for 15 percent, the industry sector 17 percent, and the service sector 68 percent in 1997. No recent information was available for French Guiana.

AGRICULTURE

Agriculture continues to play an integral, albeit declining, role in the CDF, especially in terms of generating revenue through exports. At the same time, however, none of the CDF are self-sufficient in food production, which means that they have to spend large annual amounts on importing foodstuffs. Most food is imported from France. Agriculture in the French Antilles periodically suffers from the devastating hurricanes that afflict the Caribbean. In 1998, for example, the French Antilles were affected by Hurricane George, and, in 1999 and 2000, hurricanes Jose and Lenny.

GUADELOUPE. In Guadeloupe, agriculture constituted 6 percent of GDP and employed 15 percent of the workforce in 1997, which equaled approximately 120,000. Agricultural produce includes bananas, sugarcane, tropical fruits and vegetables, cattle, pigs, and goats. Large sugar plantations that produce for both export and local consumption purposes continue to dominate, though many have been turned over to the cultivation of bananas. In 2000, the latter accounted for 82 percent of Guadeloupe's total exports, as opposed to 75 percent in 1998.

In 2000, 121,758 tons of bananas were exported, 72 percent of which were purchased by the French metropolis. Sugarcane production—Guadeloupe's second most important export—declined by 6 percent (674,822 tons) in 2000 as a result of excessive rain in cultivating regions. Melons, the third largest agricultural export, have increased enormously in production in the past 6 years, rising from 2,561 tons in 1995 to 4,939 tons in 2000.

An estimated 36 percent of the total area of the islands of Guadeloupe are cultivable arable lands, while 10 percent are pasture and 15 percent woodland (1997). Offshore fishing is a traditional source of food, and the main catches include lobster, crab, and octopus. By the end of the 1990s, 11 fishing farms were registered in Guadeloupe and experiments are under way to catch and market sea bream and grayling fish in order to respond to growing demand.

MARTINIQUE. In 1997, agriculture constituted 6 percent of GDP in Martinique and employed 10 percent of the workforce, which equaled approximately 100,000. Agricultural activity is centered on the production of sugar cane, pineapples, and bananas, mainly for industrial processing and export. In 1997, exports of bananas represented 40 percent of Martinique's total exports. Crops such as sweet potatoes, yams, manioc, beans, cabbages, and tomatoes are grown primarily for domestic consumption. The majority of farms in Martinique are privately run by **small-holders**. An estimated 48 percent of the total area of the islands of Martinique are cultivable arable lands, while 25 percent are forest, and 19 percent savannah (1997). Virtually all of Martinique's meat requirements are met by imports. Fishing of lobster, crayfish, crabs, and clams are important for domestic consumption.

FRENCH GUIANA. According to the CIA *World Factbook*, recent statistics on agricultural contribution to GDP and employment in French Guiana are unavailable (nor are they available for other sectoral contributions to GDP and employment). In 1980, however, approximately 18.2 percent of the Guianese workforce engaged in agriculture. Cultivation in French Guiana, where the land is mostly rainforest, is limited to the coastal area. Only 0.18 percent of the land is thus cultivated, with production being dominated by subsistence crops such as rice, maize, and bananas. Sugar cane is also grown for rum production, which is an important, albeit declining, export. Land tenure in French Guiana is highly unequal, with 56 percent and 3 percent of all farming operations occupying 13 percent and 57 percent of the land, respectively.

With shrimp accounting for approximately 50 percent of annual export trading value throughout the 1990s, fishing is the most important agricultural activity in French Guiana. Unfortunately, shrimp exports declined by 26.4 percent from 1999 to 2001, due, in large part, to increases in fuel prices—the largest expenditure for shrimp fishermen. Such increases meant that fishermen could not conduct their activities as often as in the past.

INDUSTRY

GUADELOUPE. In 1997, industry in Guadeloupe constituted 9 percent of GDP and provided employment for 17 percent of the labor force. Industry is largely devoted to processing agricultural products and light manufactured goods. Major industrial activities include sugar refining, rum distilling, food processing, cement and brick manufacture, box and mail/wire making, mineral water bottling, and ship repair. An industrial free-port with tax and import duty exemptions was recently established at Jarry. Guadeloupe does not possess any mineral resources.

The construction industry, which is the third largest sector of activity in the Guadeloupian economy, employs 12 percent of the workforce in Guadeloupe. Most of the construction sector is dominated by government in the form of public works. Such works provide an enormous boost to the economy and help relieve unemployment. Indeed, the 5,500 public work enterprises in the construction sector comprise 19 percent of all industrial enterprises and engage approximately 10 percent of the entire labor force.

MARTINIQUE. The industrial sector in Martinique is very similar to the industrial sector in Guadeloupe, but slightly more important to the economy in relative terms. Industry in Martinique constituted 11 percent of GDP and engaged 10 percent of the labor force in 1997. Major industries include a cement works, rum distilling, sugar refining, dairy produce, fruit canning, soft drinks manufacture, mineral water bottling and a polyethylene plant. Additionally, a major oil refinery boasts a capacity of 16,090 barrels per day (2000). As of 2000, 5 industrial zones with generous tax and import duty exemptions have been established in order to encourage light industrial development. According to *World Information.Com,* an online encyclopedic organization, the industrial sector remains underdeveloped in spite of the legislated incentives. Martinique, like Guadeloupe, does not possess any mineral resources.

The construction industry, also dominated by governmental public works in Martinique, experienced considerable growth in 2001 when total cement production rose to 243.1 thousand tons from 237.5 thousand the year before. Much of this production was designated for the building of large establishments such as a hospital and a large court.

FRENCH GUIANA. With the exception of a few small factories processing agricultural or seafood products and a few sawmills, manufacturing is virtually non-existent in French Guiana. A rocket-launching site owned by the European Space Agency at Kourou comprises one of the most important economic activities. As a result of the space center, which was built in Kourou in 1964 because of its proximity to the equator, ultra-modern buildings now dominate the city.

In terms of mining, bauxite deposits of 42 million tons and kaolin deposits of 40 million tons were recently discovered, though extraction is not economically viable in the near future due to the department's poor infrastructure. There are also reserves of silica, niobium, and tantalite.

Significantly, gold is mined by a dozen Guianese companies and over 100 small-scale miners. Official figures for the mid-1990s indicate an annual gold production of approximately 3 tons. In 2000, gold accounted for almost half of the department's exports. The United States has played an important role in boosting Guianese gold exports. In 2000, the United States, which did not import any Guianese gold in 1999, imported 7 million euros worth of gold.

According to an article that appeared in the French paper *Le Monde Diplomatique,* gold mining, which exploded in 1993 following the discovery of reserves in Maripasoula, has engendered considerable negative environmental impacts. Forest areas have been cleared, upsetting the ecosystem, and mercury waste, a threat to both fauna and humans, has been dumped in streams and rivers. The Cayode, a group of Amerindians, have protested the environmental destruction. To make matters worse, violent conflict has erupted between opposing gold prospectors, who often hire Brazilians brought into the department illegally to work for highly exploitative wages. The government has not been very receptive to those that are dissatisfied with the situation, as gold mining provides employment for many individuals who would not be able to earn a livelihood otherwise. A contentious debate as to whether certain areas with gold reserves should be set aside for **eco-tourism** has raged in Guianese politics throughout the 1990s. Thus far, the anti-restriction perspective of the miners has prevailed.

SERVICES

In 1997, the service sector in Guadeloupe constituted a whopping 85 percent of GDP and provided employment for 68 percent of the labor force. Similarly, in the same year, the service sector in Martinique constituted 83 percent of GDP and engaged 73 percent of the labor force. Many of the people employed by the service sector in the CDF work for the government in bureaucratic positions. Government and parastatal employees are paid, on average, 30 percent higher than their metropolitan French counterparts. The generous salaries, intended, in part, to boost consumption and stimulate the economy, provide an essential form of transfer to the highly dependent economies of the CDF.

According to the Australian Department of Foreign Affairs and Trade *French Antilles Fact Sheet 2000,* tourism, which accounted for 7 percent of GDP in both Guadeloupe and Martinique in 2000, has been the fastest growing sector of the economy in the French Antilles throughout the 1990s. In 2000, the number of tourists to Guadeloupe reached 623,000, a significant increase from the approximately 500,000 tourists in 1997. Unfortunately, more recent trends in tourism in Martinique have not been as positive. Indeed, the total number of tourists visiting the department declined from 993,441 in 1999 to 928,197 in 2000. This sharp downward trend illustrates the insecurity of a tourist economy, which depends on the economic well-being and whims of individuals in developed countries for revenue. In both departments, the vast majority of stop-over tourists are from France (80 to 90 percent), while most cruise ship visitors are from North America.

Tourism is an important economic activity in French Guiana with much potential for growth. The major tourist attraction is currently the space center, which received 27,293 tourists in 2000, when there were a total of 12 rocket launchings. With its exotic rainforests and beautiful mountainous scenery, however, eco-tourism could very well surpass the space center in tourist importance. Unfortunately, promises made by former French president Francois Mitterand in 1992 to create eco-parks have failed to materialize. Impediments include conflict over land with gold prospectors and, to a lesser extent, debates concerning whether restrictions should be placed on Amerindians using slash-and-burn agricultural techniques (which are detrimental to the environment). French Guiana received 451,805 tourists in 2000, a significant increase from the 422,075 tourists that visited in 1998.

With several shopping centers, markets, and restaurants in the major cities, the retail sector is relatively well developed in the CDF. **Foreign direct investment** in services has also become more prevalent, and American companies such as McDonald's, Baskin Robbins, and Subway have established operations in Martinique. The real area of growth is in the number of small and medium-sized retail outlets, however, which have increased exponentially. In 2000, there were a total of 10,324 retail outlets in the CDF. Three hundred new outlets, mostly in the leisure and supermarket sectors, were created in Guadeloupe alone. In French Guiana, 900 small enterprises were established in 2000, many of which specialized in commercial or reparation-related activities. According to INSEE, a French government statistical institute, the small enterprise commercial sector is the most dynamic engine of growth in the CDF economies.

The unemployed that do not have the resources to establish small-scale enterprises often find retail work in the **informal sector** by selling products such as fruits and small consumer commodities on the street corners. The informal sector, which is neither taxed nor regulated by the government, also offers services such as machinery and equipment repairs. Incomes acquired through the informal sector are exceedingly low.

INTERNATIONAL TRADE

The CDF trade primarily with each other, France, other EU members, and the United States. Principal exports from Guadeloupe include bananas, sugar, and rum, while imports consist of foodstuffs, fuels, vehicles, clothing and other **consumer goods**, and construction material. About 60 percent of exports are directed towards France, 18 percent to Martinique, and 4 percent to the United States. Sixty-three percent of imports come from France, 4 percent from Germany, 3 percent from the United States, 2 percent from Japan, and 2 percent from the Netherlands Antilles. Martinique's exports are mostly refined petroleum products, bananas, and rum, while imports include petroleum products, crude oil, foodstuffs, construction materials, vehicles, clothing, and other consumer goods. Around 45 percent of exports are directed towards France and 28 percent go to Guadeloupe. Sixty-two percent of imports are from France, 6 percent from Venezuela, 4 percent from Germany, 4 percent from Italy, and 3 percent from the United States. French Guiana mostly exports shrimp, timber, gold, rum, and rosewood essence, while imports consist of food (grains, processed meat), machinery and transport equipment, fuels, and chemicals. Fifty-two percent of exports go to France, 14 percent to the United States, and 6 percent to Trinidad and Tobago. Sixty-two percent of imports come from France, 7 percent from Switzerland, and 2 percent from the United States.

As agricultural exporting and **capital goods** importing departments, the CDF routinely run **balance of trade** deficits that render them highly dependent on French

Trade (expressed in billions of US$): French Guiana		
	Exports	Imports
1975	.002	.072
1980	.025	.255
1985	.037	.255
1990	.093	.786
1995	N/A	N/A
1998	N/A	N/A

SOURCE: International Monetary Fund. *International Financial Statistics Yearbook 1999.*

loans and aid to finance needed imports. Dependency on badly needed foodstuff exacerbates the trade deficits, which, for each CDF, have actually increased in recent years. In 1999, for example, the deficit in French Guiana equaled 427 million euros, whereas this figure increased to 503 million euros in 2000. In 1998, French Guiana's total **external debt** reached $1.2 billion. In terms of trade deficits, however, Martinique is in the worst position, with its deficits surpassing even the total debt of French Guiana. The department, which only had a GDP of $250 million in 1997, had a total deficit of 1.5 billion euros in 2000, a considerable increase from the total deficit of 1.4 million euros in 1999. As a result of these massive deficits, the need for the CDF to further develop their domestic industries and food-producing capacity is all the more urgent.

As departments of France, the CDF are members of the most highly integrated regional economic association in the world—the European Union (EU)—with the least barriers for the movement of goods, services, capital, and labor. Many critics have argued that less developed countries cannot engage in free trade with industrialized countries because they do not possess the ability to compete. In other words, lowering of tariffs simply means that domestic industries in developing countries will falter under competitive pressures, which, in turn, will lead to further entrenchment of the agricultural sector in the economy and a prolonging of uneven patterns of trade. At the same time, however, the CDF have benefitted within the EU as recipients of aid programs and in gaining preferential access to EU markets for agricultural produce. Unfortunately, the World Trade Organization (WTO), which binds the EU economies and most countries of the world in an international free trade arrangement, has criticized EU preferential treatment for CDF agricultural products, such as bananas. WTO members that export bananas argue that EU preferential access for the French Antilles is a violation of WTO free trade rules, which are supposed to guarantee equal access to EU markets for all WTO members on the same terms.

MONEY

As departments of France, the CDF benefit from 2 major international currencies: the French franc and the European euro. The value of the French franc is locked to the euro at F6.56 per euro. The value of the euro, in turn, fluctuates according to European market strength and supply and demand in international money markets. The European Central Bank determines **monetary policy**. Since the euro was introduced in 1999, it has steadily appreciated in value against the U.S. dollar. In 1999, 0.9386 euros equaled US$1, whereas in January 2000 the euro appreciated in value to 0.9867 euros per US$1. While a higher euro value reflects the growing strength

Exchange rates: French Guiana	
euros per US$1	
Jan 2001	1.0659
2000	1.0854
1999	0.9386
1998	5.8995
1997	5.8367
1996	5.1155

Note: Amounts prior to 1999 are in French francs per US dollar.

SOURCE: CIA *World Factbook 2001* [ONLINE].

of the EU market, less developed areas of the EU such as the CDF suffer from a high currency since it means that more money is needed to purchase their exports. This, in turn, means that their exports are less attractive. In the case of the CDF, this is especially detrimental given the already large trade deficits.

The central bank of the CDF, the **bank of issue**, is the Caisse Centrale de Co-operation Economique. There are also numerous state-owned development banks, intended to help foster business through loans and investment, in addition to several commercial banks. The former include the Societe de Credit pour le Developpement des Departement d'Outre Mer (SOCREDOM), the Caisse Regionale de Credit Agricole Mutuael, and the Societe de Credit pour le Developpement Regional Antilles Guyane (SODERAG). The latter include the Banque des Antilles Francaise, Banque Francaise Commerciale, Banque National de Paris, and Societe Generale de Banque aux Antilles.

POVERTY AND WEALTH

According to the DFAIT *A Guide for Canadian Exporters*, the elite class in the CDF is composed primarily of government employees with the most prestigious positions. This segment of society shop in very expen-

GDP per Capita (US$)					
Country	1996	1997	1998	1999	2000
French Guiana & French Antilles	N/A	N/A	6,000	N/A	N/A
United States	28,600	30,200	31,500	33,900	36,200
Brazil	6,300	6,300	6,100	6,150	6,500
Suriname	3,150	3,400	3,500	3,400	N/A

Note: Data are estimates.

SOURCE: *Handbook of the Nations*, 17th, 18th, 19th and 20th editions for 1996, 1997, 1998 and 1999 data; CIA *World Factbook 2001* [Online] for 2000 data.

sive boutiques that sell large varieties of high-quality products that are imported to the departments on jumbo jets on a weekly basis. As a result of this type of consumption, much of the money that the elites earn escapes the local economy and directly benefits France and other EU members. This is a major impediment to development, especially considering that the rationale behind awarding CDF government officials higher salaries than their metropolitan counterparts relates to increasing demand in the local economy. Supermarkets provide the same basic goods for both the elites and the middle and lower classes, though the latter must be much more cautious about what they buy. People with high incomes represent about 20 percent of the populations of the CDF, while those with middle or lower incomes constitute the remaining 80 percent.

The French government allocates a significant amount of resources to the CDF to ensure that the standard of living in the departments is similar to the standard of living in the metropolis. Consequently, the CDF enjoy some of the highest standards of living in the Caribbean and South America. Poverty is acute, but it is generally nowhere near the levels of poverty experienced by developing countries with similar economies. This notwithstanding, the standard of living in the CDF in reality falls considerably below that of the standard of living in the French metropolis. In 1997, for instance, **GDP per capita** in **purchasing power parity** in French Guiana, Martinique, and Guadeloupe equaled $6,000, $10,700, and $9,000, respectively, in contrast to the overall GDP per capita (PPP) in France, which equaled $27,975 in 1998. Evidently, there is considerable discrepancy in the social conditions between France and the CDF as a whole, not to mention within the CDF themselves.

Health care and education are generally accessible in the CDF. Free health care is provided for the poorest segments of society, while education is universally free. Furthermore, expenditure on such services has actually increased in some cases, in sharp contrast to the general decline in social expenditures in OECD countries. In Martinique, for example, total expenditure on health care increased from 583 million euros in 1999 to 610 million in 2000. Education is compulsory between the ages of 6 to 16 in the CDF and university is available for those seeking to further their education. In many cases, however, students must leave school early in order to help provide for the family.

WORKING CONDITIONS

In terms of size, the total workforce of Guadeloupe, Martinique, and French Guiana are approximately 120,000, 100,000, and 58,800, respectively (1997 est.) Labor policies are generally quite progressive, reflecting strict French labor codes that enshrine the rights of workers. There are virtually no incidents of child labor, though some children must help their parents in agricultural activities to increase household incomes. Unionization is high in the industrial sector and parts of the service sector. Agricultural workers are also unionized, though to a lesser extent. The major union federations in Guadeloupe are the General Federation of Guadeloupe Workers and the General Union of Guadeloupe Workers, while the major union federation in Martinique is the Central Union for Martinique Workers. Most unions in the CDF are strongly socialist in orientation.

By far, the most daunting problem faced by the CDF in the area of labor relates to the massive levels of unemployment characteristic of each department. Unemployment is especially acute for young workers and, to a lesser extent, women. Strikes and riots have erupted in the CDF as a result of the high unemployment rates, most notably in French Guiana in November 1996, when a general strike was triggered by student frustration with lack of prospects. The nation-wide strike lasted for 2 days, bringing the economy to a standstill.

The unemployment rate in Guadeloupe was 24 percent in 1999, though this represented a substantial improvement from the 27 percent rate in 2000. Job opportunities, particularly in the service sector, expanded by 18.7 percent in 2000 from the year before. Around 14.5 percent of all unemployed in Guadeloupe are young workers between the ages of 16 to 25 years. Unemployment rate figures suggest gender inequalities in terms of employers being more inclined to hire men. In Guadeloupe, for instance, 57.7 percent of all unemployed are women, while these figures are 53 percent and 59.3 percent, respectively, in French Guiana and Martinique. In French Guiana, the unemployment rate in 2000 was 25.8 percent—a marginal decrease of less than 1 percent from the year before. In Martinique, unemployment in absolute terms declined considerably from 48,667 unemployed in 1999 to 43,521 in 2000. The CDF are highly dependent upon the French government for job creation, and unemployment rates would be considerably higher without the support of the government service sector.

COUNTRY HISTORY AND ECONOMIC DEVELOPMENT

1493. Columbus is the first European to arrive in the islands that are now the French Antilles. In 1496, Europeans report their first sightings of South America.

1604. The French establish their first settlement in the area that is now French Guiana.

1635. The French establish their first settlements on the islands of the Antilles, and hostilities with the indigenous inhabitants escalate.

17TH CENTURY. The territories comprising the French Antilles and French Guiana become French colonies characterized by large settler plantations and African slave labor. Control over French Guiana changes several times between France, Britain, the Netherlands, and Brazil.

1848. France abolishes slavery and the liberated slaves in the French Caribbean colonies become a free labor force, though they remain exploited and land-less.

1915. France gains final domination over Guiana.

1946. The French Caribbean colonies become overseas departments with little autonomy over their own affairs. France highly subsidizes the CDF throughout the post-war period and the economies remain dependent on France for aid and transfers to this day.

1964. The Kourou space center is established in French Guiana.

1974. French Guiana is granted regional status and thus greater economic autonomy.

1982–83. The CDF receive considerable autonomy through a process of devolution.

1990s. The French government seeks to encourage industrial development through the creation of commercial zones with special tax and import duty exemptions.

1998–99. Hurricanes George, Lenny, and Jose wreak havoc in the French Antilles. The Basse-Terre declaration issued by the CDF in 1999 calls for greater departmental control over local affairs.

2001. Unemployment and dependency continue to afflict the CDF economies.

FUTURE TRENDS

The Caribbean departments of France are in a unique position in the developing world. Despite the underdeveloped nature of their individual economies, status as French departments has ensured high amounts of subsidization and transfers that have helped to maintain relatively high levels of living standards, especially in the context of South America and the Caribbean. High levels of unemployment would be even higher without the large number of jobs provided by the French governmental bureaucracy and public works. The major challenge for the CDF, therefore, relates to achieving a level of sustainable development that will end this pattern of dependency. The massive increases in the number of small- and medium-size enterprises in the commercial sector is a promising sign. Activities such as those found in the industrial sector must also be strengthened, however, while food production capacity must be increased. Terminating the pattern of unequal trade is of the utmost importance. Tourism and agricultural exports, though important, cannot be promoted as the bases of the CDF economies. Of course, sustainable development is highly elusive, and the French government will have to continue providing support and aid in a context of careful developmental planning in order to realize this goal.

DEPENDENCIES

The French Antilles and French Guiana have no territories or colonies.

BIBLIOGRAPHY

Australian Department of Foreign Affairs and Trade. *Country, Economy, and Regional Information: French Antilles.* <http://www.dfat.gov.au/geo/French_antilles/index.html>. Accessed May 2001.

Australian Department of Foreign Affairs and Trade. *Country, Economy, and Regional Information: French Guiana.* <http://www.dfat.gov.au/geo/french_guiana/index.html>. Accessed May 2001.

"Country Profile: French Guiana." *World Information.Com.* <http://www.worldinformation.com>. Accessed September 2001.

"Country Profile: Guadeloupe." *World Information.Com.* <http://www.worldinformation.com>. Accessed September 2001.

"Country Profile: Martinique." *World Information.Com.* <http://www.worldinformation.com>. Accessed September 2001.

Department of Foreign Affairs and International Trade (Canada). *The French Antilles: Martinique and Guadeloupe, A Guide for Canadian Exporters.* <http://www.dfait-maeci.gc.ca/geo/html_documents/4131-e.htm>. Accessed September 2001.

INSEE. "Antilles-Guyanne: Bilan de Guadeloupe, Martinique et Guyane." *Antiane* (No. 49, June 2001). <http:www.insee.fr>. Accessed September 2001.

Lemoine, Maurice. "Sustainable Development in French Guiana: The Politics of Gold-Prospecting." *Le Monde Diplomatique.* <http://www.monde-diplomatique.fr>. Accessed September 2001. (Available by subscription only.)

United Nations Development Programme. *Human Development Report 2000.* New York: Oxford University Press, 2000.

U.S. Central Intelligence Agency. *World Factbook 2001.* <http://www.odci.gov/cia/publications/factbook/index.html>. Accessed September 2001.

—Neil Burron

GRENADA

CAPITAL: St. George's.

MONETARY UNIT: Eastern Caribbean dollar (EC$). One EC dollar equals 100 cents. There are coins of 10, 20, and 50 cents. There are notes of 5, 10, 20, and 100 dollars.

CHIEF EXPORTS: Bananas, cocoa, nutmeg and mace, fruit and vegetables, clothing.

CHIEF IMPORTS: Food, manufactured goods, machinery, chemicals, fuel.

GROSS DOMESTIC PRODUCT: US$360 million (1999 est.).

BALANCE OF TRADE: Exports: US$55 million (1999 est.). **Imports:** US$230 million (1999 est.).

COUNTRY OVERVIEW

LOCATION AND SIZE. Grenada is an island situated between the Caribbean Sea and Atlantic Ocean, north of Trinidad and Tobago. Its total area is 340 square kilometers (131 square miles), about twice the size of Washington, D.C., and its coastline measures 121 kilometers (75 miles). Grenada has 2 dependencies in the Grenadines island chain: Carriacou and Petit Martinique. Carriacou (pronounced Carr-ycoo) lies 37 kilometers (23 miles) northeast of Grenada and is 33.5 square kilometers (13 square miles) in area, while Petit Martinique lies 4 kilometers (2.5 miles) further north and is only 486 acres in area. The capital of Grenada, St. George's, lies on the island's southwest coast and is the only town of any size.

POPULATION. Grenada's population was estimated at 89,018 in July 2000. This figure marked a drop of 0.36 percent from the previous year and a reduction of more than 2 percent from the estimated 1991 population of 91,000. Grenada's population has been declining for several decades despite positive statistics in terms of child mortality, life expectancy, and death/birth rate ratios. This is largely explained by a high rate of migration, calculated at 16.54 migrants per 1,000 population (2000). Grenadians migrate in large numbers to neighboring islands such as Trinidad & Tobago, where employment opportunities are greater, or more commonly to the United States and Canada. At current rates, Grenada's population will stand at approximately 86,000 in 2010.

Grenada's population is youthful, with 38 percent of Grenadians under the age of 15. A majority of the population lives in rural villages, and the World Bank estimates that only 37 percent are urban dwellers. The island is small enough for people to work or conduct their business in St. George's without living in the capital. About 85 percent of the population is of African decent, with smaller mixed-race and Indian communities. The latter are the descendants of indentured laborers (servants or laborers who pay an employer for transit to the employer's country, and work off their debt, often for many years) brought to the island after the abolition of slavery in 1833. English is the island's official language, though some Grenadians speak a French dialect, and Roman Catholicism, observed by 53 percent of Grenadians, is the dominant religion.

OVERVIEW OF ECONOMY

Grenada's economy has shifted significantly since the 1970s, from one almost entirely based on producing agricultural commodities for export to a much more modernized and diversified one. For many years Grenada depended on exporting 3 main crops—bananas, cocoa, and nutmeg—but fluctuating world prices, natural disasters, and the threatened removal of preferential trading agreements have forced Grenada's government to seek to broaden the island's economic base. Successive governments since the 1980s have been acutely aware that small-island states such as Grenada are extremely vulnerable to economic factors beyond their control and have hence tried to reduce over-reliance on agricultural exports. Grenada now has a small but growing manufacturing sector, a nascent financial services sector, and an important tourism sector, which is the island's main foreign exchange earner.

Grenada's movement toward economic diversification began during the short-lived People's Revolutionary Government (PRG) of 1979–83, which tried to increase manufacturing for the domestic market and look for new markets for the island's commodities. The U.S. intervention of

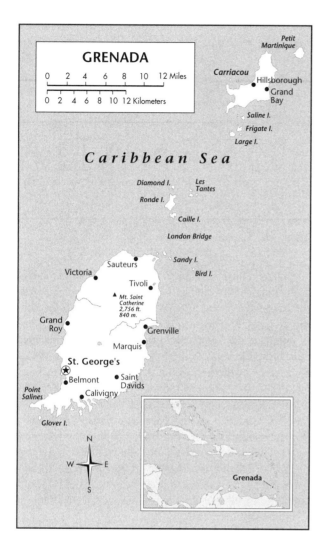

by the agricultural sector, made up of small farmers, and a small import-export sector, based in St. George's. During the PRG regime, the PRG began experiments in diversification and a mixture of **private-sector** initiatives and state intervention with an emphasis on cooperatives and central planning. Since 1983, the economy has been strongly oriented toward free-market development, with the **privatization** of several state-owned concerns and a program of structural adjustment aimed at reducing government spending.

Despite such **liberalizing** measures, Grenada's economy still faces significant problems. Its imports in 1999 were 5 times the value of its exports, creating a large **trade deficit** that is only partly offset by tourism receipts and other service income. The reduction in agricultural activity means that increasing amounts of food have to be imported, especially for the growing tourism industry. Government spending also remains high in relation to revenues. A 2000 International Monetary Fund (IMF) report expressed concerns at the high wages paid to civil servants and the large sums spent on modernizing infrastructure. There remains considerable poverty and unemployment in Grenada, with the IMF estimating that 32 percent of the population, mostly rural laborers and the unemployed, live in poverty. The country is highly indebted, with **external debt** of US$159.3 million in 2000. **Debt servicing** (money paid above the actual debt, such as interest) cost US$16.9 million in 1998, equal to one-fifth of government's annual revenue.

POLITICS, GOVERNMENT, AND TAXATION

After 2 decades of political turmoil in the 1970s and 1980s, Grenada has returned to a state of stability and constitutional government. The overthrow of autocratic and populist Prime Minister Eric Gairy in 1979 ushered in 4 years of **socialist**-oriented government until factional infighting and the murder of Prime Minister Maurice Bishop triggered the U.S. intervention of 1983. Short-term, unstable political alliances followed until 1995, when the New National Party (NNP) won a narrow majority. Led by Keith Mitchell, the NNP then won an overwhelming victory in January 1999, taking all 15 of the island's parliamentary seats.

As the leader of the majority party, Mitchell, the prime minister, was appointed by the governor general of the island, who was appointed by the Queen of England. The governor general also appoints the cabinet, on the advice of the prime minister. The **bicameral** (2 legislative chambers) parliament consists of the 15-member National Assembly, whose members are elected by popular vote to 5-year terms, and of the 13-member Senate, 10 of whose members are appointed by the government

October 1983, in which American troops invaded the island after Prime Minister Maurice Bishop was murdered by rivals within the PRG, brought a brief influx of economic aid. This assistance enabled the island to establish the **infrastructure** for small-scale manufacturing, mainly aimed at the U.S. market. In the late 1980s and early 1990s, aid and investment slowed, causing the island's economy to stagnate. Tourism grew strongly from the mid-1990s, leading to a boom in construction and other services. Economic growth, consequently, has been strong and sustained in recent years, with GDP growing by 6.8 percent in 1998 and 8.1 percent in 1999. Attracted by tax breaks and other incentives, several U.S. and European multinational companies operate in Grenada, mostly in the light manufacturing and tourism sectors. Local companies are extremely small and limited to import-export activities and **retail**. There are still several government-controlled statutory boards which represent the interests of small farmers and agricultural exporters.

Since the 1970s, Grenada's economy has passed through 3 distinct phases. Until 1979, it was dominated and 3 of whose members are appointed by the opposition. The country's legal system is based on English common law, and the system is overseen by the West Indies Associate Supreme Court, a representative of which body resides in Grenada.

The NNP is pro-private sector, favoring foreign investment in tourism and manufacturing to stimulate growth. It has also attracted former supporters of Eric Gairy and Maurice Bishop by pledging to combat unemployment and poverty. The other parties were soundly beaten in the 1999 elections and do not differ significantly in their approach to the economy.

Government policy is important in determining economic development, since the state sector remains substantial and potential foreign investors are influenced by such policy. The government has tried to reduce its **public-sector** financial commitments by reducing the number of civil servants, privatizing some assets, and converting some government agencies, such as the post office, into autonomous commercial enterprises. More controversially, it has begun to introduce performance-related pay schemes within the public sector, despite strong opposition from trade unions. The government has attempted to attract direct foreign investment by offering generous tax incentives and other financial benefits to companies interested in establishing themselves in the manufacturing and tourism sectors.

Taxation tends to be weighted towards indirect sales taxes rather than **income tax**, which the government has reduced. Government has tried to improve revenue collection through greater efficiency and has increased income from fees levied on offshore companies, particularly those in the new financial services sector. Even so, according to the Caribbean Development Bank, "Notwithstanding improvements in tax administration

departments, revenue collection continues to be undermined by widespread exemptions, high levels of tax evasion and extensive non-compliance." In other words, many Grenadians and foreign companies alike do not pay the taxes that they owe to the government. Sales taxes, according to critics, affect the poorest sectors of the Grenadian population disproportionately, but the government believes that high income taxes act as a disincentive to private enterprise.

INFRASTRUCTURE, POWER, AND COMMUNICATIONS

Grenada is a small island with a limited road infrastructure of 1,127 kilometers (700 miles), of which about one-half are paved. Rural roads are often impassable and have long been criticized by farmers in remote districts as a serious obstacle to transporting goods to collection points. There are no railways. The main port is at St. George's, where there is a cruise ship terminal. The main airport is Point Salines International Airport, near the capital, construction of which began under the PRG with extensive assistance from Cuba. There is a small airport on Carriacou. The Grenadian government is a shareholder in the regional airline, Leeward Islands Air Transportation (LIAT).

The government has invested strongly in tourism- and manufacturing-oriented infrastructure in recent years, upgrading main roads, improving port facilities, and modernizing water and sewerage systems. Little of this investment, however, has reached isolated rural districts.

There are no local oil deposits, and fuel is imported, mostly from Venezuela, for power generation. In 1998 Grenada generated 105 million kilowatt hours (kWh) of electricity and consumed 98 million kWh. The telecommunications industry is in the process of being liberalized,

Communications

Country	Telephonesa	Telephones, Mobile/Cellulara	Radio Stationsb	Radiosa	TV Stationsa	Televisionsa	Internet Service Providersc	Internet Usersc
Grenada	27,000	976	AM 2; FM 1; shortwave 0	57,000	2	33,000	14	2,000
United States	194 M	69.209 M (1998)	AM 4,762; FM 5,542; shortwave 18	575 M	1,500	219 M	7,800	148 M
Jamaica	353,000 (1996)	54,640 (1996)	AM 10; FM 13; shortwave 0	1.215 M	7	460,000	21	60,000
St. Lucia	37,000	1,600	AM 2; FM 7; shortwave 0	111,000	3	32,000	15	5,000

aData is for 1997 unless otherwise noted.
bData is for 1998 unless otherwise noted.
cData is for 2000 unless otherwise noted.

SOURCE: CIA *World Factbook 2001* [Online].

having been dominated by Cable & Wireless Grenada (a subsidiary of the large British firm Cable & Wireless PLC) for many years. There is a developed network of main-line telephones, a fiber-optic network, and growing use of mobile telephones. The advent of Call Centres Grenada, an offshore telemarketing operation, in July 2000, was evidence of the island's reliable telecommunications network. Cable & Wireless also provides Internet access.

ECONOMIC SECTORS

The importance of agriculture to Grenada's GDP has fallen steeply, from more than 26 percent in 1979 to an estimated 9.7 percent in 1996. The World Bank estimates its contribution at 8.1 percent in 1999. The 1995 agricultural census estimated that the area of cultivated land in Grenada had fallen from 61,000 acres in 1961 to 31,000 in 1995. Many young Grenadians are no longer willing to work family **smallholdings**, and this gradual abandonment of agriculture has been compounded by a crisis in the banana industry. Only nutmeg, one of Grenada's traditional export commodities, has experienced resurgence in recent years, because of rising international prices for the spice. Agriculture still accounted for an estimated 24 percent of the workforce in 1999, and many Grenadians work part-time on smallholdings for family or local consumption. Agricultural exports as a whole were valued at US$21.8 million in 1999.

Agriculture's decline has been balanced by the rising importance of industry, which has grown from 14.2 percent of GDP in 1979 to 22.2 percent in 1999, according to the World Bank. Some of this growth is accounted for by the recent opening of a plant that assem-

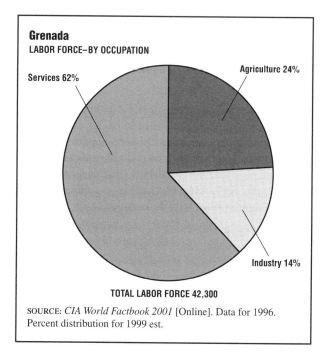

Grenada
LABOR FORCE–BY OCCUPATION

Services 62%

Agriculture 24%

Industry 14%

TOTAL LABOR FORCE 42,300

SOURCE: *CIA World Factbook 2001* [Online]. Data for 1996. Percent distribution for 1999 est.

bles electronic components for the U.S. market. There are several other such assembly plants, and Grenada has a significant agricultural processing sector, a brewery, rice mill, and cement works. Approximately 14 percent of the workforce was estimated to be employed in industry in 1999, which earned $23.1 million.

Services have also risen as a percentage of GDP, from 59.6 percent in 1979 to 76.5 percent in 1999. The nature of the service sector has changed, with a greater emphasis on tourism and financial services rather than more traditional retail and government-oriented activity. Grenada is now offering itself as a stable base for **offshore banking** and other financial services, hoping to emulate the success of other Caribbean nations such as Barbados.

AGRICULTURE

Besides food crops grown for local and tourist consumption, Grenada's 3 traditional export crops are bananas, cocoa, and nutmeg. Historically, these have been grown not on large estates, but by small farmers with properties of a few acres. The regularity of income produced by bananas, typically delivered weekly by farmers to visiting banana boats, with the high prices fetched by nutmeg, contributed to modest rural prosperity from the 1950s onwards. But since the 1990s the banana sector, in particular, has been badly affected by problems revolving around access to foreign markets. The 1997 ruling by the World Trade Organization (WTO) that the European Union (EU) was unfairly discriminating against Latin American banana producers by giving preferential access to Caribbean producers created a crisis in the in-

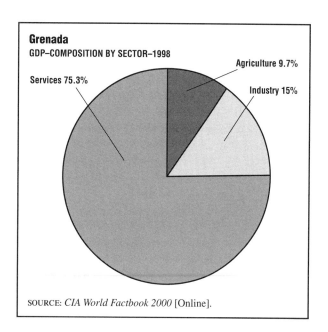

Grenada
GDP–COMPOSITION BY SECTOR–1998

Services 75.3%

Agriculture 9.7%

Industry 15%

SOURCE: *CIA World Factbook 2000* [Online].

dustry. This was worsened by complaints from the exporting company, Geest, that Grenadian bananas were unreliable in quantity and quality. The EU continues to offer preferential quotas to Caribbean producers, but Grenada's industry has declined further, despite a banana rehabilitation program initiated by the government and the Windward Islands Banana Development and Exporting Company (WIBDECO). After an 18-month suspension, banana exports resumed in November 1998.

Cocoa also suffered in the 1990s with an epidemic of mealy bug infestation, coinciding with the cancellation of a contract with a major chocolate manufacturer. Another victim of natural disasters was Grenada's fishing industry, affected first by a mysterious disease and then by Hurricane Lenny in November 1999. These factors created a sharp decline in the fishing sector, which with Japanese aid, had been expanding in the 1990s, employing an estimated 1,500 people in the coastal towns of Gouyave, Grenville, and St. George's.

Much more positive was expansion and rising prices in the nutmeg sector. Political turmoil in Indonesia, Grenada's main competitor, pushed up nutmeg prices by 72 percent in 1999 and mace (a byproduct of nutmeg) by 37.5 percent.

Some cotton is grown on Carriacou, and limes are cultivated in Grenada and Carriacou, mostly for the local market. Grenada's once important sugar industry is now confined to a small area in the south of the island, where there is a rum distillery. Fruit and vegetables are grown across the island, and what is not consumed locally is usually brought to market at St. George's.

INDUSTRY

Grenada's industry is small-scale, revolving around several zones near the capital, which cater to foreign companies in search of cheap labor. Since the 1980s, the government has tried to attract such foreign investors, with some success, and Grenada currently produces clothing, electronic components, and other **consumer goods** for export mainly to the U.S. market. This sector expanded by 10.5 percent in 1999, because of the opening of a new electronics factory. Electronic components accounted for 61.4 percent of Grenada's manufactured exports.

Other industries include brewing (where the Irish company Guinness holds a majority stake), rice milling, and agricultural processing. The recent boom in construction has also brought an increase in associated industries such as cement and furniture.

SERVICES

Tourism is the biggest part of Grenada's economy, bringing in an estimated $66.8 million in receipts in 1999.

Much of the island's tourist industry is still in local hands, and there is considerable "**trickle down**" within the economy, benefiting local farmers, restaurant owners, and taxi drivers in particular. Grenada has expanded its tourism infrastructure, and there are now approximately 2,500 hotel rooms, as well as developed cruise ship and yacht charter facilities. But despite steady growth in recent years, Grenada's tourism sector has encountered serious problems, including a 1999 decision by the Carnival cruise ship company to suspend calls at Grenada in the wake of the government's 1998 imposition of a $3 per capita landing fee.

The quickest growing service sector is offshore financial services, consisting of banking, insurance, and other services for foreign companies and individuals. It has expanded since 1996 and is expected to play an increasingly prominent role in the economy. There are 31 offshore banks and a large number of other financial interests, and despite some local opposition, the government is encouraging gaming as a tourist attraction. However, the financial service sector was damaged by allegations of financial impropriety in 2000 concerning one bank's operations. In March of 2001, the government—announcing that it was cracking down on bank fraud—closed down 17 offshore banks. Altogether, in 1999, the financial sector generated almost $5 million in revenues for the government.

Another growth sector is telemarketing and data processing, in which Grenada's literate but low-paid workforce can compete for contracts from North America. This sector, buoyed by the recent opening of a large facility on the east coast, created an estimated 1,000 jobs by 2000.

Retailing is not well developed in Grenada, with only a few large stores in St. George's and the nearby tourist areas. Most rural Grenadians depend on a weekly trip to the capital or small village stores for day-to-day essentials.

INTERNATIONAL TRADE

Until the 1990s, most bananas were shipped to Britain, Grenada's traditional trading partner. Gradually, the island has come to depend increasingly on the United States, both for its manufactured exports and imports. The United States accounted for almost 40 percent of imports (US$78.9 million) and 35 percent of exports (US$64.1 million) in 1998, according to the Caribbean Development Bank. Other important trading partners are the European Union and fellow members of the Caribbean Community (CARICOM), which provided 27 percent of imports and took 20 percent of exports in 1998.

Grenada continues to import much more than it exports, with 1999 exports of $55 million and imports of

Trade (expressed in billions of US$): Grenada

	Exports	Imports
1975	.012	.024
1980	.017	.050
1985	.023	.069
1990	.027	.105
1995	.023	.130
1998	N/A	N/A

SOURCE: International Monetary Fund. *International Financial Statistics Yearbook 1999.*

$230 million. Despite the recent upsurge in nutmeg exports, this is a source of concern to the government and international financial institutions alike. Tourism revenue and income from other services partly offset this imbalance, but Grenada is vulnerable to mounting debt and economic factors beyond its control.

MONEY

High levels of growth (6.8 percent in 1998 and 6.2 percent in 1999) reflect temporary booms in one part of the agricultural sector (nutmeg) as well as construction and services. At the same time, the government has managed to keep **inflation** under control, with consumer prices rising only 1 percent in 1999. The Eastern Caribbean dollar, a currency shared with the 7 other members of the Eastern Caribbean Central Bank (ECCB), is stable, and has been pegged at a **fixed exchange rate** of EC$2.7/US$1 for many years. This means that Grenada is less vulnerable to fluctuating **exchange rates**, although transactions with Europe have been affected by the low value of the euro. There are plans for ECCB member countries to participate in a regional stock exchange, further integrating the economies of the small islands. These plans were not yet in effect by 2001.

Exchange rates: Grenada

East Caribbean dollars (EC$) per US$1

Jan 2001	2.7000
2000	2.7000
1999	2.7000
1998	2.7000
1997	2.7000
1996	2.7000

Note: Grenadian currency has been set at a fixed rate since 1976.

SOURCE: CIA *World Factbook 2001* [ONLINE].

POVERTY AND WEALTH

There are no available statistics regarding the distribution of wealth in Grenada, but it is obvious that there is a gulf between a wealthy minority and a substantial sector of poor Grenadians. According to the World Bank, some 32 percent of Grenadians live in conditions of poverty. Recent government research suggests that most of these households are in rural areas, often in the most inaccessible and sometimes drought-ridden parts of the island. Unemployment or **underemployment** are the main problems in rural areas, especially for young adults who wish to escape what they see as the drudgery of agricultural labor. Squatting (the illegal occupation of government-owned land) is not uncommon in makeshift communities around St. George's. Some of the worst poverty is to be found on former estates, where barracks-like accommodations are still used by rural laborers. In such communities, housing conditions can be extremely rudimentary, with no sewerage and little access to other services. Clean drinking water is available throughout the island, even if poorer families have to resort to sharing a communal water pipe.

The radical PRG government of 1979–83 introduced measures to improve conditions among the rural poor, including low-cost loans for building materials and a network of village medical clinics. Some of these initiatives have been maintained since, and the current government has invested substantially in health and education. Even so, the cost of school uniforms and textbooks is often prohibitive for some families.

A prosperous middle class exists in St. George's, made up of professionals in the import-export businesses or new sectors such as tourism and data processing. Another comparatively wealthy group is made up of returning migrants, many amassing large savings after decades working in the United Kingdom and elsewhere. Private education and health facilities exist for the rich, who are accustomed to sending their children to the United States for their education. The urban elite has tended to look down on the rural majority, especially during the 1950s and 1960s when poor peasants and agricultural laborers formed the bulk of support for the eccentric populist politician, Eric Gairy.

GDP per Capita (US$)

Country	1975	1980	1985	1990	1998
Grenada	N/A	1,709	2,111	2,819	3,347
United States	19,364	21,529	23,200	25,363	29,683
Jamaica	1,819	1,458	1,353	1,651	1,559
St. Lucia	N/A	2,076	2,150	3,542	3,907

SOURCE: United Nations. *Human Development Report 2000; Trends in human development and per capita income.*

Household Consumption in PPP Terms

Country	All food	Clothing and footwear	Fuel and power[a]	Health care[b]	Education[b]	Transport & Communications	Other
Grenada	29	4	10	2	13	20	21
United States	13	9	9	4	6	8	51
Jamaica	24	7	3	1	9	8	48
St. Lucia	40	5	11	4	17	11	11

Data represent percentage of consumption in PPP terms.

[a]Excludes energy used for transport.

[b]Includes government and private expenditures.

SOURCE: World Bank. *World Development Indicators 2000.*

WORKING CONDITIONS

In 1998, the International Labor Organization estimated a workforce of 41,015, with unemployment at 15.2 percent of the economically active population. Conditions and pay, excluding the declining agricultural sector, are better in Grenada than in many other Caribbean countries. This is because of a relatively strong and effective trade union movement, which defends the interests of workers in the public and private sectors. Unions have been particularly active in negotiating conditions for civil servants such as teachers and doctors. In manufacturing, pay rates are much higher than in such competitor countries as Haiti or the Dominican Republic. The Grenada Industrial Development Corporation, for instance, suggests workers in the electronic components plants can earn a weekly salary of between $100 and $250, at least 3 times that in lower-wage countries. Grenada's laws include protection against wrongful dismissal, the right to join unions, and many other basic workers' rights. Attempts by companies to violate such rights have caused strikes in the past.

For small farmers and rural laborers, conditions and pay are poor. Unions representing agricultural workers were powerful in the 1950s and 1960s, but have lost much of their influence. Wages have fallen dramatically in comparison to the manufacturing and services sector. Farming is now the preserve of older Grenadians or carried out on a part-time family basis. There is little or no child labor in Grenada, with the exception of this sort of farm work, while women are well represented in all areas of the economy and professions.

COUNTRY HISTORY AND ECONOMIC DEVELOPMENT

1498. Columbus sights and names Grenada on his third expedition.

1650. First permanent European settlement on island.

1783. British win control over island after colonial competition with France.

1951. First electoral success of populist politician Eric Gairy.

1974. Independence from the U.K.

1979. Gairy overthrown by bloodless coup, followed by formation of People's Revolutionary Government.

1983. U.S. military intervention after murder of Prime Minister Maurice Bishop.

1996. Launch of offshore financial services sector.

1999. New National Party wins second term with 15 out of 15 seats.

FUTURE TRENDS

Grenada's economy seems likely to move further away from agriculture and toward tourism and manufacturing, especially when the temporary boom in nutmeg exports comes to an end. It is likely that the government will encourage growth in these newer sectors by offering new incentives to foreign companies. The success or failure of the first telemarketing ventures will determine the future of high-tech investment in Grenada and similar Caribbean economies. Grenada will be less affected than other Eastern Caribbean islands by the decline in the banana industry or an eventual collapse, and in this sense its economic future is relatively hopeful.

The main problems for the government will involve narrowing the wide trade deficit and reducing the **national debt**. There is much work to be done in redistributing wealth away from a small minority toward the many Grenadians who continue to live in poverty. The NNP has the political support to make progress in these areas and has the capability to introduce effective poverty-alleviation programs. Nevertheless, much depends on the health of the U.S. and European economies, which are critical to the continuing growth of Grenada's tourism industry. If there is a slowdown in this sector, government revenue will decline and so will its ability to achieve its social objectives.

DEPENDENCIES

Grenada has no territories or colonies.

BIBLIOGRAPHY

Belgrafix. "Government Closes 17 Offshore Banks." <http://www.belgrafix.com>. Accessed June 2001.

Brizan, George. *Grenada, Island of Conflict: From Amerindians to People's Revolution, 1498–1979.* London: Zed Books, 1984.

Caribbean Development Bank. *Annual Report 1999.* Barbados: Caribbean Development Bank, 2000.

Economist Intelligence Unit. *Country Profile: OECS.* London: Economist Intelligence Unit, 2000.

Ferguson, James. *Grenada: Revolution in Reverse.* London: Latin America Bureau, 1990.

International Monetary Fund. "Grenada and the IMF." <http://www.imf.org/external/country/GRD/index.htm>. Accessed July 2001.

U.S. Central Intelligence Agency. *World Factbook 2000.* <http://www.odci.gov/cia/publications/factbook/index.html>. Accessed July 2001.

—James Ferguson

GUATEMALA

Republic of Guatemala
República de Guatemala

CAPITAL: Guatemala City.

MONETARY UNIT: Quetzal (Q). One quetzal is equal to 100 centavos. There are coins of 1, 5, 10, and 25 centavos, as well as paper bills in the amounts of 50 centavos and 1, 5, 10, 20, 50, and 100 quetzals.

CHIEF EXPORTS: Coffee, sugar, bananas, fruits and vegetables, meat, apparel, petroleum, electricity.

CHIEF IMPORTS: Fuels, machinery and transport equipment, construction materials, grain, fertilizers, electricity.

GROSS DOMESTIC PRODUCT: US$47.9 billion (purchasing power parity, 1999 est.).

BALANCE OF TRADE: Exports: US$2.4 billion (f.o.b., 1999). **Imports:** US$4.5 billion (c.i.f., 1999).

COUNTRY OVERVIEW

LOCATION AND SIZE. Located in Central America at the southern tip of Mexico between the Caribbean Sea and the Pacific Ocean, Guatemala has a total area of 108,890 square kilometers (42,042 square miles), slightly smaller than that of the state of Tennessee. Belize, Honduras, El Salvador, and Mexico all share land boundaries with Guatemala that total 1,687 kilometers (1,048 miles) in length, while Guatemala's coastline along the Pacific Ocean and the Caribbean Sea totals 400 kilometers (249 miles). Guatemala City, the national capital and home to 2 million Guatemalans, is located in south-central Guatemala, less than 100 kilometers (62 miles) from the Pacific Ocean.

POPULATION. As of July 2000, Guatemala's population was estimated at 12,639,939. There are approximately 484 persons to every square kilometer of the country (1,253 persons per square mile), making Guatemala the second most densely populated nation in Central and South America. (El Salvador is the only nation in the region with a higher population density.) Guatemala also has an extremely high rate of population growth; if the

population were to continue at its current growth rate of 2.9 percent per year, the total number of people living in the nation would double in 24 years. Population projections estimate that Guatemala's population will reach 16,295,000 by 2010. The fertility rate in Guatemala is the highest in Latin America, with an average of 5 children born to each Guatemalan woman during her lifetime. Although the Guatemalan government has officially recognized that the national birth rate is high, it has done little to encourage family planning or birth control among its populace. The reluctance of the Guatemalan government to institute population control policies can be partly attributed to its strong ties with the Catholic Church, while resistance to family planning among the general populace can be partially imputed to the civil unrest of the 1980s, which provoked a distrust of foreign-initiated programs (including family planning programs).

In stark contrast to most Latin American countries, Guatemala has a populace that is concentrated mainly in rural areas. Only 39 percent of its population is urban (though urbanization is accelerating). The sizeable rural population is linked to the large indigenous (Amerindian) presence in Guatemala; persons descended from the Mayan Indians account for 56 percent of the nation's total population, making Guatemala the Latin American nation with the largest indigenous population relative to total population. The other 44 percent of the national population is mestizo (of mixed Amerindian-Spanish descent, also called *ladino* in local Spanish). Despite the concentration of the population in rural areas, close to 80 percent of physicians are located in the metropolitan area, making health care difficult to access for rural inhabitants. Additionally, water supply and sanitation services reach 92 percent and 72 percent of the urban population respectively, while in rural areas they reach marginally more than 50 percent of the population. These facts betray a broader phenomenon of rural disadvantage that

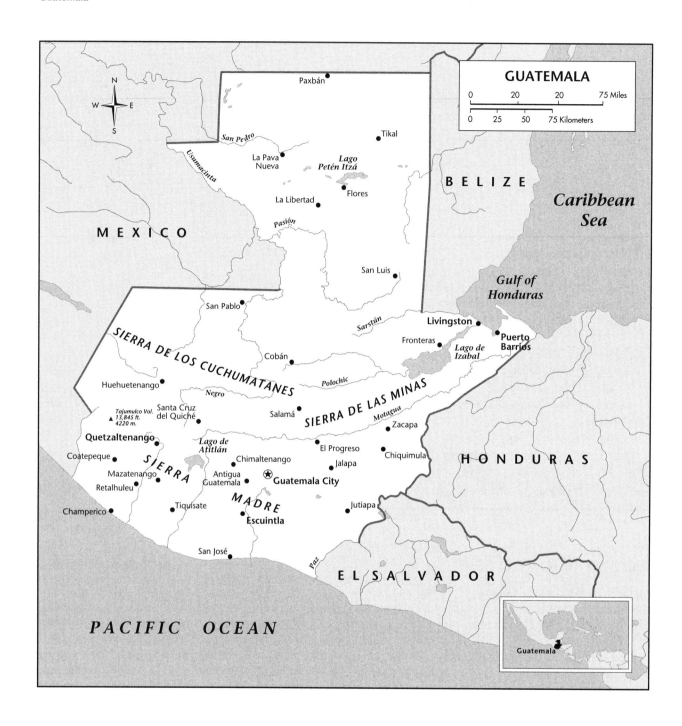

extends to the economic, political, and social realms of Guatemalan life.

OVERVIEW OF ECONOMY

Known for its varied landscape, fertile soil, and tropical climate, Guatemala has its economic roots in the coffee and banana plantations that started up around 1860 and remained the major focus of economic activity for almost a century. Until 1950, coffee and bananas alone accounted for 90 percent of the value of Guatemala's total exports. After World War II, the practice of commercial farming spread, and the production of cotton, sugar,

and livestock became an integral part of the national economy. Augmented by mining and manufacturing activity, the economy continued to expand and diversify during the 1960s and 1970s. The debt crisis of the 1980s led to sinking export prices, **inflation**, and declining product values, but the Guatemalan economy gained new life in the 1990s, particularly after the signing of the 1996 Peace Accords that put an end to Guatemala's 36-year internal conflict. Currently, Guatemala has the highest GDP in Central America and continues to enjoy strong growth rates. The major forces acting upon Guatemala's economy at present are the fluctuating international demand for primary resources, the actions of political elites, and the implementation of **liberalization** measures (including **privatizations**, trade and investment reforms, and tax reform).

Guatemala has achieved a fairly good balance between the agricultural, manufacturing, and service sectors of its economy. In agriculture, it is the third largest exporter of coffee in the world and a major exporter of bananas and sugar, while its manufacturing sector depends chiefly on the apparel, construction, mining, and energy industries. The service sector, which composes the largest segment of Guatemala's GDP, embraces telecommunications, tourism, and other technological enterprises. Guatemala, though not a net exporter of petroleum, is the only oil-producing nation in Central America, and the possibility of investing more intensively in oil and natural gas in the future is a viable one. Unfortunately, the **infrastructure** needed to develop Guatemala's natural resources is sorely lacking at present, with low telephone density, scarce access to electricity, and poor road networks outside of Guatemala City posing impediments to entrepreneurial investments.

The **macroeconomic** indicators often used to measure a nation's economic status speak well of Guatemala's economy. Inflation and currency **devaluation** have remained steady (excepting the debt crisis of the 1980s, when they were pushed beyond acceptable levels), the **foreign debt** of US$4.4 billion is manageable, and the GDP has grown steadily for the last decade, following a period of stunted growth during the 1980s. The political climate is also ripe for foreign investment, as the war between the Guatemalan government and the Guatemalan National Revolutionary Unity (URNG) guerrilla group came to an end in 1996. Recent privatizations have lessened the role of the government in the Guatemalan economy, easing the financial burden on the state and providing an immediate source of income from the sale of the previously state-owned enterprises. Furthermore, the government has adopted plans to dollarize its economy, following the path taken by other Latin American countries, including Ecuador, El Salvador, and Panama. Dollarization (the adoption of the U.S. dollar as the official monetary unit by another country) is generally viewed in a positive light by foreign investors, as it holds interest rates to lower levels and promises to eliminate devaluation.

While macroeconomic indicators paint a hopeful picture of Guatemala's economic situation, the conditions that exist within the nation provide far less cause for optimism. Poverty and inequality are endemic in Guatemala and are linked to the nation's other socio-economic problems, which include an inadequate education system, widespread health and sanitation deficiencies, and high rates of crime and violence. These issues have contributed to political turmoil in the past, and while Guatemala is

no longer plagued by civil war, there is still great unrest and tension within the nation that could threaten political and economic stability in the future. International agencies and foreign governments are dispensing aid to Guatemala more willingly now than during the nation's civil war, but these funds are not large enough to promote change in a system that is deeply rooted in unequal distribution of land and wealth.

POLITICS, GOVERNMENT, AND TAXATION

Guatemala is a constitutional democratic republic that is divided into 22 departments and governed by a 3-branch system, consisting of the executive, legislative, and judicial. The legislative branch consists of the National Congress, a 1-house legislature composed of 116 members, while the judicial branch is headed by the Supreme Court of Justice. The president serves as both the chief of state and the head of government and has the authority to appoint departmental governors and cabinet members.

Current president Alfonso Portillo of the Guatemalan Republican Front (FRG) was elected by a landslide victory in his December 1999 campaign against candidate Oscar Berger of the National Advancement Party (PAN). The FRG and the PAN are the 2 major political parties active in Guatemala today; a third party, the New Nation Alliance (ANN), plays a minor role in the nation's political races. The PAN (the party to which Portillo's predecessor Alvaro Arzú belonged) is conservative and business-oriented while the FRG is conservative and populist, at least according to the platform Portillo used to win the presidency. Both parties support rigorous economic programs that put emphasis on fiscal discipline and macroeconomic stability, but Portillo and the FRG also support policies that work to the benefit of economically disadvantaged Guatemalans. Among the policies proposed by Portillo during his first year as president were a hike in the minimum wage, the decentralization of political power, and others with similar populist themes. However, Portillo's proposals were not met with a spirit of cooperation in Congress, and little has been done to better the situation of the poor since he took office in early 2000.

The Guatemalan government traditionally has not exerted a great amount of control on the economy through regulations or other interventionist measures, preferring to keep its involvement minimal, as evident in the fact that the **private sector** generates more than 85 percent of the GDP. This hands-off approach has been bolstered by recent decisions to privatize the state telecommunications, electric generation, and electric distribution companies, as well as by new policies that lift restrictions and regulations on trade and investment in Guatemala. The government has also been frugal in its support of public and social programs; Guatemala's education and health systems leave much to be desired, often to the detriment of disadvantaged Guatemalans.

The tax system is currently undergoing reform as the Guatemalan government attempts to make taxation a more lucrative tool. In 1996, Guatemala's tax revenue accounted for just 8 percent of its GDP, putting it at the second lowest rate in the Western hemisphere. The peace accords signed in 1996 called for an increase that would bring tax revenues up to 12 percent of the GDP by 2000, providing greater funding for social programs. Unfortunately, the parties who signed on to this fiscal pact (government, social organizations, and business leaders) have not all given it their steadfast support, and tax revenues for 2000 only amounted to slightly more than 10 percent of the GDP. Among the taxes on which Guatemala relies for revenue are customs **duties**, sales taxes, and excises on liquor and tobacco. Additional taxes under discussion for reform or implementation in Guatemala currently include the **value-added tax** and new taxes to be applied to a variety of industries.

INFRASTRUCTURE, POWER, AND COMMUNICATIONS

An underdeveloped infrastructure is one of the main obstacles to investment and economic development in Guatemala. Public and private investment is disproportionately concentrated around Guatemala City because of the lack of infrastructure connecting the capital to other regions of the country. Not only is much of Guatemala's 12,795 kilometer (3,519 mile) highway network in poor condition, its electricity and telephone density is low, and all of its television stations and newspapers are concentrated in Guatemala City. Additionally, 3 ports (Champerico, Puerto Barrios, and San Jose) handle the bulk of Guatemalan exports, and La Aurora Airport is the only national airport with full capacity for both freight and passengers. These facilities are approaching their breaking points and will need to be expanded soon in order to keep up with growing trade and travel. Overall, major renovation of the country's infrastructure is necessary if trade is to continue uninterrupted.

Telephones are not as available in Guatemala as would be desirable for the purposes of business and general efficient communication. There were 430,000 main telephone lines installed in Guatemala in 1997, but this number still left Guatemala trailing several Central American countries in proportionate terms. Use of cell phones is growing at a remarkable rate, having increased by 2,047 percent between 1993 and 1997, while the number of regular phone lines in the nation increased by only 86.1 percent during the same span of time. In 1998, the government decided to privatize the state telephone company along with several other enterprises. So far, the privatization has not brought about as much progress in infrastructure as outside investors had hoped; the U.S. Department of State's *FY 2000 Country Commercial Guide: Guatemala* states, "It is not clear that the new owners of the recently privatized telephone company will undertake the investment needed to extend basic telephony to those areas currently underserved."

Electricity has also undergone significant changes due to recent privatizations. Both the major state electricity distribution company and selected assets of the state-owned electricity production company were auctioned off to private bidders in 1998, provoking anticipation of higher electricity prices but also feeding hopes of improved service, mainly among businesses and professionals.

ECONOMIC SECTORS

Guatemala's economy, while still largely dependent on the income and employment provided by the agricultural sector, has been successful in developing its manufacturing and service sectors, thereby remaining competitive within the global market. Among the products and

Communications

Country	Newspapers	Radios	TV Sets[a]	Cable subscribers[a]	Mobile Phones[a]	Fax Machines[a]	Personal Computers[a]	Internet Hosts[b]	Internet Users[b]
	1996	1997	1998	1998	1998	1998	1998	1999	1999
Guatemala	33	79	126	28.5	10	N/A	8.3	1.26	65
United States	215	2,146	847	244.3	256	78.4	458.6	1,508.77	74,100
Mexico	97	325	261	15.7	35	3.0	47.0	23.02	1,822
El Salvador	48	464	675	N/A	18	N/A	N/A	1.17	40

[a]Data are from International Telecommunication Union, *World Telecommunication Development Report 1999* and are per 1,000 people.
[b]Data are from the Internet Software Consortium (http://www.isc.org) and are per 10,000 people.

SOURCE: World Bank. *World Development Indicators 2000.*

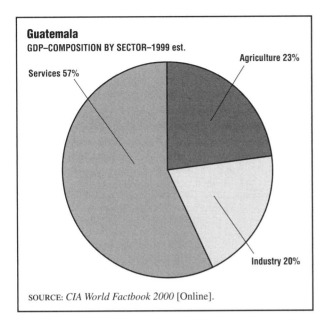

Guatemala
GDP–COMPOSITION BY SECTOR–1999 est.

Services 57%

Agriculture 23%

Industry 20%

SOURCE: *CIA World Factbook 2000* [Online].

decrease in agriculture's contribution to the GDP. This trend away from agriculture is generally viewed by development economists as a positive occurrence, since prices of agricultural products on the international market are subject to sharp, sudden declines and can create economic instability. Overall, the structure of Guatemala's economy is stable and fairly well balanced, providing it with a necessary foundation for expansion in the future.

AGRICULTURE

Although Guatemala is trying to expand its manufacturing activities to reduce economic dependence on agriculture, the agricultural sector is a crucial component of Guatemala's export and domestic economies, accounting for 23 percent of GDP (US$11 billion) in 1999 and employing 50 percent of the **labor force** (1.7 million workers).

COFFEE. One of Guatemala's original commercial developments in the 19th century, coffee production is still of vital importance to the national economy. In 1998, coffee exports brought in US$586.3 million, almost double the amount of sugar, the next most profitable agricultural export. Guatemala's production of coffee is equally important in the global economy, as Guatemala is the world's third largest exporter of coffee. Because large-scale operations are needed to produce vast quantities of coffee for export, most Guatemalan coffee is harvested at large plantations along the southern border of the highlands.

SUGAR. After coffee, sugar is Guatemala's most profitable crop, earning US$315.3 million on the world market in 1998. Sugar has also shown promise as an expanding industry in Guatemala, particularly because it can be produced in raw form or processed within the country prior to export, augmenting its value.

BANANAS. Bananas remain one of Guatemala's top agricultural exports, grabbing US$190.4 million in revenue in 1998. Like other developing countries that export bananas, Guatemala has recently encountered problems on the international market, including declining prices and a European Union policy that places new restrictions on its imports of bananas. Additionally, conflicts between Guatemalan banana workers and the companies that contract them have led international fruit companies to move their headquarters from Guatemala to Ecuador, where labor is unorganized and therefore cheaper. All of these factors have contributed to the recent decline of the banana industry in Guatemala.

services most important to Guatemala's economy are coffee, sugar, cotton, bananas, apparel, food processing, and tourism. Some of these industries date back to the early post-independence era, while others are just beginning to blossom. Tourism, for instance, was severely impeded until recently, when the Guatemalan peace accords were signed and the process of demilitarization commenced.

A look at Guatemala's economic sectors over the past thirty years shows that while there has been movement between the agricultural, industrial, and service sectors, that movement has not been uni-directional. Instead, the only well-established pattern seems to be the gradual

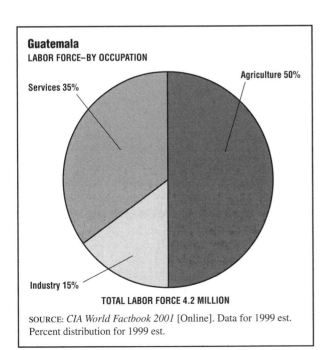

Guatemala
LABOR FORCE–BY OCCUPATION

Services 35%

Agriculture 50%

Industry 15%

TOTAL LABOR FORCE 4.2 MILLION

SOURCE: *CIA World Factbook 2001* [Online]. Data for 1999 est.
Percent distribution for 1999 est.

INDUSTRY

Industry in Guatemala, which includes food processing, publishing, mining, and the manufacture of textiles, clothing, cement, tires, and pharmaceuticals, comprises 20 percent of the GDP (US$9.6 billion) and employs about 15 percent of the total workforce (500,000 workers). After growing steadily during the 1960s and 1970s, manufacturing slowed during the debt crisis of the 1980s but picked up again during the 1990s.

TEXTILES AND APPAREL. More than 80,000 Guatemalans are currently employed by the apparel industry, most of whom are young women. The apparel industry has experienced growth over the past decade, but international attention directed to the poor working conditions within apparel-for-export factories or *maquilas* has resulted in the closing of some major plants, including the Phillips-Van Heusen factory that used to be located in Guatemala. So long as labor remains cheap and accessible in Guatemala, the apparel industry is likely to continue expanding. The United States provides a sizeable market for Guatemala's apparel exports, importing more than US$1 billion worth of apparel in 1998 alone.

MINING AND OIL. Combined with production of energy (mainly from petroleum), mining contributes roughly 3 percent of Guatemala's GDP. Antimony, copper, nickel, iron, and tungsten are all mined in Guatemala, though not in great quantities. Surveys of Guatemala's subsurface have revealed that the nation has a wealth of mineral resources, indicating that, given the right investment interest, mining could become a more prominent part of Guatemala's economy in the future. Guatemala, the only oil-producing country in Central America, has been extracting oil from its Petén Basin since the early 1980s, though it does not extract nearly enough to be a net exporter of petroleum.

SERVICES

TOURISM. The service industry contributes the largest segment of Guatemala's GDP (57 percent, or US$27.3 billion) and employs about 35 percent of the nation's total workforce (1.2 million workers). While the service sector encompasses several different industries like **retail**, financial services, transportation, and computer services, the most profitable component is tourism. Because of its agreeable climate and diverse landscape, as well as its Mayan ruins, Guatemala is becoming a popular travel destination in the post-conflict period. In light of the high profit margins associated with tourism receipts, the government is making solid efforts to expand tourism and attract more foreign visitors to Guatemala.

INTERNATIONAL TRADE

The United States, Latin America, and Europe are the most frequent destinations for Guatemala's exports, composing 51.5 percent, 26.6 percent and 11.3 percent

Trade (expressed in billions of US$): Guatemala		
	Exports	Imports
1975	.624	.733
1980	1.520	1.598
1985	1.057	1.175
1990	1.163	1.649
1995	2.156	3.293
1998	2.582	4.651

SOURCE: International Monetary Fund. *International Financial Statistics Yearbook 1999.*

of the export market respectively in 1998. In addition to its membership in the Central American Common Market trade group, Guatemala also holds free trade agreements with Panama, Chile and the Dominican Republic. Guatemala exports a wide variety of products with a mainly agricultural base, while it imports goods of an industrial nature, including machinery, road vehicles and apparel. This combination of exports and imports reflects Guatemala's position as a developing country that must rely partially on outside advancements to sustain and promote industrial activities within its own economy. As Guatemala becomes more developed and expands its manufacturing sector, it should depend less on industrial imports from the United States and other developed nations.

Guatemala has consistently imported more than it has exported over the past 25 years, but this trend has sharpened over the past 5 years or so, with imports surpassing exports by significant margins and resulting in a considerable **trade deficit**. In 1998, Guatemala exported only US$2.582 billion worth of goods while importing US$4.651 billion worth. Increasing imports can be a sign that the Guatemalan economy is strong enough to afford large quantities of goods from abroad, but they can also throw off the stability of the nation's trade regime if not matched by growth in exports.

The unprecedented level of Guatemala's imports in 1998 might also be a result of the end of *la violencia*, or the civil war, in 1996. The political space created by the peace agreement may have encouraged deeper interaction between Guatemala and the global market and may have opened up new trade opportunities with economic players who had previously withheld their trade partnership as a political gesture.

MONEY

Despite its 36-year internal conflict (1960–96) that was characterized by political instability and mass killings, Guatemala maintained a functional economy throughout the second half of the 20th century. The

Exchange rates: Guatemala

quetzales (Q) per US$1

Jan 2001	7.8020
2000	7.7632
1999	7.3856
1998	6.3947
1997	6.0653
1996	6.0495

SOURCE: CIA *World Factbook 2001* [ONLINE].

1960s and 1970s brought a healthy dose of economic development to Guatemala, resulting in impressive economic growth figures (average annual growth totaled 5.5 percent over the 20-year span of time). The 1970s in particular proved to be very important economic years, as Guatemala focused its attention on expanding the manufacturing sector in order to soften its dependence on agricultural exports. As a result, manufacturing expanded at an annual rate of more than 6 percent from 1970 to 1979. Like other Latin American countries, Guatemala was adversely affected by the foreign debt crisis of the 1980s; inflation grew to an average annual rate of 16.5 percent, and the nation's foreign debt tripled to more than US$4.7 billion. Nonetheless, Guatemala's economy staged a recovery in the 1990s that brought back healthy rates of growth and inflation. In 1999, the country experienced a mild **recession**, but the effects are expected to be temporary and surmountable.

The Guatemalan quetzal has never experienced a period of hyperinflation or intensive devaluation like many other Latin American currencies have encountered. Instead, the devaluation of the quetzal in respect to the U.S. dollar has occurred gradually; from 1983 to 2000, for example, the value of the quetzal dropped 70 percent, an average annual rate of slightly more than 4 percent. Despite the relative consistency the quetzal has experienced on the world market, Guatemalan officials are planning to dollarize the economy, eventually eliminating the quetzal in order to implement the U.S. dollar as the official national currency. The first step of the dollarization process took place on 1 May 2001, when the U.S. dollar was first allowed to circulate as legal tender. Guatemalan economists and government officials hope that by adopting the U.S. dollar, they can make Guatemala more attractive to foreign investors and effectively eliminate the phenomenon of currency devaluation. Dollarization should also encourage discipline within the banking sector, which, under the jurisdiction of the Superintendency of Banks, currently functions according to rather loose regulations and has encountered several bankruptcies.

POVERTY AND WEALTH

Although Guatemala enjoys the highest GDP in Central America, unequal distribution of wealth and rapid population growth within the nation have given Guatemala one of the highest poverty rates in Latin America. More than 75 percent of the national population lives below the poverty line, and the extent of poverty is even more severe among the rural and indigenous populations. In 1989, about 93 percent of the indigenous population in Guatemala were living in poverty and 91 percent in extreme poverty, whereas only 66 percent and 45 percent of the non-indigenous population were living in those respective conditions. Guatemala's income distribution is among the most unequal in the world, with the wealthiest 10 percent of the population owning nearly 50 percent of the national wealth and the poorest 10 percent owning less than 1 percent. As a result, there is a very small middle class in Guatemala, and political power rests almost exclusively with elite groups. Land, just like monetary wealth, is concentrated in the hands of the few, making it very difficult for poor rural workers to improve their financial situation, as the amount of land they own or have access to is minimal.

While the economic policies implemented during the 1990s in Guatemala produced manageable **inflation rates** and healthy economic growth, they did not bring about greater economic equality or help to reduce poverty. Economic reforms in Guatemala have been aimed at improving macroeconomic indicators, sometimes to the disadvantage of social spending, as with the reduction of the **public sector** deficit from 1990 to 1996, which was accomplished through spending cuts. Although some government leaders (such as current president Alfonso Portillo) have run for office on populist platforms, little has been done to improve the situation of the poorest segments of the population.

The poor in Guatemala do not have easy access to good health care, particularly because health-care facilities and experts are focused in metropolitan areas. This factor, combined with the negative health effects of pesticides and the low availability of drinking water and waste disposal services in rural areas, results in a higher

GDP per Capita (US$)

Country	1975	1980	1985	1990	1998
Guatemala	1,371	1,598	1,330	1,358	1,533
United States	19,364	21,529	23,200	25,363	29,683
Mexico	3,380	4,167	4,106	4,046	4,459
El Salvador	1,779	1,596	1,333	1,378	1,716

SOURCE: United Nations. *Human Development Report 2000;
Trends in human development and per capita income.*

Distribution of Income or Consumption by Percentage Share: Guatemala

Lowest 10%	0.6
Lowest 20%	2.1
Second 20%	5.8
Third 20%	10.5
Fourth 20%	18.6
Highest 20%	63.0
Highest 10%	46.6

Survey year: 1989
Note: This information refers to income shares by percentiles of the population and is ranked by per capita income.

SOURCE: *2000 World Development Indicators* [CD-ROM].

occurrence of health problems in rural areas than in urban centers. There are signs that the issue of health care has started to receive greater political and social attention in Guatemala. In 1996, about 13 percent of the government's budget was devoted to health, whereas in 1992 the amount allocated for health care was only 6.6 percent of the overall budget. Additionally, the government recently initiated a health sector reform to provide health services to all Guatemalans who currently lack access to health care; the minimum health services available under this plan include care of pregnant women, child health care, and emergency and disease care.

Education presents another problem for poor Guatemalans, as some parents call on their children to work long hours to contribute to the family income, preventing them from attending school. This phenomenon occurs most often in rural areas, where families engage in **subsistence farming** or work for larger landowners, and the amount of manual labor available determines a family's total income. Unfortunately, children who have to work instead of attending school miss out on the education that is almost always necessary for economic advancement. Although school attendance is compulsory for 6 years by government mandate, only 41 percent of school-aged children in Guatemala attend classes, and only 55.6 percent of the total population are literate.

WORKING CONDITIONS

The conditions under which most Guatemalans work are less than desirable and often in violation of Guatemalan law. According to the nation's labor laws, the minimum daily wage is US$3.00 for agricultural workers, US$3.30 for workers in commerce, US$3.38 for construction workers, and US$6.00 for specialized labor. The workweek consists of 44 hours for day-shift workers and 36 hours for night-shift workers. Overtime work is to be compensated with time-and-a-half pay, and children under the age of 18 are not to work overtime. In terms of workplace conditions, employers are to ensure healthy and safe environments for their workers by providing adequate bathroom facilities and on-hand medical care. If 25 percent of the employees at a given workplace request to organize a trade union, they have the right to do so freely.

Work conditions in Guatemala's agricultural and industrial sectors often fail to meet the government's specified requirements. More than 80,000 Guatemalans, most of them young women, work at *maquilas* (apparel-for-export factories), often in unsafe and unhealthy (not to mention illegal) conditions. Among the labor law violations common to *maquilas* are forced overtime, employment of children as young as 13 years old, and bathrooms that remain locked for most of the workday. Equally poor conditions exist for workers in the agricultural sector, where the need to meet daily quotas leads to the coercive employment of children as young as 6 years old by their parents, who do not receive compensation unless they reach the fixed quota. Much agricultural employment is seasonal and occurs at off-site locations, where housing facilities are generally poor; at some cotton plantations, the housing provided for workers consists of bare wooden constructions without bedding or furniture. Wages for agricultural and industrial workers often fail to meet minimum wage requirements, and average income is sometimes less than the cost of a basic food basket for a family of 5, meaning that wages are set at starvation levels.

Despite the treacherous conditions that exist for unskilled workers, fewer than 15 percent of all workers are unionized. This fact has much to do with the abuses that have been committed against trade union members and leaders over the past half-century. Military and civilian governments since the 1950s have held union organizations in contempt and have committed serious human rights abuses and "disappearances" against union leaders. Amnesty International has documented that between 1976 and 1996 (the final 20 years of Guatemala's internal war), thousands of trade unionists were tortured and killed, or "disappeared," because of their union activities. This hostile attitude towards labor organizations continues today and acts as a significant deterrent to trade union mobilization.

One major reason that work conditions are so poor and unions so weak is that work is hard to come by in Guatemala. While open unemployment affects about 7 percent of the population, total unemployment lingers around 37 percent; as a result, close to 1 million Guatemalans work in the **informal economy**, augmenting the formal economy's workforce of 3.5 million. Additionally, the culture of violence that developed during Guatemala's civil war has not yet been eliminated, so threats and coercion are common workplace elements. Not all forms of employment in Guatemala are undesirable; jobs in urban areas and in the service sector provide stable and healthy conditions and livable wages. Too often, however, working conditions do not correspond to the standards set by the Guatemalan government, and of the groups impacted by this disregard for labor laws, unskilled, rural workers suffer the gravest consequences.

COUNTRY HISTORY AND ECONOMIC DEVELOPMENT

1524. Pedro de Alvarado of Spain invades Guatemala.

1528. Alvarado defeats Guatemalans, and Spanish rule begins.

1786. Spaniards separate Chiapas, Honduras, and Nicaragua from the province of Guatemala.

1821. Guatemala, along with Central America, declares its independence from Spain.

1823. Guatemala joins with other nations to form the United Provinces of Central America.

1840. Guerilla group led by Rafael Carrera overthrows president of United Provinces, resulting in the abolition of the federation.

1850s. Guatemala embarks upon a long period of undemocratic rule, marked by a series of dictatorships, military governments, coups, and insurgencies that continue until the mid-1980s.

1901. United Fruit Company establishes itself in Guatemala, becoming the first transnational corporation in the country.

1944. The "October Revolutionaries," a group of students, liberal professionals, and military dissidents, overthrow General Jorge Ubico's dictatorship.

1945. Guatemala joins the United Nations.

1948. Guatemala joins the Organization of American States.

1952. Communist Guatemalan Labor Party gains legal status and institutes agrarian reforms that distribute unused lands to peasants.

1954. U.S. CIA deploys "Operation Success" with help from domestic forces, invading Guatemala and overthrowing President Jacobo Arbenz.

1960. Rebel Armed Forces (FAR) forms; civil war over economic and land issues commences.

1966. United States sends in Green Berets and directs counterinsurgency campaign in Guatemala; Mano Blanca and other Guatemalan death squads form.

1970s. Manufacturing expands markedly in Guatemala, growing at an annual rate of 6.2 percent.

1978. United States bans the sale of arms to Guatemalan government.

1980. Spain breaks off diplomatic relations with Guatemala after a government massacre in which Indian protestors were burned inside of the Spanish Embassy. Debt crisis strikes Guatemala; high inflation and foreign debt accumulation ensue.

1981. Guatemalan army initiates counteroffensive, destroys over 400 Indian villages in 2 years.

1982. Guerrilla Army of the Poor (EGP), Organization of Armed People (ORPA), and Rebel Armed Forces (FAR) combine to form the Guatemalan National Revolutionary Unit (URNG). Efrain Rios Montt overthrows General Angel Anibal Guevara presidency.

1983. Military overthrows Rios Montt. United States resumes sale of arms to Guatemala.

1985. Marco Vinicio Cerezo is elected, becoming the first civilian president in 15 years. United States reinstates official economic and military aid to Guatemala.

1987. Central American Peace Accord is signed.

1990. United States again cuts off military aid and arms sales to Guatemala.

1991. Economic recovery begins; Guatemala regains healthy inflation rates and experiences consistent growth.

1994. Guatemalan government and guerrillas sign agreements on human rights, resettlement, historical clarification, and indigenous rights. United Nations Human Rights Verification Mission in Guatemala (MINUGUA) is formed.

1996. Alvaro Arzú, member of National Advancement Party, is elected president. Guatemalan government and guerillas sign peace accord, ending 36-year conflict.

1997. URNG demobilizes and becomes political party.

1999. Alfonso Portillo, member of Guatemalan Republican Front, is elected president.

FUTURE TRENDS

Having finally negotiated an end to its decades-long civil war in December of 1996, Guatemala is currently attempting to construct a peaceful and democratic political environment that will foster greater economic growth and prosperity. This task has proven more difficult than anticipated, partly due to the vestiges of violence and distrust left over from the war and partly because of continuing problems with corruption, a weak justice system, and poor political representation. If such obstacles to functional democratic governance can be overcome and

Guatemala can develop a stable and more attractive atmosphere for investment, diversification of exports and economic growth should follow. Even during the period of internal political turmoil from 1960–96, Guatemala's economy experienced growth and manageable inflation rates, suggesting that the opportunities proffered by peace and demilitarization could provide the necessary impetus for economic progress.

Even so, sustaining a healthy and growing economy will require more than the absence of internal conflict and the presence of a more democratic political culture. To achieve the economic stability necessary to be competitive within the global economy, Guatemala will have to exercise fiscal discipline, privatize some of its state-owned companies, liberalize its trade regime, reform its banking sector, and explore new options for production and export. A series of economic liberalization measures initiated under the Arzú administration (1996–99) introduced privatization and lifted restrictions on trade and investment, but the process of liberalization must be embraced and continued by current and future administrations in order to bring about economic stability and progress. In respect to new production and export options, the most promising prospects for economic expansion in Guatemala are the textile and apparel industries, as well as the non-traditional export industries of shrimp farming and cut flowers. Guatemala also has proven natural gas and oil reserves that could attract substantial amounts of capital from foreign or domestic investors.

Poverty and deep-seated inequality have been the most stubborn and devastating economic problems for Guatemala in the past, and they will likely continue to afflict Guatemala, even assuming economic growth and expansion on the national level. Unequal distribution of wealth and land within the country over time has led to the present dire scenario, in which more than 60 percent of the Guatemalan population subsist on less than US$2.00 a day. Because the current political system lacks representation on the left and is dominated by 2 conservative parties (PAN and FRG), the interests of the poor and underprivileged are not likely to receive due attention in the political arena until a viable left-of-center party forms. While some of the policies proposed by President Alfonso Portillo at the beginning of his term (2000-present) would have benefited the working class, they have not been passed into law because of lack of support in Congress. International agencies and foreign governments continue to provide aid to Guatemala for poverty relief and other development initiatives, but these funds are not large enough to significantly mitigate the effects of widespread poverty, unequal distribution of wealth, and a rapidly growing population. Unless Guatemala gives serious political attention to the issues of inequality and population growth, the economic future of Guatemalans will be bleak.

DEPENDENCIES

Guatemala has no territories or colonies.

BIBLIOGRAPHY

Banco de Guatemala. "Guatemala: Algunas variables macroeconomicas, años 1950–1999." <http://www.banguat.gob.gt/ver.asp?id'/indicadores/hist03>. Accessed March 2001.

BASICS/USAID. "Guatemala: Country Achievement Summary." <http://www.basics.org/summaries/Guatemala.htm>. Accessed January 2001.

Canadian Foundation for the Americas. "Guatemala Under the FRG: Peace at a Crossroads." <http://www.focal.ca/images/pdf/guatemala.pdf>. Accessed March 2001.

Country Watch. "Guatemala: Economy." <http://www.countrywatch.com/files/069/cw_topic.asp?vCOUNTRY=069&TP=ECO>. Accessed March 2001.

Pan American Health Organization. "Guatemala: Basic Country Health profiles, Summaries 1999." <http://www.paho.org/English/SHA/prflgut.htm>. Accessed February 2001.

Population Reference Bureau. "2000 World Population Data Sheet: Central America." <http://www.prb.org/pubs/wpds2000/wpds2000_CentralAmerica.html>. Accessed March 2001.

USAID Bureau for Latin America and the Caribbean. *Latin America and the Caribbean: Selected Economic and Social Data.* Washington, D.C.: USAID, 1999.

U.S. Central Intelligence Agency. "The World Factbook: Guatemala." <http://www.cia.gov/cia/publications/factbook/geos/gt.html>. Accessed February 2001.

U.S. Department of State. "Background Notes: Guatemala." <http://www.state.gov/www/background_notes/guatemala_0500_bgn.html>. Accessed March 2001.

—Heidi Jugenitz

GUYANA

Cooperative Republic of Guyana

CAPITAL: Georgetown.

MONETARY UNIT: Guyanese dollar (G$). One Guyanese dollar equals 100 cents. Notes come in denominations of 20, 100, 500, and 1,000 dollars. Coins come in denominations of 1, 5, 50, and 100 cents. U.S. currency is also accepted in Guyana.

CHIEF EXPORTS: Sugar, gold, bauxite/alumina, rice, shrimp, molasses, rum, and timber.

CHIEF IMPORTS: Manufactures, machinery, petroleum, and food.

GROSS DOMESTIC PRODUCT: US$3.4 billion (purchasing power parity, 2000 est.).

BALANCE OF TRADE: Exports: US$570 million (f.o.b., 2000 est.). Imports: US$660 million (f.o.b., 2000 est.).

COUNTRY OVERVIEW

LOCATION AND SIZE. Guyana is situated on the northeast coast of Latin America, along the Atlantic Ocean. It shares a 600-kilometer (373-mile) border with Suriname to the east, a 743-kilometer (462-mile) border with Venezuela to the northwest, and a 1,119-kilometer (695-mile) border with Brazil to the south and southwest. Guyana covers 214,970 square kilometers (83,000 square miles), making it slightly smaller than the U.S. state of Idaho. Approximately 196,850 square kilometers (76,000 square miles) of Guyana's area is land and 18,120 square kilometers (7,000 square miles) is water. The coastline of Guyana totals 459 kilometers (285 miles). The capital, Georgetown, is located on the coast.

Guyana has 3 distinct geographical zones. It has a narrow coastal belt that is just over 25 kilometers (16 miles) in width. Much of the coastal belt is below sea level, which makes it good for sugar and rice production. Approximately 90 percent of the Guyanese population lives in this region. The high savannah uplands are located further inland. These are mostly thickly forested, hilly, tropical areas where the country's bauxite, dia-

monds, gold, manganese, and other minerals are found. The highest point is Mount Roraima, which rises to 2,835 meters (9,302 feet). The river basin hosts Guyana's massive rivers, namely the Demerara, Berbice, Courantyne, and Essequibo. Rapids, bars, and other obstacles make navigation very difficult on these waters.

POPULATION. The population was estimated at 697,181 in 2001, with an average annual growth rate of 0.07 percent in the same year. Recently the population has been falling as a result of out-migration. Half of Guyana's population is descended from Indian workers of the Dutch West Indian Company who first settled there in 1620. One-third of the population descends from native Africans who were brought as slaves in the 18th century. The rest are mostly Amerindians, Europeans, Chinese, and people of mixed races.

Guyana has the highest proportion in South America of people who live in rural areas, with only 35 percent living in urban areas in 1995. English is the official language, although Hindi and Urdu are used by the Indian community. There is religious diversity in Guyana; Protestants constitute 34 percent of the population, 34 percent are Hindu, Catholics are 18 percent, and 9 percent are Muslim.

OVERVIEW OF ECONOMY

Guyana is one of the poorest countries in South America, with a per capita income of US$4,800 in 2000 (figured at **purchasing power parity**). After gaining independence from Great Britain in 1966, Guyana followed a **socialist** model of development. The bauxite, timber, and sugar industries were **nationalized** in the first half of the 1970s, and by 1976 the state controlled 75 percent of the country's economy. At the same time, regional integration was implemented through the Caribbean Common Market (CARICOM), the Latin American Economic

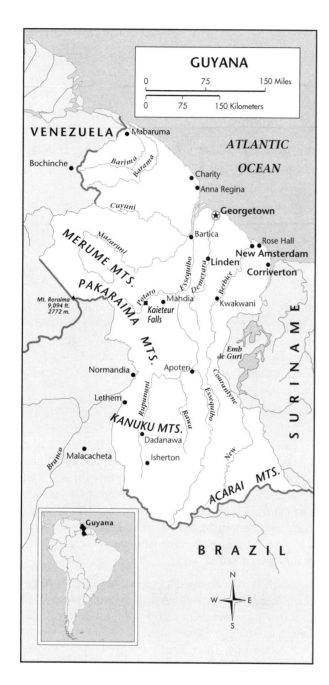

the rationed commodities and foreign exchange could be purchased, but at prices higher than the official prices. During the 1980s the **real gross domestic product** (GDP) continually declined, falling at a yearly average of 2.8 percent, mainly due to economic mismanagement. With the rising share of foreign interest payments, gross national income declined at an even faster rate of 4.9 percent a year.

Technical, organizational, and financial problems in Guyana's key sectors (sugar, rice, and bauxite production) and falling world demand led to stagnation in output and a consequent decline in government revenues in the late 1980s. Inflation accelerated, and there was an increased reliance on external borrowing. While new investments were being made in the public industrial sector, the nation's **infrastructure** was being neglected and steadily deteriorated.

By 1988 output was only 68 percent of the 1976 level. Since Guyana's **external debt** is denominated in U.S. dollars, if the exchange rate is reduced (such as by the **devaluation** in 1989), the value of the debt expressed in Guyanese dollars increases. In 1989, total debt become over 600 percent of the GDP. The severe decline in living standards led to a major migration of talented Guyanese to lucrative jobs abroad.

In 1988, the government adopted an Economic Recovery Program (ERP) that called for a major redirection in government policy. Specifically, there was a greatly reduced role in the economy by the **public sector** and a removal of price and exchange controls that led to shortages and unofficial markets.

Few countries have undertaken such a dramatic turnaround in economic policies, and even fewer have implemented such a program with so much speed and determination. Because of the government's efforts, a support group of donors was organized, and Guyana was able to secure financing to clear debts to the multilateral agencies. The government was also able to agree with the International Monetary Fund (IMF), the World Bank, and the Caribbean Development Bank (CDB) on major programs of support. Guyana also reached agreement with the Paris Club (a group of creditor countries who lend to developing countries) on a major program of **debt relief**.

The government has continued to implement the ERP despite the 1998 drought that severely affected the economy. The GDP growth in 1997 was estimated at 6.3 percent. However, the drought caused the growth rate to fall to -1.5 percent in 1998, but there has been a modest recovery to 1.8 percent in 1999 and 3 percent in 2000.

POLITICS, GOVERNMENT, AND TAXATION

The original inhabitants of what is now Guyana were the Arawaks. They were displaced from the area by the

System (SELA), and the Caribbean Merchant Fleet. In 1980 Guyana granted authorization for transnational corporations to carry out oil and uranium explorations.

By 1988 the government controlled over 80 percent of recorded import and export trade and 85 percent of total investment. The government attempted to set prices and fix the **exchange rate** for currency. With **inflation**, prices and the exchange rate were soon rendered unrealistically low. At the low prices, more commodities and more foreign exchange were demanded than could be supplied. There were shortages of supplies, and the government instituted a system of rationing. Unofficial markets (sometimes called parallel or **black markets**) emerged, where

Caribs, warriors who dominated the region before moving on. Both the Arawaks and the Caribs were nomadic, moved primarily in clans of 15–20 people, and lived by fishing and hunting.

Attracted by the legend of El Dorado—a fabled city that was thought to be full of gold and precious jewels—the Dutch built the first fort in present-day Guyana in 1616. They divided Guyana into 3 colonies: Demerara, Berbice, and Essequibo. The territory was captured by Britain in 1796 and renamed British Guiana.

Beginning in 1950, an anti-colonial struggle was spearheaded by the People's Progressive Party (PPP), led by Cheddi Jagan and Forbes Burnham. After the success of the PPP in the elections of 1953 and the introduction of a socialist program, however, the British government suspended the constitution and sent troops into Georgetown. Some members of the PPP were detained or confined to their homes. By the time internal autonomy was granted in 1961, Burnham had split with Jagan to form a more moderate People's National Congress (PNC). After years of struggle and violence, Britain recognized Guyana as an independent state within the British Commonwealth on 26 May 1966. Burnham served as the first prime minister.

On 23 February 1970, Guyana became the first ever Cooperative Republic, with Arthur Chung as its first non-executive president. In October 1980, Prime Minister Forbes Burnham declared himself the executive president. About 2 months later his party, the PNC, won a large majority of votes in the National Assembly election, which was widely condemned as being rigged. It was declared that Burnham was duly elected as president.

When Burnham died in August 1985, Prime Minister Desmond Hoyte succeeded him as president. Like his predecessor, Hoyte was declared duly elected when the PNC gained a large majority during the 1985 election for the National Assembly, although the results were again disputed. However, desperate economic circumstances forced Guyana to seek external aid that came with the condition of restoring credible elections. Cheddi Jagan finally gained power in 1992. Following his death in March 1997, his wife, Janet Jagan, was sworn in as president on 24 December 1997. When Janet Jagan resigned in 1999, Bharrat Jagdeo assumed the presidency.

In 1980 a new constitution was adopted. The constitution established an executive president and a National Assembly, which consists of 53 elected members and 12 members appointed by local government councils. Elections for 5-year terms are held under a single list system of **proportional representation**, with the whole of the country forming one electoral area and each voter casting a vote for a party list of candidates. Guyana has 10 administrative regions.

The tax system in Guyana is poorly administered, and the level of collection is far below the system's potential. Evasion, avoidance, and corruption are rampant. For example, in 1991 tax revenue from the **private sector** amounted to only 21 percent of the GDP. Many firms enjoy overly generous tax and **tariff** holidays as part of the government's attempt to encourage new investment through incentives. Corrupt revenue officials issue lower tax demands as the result of bribery.

Sales taxes are very high for some products (up to 150 percent), though other sectors, such as services, are ignored entirely. Fees charged for public services, which often have not been adjusted for inflation, are very low or simply remain uncollected or are non-existent. The present tariff structure remains protective. While it follows the CARICOM structure, the top tariff rate of 45 percent is high by present standards in Latin America. Many other Latin American countries have reduced tariffs to a maximum of 20 percent. It has been estimated that the system of tariff protection and fiscal incentives cost the country G$150,000 for every job created. However, the Economic Recovery Program (ERP) launched in 1988 began to reverse these policies. It eliminated import licensing, reduced tariffs, and began an overhaul of the entire tax system. Corporate **income tax** is relatively high at 45 percent. The tax rate on capital gains is 20 percent, and interest and dividends paid by non-resident companies are subject to a 15 percent withholding tax.

INFRASTRUCTURE, POWER, AND COMMUNICATIONS

Most public sector infrastructure necessary to support the private sector has deteriorated almost to the point of non-existence. Power and water supplies are so erratic that many large private sector firms have invested in their own generators and water sources. The road system has deteriorated, particularly the critical farm-to-market network of feeder roads. In 1996 it was estimated that there were 7,970 kilometers (4,953 miles) of highways, of which only 590 kilometers (367 miles) were paved. Passenger cars numbered 24,000 in 1993, and there were approximately 9,000 commercial vehicles. The sea wall system, which protects the most productive agricultural land, has been breached in several places and patched temporarily but needs major reconstruction. Even in urban areas most of the population lacks access to safe water supplies.

Social services are inadequate to meet the needs of the population. Schools lack basic repairs, books, equipment, and supplies. Hospitals operate with most equipment not working, with no drugs to dispense, insufficient budgets for food, and the inability to carry out simple diagnostic tests, such as X-rays or blood tests. In 1994, there were 30 hospitals (5 private), 162 health centers,

Communications

Country	Telephones[a]	Telephones, Mobile/Cellular[a]	Radio Stations[b]	Radios[a]	TV Stations[a]	Televisions[a]	Internet Service Providers[c]	Internet Users[c]
Guyana	70,000 (2000)	6,100 (2000)	AM 3; FM 3; shortwave 1	420,000	3	46,000	3	3,000
United States	194 M	69.209 M (1998)	AM 4,762; FM 5,542; shortwave 18	575 M	1,500	219 M	7,800	148 M
Brazil	17.039 M	4.4 M	AM 1,365; FM 296; shortwave 161 (1999)	71 M	138	36.5 M	50	8.65 M
Suriname	64,000	4,090	AM 4; FM 13; shortwave 1	300,000	3 (2000)	63,000	2	10,000

[a]Data is for 1997 unless otherwise noted.
[b]Data is for 1998 unless otherwise noted.
[c]Data is for 2000 unless otherwise noted.

SOURCE: CIA *World Factbook 2001* [Online].

and 14 health posts. In 1997 there were 38.8 hospital beds per 10,000 persons.

Guyana has a small government-owned railway in the northwest region, while the Guyana Mining Enterprise operates a standard gauge railway of 133 kilometers (82.6 miles). The private line runs from Linden, located on the Demerara River, to Huhi and Coomacka. There is an international airport at Georgetown. Guyana has 4 ports, with the major shipping port located in Georgetown. Guyana has an **Exclusive Economic Zone** (EEZ) of 200 nautical miles.

There is an inland public telegraph and radio communication corporation. In 1997, there were 55,100 telephone main lines (65.2 per 1,000 population). Cellular phone subscribers numbered 1,200 in 1995, and there were 85 post offices. In 1998, electricity production was 325 million kilowatt hours (kWh). More than 98 percent of electricity was produced from fossil fuels and less than 2 percent from hydropower.

Guyana has no domestic petroleum resources. The National Energy Authority (GNE) imports all petroleum products other than those required by the bauxite industry, largely through a Venezuelan line of credit. At present some exploration activity is going on both offshore and in southern Guyana, but no commercially viable resources have yet been located.

ECONOMIC SECTORS

Upon gaining independence, Guyana followed a socialist strategy for development. Major productive sectors were controlled either through government investment or through **price controls** and foreign exchange rationing. Since 1990 Guyana has pursued an economic policy where state control has been reduced by **privatization**.

Agriculture accounted for approximately 35 percent of the GDP in 1998, with the main products being sugar, coffee, cocoa, coconut and edible oils, copra, fruit, vegetables, and tobacco. In 1995, the total area of forestland totaled 18.58 million hectares (46 acres). Guyana and neighboring Suriname were the world's most heavily forested countries in 1995. About 25 percent of the country's energy needs are met by woodfuel. Timber production in 1996 was 580,000 cubic meters. Total fish catches in 1995 came to approximately 46,000 metric tons, of which more than 98 percent was from marine sources.

Industry generated 32.5 percent of the GDP in 1998, with the main activities being agro-processing (sugar, rice, timber, and coconut) and mining (gold and diamonds). There is a light manufacturing sector, and tex-

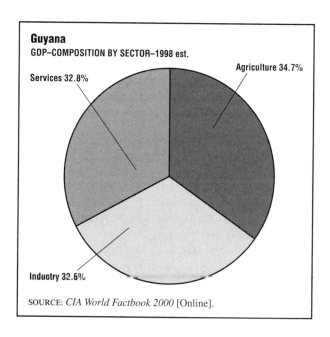

Guyana
GDP–COMPOSITION BY SECTOR–1998 est.

Services 32.8%
Agriculture 34.7%
Industry 32.5%

SOURCE: *CIA World Factbook 2000* [Online].

tiles and pharmaceuticals are produced by state and private companies.

Services accounted for about 33 percent of the GDP in 1998. The service sector is comprised mainly of banking and financial services, post and telecommunications, transport, tourism, hotels and restaurants, and public administration.

AGRICULTURE

Guyana has a rich and potentially very productive agriculture sector that can make major contributions to the recovery of the economy. There is scope for expansion, as a considerable amount of suitable land is currently not being cultivated. Guyana is mostly self-sufficient in food.

The main agricultural exports are sugar, rice, and shrimp. Sugar production has risen from 162,573 metric tons in 1991 to 280,066 metric tons in 1996. Approximately 255,655 metric tons of sugar were produced in 1998 despite the severe drought. Most of the sugar is exported to Europe under the Lomé Convention (an agreement by the European Union under which preferential trade terms are offered to certain developing countries). Most of the rice is produced by small-scale farmers, unlike sugar production, which is mainly a plantation activity. Other agricultural products are coffee, cocoa, cotton, coconut, copra, fruit, vegetables, and tobacco.

There is some cattle ranching, and pigs, sheep, and poultry are also raised. The fishing industry, which supplies both the domestic and export markets, is expanding. A big fisheries complex that is being constructed on the Demerara River will provide freezing and packing facilities. Forestry covers around 75 percent of the country. Large areas are, therefore, inaccessible, and agricultural development is hindered by the lack of electricity and economic transport.

Most agricultural output is derived from a thin belt of land close to the sea, most of which is below sea level. The sea wall system, which prevents inundation at high tide, is in danger of collapse due to lack of maintenance and wave damage during storms. Repairs to the sea wall are critical, and the immediate action program will cost about US$36 million, a large sum relative to the Guyanese economy.

The country's drainage and irrigation systems are in need of repair and currently are poorly managed. The divestment of state-owned land and the provision of adequate land titles to privately owned farms is a daunting but essential task if the market system is to raise agricultural productivity.

Agriculture provides the raw materials for Guyana's agro-based industries. The major crops include rice, sugar, coffee, cocoa, coconuts, edible oils, copra, fruit, vegetables, and tobacco. Livestock include cattle, sheep, pigs, goats, and chickens.

INDUSTRY

The main industries in Guyana are agro-processing (sugar, rice, timber, and coconut) and mining (gold and diamonds). There is a light-manufacturing sector, and textile and pharmaceuticals are produced by state and private companies. Manufacturing constituted 7.3 percent of the GDP in 1996. Manufacturing output declined at 3.9 percent annually between 1977 and 1987. The manufacturing sector then recovered through a government reform program and expanded at 8.8 percent annually between 1988 and 1998. About 75 percent of production is comprised of processing primary products (rice, coconut, sugar, bauxite, gold, diamonds, and timber). There are also many small workshops and factories producing flour, footwear, clothing, soap, cigarettes, and soft drinks. Mining and quarrying contributed about 16.5 percent of the GDP in 1996. Outdated equipment and the industry's indebtedness have hampered the bauxite/alumina industry.

SERVICES

Guyana has a small but significant tourism sector, which generated about US$39 million from 93,000 visitors in 1997. Many of the tourists were expatriate Guyanese. Guyana has great potential for adventure and nature-watch holidays, with the Kaieteur Falls especially offering considerable tourist potential. Hotel accommodation is available in Georgetown but does not meet demand. There are camps and resorts in the interior of the country, most of which are connected with Georgetown hotels. Tours by light aircraft are also available.

INTERNATIONAL TRADE

Guyana's economic situation remains constrained by its difficulties in external payments, although exports are beginning to respond to recent adjustments in the exchange rate. In 1991, the current account deficit amounted to 52 percent of the GDP. Guyana's external debt in early 1998 was US$1.65 billion. Interest payments on external debt took up 20 percent of export earnings in 1998.

In 1991, total exports increased by 17 percent largely because of better results in the bauxite, sugar, and rice sectors. Imports, however, increased by the same amount, reflecting an increase in the level of investment, particularly in the public sector and general recovery of the economy. By 2000, exports were valued at US$570 million and imports at US$660 million.

Principal commodities exported in 1996 were sugar, US$150.7 million; gold, US$105.9 million; rice, US$93.7

Trade (expressed in billions of US$): Guyana

	Exports	Imports
1975	.357	.342
1980	.396	.365
1985	.206	.226
1990	.251	.311
1995	.467	.528
1998	.485	N/A

SOURCE: International Monetary Fund. *International Financial Statistics Yearbook 1999.*

GDP per Capita (US$)

Country	1975	1980	1985	1990	1998
Guyana	873	819	626	554	825
United States	19,364	21,529	23,200	25,363	29,683
Brazil	3,464	4,253	4,039	4,078	4,509
Suriname	888	930	801	787	N/A

SOURCE: United Nations. *Human Development Report 2000; Trends in human development and per capita income.*

million; and bauxite, US$86.0 million. Other important exports include shrimp, timber, and rum. The main export markets in 1998 were the United States (25 percent), Canada (24 percent), the United Kingdom (19 percent), Netherlands Antilles (11 percent), and Jamaica (5 percent).

Most imports consist of **capital goods** (about 45 percent of the total in 1990) and **intermediate goods** (42 percent). Fuels and lubricants are the principal intermediate goods. Imports in 1998 came from the United States (28 percent), Trinidad and Tobago (21 percent), Netherlands Antilles (14 percent), the United Kingdom (7 percent), and Japan (8 percent).

MONEY

The unit of currency is the Guyanese dollar (G$), which is divided into 100 cents. The Guyanese dollar became a floating currency in 1991 in order to curb the large-scale illegal trade in foreign currency. It then depreciated rapidly from G$40=US$1 in 1990 to G$143=US$1 at the start of 1995. The value of the Guyanese dollar held steady from 1995 to 1997. It began to fall again in 1998 due to falling commodity prices and domestic political uncertainty. By mid-2001 it had depreciated to G$180.5=US$1. The depreciation meant that, as compared with 1990, imported goods cost over 4 times as much. There has been a major push to make do with locally produced substitutes for imports. For ex-

ports, the revenue in Guyanese dollars for producing a kilogram of gold became more than 4 times greater, providing a major incentive to produce more for export.

POVERTY AND WEALTH

It is difficult to know exactly the nature and the extent of poverty in Guyana. Since the 1980s, thankfully, out-migration has resulted in a low population growth rate, so a growing population is not among Guyana's problems. At the same time, the real GDP has fallen by 24 percent, and consumption spending has fallen by 22 percent. The incidence of underweight children suggests that about 16 percent of the population was below the dollar-a-day poverty line in 1998.

The measure of per capita GDP using the purchasing power parity conversion (which makes allowance for the low price of basic commodities in Guyana) was US$4,800 in 2000 which puts Guyana near the top of the low-income group of countries. The United Nations Human Development Index (which combines measures of income, health, and education) ranked Guyana as 96th out of 174 countries in 1998, and Guyana was judged to have a medium level of human development. Thus, Guyana is placed among those countries with levels of income, health provision, and educational facilities that

Exchange rates: Guyana

Guyanese dollars (G$) US$1

Nov 2000	184.1
2000	182.2
1999	178.0
1998	150.5
1997	142.4
1996	140.4

SOURCE: CIA *World Factbook 2001* [ONLINE].

Distribution of Income or Consumption by Percentage Share: Guyana

Lowest 10%	2.4
Lowest 20%	6.3
Second 20%	10.7
Third 20%	15.0
Fourth 20%	21.2
Highest 20%	46.9
Highest 10%	32.0

Survey year: 1993
Note: This information refers to expenditure shares by percentiles of the population and is ranked by per capita expenditure.

SOURCE: *2000 World Development Indicators* [CD-ROM].

are mid-way between the high human development countries of Europe and North America and the countries that are the poorest and most deprived.

WORKING CONDITIONS

The **labor force** was 245,492 in 1992 with an unemployment rate of 12 percent, a rate that remained the same in 1999. However, the majority of the population relies on agriculture for their livelihoods, and there is probably considerable "disguised unemployment" in small-scale farming. There is relatively little work to do for much of the year in **subsistence farming**, and the work is shared among the family members. During planting and harvesting there is more work to be done, and everyone is more fully occupied. Even in these periods, however, there may be more than enough labor to do the tasks, and the work is again shared by many. Everyone who shares the work appears to have an occupation in agriculture, but in fact workers are not engaged full time for the entire year, hence the "disguised unemployment."

There is no regulation of working conditions in the small-scale farming sector. In other sectors of the economy regulation is not enforced, and minimum wage levels have been rendered obsolete by inflation. Guyanese workers generally possess very low skills levels, as most skilled workers have left the country for better jobs elsewhere. There are active labor unions that exist in nearly every organized industry, but they have not been very effective in attaining better conditions for their laborers.

COUNTRY HISTORY AND ECONOMIC DEVELOPMENT

1600. The Dutch begin to settle along the coast of Guyana.

1796. The Dutch are ousted by the British.

1831. Britain consolidates the area as the colony of British Guiana.

1966. Guyana becomes a self-governing dominion within the British Commonwealth; Forbes Burnham becomes prime minister.

1968. Burnham's People's National Congress (PNC) wins electoral victory following the controversial enfranchisement of overseas Guyanese. The United Force (UF) leaves the coalition, protesting irregularities in the elections.

1970. Guyana is proclaimed a Cooperative Republic; the post of governor-general is abolished. Supreme Court Justice Arthur Chung is elected president.

1971. The Demerara Bauxite Company is nationalized.

1973. Legislation is passed permitting preventive detention without trial and restricting freedom of movement.

1974. By the Declaration of Sophia, the PNC is transformed into a socialist party committed to nationalization of all foreign enterprises and redistribution of land.

1975. The Reynolds Guyana Mines are nationalized.

1976. The Booker Sugar Estates are nationalized. The government announces plans to nationalize the school system.

1977. Burnham rejects the plan of Cheddi Jagan, leader of the opposition People's Progressive Party (PPP), for a national coalition government. A strike by sugar workers becomes violent as the government uses police force to break it.

1978. Jonestown, Guyana is the scene of a mass suicide by over 900 members of the People's Temple commune, led by U.S. cultist, Jim Jones.

1980. Guyana adopts the presidential form of government when a new constitution is approved; Burnham becomes the first president under the new constitution.

1985. Burnham dies and is succeeded in office by Hugh Hoyte, who promises to continue Burnham's leftist policies. In national elections, Hoyte is elected president, and the PNC wins with a massive majority.

1990. Guyana accepts IMF conditions and begins receiving assistance. The World Bank and the Caribbean Development Bank resume lending.

1991. Guyana becomes a member of the Organization of American States (OAS).

1992. In elections held in October, the PPP/Civic Congress, still led by Dr. Cheddi Jagan, wins 54 percent of the vote and gains 28 seats. The PNC wins 23 seats and 2 seats are won by other parties.

1997. Jagan dies from a heart attack in March. Elections held in December are won by the PPP/Civic Congress with 56 percent of officially counted votes. Jagan's widow becomes Guyana's first female president.

1998. Violent PNC-supported protests over election results rock the country in mid-January. The PNC agrees to join parliament in July following a CARICOM summit in St. Lucia.

1999. An agreement between members of the PPP/Civic Congress and PNC is reached to draft a new constitution focusing on limiting the powers of the president and making the electoral process more transparent. President Jagan resigns in August because of illness and nominates Bharrat Jagdeo as president.

2001. National Assembly elections give the PPP/Civic Congress 35 seats, the PNC 27 seats, and other parties 4 seats.

FUTURE TRENDS

The long-term outlook for Guyana continues to be discouraging. The problems of shortages caused by setting prices and fixing the exchange rate have ended with the abolition of these regulations, but economic recovery will remain slow until the government earns the full confidence of the international community. The country still suffers from the accumulated costs of past policies, including an external debt that is over 240 percent of the GDP and a very low per capita income in comparison to the rest of Latin America and the Caribbean.

Severe drought and political turmoil caused Guyana to report a negative growth rate of -1.5 percent in 1998, following 6 straight years of growth of 5 percent or higher. Growth rebounded to 1.8 percent in 1999 and 3 percent in 2000. Underlying factors in the GDP growth have included expansion in the key agricultural and mining sectors, a more favorable atmosphere for business initiative, a realistic exchange rate, a moderate **inflation rate**, and continued support from international organizations. President Jagdeo, the former finance minister, is taking steps to reform the economy, including drafting an investment code and **restructuring** the inefficient and unresponsive public sector. Problems hindering the economy include a shortage of skilled labor and an inadequate and poorly maintained transportation system. Electricity has been in short supply, but the privatization of the sector in 1999 is expected to improve prospects.

Guyana is rich in minerals, especially bauxite, gold, and diamonds. In comparison to general worldwide deforestation, Guyana has suffered little and until 1990, only a small fraction of the extensive forests had been felled. An improved infrastructure will harness the potential in mining and forestry and enable Guyana to experience steady progress.

DEPENDENCIES

Guyana has no territories or colonies.

BIBLIOGRAPHY

Economist Intelligence Unit. *Country Profile: Guyana.* London: Economist Intelligence Unit, 2001.

Embassy of the Republic of Guyana, Washington, D.C. <http://www.guyana.org/govt/embassy.html>. Accessed October 2001.

Guyana News and Information. <http://www.guyana.org>. Accessed October 2001.

Jeffrey, Henry B. *Guyana: Politics, Economics, and Society: Beyond the Burnham Era.* Boulder, Colorado: Rienner Publishers, 1986.

U.S. Central Intelligence Agency. *World Factbook 2001.* <http://www.odci.gov/cia/publications/factbook/index.html>. Accessed September 2001.

U.S. Department of State. *FY 2001 Country Commercial Guide: Guyana.* <http://www.state.gov/www/about_state/business/com_guides/2001/wha/index.html>. Accessed October 2001.

—Allan C. K. Mukungu

HAITI

CAPITAL: Port-au-Prince.

MONETARY UNIT: The Haitian gourde. One gourde equals 100 centimes. There are coins of 5, 10, 20, and 50 centimes. There are notes of 1, 2, 5, 10, 50, 100, 250, and 500 gourdes.

CHIEF EXPORTS: Manufactured goods (clothing, sports goods), coffee, oils, mangos.

CHIEF IMPORTS: Food, machinery and transport equipment, fuels.

GROSS DOMESTIC PRODUCT: US$9.2 billion (purchasing power parity, 1999 est.).

BALANCE OF TRADE: Exports: US$322 million (f.o.b., 1999). **Imports:** US$762 million (c.i.f., 1999).

---

270 persons per square kilometer (699 per square mile) in 1997. Land shortages and urban overcrowding have led to many Haitians attempting to **emigrate**, either to the neighboring Dominican Republic or to the United States. The net migration rate stood at 2.97 persons per 1,000 in 2000. The capital, Port-au-Prince, had an estimated population of 850,000 in 1995, but much settlement in slum areas is unregulated, and the population probably exceeds 1 million.

Haiti's population is a young one, with 41 percent estimated to be between 0 and 14 years of age in 2000. Most Haitians are of African descent, with approximately 95 percent of the population defined as black. The remaining 5 percent is comprised of mulattos (people of mixed European and African ancestry), and a small community descended from immigrants from the Middle East.

OVERVIEW OF ECONOMY

Haiti has long been the poorest country in the Western Hemisphere, a consequence of its unique historical development, generations of misrule, and declining natural resources. Since its slave revolution and war of independence, which culminated in the founding of the nation in 1804, the country's economy has been dominated by small-scale agricultural production. Rural overpopulation, the increasing division of small farms, and disastrous ecological degradation caused by tree felling and soil erosion have destroyed the traditional economy in some parts of the country and threaten it in others. Traditionally, most small farmers and peasant laborers have had little to do with the state, other than to pay taxes on export commodities such as coffee. The machinery of government, the political parties, and the country's business and cultural life are almost exclusively concentrated

COUNTRY OVERVIEW

LOCATION AND SIZE. Haiti occupies the western third of the island of Hispaniola, between the Atlantic Ocean and Caribbean Sea, which it shares with the Dominican Republic. Haiti has an area of 27,750 square kilometers (10,714 square miles), slightly smaller than Maryland. It shares a border of 275 kilometers (171 miles) with the Dominican Republic and has a coastline of 1,771 kilometers (1,100 miles). Its capital and largest city, Port-au-Prince, is in a bay on the country's southwestern coast.

POPULATION. Haiti's population was estimated at 6,867,995 in July 2000, showing a growth rate of 1.39 percent and a total rise of 36 percent since the last official census of 1982, when the population stood at 5,053,792. The country's demographic statistics reveal the effect of extreme poverty and an HIV/AIDS epidemic. These conditions have reduced life expectancy to 49.2 years, contributed to high infant mortality and general death rates, and slowed population growth. At current growth rates, Haiti's population will stand at approximately 7 million in 2010.

Despite slow growth rates, Haiti is one of the most densely populated countries in the world, estimated at

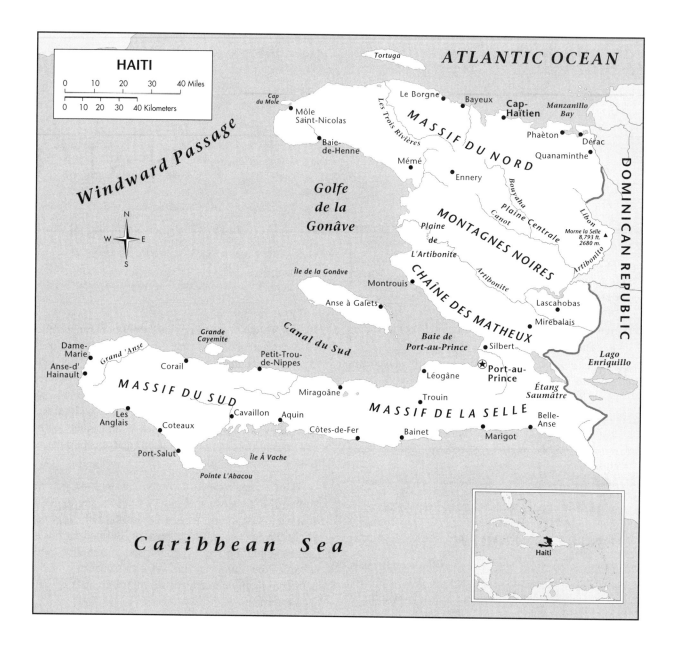

in Port-au-Prince, a small city until the 1950s but now a rapidly growing area of shantytown development (shantytowns are dwellings constructed primarily of found materials, including cardboard and pieces of metal). A huge gulf has existed between a poor, black, peasantry, who are mainly illiterate and Creole-speaking, and a small, lighter-skinned, urban elite who speak French and, increasingly, English.

In the 1970s the dictatorship of Jean-Claude Duvalier tried to capitalize on Haiti's huge unemployment and low wage rates by inviting foreign companies, principally from the United States, to establish manufacturing bases near Port-au-Prince. In the 1980s this sector grew substantially, producing clothing, sports goods, and electronic parts for the North American market. However, intense political turmoil in the late 1980s and 1990s,

coupled with the deterioration of the country's **infrastructure**, has since reduced the number of foreign companies operating in Haiti.

Haiti is, therefore, a country of largely impoverished peasant farmers and urban slum dwellers, with a small minority of lighter-skinned, wealthier people who tend to control import-export businesses, the financial sector, and a small tourist industry. There are few national companies, but family-run enterprises, often working as agents for U.S. businesses, dominate commerce. Since the 1950s Haiti has also been dependent on foreign aid, although its political violence and occasional periods of international isolation have often prevented that aid from reaching its intended beneficiaries. Government expenditures far exceed government revenues through taxation, and this shortfall is usually met by grants and loans from multinational agencies, totaling US$353 million in 1998 alone. Haiti's **foreign debt** stood at approximately US$1 billion in 1997.

In recent years Haitian governments have come under pressure from international aid agencies to **liberalize** the economy in return for continuing aid. Successive governments had retained control over important sectors of the economy, leading to huge inefficiency and persistent corruption. Several state **monopolies**, such as cement and the national flour mill, have been **privatized**, and others are expected to be sold off. These moves have increased unemployment as private owners cut payrolls.

Haiti's economy is essentially a survival one, where unemployment was officially estimated at 70 percent in 1999 and the **informal sector** provides the only work opportunities for most urban Haitians. In the countryside, many peasants operate almost outside the official cash economy, aiming for self-sufficiency and small surpluses for sale or **barter** at the many rural markets across the country. Not surprisingly, with approximately 80 percent of Haitians living in absolute poverty, pressures to emigrate, usually illegally, are strong. Other Haitians choose to cross the border into the Dominican Republic to work on sugar plantations or as manual laborers, for low wages. **Remittances**, estimated at US$150 million annually sent home from family members living abroad, are a vital means of support for many communities. Another unregulated source of income, earned by a small clique of influential individuals, derives from Haiti's importance as a trans-shipment point for cocaine and other narcotics en route from South America to the United States.

POLITICS, GOVERNMENT, AND TAXATION

Haiti's political system is notoriously volatile and prone to violence. Since gaining its independence from France in 1804, the country has experienced little democracy and has suffered at the hands of many dictators and corrupt regimes. The most enduring of these dictatorships was that of François "Papa Doc" Duvalier (1957–71) and his son Jean-Claude "Baby Doc" (1971–86). Since the overthrow of Jean-Claude Duvalier, the country has been ruled by a succession of unstable governments and military juntas. The political landscape changed dramatically in 1991 with the presidency of Jean-Bertrand Aristide, a radical Catholic priest, who was elected by a landslide majority in the country's first free elections. He was ousted by the military after only 8 months and spent 3 years in exile before being returned to power by a joint United Nations/United States military force in 1994. In the meantime, Haiti suffered a 3-year period of political repression, compounded by increased economic hardships as the result of an international economic **embargo** orchestrated by the Organization of American States (OAS) and the United Nations (UN). In December 2000 Aristide again won election by an overwhelming majority.

The dominant political force in Haiti today is Aristide's Fanmi Lavalas (FL), which means "landslide family" in Creole. The FL has an extended network of activists but is held together by the charismatic personality of Aristide, who won 91.8 percent of the vote in the November 2000 elections. Other political groupings are weak and unpopular in comparison. The main group is the Organization of People in Struggle (OPL), formerly allied to Aristide but now bitterly opposed to FL. All other parties boycotted the 2000 presidential elections, claiming that intimidation and electoral malpractice were rife. By early 2001 FL was in control of 103 out of 110 seats in the Senate and Chamber of Deputies.

Aside from its promotion of Aristide as a "savior," FL tends to vacillate between supporting the rural economy through infrastructural investment and state **subsidies**, and pursuing a course of liberalization and privatization. In the wake of Aristide's return to power in 1994, for instance, the government presided over the removal of many trade barriers and the beginning of a privatization program, but Aristide later criticized these measures. Aristide's populist appeal runs counter to the demands placed on his government by international donors, who wish to see the Haitian economy further opened to foreign investment.

Revenue collection in Haiti has always been inefficient and plagued by corruption and tax evasion. Aristide's threats to tax the tiny wealthy minority were instrumental in his overthrow in 1991. **Indirect taxes** and excise **duties** were 3 times greater than **income tax** receipts in 1997, while punitive taxes have traditionally been levied on export commodities such as coffee.

Because the government is heavily dependent on foreign aid, its ability to forge independent economic policy is limited by donor demands for agreed economic programs as a precondition for releasing aid. The main policy of the FL government focuses on land distribution and attempts to regenerate agricultural production damaged by low productivity and environmental degradation. The government also promises higher wages in the small manufacturing sector, a proposition that has caused several companies to relocate to the Dominican Republic.

INFRASTRUCTURE, POWER, AND COMMUNICATIONS

Haiti's infrastructure is primitive and poorly maintained, the result of decades of under-investment and environmental damage. Most roads, even those linking

Communications

Country	Newspapers	Radios	TV Sets[a]	Cable subscribers[a]	Mobile Phones[a]	Fax Machines[a]	Personal Computers[a]	Internet Hosts[b]	Internet Users[b]
	1996	1997	1998	1998	1998	1998	1998	1999	1999
Haiti	3	55	5	N/A	0	N/A	N/A	0.00	6
United States	215	2,146	847	244.3	256	78.4	458.6	1,508.77	74,100
Jamaica	62	480	182	73.1	22	N/A	39.4	1.04	60
Dominican Republic	52	178	95	15.5	31	0.3	N/A	7.63	25

[a]Data are from International Telecommunication Union, *World Telecommunication Development Report 1999* and are per 1,000 people.

[b]Data are from the Internet Software Consortium (http://www.isc.org) and are per 10,000 people.

SOURCE: World Bank. *World Development Indicators 2000.*

Port-au-Prince to other large towns, are often impassable to ordinary vehicles. Of a total of 4,160 kilometers (2,585 miles) of roads, only 1,011 kilometers (628 miles) are paved, and these are frequently pot-holed and damaged by landslides. There is no railway other than a stretch attached to an ex-sugar plantation. Several ports are capable of dealing with container shipping, but most foreign trade passes through Port-au-Prince. Port-au-Prince International Airport is situated 5 miles from the capital and has regular connections with North America and Europe. The only other modern airport is near Cap-Haïtien, in the north of the country.

Deforestation and the resulting soil erosion have silted up Haiti's main hydroelectric power generating system. The 677 million kilowatt hours (kWh) of electrical power consumed in 1998 was barely enough to keep industries going, and most wealthy people and companies have private generators. Only 10 percent of city dwellers and 3 percent of the rural population have access to electricity. The main fuel is charcoal, produced by **smallholders** at often enormous environmental cost.

Poor road conditions have had disastrous effects on farmers, who face serious problems in taking their goods to markets and towns. The crumbling infrastructure, erratic power supplies, and constant threat of unrest have also been cited by foreign manufacturers as a discouragement to locating companies in Haiti. What little public transport there is consists of tap-taps, colorfully painted buses that link towns and villages.

Telephone and television access is almost non-existent in the countryside, while mobile phones and Internet connections are the preserve of the wealthy minority and business interests in the capital. In 1996 there were only 60,000 phone lines recorded in the country. The state-owned Téléco company is highly profitable as it holds a monopoly on the lucrative business in international calls.

ECONOMIC SECTORS

Haiti is a traditionally agricultural economy, and almost two-thirds of the workforce (over 2 million people) are employed in farming, much of it on tiny properties. But agriculture, which is plagued by primitive techniques, soil erosion, and low commodity prices, contributed only 32 percent to the GDP in 1998. It also provided less than half of the country's food needs and less than 10 percent of export earnings. The agricultural sector is in deep crisis and is the first priority of the Aristide administration.

Industry is mainly based on low-wage assembly plants producing goods for export to the United States. Contributing 20 percent to the GDP in 1998, manufacturing was badly hit by the political turmoil of the 1980s and 1990s but has stabilized somewhat since 1994. About 35,000 people, or 1 percent of the total workforce, are employed in the export sector, while the domestic mar-

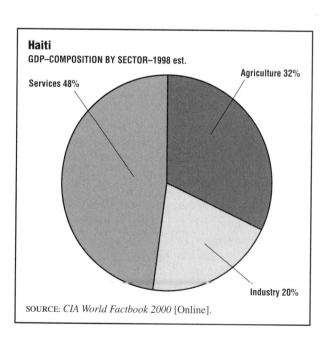

Haiti
GDP–COMPOSITION BY SECTOR–1998 est.

Services 48%

Agriculture 32%

Industry 20%

SOURCE: *CIA World Factbook 2000* [Online].

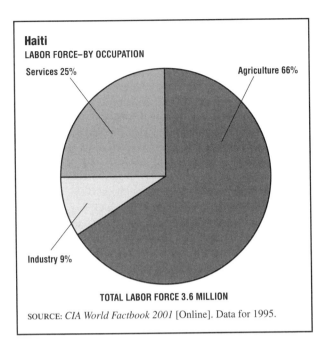

Haiti
LABOR FORCE–BY OCCUPATION

Services 25%

Agriculture 66%

Industry 9%

TOTAL LABOR FORCE 3.6 MILLION

SOURCE: *CIA World Factbook 2001* [Online]. Data for 1995.

ket is so small and poor that only essentials such as cooking oil, cement, and beverages are produced locally.

Services accounted for 48 percent of the GDP in 1998 and largely involved **retail**, transportation, and government services. Approximately a million people work in trade, transport, and personal services, many of them as domestic servants. Haiti's once important tourism sector collapsed in the 1980s due to political unrest and fears about HIV/AIDS.

AGRICULTURE

Declining soil fertility, natural disasters, and cheap imports from abroad have all contributed to agriculture's decline. It is calculated that only one-third of Haiti's land is arable, but nearer one-half is under cultivation, adding to deforestation and soil erosion. The land is often too mountainous to produce sufficient yields while, in the more fertile valleys, disputes over land ownership have often led to violence. Technology is largely lacking.

The main export crop is coffee, but it contributed less than 6 percent of earnings in 1999. Many small-scale coffee farmers have switched to food crops because of high taxes and exorbitant percentages demanded by the middlemen who buy the coffee from the peasants to sell on the international market. Other small export crops include mangos and essential oils for the cosmetics and pharmaceutical industries in the United States. **Subsistence farming** is also in decline, hit by an influx of rice and wheat, some of it smuggled in from the Dominican Republic and some sent to the country as humanitarian aid. Most of what is produced by small farmers is con-

sumed or sold locally, but Haiti's main imports continue to be basic foodstuffs.

INDUSTRY

Haiti's industrial sector is almost exclusively export-oriented, revolving around assembly plants producing **consumer goods** for the U.S. market. In the 1970s and 1980s this sector grew rapidly, and Haiti was briefly one of the leading producers of baseballs and other sporting goods, with 60,000 people employed around Port-au-Prince. The political violence of the late 1980s and 1990s and particularly the embargo imposed on the military regime between 1991 and 1994 severely affected this sector, and many companies relocated to the Dominican Republic or Mexico.

By 1999 the manufacturing sector was estimated to employ 35,000 workers, mostly women, producing clothing, toys, and electronic parts. The value of manufactured exports in 1999 was estimated at almost US$250 million and accounted for most overall exports.

Other manufacturing takes place on a small scale and is either directed at the small local market or involves artisans who produce goods such as artworks, furniture, and souvenirs, which are normally exported to tourist destinations elsewhere in the Caribbean.

SERVICES

Haiti has long had a large and unproductive government service sector, a legacy of the Duvalier dictatorship, which created government jobs for its supporters. Social services, however, are almost non-existent, and recent governments have come under pressure to reduce the state payroll through privatization and by firing workers or giving them early retirement.

Retail and transportation are both labor-intensive and largely primitive economic sectors, with large numbers employed in informal vending and rural markets. There are few modern retail outlets in Haiti, and most rural dwellers depend on their own food production and basic items bought at markets or village stores.

In the 1980s, tourism was a relatively important sector, providing Haiti's second largest source of foreign exchange, but the industry was destroyed by adverse publicity about political violence and the dangers of HIV/AIDS in the country. Some hotels have survived by catering to the large numbers of aid workers and other foreign staff who are posted to work in Haiti, but tourism as such has yet to recover. Tourist arrivals numbered 146,367 in 1998, and cruise ships now call at a specially constructed beach resort, Labadee, in the north of the country. The government has invested in promoting the southern town of Jacmel and the northern area around Cap-Haïtien as tourist destinations.

Trade (expressed in billions of US$): Haiti		
	Exports	Imports
1975	.080	.149
1980	.226	.375
1985	.168	.442
1990	.160	.332
1995	.110	.653
1998	.175	.797

SOURCE: International Monetary Fund. *International Financial Statistics Yearbook 1999.*

INTERNATIONAL TRADE

Haiti's manufactured exports go almost exclusively to the United States, which accounted for 86 percent of exports in 1998. The rest, in the form of coffee and essential oils, was exported to the European Union (EU). The United States is also the source of most of Haiti's imports and provided 60 percent of the country's import requirements in 1998. In 1999, Haitian exports totaled US$322 million, against imports of US$762 million, creating a substantial deficit of US$440 million.

During the embargo of 1991–94, U.S. trade with Haiti dropped substantially, creating increased hardship in the country and stimulating the growth of a large contraband trade from the Dominican Republic. Trade with Haiti's neighbor is still an important part of the informal sector, but little of this activity appears on official financial records.

Haiti's **trade deficit** is partly offset by international aid and partly by remittance payments sent back by Haitians living and working overseas.

MONEY

Following a period of U.S. occupation (1915–34), Haiti's currency, the gourde, was tied at a rate of 5 to the U.S. dollar. Dollars have always circulated freely in Haiti and are often preferred by retailers and others to the lo-

cal currency. In 1991, the Aristide administration finally severed the official **exchange rate** and let the gourde float. It fell from 7.5 to the dollar in 1991 to 16.2 in 1995 and 22.5 in 2000. This means that the cost of many basic imported goods has risen dramatically for Haiti's poorest sectors.

Haiti experienced high levels of **inflation** during the embargo of the early 1990s, reaching 39.3 percent in 1994. This rate was reduced to 15.4 percent in 1998 and has remained stable since. Growth in the GDP has been modest in recent years. In 1995, in the wake of Aristide's return and an influx of foreign aid, the GDP grew by 4.4 percent, but this fell to 2.7 percent in 1996 and then contracted by 0.9 percent the following year. The GDP growth in 1999 was estimated at 2.4 percent.

The Banque de la République d'Haïti is the country's central bank. It issues currency and holds the government reserves. There are 9 commercial banks, as well as U.S., Canadian, and French banks. Most Haitians, however, never use a bank, dealing only in cash and investing their savings in a tangible asset.

POVERTY AND WEALTH

No recent statistics exist, but it is widely accepted that Haiti is not merely the poorest country in the Western Hemisphere but also one of the most unequal. A small elite of no more than several thousand families is extremely wealthy, including many millionaires among their number. In stark contrast, an estimated 80 percent of Haitians live in absolute poverty. There is a small middle class comprised of civil servants and other state-sector employees, but a vast gulf exists between a tiny rich minority and the overwhelmingly poor majority. Class and color have overlapped ever since Haitian independence, with the lighter-skinned minority occupying positions of political and economic power. This status quo was challenged by the Duvalier dictatorship, which promoted some of its black supporters into a growing middle class.

The country's wealthy are clustered around the cooler mountainside suburb of Pétionville, where French

Exchange rates: Haiti	
gourdes per US$1	
Jan 2001	23.761
2000	22.524
1999	17.965
1998	16.505
1997	17.311
1996	15.093

SOURCE: CIA *World Factbook 2001* [ONLINE].

GDP per Capita (US$)					
Country	1975	1980	1985	1990	1998
Haiti	500	607	527	481	370
United States	19,364	21,529	23,200	25,363	29,683
Jamaica	1,819	1,458	1,353	1,651	1,559
Dominican Republic	1,179	1,325	1,325	1,366	1,799

SOURCE: United Nations. *Human Development Report 2000; Trends in human development and per capita income.*

restaurants and luxury car concessions cater to expensive tastes. Education and medical services are entirely private, and the children of the elite tend to be educated abroad, either in Paris or the United States. Shopping trips to Miami are commonplace, and most of the richest families hold dollar bank accounts in the United States.

Life for the rural and urban poor could not be more different. Most Haitians live in small, often remote, villages or isolated settlements, with no access to electricity, clean water, or social services. Some rudimentary education is offered by church and other charitable organizations, but the distances children must travel to school, the costs of books and uniforms, and the necessity for them to work from an early age means that illiteracy is estimated at over half of the adult population. Illness can often spell financial disaster, as meager savings or investments such as a pig must be sold to pay for medicines. In some areas large numbers of people are dependent on aid agencies for food supplies.

Existence in the teeming slums of Port-au-Prince is perhaps even grimmer, with overcrowding, disease, and squalor widespread. Those who work can expect to earn no more than US$2 a day, hardly enough to buy food, let alone other necessities. The majority, however, must scrape some sort of living from the informal sector. Figures for child mortality, communicable diseases, and life expectancy reveal the country's poverty and deprivation. According to the Pan-American Health Organization, approximately 380,000 Haitians—over 5 percent of the population—were infected with HIV/AIDS by 2000.

WORKING CONDITIONS

In 1997 the unemployment rate was estimated at 70 percent. Some Haitians have jobs in the formal sector. Yet most are low-wage manufacturing jobs where conditions are basic and trade unions discouraged. International agencies have cited many cases of abusive practices by managers and employers in this sector, where women are employed to stitch clothing or assemble toys for export. Conditions in agriculture are no better, and most small farmers work long hours in highly primitive conditions to produce a precarious livelihood for their families.

The informal sector encompasses almost every area of economic activity from street selling and garbage recycling to taxi driving and handicraft manufacturing. Nearly all this activity is unregulated, and workers have no rights or security whatsoever. There are no effective laws to protect workers' rights, and trade unions are small and divided. The most powerful organizations are those neighborhood or peasant groups which are usually linked to Fanmi Lavalas and which sometimes take militant action against exploiters.

COUNTRY HISTORY AND ECONOMIC DEVELOPMENT

1492. Spanish explorer Christopher Columbus lands on the island of Hispaniola. Spain eventually battles the Arawak Indian population on the islands and establishes a colony.

1697. Spain cedes to France the western part of Hispaniola and founds the colony of Saint-Domingue (which later becomes Haiti). France turns the colony into the center of its slave trade.

1804. Haiti gains independence after a 12-year war against the French led by Touissant L'Ouverture.

1915–34. The United States occupies Haiti in the name of regional security.

1958–71. François "Papa Doc" Duvalier rules the country as a dictator, and the country's economy collapses.

1971–86. Jean-Claude "Baby Doc" Duvalier continues the dictatorship but encourages the development of manufacturing and tourism.

1986. Opposition groups force Duvalier to flee the country, leading to several years of instability and military rule.

1990. Jean-Bertrand Aristide is chosen president in elections overseen by the United Nations. About 9 months later, in 1991, the military ousts Aristide and places its candidate in office. The international community condemns these actions, leading to international isolation for Haiti.

1994. U.S. and, later, United Nations troops enter Haiti to help the nation return to democratic rule. Aristide is returned to serve the remainder of his term in office.

1995. In new elections, from which Aristide is barred, Aristide associate René Préval wins the presidency. His presidency is marred by violence and instability.

2000. Aristide wins the presidency in elections that are plagued by accusations of fraud, but he returns a semblance of political stability to the country.

FUTURE TRENDS

Haiti faces seemingly insurmountable problems in the years to come. Its environment is damaged, probably beyond repair, and its agricultural sector will require huge investment for regeneration. There is no sign that the country's ecological disaster can be reversed. The government's proposed land reform program would have to guarantee viable farms for many more producers, with assistance with technology. The manufacturing sector will also face huge problems, most notably in competition from other low-cost economies such as the Dominican Republic.

Much will depend on the political relationship forged between the Haitian government and the Bush administration, which contains political figures hostile to Aristide and his populism. Haiti will remain dependent on foreign aid in the future and will look to the EU to pay for joint projects with the Dominican Republic. The country's greatest obstacle to sustainable development, however, remains its stubbornly high levels of poverty and deprivation, leading to huge social inequalities and political volatility.

DEPENDENCIES

Haiti has no territories or colonies.

BIBLIOGRAPHY

Arthur, Charles, and Michael Dash, editors. *Libète: A Haiti Anthology*. London: Latin America Bureau, 1999.

Economist Intelligence Unit. *Country Profile: Dominican Republic, Haiti and Puerto Rico*. London: Economist Intelligence Unit, 2001.

McFadyen, Deidre, et al., editors. *Haiti: Dangerous Crossroads*. Boston, MA: South End Press, 1995.

U.S. Central Intelligence Agency. *World Factbook 2000*. <http://www.odci.gov/cia/publications/factbook/index.html>. Accessed August 2001.

U.S. Department of State. *FY 2000 Country Commercial Guide: Haiti*. <http://www.state.gov/www/about_state/business/com_guides/2000/wha/index.html>. Accessed September 2001.

Welcome to the Embassy of the Republic of Haiti, Washington, D.C. <http://www.haiti.org>. Accessed September 2001.

—*James Ferguson*

HONDURAS

Republic of Honduras
República de Honduras

CAPITAL: Tegucigalpa.

MONETARY UNIT: Lempira (L), also known as the peso. One lempira equals 100 centavos. Coin denominations include 1, 2, 5, 10, 20, and 50 centavos, and notes include 1, 2, 5, 10, 20, 50, and 100 lempiras.

CHIEF EXPORTS: Coffee, bananas, shrimp, lobster, meat, zinc, lumber.

CHIEF IMPORTS: Machinery and transport equipment, industrial raw materials, chemical products, fuels, foodstuffs.

GROSS DOMESTIC PRODUCT: US$5.25 billion (purchasing power parity, 1998 est.).

BALANCE OF TRADE: **Exports:** US$1.2 billion (1999 est.). **Imports:** US$2.7 billion (1999 est.).

COUNTRY OVERVIEW

LOCATION AND SIZE. Honduras is located in Central America. Its northern border, between Guatemala and Nicaragua, lies along the Caribbean Sea. The southwestern tip of the country, between El Salvador and Nicaragua, borders the northern Pacific Ocean. Slightly larger than Tennessee, Honduras has an area of 112,090 square kilometers (43,278 square miles).

POPULATION. In July of 2000 the population of Honduras was estimated at 6.25 million, with an annual growth rate of 2.52 percent. In 2000, for every person who died in Honduras, approximately 6 were born. The birth rate during this period was 32.65 per 1,000, the death rate 5.31 per 1,000.

Approximately 90 percent of Hondurans are ethnic mestizo (mixed Amerindian and European). The remainder of the population is primarily Amerindian (7 percent). Blacks make up 2 percent of the population, while 1 percent of the country is white.

A significant portion of the Honduran population— about 43 percent—is under the age of 15. Approximately

54 percent are between the ages of 15 and 64. Those over 65 account for only 3 percent of the population. The life expectancy for males in Honduras is 67.91 years, while females are expected to live slightly longer, to 72.06 years.

OVERVIEW OF ECONOMY

The Honduran economy, one of the least developed in Latin America, has traditionally been fueled by the export of bananas and coffee. In the 1980s these crops accounted for between one-half and two-thirds of the country's total exports. Such a narrow export base limited growth and left the entire economy vulnerable to changing market conditions and poor weather, so in the 1990s moves were made toward economic diversification. The production of nontraditional exports such as melon, pineapple, and shrimp increased; the manufacturing industry grew; and the services sector, once fairly limited, emerged as a vital component of the economy. This diversification helped the Honduran economy withstand the effects of Hurricane Mitch, which swept through the country in October of 1998, devastating the agricultural sector. In the northern Sula Valley, the hurricane destroyed 70 percent of the banana plantations and brought heavy losses to basic grains. Coffee production was cut by about 20 percent. Despite these losses, the economy still gained 3 percent in 1998, led by strong performances in the manufacturing and services industries. The 3 percent growth was considered solid given the severity of the hurricane, which killed 7,000 people, destroyed 200,000 homes, and left 1.5 million Hondurans temporarily homeless. The damage caused by Mitch was estimated at US$5 billion, equivalent to 95 percent of the country's **gross domestic product** in 1998.

Honduras, despite moves to improve its economy, still depends on international aid and imported goods to meet consumer and fiscal demands. This dependence was

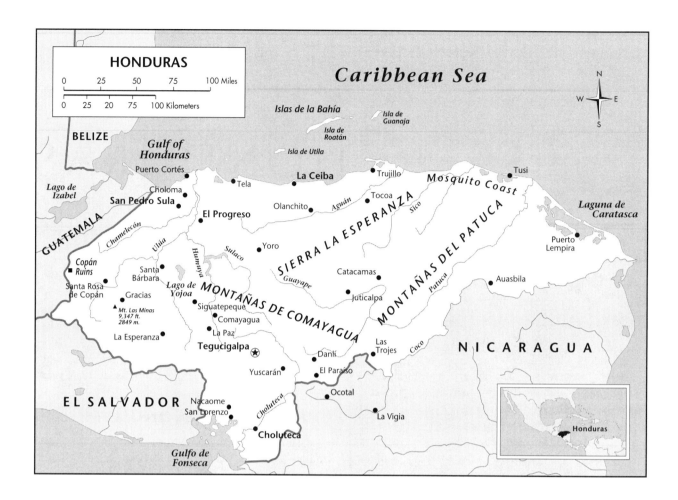

heightened by Hurricane Mitch. The storm put domestic production on hold, increasing the need for imported goods and loans to help finance reconstruction. By 1999 Honduras was US$4.4 billion in debt, most of it owed to multilateral lending agencies and the United States. In 1999, in exchange for **debt relief** of nearly US$1 billion, the Honduran government agreed to **restructure** the economy along lines agreed to by the International Monetary Fund (IMF). As part of the **structural adjustment program**, Honduras agreed to **privatize** certain sectors of the economy. It also made a commitment to fight poverty and corruption, reform social security, strengthen the financial sector, and improve education and health care for the poor.

To spur the economy and increase foreign investment, the Honduran government, under President Carlos Roberto Flores Facusse, pledged in 1999 to accelerate the privatization programs which had stalled under the previous administration. Earlier privatization initiatives and the expansion of the tourist and manufacturing industries led to an increase in foreign investment in Honduras in the 1990s. Foreign investment in 1993 amounted to US$27 million. By 1999, that figure had grown nearly 10 times to US$230 million. Investment in Honduras will likely continue to increase as privatization initiatives move forward and industries expand. In the medium term

Honduras will rely on close to US$3 billion in multilateral funding to assist in reconstruction costs and poverty alleviation programs.

POLITICS, GOVERNMENT, AND TAXATION

Since gaining its independence from the Spanish empire in 1821, Honduras has been plagued by political and financial instability. Changes of government have often been accompanied by violence and bloodshed. Rebellions, coups, and civil wars characterized much of the 20th century.

Two parties, the Partido Liberal (PL) founded by Celeo Arias in the 1880s, and the Partido Nacional (PN) established in 1902 by Manuel Bonilla, have dominated Honduran politics for the last century and continue to play a predominant role. The PN, which garners support from the military, is the more conservative of the parties, with strongholds in less-developed rural areas. The PL is more to the political left and draws support from an urban base, although it has a constituency among rural landowners as well.

Honduras has spent much of its independence under military rule. A break in military control occurred in 1955 when a group of military reformers staged a coup and installed an interim government, paving the way for constitutional elections. In 1957, a civilian, Ramon Morales, was elected to a 6-year term as president. Morales introduced agrarian reforms and social welfare legislation, including social security provisions. He also introduced a labor code to protect the rights of workers, and took Honduras into the Central American Common Market, a **free trade zone** made up of 5 Central American countries. In 1963 a military coup prevented Morales from running for a second term. General Oswaldo Lopez Arellano became the country's leader and placed agricultural development and the banking system under government control.

The military ran the country until 1981, when Honduras was returned to civilian rule. In 1982 a new constitution was drafted, and in 1986 Roberto Suazo Cordoba of the Liberal Party was elected president, marking the first peaceful transition of power between civilians in over 30 years.

The Liberal Party held the presidency for 4 years. Then, in 1990 the Nationalists took over with the election of Rafael Leonardo Callejas. Callejas moved to bring the military under civilian control, and instituted fiscal reforms to stabilize the economy, concentrating primarily on deficit reduction and currency stabilization. His presidency, however, was marred by allegations of corruption. Despite his reforms, the Liberal Party, under the leadership of Roberto Reina, regained the presidency in 1994. Under Reina the economy improved, with growth reaching 5 percent in 1997. International reserves were increased, and **inflation** dropped to 12.8 percent a year.

The current president of Honduras is Carlos Flores Facusse, a member of the Partido Liberal. In November 1997 he was elected to a 4-year term which began in January of 1998. His party holds over half the seats in the 128-seat National Congress. The Honduran government remains highly centralized despite slow-moving reforms to increase the power and participation of local municipalities.

Efforts to decentralize the political system (to give more power to the leaders of local governments) have been accompanied by economic reforms, with the government loosening its control over various economic operations, including those in the financial sector. In 1997, the Central Bank of Honduras was given greater independence in an effort to strengthen the country's financial system. In 2000 mandatory currency reserves were lowered from 25 percent to 19 percent. The government hopes that lowering reserve requirements and giving banks higher **liquidity** will increase loan disbursements and stimulate the economy.

Flores has also instituted a series of tax reforms designed to boost private investment and reduce the fiscal deficit. Flores reduced export **tariffs**, most notably in the banana sector, cutting **duties** from 50 cents a box to 4 cents. He also lowered the business **income tax** from 42 percent in 1997 to 25 percent in 1999. In order to offset losses from the cuts, the administration raised the sales tax from 7 percent to 12 percent. Flores has also undertaken efforts to increase privatization. The state-owned telecommunications company, Empresa Hondurena de Telecomunicaciones (Hondutel), and the state-owned electric company, Empresa Nacional de la Energia Electrica (ENEE) are prime candidates for privatization.

INFRASTRUCTURE, POWER, AND COMMUNICATIONS

In 1998 mudslides and flooding caused by Hurricane Mitch devastated the Honduran **infrastructure**. Nearly half of the country's road network was damaged by the storm. Over 160 bridges were destroyed. Approximately 50,000 telephone lines went down. Water and sewage pipes were damaged, as were seaports, airports, and schools throughout the country.

Honduras has 9,074 miles of primary, secondary, and municipal roads. About 18 percent of them are paved. The country has 2 main highways. The north-south highway

Communications

Country	Newspapers	Radios	TV Sets[a]	Cable subscribers[a]	Mobile Phones[a]	Fax Machines[a]	Personal Computers[a]	Internet Hosts[b]	Internet Users[b]
	1996	1997	1998	1998	1998	1998	1998	1999	1999
Honduras	55	386	90	N/A	5	N/A	7.6	0.19	20
United States	215	2,146	847	244.3	256	78.4	458.6	1,508.77	74,100
Mexico	97	325	261	15.7	35	3.0	47.0	23.02	1,822
Nicaragua	30	285	190	40.2	4	N/A	7.8	2.21	20

[a]Data are from International Telecommunication Union, *World Telecommunication Development Report 1999* and are per 1,000 people.

[b]Data are from the Internet Software Consortium (http://www.isc.org) and are per 10,000 people.

SOURCE: World Bank. *World Development Indicators 2000.*

connects the capital, Tegucigalpa, with San Pedro Sula. The Pan-American highway runs parallel to the Pacific coast and connects Honduras to Nicaragua and El Salvador. While road construction has remained stagnant over the past 5 years, the number of automobiles has substantially increased. There were 273,927 registered vehicles in Honduras in 1995. By 1999, that number had risen to 417,431, increasing traffic and congestion, especially in urban areas. There are also about 600 miles of rail lines to accommodate overland traffic.

The main Honduran port is Puerto Cortes on the northern coast. With 4,000 square feet of docking space capable of accommodating 10 vessels at a time, Puerto Cortes handles over half the country's export trade, on and off-loading 14 to 25 containers of goods an hour. Consistent with its larger privatization efforts, the Flores administration is seeking to open Honduran ports to **private sector** participation.

The 4 international airports in Honduras have already been turned over to private management. A U.S.-Honduran consortium led by the San Francisco International Airport (SFIA) will run the airports for the next 20 years. Under the terms of the agreement with the Honduran government, the consortium will invest US$120 million in the airports over the next 20 years, making physical improvements and raising the standards of efficiency, safety, and services.

The telecommunications infrastructure was greatly expanded in the 1990s. Empresa Hondurena de Telecomunicaciones (Hondutel), the state-owned telecommunications firm, increased the number of phone lines from 87,311 in 1990 to 373,032 in 1998. In 2000, as part of its structural adjustment agreement with the IMF, the Honduran government attempted to partially privatize Hondutel by selling 51 percent of the company's shares to the private sector. However, an October auction produced only a single bid for the shares. Telefonos de Mexico offered to pay US$106 million for the majority stock, but that offer was soundly rebuffed by Honduran privatization officials who set the minimum selling price at US$300 million. As part of the takeover agreement, any company which purchases the shares in Hondutel will be required to install 23,500 pay phones and add 600,000 kilometers of fixed lines in Honduras by the end of 2005. Honduran officials are seeking buyers in the United States and Europe, hoping to possibly attract an international consortium to take over company operations.

In 1999 Hondurans received about two-thirds of their energy from state-owned hydroelectric plants, with thermal plants providing the rest. Energy demands are increasing by about 12 percent a year, driven upwards by a widening industrial base and a rural electrification program. The heavily indebted state-run energy corporation, Empresa Nacional de la Energia Electrica (ENEE), is in-

creasingly turning to private sources for help in meeting the country's growing energy needs. The Flores administration has expressed a commitment to privatize the state-run power plants, both hydroelectric and thermal, which together provided over three-quarters of the country's energy in 1999.

ECONOMIC SECTORS

Honduras has traditionally had a limited industrial capability, relying primarily on agricultural exports like bananas and coffee for the bulk of its foreign exchange. In the 1990s this began to change as Honduras made aggressive moves to shore up its economy by diversifying exports and broadening its industrial base. The services sector was also targeted for growth, resulting in the rapid expansion of the tourist industry.

Honduras is thought to have extensive mineral deposits which have yet to be exploited, indicating the potential for growth in the mining industry. Seeking to capitalize on the situation, the Flores administration passed legislation to increase foreign investment in the sector. However, some of Honduras's most fertile mining grounds are located near the Nicaraguan border and, as land disputes between the nations are common, this has led to political complications and has stifled industry expansion.

Growth in the manufacturing sector, led by the expansion of the maquila (offshore assembly for **re-export**) industry, has been most pronounced. The re-export business was one of the few areas of the economy to escape Hurricane Mitch virtually unscathed.

Agricultural activity, which registered substantial declines after Hurricane Mitch, is not expected to fully

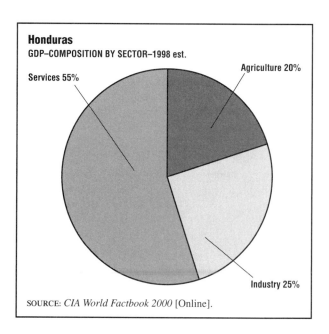

Honduras
GDP–COMPOSITION BY SECTOR–1998 est.

Services 55%
Agriculture 20%
Industry 25%

SOURCE: *CIA World Factbook 2000* [Online].

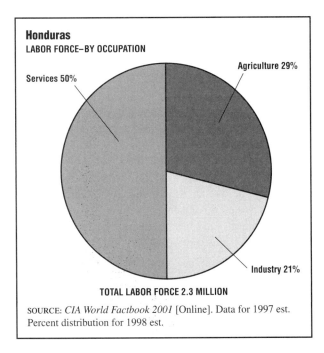

Honduras
LABOR FORCE—BY OCCUPATION

Services 50%

Agriculture 29%

Industry 21%

TOTAL LABOR FORCE 2.3 MILLION

SOURCE: *CIA World Factbook 2001* [Online]. Data for 1997 est. Percent distribution for 1998 est.

recover before 2001. The severe damage wrought by the storm to traditional export crops has increased the pace of agricultural diversification. The cultivation of melons, pineapples, sugar cane and African palm were expanded in the wake of the storm.

AGRICULTURE

Despite declines in production caused by Hurricane Mitch, agriculture continues to dominate the Honduran economy, supplying in 1999 over 60 percent of the jobs and over half of all merchandise export earnings. That year, out of a working population of 2.13 million people, 834,900 of them held agricultural jobs. Coffee and bananas have traditionally made up the bulk of Honduras's agricultural exports.

Coffee is produced in 14 of the country's 18 provinces by 70,000 independent producers. Over the last decade, the coffee industry has been beset by financial problems. Some of these problems have resulted from poor weather. In 1998, prior to Hurricane Mitch, Honduras was the tenth largest coffee producer in the world. The damage caused by Hurricane Mitch contributed to an 11 percent decline in coffee production in 1999. Other problems came as a result of the structure of the industry itself. With so many small producers, quality control was hard to maintain. This caused great price volatility and made revenues less dependable. Furthermore, many small coffee producers and exporters took out loans before the hurricane, putting them in debt to the Central Bank following the destruction of their crops. Government **subsidies** to assist coffee farmers have been slow in coming, adding to the coffee industry's problems.

Banana production, which takes place on the northern coast, is controlled primarily by the subsidiaries of 2 U.S. conglomerates, Chiquita and Dole. These companies have established effective **monopolies** over the banana export trade in Honduras. However, legal challenges to the monopolies are growing more frequent.

Like the coffee sector, the banana sector had its share of trouble in the 1990s. Between 1991 and 1994, production was affected by strikes and floods. The industry recovered in 1995, but was then devastated in 1998 when Hurricane Mitch destroyed a majority of the banana plantations. In 1999, production fell by over 70 percent. Banana exports are not expected to reach pre-hurricane levels until 2001 or 2002. A reduction in the banana export tax from 50 U.S. cents per box to 4 cents will likely help boost the recovery.

With bananas and coffee proving highly susceptible to price volatility, bad weather, and labor unrest, Honduras has made efforts to diversify its agricultural exports. The development of nontraditional crops such as melon, pineapple, sugarcane, and African palm has expanded since the mid-1990s. Between 1995 and 1999, African palm production rose 50 percent. Sugar production during the same period increased from 67.5 million bags, to 82.8 million bags, reaching a high in 1998 of 89.4 million bags. In the wake of the hurricane, the pace of diversification increased with many banana farmers turning over some of their fields to the production of nontraditional crops.

During the 1990s commercial shrimp farming emerged as one of Honduras's most dynamic industries, posting steady gains in production and revenue between 1995 and 1998. Volume and earnings fell slightly in 1999 after Hurricane Mitch, but the industry quickly recovered. Shrimp is the third most important agricultural export after bananas and coffee, generating revenues of US$153 million in 1999.

INDUSTRY

MINING. The mining industry in Honduras has achieved noticeable growth in recent years, with output increasing by 7 percent in 1999. However, between 1995 and 1999 the industry's contribution to the gross domestic product remained steady at around 2 percent. Honduras's primary mineral exports are silver, lead, and zinc. With a substantial portion of the country's mineral deposits still unexploited, the potential for growth in the sector is high. Attempts to expand the industry, however, have been complicated by political and environmental factors. Despite new mining laws, which were introduced by the Flores administration in 1998 to increase investment in the sector, foreign companies have been hesitant to operate in Honduras. The Canadian company Greenstone had to abandon its operations in the Copan region near the border with Nicaragua, in 1999 because of territorial disputes between Nicaragua and Honduras. Mining interests near Tegucigalpa have been opposed by environmental groups, offering another setback to the industry.

MANUFACTURING. Unlike the mining industry, the manufacturing sector has experienced unimpeded growth over the last decade, with the most dramatic expansion being in the maquila industry. The industry produced about US$545 million in foreign exchange earnings in 1999 (just over 18 percent of the gross domestic product at market prices), exceeding agriculture proceeds to become the single largest export category. The number of workers in the sector grew from 9,000 to 120,000 between 1990 and 1998. A majority of these workers—70 percent—were women aged 15 to 26. Between the years 2000 and 2005, the industry will likely expand by another 80,000 workers, with new investment expected to reach US$700 million.

Growth in maquila can be attributed to a number of factors, including favorable tax provisions, a solid manufacturing infrastructure, and low wage costs. A series of laws passed between 1975 and 1999 granted national and foreign companies tax and duty exemptions in specified areas called free zones. This made the maquila industry more lucrative for domestic companies and established Honduras as a particularly attractive base of operations for foreign firms.

In May 2000 the U.S. Congress decided to eliminate an 18 percent duty on finished apparel from Africa, the Caribbean, and Central America, making Honduran maquila producers more competitive. As investment and labor increases, the maquila sector will likely diversify and begin performing more technical operations, such as the cutting and dying of fabrics. As it stands now, a majority of these operations take place in the United States.

In July 2000 Honduras was granted North American Free Trade Agreement (NAFTA) parity for its exports, meaning it would receive the same trade benefits as signatories of NAFTA even though it was not an actual party to the agreement. Although NAFTA parity had been granted to other Central American and Caribbean countries, Honduras was in an especially good position to benefit from enhanced access to American markets. Its port facilities are some of the most developed in Central America, and its proximity to American markets facilitates high levels of trade.

SERVICES

TOURISM. Tourism is one of the fastest growing industries in Honduras. The country hosts a variety of attractions including beaches and coral reefs, historic colonial cities, Mayan ruins, and lush national parks. Revenues from tourism rose steadily in the 1990s, from US$30.6 million in 1991 to US$185 million in 1999. In 1994 Honduras had around 230,000 recreational visitors. By 1999 the number had increased to 375,000.

The government has attempted to expand the tourist industry in part through large-scale development projects. A plan emerged in the late 1990s to allow foreign nationals to own land and operate tourist-related businesses within 40 miles of the coast. This plan was vigorously opposed by the coastal Amerindians who feared the development would disrupt their livelihoods. Amerindians may be a minority in the overwhelmingly mestizo population, but they have grown more vocal in recent years. In 2000 Congress rejected the measure that would have allowed foreigners to run tourist operations in the coastal regions. Clashes over coastal development between the government and indigenous groups will likely continue.

FINANCIAL SERVICES. When financial services in Honduras were **liberalized** in the 1990s, the banking industry underwent a period of expansion. By the end of the decade, the sector had begun to consolidate. After the 1999 collapse of Banco Corporativo, Bancahsa and Banco del Ahorro Hondureno merged to create the largest bank in the country. By the late 1990s, financial assets in Honduras had been consolidated into the hands of a few large banks. With most the 19 finance houses and 11 insurance companies being grouped under **holding companies** with common shareholders, banks can easily shift assets in response to changing market forces and new regulations.

Only 2 foreign banks operate out of Honduras: Lloyds Bank and Citibank, the latter of which owns Banco de Honduras. The country's 2 stock exchanges—one in the capital, Tegucigalpa, and the other in San Pedro Sula—run mainly short-term credit operations.

In an effort to shore up confidence in the banking system and stem **capital flight** (the movement of financial assets from domestic markets to foreign countries), the Banco Central de Honduras (the central bank) in 1995 authorized the holding of U.S. dollar accounts in Honduran banks. Import and export operations benefited from the move. In another measure to retain capital, insurance companies were allowed to issue policies in U.S. dollars, having been formerly restricted to providing coverage in lempiras.

INTERNATIONAL TRADE

Honduras conducts a majority of its trade with the United States. In 1999 over one-third of Honduras's exports went to America, not including merchandise produced in the maquila sector. Although technically a func-

Trade (expressed in billions of US$): Honduras

	Exports	Imports
1975	.295	.400
1980	.829	1.009
1985	.780	.888
1990	.831	.935
1995	1.220	1.643
1998	1.533	2.500

SOURCE: International Monetary Fund. *International Financial Statistics Yearbook 1999.*

tion of manufacturing, Honduras lists maquila as a service export instead of a product export. With maquila exports included, the United States received over 70 percent of total Honduran exports. Nearly half of Honduras's imports—about 47 percent—came from the United States (over 60 percent with maquila). Other trading partners included Germany, El Salvador, Nicaragua, Guatemala, Mexico, and Japan.

During the 1980s coffee and bananas in Honduras accounted for a majority of total exports. Over the past decade, exports were diversified. By 1999, due to a widening agricultural base and the effects of Hurricane Mitch, which destroyed much of the banana crop, the export share of coffee and bananas had been reduced to 25 percent.

In 1999 coffee and shellfish were the leading export earners. Coffee receipts came to US$256.1 million, and shellfish exports generated US$193.2 million. Revenues from banana exports, which were US$279.8 million in 1996, fell in 1998 to US$175.7 million. After Hurricane Mitch, banana receipts dropped to US$37.7 million.

The Honduran government in the 1980s instituted policies to curb imports. This led to pent-up demand, and a decade later when trade was liberalized, import levels rapidly rose, exceeding export levels and widening **trade deficits**. The situation was exacerbated by Hurricane Mitch, which lowered export production and raised the demand for imported goods. By 1999, trade deficits, excluding maquila value, had widened by 60 percent to US$1.48 billion (US$764.2 million with maquila).

Honduras is looking to expand its regional trading relationships in order to lessen its economic dependence on the United States. Honduras, along with El Salvador and Guatemala, established a trade agreement with Mexico in June 2000 which was meant to reduce tariffs on industrial and agricultural products and give Central American countries enhanced access to Mexican markets. In 1993 Honduras also entered into a free-trade agreement with Guatemala, El Salvador, and Nicaragua. Central Ameri-

can policy makers hoped the creation of the free-trade area, known as the Group of Four (G4), would make the region more competitive in the world economy. Efforts to expand regional trade have been partly successful. In Honduras, exports to G4 countries rose from 13 percent of the total in 1997 to 17 percent in 1999. However, border disputes between Honduras, Nicaragua, and El Salvador could potentially complicate the agreement.

Problems arose in 1999 when Honduras recognized Colombia's right to a stretch of maritime land off the coast of Nicaragua. Nicaragua, claiming ownership of the land, responded by levying a 35 percent surcharge on all Honduran imports. The dispute, which is still unresolved, has left relations between the countries strained. Disputes in other areas between the countries have led to violence. Military clashes have occurred over fishing rights in the Gulf of Fonseca, and in recent years Honduras has also clashed with El Salvador over contested land in the province of La Paz.

MONEY

Between 1919 and 1990, the lempira maintained an artificially fixed rate against the U.S. dollar at L2.0:US$1. This meant the Honduran economy was vulnerable to shifts in U.S. **monetary policy**. Furthermore, the printing of domestic currency was constrained by the need to keep local money supplies in line with U.S. dollar reserves. In March of 1990, in an effort to give the Central Bank and the Honduran government more control over the country's fiscal development, the fixed rate was removed and the value of the lempira sharply declined. By the end of that year, the **exchange rate** had risen to L5.3:US$1. The government tried to support the currency by strictly enforcing laws which required exporters to **repatriate** foreign exchange earnings (meaning exporters selling to the United States, for instance, would have to convert their profits from dollars to lempiras when placing them back in Honduran banks). However, these efforts were insufficient and the lempira continued its downward slide throughout the first half of the 1990s. In 1994, in a further attempt to stabilize the currency, the Central Bank

Exchange rates: Honduras

lempiras (L) per US$1

Dec 2000	15.1407
2000	15.1407
1999	14.5039
1998	13.8076
1997	13.0942
1996	12.8694

SOURCE: CIA *World Factbook 2001* [ONLINE].

established a public U.S. dollar auction system. In this system the Central Bank sold American dollars to domestic commercial banks at a slightly elevated exchange rate. This allowed the Central Bank to make money on the exchange, and by pulling lempiras out of the system (taking them from commercial banks in exchange for dollars) it lowered the supply of domestic currency, thereby raising its price. By the end of 1995, the lempira's decline had begun to slow, improving the performance of the external sector and boosting investor confidence. By 1999 the lempira had steadied at L14.5:US$1, representing a 3.3 percent appreciation against the U.S. dollar in real terms for the year.

POVERTY AND WEALTH

Hurricane Mitch devastated Honduras in 1998, causing over 7,000 deaths. Over 1.5 million people were left homeless by the storm. Thousands of buildings were destroyed, and roads and bridges were washed away. The economy came to a near standstill, worsening the effects of already endemic poverty.

Since 1998, the government of Honduras has committed to a development strategy which was coordinated in conjunction with the World Bank and IMF. The World Bank is currently supporting a US$30 million Social Investment Fund aimed at alleviating poverty through the improvement of the country's infrastructure at the community level. The project includes self-help programs for the poor and involves the construction of numerous schools in rural areas. The World Bank has also initiated a US$25 million nutrition and health program for 255,000 poor women and children. The program's goals include the establishment of up to 160 health care centers with a priority given to rural areas.

The infant mortality rate in 2001 was high at 36 deaths per 1,000 live births. Approximately 25 percent of children were suffering from malnutrition. Despite World Bank initiatives, Honduras remains one of the poorest countries in the Americas with an estimated gross domestic product of US$6.5 billion in 2001. More than 53 percent of the population live below the poverty line,

Distribution of Income or Consumption by Percentage Share: Honduras	
Lowest 10%	1.2
Lowest 20%	3.4
Second 20%	7.1
Third 20%	11.7
Fourth 20%	19.7
Highest 20%	58.0
Highest 10%	42.1

Survey year: 1996
Note: This information refers to income shares by percentiles of the population and is ranked by per capita income.

SOURCE: *2000 World Development Indicators* [CD-ROM].

42 percent of the population do not have access to safe drinking water, and a quarter of the population are illiterate. Over 50 percent of Honduras's rural population are agricultural workers who own no land or are small-scale landowners who have less than 5 hectares. Land reform that provides technical as well as financial assistance in the form of micro credit (small-scale loans) could reduce poverty in Honduras by allowing farmers to earn income, be self sufficient, and increase overall production.

WORKING CONDITIONS

After a 1954 banana strike, trade unions emerged as a major force in Honduran politics. In 1999, with 14 percent of its **labor force** organized, Honduras was the most heavily unionized country in Central America. Still, the strength of unions diminished in the 1990s. Despite the labor movement's opposition to privatization, the Flores administration remained committed to economic reforms that would give up state-owned companies to the private sector, while union calls for higher wages were ignored.

While the law in Honduras grants workers the right to form and join unions, there have been cases reported of employers seeking to disrupt union activities by harassing or firing union sympathizers. As of 1999, the labor court in Honduras was considering numerous appeals by workers who claimed to have been fired by their companies for engaging in union activities.

Forced labor is forbidden by law, but there have been some cases reported of forced overtime in the maquila sector, particularly for women. Child labor is prohibited as well. Children under 14 years old are barred from the workforce, even if they have parental permission to work. Allowing a child to work illegally is punishable by up to 5 years in prison; however, frequent violations occur in rural districts. According to a human rights report issued in 1999 by the U.S. State Department, an estimated 350,000 children in Honduras work illegally.

GDP per Capita (US$)					
Country	1975	1980	1985	1990	1998
Honduras	614	733	681	682	722
United States	19,364	21,529	23,200	25,363	29,683
Mexico	3,380	4,167	4,106	4,046	4,459
Nicaragua	999	690	611	460	452

SOURCE: United Nations. *Human Development Report 2000; Trends in human development and per capita income.*

The labor force in Honduras is mostly unskilled. The general level of education is low and training is limited. Children between ages 7–13 receive free, compulsory education, but in order to continue after the age of 13 tuition is required. A majority of families cannot afford to pay for education, and instead of continuing with school, most children move into the labor force after they turn 14. In 1999, out of 841,236 children aged 15 to 19, only 187,561 were receiving regular schooling. The illiteracy rate in Honduras is around 19 percent. Public spending on education, traditionally low in Honduras, has declined in recent years, falling to 4.1 percent of the gross domestic product in 1999.

In January 1998 the average minimum wage in Honduras was raised 17 percent. In 1999 it was hiked another 25 percent, and in 2000, the wage was raised again, this time by 8 percent. The wage varies from sector to sector, the lowest being US$2.12 a day in non-export agriculture. The highest minimum wage is paid in the export sector, where workers receive at least $3.47 a day. Even the highest minimum wage is insufficient to provide a standard of living over the poverty line.

The maximum workday is 8 hours. Workers cannot be required to work more than 44 hours in a week, and they must be given at least one 24-hour rest period every 8 days. The labor code stipulates that workers be given 10 days of paid vacation after 1 year of work, and 20 days after 4 years of work. These laws, however, are often ignored. Demand for jobs is so high that workers cannot afford to complain.

COUNTRY HISTORY AND ECONOMIC DEVELOPMENT

1502. Christopher Columbus visits Honduras on his third voyage to the New World.

1524. Spanish colonization of Honduras begins.

1537. Native Honduran Chief Lempira murdered by the Spaniards.

1821. Honduras gains independence from Spain and joins the Central American Federation.

1830. Francisco Morazan becomes the nation's first president.

1842. The Central American Federation falls apart. Morazan is murdered.

1870s. A revolution takes place. Church and state are separated under Marco Aurelio Soto.

1880s. Partido Liberal, one of the dominant political parties, is founded by Celeo Arias.

1899. First banana concession is granted to Vicaro brothers, later becoming Standard Fruit (Dole).

1902. Manuel Bonilla establishes the Partido Nacional.

1907. The Cuyamel Fruit Company is set and is later bought by United Fruit (Chiquita).

1929. Honduras becomes the largest banana exporter in the world.

1954. A banana workers strike establishes unionized labor and gains recognition from the government.

1956. The Honduran military takes control of the government.

1957. Civilian rule is restored. Ramon Villeda Morales is elected president.

1957. Morales promotes social reforms, and Honduras joins the Central American Common Market.

1963. Statist General Oswaldo Lopez Arellano takes control of the government in a military coup.

1981. Honduras again returns to civilian rule.

1982. Debt crisis sparks fiscal austerity.

1989. Rafael Leonardo Cellejas of the Partido Nacional is elected president. He makes moderate reforms.

1994. Carlos Roberto Reina of the Partido Liberal becomes president, inheriting wide **public sector** debt.

1998. President Carlos Flores Facusse (PL) decentralizes the government and privatizes the economy.

1998. Hurricane Mitch hits Honduras with devastating force.

1999. Honduras receives US$3 billion in loans to help finance reconstruction after Hurricane Mitch.

2000. Honduras qualifies for debt relief under the Debt Initiative for Heavily Indebted Poor Countries (HIPC).

FUTURE TRENDS

Honduras is still recovering from Hurricane Mitch, which swept through the country in 1998, interrupting the implementation of much-needed reforms, including decentralization and privatization programs. As the country rebuilds itself, and those reforms get back on track, Honduras could experience a period of solid economic growth.

The offshore manufacturing sector will continue to expand, and competitive access to American markets will keep export revenues high. Mining production could increase as well, which, along with the growth in manufacturing, could widen the export base, raise trade revenues, and generate foreign investment. Increased activity in the tourist sector will also play an important role in the country's economic revitalization. However, regional disputes still threaten to undermine the Honduran economy.

The ongoing land dispute between Nicaragua and Honduras flared up again in 1999 when Honduras recognized Colombia's right to a stretch of maritime land claimed by Nicaragua. Nicaragua, in retaliation, imposed a 35 percent tariff on all Honduran imports. Honduras, in turn, has threatened to impose trade **sanctions** on Nicaragua effective April 2000 if the tariffs are not lifted. The case has been taken up by the International Court of Justice in the Netherlands but will likely take years to resolve. In the meantime, Honduran exporters will suffer high regional tariffs, costing millions of dollars and stifling domestic growth.

On the political front, the Honduran democratic process will be put to the test in November 2001 when the country's next presidential election is set to be held. The 2 main parties are fiercely competitive and regard one another with hostility. The level of acrimony between them was heightened by a recent dispute over the eligibility of candidates. The dispute threatens to jeopardize political stability and plunge Honduran politics back into violence.

Honduras may benefit from the joint initiative developed by the World Bank and the IMF, known as the Debt Initiative for Heavily Indebted Poor Countries. The program provides debt relief for poor countries who, in exchange, commit to economic reforms. Reforms in Honduras have been opposed by the unions, but union influence has waned and, so far, the reforms are proceeding. The reforms include privatizing the telecommunications industry as well as power production in order to meet the terms of a 3-year poverty reduction program signed with the IMF in April 1999. It has been estimated that relief from the HIPC program will save Honduras nearly US$1 billion over 20 years.

DEPENDENCIES

Honduras has no territories or colonies.

BIBLIOGRAPHY

Economist Intelligence Unit. *Country Profile: Honduras, 2000.* London: Economist Intelligence Unit, 2000.

International Monetary Fund. *Interim Poverty Reduction Strategy Papers.* <http://www.imf.org/external/NP/prsp/2000/hnd/01/>. Accessed August 2001.

U.S. Central Intelligence Agency. *CIA World Factbook 2000: Honduras.* <http://www.odci.gov/cia/publications/factbook/geos/ho.html>. Accessed August 2001.

U.S. State Department: Bureau of Democracy, Human Rights, and Labor. *1998 Human Rights Report: Honduras Country Report.* Released February 1999. <http://www.usis.usemb.se/human/human 1998/honduras.html>. Accessed August 2001.

U.S. State Department: Bureau of Western Affairs. *Background Notes: Honduras, March 1999.* <http://www.state.gov/www/background_notes/honduras_0399_bgn.html>. Accessed August 2001.

U.S. State Department. *Country Report, Honduras, Bureau of Economic Policy and Trade Practices.* <http://www.state.gov/www/issues/economic/trade_reports/1999/honduras.pdf>. Accessed August 2001.

World Bank. *World Bank Development Report.* Washington D.C.: World Bank Group, 2000.

—John Mazor

JAMAICA

CAPITAL: Kingston.

MONETARY UNIT: Jamaican dollar (J$). One Jamaican dollar equals 100 cents. There are coins of 1, 5, 10, and 25 cents, and 1 dollar. There are notes of 2, 5, 10, 20, 50, and 100 dollars. In 1999 the exchange rate of Jamaican to U.S. dollars was J$42.25=US$1.

CHIEF EXPORTS: Bauxite, alumina, sugar, bananas, rum.

CHIEF IMPORTS: Machinery and transportation equipment, construction materials, fuel, food, chemicals, fertilizers.

GROSS DOMESTIC PRODUCT: US$8.8 billion (purchasing power parity, 1998 est.).

BALANCE OF TRADE: **Exports:** US$1.303 billion (f.o.b., 1998). **Imports:** US$3.273 billion (c.i.f., 1998).

COUNTRY OVERVIEW

LOCATION AND SIZE. The largest English-speaking island in the Caribbean Sea, Jamaica is about 160 kilometers (90 miles) south of Cuba and has an area of 10,990 square kilometers (4,243 square miles) and a total coastline of 1,022 kilometers (634 miles). Comparatively, the area occupied by Jamaica is slightly smaller than the state of Connecticut. Jamaica's capital city, Kingston, is located on the country's southeastern coast.

POPULATION. The population of Jamaica was estimated at 2,652,689 in July of 2000, an increase of 7.5 percent from the 1990 population of 2,466,100. In 2000 the birth rate stood at 18.51 per 1,000 while the death rate stood at 5.51 per 1,000. With a projected annual population growth rate of 0.9 percent between 1997 and 2015, the population is expected to reach 2.9 million by the year 2015.

The Jamaican population is primarily of African descent (90.9 percent), with mixed race people making up 7.3 percent of the population, East Indians making up 1.3

percent, and several other ethnic groups rounding out the total. The population is generally young, with 30 percent below the age of 14 and just 7 percent of the population older than 65. A majority of Jamaicans—54.7 percent—lived in urban areas in 1997, up more than 10 percent from 1975; it is expected that by 2015 more than 63 percent of the population will live in urban areas. The capital city of Kingston and its suburbs are home to the largest number of Jamaicans.

Jamaica became the first Caribbean nation to implement a population policy. The National Population Policy, adopted in 1983, was designed to control the growth, health, and concentration of the population. Mainly, the policy focuses on limiting the birth rate by encouraging the use of contraception, and increasing the quality and length of Jamaicans' lives by addressing treatments for chronic diseases like AIDS and by reducing the number of violent deaths. In addition, the policy considers issues of migration, including urban growth, sustainable environmental plans, and other housing and transportation issues. The major funding for the implementation of this policy comes from international sources. Grants have come from the United States Agency for International Development (USAID), United Nations Fund for Population Activities (UNFPA), and United Nations International Children's Emergency Fund (UNICEF); the World Bank is the largest loan provider.

OVERVIEW OF ECONOMY

Tourism and bauxite and alumina production dominated Jamaica's economy in 2001, but the island's early economy was centered around the production of one thing: sugar. The English colonists who occupied the island in 1655 imported slave labor and developed large sugar plantations. For the colony's first 2 centuries sugar production dominated the economy, but the end of slavery in 1834 and the beginning of banana production ended this monoculture (dependence on a single crop). Nevertheless, sugar remained Jamaica's dominant export until the 1950s.

Jamaica entered the 20th century as a crown colony of England, which meant that it was administered by officials from England. Jamaica received limited self rule

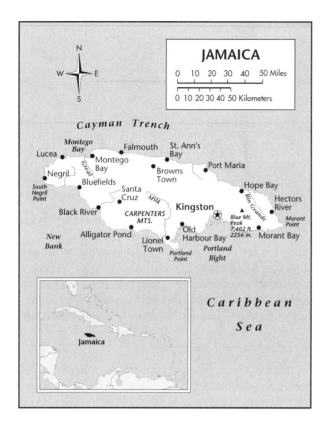

in 1944, but the growing power of the country's black majority was acknowledged in 1962 with the island's peaceful claim of independence. Since claiming its independence, Jamaica has struggled to create a stable, diversified economy. By the end of the 20th century, Jamaica had not yet created a truly vibrant economy and remained heavily dependent on the United States and Europe for imported goods, and on international lending agencies for financial assistance.

Jamaica is primarily a free-market economy with some state control; despite occasional political violence, it has a fairly stable, 2-party political system and the strong economic support of the United States, Canada, and the European Union. The economy's main exports are bauxite, alumina, sugar, and bananas, but the greatest single contributor to the national economy is tourism. Mining is largely conducted in the island's central highlands, and tourist activities are concentrated on the island's north and west coasts; farms—many of them quite small—are spread throughout the island. Limited manufacturing, **retail** trade, and services are centered around the urban centers of Kingston and Montego Bay. Because of its limited productive capacity, the island nation is heavily dependent on imported goods and on foreign **debt relief** to sustain its struggling economy.

Neither mining nor tourism is capable of providing enough jobs to counteract long-standing problems with unemployment. Unemployment reached nearly 40 percent in the 1970s under the democratic **socialist** government of Michael Manley. Even under the more conservative regimes of later governments, unemployment often hovered around 20 percent. In 1998 unemployment stood at 15.5 percent; by contrast, the unemployment rate in the United States in 1999 was just 4.2 percent.

Despite its economic difficulties—trade imbalance, high unemployment, underdeveloped commercial sector—Jamaica is largely perceived by the outside world as an island paradise. Tourists from North America, Europe, and Japan flock to the sunny Caribbean island in the winter, and they find luxurious hotels and many businesses dedicated to serving their needs.

POLITICS, GOVERNMENT, AND TAXATION

As a member of the British Commonwealth, Jamaica's government follows the Westminster Parliamentary model. The British queen is represented by the governor general, who acts as head of state, while the prime minister serves as head of the government. Voters elect members of the House of Representatives, and the leader of the majority becomes the prime minister.

Since earning its independence from England in 1962, Jamaica has been governed alternately by the 2 major political parties, the left-leaning People's National Party (PNP) and the more conservative, pro-business Jamaica Labour Party (JLP). Unlike in the United States, where transitions between the 2 major parties have not marked major swings in policy, Jamaica's 2 parties have often offered conflicting programs for managing the economy and have resorted to violence in opposing each other. Throughout the 1970s and 1980s, both parties aligned themselves with rival gun gangs and fought their political battles in the streets as well as at the ballot box. The taint of political violence has touched nearly every election in Jamaican history. In 1995 a new party, the National Democratic Movement (NDM), broke onto the political scene.

From 1972 to 1980 the PNP, under prime minister Michael Manley, adopted democratic socialism as its ruling platform and instituted state control over economic activities. The PNP had little success, as the widespread prosperity of the 1960s gave way to high **inflation**, unemployment, and great civil unrest and violence. During the 1970s Jamaica became a debtor nation and has remained so ever since. The more conservative JLP won control of the government in 1980 and maintained power until 1989. This pro-business party, led by Edward Seaga, withdrew state control from many industries and encouraged closer economic ties with the United States. Such controls were encouraged, even demanded, as a condition of loans made by the World Bank and the International Monetary Fund (IMF). Under Seaga, the economy recovered some of its strength. Nevertheless, Seaga's implementation of austerity measures demanded by the IMF as part of Jamaica's debt maintenance eroded his popularity, and in 1989 the PNP returned to power, again under the leadership of Manley. After Manley's retirement in 1992, Percival J. Patterson assumed the position of prime minister and led the party to an unprecedented third consecutive victory in the 1997 elections.

With socialist economic principles largely discredited by the collapse of the Soviet Union, the PNP generally continued the pro-business programs of the JLP in the 1990s. A crisis in the financial sector which shook the Jamaican economy between 1994 and 1996 prompted the PNP to place this sector under close government supervision, raising fears that the party was returning to more state control of the economy. Yet the PNP's efforts did little to correct the poor health of the economy—as measured by mounting government debt, little or no growth in GDP, continued high **inflation rates**, and the declining value of the Jamaican dollar—and could not contain rising levels of street violence and the drug trade. Though analysts expect that the Jamaican economy may begin to rebound in 2001, it may be too late for the PNP to maintain power.

The major source of government revenue comes from taxes. According to the U.S. State Department *Country Commercial Guide for 2001*, 36 percent of Jamaica's revenues come from **income tax**, 20 percent come from a **value-added tax**, and the remainder from customs **duties** and other sources. The highest marginal tax rate on Jamaican taxpayers stood at 25 percent for incomes over US$2,712 in 1999; while the tax rate percentage is low compared to other countries, the level of the income taxed at this rate is also quite low, which means that a fairly high percentage of Jamaicans are taxed at the highest rate. The highest marginal tax rate on corporations in the same period was 33 percent. Customs taxes are collected under the Common External Tariff (CET) policy enacted by the CARICOM (Caribbean Common Market). The CET is intended to encourage trade among Caribbean nations by placing a **tariff** of between 0 and 30 percent on goods imported from outside the CARICOM.

The declining value of the Jamaican dollar forced the government to increase the burden of taxes on the Jamaican public. During the financial crises of the late 1990s, the government raised the tax rate on such goods as gasoline, cigarettes, and alcohol, sparking widespread protests. When the government raised taxes on petroleum products in April 1999, for example, riots paralyzed the island for 3 days. To stop the violence, the government reduced the tax increases.

INFRASTRUCTURE, POWER, AND COMMUNICATIONS

Jamaica enjoys an extensive though aging **infrastructure** which has received much government attention in the 1990s. The small island is served by a network of over 18,700 kilometers (11,620 miles) of roads, 13,100 kilometers (8,140 miles) of which are paved. With growing numbers of licensed automobiles in the 1990s, the road system, especially in urban areas, has become highly congested. A major highway development project between Montego Bay and Negril began in 1999, but has since been suspended because of financial problems experienced by the contractor.

The nation's rail system is troubled—in 1992 the state-owned Jamaica Railway Corporation ceased operation and the few operating rail lines are used only for

Communications

Country	Telephones[a]	Telephones, Mobile/Cellular[a]	Radio Stations[b]	Radios[a]	TV Stations[a]	Televisions[a]	Internet Service Providers[c]	Internet Users[c]
Jamaica	353,000 (1996)	54,640 (1996)	AM 10; FM 13; shortwave 0	1.215 M	7	460,000	21	60,000
United States	194 M	69.209 M (1998)	AM 4,762; FM 5,542; shortwave 18	575 M	1,500	219 M	7,800	148 M
Cuba	473,031 (2000)	2,994	AM 169; FM 55; shortwave 1	3.9 M	58	2.64 M	4 (2001)	60,000
St. Lucia	37,000	1,600	AM 2, FM 7, shortwave 0 (1998)	111,000	3	32,000	15	5,000

[a]Data is for 1997 unless otherwise noted.
[b]Data is for 1998 unless otherwise noted.
[c]Data is for 2000 unless otherwise noted.

SOURCE: CIA *World Factbook 2001* [Online].

transporting bauxite and alumina—but the government is pursuing efforts to modernize the country's railways. An Indian agency responsible for the rehabilitation of track line, locomotives, and stations, and the acquisition of new technology and equipment is working to improve Jamaica's rail service. In addition, the government announced upcoming commuter services from Kingston to Spanish Town and Linstead in early 2001.

Jamaica has 2 major airports: the Norman Manley International Airport in Kingston and the Sangster International Airport in Montego Bay, both of which are quite modern. The latter was slated for **privatization** by the end of 2000. Ten major airlines provide service to Jamaica, and are responsible for carrying many of the country's tourists. The ports of Kingston and Montego Bay are world-class sea ports; in fact, the port of Kingston was estimated to be the seventh largest transshipment port (a port in which goods arrive to be distributed by other means) in the world, according to the EIU *Country Profile* for 1997–98. However, Jamaica has lost some international shipping business due to the high cost of shipping operations in the country.

Electrical power is supplied to Jamaicans by the state-owned Jamaica Public Service Company, which has the capacity to produce 656.2 megawatts of power. Because the nation has no natural fuel reserves, over 95 percent of the country's power is generated from imported fuel oil, which accounted for 15 percent of all imports in 1996. Though generally reliable, the 110-volt power system has been subject to occasional power shortages and blackouts.

Telecommunications services in Jamaica are thoroughly modern. Telephone service is provided by Cable and Wireless of Jamaica Limited; although Cable and Wireless held a **monopoly** at the beginning of the 21st century, the government allowed for domestic competition in 2001, with plans for the market to be fully competitive by 2003. In addition, 2 foreign companies bought licenses to introduce mobile phone service to the country: Cellular One Caribbean, a St. Maarten-based U.S. company, and Mossel Limited, an Irish firm. According to the EIU *Country Profile* for 1997–98, the country had 331,816 telephone lines and was adding new lines at the rate of 60,000 a year. In 1999 the country also had 6 Internet service providers.

ECONOMIC SECTORS

Jamaica's economic sectors reflect the small size of the country, which places real limits on the availability of natural resources, population, and domestic markets. During the late 1990s, Jamaica's economy suffered from a variety of setbacks that hampered the growth of its goods-producing sectors—all of which experienced declines, with the exception of agriculture. The economy is

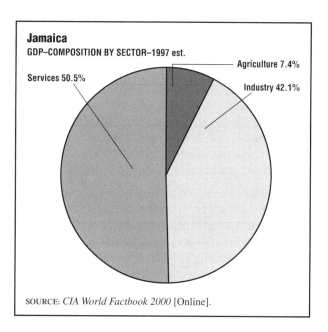

Jamaica
GDP–COMPOSITION BY SECTOR–1997 est.

Services 50.5%
Agriculture 7.4%
Industry 42.1%

SOURCE: *CIA World Factbook 2000* [Online].

still reeling from the crisis experienced in the financial sector in 1996, although the government's intervention to stabilize the banking system led to a growth of 4.8 percent in the services sector in 1999. Increasing political violence also held back growth in the tourist industry. Jamaica's economy relies heavily on trade with other countries, so changes in the preferential trade regimes it enjoyed with the United States and the European Union, combined with an overvalued currency, has significantly shrunk its export market.

Recognizing these obstacles, Jamaica has targeted certain economic sectors to fuel the economy's growth.

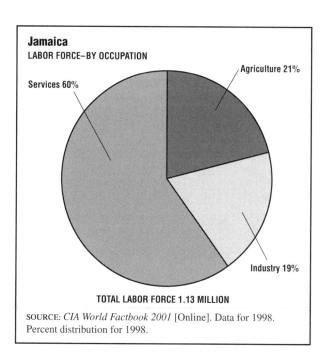

Jamaica
LABOR FORCE–BY OCCUPATION

Services 60%
Agriculture 21%
Industry 19%

TOTAL LABOR FORCE 1.13 MILLION

SOURCE: *CIA World Factbook 2001* [Online]. Data for 1998. Percent distribution for 1998.

Jamaica's 15-year plan called the National Industrial Policy, adopted in 1996, identified tourism, shipping and port services, apparel, agricultural processing, minerals, bauxite, and alumina as industries to target for export growth and expansion. The World Trade Organization (WTO) highlighted the services sector, especially tourism, as critical to Jamaica's development.

AGRICULTURE

Agricultural production is an important contributor to Jamaica's economy, accounting for 7.4 percent of GDP in 1997 and providing nearly a quarter of the country's employment. Sugar, which has been produced in Jamaica for centuries, is the nation's dominant agricultural export, but the country also produces bananas, coffee, spices, pimentos, cocoa, citrus, and coconuts. In addition to legal agricultural production, Jamaica is also a major producer of marijuana, known locally as *ganja*, which contributes a great deal of money to the **informal economy**. Agricultural production of all sorts has been subject to the region's tumultuous weather, which includes seasonal hurricanes and occasional drought. In addition to **cash crops**, Jamaica also produces a wide variety of produce for domestic consumption.

In 1996 the country produced 237,943 metric tons of sugar, its highest output since 1980. Of this total, 181,183 metric tons of sugar were exported, earning US$109 million. The European Union (EU) was the major purchaser of Jamaican sugar, thanks to standard export quotas granted to Jamaica. The United Kingdom was the single largest purchaser of Jamaican sugar, purchasing 86.5 percent in 1996.

The bulk of Jamaican sugar is produced on large sugar plantations, though small and medium-sized businesses do contribute between 30 and 40 percent of the bulk sugarcane converted on the plantations. Productivity in the Jamaican sugar industry is low due to outdated equipment, inefficient management, and an aging workforce. Losses in this economic sector, prompted in part by a severe drought in 1997, forced the government to offer the sector a US$100 million assistance package late in 1997.

The EU previously offered Jamaica an annual quota of 105,000 metric tons on bananas (which means that they agree to purchase a defined amount of bananas each year), but the WTO ruled in 1995 that the EU went against free trade legislation by giving preference to Caribbean banana exports. As will be the case with many Caribbean nations which rely on strong banana exports, this ruling is expected to negatively affect Jamaica's banana industry as the preferential market is phased out. From a low in 1988 following Hurricane Gilbert, Jamaican banana production reached 88,917 metric tons in 1996 and earned US$44.1 million. Banana producers, who are generally small farmers, hope to increase their output by increasing efficiency and extracting higher yields per acre.

The remainder of Jamaica's agricultural production is divided among a number of smaller export products, including cocoa, coffee (Jamaican Blue Mountain coffee is prized throughout the world), copra (coconut flesh), and pimentos. Production of these minor crops climbed in the early 1990s, though they were also affected by the drought of 1997. Food production for domestic consumption—generally conducted by small farmers selling their goods in local markets—also climbed during the early 1990s. Despite this increased production, Jamaica imports the majority of the food it consumes, which keeps food prices high throughout the country.

Though it is not recorded on any official reports on agricultural production and exports, marijuana is an important cash crop for many Jamaican farmers. Many small farmers plant marijuana between their other crops and an efficient farmer can expect to earn thousands, even tens of thousands, of Jamaican dollars off a small plot of land. Farmers sell their crop to drug dealers, who risk arrest to supply high U.S. demand for the illegal drug. The profits earned from the drug trade, in turn, fuel corruption and bribery among local police and politicians.

Though Jamaica's location would suggest that the island would have a booming fishing industry, actual fishing production has remained relatively stagnant throughout the 1980s and 1990s, rarely reaching even 50 percent of government targets. In fact, the island imports between US$15 and $20 million in fish annually.

INDUSTRY

MINING. Bauxite and alumina, raw materials used in the production of aluminum, are the country's main exports. During the 1960s Jamaica was the world's largest producer of bauxite, a position it held until the 1980s. Today, Jamaica is the world's third largest producer of bauxite, after Australia and Guinea, and has estimated reserves of more than 1.9 billion metric tons. The majority of the bauxite exported from Jamaica is first converted into alumina, though roughly 30 percent of bauxite is exported in its raw form. Bauxite is taken from mines to processing plants by truck and rail, but, because the island lacks sources of cheap energy, the final and most profitable conversion process that turns bauxite/alumina into aluminum must take place overseas.

Bauxite production first became a factor in Jamaica's economy in the 1950s. Between 1950 and 1960, the contribution of bauxite production to the nation's GDP grew from less than 1 percent to 9.3 percent. By 1970, mining's contribution to GDP reached 15.7 percent. In the years since, the industry's contribution to Jamaica's GDP remained at about 10 percent. Historically, the mining of bauxite was overseen by large American and Canadian aluminum companies such as Alcoa and Alcan, and final processing of the ore took place in their plants elsewhere. In the 1980s and 1990s, however, foreign companies withdrew from the island, and the government bought into the industry, thus keeping profits at home.

In the late 1990s, the bauxite/alumina industry employed about 5,000 people in the country's most highly paid economic sector. According to the U.S. State Department's *Country Commercial Guide*, the industry produced 12.6 million tons of bauxite and alumina in 1998, its highest level of production in over a decade. However, production declined by 7.3 percent to 11.79 million tons in 1999; some of the lost volume is due to an explosion at a Louisiana refinery which handles two-thirds of Kaiser Jamaica Bauxite Company's exports. The loss was offset by an increase in the price of bauxite on international markets, but shifting world demand for aluminum and variations in oil prices have made profits from the industry quite variable over the years. Fortunately, tourism helps bring in foreign dollars when bauxite profits decline.

In addition to bauxite, Jamaica has substantial reserves of several other important minerals, including limestone, gypsum, silica, and marble. Extensive, high-quality limestone reserves estimated at 50 billion tons provide an ample base for exports, though limestone production has, in fact, been rather small. Gypsum, which has been mined in eastern Jamaica since 1949, is another important export mineral. While some gypsum is used locally in the manufacture of tiles and cement, most is shipped unprocessed to the United States and Latin America.

MANUFACTURING. The manufacturing sector is an important, though declining, contributor to the Jamaican economy. Though manufacturing accounted for 19.6 percent of GDP in 1988, it had fallen to 18.1 percent in 1996. Total employment in manufacturing in 1996 stood at 100,400 people, or 8.7 percent of the **labor force**. Forces contributing to the shrinkage of the manufacturing sector include the sinking price of imports, increases in domestic wages, and, in the mid-1990s, increased competition from Mexico in the garment industry following the passage of the North American Free Trade Agreement (NAFTA), which granted Mexican products preferential treatment in U.S. markets.

Historically, Jamaican companies have processed sugar, food, beverages, and tobacco; produced chemicals, metals, and construction materials; and assembled electrical appliances and apparel. Many of these companies were set up to encourage **import substitution**,

which meant that they were designed to produce goods that had previously been imported. Beginning in the 1980s, however, apparel production became the dominant manufacturing activity in the nation, employing 35,000 people in the early 1990s. Production was greatly increased when U.S. companies began exporting their apparel assembly to countries such as Jamaica, which could assemble clothing at far lower prices than in the United States. The value of apparel exports reached US$292 million in 1995, making it the nation's second most valuable export next to alumina.

SERVICES

TOURISM. Tourism is vitally important to the health of the Jamaican economy, contributing approximately US$1.23 billion to the economy in 1999. Beginning in the 1960s, economic prosperity in the major Western countries and declining international air fares helped make Jamaica a major tourist destination. By the early 1970s tourism competed with the bauxite industry as the country's dominant source of income. After a brief decline in tourism in the late 1970s and early 1980s—due largely to internal unrest—tourism has expanded dramatically through the late 1980s and into the 1990s. The number of tourist arrivals has risen from 846,716 in 1983 to 1.82 million in 1996. Of these visitors, roughly 65 percent of tourists stay in Jamaican hotels, apartments, guest houses, and other lodging, while the majority of the remainder visit from cruise ships anchored offshore. Two-thirds of tourists to Jamaica in 1999 were from the United States.

Jamaicans have responded to this influx of tourists by constructing a range of lodging options and by investing in the infrastructure—roads, docks, services, and airports. According to the U.S. Department of State *Country Commercial Guide*, Jamaica had a total room capacity of 22,715 in 1998 and was planning to add another 1,289 rooms between 2000 and 2001. Important development projects included the opening of the Ritz-Carlton hotel complex in the Montego Bay area, in addition to 3 other hotels before 2001. In the late 1990s, however, Jamaica began experiencing slight declines in tourist visits, thanks to unfavorable **exchange rates**, increasing competition for tourist dollars by other Caribbean destinations, and heightened fears that tourists might be affected by the rising political and gang violence in the country.

The tourist economy employs 84,300 people directly and it is estimated that another 170,000 people are engaged in tourism-related activities. Most tourist activity is centered on the northern coast of the island, which is more accessible to cruise ships departing from the United

States, and in the communities of Montego Bay, Port Royal, and Kingston.

FINANCIAL SERVICES. The other major component of Jamaica's service industry, beside tourist services, is the financial services industry. The early 1990s saw a rapid expansion in banking, investment, and insurance services fueled by an influx in capital and a lack of sufficient oversight by government regulatory agencies. In the mid-1990s, however, the entire financial services sector entered a period of severe crisis. Banks found themselves suffering from poor lending decisions as many of their loans were not repaid. Insurance companies who had invested in or owned banks were affected, as were other branches of the financial services sector.

In 1996 the Jamaican government took over the nation's fourth-largest bank, Century National Bank, in order to stave off its failure, and trust in the banking industry in general declined, prompting customers to attempt to withdraw their funds. By 1997 the government was forced to assume partial ownership of 5 of the nation's 6 largest locally-owned commercial banks with a rescue package valued at US$276 million, or 4.5 percent of GDP. The government agency entrusted with regulating the industry, the Financial Sector Adjustment Company, hoped to provide both the funding and the management skills necessary to rescue the industry, but by the late 1990s these changes had not yet taken affect.

RETAIL. The absence of large commercial centers, other than Kingston and its suburbs and the tourist center at Montego Bay, has resulted in a poorly developed retail sector in Jamaica. While Kingston is home to a variety of retail stores, including fast-food franchises such as Burger King and McDonald's, the majority of the towns in the interior of the country have small shops, farmer's markets, and temporary roadside stands.

INTERNATIONAL TRADE

Over the past several decades, Jamaica has relied more and more on imports. The value of imports in 1998 was more than double the value of exports. Jamaica exports and imports the majority of its goods from the United States. The United Kingdom was Jamaica's second largest single trading partner, with US$192 million in exports in 1995, or 13 percent; the remainder of the European Union countries received US$219 million, or 15 percent. Other major recipients of Jamaican goods were Canada, Norway, and the various CARICOM countries.

Imports of foreign goods were also dominated by the United States. In 1995, Jamaica imported US$1,399 million in goods from the United States, representing 49 percent of all imports (this number climbed to 52 percent in 1999). Major imports were **consumer goods**, including

Trade (expressed in billions of US$): Jamaica		
	Exports	Imports
1975	.815	1.122
1980	.963	1.095
1985	.566	1.111
1990	1.135	1.859
1995	1.414	2.757
1998	1.303	3.273

SOURCE: International Monetary Fund. *International Financial Statistics Yearbook 1999.*

food, fuels, and other raw materials. CARICOM countries accounted for US$255 million in imports, or 9 percent, in 1995, while the United Kingdom (US$240 million, or 8.5 percent), Norway (US$184 million, or 6.5 percent), other EU countries ($112 million, or 4 percent), and Canada (US$99 million, or 3.5 percent) accounted for the remainder of imports. Imports rose dramatically through the 1990s, from US$1.799 billion in 1991 to US$3 billion in 1999. Much of the rise in imports can be attributed to large purchases of **capital goods** by the government, expanding demand for consumer goods, and to major purchases made by Air Jamaica, the country's major airline.

The United States has increased in importance as Jamaica's dominant trading partner throughout the 1990s. In 1990, the United States accounted for 28 percent of Jamaica's exports and 49 percent of its imports; by 1999, those numbers had risen to 42 percent and 52 percent, respectively. Major exports are bauxite and alumina, food, and garments assembled in Jamaica. As Jamaica's trade with the United States increased, its trade with fellow members of CARICOM, the Caribbean Common Market, decreased from 8.3 percent of exports and 21.7 percent of imports in 1990 to 4 percent and 9 percent, respectively, by 1995. This lack of trade within CARICOM signals the group's inability to stimulate the regional economy despite the proximity and the lack of trade restrictions between member nations.

Exchange rates: Jamaica	
Jamaican dollars (J$) per US$1	
Jan 2001	45.557
2000	42.701
1999	39.044
1998	36.550
1997	35.404
1996	37.120

SOURCE: CIA *World Factbook 2001* [ONLINE].

The substantial and growing trade imbalance that Jamaica endured over the years has been partially offset by the input of tourist dollars and of monies sent home by Jamaicans working abroad. Nevertheless, Jamaica continues to run a **trade deficit** which forces it to borrow heavily to pay for its consumption.

MONEY

The value of the Jamaican dollar has slowly declined on the world market over a period of 30 years, making it increasingly difficult for the average Jamaican to afford imported goods. In 1977 the Jamaican dollar was valued at 90.9 cents for every U.S. dollar; by December of 1999 the value of the Jamaican dollar had collapsed to J$42.25 for every U.S. dollar. The International Monetary Fund (IMF) classifies the Jamaican exchange rate as freely floating, which means that the value of the Jamaican dollar is determined by supply and demand in the foreign exchange market and not by government control. The government, however, has tried to stabilize the price of the Jamaican dollar under IMF supervision in order to stabilize its economy. These stabilization efforts have subjected Jamaicans to periods of high inflation, economic **recession**, and mounting **national debt**. In 1999 **debt service** accounted for J$97.5 billion, or 58.1 percent of the budget. Even so, Jamaica's debt is lower than that of many other Caribbean nations.

Jamaica has a single stock exchange, the Jamaica Stock Exchange (JSE), which began operations on 3 February 1969. During its first year of operation the JSE had 34 member companies with a total **market capitalization** of J$146 million. The JSE had as many as 51 member companies during the financial services boom of the mid-1990s, but dropped back down to 45 companies in 1999. That same year the total market capitalization of the companies trading on the JSE was J$104 billion.

POVERTY AND WEALTH

When it comes to wealth, Jamaica is a land of extremes. On the northern coast—home to tourism—and in the suburbs of Kingston, wealthy Jamaicans live in first-rate housing, visit shopping centers featuring the best imported goods, and enjoy an elevated standard of living. Living in such suburbs as Cherry Gardens, Arcadia Gardens, and Forest Hills, the wealthy send their children to private schools and to universities abroad, and employ private security forces. Yet not far from these wealthy enclaves a significant number of poor Jamaicans live in squalor, with poor housing, limited food supply, and inadequate access to clean water, quality health care, or education. Kingston's poor congregate in the slum districts of Trench Town, Jones Town, and Denham Town, where

GDP per Capita (US$)					
Country	1975	1980	1985	1990	1998
Jamaica	1,819	1,458	1,353	1,651	1,559
United States	19,364	21,529	23,200	25,363	29,683
Haiti	500	607	527	481	370
St. Lucia	N/A	2,076	2,150	3,542	3,907

SOURCE: United Nations. *Human Development Report 2000; Trends in human development and per capita income.*

water supplies are often polluted and violent youth gangs clash with police for control of the streets.

The wealth is distributed largely along racial lines, reflecting Jamaica's slave-plantation heritage. The descendants of black slaves tend to be among the poorest classes in Jamaica, while white and mixed-race descendants of plantation owners and traders tend to be better off. These extremes are reflected in the nation's distribution of income: in 1996 the wealthiest 20 percent of Jamaicans controlled 43.9 percent of the wealth, while the poorest 20 percent controlled only 7 percent. In fact, the poorest 60 percent controlled just 34.3 percent of wealth. Due in large part to the decline of services in urban slums, the percentage of people with access to safe water has declined from 96 percent in the period from 1982–85 to 70 percent in the period from 1990–96; access to sanitation facilities (plumbed toilets) has dropped from 91 percent to 74 percent in the same period.

Jamaica's rural poor also face difficult circumstances, for many workers must try to grow their own crops or participate in the informal economy —in some cases, the drug trade—in order to survive. Both the rural and urban poor have suffered from the long decline in the quality of social services provided to Jamaicans. Though the British built a well-developed health and education system on the island in the post-

Distribution of Income or Consumption by Percentage Share: Jamaica	
Lowest 10%	2.9
Lowest 20%	7.0
Second 20%	11.5
Third 20%	15.8
Fourth 20%	21.8
Highest 20%	43.9
Highest 10%	28.9

Survey year: 1996
Note: This information refers to expenditure shares by percentiles of the population and is ranked by per capita expenditure.

SOURCE: *2000 World Development Indicators* [CD-ROM].

Household Consumption in PPP Terms

Country	All food	Clothing and footwear	Fuel and power[a]	Health care[b]	Education[b]	Transport & Communications	Other
Jamaica	24	7	3	1	9	8	48
United States	13	9	9	4	6	8	51
Cuba	N/A	N/A	N/A	N/A	N/A	N/A	N/A
St. Lucia	40	5	11	4	17	11	11

Data represent percentage of consumption in PPP terms.
[a]Excludes energy used for transport.
[b]Includes government and private expenditures.

SOURCE: World Bank. *World Development Indicators 2000.*

World War II years, a lack of government funding for schools and hospitals has meant that these services have declined in quality over the years. Despite this deterioration, 93 percent of Jamaican primary-level students are enrolled in school, and a government-funded health-care system ensures that Jamaicans have access to adequate health care.

Jamaica's high inflation and dependence on imports—especially for food, gasoline, and clothing—has meant that the poor have had to spend a high amount of their relatively small incomes on the necessities of life. Despite governmental food **subsidies** for the poor, similar to food stamp programs (vouchers that can be exchanged for food in grocery stores) in the United States, most poor Jamaicans spend more than half of their income on food and beverages. The difficulty that many Jamaicans face to earn a living on the island has contributed directly to the high **immigration** rate of the country and to its very low population growth. Despite the difficulties faced by Jamaica's poor, a study conducted by the Overseas Development Council judged that Jamaica's quality of life was better than both Mexico and Venezuela and equal to that of neighboring Trinidad and Tobago.

WORKING CONDITIONS

In the last years of the 1990s the Jamaican labor force has been shrinking, to an estimated 1,120,000 workers in 1999. The official unemployment rate for 1999 was 15.7 percent, down 1 percent from the year before. But the declining unemployment rate does not necessarily mean that opportunities for workers are increasing. Many of those leaving the workforce to retire are older, more highly skilled workers, while those entering the workforce are younger and unskilled. Job training and secondary education in Jamaica are generally poor, thus much of the younger workforce cannot expect high-paying jobs. Unemployment remains particularly high among women and younger workers.

Before there were even political parties in Jamaica there was a labor union: the Bustamante Industrial Trade Union, formed in 1938 to protect the rights of Jamaican workers. In the 1990s the U.S. State Department estimated union membership in Jamaica's 70 labor unions at around 20 percent of the employed workforce. The government of Jamaica supports workers' rights conventions promoted by the International Labour Organisation (ILO) and has set conditions governing industrial and human relations, established minimum wage standards, and protected low-wage workers from paying income tax. The 40-hour work week is the standard, and Jamaica has no history of child labor problems. In 1999, the government-mandated minimum wage increased to J$1,200 a week, and no income tax was required on wages lower than J$100,464 a year. In addition, the government provides social security benefits that include a retirement pension, pay for on-the-job injuries, food stamps, rehabilitation, and training. These latter benefits are considered substandard, however, and represent a tiny portion of federal spending.

Despite the protections offered by unions and government regulations, conditions for workers in Jamaica are not ideal. First, labor actions—strikes, slow downs, and protests—have frequently disturbed work life; in 1996 there were a total of 195 such disputes, up 7.7 percent from 1995. Second, the educational and training system in Jamaica is of such low quality that few workers have the skills to secure higher paying skilled jobs. (In 1998 adult illiteracy rates stood at 18 percent for men and 10 percent for women, significantly higher than elsewhere in the Caribbean.) Thus many workers seek earnings in the informal sector, which includes jobs as street vendors but also in the illegal drug trade. Finally, the close connection between labor unions and political parties has meant that union jobs are often granted as political favors, and that fights for jobs and votes have often turned violent. Industrial and political violence has been a recurring feature in Jamaican life since the 1970s and has helped decrease the attraction of Jamaica for those looking to locate factories in the country.

COUNTRY HISTORY AND ECONOMIC DEVELOPMENT

1494. Jamaica is discovered by Christopher Columbus, and comes under the control of Spain in 1509.

1655. England establishes a colony on Jamaica, which is confirmed by the Treaty of Madrid in 1670. The English begin importing slaves to harvest sugar on large plantations.

1807. England bans the slave trade, ending the flow of African slaves into Jamaica.

1834. England abolishes slavery in its colonies, forcing sugar plantation owners to change their labor relations and granting more power to the island's largely black population.

1865. The Morant Bay Rebellion against the authoritarian rule of white colonial leaders is crushed, but British authorities decide to rule Jamaica as a crown colony, which means that it is administered by British officials.

1938. Labor leader Alexander Bustamante helps establish the first trade union in the Caribbean region, the Bustamante Industrial Trade Union (BITU). In the same year Norman Washington Manley forms Jamaica's first political party, the People's National Party (PNP).

1943. Alexander Bustamante forms the nation's second political party, the Jamaica Labour Party (JLP).

1944. England grants Jamaica a new constitution allowing for the election of a governor by all citizens. Jamaica is now self-governed.

1958–61. The West Indies Federation attempts to join Caribbean nations in a single political entity, but is undermined by competition between Jamaica and Trinidad, the federation's 2 largest members.

1962. Jamaica is granted its independence from England on 5 August 1962, and becomes an independent state within the British Commonwealth.

1968. Jamaica joins Caribbean Free Trade Association (CARIFTA), hoping to enlarge the regional market for its goods.

1973. Jamaica becomes a founding nation of the Caribbean Common Market (CARICOM), a union of Caribbean nations dedicated to ensuring the free flow of goods between countries. CARICOM has never received sufficient support from member countries to operate effectively.

1973–74. The worldwide oil crisis undermines Jamaica's economy and puts the nation on the path to lasting trade imbalances and debt.

1988. Hurricane Gilbert devastates the island's agricultural sector, causing damage that continues to affect the economy into the 1990s.

1995. Bruce Golding helps found the National Democratic Movement (NDM), the nation's third major political party.

FUTURE TRENDS

Jamaica entered the 21st century under a cloud of economic decline. For the better part of 3 decades, despite some successes at increasing tourism and exports and curbing imports, the nation has been fighting a losing battle with inflation, mounting debt, and the declining value of the Jamaican dollar. In real terms, this has meant that the quality of life for the average Jamaican has undergone a slow but steady decline. The government enacted policies in the early 1990s to stabilize the economy and appeared to be making progress toward that goal. However, the financial collapse of the mid-1990s caused significant setbacks. Following policies outlined by the World Bank, the IMF, and other lending agencies, the government hopes that its program of lowering interest rates, encouraging tourism, and encouraging exports can help the economy. Yet nearly 20 years of following policies outlined by lending agencies has not yet led Jamaica out of its economic decline. Whether the Jamaican economy will rebound depends heavily on continued world prosperity in the early part of the 21st century, especially in areas related to Jamaica's main revenue producers, and on the government's ability to ride out the social backlash against needed austerity measures.

DEPENDENCIES

Jamaica has no territories or colonies.

BIBLIOGRAPHY

Bayer, Marcel. *Jamaica: A Guide to the People, Politics and Culture.* London: Latin American Bureau, 1993.

"The Caribbean's Tarnished Jewel." *The Economist.* 2 October 1999.

Economist Intelligence Unit. *Country Profile: Jamaica, Barbados, 1997–98.* London: Economist Intelligence Unit, 1998.

U.S. Department of State. *FY 2001 Country Commercial Guide: Jamaica.* <http://www.state.gov/www/about_state/business/com_guides/2001/wha/jamaica_ccg2001.pdf>. Accessed September 2001.

World Trade Organization, Ministry of Foreign Affairs and Foreign Trade. "Jamaica: 1998." <http://www.wto.org/English/tratop_e/tpr_e/tp85_e.htm>. Accessed September 2000.

—*Tom Pendergast*

MEXICO

CAPITAL: Mexico City.

MONETARY UNIT: New peso (peso, or NM$). One peso equals 100 centavos. Coins are in denominations of NM$1, 2, 5, 10, and 20, as well as 5, 10, and 20 centavos. Paper currency is in denominations of NM$10, 20, 50, 100, 200, and 500.

CHIEF EXPORTS: Manufactured goods, oil and oil products, silver, coffee, and cotton.

CHIEF IMPORTS: Metal-working machines, steel mill products, agricultural machinery, electrical equipment, car parts for assembly, repair parts for motor vehicles, aircraft and aircraft parts.

GROSS DOMESTIC PRODUCT: US$865.5 billion (purchasing power parity, 1999 est.).

BALANCE OF TRADE: Exports: US$136.7 billion (f.o.b., 1999 est.). **Imports:** US$142.06 billion (f.o.b., 1999 est.).

COUNTRY OVERVIEW

LOCATION AND SIZE. Mexico is a country located in North America and is bordered by the United States to the north, Belize and Guatemala to its south, the Gulf of Mexico to its east and the North Pacific Ocean to its west. The country's total area is 1,972,550 square kilometers (761,601 square miles), or nearly 3 times the size of Texas. Its capital, Mexico City, is located in the south-central part of the country.

POPULATION. As of July 2000, the population of Mexico was estimated to be 100,349,766. This is 19,099,766 more than the 1990 population of 81,250,000, reflecting a ten-year increase of 23.5 percent. In 2000, the birth rate was estimated to be 23.15 per 1,000. This was more than 4 times the death rate of 5.05 per 1,000. Based on a projected annual growth rate of 1.8 percent, the population is expected to number approximately 120 million by the year 2010.

People of Indian/Spanish heritage (mestizo) are estimated to account for 50 to 60 percent of the population

of Mexico. Indians are from 25 to 30 percent, Caucasians from 9 to 15 percent, and Africans are a very small part of the population. These estimates of racial groupings are tenuous at best because Mexicans do not characterize themselves in racial terms. Groups are defined culturally so that the term "mestizo" means someone who is culturally Mexican in language, dress, and perspective. Someone who does not speak Spanish but speaks an Indian dialect and dresses in traditional Indian wear would be considered Indian, even if that individual were Caucasian. Accordingly, during the course of one's life, it is possible for someone to change their ethnic grouping by simply adopting the language and habits of another ethnic group. Indeed, in Mexico an increasing number of Indians are becoming mestizos by adopting the Spanish language and de-emphasizing their Indian customs.

The Mexican population is also a relatively young population; 4 percent are older than 65 while 34 percent are under 14. It is also an urban population; 70 percent of the population lives in urban areas while 30 percent lives in rural areas (50 percent lived in rural areas in 1950). The 3 largest cities in Mexico are Mexico City, Guadalajara, and Netzahual-coyotl. Mexico City is the largest metropolis in the world, with population estimates ranging between 18 and 20 million. In 1999, Guadalajara and Netzahual-coyotl were estimated to have populations of 1.65 million and 1.25 million people, respectively.

The nature of the population of Mexico is notable in at least 2 other respects. First, in 1973 Mexico became the first country in Latin America to adopt a population control policy. The policy was needed because from 1940 to 1970, Mexico's population had increased by 250 percent. Overcrowding in cities and unemployment were serious problems. Indeed, Mexico had become a victim of its own success. The Mexican death rate had decreased as a result of advances in preventive

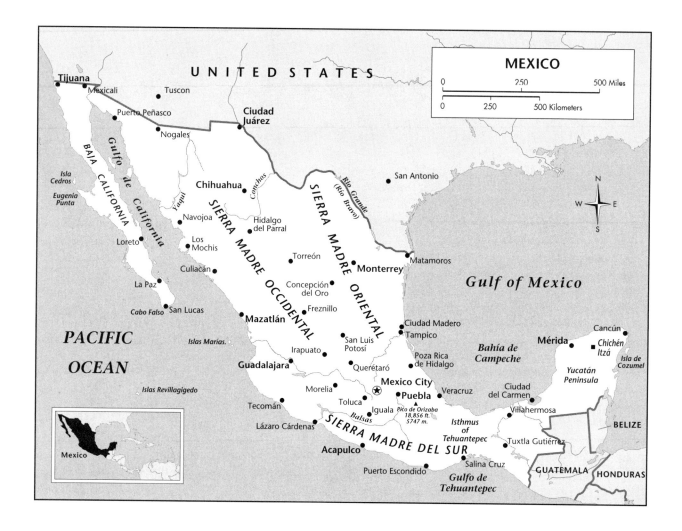

medicine and sanitation, making it possible to control such diseases as yellow fever. The death rate was 33.2 per 1,000 members of the population in 1905, but by 1970 it was 10.1 per 1,000. Despite this decrease in the death rate, the fertility rate (the number of children born to each woman) had remained constant during this time. The end result was an increase in the population so that it grew an average of 3.4 percent per year from 1960 to 1970. Since the institution of the population policy, the rate of growth of the population has gradually decreased to an average of 1.8 percent per year (1995–2000). The second respect in which the population of Mexico is interesting has to do with the sizeable net migration of Mexicans to the United States. Estimates from 1990 are that there were 13.5 million people of Mexican origin living in the United States. Of those 13.5 million, 4 to 5 million had been born in Mexico. Unfortunately, because of the problem of unemployment from overpopulation, a number of Mexicans have come to the United States illegally in the recent past. By 1996, 2.7 million Mexicans were estimated to be living in the United States illegally. Indeed, the number of Mexicans coming to the United States legally is roughly equivalent to the number entering the

country illegally (approximately 150,000 per year). Unfortunately, **immigration** authorities face a never-ending battle because many expelled immigrants simply return as soon as they are deported from the United States.

OVERVIEW OF ECONOMY

The Mexican economy is both complex and very much in transition. There are at least 3 transitions that are worth noting. The first is the economy's transition from an agricultural economy to an industrial one. In 1940, agriculture accounted for 19 percent of **GDP** and employed 65 percent of the **labor force**. However, in 1999 agriculture accounted for 5 percent of GDP and employed 23 percent of the labor force. In contrast, manufacturing and services accounted for 88 percent of GDP in 1999 and employed approximately 70 percent of the labor force. The most important catalyst for such a dramatic change is Mexico's involvement in World War II in the early 1940s. As a member of the Allies, Mexico began supplying its fellow Allies with war equipment and supplies and, because of the decreased availability of **consumer goods** from other nations, supplied its own population with consumer goods as well. Since then, both government and private citizens have furthered Mexico's industrial development.

The second transition that characterizes the Mexican economy is a shift from a closed to an open economy. Although after World War II the government pursued a successful policy of industrializing the economy, that policy was buttressed by efforts to keep the Mexican economy closed. For example, the government pursued a policy of encouraging Mexican manufacturers to engage in **import substitution**. Part of that policy required that the government set up barriers (such as **tariffs**) to the importation of those same items. All of this changed in 1985 when the government decided to pursue a policy of promoting Mexican exports and decreasing barriers to imports into Mexico. This commitment to an open economy was crystallized when Mexico signed the North American Free Trade Agreement (NAFTA) in 1992. Under that agreement, Mexico has committed itself to eliminating the trade barriers that exist between it and the United States and Canada by the year 2009. At the time Mexico signed NAFTA, its economy was dominated by small to medium-sized companies. NAFTA opened the door for large U.S. and Canadian companies to open branches or offices in Mexico, which would bring more jobs to the country.

The third transition that characterizes the Mexican economy is a change from an economy that pursues public ownership to one that pursues private ownership. In the 1970s and 1980s the government assumed a large amount of **foreign debt** and much of that money was used to purchase businesses—many of which were run inefficiently—by the government. The vast majority of these businesses were sold by the government in the 1990s. Although Mexico continues to wrestle with its foreign debt, which as of 1999 was US$161 billion, its debt is now a reasonable amount of debt when compared to that of other Latin American countries. For instance, Mexico's economy is 5 times as large as Venezuela's, but Mexico has only 4 times the amount of debt that Venezuela has.

At the beginning of the new millennium, the Mexican economy is vibrant, with fully functioning agricultural, services, industry, and banking sectors. Mexico has demonstrated to the world that it can sustain itself. But Mexico continues to be plagued by persistent problems of the poverty and **underemployment** of a large segment of its population. These problems pose the greatest challenges to the country's economic future.

POLITICS, GOVERNMENT, AND TAXATION

Under its present (1917) constitution, Mexico is a federal republic with 1 Federal District and 31 states. The president, presently Vincente Fox Quesada, elected in 2000, serves for a 6-year term. There is no vice-president. The president cannot run for reelection to succeed himself or herself. However, the president can run for re-election at a later date. The president selects a cabinet that presently consists of 19 secretaries. The Mexican congress has an upper chamber and lower chamber. The Senate is the upper chamber and consists of 128 senators who are elected to 6-year terms. The Chamber of Deputies is the lower chamber and consists of 500 deputies who are elected to 3-year terms. Although 90 percent of legislation is initiated by the president, it is the responsibility of the legislature to discuss and approve this legislation as well as presidential appointments to high office. The judicial system in Mexico is divided into state and federal components. The Supreme Court of Justice is the highest court in the land. There are 21 magistrates and 5 auxiliary judges on this court. These judges are appointed for life by the president, subject to the approval of the Senate. The judges on the Supreme Court appoint the judges of the lower federal courts. Although the judges on the Supreme Court are independent of the president and are appointed for life, there is a tradition in Mexico that all federal judges tender their resignation at the start of the term of the new president. Local government officials are elected by local elections.

The election of Vincente Fox Quesada, a former Coca-Cola executive, as president of Mexico in July of 2000 made headlines around the world. For the first time in 71 years, the presidency was not held by someone from the Institutional Revolutionary Party or the PRI (Partido Revolucionario Institucional). The PRI is the political party that was formed to embody the principles of the Mexican Revolution. The term "Revolution" is a term that refers to the military overthrow of Mexico's last major military dictator, Porfirio Díaz, in 1910. In 1917, after 7 years of civil war, those who favored the Constitutionalist Revolution led by Venustiano Carranza prevailed in putting together a new constitution for Mexico. The Constitution of 1917 was a remarkably advanced document for its time. It sought to assert not only the political but the economic and social rights of the Mexican people. For example, in addition to establishing a federal government, there are clauses within the Constitution that guarantee free compulsory education, minimum wages, the right of labor to organize and strike, social security, national ownership of resources that are below the ground, and land reform.

In 1929, a Mexican president by the name of Plutarco Elías Calles formed a political party, the National Revolutionary Party to govern in the name of the Revolution. The name of the party was changed in 1946 to the PRI. From 1929 until 1988, Mexico had, in effect, a one-party political system. The system succeeded for at least 2 reasons. First, the party contained political competition by allowing competing interests and factions to organize themselves into "sectors" within the party (the labor and military sector). Second, the PRI in effect provided something for everybody. Those who would otherwise have led rebellions against the establishment had no reason to do so because they could achieve political and economic mobility within the PRI. A political monopoly was maintained by the PRI by matching techniques (such as fraud and bribery) to the appropriate circumstance.

In the 1988 elections, the PRI won the presidency by 50.4 percent of the vote, its lowest winning margin ever. Fully one-third of the seats in the Chamber of Deputies went to opposition parties. In 1997, the PRI lost its majority in the Chamber of Deputies. In 2000, for the first time in Mexican history, the PRI lost the presidential election to an opposition party, the right of center National Action Party (Partido Acción Nacional or PAN). Some have argued that the PRI lost its political monopoly because there are few living Mexicans who remember what the Revolution of 1910 was all about. Others have argued that because the Mexican economy fell upon hard times in the 1980s it became difficult for the PRI to provide something for everyone. More importantly, in the early 1980s the public image of the PRI was badly tarnished with the public disclosure of the corruption and excesses of PRI government officials (for instance, a "gift" of a US$2 million house from the labor unions to President Portillo). After these disclosures, those career politicians who had benefitted from the excesses of the Portillo years found that their political careers were badly derailed. To bolster the image of the PRI, the succeeding president, Miguel de la Madrid Hurtado, appointed a number of **technocrats** to his cabinet. This tension between the technocrats ("technicos")—people who had professional backgrounds and for the most part had never run for political office—and the career politicians ("politicos") came to a head when de la Madrid nominated a technocrat, Carlos Salinas de Gortari, to succeed him as president. In response to this nomination, arguing that the PRI had departed from its populist roots, 2 PRI officials (Cuauhtemoc Cardenas and Porfirio Muñoz Ledo) split from the party by forming the left of center Party of the Democratic Revolution (Partido de la Revolución Democrática or PRD). Although the PRD fielded Cardenas as its candidate, Salinas subsequently won the presidency by 50.4 percent of the popular vote.

Significantly, the free-market, pro-business policies begun by the de la Madrid administration in 1982 have continued since that time into the Fox administration of 2000. The difference is that Fox's political party, PAN, is a party that is economically and socially conservative. From 1982 until 2000, the policies pursued by PRI presidents were certainly economically conservative. For example, Salinas opened the Mexican economy to market forces by signing the North American Free Trade Agreement (NAFTA) in 1992. This agreement, which went into effect in 1994, decreased trade barriers between Mexico, Canada, and the United States. Additionally, the number of enterprises owned by the government went from 1,155 in 1982 to 215 in 1994, representing a significant decline in government involvement in and regulation of economic activity. It is difficult, however, to characterize the social policies of PRI officials over the last 20 years as necessarily conservative. For example, the response of the Salinas administration to a rebel uprising in Chiapas in 1994 was to negotiate with the rebels rather than confront them.

Over the past 20 years there have also been some significant reforms in the Mexican tax system in an effort to increase government revenues. For example, the government has put in place a **value-added tax** (VAT) in addition to the income (corporate and personal) and sales taxes that already exist in the country. In addition to the VAT, Mexico has a personal tax system with remarkably low rates. For example, the highest rate of personal **income tax** is approximately 25 percent. Despite these changes over the past 20 years, Mexico has not succeeded in increasing its tax revenues. The Mexican government's tax revenues when expressed as a percentage of GDP (the tax revenue rate) is approximately 11 percent (that same rate in the United States is approximately 28 percent). This rate is low because individuals and businesses do not comply with the tax laws. Because of low tax revenues, the government has relied on the revenues it receives from the country's oil **monopoly** (PEMEX). One source has estimated that up to 40 percent of the government's revenue may come from monies it receives from PEMEX.

INFRASTRUCTURE, POWER, AND COMMUNICATIONS

The highway network in Mexico is one of the most extensive in Latin America. Indeed, all areas of the country are linked by it. As of 1997, Mexico had 323,761 kilometers (201,185 miles) of highways of which 96,205 kilometers (59,792 miles) were paved. There were also 6,335 kilometers (3,937 miles) of expressways. The most traveled highways link 3 of Mexico's most populous cities (Mexico City, Guadalajara, and Monterrey) in the form of a triangle. Mexico's highway system is extensive, but poorly maintained because of lack of government funds. The government has responded to this problem by granting concessions to companies to build toll roads. However, construction cost overruns have led to high tolls and reduced traffic on these roads. In 1994, the Mexican government revoked a number of these concessions and offered financial assistance to some of the construction companies.

Mass transit within Mexico is modest, although the bus service between cities is extensive. Mexico City's

Communications

Country	Newspapers	Radios	TV Sets[a]	Cable subscribers[a]	Mobile Phones[a]	Fax Machines[a]	Personal Computers[a]	Internet Hosts[b]	Internet Users[b]
	1996	1997	1998	1998	1998	1998	1998	1999	1999
Mexico	97	325	261	15.7	35	3.0	47.0	23.02	1,822
United States	215	2,146	847	244.3	256	78.4	458.6	1,508.77	74,100
Brazil	40	444	316	16.3	47	3.1	30.1	18.45	3,500
Canada	159	1,077	715	263.8	176	33.3	330.0	422.97	11,000

[a]Data are from International Telecommunication Union, *World Telecommunication Development Report 1999* and are per 1,000 people.

[b]Data are from the Internet Software Consortium (http://www.isc.org) and are per 10,000 people.

SOURCE: World Bank. *World Development Indicators 2000.*

subway system opened in 1969. As of 1993, the system had 8 lines and 135 stations covering 98 miles. By the year 2010 the system will have expanded to 15 lines covering 196 miles. Guadalajara's subway system opened in the early 1990s. Despite the availability of mass transit, cars still crowd the roadways in urban areas like Mexico City. The country's **infrastructure** has not expanded along with the greater number of cars in its major cities. The end result is chronic traffic congestion and thick smog.

The railway system within Mexico is extensive, consisting of 30,952 kilometers (19,233 miles) of rail lines as of 1998. The Mexican National Railways (Ferrocarriles Nacionales Mexicanos—FNM) was a state-owned company that carried 80 percent of the rail traffic and operated on 70 percent of the tracks. Many Mexican companies did not use the railway system to transport cargo because they considered it inefficient and outdated. In 1997, the government began to **privatize** the FNM, a process which was completed by the end of 1999. Because the process of privatization was only recently completed, it will take time to determine whether it has addressed the ills that had beset Mexico's railway system.

As of 1999, Mexico was estimated to have 1,806 airports of which 233 had paved runways. Much like it has done with its railways, Mexico has recently gone through the process of privatizing its main airports. There are 35 airports in Mexico that carry 97 percent of the passenger traffic. The process of privatizing those airports was begun in 1998 and was completed by the end of 1999. The only exception to privatization is the Benito Juarez International Airport in Mexico City (Mexico's main airport) which remains under government control. Privatization has benefitted Mexico's airlines. Only 2 of Mexico's more than 70 domestic airlines are known internationally—Aeromexico and Mexicana—both of which were privatized in 1989. Since that time, Aeromexico has lost its reputation as "Aeromaybe" because of its unreliability and has developed a reputation for on-time performance. However, in 1995, confronted with the possibility of the financial collapse of these 2 airlines allegedly because of

financial mismanagement, the 2 airlines were placed in a **holding company** (Cintra). Cintra will soon be broken up and its 2 airlines sold to foster competition in the industry. American airline companies are poised to become investors in the new Mexican airlines. Finally, it should be noted that Mexico has privatized not only its airports and airlines, but its seaports as well.

In 1998, 176.05 billion kilowatts (bkw) of electricity were produced in Mexico while the country consumed 164.76 bkw of electricity in that same year. Of the electricity produced, 78 percent was produced from fossil fuels while 14 percent was hydro-electrical energy. In the 1960s, the government **nationalized** the country's electricity-producing companies. As of 1992, 90 percent of the electricity produced in Mexico was produced by the country's Federal Electricity Commission. All of that began to change in 1991 when the laws were changed to allow private companies to produce electricity for their own consumption and for sale to the Commission. The laws were again changed in 1997, this time empowering the Commission to award permits to private companies to build power plants that produce electricity for sale to the public. As of July 2000, 9 such permits had been issued by the Commission.

Presently, the telecommunications industry in Mexico is dominated by 1 company—Telmex (Mexican Telephone or Telefonos de Mexico). Telmex was privatized in 1990 and by 1999 had increased the number of telephone lines in Mexico by 104 percent. Despite the increase in available lines, there has been little improvement in the services rendered by Telmex. Relative to other large Latin American economies, Mexico continues to have one of the lowest numbers of telephones per capita. Improvements to the telecommunications within the country may come as Telmex adjusts to new rules by Cofetel (Comisión Federal de Telecomunicaciones), the telecommunications industry regulator, and competition from other telephone companies and cellular telephone companies. In 1999, there were 6.94 million cellular telephone subscribers in Mexico.

Radio, television, and Internet usage in Mexico are prevalent. Mexico had 2.45 million Internet users as of 1999. The government owns and runs a number of radio networks. There are over 20 private radio networks spanning over 700 radio stations in Mexico. Televista (Mexican Telesystem or Telesistema Mexicano) is the dominant television company in Mexico, with an estimated 80 percent share of the television audience. There are over 326 television stations in Mexico and most of them are owned or associated with Televista. Some television stations are affiliated with the government's television station (Mexican Institute of Television).

ECONOMIC SECTORS

The Mexican economy is primarily a service economy to the extent that 66 percent of GDP and over 50 percent of employment in 1999 was accounted for by the services sector. Much of the decline in agricultural employment over the past 60 years has been picked up by the services sector. Hospitality, personal, and professional services account for most of the services that are performed within the economy.

The manufacturing sector is the next most important sector with 20.8 percent of GDP and approximately 17 percent of the labor force in 1999. The notable activity in this sector has to do with the success of the *maquiladora* plants in Mexico. Maquiladora plants are plants that exist along the Mexican-American border that receive inputs from American plants and produce items that can be exported or sold within Mexico. It has been estimated that these plants generated 49 percent of Mexico's manufacturing output in 1999.

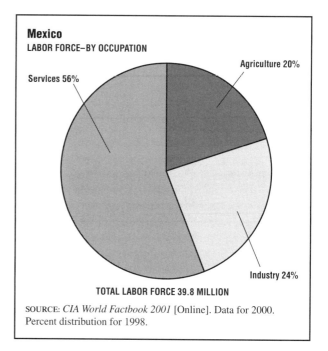

Mexico
LABOR FORCE–BY OCCUPATION

Services 56%

Agriculture 20%

Industry 24%

TOTAL LABOR FORCE 39.8 MILLION

SOURCE: *CIA World Factbook 2001* [Online]. Data for 2000. Percent distribution for 1998.

The third-most important sector in Mexico is agriculture, which accounted for 5 percent of GDP in 1999 yet employed 23 percent of the labor force. As discussed previously, the industrialization of the Mexican economy has resulted in a decrease in the importance of this sector since 1940. However, the sector continues to provide employment for a significant portion of the Mexican labor force.

Mining makes up a small portion of the economic output of the country, accounting for only 1.2 percent of GDP and employing approximately 0.3 percent of the labor force in 1999. The great significance of this sector stems from the government's reliance on revenues from the country's oil company for a substantial portion of its revenue.

AGRICULTURE

In 1999, agriculture employed 23 percent of Mexico's labor force but accounted for only 5 percent of Mexico's GDP. Crop production was and continues to be the most important agricultural activity in Mexico, accounting for fully 50 percent of agricultural output. Domestically, the most important crops for consumption purposes are wheat, beans, corn, and sorghum. The most important crops for export purposes are sugar, coffee, fruits, and vegetables. Mexico continues to be one of the top producers of crops in the world. In 1999, the crops produced in greatest number in Mexico were sugar cane (46.81 billion tons), corn (15.72 billion tons), sorghum (5.59 billion tons), wheat (3 billion tons), and beans (1.04 billion tons). Fruits and vegetables are the most eco-

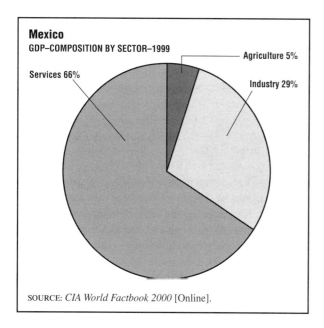

Mexico
GDP–COMPOSITION BY SECTOR–1999

Services 66%

Agriculture 5%

Industry 29%

SOURCE: *CIA World Factbook 2000* [Online].

nomically significant agricultural products exported by Mexico. For example, in 1998 Mexico's export of fruits and vegetables to the United States generated revenues of US$2.86 billion while meat and fish exports generated US$.71 billion, and coffee and cocoa US$682 million.

In comparison to its crop production, livestock accounts for 30 percent of Mexico's agricultural output. In 1999, livestock or livestock products produced in greatest number were milk (8.96 billion liters), poultry (1.72 billion tons), eggs (1.63 billion tons), and beef (1.39 billion tons). Mexico is not self-sufficient in the production of meat and fish. In 1998 it imported US$1.05 billion of meat and fish from the United States.

There are at least 3 reasons why Mexico has enjoyed some success in its crop production over the past 5 years. First, there is much land that is available to grow crops. Mexico has been able to increase the land that it uses for crops from 3.70 million acres in 1950 to 8.64 million acres in 1965 because of irrigation programs instituted by the government in the 1940s and 1950s. Second, there have been changes in the land ownership system that were instituted by President Salinas in 1992. Under the Constitution of 1917, land was distributed by the government to a community of peasants called an *ejido*, whose members owned the land but could not lease or sell it. In the face of increasing importation of food and decreased agricultural output, President Salinas was successful in getting the Mexican Constitution amended to give the members of the ejido the right to lease or sell the land if most of the members of the ejido agreed to do so. The purpose of this change was to allow ejidos to combine to form large efficient farms. Millions of acres of ejido land have now been transferred and a substantial amount of money has now been invested in the agricultural sector by private investors in their efforts to buy or lease ejido land. A third reason why Mexico has enjoyed an increase in crop production over the past few years is because under the Procampo program, the government now makes cash payments directly to farmers and they can then determine which crops they want to produce. The program has encouraged Mexican farmers to produce crops like wheat and sorghum as well as fruits and vegetables instead of the more profitable corn and beans. This program will be phased out from 2003 to 2008.

Although Mexico's agricultural production has increased over the past few years, there are some who would argue that there is still much work to be done in the Mexican agricultural sector. The growth rate in the agricultural sector has recently been below the growth rate of the rest of the Mexican economy. The sector has gone from a high of 5.8 percent of GDP in 1993 to its present low of 4.5 percent of GDP in 1999. In addition, Mexico exported more than it imported in agricultural products from 1992 through 1997. In 1998 it imported

US$845 million more than it exported; its net agricultural imports were US$364 million in 1999. But the changes instituted in the early 1990s have had positive effects and will continue to offer a positive trend for the agricultural sector.

INDUSTRY

MINING. Fuel and nonfuel mining accounted for 1.2 percent of Mexico's GDP in 1999. Traditionally, the sector has employed a small percentage of the workforce. For example, in 1997 it employed 0.3 percent of the Mexican labor force. Despite these small numbers, fuel mining is important in Mexico because the oil revenue that the government receives from the state oil company Pemex (Petróleos Mexicanos) is a large part of its budget (32.5 percent in 1999). Further, oil is an important component of the country's export revenues (7.3 percent in 1999). Indeed, in 1999, it ranked fifth in the world in terms of the oil that it produced (3.34 million barrels/day). Its oil reserves are estimated to be 58.2 billion barrels of oil (40 years of production), some of the highest reserves in the world. Most (56 percent) of these reserves are located in the Gulf of Mexico. The remaining reserves are found in southern Mexico (Chiapas).

The first oil well was drilled in 1869. The Constitution of 1917 gave the Mexican government the right to all Mexican subsoil resources including oil. Accordingly, in 1938 the government nationalized the petroleum industry. Foreign companies were compensated for their holdings in 1943.

From 1957 to 1971 Mexico's industrial sector grew to such an extent that the country became a net importer of oil. The increasing demand for oil by the Mexicans exceeded the production of oil by the state. However, production of oil increased significantly in 1972 when sizeable oil deposits were discovered in the southern Mexico.

In 1995, the government privatized the exploration for natural gas and since then several companies have been given permits to explore for natural gas in Mexico. Non-fuel mining accounted for only 1.1 percent of GDP and 0.3 percent of exports in 1999. In the same year, the top 4 minerals mined were silver (1.06 million pounds), gold (1,039 pounds), copper (321,000 tons), and zinc (321,000 tons). Silver is the most valuable mineral mined in Mexico. Indeed, Mexico is the leading silver producer in the world, producing more than 16 percent of the world's silver. Most of this silver is mined in the country's "Silver Belt," a region that extends from the central part of the country into the northeast. Mexico is one of the world's top producers of copper as well.

MANUFACTURING. Manufacturing has provided an enormous boost to the Mexican economy since the 1980s, increasing from 25 percent of total exports in 1982 to nearly 90 percent in 1999. In 1999, manufacturing accounted for 20.8 percent of GDP and employed 16.9 percent of the labor force in 1997. The top 4 categories of items manufactured in 1999 were metal products, machinery, and equipment (29.9 percent of manufacturing output); food, beverages, and tobacco (24.7 percent); chemicals, petroleum products, rubber, and plastics (15.1 percent); and clothing and footwear (8.4 percent). These top 4 categories also employed 83 percent of the labor force. Although manufacturing output grew by 5.2 percent per year on average from 1994 to 1999, it is important to note that metal products, machinery, and equipment grew by an average of 9.2 percent per year during that same period.

The growth of the manufacturing sector reflects Mexico's shift from a country concerned with only supplying and protecting its own needs to one that vigorously pursues other markets. Indeed, the story of Mexican manufacturing is about the surrender of nationalism for globalism. In the early 1950s, under a policy of import substitution, the government provided incentives for manufacturers to produce the items that Mexican consumers were importing (thereby "substituting" Mexican goods for imports). This policy worked, and Mexican manufacturing output grew by 9 percent in the 1960s and 7 percent in the 1970s. However, by 1982 total government spending was so large that it was equivalent to 47 percent of the Mexican GDP. Additionally, the government was spending more than it was taking in and that **budget deficit** was equivalent to 18 percent of GDP. This spending produced a drag on the economy and consumer demand decreased. Manufacturing output, which depended on consumer demand, decreased as well (down 10 percent from 1981 to 1983, and 6 percent in 1985).

In view of the preceding realities, in 1985 the administration of President de la Madrid changed Mexico's policy from one of import substitution to one of export promotion. Clearly, the manufacturing sector has benefited nicely from this change in policy, especially the maquiladora sector, which is made up of factories that are located along the American/Mexican border. The factories on the Mexican side accept materials often from American factories on the American side of the border, assemble them and then either **re-export** them or ship them internally for sale to Mexican consumers. Maquiladoras manufacture automobile engines, and electronic equipment such as stereos, televisions, and household appliances. American companies benefit from this arrangement because of the lower cost of labor in Mexico. It has been estimated that 49 percent of Mexican manufacturing output was produced by the maquiladora sector in 1999. In the same year, there were 3,436 maquiladora plants that employed 1.2 million Mexicans, or roughly 20 percent of the manufacturing labor force. Some of the items pro-

duced by these plants included clothing and textile products (1,035 plants) and electronic parts and materials (533 plants). Mexico City and its suburbs, Guadalajara, and Monterrey are also centers of a great deal of manufacturing output.

Forcing Mexican manufacturers to compete in an open economy is a policy that has had costs as well as benefits. Specifically, the manufacturing sector has enjoyed robust growth in output and exports, but many manufacturing enterprises that were once protected from competition by the Mexican government through tariffs are no longer protected. Because a very large percentage of Mexican manufacturers are small with fewer than 250 workers, some of them have not been able to withstand the pressures of competing in an international marketplace. However, the increase in manufacturing output over the past 5 years suggests that the surviving manufacturers are doing well.

SERVICES

Some 66 percent of GDP is generated by services in the Mexican economy. The sector also employs the majority of workers in the labor force, having employed 53 percent of workers in 1997. An analysis of the numbers of people who are employed within the services sector gives one a sense for the types of services that predominate within Mexico and their degree of labor intensiveness. In 1997, the category that employed the greatest number of workers was the community, social, and personal services category (8.8 million people). Next largest, at 7.8 million people, was the trade, restaurant, and hotel business. The transport, storage, and communications industries employed 1.5 million people. Finally, the finance, insurance, real estate, and business services industries employed 1.4 million people.

TOURISM. Because 7.8 million people (or 21 percent of those employed) in 1997 worked in the restaurant or hotel business, one could conclude correctly that tourism is big business in Mexico. It has been estimated that in 1997 the tourism industry employed 1.8 million people directly. The country has over 8,000 hotels with over 322,000 hotel rooms with another 88,000 nontraditional guest facilities such as villas. Tourists are attracted to popular tourist resorts in places like Cancun and Acapulco, but they often go to visit the monuments and shop in Mexico City as well. American tourists also visit Mexico's border towns. For example, in 1990 Americans made 70 million visits to Mexican border towns, while Mexicans made 88 million visits to American border towns in that same year. It has been estimated that in an average year over 80 percent of tourists to Mexico come from the United States. These American tourists spend quite a bit of money; 10 million tourists spent US$5.4 billion in 1999.

RETAIL AND FINANCIAL SERVICES. What is remarkable about the Mexico of today is that one can step inside an air-conditioned shopping mall and find most of the amenities of modern life, from televisions to toothpaste. Monterrey, a major city far to the north of Mexico City, typifies this kind of consumer choice. Although finding such a facility in Mexico City or its posh western suburbs especially has not been such an unusual occurrence, the increasing appearance of such **retail** facilities today in other cities in Mexico speaks volumes about what has happened to retail trade in Mexico in the 1990s. In fact, it has been estimated that up to 45 percent of retail sales in Mexico are made in such large facilities. The remaining 55 percent of retail sales continue to be made by small family-operated businesses. The reason for this change in the 1990s is simple. The opening of the Mexican economy in the 1990s resulted in an influx of foreign retailers. Many Mexican retailers that were not purchased by larger foreign companies have now moved out of the largest urban center to service the smaller Mexican cities. Mexico is now a country with department stores, shopping malls, and discount clubs. It is increasingly beginning to resemble its large American neighbor. Retail sales have been increasing steadily in Mexico each year since 1996.

Mexico's banking system is a remarkably well-developed one. The central bank, the Bank of Mexico, is an independent agency of the government that performs the traditional functions of a central bank. Specifically, it dictates to member banks the amount of money they must keep in reserve and it regulates the nation's money supply. In 1982, in the wake of Mexico's **recession** and in an effort to contain the flight of capital out of Mexico, the nation's private banks were nationalized by the government. All banks were privatized again by 1992 and as of 1999 there were 39 commercial banks operating in Mexico. As of 1994, the government has allowed Canadian and U.S. banks to open branches in Mexico. Although the banking system is no longer in a state of crisis, the fact remains that all is not well with the Mexican banking system. **Bad loans** are the critical problems facing Mexican banks. The government has intervened here by setting up a fund to take over the bad debts of banks. This fund had absorbed US$89 billion of debt as of 1999. It is becoming clear that only a small fraction of these debts will be recovered by the government. The matter of what to do with these loans has become an issue of political negotiation.

INTERNATIONAL TRADE

Mexico has dramatically changed its approach to international trade. Over the past 25 years Mexican exports have moved successfully from a reliance on oil (oil was 76 percent of export revenue in 1982) to a reliance on

Trade (expressed in billions of US$): Mexico		
	Exports	Imports
1975	2.904	6.580
1980	18.031	22.144
1985	26.757	19.116
1990	40.711	43.548
1995	79.542	75.858
1998	117.500	130.811

SOURCE: International Monetary Fund. *International Financial Statistics Yearbook 1999.*

manufacturing (manufacturing was 89 percent of export revenues in 1999). The success of this shift has come primarily from the maquiladora program, which started in the 1960s but which was greatly increased by the NAFTA agreement in 1994.

As Mexico has changed its approach to international trade, its **balance of trade** has also changed. Before 1981, Mexico suffered from a trade deficit. During this time, the Mexican government was committed to a policy of "defending" the peso by setting the value of the peso at a high level—unrealistically high in this case—as a matter of national pride. But because the price of pesos was too high, people were unwilling to buy pesos with other currencies at the official **exchange rate**. Therefore, the main way for the Mexican government to get foreign currency so that it could trade with other countries was to borrow it. By the early 1980s, the government had amassed a large foreign debt to other countries. What is worse is that oil revenues, the main source of revenue to the government, decreased with the drop in world oil prices in the late 1970s. Things got so bad that by 1982 the Mexican government announced that it could no longer even pay the interest on the debt that it owed. As a result of this more expensive peso, Mexicans were able to buy more goods from outside of Mexico because they could get more dollars for their peso. So imports into Mexico increased. By the same token, buyers outside of Mexico were less willing to buy Mexican goods because the peso was too expensive relative to their currencies. As a result, although exports out of Mexico increased before 1981, imports increased faster than exports, leading to a trade deficit.

Nationalism gave way to economic reality and in 1982 the government devalued the peso. But the Mexican government went even further, deciding in 1985 to pursue growth of the economy through exports. On the export side, in addition to its **devaluation** of the peso, the government gave Mexican manufacturers various incentives to export. On the import side, the government followed a policy of **liberalizing** trade by removing the restrictions (e.g., licenses) that it had placed on countries wanting to export to Mexico. This policy made it easier for Mexican manufacturers to get the inputs they needed for their manufacturing processes. The result was that exports exceeded imports from 1982 to 1989. However, in 1990 Mexico became a victim of its own success. The growth of the economy generated an internal demand for goods that resulted in an increase in imports into Mexico. In addition, the price of pesos was now high relative to other currencies, probably because the demand for pesos was high. The expensive peso resulted in a slower rate of increase of Mexican exports. So in 1990 Mexico experienced a trade deficit. This deficit persisted until the Mexican government once again devalued the peso in 1994. That devaluation made possible a trade surplus from 1995 to 1997. Since then, however, the economy has once again experienced a trade deficit.

A great deal of Mexico's trade situation depends on the United States, its largest trading partner. Exports to the United States reached a high of 88.4 percent of Mexico's total exports in 1999. In 1999, Canada received the next highest percentage of Mexico's exports (1.7 percent). In addition, Mexico imports most of its products from the United States, almost 75 percent in 1995. Some argue that the increase in Mexico's exports to and imports from the United States over the past 5 years have come as a result of the North American Free Trade Agreement (NAFTA), which was entered into by Mexico, the United States, and Canada in 1994. NAFTA gradually abolishes the trade barriers (for example, import tariffs) between the countries over a 15-year period, resulting in one single economic market with a population of over 400 million people and a **gross domestic product** of over US$6 trillion.

But Mexico is not willing to be wholly reliant on the United States. Mexico entered into a free trade agreement with the European Union (EU) in July of 2000 that commits the parties to eliminate their trade barriers over 10 years. With its agreement with the EU, Mexico becomes the only country other than Israel to have special access to the European and North American markets.

In addition to the flow of imports and exports in Mexico, a very positive role in the international accounts has been played by **remittances** of Mexicans who are living abroad (mostly in the United States). These transfers (US$6.3 billion in 1999) are treated in the international accounts in the same manner as Mexican exports are treated.

MONEY

For approximately 30 years (from the 1940s to the 1970s), Mexico had an average annual growth rate of 6 percent, **inflation** of less than 10 percent, and very little debt to the outside world. However, over the next 30 years (1970s to the present) there were 2 economic crises

Exchange rates: Mexico	
Mexican pesos (Mex$) US$1	
Jan 2001	9.7701
2000	9.4556
1999	9.5604
1998	9.1360
1997	7.9185
1996	7.5994

SOURCE: CIA *World Factbook 2001* [ONLINE].

that brought the economy to the brink of collapse (in 1982 and 1995). During these crises, the economy experienced significant inflation (159 percent in 1987), unemployment, and a recession of 7 percent in 1995 (the largest since the Great Depression of the 1930s). Mexico's troubles stem from 2 successive administrations (Presidents Echeverría in 1970 and Lopez Portillo in 1976) which pursued political and expansionist policies that exceeded the limitations of the Mexican economy. These policies left the economy in shambles with a large **external debt** and a number of poorly functioning, corrupt, and inefficient government agencies. The administrations that have come to power since 1982 have labored mightily to undo the damage that was done to the Mexican economy from 1970 to 1982. It is useful to consider briefly the strategy pursued by each administration since 1982.

In 1982, President de la Madrid inherited a government with a deficit equal to 18 percent of GDP and government spending that was 47 percent of GDP. Immediately, his administration faced an upcoming foreign debt payment of US$10 billion for which it had no funds. Indeed, high oil prices in the 1970s had given prior administrations the illusion of continued government revenues, but these dissipated in the early 1980s when oil prices collapsed. In 1982, the incoming de la Madrid administration declared the situation an emergency and instituted measures that included an increase in taxes and interest rates, and a cut of the federal budget. The U.S. government intervened with a US$1 billion loan guarantee and by pressuring banks to postpone their receipt of the US$10 billion debt repayment. The Mexican government also **restructured** its foreign debt with the International Monetary Fund so that it paid a lower interest rate on its debt over a longer period of time. The peso was also devalued by the government a number of times. These early efforts by the de la Madrid administration did not bear fruit. For example, the Mexican economy contracted by 5 percent in 1983, grew by 3.5 percent in 1984, but contracted again by 1 percent in 1985.

However, 3 events occurred in the mid-1980s that ultimately yielded positive results for the Mexican economy. First, the de la Madrid administration made a deliberate decision in 1985 to promote Mexican exports and liberalize trade. The success of that policy in increasing Mexico's exports has been previously discussed in the section on international trade. Second, the Baker Plan (named after U.S. Treasury Secretary James A. Baker), implemented in 1986, allowed Mexico to reschedule US$43.3 billion of its US$52.2 billion foreign debt. It also provided the Mexican government with US$12.5 billion in new credit. The final event was the Economic Solidarity Pact that the government entered into with the various sectors of the economy (including business and labor) in 1987 wherein all agreed to try to limit wage and price increases. The government for its part agreed to such things as a cut in spending and a more restrictive **monetary policy**. All 3 of these events yielded results and by 1988, Mexico's **inflation rate** was 52 percent, down from a high of 159 percent in 1987.

In 1988, the Salinas administration continued many of the policies of the de la Madrid administration. Companies were privatized; as of 1993, 390 (63 percent) of the companies that had been held by the government in 1988 had been sold. Tax collection improved and in 1995 the government ran a surplus of 815 million pesos. Inflation was controlled initially and by 1994, the rate of inflation was 7 percent. However, in its pursuit of trade liberalization, the government mismanaged its currency. Current account deficits (imports greater than exports) progressed to a point where the government was without international reserves to pay for imports. In December of 1994, the incoming government of President Zedillo was forced to devalue the peso. Inflation and unemployment resulted. The economy contracted by 6.2 percent in 1995. However, the Mexican government was able to borrow or obtain credit guarantees of US$48 billion in 1995.

The Mexican economy has recovered quickly since 1995 through the pursuit of traditional economic policies. The Zedillo administration cut government spending and increased taxes. Accordingly, the rate of inflation went from 52 percent in 1995 to 27.7 percent in 1996. Privatization efforts will continue with the Fox administration that came into power in December of 2000. The growth numbers for the Mexican economy have looked impressive since 1996 with GDP growth in that year of 5.2 percent, 6.8 percent in 1997, 4.8 percent in 1998, and 3.7 percent in 1999. Inflation has also been controlled, with inflation in 2000 at 8.96 percent, the lowest annual inflation rate since 1994. Unemployment in October of 2000 fell to an all-time low of 1.97 percent. It is curious that the 19 year-old Mexican Stock Exchange (Bolsa Mexicana de Valores) did not respond to all of this good economic news in 2000. The Bolsa's stock index finished the year with a loss of 20.7 percent at 5,652 points. One possible explanation for this is that stock exchanges throughout the world tend to move in tandem and that

GDP per Capita (US$)					
Country	1975	1980	1985	1990	1998
Mexico	3,380	4,167	4,106	4,046	4,459
United States	19,364	21,529	23,200	25,363	29,683
Canada	14,535	16,423	17,850	19,160	20,458
Brazil	3,464	4,253	4,039	4,078	4,509

SOURCE: United Nations. *Human Development Report 2000; Trends in human development and per capita income.*

the Bolsa lost value as did other stock exchanges throughout the world in 2000. It is worth noting, however, that the Bolsa continues to be one of the fastest growing stock exchanges in the world. Its index was valued at 1,500 points in 1995 after the peso crisis. Its close at 5,652 points in 2000 implies a 55 percent annual growth rate from 1995 to 2000. There are hundreds of Mexican companies presently traded on the exchange.

POVERTY AND WEALTH

Social stratification in Mexico persists to the present day. Historically the members of the upper class were those who owned the land that the lower class cultivated. This changed with the Mexican Revolution of 1910. It has been estimated that as a result of the Revolution, the Mexican government redistributed 50 percent of the land held by the landed gentry. Today, land ownership continues to form the basis for wealth in Mexico. However, the economy's industrial transformation means that industrialists and politicians are also likely to number among the wealthy. Unfortunately, only 10 percent of Mexicans are wealthy. Another 30 percent are middle class. Fully 60 percent of Mexicans are poor, including peasants and industrial workers. The country's income is very unevenly distributed. The wealthy 10 percent of the population owns 38 percent of the country's income, the

Distribution of Income or Consumption by Percentage Share: Mexico

Lowest 10%	1.4
Lowest 20%	3.6
Second 20%	7.2
Third 20%	11.8
Fourth 20%	19.2
Highest 20%	58.2
Highest 10%	42.8

Survey year: 1995
Note: This information refers to income shares by percentiles of the population and is ranked by per capita income.

SOURCE: *2000 World Development Indicators* [CD-ROM].

Household Consumption in PPP Terms

Country	All food	Clothing and footwear	Fuel and power[a]	Health care[b]	Education[b]	Transport & Communications	Other
Mexico	30	6	4	2	7	5	46
United States	13	9	9	4	6	8	51
Brazil	22	13	18	15	34	4	−6
Canada	14	5	10	4	21	9	38

Data represent percentage of consumption in PPP terms.
[a]Excludes energy used for transport.
[b]Includes government and private expenditures.

SOURCE: World Bank. *World Development Indicators 2000.*

middle 30 percent of the population has 36 percent, while the remaining 60 percent gets 26 percent of the country's income.

One need look no further than the indexes of health, education, and housing to understand that there are great disparities between the wealthy and poor in Mexico. With respect to health, the Mexican population has on average done well. In 1940, average life expectancy and infant mortality were respectively 42 and 125 per 1,000 live births. By the year 2000, those statistics had changed to 75.3 and 25 per 1,000 live births. But disparities persist; life expectancy is lower by 10 to 15 years and infant mortality can be twice as high in the poorer southern states like Chiapas. Health care is substantially free for all Mexican citizens. The Mexican Institute of Social Security runs hospitals and clinics that are available to workers in the formal sector. Mexicans who are not in the formal labor force are able to receive medical care from a number of different governmental agencies. Yet the reality is that receiving health care from a nurse in a rural clinic is quite different from receiving health care from an expensive specialist in the United States, an option often exercised by the wealthy in Mexico. The disparities in the nation's health statistics reflect this reality.

With respect to education, it is important to note that 89.6 percent of the population is literate. In fact, the educational system within Mexico is extensive. Education is compulsory through to the equivalent of the ninth grade. At least 1 public university can be found within each state. Mexico City boasts the country's largest public university, the National Autonomous University of Mexico, with over 275,000 students. The campus is also the repository of the country's national library. Yet public schools in Mexico have significant problems. The quality of instruction is low, the bureaucracy is ineffective, and students do not stay in school (only 60 percent of Mexican children complete primary school). Experts agree that the system does a poor job of preparing Mexican citizens to compete in a global economy. However, the disparity between rich and poor is evident here. In

Mexico, the rich are more likely to be educated. They are more likely to have attended the country's better private schools, and schools in the United States, whereas in the rural villages the state may not provide education beyond the sixth grade.

The housing situation in Mexico also provides a dramatic illustration of the disparity between rich and poor in the country. Even within Mexico City it is possible to see numerous examples of the country's housing shortage. In the community of Netzahual-coyotl, on the eastern outskirts of Mexico City, over 1,000,000 lower-class Mexicans live in single-room brick structures erected on land that floods when it rains. They have few public services. By contrast, the elite western suburbs of Mexico City allow the wealthy to live with all of the amenities of modern life.

In the modern era, persistent poverty has been one of the abiding problems of the Mexican economy. The economy has few safety nets; there is no unemployment compensation and the poor do not receive welfare payments. Economic policies that have worsened things like inflation have eroded the **real wages** of the poor. Each incoming Mexican administration, it seems, has proposed a new government program to address the needs of the poor. Sometimes the programs have worked temporarily and sometimes not at all. And if the nation's income distribution and housing pattern is any indication, the situation appears to be worsening. While education is the ticket to upward social mobility in Mexico, it is not at all clear that the state is providing educational opportunities for the poor.

WORKING CONDITIONS

The conditions under which someone works in Mexico depend on whether or not that person is a member of the formal labor force or is employed in the **informal sector**. Formal workers are those who have registered with the Mexican Institute for Social Security as workers. They and their employers make payments into a fund that pays for—among other things—health care. These workers also receive the protection of the country's minimum wage and labor laws. In 1999, the formal labor force was 41.41 million workers with an unemployment rate of 2.5 percent, down from 6.5 percent in 1995. Individuals working less than 35 hours per week (the **underemployed**) totaled 19.1 percent of the labor force. Informal workers, estimated at up to 40 percent of the labor force, are unregistered workers, and include Mexico's hundreds of thousands of street vendors. These individuals are not entitled to the benefits received by formal workers.

The minimum wage in Mexico is set annually by a commission that has representatives from government, business, and labor. The commission seeks to increase the minimum wage by an amount that will account for the next year's anticipated inflation. There are 3 different minimum wages corresponding to different geographic areas. The highest wage is in Mexico City (NM$40.35 a day or approximately US$4.25 per day). Unfortunately, the country's inflation has on average been higher than the increase in the minimum wage. For example, at the beginning of 1995, the commission increased the minimum wage by 21 percent. However, the currency crisis in that year caused inflation to increase by more than 50 percent. So it is that in 1987, the minimum wage covered 94 percent of a worker's basic necessities. By 1995, it covered only 35 percent of those necessities. The reality is even worse because estimates of noncompliance with the minimum wage law vary from 30 to 80 percent of employers, depending on the location of the business. In view of this economic reality, one of the important developments in Mexico's labor force has been the number of women who have joined the labor force in the past 20 years. Married women in particular have joined the labor force because of the erosion of the real wages of their husbands. Unfortunately, the wages of women have lagged far behind those of men.

The economic woes that confront Mexican workers stand in sharp relief to the progressive labor laws and infrastructure that are available for their protection. For example, Mexican labor laws guarantee workers such things as 1 day off each week, and 8 days of vacation per year. The minimum age for work is 14 years of age, and child labor laws prohibit children from working certain jobs and certain hours. Labor unions are the most visible component of Mexico's labor infrastructure. Although there are only a few professionals who are organized, it has been estimated that over 90 percent of industrial workers are part of a union if they work for a business with at least 25 employees. The country's unions are organized at the local, regional, state, and national level. The national labor organization is called the Congress of Labor and fully 85 percent of unionized workers belong to it. The unions do provide a voice for the workers in Mex-

ican society although some question their effectiveness. Indeed, the realities of the Mexican economy over the past 20 years has forced the unions to make major wage concessions. Privatization has resulted in the elimination of thousands of union jobs. One can imagine, however, that the situation for Mexican workers would have been far worse but for the presence of Mexico's labor unions.

COUNTRY HISTORY AND ECONOMIC DEVELOPMENT

1100s. Aztec civilization begins with first Aztec arrivals in the Valley of Mexico.

1502–20. Montezuma reigns. The empire is organized into a bureaucracy with provinces, governors, and taxation.

1519–20. Montezuma is conquered by Hernan Cortés.

1521–1700. New Spanish colony prospers. Natives are destroyed with overwork and European diseases. Colony begins to founder economically.

1821. Conservatives persuade Spanish officer and creole Augustin de Iturbide to negotiate with guerilla leader Vicente Guerrero for Mexican independence. Agreement called Plan of Iguala declares Mexican independence.

1822. Combined rebel and royal troops control Mexico. Iturbide proclaimed emperor Augustin I, but is deposed. General Antonio Lopez de Santa Anna declares Mexico a republic.

1824. Iturbide is assassinated, and Guadelupe Victoria is elected Mexico's first president.

1833. Santa Anna elected president.

1836. Santa Anna gets new constitution that eliminates states' rights. U.S. immigrants to Mexican territory of Texas declare it an independent republic. Texas garrison at the Alamo destroyed by Santa Anna but he is ultimately defeated. He refuses to recognize Texas as an independent republic.

1845. United States annexes Texas. Santa Anna is overthrown.

1847. Mexican-American War. U.S. wins, gets upper California, New Mexico, and pays Mexico US$15 million.

1857. Constitution of 1857 passes.

1858–61. Conservatives and liberals fight War of the Reform.

1861. Conservatives in exile persuade Napoleon III to set up a monarchy in Mexico. Mexico suspends payments on its foreign debt and is invaded by combined forces of Spain, France, and Britain. Britain and Spain leave over dispute on how to divide Mexican assets.

1863. French stay and take the city of Puebla and then Mexico City. President Benito Juarez leaves the city.

1866–67. Napoleon declares campaign a costly failure and pulls out French troops. Juarez amasses sizeable Mexican army, retakes Mexico City, and becomes president again. Maximillian is captured at Querétaro and is executed.

1876. General Jose de la Cruz Porfirio Díaz becomes president by leading revolt. He engages in rational planning, but also repression of political opposition. The economy is modernized, and the U.S. and Europeans help build infrastructure.

1906. New Mexican middle class and new generation of Mexicans ("Regeneration Movement") become politically active and critical of government. Many are jailed.

1908. Díaz is elected to seventh term. Mexico celebrates 100 years of independence. Activist Francisco Madero calls for Rebellion which begins in Puebla and spreads throughout Mexico.

1911. Díaz resigns after attack on Ciudad Juarez. Madero is elected president.

1913–28. Era of political turmoil and assassinations. The United States intervenes again in Mexican politics.

1928. Emilio Portes Gill is appointed president.

1929. Plutarco Elias Calles forms National Revolutionary Party, Mexico's first official political party.

1934–40. Lazaro Cardenas becomes president. He expropriates and redistributes private land to peasants, and expropriates oil company assets and railroads. He sends Calles into exile.

1940–46. Manuel Avila Camacho becomes president. Mexico joins Allies; it has limited military involvement but becomes a significant supplier of material. Mexican industry develops.

1946–70. Presidencies of Aleman (1946), Ruiz (1952), Lopez (1958), Díaz (1964) all characterized by increased industrialization and urbanization. Political party renamed PRI (Partido Revolucionario Institucional) by Aleman with all presidents during this time a member of the party. Nationwide voting rights for women granted in 1958.

1970–76. Presidency of Luis Echeverria Alvarez characterized by leftist rhetoric, alienation of upper classes, and expansion of federal bureaucracy. US$80 billion of foreign debt financed on basis of significant oil deposits found.

1976–82. Presidency of José Lopez Portillo y Pacheco with further increases in foreign debt, inflation, and

government corruption. Oil **glut** leads to collapse of oil prices. Minority political parties increase in Mexican Congress.

1982–88. Presidency of Miguel de la Madrid Hurtado institutes austerity measures, devalues peso, restructures foreign debt. Economy goes into recession.

1988–94. Presidency of Carlos Salinas de Gortari attempts to control corruption, continues to decrease spending, and launches other austerity measures. Mexico signs North American Free Trade Agreement. Rebellion in Chiapas is suppressed, with more than 145 killed. PRI presidential candidate is assassinated (Donald Luis Colosio Murrieta).

1994–2000. Presidency of Ernesto Zedillo Ponce de Leon devalues peso again and gets rescue package from the United States; economy goes into recession. The government privatizes a number of government industries, inflation is controlled, and growth established by the end of his term. The PRI loses majority in Mexican Congress.

2000. President Vicente Fox Quesada becomes the first non-PRI president elected in 70 years. Fox promises to eliminate government corruption and continue austerity measures.

FUTURE TRENDS

As the Mexican people prepare to celebrate the 100th anniversary of their Revolution and the 200th anniversary of their independence in the year 2010, it is clear that there are at least 3 important economic issues that they and their leadership will have to address. First, what is the most effective way to prepare the Mexican labor force to compete in a global economy? Second, what are the ways in which the Mexican economy can generate more and sufficient employment for the Mexican people? Finally, what are the ways to achieve a more equal distribution of income with the Mexican economy? To be sure, the answers to these questions are remarkably complicated ones. However, it is encouraging to note that the actions taken by the Mexican government have yielded positive results in terms of the growth rate of the Mexican economy. Certainly, the transitions of the Mexican economy from a closed one to an open one, from an agricultural to an industrial one, and from one that values public ownership to one that values private ownership are all steps in the right direction. What remains to be seen is whether these steps are progressing rapidly enough.

DEPENDENCIES

Mexico has no territories or colonies.

BIBLIOGRAPHY

Blanchard, Olivier. *Macroeconomics,* second edition. Upper Saddle River, NJ: Prentice Hall, 2000.

Economist Intelligence Unit. *Country Profile 2000: Mexico.* London: Economist Intelligence Unit, 2000.

International Monetary Fund. *International Financial Statistics Yearbook.* Washington, D.C.: International Monetary Fund, 2000.

Miller, Frank. "Mexico: The People." *The Encyclopedia Americana International Edition.* Danbury, CT: Grolier, 1999.

U.S. Central Intelligence Agency. *World Factbook 2000.* <http:// www.odci.gov/cia/publications/factbook/index.html>. Accessed August 2001.

U.S. Department of State. *FY 2001 Country Commercial Guide: Mexico.* <http://www.state.gov/www/about_state/business/ com_guides/2001/wha/index.html>. Accessed September 2001.

U.S. Library of Congress. *Mexico: A Country Study.* <http:// lcweb2.loc.gov/frd/cs/mxtoc.html>. Accessed December 2000.

—Linz Audain

NETHERLANDS ANTILLES AND ARUBA

COUNTRY OVERVIEW

LOCATION AND SIZE. The Netherlands Antilles are a federation of 2 Caribbean island groups some 806 kilometers (500 miles) apart. The first group, known as the Dutch Leeward Islands, comprises Curaçao and Bonaire, and is located about 81 kilometers (50 miles) off the northern coast of Venezuela. The second group, known as the Dutch Windward Islands (confusingly, because they are part of the larger Leeward Island chain), is about 242 kilometers (150 miles) east of Puerto Rico, and in-

cludes Saba, Sint Eustatius, and Sint Maarten (the southern half of the island of Saint-Martin). The combined area of the 5 islands is 958 square kilometers (370 square miles), or about 5 times the area of Washington, D.C.

Curaçao is the largest island (461 square kilometers, or 178 square miles) and home to the federation's capital, Willemstad (pop. 24,235 in 1992), the islands' commercial and industrial center. Blessed with the world's seventh largest natural harbor and the largest in the region, Curaçao was once the base for Dutch trade activity in the region and the site of a major slave market. Since the early 20th century it has been sustained by its oil refining industries, which include 1 of the largest refineries in the world. Its terrain is volcanic and semi-arid, and its climate tropical.

Bonaire (290 square kilometers, or 112 square miles), some 32 kilometers (20 miles) to the west, is better served environmentally and includes a scenically spectacular coastline and several fine beaches, the bases jointly of its tourist industry. Bonaire's main town is Kralendijk.

In the northern group the principal territory is Sint Maarten (52 square kilometers, or 20 square miles), the Dutch portion of the island of Saint-Martin (96 square kilometers, or 37 square miles), which, since its dual occupation by French and Dutch forces in 1648, has been split into 2 parts. Northern Saint-Martin belongs to French Guadeloupe, and it shares with its Dutch neighbor the Netherlands Antilles' only border, 10 kilometers (6.3 miles) long. The island has the distinction of being the smallest in the world shared by 2 nations. Mountainous and arid, the island's beaches and picturesque scenery have made tourism its main industry. The principal town of Dutch Sint Maarten is Philipsburg.

Sint Eustatius, known by its inhabitants as "Statia," and Saba (21 and 13 kilometers, or 8 and 5 square miles, respectively) are also noted for their rugged scenery. The islands too, unlike Curaçao and Bonaire, lie in the Caribbean hurricane belt and are periodic targets in the July to October hurricane season. All of Sint Eustatius's inhabitants live in the island's capital, Oranjestad. Saba's capital is the tiny village of The Bottom. Its central

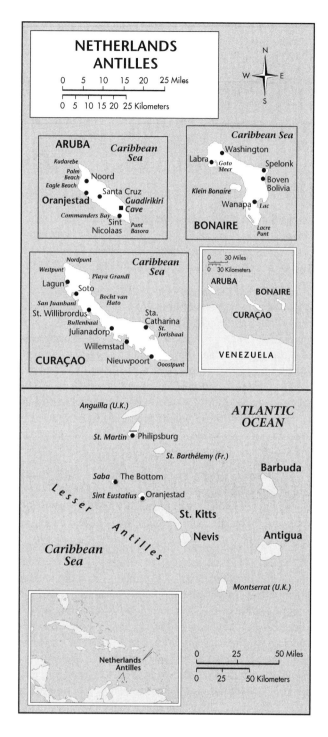

NETHERLANDS ANTILLES

volcanic cone, Mount Scenery, at 879 meters (2,885 feet) is not only the highest peak in the Netherlands Antilles, but in the entire Kingdom of the Netherlands.

Aruba lies about 65 kilometers (40 miles) west of Bonaire. Its land area is 193 square kilometers (74.5 square miles), slightly larger than Washington D.C., with a coastline of 69 kilometers (42.6 miles). It shares the dry sub-tropical climate of its neighbor the Netherlands Antilles, and like Bonaire and Curaçao relies on desali-

nated seawater for drinking water. But its geography tends to be flatter; its highest point is Mt. Jamanota at 188 meters (616 feet). The capital and main port is Oranjestad (1991 pop. 20,045).

POPULATION. The Netherlands Antilles' combined population was estimated in 2000 at 210,134. Of these more than two-thirds (146,100 or 69.5 percent) lived on Curaçao, while Bonaire's inhabitants numbered 11,000 (5.2 percent), Sint Maarten's 29,500 (14.0 percent), Sint Eustatius's 1,861 (0.9 percent), and Saba's around 1,100 (0.5 percent). Relatively good health conditions (compared to its Caribbean neighbors) have given Antilleans a life expectancy of 74.72 years.

The Antillean national birth rate of 16.94 per 1,000 has produced a growth rate of 1.01 percent per annum—considerably above its economic growth rate of -4.4 percent (2000). This fact has contributed to the worryingly high rate of **emigration**, especially in the 17-to-30-year-old age group. The Netherlands, which receives 80 percent of emigrants, has 100,000 Antilleans. For the islands the long-term consequences of emigration are very serious, and it is a problem both Dutch and Antillean governments are concerned to address—especially as the flow shows signs of quickening: 3.0 percent of Antilleans emigrated in 1998, jumping up to 3.5 percent in 1999, and to as much as 4.1 percent (8,420 people) in the first 10 months of 2000 alone. The skewing effect this has on the population can be seen in the islands' age distributions. In the Windward Islands, where employment is high, those over 60 constitute 5 percent of the population; in Curaçao, where emigration has been heaviest, they are 11 percent. By 2017, if the rates of loss remain the same, 20 percent of Curaçao's population could be over 60. The effect of this on the island's already strained social services could be devastating.

Aruba's population stands at 69,539, and its demographic statistics, when compared to the Netherlands Antilles, reflect its generally greater prosperity. The life expectancy is 78.37 years at birth. The birth rate is 13.1 births per 1,000 of population, with a growth rate of 0.7 percent (2000 est.)—well within the economic growth rate of 3 percent (1998). In fact, not only does Aruba enjoy near **full employment**, it has often been obliged to import additional labor from neighboring islands. Nearly one-third of Arubans live in the capital Oranjestad.

Ethnically the Netherlands Antilles and Aruba are a diverse mix. The mushrooming of the oil industry in the 1920s attracted workers from around the Caribbean, doubling the population and further expanding what was already a broad ethnic base. Around 50 nationalities are represented, with Dutch, African, Spanish, Jewish Portuguese, Lebanese, and Chinese origins being the most common. What survived of the indigenous Arawak Indian community was absorbed in the early 20th century;

no full-blooded Indians remain. Religions are similarly diverse, with Roman Catholicism, various forms of Protestantism, Judaism, and Seventh-Day Adventism all represented. The official language of both countries is Dutch, but Papiamento, a hybrid of Spanish, Dutch, English, and Portuguese is also spoken, especially in the (southern) Leeward Group, while English tends to dominate in the (northern) Windwards.

OVERVIEW OF ECONOMY

Mountainous and barren, with few natural resources or advantages, the Netherlands Antilles and Aruba nevertheless enjoy 2 of the more affluent economies in the Caribbean region. This relative prosperity is founded on their one overriding asset: location. In the early 19th century the islands, conveniently poised between the Caribbean islands and the South American mainland, thrived as the clearing house of the Dutch slave trade. When slavery was outlawed in 1863 this industry collapsed. But with the discovery of Venezuela's massive Maracaibo oil reserves in the early 20th century, the islands' advantageous location (just off the Venezuelan coast) again proved to their economic making. In 1918 the world's largest oil refinery was built on Curaçao, and in 1929 another huge refinery was constructed on Aruba. Aruba and the Netherlands Antilles still serve as major refining and transshipping bases for the Venezuelan oil industry, a role that has given the Netherlands Antilles a **gross domestic product per capita** of US$11,800 (1998 est.).

But in the case of the Netherlands Antilles, this narrow economic focus has also left it vulnerable, and the contraction of the South American oil industry in the 1980s led to increasing economic difficulty. As a service-oriented economy, the Netherlands Antilles relies on its "invisible" earnings from tourism, offshore financial services, and shipping to offset their huge **trade deficit**, which was US$1,013.7 billion in 1998. The trade deficit has been difficult to manage. In the 1990s, a combination of hurricane damage, weak investment levels, and fluctuating oil prices increased the debt. Plans drawn up in conjunction with the Dutch government and the International Monetary Fund (IMF) aimed at attacking the deficit, raising revenue, and decreasing expenditure. But the price of such plans—reduced government services, **privatizations**, and redundancies—have made them difficult to implement. Predictions that the country would begin to reemerge in the 2000s from the **recession** that dogged it in the previous decade have proved to be premature.

Aruba has fared better. Although like the Netherlands Antilles it is heavily dependent on oil refining, transshipment, and service industries such as banking,

Aruba has been more successful in developing tourism as an alternative economic base. This combined with more conservative fiscal management—despite some heavy deficits in the late 1990s—has seen the **real GDP** growth in the 1991 to 1997 period of around 5.6 percent per annum. Its principal sources of income continue to be tourism and oil transshipment, both industries showing solid growth. With Aruba's annual GDP per head at US$22,800—more than 6 times, for example, that of its Caribbean neighbor Jamaica—Arubans are estimated to be among the most affluent people in the Caribbean region.

POLITICS, GOVERNMENT, AND TAXATION

First inhabited by Arawak and Carib Indians, the islands of Aruba and the Netherlands Antilles were taken by the Spanish in the 16th century, falling in turn to the Dutch in the course of the 17th century. The Dutch used them as trading posts, and by the 17th century the mercantile ports of Sint Eustatius and Curaçao were 2 of the 3 richest in the Caribbean (with Port Royal in Jamaica). After multiple changes of hands, the 6 islands were finally secured by the Netherlands under the Treaty of Paris in 1816 and officially constituted as the Netherlands Antilles in 1845. Autonomy from the Netherlands came in 1956.

In 1986 Aruba, resentful of Curaçaoan political dominance, left the federation to seek its own free-standing membership in the Dutch overseas community. Fears in the 1980s that the Netherlands Antilles might fragment further as other islands sought autonomy were partially resolved in a nation-wide referendum in November 1993 in which all 5 remaining islands opted for continued union. However, a further referendum held in Sint Maarten in June 2000 found 67 percent of its inhabitants in favor of separating from the federation. Such a partition can only be undertaken with the cooperation of the other islands, but it remains a source of on-going uncertainty. The Dutch government is content to let the islands decide their own future but is eager for them to develop economic self-sufficiency. Aruba, according to the provisions of its 1986 secession from the Netherlands Antilles, would have become completely independent of the Dutch kingdom in 1996. In 1995, however, this provision was permanently shelved by the Aruban legislature.

Constitutionally the Netherlands Antilles and Aruba are autonomous parliamentary states within the Kingdom of the Netherlands. Their head of state is the Dutch sovereign (Queen Beatrix), who is represented in each country by a governor, appointed by The Hague, but since the 1960s a native-born islander. The Netherlands also administers the islands' foreign affairs and defense arrangements and appoints their senior judges. Internal affairs—including finance, police, telecommunications, education and health—are left to the prime minister of each country, his cabinet (made up of 9 ministers in the Netherlands Antilles and 7 in Aruba), and the parliament, or Staten, which appoints them (22 members in the Netherlands Antilles and 21 in Aruba). In the Netherlands Antilles each island replicates this system in miniature, with each having a lieutenant-governor to represent the Dutch crown, each with an island council, and each with a regional legislature which appoints it. Elections are by **proportional representation**, suffrage is universal, and electoral terms are 4 years long.

Politics in Netherlands Antilles tend to be island based. Seats in the Staten are distributed by island: 14 from Curaçao, 3 each from Sint Maarten and Bonaire, and 1 each from Saba and Sint Eustatius. Reconciling the various island interests is an often precarious exercise and made more complicated by the proliferation of parties and the tendency of the federation's proportional representation system to produce coalition governments. Although some stability is afforded by Curaçao's control of the Staten—a consequence of its numerical dominance—this has also generated resentment in the other islands. The 2 main parties are both Curaçao-based: the Antillean Restructuring Party (Partido Antía Restrukturá or PAR) and the National People's Party (Partido Nashonal di Pueblo or PNP). The prime minister as of 2001 was Miguel Pourier, leading a coalition that includes 18 of the 22 Staten members, the country's broadest ever.

Aruban governments also tend to be multi-party. The prime minister as of 2001 was Jan Hendrik Emman, leading a coalition of his own Aruban People's Party (Aubaanse Volkspartij or AVP) and the Aruban Liberal Party (Organisacion Liberal Arubano or OLA). Pressing political issues, as in the Netherlands Antilles, turn on the government's program of fiscal austerity, including health-care reform and its controversial planned privatization of the state telecommunications company, Setar.

Both countries rely heavily on **income tax** for their revenue collection, with important supplements provided by port dues. Tax reform in the Netherlands Antilles, designed to stimulate business growth, has included the reduction of corporate tax rate to 30 percent in 1999 and the raising of the personal tax threshold. Revenue in 1999 totaled US$707.8 million, of which 88 percent (US$622.6 million) comes from taxes. Aruba's revenue in the same year came to US$361.1 million, of which 83 percent (US$299.1 million) came from taxes.

INFRASTRUCTURE, POWER, AND COMMUNICATIONS

The 5 small islands of the Netherlands Antilles have no railroad and only 602 kilometers (373 miles) of roads between them, of which only 300 kilometers (186 miles) are paved. And yet given their size, they are, in fact, unusually well served. Even the tiny and impossibly precipitous Saba boasts "The Road," 31 kilometers (19 miles) of winding roadway built in early 1940s and one of the region's engineering marvels. Most of this development, however, has occurred since the 1960s. Saba's dock was only built in 1963; until then everything reaching the island had to be rowed ashore through the surf. It was not until the 1960s that all of islands received public electricity and water supplies.

Inter-island traffic has made sea and air connections a vital means of communication, as well as vital parts of the economy. Curaçao is blessed with one of the largest natural harbors in the world, and the port has become not

Communications

Country	Telephones[a]	Telephones, Mobile/Cellular[a]	Radio Stations[b]	Radios[a]	TV Stations[a]	Televisions[a]	Internet Service Providers[c]	Internet Users[c]
Netherlands Antilles	76,000 (1995)	13,977 (1996)	AM 9; FM 4; shortwave 0	217,000	3	69,000	6	2,000
United States	194 M	69.209 M (1998)	AM 4,762; FM 5,542; shortwave 18	575 M	1,500	219 M	7,800	148 M
Jamaica	353,000 (1996)	54,640 (1996)	AM 10; FM 13; shortwave 0	1.215 M	7	460,000	21	60,000
St. Lucia	37,000	1,600	AM 2; FM 7; shortwave 0	111,000	3	32,000	15	5,000

[a]Data is for 1997 unless otherwise noted.
[b]Data is for 1998 unless otherwise noted.
[c]Data is for 2000 unless otherwise noted.

SOURCE: CIA *World Factbook 2001* [Online].

only a major center for the transshipment of Caribbean oil, but an important dry dock for ship repairs. The port annually handles around 850,000 metric tons of cargo, and the foreign exchange earnings it generates are a crucial component of the Antillean economy. Also economically central is the ailing national carrier, Antillean Airlines (ALM), scheduled for privatization. Each of the islands has an airport, with international access via Hato Airport in Curaçao and Juliana Airport in Sint Maarten, both major hubs for their respective regions. There are also plans to upgrade Bonaire's airport to receive international flights. Nevertheless, the federation's fragmentation into widely separated parts, in which separate infrastructures are required for each island and communication between islands is cumbersome and expensive, is a continual economic drain.

The islands boast 76,000 telephones (1995), and 11,727 cellular telephones (1995)—one for each 2.8 and 17.9 Antilleans, respectively. Energy provision is good, and more than 97 percent of Antillean households have electricity (93 percent with a refrigerator). Generating capacity runs to 200 megawatts, all of it produced from imported fossil fuels. In 1999 the islands' final power consumption equaled around 2.67 million tons of oil.

The picture for Aruba is much the same: 802 kilometers (497 miles) of roads, 513 kilometers (318 miles) of them paved (mostly the perimeter coastal roads); 27,000 telephones and 1,718 cellular phones (one for each 2.5 and 40.5 Arubans respectively, as of 1995). Moves are underway to sell the state telecommunications utility, Setar, but these have faced stiff resistance from the country's labor groups. Like the Netherlands Antilles, Aruba relies heavily on its ports and air connections. Its 3 ports are Oranjestad, the main commercial and cruise ship facility; Sint Nicolas, used by the oil industry; and Barcadera, opened in 1962 to serve the industrial zone on the leeward coast. The island has 2 airports, with international facilities at Oranjestad. **Deregulation** of the air market included the sale in 1998 of 70 percent of the government's share in the bankrupt national carrier Air Aruba. Continued difficulties in the company, however, forced it to cease operations in October 2000.

Aruba's electricity generating capacity of 125 megawatts gives almost universal access to electricity. Like the Netherlands Antilles, power generation relies on fossil fuels. Aruba's total power consumption in 1999 came to the equivalent to 210,000 tons of oil, around 0.02 percent of the island's oil production.

ECONOMIC SECTORS

Tourism, offshore financial services, shipping and oil refining are the primary Aruban and Antillean eco-

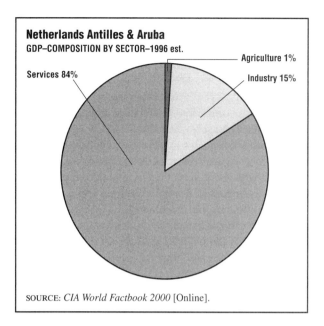

Netherlands Antilles & Aruba
GDP–COMPOSITION BY SECTOR–1996 est.

Services 84%
Agriculture 1%
Industry 15%

SOURCE: *CIA World Factbook 2000* [Online].

nomic sectors. Petroleum processing continues to be central. Having survived the industry's slowdown during the oil **glut** of the 1980s, its future looks relatively secure. For growth, however, the Netherlands Antilles are obliged to look to tourism, and other service sectors like finance and banking. Industry accounts for 15 percent of the GDP and 13 percent of the Antillean workforce, and services for 84 percent of the GDP and 86 percent of the workforce (with three-quarters of these working for the government). The same constellation of sectors predominate in Aruba.

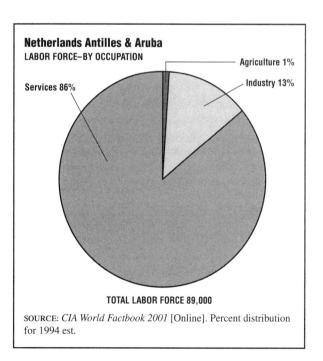

Netherlands Antilles & Aruba
LABOR FORCE–BY OCCUPATION

Services 86%
Agriculture 1%
Industry 13%

TOTAL LABOR FORCE 89,000

SOURCE: *CIA World Factbook 2001* [Online]. Percent distribution for 1994 est.

AGRICULTURE

The rugged, rocky terrain of the Windwards' and the Leewards' poor soil and arid climate leave little scope for agriculture in either group. Various plantation crops have been pursued over the centuries—sugar, cotton, and tobacco especially. But efforts were always a struggle and had been largely abandoned by the 19th century. Aruba and Curaçao were used for ranching in the 18th and 19th centuries, but ranching too could never really compete with the islands' harsh environment. Only 10 percent of the Netherlands Antilles is arable, and its crop production—mostly fruits and vegetables, with some aloes, sorghum, and peanuts—are consumed entirely by the domestic market. Woodlands are almost non-existent and fishing scarce; only Sint Maarten has a small commercial fishing sector. Consequently, both Aruba and the Netherlands Antilles are heavily reliant on food imports. All in all, agriculture contributes less than 1 percent of the Antillean GDP and accounts for 1 percent of the workforce. In Aruba agriculture is even more marginal, occupying only 7 percent of available lands and 0.6 percent of the workforce.

INDUSTRY

Industrial activity in the Netherlands Antilles is overwhelmingly concentrated on one product: oil. Originally a center for oil refining—the Shell refinery on Curaçao is one of the biggest in the world—diversification in the 1970s expanded operations into transshipment and storage, with the terminal at Bullenbaai becoming one of the largest bunkering ports in the world. But the oil glut in the 1980s, followed by a world-wide recession, hit the island hard when Shell sold its stake in the refinery in 1985. The operation was rescued by the intervention of the Antillean government, which bought the plant and negotiated a lease agreement with the Venezuelan state oil producer, Petróleos de Venezuela. In 1995, after a series of short-term leases, a 20-year agreement was signed. The industry faces heavy competition from the United States and continues to suffer the vagaries of a fluctuating world oil market, but the long-term partnership with Petróleos de Venezuela and strengthening international demand for oil suggest a relatively healthy forecast.

Prospects are even better in Aruba. The reopening by Coastal Oil (U.S.) in 1993 of the massive Exxon refinery at Sint Nicolas at the eastern end of the island, the bedrock of the island's prosperity since it was opened in 1929 and which had been closed in 1985, provided an enormous new source of jobs and foreign exchange and has considerably spurred the economy. Production capacity is around 150,000 barrels per day.

Manufacturing is a limited sector in both countries. In the Netherlands Antilles the industry is concentrated almost entirely on Curaçao and Bonaire, with products including paper, plastics, and textiles. The **tariffs** that protect the sector, however, are under attack from importers and whether these industries can survive their removal remains to be seen. The 68-acre export-oriented industrial **"free zone"** around Hato International Airport in Curaçao, founded in 1984, is devoted almost entirely to oil processing. Bonaire's 9,000 acre industrial salt farm is managed by the Antilles International Salt Company and has become a significant part of that island's economy.

Aruba's manufacturing base is more diversified and includes the repair and assembly of machinery and transport equipment, crafts and art collectibles, and animal products. The island's free zone has shown dynamic growth, with exports through the program increasing by 60 percent in the 1994 to 1997 period and reaching an earnings total of US$247 million.

SERVICES

TOURISM. Tourism is a crucial industry for both the Netherlands Antilles and Aruba, and most of their economic growth since the 1960s has come from this sector.

Curaçao's quaint Dutch-style towns and stark, cactus-dotted interior, coral reefs, and brilliantly blue waters draw around 225,000 stay-over tourists per annum, with a roughly equal number from the cruise ship trade (223,788 and 171,675, respectively, in 1995). Around 30 percent come from the Netherlands, 15 percent from the United States, and 14 percent from Venezuela. Most of the island's hotel facilities are luxurious. Sint Maarten, renowned for its beaches and **duty**-free shopping, is one the Caribbean's top cruise-ship destinations and attracts 2 million visitors annually. Since the first hotel was opened in 1955, development has been rapid and extensive, and the island boasts an array of expensive hotels, restaurants, casinos, and boutiques. Saba's lack of a port has made development difficult, and the tourist trade is low-key, with around 25,000 visitors annually, about 65 percent making overnight stays, the rest being day-trippers (1992). The island's major attraction is the diving at its Marine Park, established in 1987 to protect the island's exceptionally diverse marine environment. Bonaire also relies heavily on its diving attractions, which draw 44 percent of the island's visitors, though wind-surfing and bird-watching are also becoming important. Cruise ship calls are another key source of income, with visits rising from 18 ships in 1998–99 to 61 in 1999–2000. Sint Eustatius's tourist development has long been hindered by its lack of beaches and its poverty; it is the poorest of the Antillean islands. Attempts to capitalize on its diving opportunities have met with mixed success, with tourist arrivals declining from 10,000 in 1994 to around 8,500 in 1997, though showing some signs of recovery in 1998–99.

But Caribbean tourism is a highly contested trade, and the Antillean industry in particular is not without its problems. The Antillean islands are handicapped by having relatively few beaches. Most of the best ones are on Sint Maarten, but Sint Maarten is prone to hurricane damage and was badly affected by severe storms in 1995 and 1998 that seriously disrupted its tourism sector. Competition from other Caribbean islands has also put pressure on tourist arrivals, especially the numbers of cruise ship visitors from the United States. Steps being taken to address this issue include the renovation of Willemstad's port—sponsored by the Netherlands and European Union—and the construction, begun in 1998, of a new pier to handle larger cruise ships. Several new hotel facilities on Curaçao are also planned. Progress is also being made in Bonaire, where the exceptional diving opportunities are starting to attract significant numbers of tourists. The islands' total earnings from tourism in 1998 were US$749.5 million, or 31 percent of the GDP.

Aruba's tourist industry is even more developed. The decision to promote the industry was taken at the IMF's prompting in the wake of the crisis that followed the closing of the island's oil refinery by Exxon in 1985. Since then Aruba has almost quadrupled the number of its hotel rooms (from around 2,000 in 1985 to 7,103 by 1996), becoming one of the most popular tourist destinations in the Caribbean. One-third of the island's jobs are related to the industry, with 14,825 Arubans in 1999 in full-time tourism-related employment. The island attracts around 650,000 stay-over visitors per annum, producing receipts totaling US$715 million, or 41 percent of the GDP (1998).

FINANCIAL SERVICES. It was the flight of Dutch business capital offshore during the World War II, much of it to the Netherlands Antilles, that was the beginning of the Antillean **offshore banking** sector. As of 1995 some 21,000 companies were listed on the offshore register, including 39 international banks. The industry employs around 2,500 Antilleans and is responsible for 23 percent of GDP. The local financial sector has 16 commercial banks, 2 savings banks, 21 savings and credit funds, and 26 credit unions. The remaining 45 banks are exclusively for offshore business.

But here too stresses have been felt. The repeal of a withholding tax by the United States in 1984 removed many of the islands' tax advantages. Shortly afterwards the United States and Britain cancelled their double taxation treaties (allowing U.S. businesses to trade in the euro-dollar market directly, without "diversion" through the Netherlands Antilles), further compounding the damage. The result for the islands was a dramatic slump in their financial services sector. The subsequent deregulation of the industry brought steady recovery in the 1990s, and the islands have sought new business in the captive insurance and mutual funds market. But evidence that the

islands may be serving as a **money-laundering** venue for the illicit drugs trade has strained relations with the United States and placed the industry under something of a cloud. To allay fears a reporting center was established in Curaçao in 1997 to monitor all large banking transactions, and closer cooperation with the U.S. Drug Enforcement Agency has made available funds to allow even closer supervision.

Aruba's offshore banking sector is also important. Targeted for development, the sector was deregulated in the 1980s and more effective legislation was enacted. In an effort, however, to prevent the island from being used to launder drug money, some of the sector's openness was stopped, and in 1998 the State Ordinance on the supervision of the credit system was set in place to consolidate the central bank's powers as the industry's monitor.

RETAIL. Relatively high standards of living and the high concentration of consumers have greatly benefitted the islands' **retail** sector, especially on the larger islands. Aruba and Curaçao are equipped with a wide variety of restaurants, shops, malls, and supermarkets selling goods from around the world. Tourism has provided an additional stimulus. Sint Maarten's status as a duty-free port—a continuation of its old trading center heritage—has made shopping one its main attractions, and its more than 500 duty-free stores carry a full array of jewelry, perfumes, handbags, leatherwear, and electronic goods.

INTERNATIONAL TRADE

Lacking a developed agricultural and manufacturing sector, the Netherlands Antilles are wholly dependent on imports for their food, raw materials, and manufactured goods. And typical of the smaller Caribbean island states, such imports significantly exceed the value of exports. In 1998 this imbalance ran to over US$1 billion. The country is especially susceptible to increases in the price of oil, which constitutes 64 percent of its imports; the remaining 36 percent is made up of food and manufactures. Import partners include Venezuela (35.3 percent), the

Trade (expressed in billions of US$): Netherlands Antilles		
	Exports	Imports
1975	2.395	2.956
1980	5.162	5.676
1985	1.031	1.388
1990	1.789	2.146
1995	N/A	N/A
1998	N/A	N/A

SOURCE: International Monetary Fund. *International Financial Statistics Yearbook 1999.*

United States (21 percent), Mexico (9.8 percent), Italy (5.4 percent), the Netherlands (4.8 percent), and Brazil (3.1 percent).

Petroleum makes up 98 percent of all Antillean exports. Even more so than with the import market, the export trade is overwhelmingly regional, with customers including the United States (17.5 percent), Guatemala (8 percent), Costa Rica (6.5 percent), the Bahamas (4.6 percent), Jamaica (4.1 percent), and Chile (3.4 percent).

Aruba also leans heavily on imported food and manufactures but has been more successful at containing its deficits. A lowering in the demand for oil in the international market in the 1980s caused the trade imbalance to tilt heavily into deficit, but recovery of sales has seen the import-export gap narrow by a dramatic 80 percent from 1999 to 2000, falling from a trade deficit of US$298.8 million to US$60.3 million. The main customer of Aruban exports is the United States, which in 1998 took 53.2 percent of its goods; other important partners are Colombia (14.9 percent), and the Netherlands (8.8 percent). The United States is also the primary supplier of imports to Aruba (55.5 percent), with the Netherlands (12.3 percent) and Japan (3.5 percent) also significant.

MONEY

Debt continues to pose a significant problem for the Netherlands Antilles, ballooning by the end of 1998 to a massive US$1.75 billion. An appeal to the IMF produced a **structural adjustment program** that is heavily geared toward debt reduction, and through a combination of cutting its costs and raising its income the governmental aims by 2002 to reduce its **budget deficit**, which in 1998 hovered at 5.3 percent of the GDP, to 2 percent of the GDP. But maintaining parity between the country's sizable trade deficit and its invisible services earnings is a juggling act that is easily upset by glitches and ticks in the world economy. Shortfalls usually have to be supplied by borrowing—usually from the Dutch government

and **private sector**. In 1999 talks began with the Dutch about possible debt restructuring or forgiveness. A 117-percent jump in the price of oil in 2000, which inflated the annual deficit by 13.6 percent, has now made these urgent. Rises in the world prices of oil have also accelerated **inflation**, which—climbing through the late 1990s—reached 6.6 percent in 2000.

Aruba's debt problems are more manageable. In 1998 the total external **foreign debt** was US$199.5 million, a rise of 11 percent over the 1998 level of US$180 million. Like the Netherlands Antilles, Aruba is vulnerable to high oil prices, which lift its import bill and inflates its currency. In 1999 inflation sat at 2.9 percent.

Since 1971 both the Netherlands Antilles and Aruba have adhered to the "dollar standard," with each pegging its guilder at US$0.56 (US$1.00=G1.79). Their central banks, therefore, play an important role in ensuring that each country has sufficient **foreign exchange reserves** to maintain the standard. In 2000 the Central Bank of the Netherlands Antilles held reserves equaling 1.6 months of import coverage, which was 2.4 months below the international norm; the Central Bank of Aruba held 5 months' worth.

POVERTY AND WEALTH

Mounting economic problems are exposing deep rifts in Antillean society. The islands' multicultural composition obscures an ethnic hierarchy, the source of continuing tensions. Traditionally the islands' elite have been its white settlers and administrators, with the largely Jewish Portuguese and Lebanese mercantile class in a secondary position, and the black majority at the bottom. The explosive race riots of 1969 drew critical attention to this division, but even 30 years later Antillean blacks are far from achieving social equality.

The federation continues, in fact, to be ruled by a small circle of political insiders, who monopolize the government, staff its bureaucracy, and control its industry. In Aruba this elite is made up of just a few powerful fami-

---

Exchange rates: Netherlands Antilles

Netherlands Antillean guilders, gulden, or florins and Aruban florins per US$1

2001	1.790
2000	1.790
1999	1.790
1998	1.790
1997	1.790
1996	1.790

Note: Currency rates have been fixed since 1989.

SOURCE: CIA *World Factbook 2001* [ONLINE].

GDP per Capita (US$)

Country	1996	1997	1998	1999	2000
Netherlands Antilles & Aruba	9,800	11,500	11,800	N/A	11,400
United States	28,600	30,200	31,500	33,900	36,200
Jamaica	3,260	N/A	3,300	3,350	3,700
St. Lucia	4,400	4,100	4,300	N/A	4,500

Note: Data are estimates.

SOURCE: *Handbook of the Nations*, 17th, 18th, 19th and 20th editions for 1996, 1997, 1998 and 1999 data; CIA *World Factbook 2001* [Online] for 2000 data.

INTRODUCTION
TO WORLD CURRENCY

The following insert contains color photographs of paper currency from around the world. Where possible, the most recent issue and lowest denomination was selected to show the bank notes of the countries represented in this encyclopedia. As of the year 2002, approximately 169 countries issued their own paper money.

Bank notes are more than a measuring system for value to be used as payment for goods and services. In many instances a banknote is a graphic reflection of a country's history, politics, economy, environment, and its people. For example, many bank notes depict plant life such as flowers and trees, as well as birds and other animals native to that geographic region. The 5-lats note of Latvia has a giant oak tree on the front, while the 25-rupee note of Seychelles and the 5-guilder note of Suriname both show flowers from the homeland. Birds adorn notes from São Tomé and Príncipe, Papua New Guinea, and Zambia. Large animals such as the mountain gorillas on the 500-franc note from Rwanda, the white rhinoceros on the 10-rand note from South Africa, and the bull elephant on the 500-shilling note of Uganda are commonplace.

Famous rulers and political figures from history are prevalent. Sir Henry Parkes, a famous 19th-century statesman, graces the front of the 5-dollar note from Australia; and Canada's Sir John Alexander MacDonald, a noted Canadian prime minister from the same time period, appears on the front of the 10-dollar Canadian note. Mieszko I, a medieval prince credited with being the founder of Poland in 966, is on the 10-zloty note from that country. Bank notes also reflect the power of more contemporary rulers, as exemplified by the image of Iraq's current president, Saddam Hussein, on that country's 50-dinar note, issued in 1994. Malaysia's paramount ruler and first chief of state, Tunku Abdul Rahman, is on the front of that country's 1-ringgit note and all notes of all denominations issued since 1967.

Architectural vignettes are common on world notes. Islamic mosques with minarets can be found on the 5000-afghani note from Afghanistan, as well as the 25-piaster note from Egypt, indicating the prevalent Islamic religious influence in those 2 countries. The 5-pound 1994 regular issue note from Ireland shows the famous Mater Misericordiae Hospital in Ireland, where Sister Catherine McAuley, founder of the Sisters of Mercy religious order, served in the area of health care. The depiction of religious figures is common on European notes. Examples include St. Agnes of Bohemia on the 50-koruna note of the Czech Republic, St. John of Rila on the 1-lev note of Bulgaria, and the Archangel Gabriel on the 50-denar note of Macedonia.

Artists, authors, scientists, and musicians are also honored on many bank notes. James Ensor (1860–1949), an innovative painter and etcher, is shown on the 100-franc note from Belgium, while Baroness Karen Blixen (pen name Isak Dinesen), the famed Danish author of *Out of Africa* is found on the 50-krone note of Denmark.

Several notes commemorate the new millenium, significant local events, or anniversaries. The front of the 2000-leu commemorative note from Romania has an imaginative reproduction of the solar system as a reference to the total solar eclipse of 11 August 1999. Another example of a commemorative note is the 200-rupee note from Sri Lanka. The note was issued 4 February 1998 to commemorate the 50th anniversary of independence as a self-governing Dominion of the British Commonwealth.

As of 2002, 15 countries did not issue or use their own paper currency, but allowed the bank notes of neighboring countries as well as U.S. currency to circulate freely in their local economies. Many of these countries are relatively small in size with economies to match. Countries such as San Marino, Monaco, Liechtenstein, and Vatican City are tourist-oriented and do not see a need to issue their own homeland currency. Five of these fifteen countries—namely Marshall Islands, Micronesia, Palau, Panama, and Puerto Rico—all use the U.S. dollar as their monetary unit of exchange. As of March 2001, Ecuador and El Salvador had joined the above-mentioned countries in adopting the U.S. dollar. Countries struggling with hyperinflation (uncontrolled inflation marked by the sharp devaluation of the homeland currency) may choose to use the U.S. dollar in place of their own currencies in an attempt to stabilize their economy by linking it directly to the strength and stability of the

U.S. economy. Countries that use U.S. dollars in conjunction with sound economic policies can usually expect to control and/or minimize inflation. The complete adoption of the U.S. currency has been more successful than the practice of pegging the value of local currency to the U.S. dollar according to a fixed ratio, an approach attempted recently by Argentina to disastrous effect. Even those countries that have not completely adopted the U.S. dollar as their currency often have economies operating freely with both their own national and the U.S. currencies. The strength of the U.S. dollar has also made it the currency of choice in the global black market.

Another trend that will probably continue into the future is the joining together of several neighboring countries to form a central bank issuing a common currency. The primary objective of these economic and monetary unions is to eliminate obstacles to free trade, creating a single unified marketplace. This grouping together tends to strengthen the economy and currency of the member countries as well as providing a cost savings in currency production. While such economic partnerships have occurred throughout history, more recent examples began in the early 1950s with the union of the East Caribbean States, followed by the Central African States, French Pacific Territories, and West African States. The most recent and highly publicized example is the European Monetary Union (EMU), composed of 12 European member countries—namely Austria, Belgium, Finland, France, Germany, Greece, Ireland, Italy, Luxembourg, the Netherlands, Portugal, and Spain. On 1 January 2002, the EMU, through its newly formed central bank, replaced the participating countries' homeland currencies with a new common currency called the *euro*. An example of the 10-euro note is shown on the following currency insert pages. Those countries that had pegged their currencies to an EU member's currency prior to the euro's adoption (as several Francophone countries in Africa did with the French franc) now peg their currency to the euro.

It should be mentioned that, in contrast to this recurring trend of country unification for economic and monetary purposes, there are several countries with isolationist governments that have done just the opposite in order to limit the influence of the international community on their economies and populations. For example, Iraq and Syria have made it illegal to use or export their currency outside of their homelands. Several other nations embraced this isolationist attitude through the use of trade voucher and tourist certificates in place of currency, thus keeping their national circulating bank notes from being used or exported by visitors to their country. China, Bulgaria, and Poland are examples of countries that issued what they termed "foreign exchange certificates" for this specific purpose. However, this practice has largely been discontinued, with the exception of Cuba, which still uses a similar certificate first issued in the mid-1980s.

So what does the future have in store for the economies of the world? Trends indicate most countries in the world want free, open, and balanced trade with a strong, stable, and growing economy, free of hyperinflation. More countries are achieving this goal by unifying in regional economic partnerships such as the European Union, or by clearing the barriers to free trade through agreements such as NAFTA (North American Free Trade Agreement). As the use of the U.S. dollar increases throughout the Americas, some economists predict that this region will follow in the footsteps of Europe in terms of establishing a common currency under a central bank. The Asian and Middle-Eastern regions are also likely candidates for similar regional economic partnerships given the prevalence of established trade agreements already in existence among those countries. As the globalization of trade necessitates closer economic ties between countries, it is not inconceivable that a single central bank and common currency will eventually unite the countries of the world. While that development is still only a remote possibility at this point, there is little doubt that nations' increased dependence on international trade for economic prosperity will promote a currency policy conducive to closer trade ties and cross-border partnerships.

—Keith S. Bauman, professional numismatist
International Bank Note Society
American Numismatic Association
Professional Currency Dealers Association

Afghanistan

Albania

Algeria

Andorra
(used both Spanish and French currency until the
adoption of the euro in January of 2002)

Angola

Antigua and Barbuda
(shares currency with other East Caribbean States)

Argentina

Armenia

Aruba

Australia

Austria
(adopted the euro as of January 2002)

Azerbaijan

The Bahamas

Bahrain

Bangladesh

Barbados

Belarus

Belgium
(adopted the euro as of January 2002)

Belize

Benin
(shares currency with other West African States)

Bhutan

Bolivia

Bosnia and Herzegovina

Botswana

Brazil

Brunei Darussalam

Bulgaria

Burkina Faso
(shares currency with other West African States)

Burma (Myanmar)

Burundi

Cambodia

Cameroon
(shares currency with other Central African States)

Canada

Cape Verde

Central African Republic
(shares currency with other Central African States)

Chad
(shares currency with other Central African States)

Chile

China

Colombia

Comoros

Democratic Republic of the Congo

Republic of the Congo
(shares currency with other Central African States)

Costa Rica

Côte d'Ivoire
(shares currency with other West African States)

Croatia

Cuba

Cyprus

Czech Republic

Denmark

Djibouti

Dominica
(shares currency with other East Caribbean States)

Dominican Republic

Ecuador

Egypt

El Salvador

Equatorial Guinea
(shares currency with other Central African States)

Eritrea

Estonia

Ethiopia

European Union (EU)

Fiji

Finland
(adopted the euro as of January 2002)

France
(adopted the euro as of January 2002)

French Guiana, Martinique, and
Guadeloupe
(used the Fench currency until the adoption of the
euro in January 2002)

French Polynesia

Gabon
(shares currency with other Central African States)

The Gambia

Georgia

Germany
(adopted the euro as of January 2002)

Ghana

Greece
(adopted the euro as of January 2002)

Grenada
(shares currency with other East Carribbean States)

Guatemala

Guinea

Guinea-Bissau
(shares currency with other West African States)

Guyana

Haiti

Honduras

Hong Kong

Hungary

Iceland

India

Indonesia

Iran

Iraq

Ireland
(adopted the euro as of January 2002)

Israel

Italy
(adopted the euro as of January 2002)

Jamaica

Japan

Jordan

Kazakhstan

Kenya

Kiribati
(uses the Australian currency)

North Korea

South Korea

Kuwait

Kyrgyzstan

Laos

Latvia

Lebanon

Lesotho

Liberia

Libya

Liechtenstein
(uses the Swiss currency)

Lithuania

Luxembourg
(adopted the euro as of January 2002)

Macau

Macedonia

Madagascar

Malawi

Malaysia

Maldives

Mali
(shares currency with other West African States)

Malta

Marshall Islands
(uses the U.S. currency)

Mauritania

Mauritius

Mexico

Micronesia
(uses the U.S. currency)

Moldova

Monaco
(used the Frency currency until the adoption of the
euro in January 2002)

Mongolia

Morocco

Mozambique

Namibia

Nauru
(uses the Australian currency)

Nepal

The Netherlands
(adopted the euro as of January 2002)

Netherlands Antilles

New Zealand

Nicaragua

Niger
(shares currency with other West African States)

Nigeria

Norway

Oman

Pakistan

Palau
(uses the U.S. currency)

Panama
(uses the U.S. currency)

Papua New Guinea

Paraguay

Peru

Philippines

Poland

Portugal
(adopted the euro as of January 2002)

Puerto Rico
(uses the U.S. currency)

Qatar

Romania

Russia

Rwanda

San Marino
(used the Italian currency until the adoption of the
euro in January of 2002)

São Tomé and Príncipe

Saudi Arabia

Senegal
(shares currency with other West African States)

Seychelles

Sierra Leone

Singapore

Slovakia

Slovenia

Solomon Islands

Somalia

South Africa

Spain
(adopted the euro as of January 2002)

Sri Lanka

St. Kitts and Nevis
(shares currency with other East Caribbean States)

St. Lucia
(shares currency with other East Caribbean States)

St. Vincent and the Grenadines
(shares currency with other East Caribbean States)

Sudan

Suriname

Swaziland

Sweden

Switzerland

Syria

Taiwan

Tajikistan

Tanzania

Thailand

Togo
(shares currency with other West African States)

Tonga

Trinidad and Tobago

Tunisia

Turkey

Turkmenistan

Tuvalu
(uses Australian currency)

Uganda

Ukraine

United Arab Emirates

United Kingdom

United States

Uruguay

Uzbekistan

Vanuatu

Vatican City
(used the Italian currency until the adoption of the
euro in January of 2002)

Venezuela

Vietnam

Yemen

Yugoslavia

Zambia

Zimbabwe

lies. Politics is informal, and appointments are made on the basis of contacts and patronage. The result in both countries has often been ineffective and unresponsive leadership and sometimes even flagrant corruption. Another byproduct has been the unequal distribution of resources. The same elite which controls the islands' politics also controls their wealth. The richest 20 percent Curaçaoans, for example, have an income 9.8 times that of the poorest 20 percent. This discrepancy has greatly contributed to the polarization of politics in the islands.

WORKING CONDITIONS

Of the roughly 66,000 strong Antillean workforce as many as 11,000 are unemployed, a result of the economy's steady slowdown since the 1980s. In 1995 the unemployment rate was posted at 13.1 percent; by 1998 deepening economic difficulties had pushed it to 16.7 percent. And plans to rein in government spending by cutting back the civil service will further add to the problem. Relations between the labor movement and the government have consequently become more tense as the level of social welfare is decreased and insecurity in the workforce mounts.

But conditions on the islands vary markedly. Curaçao is the most industrialized of the islands and home to much of the federation's wealth, but it has also suffered some of its most serious problems. The oil boom in the mid-20th century swelled Curaçao's population from around 33,000 in 1915 to 145,000 in 1975 and transformed the island. But the contraction of the industry in the 1980s, combined with the introduction of less labor-intensive production techniques, has created a serious labor surplus. Economic restructuring, a condition of continued Dutch support, has tended to make the situation—at least for the short-term—even worse. The government is committed to cutting the civil service by 30 percent, while staff losses at ALM are also expected to run to 30 percent. The result is a considerable degree of social stress, accompanied by a widening disparity between those who have been able to benefit from economic deregulation and those who have suffered (such as the unemployed). Emigration has diffused some of the tension, but this is far from being an adequate long-term solution—either for the Antillean economy or for those Antillean immigrants to the Netherlands, many of whom face considerable problems of adaptation and integration. Emigration too is increasingly coming from the Netherlands Antilles' educated middle classes, creating a serious skills shortage at precisely the time when the country is looking to develop new industries and markets.

Sint Maarten's situation is somewhat different. In the space of 30 years tourism development turned this once sparsely populated and sleepy island into a major tourist hub and a source of jobs for Antilleans from throughout the Caribbean. But many of these workers come illegally, forming a growing under-class. The distribution of tourism's proceeds has also tended to be skewed, going mostly to those who own the shops, restaurants, and guesthouses, at the expense of those who work in them. Similar divisions are also developing on Bonaire and Saba, where tourism investment has also been heavy. Sint Eustatius, where tourism remains in its infancy, preserves the atmosphere of the "old" Antilles. But as the poorest of the islands, it is dependent for its income on **remittances** from the Dutch government and money sent home by former residents forced to leave to find work.

Aruba's problems are less pressing, but here too economic adjustments—a new health insurance program, government divestment, and the failure of Air Aruba—threaten job security and have caused heated debate. Aruba's more robust economy has kept unemployment in its 41,500 strong workforce to a minimum, often requiring it to import labor to meet local demand. But with a population density of 1,142 people per square mile, the influx of foreign workers, combined with poor home mortgage financing availability, has produced a serious housing shortage, especially for those in lower income groups. Addressing this problem is a government priority.

The **labor forces** of both countries tend to be well educated, as well as multi-lingual. The Antillean government's investment in education is substantial—16 percent of its annual budget in 1994—and has given the Netherlands Antilles a high literacy rate of around 98 percent. The islands also have their own university, an adjunct branch of the University of the West Indies, located in Curaçao. But unemployment has tended to discourage higher education, resulting in poor school retention rates at the secondary and tertiary levels. This situation combined with emigration have contributed to the islands' growing skills deficit. Aruba's investment in education has also been extensive (16.9 percent of the GDP in 1994), with similar results (97 percent literacy). In 1988 the University of Aruba law school was founded; in 1993 courses on finance and economics were added.

COUNTRY HISTORY AND ECONOMIC DEVELOPMENT

1493. Columbus explores Sint Maarten.

1499. Alonso de Ojeda and Amerigo Vespucci visit Aruba, Bonaire and Curaçao.

1499–1634. Spanish dominate the area.

1621. Dutch West Indies Company is founded.

1632. Dutch settle Saba and Sint Eustatius.

1636. The Dutch take Aruba.

1648. The Dutch occupy Sint Maarten.

1792. Dutch West Indies Company is dissolved.

1797. Slaves rebell on Curaçao.

1805–16. Aruba falls under English control during Napoleonic wars.

1845. The "ABC" Islands, Aruba, Bonaire and Curaçao are brought together with the "3 Ss"—Saba, Sint Eustatius, and Sint Maarten—to form the Netherlands Antilles.

1863. Slavery is abolished in the Dutch West Indies.

1954. Autonomy ("status aparte") from the Netherlands is achieved.

1969. Curaçao race riots occur.

1986. Aruba leaves the Netherlands Antilles federation.

1995. Aruba decides indefinitely to postpone independence from the Netherlands, scheduled in 1986 for 1996.

2000. Sint Maarten votes to leave the Netherlands Antilles federation.

FUTURE TRENDS

Aruba and the Netherlands Antilles still possess a variety of solid assets: a strategic location, stable governments, flexible workforces, and positive tax and regulatory environments. Core sectors—oil refining and transshipment, tourism, and offshore financial services—remain sound, with tourism even showing signs of growth. Although the Antillean government's policy of tight fiscal discipline and **public sector** restructuring has proved controversial, provoking strikes and demonstrations, the deficit has been reduced by US$3.9 million in 2000 over its US$89.4 million 1999 level.

Nevertheless, problems remain acute. Both countries remain heavily indebted: Aruba carries a debt of US$1.63 billion (41 percent of the GDP), the Netherlands Antilles, US$1.68 billion (73 percent of the GDP). While Aruba has been able to maintain positive growth, in 2000 the Netherlands Antilles economy shrank 4.4 percent. The Antillean government's strict **fiscal policy**, moreover, has tended to exacerbate rather than improve the country's recession, with unemployment a serious concern and emigration reaching near-crisis proportions. The federation's economic future is highly troubled.

Both countries crucially benefit from their continued connection to the Netherlands, a source of valuable economic aid as well as technical help. The Netherlands Antilles receives US$80 million a year from the Dutch government, as well as the loan of 170 Dutch tax and finance experts. Such dependence has made Antilleans anxious to maintain ties. A 1999 poll showed more than half the population actually wanted greater Dutch involvement; even in Sint Maarten (according to a 2000 survey) only 15 percent were for independence. Whether support will continue indefinitely, however, is unclear. The Netherlands gives more money to the federation than it does to any other nation, and its willingness to continue to do so has been placed under some strain, with The Hague threatening in July 2000 to suspend **subsidies** if the Antillean government did not contain its deficit. The eventual withdrawal of Dutch support is a contingency both the Netherlands Antilles and Aruba must plan around, making, for the Netherlands Antilles in particular, a grim economic prognosis even grimmer.

DEPENDENCIES

Netherlands Antilles and Aruba have no territories or colonies.

BIBLIOGRAPHY

Aruba Ministry of Economic Affairs and Tourism. December 1997. <http://www.arubaeconomicaffairs.com>. Accessed 1 March 2001.

Curaçao Chamber of Commerce and Industry. "Key Statistics. 1998." <http://www.iseeyou.com/kvk/kvk5.html>. Accessed 10 April 2001.

Economist Intelligence Unit. *"Country Profile: Bahamas, Barbados, Bermuda, British Virgin Islands, Netherlands Antilles, Aruba, Turks and Caicos Islands, Cayman Islands."* 2000. <http://db.eiu.com/report_dl.asp?mode=pdf&valname= CPAAWB>. Accessed 1 March 2001.

Economist Intelligence Unit. *"Country Report: Bahamas, Barbados, Bermuda, British Virgin Islands, Netherlands Antilles, Aruba, Turks and Caicos Islands, Cayman Islands."* December 2000. <http://db.eiu.com/report_dl.asp?mode= pdf&valname=CRAAWC>. Accessed 1 March 2001.

Goslinga, Cornelis Christiaan. *A Short History of the Netherlands Antilles and Suriname.* The Hague and Boston: M. Nijhoff, 1979.

Ministerie van Binnenlandse Zaken en Koninkrijksrelaties. *"Aruba en de Nedelandse Antillen."* <http://www.minbzk.nl>. Accessed 10 April 2001.

NRC Handelsblad. *Dossier Nederlandse Antillen.* <http://www .nrc.nl/W2/Lab/Antillen/inhoud.html>. Accessed 10 April 2001.

—*Alexander Schubert*

NICARAGUA

Republic of Nicaragua
República de Nicaragua

CAPITAL: Managua.

MONETARY UNIT: Gold córdoba (C$). One gold córdoba equals 100 centavos. Coins include denominations of 5, 10, 25, and 50 centavos, and 1 and 5 córdobas. Notes include 1, 2, 5, 10, 20, 50, 100, 500, 1,000, 5,000, 10,000, 20,000, 50,000, 100,000, 500,000, 1,000,000, 5,000,000, and 10,000,000 córdobas.

CHIEF EXPORTS: Coffee, shrimp and lobster, cotton, tobacco, beef, sugar, bananas, gold.

CHIEF IMPORTS: Machinery and equipment, raw materials, petroleum products, consumer goods.

GROSS DOMESTIC PRODUCT: US$2.3 billion (purchasing power parity, 1998 est.).

BALANCE OF TRADE: Exports: US$573 million (f.o.b., 1998). **Imports:** US$1.5 billion (c.i.f., 1999).

COUNTRY OVERVIEW

LOCATION AND SIZE. Nicaragua is the largest Central American country with borders on the Caribbean Sea and the Pacific Ocean. The nation's borders are 1,231 kilometers (765 miles) long. To the north, the country has a border of 922 kilometers (573 miles) with Honduras. To the south, Nicaragua has a border of 309 kilometers (192 miles) with Costa Rica. Its combined coastline is 910 kilometers (565 miles) in length. Nicaragua's total area is 130,688 square kilometers (50,446 square miles). This includes 120,254 square kilometers (46,430 square miles) of land and 9,240 square kilometers (3,568 square miles) of water. The country is slightly larger than the state of New York. Nicaragua's capital is Managua, which is in the west-central region of the country. The population of Managua is approximately 1 million.

POPULATION. The population of Nicaragua is 4,812,569, according to a July 2000 estimate. This represents substantial growth over the 1990 population of 3,871,000. The current population growth rate is 2.2 percent. In 2000, there were 28.26 births per 1,000 people,

and the nation's fertility rate was 3.27 children born per woman. The country's mortality rate was 4.9 deaths per 1,000 people. With a high birth rate and low mortality rate, Nicaragua's population is quickly growing. About 40 percent of the population is under the age of 15. The nation does have a high infant mortality rate of 34.79 deaths per 1,000 live births and it loses people to **emigration** (1.35 people per 1,000). Nonetheless, the population is expected to exceed 5 million by 2005. The life expectancy for males in Nicaragua is 66.81 years and 70.77 years for females.

The largest ethnic group in Nicaragua are the mestizos (mixed ethnic backgrounds, mainly Spanish and Native American). Mestizos make up 69 percent of the population, whites comprise 17 percent, blacks 9 percent, and Native Americans 5 percent. The population of the country is 54 percent urban, but the overall population density is low with 33 people per square kilometer.

OVERVIEW OF ECONOMY

Nicaragua is one of the poorest countries in the Western Hemisphere. It has a low **gross domestic product (GDP) per capita** of US$460 per year, a very large **external debt**, and high **inflation**. In 1999, it was estimated that almost one-half of the country's population lived below the poverty line. Inflation, while still high at 12 percent, has decreased from 16 percent in 1998. In addition, the country has qualified for **debt relief** under a program known as Highly Indebted Poor Countries (HIPC), a program developed by the World Bank and supported by the world's most highly developed nations, including the United States and Japan.

To a large degree, the country's economy is still based on agriculture. Nicaragua's manufacturing base is small and the country is dependent on imports of foreign goods,

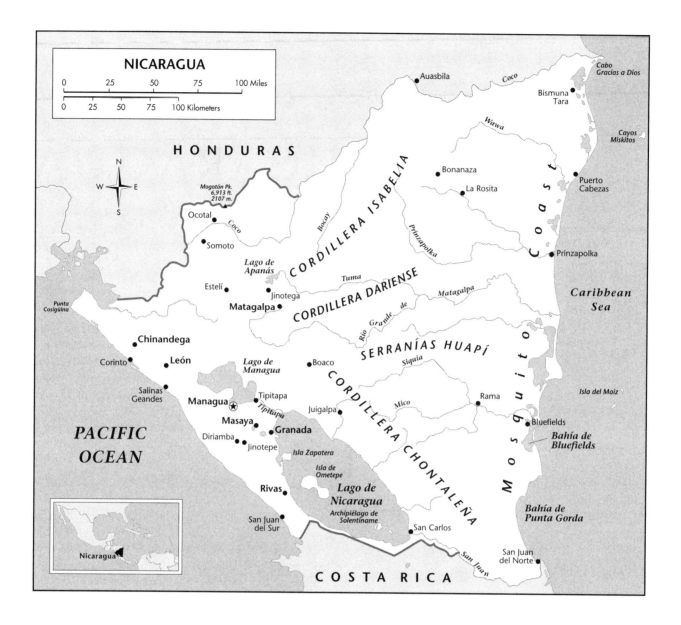

especially consumer products. The fastest growing segment of Nicaraguan industry is clothing manufacturing. The service sector is also increasing in Nicaragua. Financial services, transport, telecommunications, and tourism are growing in size and as percentages of GDP. Tourism now ranks as the third largest source of foreign capital.

Nicaragua began a period of economic reform and **restructuring** in 1991, and this restructuring continues. From 1979 through 1991, Nicaragua was under the control of the Sandinistas, a **Marxist**-based political regime, and the nation underwent a significant period of economic decline.

The United States is Nicaragua's main trading partner. Since 1990 the United States has provided US$1 billion in aid and assistance to Nicaragua. In 1996, foreign aid accounted for 22 percent of GDP. In 1999, Nicaragua received pledges of US$1.4 billion in new aid.

POLITICS, GOVERNMENT, AND TAXATION

The country is now a democratic republic. The nation's president is both the head of state and the leader of the government. The president is elected for a 5-year term and chooses the cabinet ministers. The legislature is a single-chamber body that has 93 members who are also elected for 5-year terms. The legislature is known as the National Assembly. The Supreme Court is composed of 16 magistrates who are elected to 7-year terms by the National Assembly.

Nicaragua has 35 registered political parties and factions, but the country is dominated by just 2: the Liberal Alliance, and the Sandinista National Liberation Front (FSLN). The Liberal Alliance is a coalition of 5 moderate to conservative parties that support economic reforms. The FSLN controlled Nicaragua from 1979 to 1990 under a dictatorial government.

Since 1990, the government has undertaken a variety of reforms to restructure the economy and **liberalize** the nation's political system. From 1995–96, there were broad reforms of the army and the national police force, including reductions in military spending. The country now spends about 1.2 percent of its GDP on defense (US$26 million in 1998). Programs have resulted in the **privatization** of 351 state-owned companies. Foreign investment in the country has increased dramatically to US$446 million in 2000.

Nicaragua's **national debt** is US$6.5 billion, making it one of the most highly-indebted nations in the world on a per capita basis. The country's debtors have pledged US$1.2 billion in debt relief under the HIPC and other aid programs. In 2000, government spending accounted for 33.7 percent of GDP. In 1998, the government's revenues were US$527 million while its expenditures were US$617 million. The main sources of government revenue are an **income tax** of 25 percent, a general sales tax of 15 percent, a luxury tax on certain products, corporate taxes, and **tariffs** on imported goods.

INFRASTRUCTURE, POWER, AND COMMUNICATIONS

The country's **infrastructure** has improved since 1990, but it still needs considerable upgrades and improvements. Nicaragua has 16,382 kilometers (10,180 miles) of roadways, including 1,818 kilometers (1,130 miles) of paved roads. Only about one-third of all roads are considered to be in good condition, while the remaining two-thirds are only in marginal or poor condition. The country spends less on highway construction than any other Latin American country.

Nicaragua has no major rail lines. The country does have 2,220 kilometers (1,380 miles) of navigable waterways and there is considerable traffic on some of these routes. The government has entered into a US$1.5 billion agreement with a private consortium to allow the construction of a 377-kilometer (234-mile) railway system from the Atlantic coast to the Pacific region and the development of 2 ports. Air traffic has increased dramatically in Nicaragua. The nation has 182 airports, but only 11 have paved runways. Managua International Airport in the capital is the largest airfield.

The nation is dependent on energy imports, mainly oil. In 1998, total electric production in Nicaragua was 2.714 kWh. Fossil fuels provided 53.43 percent of energy use, while hydroelectric provided 35.34 percent. The country's telephone system is operated by the government-owned company ENITEL. Private companies have been granted licenses to provide cellular service. In 1998, there were 10,000 mobile phones in use. Telephone-density is currently only 3 phones per 100 people. Nicaragua now has 5 Internet service providers.

ECONOMIC SECTORS

Nicaragua is undergoing a transition from an economy based on agriculture to one based on industry and services. In 1998, agriculture still accounted for 34 percent of GDP and 42 percent of employment. The industrial sector of the Nicaraguan economy is small compared with agricultural and services. In 1998, industry provided 22 percent of the country's GDP. It also provided 15 percent of employment. The service sector is the fastest growing segment of the Nicaraguan economy. In 1998, services were also the largest sector of the economy. As a group, they accounted for 44 percent of the country's GDP and 43 percent of the workforce.

AGRICULTURE

Agriculture provides a significant level of GDP and employment and two-thirds of the nation's exports. In 1998, the total value of agricultural exports was US$357.2 million and imports totaled $246.9 million. Agricultural workers earn an average of US$119.23 per month and are the lowest paid workers of any economic sector.

Communications

Country	Newspapers	Radios	TV Sets[a]	Cable subscribers[a]	Mobile Phones[a]	Fax Machines[a]	Personal Computers[a]	Internet Hosts[b]	Internet Users[b]
	1996	1997	1998	1998	1998	1998	1998	1999	1999
Nicaragua	30	285	190	40.2	4	N/A	7.8	2.21	20
United States	215	2,146	847	244.3	256	78.4	458.6	1,508.77	74,100
Mexico	97	325	261	15.7	35	3.0	47.0	23.02	1,822
Honduras	55	386	90	N/A	5	N/A	7.6	0.19	20

[a]Data are from International Telecommunication Union, *World Telecommunication Development Report 1999* and are per 1,000 people.
[b]Data are from the Internet Software Consortium (http://www.isc.org) and are per 10,000 people.
SOURCE: World Bank. *World Development Indicators 2000.*

Nicaragua

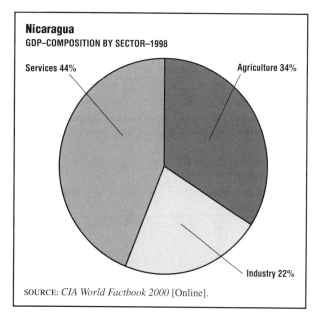

Nicaragua
GDP–COMPOSITION BY SECTOR–1998

Services 44%

Agriculture 34%

Industry 22%

SOURCE: *CIA World Factbook 2000* [Online].

In 1998, Hurricane Mitch caused extensive damage to the nation's agricultural sector, including the destruction of crops and farm facilities and equipment. Damages from the hurricane totaled US$6 million in equipment and infrastructure. In addition, Mitch destroyed 59,000 acres of pasture and crop land and caused the deaths of 81,000 head of cattle. Because of Mitch, agricultural production in Nicaragua declined by 3.3 percent in 1998.

CROP PRODUCTION. Farms are divided between small, family-owned subsistence units that are usually less than 10 acres in size and large plantations that produce crops for export. In 1999, the nation produced 4.385 million

metric tons of crops. The largest single crop was sugar cane with 3.749 million metric tons. Other significant crops were corn (302,000 metric tons), rice (136,850 metric tons) and bananas (68,830 metric tons). Although coffee production only amounted to 65,000 tons, it was one of the main cash export crops.

LIVESTOCK. The major livestock products are beef and veal, chicken, lamb, and pork. In 1999, the nation had to import US$219,000 worth of cattle from the United States for breeding purposes to repopulate herds. In addition, the nation's largest slaughterhouse was forced to close in 1999 because of financial difficulties resulting from Mitch. As a result, beef production only grew by 0.7 percent in 1999.

FISHERIES. The fisheries industry in Nicaragua includes oceanic catches from the Caribbean and Pacific Ocean, freshwater fish from the nation's numerous rivers and lakes, and farm-raised species. The most profitable catches are shrimp and lobster which are both ocean-caught and farm raised. In the Caribbean, snook accounts for half of all catches, while red snapper provides two-thirds of Pacific harvests. Grouper, catfish, croaker, shark, flounder, and tuna are also caught. Over 80 percent of the fish caught for export come from the Caribbean.

FORESTRY. The nation has 65 different commercially valuable species of trees. Among the most valuable species are pine, rosewood, mahogany, and cedar. There is a history of abuse by timber companies. In 1998, overcutting of forests led the Ministry of Environment and Natural Resources to declare a 5-year moratorium on harvesting cedar and mahogany.

INDUSTRY

Nicaragua currently has a lower level of industrialization than it did before the Sandinista regime took power in 1979. For instance, although Nicaragua was the world's fourteenth largest gold producer, gold now only accounts for 1 percent of GDP and the nation has fallen behind such small producers as Panama. Manufacturing, mining, and construction form the main core of Nicaraguan industry.

MANUFACTURING. The manufacture of **consumer goods**, such as clothing, shoes, and processed foods, is the fastest growing component of this sector. Manufacturing is the main sector of industry and in 1998 provided 19 percent of GDP (while total industry provided 22 percent). In 1999, woven apparel exports increased by 17.4 percent and had a total value of US$219 million, while knit apparel was worth US$58 million. Workers in manufacturing earn an average of US$183.95 per month.

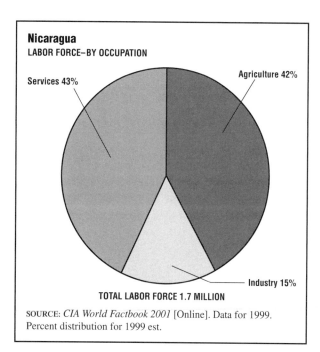

Nicaragua
LABOR FORCE–BY OCCUPATION

Services 43%

Agriculture 42%

Industry 15%

TOTAL LABOR FORCE 1.7 MILLION

SOURCE: *CIA World Factbook 2001* [Online]. Data for 1999. Percent distribution for 1999 est.

274

MINING. During the 1970s, mines produced over US$100 million a year for the nation. Current estimates are that Nicaragua has 3.8 million ounces of gold and 4.9 million ounces of silver available for exploitation. In 1994, production was at 1,241 kilograms, but by 1999, production had risen to over 1,800 kilograms. Silver production has remained constant throughout the 1990s at 2 metric tons per year. Miners are among the highest paid industrial workers in manufacturing, earning an average of US$229.43 per month.

CONSTRUCTION. Increased government spending on infrastructure, the growing economy, and the need for new commercial and residential buildings propelled the construction industry growth by 22 percent in 1999. The industry was worth $131.9 million that year. Construction workers earn an average of US$166 per month.

SERVICES

The service sector continues to grow in Nicaragua, but this component of the economy is constrained by a lack of educated and skilled workers. In addition, the continued existence of government **monopolies** in some fields also limits growth and has prevented foreign companies from entering the market. Workers in the service sector earn an average of US$133 per month, although the official minimum wage for the sector is US$47.95 per month.

FINANCIAL SERVICES. Employees in the financial services sector are the most highly skilled and earn an average of US$300 per month. The country has 10 private banks and 2 state-owned banks. There are also 2 finance companies and a leasing firm. The nation's financial sector was valued at US$1.4 billion. There are 2 foreign-owned banks in Nicaragua: 1 Salvadoran (Banco Caley Dagnell) and 1 Guatemalan (Banco Sur). No major U.S. or European banks have established a presence in the country. The state-owned insurance company continues to dominate the market and has 75 percent of business. Because of the dominance of the state insurance company, no foreign firms have entered the market.

TELECOMMUNICATIONS. The telecommunications market in Nicaragua is expected to expand rapidly. For instance, the number of mobile phone customers has increased from less than 4,000 in 1996 to over 10,000. In 1995, Alfanumeric and Mobile Phone began offering pager service and currently there are 6 paging firms with 20,000 customers.

RETAIL AND FOOD SERVICES. Fast-food franchises are expanding rapidly in Nicaragua. There are currently 25 different national and international franchisers operating in the country, including McDonald's, TGI Friday's, Subway, Domino's Pizza, and Pizza Hut. Between 1998 and 2001, there was US$21.6 million spent on new franchises, including the establishment of 65 new restaurants.

TOURISM. Tourism is Nicaragua's third largest source of foreign currency. In 1999, it provided revenues of US$105 million. In 2000, approximately 468,000 tourists visited the country, an increase of 15 percent over the previous year. The number-one source of foreign tourists for Nicaragua is Honduras, while the United States comes in at number-two. Because of the potential value of tourism, by 1998 the number of hotel rooms in the country had doubled. Tourists are drawn to the nation because of the low travel and lodging costs. The undeveloped nature of the country also means that many natural and wildlife areas remain undisturbed by human development.

INTERNATIONAL TRADE

Nicaragua is a member of the Central American Common Market and is negotiating an agreement with the **free trade zone** of the southern American nations (MERCOSUR). In 1997, Nicaragua signed a free trade agreement with Mexico. The nation also has bilateral trade agreements with the United States, Spain, Taiwan, Denmark, the Netherlands, and the United Kingdom. The nations that export the most products to Nicaragua are the United States with 35 percent of goods and services, Germany with 13 percent, El Salvador with 10 percent, Spain with 4 percent, Costa Rica with 4 percent, and France with 2 percent. Nicaragua's main import markets are the United States at 31 percent, Costa Rica at 11 percent, Guatemala at 8 percent, Venezuela at 6 percent, El Salvador at 5 percent, and Mexico at 4 percent.

A major component of the government's effort to promote foreign trade and attract new investment has been the establishment of free trade zones. Business in these zones has increased 30 percent as has employment since 1997. The 5 current zones have 19 international and 11 Nicaraguan companies in them and produce US$198 million in goods and services for export. These zones employ 28,183 people.

Trade (expressed in billions of US$): Nicaragua		
	Exports	Imports
1975	.375	.517
1980	.451	.887
1985	.302	.964
1990	.331	.638
1995	.526	.962
1998	.573	1.492

SOURCE: International Monetary Fund. *International Financial Statistics Yearbook 1999.*

Exchange rates: Nicaragua

gold cordobas (C$) per US$1

Nov 2000	12.96
2000	12.69
1999	11.81
1998	10.58
1997	9.45
1996	8.44

SOURCE: CIA *World Factbook 2001* [ONLINE].

GDP per Capita (US$)

Country	1975	1980	1985	1990	1998
Nicaragua	999	690	611	460	452
United States	19,364	21,529	23,200	25,363	29,683
Mexico	3,380	4,167	4,106	4,046	4,459
Honduras	614	733	681	682	722

SOURCE: United Nations. *Human Development Report 2000; Trends in human development and per capita income.*

MONEY

Inflation has seriously eroded the value of the nation's money, the córdoba. In 1991, inflation reached 750 percent which made the currency relatively worthless since what had previously cost 1 córdoba cost 750 córdobas. Although inflation has been reduced to 12 percent, it is still high by international standards. For example, the rate of inflation in the United States in 2000 was 3.4 percent. In 1999, it took 12.29 córdobas to equal US$1. In 1995, the rate was 7.55 córdobas per US$1. Inflation has been the main reason for the decline in value of the córdoba.

The country's stock market, known as the Bolsa de Valores de Nicaragua, was established in 1993 and began operations in 1994. By 1997, the exchange was worth US$690 million. However, unlike in most countries where the stock market is dominated by private companies, in Nicaragua government-issued bonds accounted for 81 percent of trades while private-company securities only accounted for the remaining 19 percent of volume. The nation has 10 brokerage firms, all of which are associated with local banks.

POVERTY AND WEALTH

Nicaragua is one of the poorest nations in the Western Hemisphere. Despite improvements in the nation's economy and the implementation of government programs, almost half of the population lives in poverty. These factors have only reduced poverty in the nation from 50 percent of the population to 48 percent (or about 2.3 million people) since 1995. The nation's official poverty line is US$350 in income per year. Of the nation's poor, 17 percent live in extreme poverty, earning less than US$185 per year.

The middle and upper classes of Nicaragua live lifestyles that are comparable to those in the United States. For instance, they own American and European-built cars, use mobile phones, and their homes have all of the amenities of the American middle-class, including electric appliances and conveniences. The wealthiest 10 percent of the population controls 39.8 percent of the nation's wealth (the poorest 10 percent only controls 1.6 percent of wealth).

WORKING CONDITIONS

In 1999, the nation's unemployment rate was 10.5 percent, the lowest level since the 1970s. With 1 out of 10 Nicaraguans unemployed, the competition for jobs is intense. Many Nicaraguans find themselves forced to take jobs for which they are overqualified. In 1999, the **underemployment** rate was 36 percent. The nation's constitution guarantees workers the right to organize and join unions. Overall union membership is declining because of the competition for jobs and the increasing number of foreign companies entering the country (many of these firms are resistant to unionization because of the increased labor costs).

Child labor is forbidden by law. The 1996 Labor Law raised the minimum age to employ children from 12 to 14 years old. Parental permission is required for anyone under the age of 16. However, estimates are that as many as 42 percent of children between the ages of 6 and 9 work. A 1999 government study found that 6,219 children in Managua work in occupations such as car washers, street vendors, and beggars.

Distribution of Income or Consumption by Percentage Share: Nicaragua

Lowest 10%	1.6
Lowest 20%	4.2
Second 20%	8.0
Third 20%	12.6
Fourth 20%	20.0
Highest 20%	55.2
Highest 10%	39.8

Survey year: 1993
Note: This information refers to expenditure shares by percentiles of the population and is ranked by per capita expenditure.

SOURCE: *2000 World Development Indicators* [CD-ROM].

The minimum wage varies from sector to sector. The monthly minimum wage for agriculture is set at US$36, fisheries at US$56, manufacturing at US$48, government at US$44, restaurants and hotels at US$72, construction at US$96, mining at US$68, and banking at US$80. Except for the construction, banking, hotel, and mining sectors, the minimum wage does not provide enough income for an average family to live. As a result, many workers supplement their wages in the **informal economy**.

COUNTRY HISTORY AND ECONOMIC DEVELOPMENT

20,000–10,000 B.C. Native Americans settle in the region.

1502. Columbus lands on the Caribbean coast of Nicaragua.

1524. Hernandez de Cordoba establishes the first Spanish colonies in Nicaragua, including 2 of the present-day principal cities of Leon and Granada.

1740–86. The Mosquito Coast region becomes a British protectorate. The British continue to exert influence on the region well into the 20th century.

1821. Nicaragua becomes independent of Spain; first as part of the Mexican Empire and then as a member of the federation, the United Provinces of Central America.

1838. Nicaragua becomes an independent republic.

1848–60. The British control the port of San Juan del Norte.

1850s. Many Americans travel through Nicaragua on their way to the gold fields of California.

1855–57. American William Walker seizes the presidency, but is overthrown in 1857 by a coalition of 5 Central American nations.

1909. The United States provides support for a conservative revolt after American businesses and property are threatened in the Bluefields region.

1912–33. With the exception of a 9-month period from 1925–26, U.S. troops are stationed in Nicaragua.

1936. General Anastasio Somoza Garcia takes control of the government. This initiates 40 years of rule by the Somoza family.

1972. A massive earthquake devastates the nation, leaving 6,000 dead and over 300,000 homeless.

1979. Led by the Sandinistas, a popular uprising overthrows the Somoza dynasty.

1981. The United States suspends economic aid after the Sandinistas begin privatizing property and businesses.

1985. The United States imposes an economic **embargo** in Nicaragua because of its support for Marxist Central American revolutionary groups. The United States also begins support for anti-Sandinista rebels, known as Contras.

1990. Under international pressure, the Sandinistas agree to open elections in which the opposition candidate Violetta Chamorro is elected.

1994. The nation's stock market begins operations.

1996. Former Managua Mayor Arnoldo Aleman, leader of the moderate-conservative Liberal Alliance, defeats the Sandinista candidate to become president.

1998. Hurricane Mitch devastates the nation, causing 4,000 deaths and widespread economic disruption.

2000. Nicaragua qualifies for debt-relief under the HIPC program.

FUTURE TRENDS

Nicaragua faces a host of problems as it continues to recover from the economic problems of the Sandinista period. Despite some debt relief and forgiveness through the HIPC and other aid programs, the nation continues to have one of the highest debt per capita ratios in the world. The nation's main opposition party, the Sandinistas, actively seeks to undermine economic reforms.

On the other hand, there are a variety of positive signs that the economy will continue to improve. Inflation and unemployment have decreased dramatically over the past decade. From 1998–2000, the economy added 250,000 new jobs. In addition, a number of foreign companies have begun to invest in Nicaragua, especially in the services sector. The government's aggressive development of free trade zones will also continue to attract more foreign companies. One of the most promising potential developments for the nation would be the construction of a railway linking the Caribbean and Pacific coasts and offering an alternative to the overburdened Panama Canal.

DEPENDENCIES

Nicaragua has no territories or colonies.

BIBLIOGRAPHY

Babb, Florence E. *After Revolution: Mapping Gender and Cultural Politics in Neoliberal Nicaragua.* Austin: University of Texas Press, 2001.

Close, David. *Nicaragua: The Chamorro Years.* Boulder: Lynne Rienner Publishers, 1999.

U.S. Central Intelligence Agency. *The World Factbook 2000.* <http://www.odci.gov/cia/publications/factbook/geos/nu.html>. Accessed April 2001.

U.S. Department of State. *Background Notes: Nicaragua.* <http://www.state.gov/www/background_notes?nicar_0009_bgn.html>. Accessed April 2001.

————. *FY 2001 Country Commercial Guide: Nicaragua.* <http://www/ipade.mx/econ/Paises/nicaragua.pdf>. Accessed April 2001.

————. "Nicaragua." *2000 Country Reports on Human Rights Practices.* <http://www.state.gov/g/drl/rls/hrrpt/2000/wha/index.cfm?docid=813>. Accessed April 2001.

—Tom Lansford

PANAMA

Republic of Panama
República de Panamá

CAPITAL: Panama City.

MONETARY UNIT: Balboa (B). One balboa equals 100 centésimos. Panama only issues coins in denominations of 5, 10, 25, and 50 centésimos and 1 and 5 balboas. The U.S. dollar is distributed freely throughout the country and is legal tender.

CHIEF EXPORTS: Bananas, shrimp, sugar, coffee.

CHIEF IMPORTS: Capital goods, crude oil, foodstuffs, consumer goods, chemicals.

GROSS DOMESTIC PRODUCT: US$21 billion (purchasing power parity, 1999 est.).

BALANCE OF TRADE: Exports: US$4.7 billion (f.o.b., 1999). **Imports:** US$6.4 billion (f.o.b., 1999).

COUNTRY OVERVIEW

LOCATION AND SIZE. Panama is located in Central America between Costa Rica to the north and Colombia to the south. It is at the southern end of the Central American isthmus (a narrow piece of land that connects two larger land areas) and forms the land bridge between North and South America. The nation is S-shaped and runs from east to west with a length of 772 kilometers (480 miles) and a width that varies from 60 to 177 kilometers (37 to 110 miles). Panama has an area of 77,381 square kilometers (29,762 square miles) which makes it slightly smaller than South Carolina. This area consists of 75,990 square kilometers (29,340 square miles) of land and 2,210 square kilometers (853 square miles) of water. The nation borders the Caribbean Sea on one coast and the Pacific Ocean on the other. The 80-kilometer (50-mile) Panama Canal cuts the nation in half and joins the Atlantic and Pacific Oceans. The combined coastlines of Panama are 2,857 kilometers (1,786 miles) long. The nation's border with Costa Rica is 330 kilometers (205 miles), and its border with Colombia is 225 kilometers (140 miles) in length. Panama's capital and largest city, Panama City, with a population of 827,828, is located on the Pacific coastline of the country. The second largest city is Colón, located on the Atlantic coast. Colón has a population of 140,908.

POPULATION. The population of Panama was calculated to be 2,808,268 according to a July 2000 estimate. The country's population growth rate was 1.34 percent in 2000. The Panamanian population is growing rapidly. In 1970, the nation's population was approximately 1.5 million, but by 1990, the population had grown to about 2.2 million. Current estimates have the population expanding to 3.2 million by 2010. There were 19.53 births per 1,000 people, and the Panamanian fertility rate was 2.32 children born per woman. The nation's mortality rate was 4.95 deaths per 1,000 people. Panama has a high infant mortality rate due to the rudimentary health-care system and high incidence of poverty. In 2000, there were 20.8 deaths per 1,000 live births. The country has a high **emigration** rate and in 2000, 1.16 out of every 1,000 Panamanians emigrated to other nations. Emigration is frequent because of the lure of higher-paying jobs in places such as the United States (the main destination for Panamanian emigrants). Life expectancy in Panama is 72.74 years for males and 78.31 years for females.

The majority of the Panamanian population is young. In 2000, the largest age group in Panama was the 5 to 14 age group with about 550,000 people. In comparison, those over the age of 60 number only 240,000. By 2025, the demographics of the nation will have shifted, and the largest single group of people will be in the age group 30 to 39, and by 2050, the largest group will be over those over the age of 55.

The majority of the population is mestizo (mixed ethnic backgrounds, mainly Spanish and Native-American). Mestizos makeup 70 percent of the population. Other ethnic groups include Africans (14 percent), whites (10 percent), and Native Americans (6 percent). Members of ethnic minorities and the nation's Native American

Worldmark Encyclopedia of National Economies

279

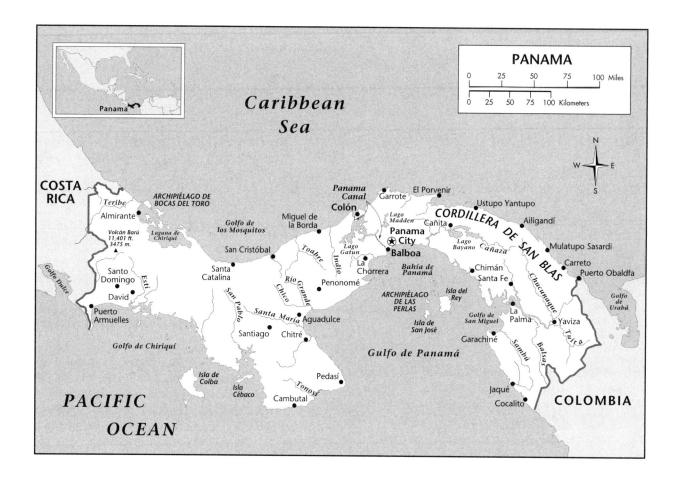

population face discrimination in employment, housing, and politics. The culture and society of Panama is mainly Spanish-Caribbean. Spanish is the official language, but much of the population also speaks English. This is especially true of West Indian descendants. English is also commonly used in business. Almost 85 percent of the population is Roman Catholic; the remaining 15 percent are Protestant.

The majority of the population is urban; almost 60 percent of people live in towns or cities, especially in the metropolitan areas around Panama City and Colón. About 50 percent of Panamanians live in the corridor that runs from Colón on the Caribbean Coast to Panama City on the Pacific. Only about 25 percent of the land is inhabited. The nation has a population density of 36.6 per square kilometer, compared to that of the United States which is 28.4 per square kilometer.

OVERVIEW OF ECONOMY

Panama has a long history as a trading area. In 1501, the Spanish began exploring the area that is now Panama in search of gold and silver. Panama soon became one of the main crossroads for the trade between Spain and its colonies in Central and South America, including Mexico, Peru, and Cost Rica. Gold and silver were transported

to Panama and then shipped to Spain abroad ships. This route became known as the Camino Real or Royal Road.

The modern economic history of Panama has been dominated by efforts to construct a canal across the isthmus. The Panama Canal currently forms the backbone of the Panamanian economy. In addition to revenues from the tolls, maintenance work, and general operations of the canal, a variety of businesses and industries have emerged to support the trade goods going through the canal, including storage warehouses, refueling stations, and repair facilities. In order to capitalize on the importance of the canal, the government has long supported the establishment of free trade areas where goods can be transshipped without **tariffs** or taxes. The U.S.-built 80-kilometer (50-mile) canal opened in 1914. The United States paid Panama US$10 million for the rights to construct the canal and then a base of US$250,000, plus **inflation**, annually for the right to operate the canal. In 1999, the United States turned control of the canal over to the Panamanians. Ships going to Japan from the east coast of the United States save 3,000 miles by using the canal, and ships sailing from Europe save 5,000 miles traveling to Asia.

Because of the Panama Canal, the nation's small geographic size, and small population, Panama's economy is centered on services. The main elements of this sector include services related to the transshipment of goods across the canal: banking, insurance, and international trade. The Colón **Free Zone** is the world's second largest free trade area after Hong Kong. The agricultural sector is small, but it accounts for the majority of the country's exports. The main Panamanian industries are construction, petroleum refining, brewing, paper and paper products, clothing, furniture, the production of cement and other construction materials, and sugar milling. While the Panamian economy is structured around the services in the Canal Zone, the nation does have a variety of economically-advantageous natural resources including timber, precious minerals, and seafood.

Since 1991, the Panamanian economy has been increasing by 5 to 8 percent annual growth (as measured by the GDP). However, growth slowed toward the end of the decade. In 1997, the GDP grew at a rate of 4.5 percent. The rate slowed to 3.2 percent in 1999 and to 2.6 percent in 2000. Economic growth was greatly affected by the economic and political reforms which followed the restoration of democracy in 1991. The nation's per capita GDP has increased from US$3,198 in 1997 to US$3,513 in 2000 to give Panama the highest **GDP per capita** in Central America. Panama's prosperity is directly attributable to the canal.

In 1999, the United States withdrew from the 50-mile wide Canal Zone that it had maintained since 1914. This withdrawal provided the Panamanian government with 364,000 acres of land and 5,000 buildings. In 2000, the canal provided the government with $569 million in tolls. However, the U.S. withdrawal also meant the loss of numerous jobs and $175–350 million in funds that were spent by U.S. military forces in the region. Most of the lost jobs were service sector jobs that had provided for the U.S. forces. Examples include domestic help, restaurant workers, and **retail** employees. After the withdrawal of the United States from the canal, many Panamanians found that their own government paid less than the Americans had. Unemployment and **underemployment** continue to cause problems for the economy. In 2000, unemployment in Panama was 11.6 percent, down from 13.6 percent in 1998. Underemployment affects approximately 25 to 30 percent of the working population.

There is also a large informal or **black market** economy. Estimates are that the **informal economy** may be worth as much as US$2 billion annually. Among the main components of this sector of the economy are the illegal drug trade and various types of personal services including maintenance work, household help, and transportation.

Panama is dependent on foreign trade. In 1996, the nation joined the World Trade Organization (WTO). Membership allowed Panama to export goods to other members of the WTO with substantially reduced tariffs

and import **duties**. During the 1990s, there were broad efforts to **privatize** government-owned companies and firms; however, the current administration has slowed or halted these programs in order to prevent further increases in unemployment. In addition, to the withdrawal of U.S. forces, which created an increase in unemployment, the slowdown in the U.S. economy has also caused an economic slowdown in Panama since the United States is one of the nation's largest trading partners.

Panama is a net recipient of foreign aid. Each year the country receives approximately US$200 million in aid. Panama has a substantial **foreign debt** which in 2000 was US$7 billion. When the nation joined the WTO, it renegotiated some of its debt and reduced interest rates. However, payments on the debt continue to be a drain on the government's revenues. Currently, about 15 percent of the budget to devoted to debt management.

POLITICS, GOVERNMENT, AND TAXATION

For most of the 20th century, Panama was a constitutional democracy. However, a coup in 1968 brought the military to power. During the 1980s, Panamanian General Manuel Noriega assumed control of the government. After diplomatic and economic pressure failed to remove Noriega, U.S. president George Bush used American troops to remove the dictator from power and restore democracy in 1991 in a military operation known as "Just Cause."

Panama is now a constitutional representative democracy. The government is divided into 3 branches: executive, legislative, and judicial. The executive branch is led by an elected president who serves as both the head of state and the head of the government. The president is elected for a 5-year term and appoints the national cabinet. There are also 2 elected vice-presidents who also serve 5-year terms. The legislative branch of government is made-up of a 1 chamber legislature. It has 71 members who are elected for 5-year terms. The judicial branch consists of a national supreme court, 5 superior courts and 3 courts of appeal. The judicial system is plagued by corruption and inefficiency.

The largest political party in Panama is the Democratic Revolutionary Party (PRD). The PRD is conservative on economic matters and appeals mainly to the country's young and urban poor. The Arnulfista Party (PA) is the party of the nation's current president and its base is among the Panama's rural population. The Popular Block is a coalition of former Christian Democrats and pro-business groups, as is the National Liberal Republican Movement and Democratic Change. These parties appeal to the middle and upper classes and tend to have strong ties to the business community.

In 1997, the government's budget was US$2.4 billion and it had revenues of US$2.4 billion. Government spending accounts for about 30 percent of the nation's GDP. In 1999, Panama's official foreign debt exceeded US$7 billion. Currently there are over 50 different forms of taxes, but plans are underway for reforms to reduce that number to 10. These reforms are designed to simplify the tax code in order to increase efficiency and make the tax system more friendly to business with reductions in some forms of corporate taxes. The maximum personal **income tax** is 33 percent, and the maximum corporate tax rate is 30 percent. The government's tax collection system is very inefficient, and collection rates of some forms of taxes fall below 50 percent.

Because of its history of military interference in the government, the nation adopted a constitutional amendment in 1994 which abolished the military. Security is now in the hands of the national police force, the coast guard, and a national air service. In 1997, the government spent 1.9 percent of the nation's GDP on security or about US$132 million. About 150,000 people work for the government in some capacity.

During the 1990s, the government was engaged in a variety of programs to **liberalize** the economy. It enacted reforms in banking, labor regulation, and taxes. In 1996, the government passed the first anti-**monopoly** laws. This legislation created 4 special commercial courts to hear cases related to patent, trademark, and anti-trust cases. It also created a consumer protection agency known as the Free Competition and Consumer Affairs Commission. New laws levy fines against companies that engage in practices that are harmful to consumers, including the sale of expired products and price fixing. However, there remain a number of problems in Panamanian business law. For instance, there is no bankruptcy law that allows companies to **restructure** themselves rather than go out of business.

A number of previously government-owned businesses were privatized. These include the ports of Cristobal and Balboa; the nation's telecommunications company, INTEL; power generation facilities; and a cement company. In addition, the government has privatized the nation's 17 casinos and slot-machine companies. Plans to privatize the electric and water companies were halted by a new government in 1999. Because the nation uses the U.S. dollar, it cannot control its **monetary policy**.

INFRASTRUCTURE, POWER, AND COMMUNICATIONS

The nation's **infrastructure** is relatively well developed. Roads in the urban areas are generally good, but in the rural areas of the nation they remain poor. Panama has 11,258 kilometers (6,996 miles) of roads, but only 3,783 kilometers (2,350 miles) are paved. Plans are underway for the construction of 2 major superhighways that will be funded through tolls. In addition, there are 355 kilometers (220 miles) of railways. The government is in the midst of a program to privatize the nation's main railway, the Panama-Colón Railroad. In addition, a **joint venture** between the U.S. companies, Kansas City Southern Industries and Mi-Jack Products, is investing US$73 million to rebuild a rail line parallel with the canal and across the nation. There are 105 airports in the country, but only 41 have paved runways. The withdrawal of the Americans from the Canal Zone has provided the government with a former military airfield that can serve as a major international airport. There are 130 kilometers (81 miles) of crude oil pipelines in Panama.

In addition to the 80-kilometer (50-mile) Panama Canal, the country has 800 kilometers (497 miles) of navigable waterways, although most of these can only be used by shallow-draft vessels. The major ports in Panama are Balboa, Cristobal, Coco Solo, Manzanillo, and Vacamonte. The international shipping terminal in Manzanillo is the largest container port in Latin America. Hutchison Port Holdings of Hong Kong has initiated a $150 million port project to develop a port facility on the Pacific side of the Panama Canal. Panama allows ships of other na-

Communications

Country	Newspapers	Radios	TV Sets[a]	Cable subscribers[a]	Mobile Phones[a]	Fax Machines[a]	Personal Computers[a]	Internet Hosts[b]	Internet Users[b]
	1996	1997	1998	1998	1998	1998	1998	1999	1999
Panama	62	299	187	N/A	29	N/A	27.1	2.97	45
United States	215	2,146	847	244.3	256	78.4	458.6	1,508.77	74,100
Mexico	97	325	261	15.7	35	3.0	47.0	23.02	1,822
Costa Rica	94	271	387	13.8	28	2.3	39.1	10.41	150

[a]Data are from International Telecommunication Union, *World Telecommunication Development Report 1999* and are per 1,000 people.
[b]Data are from the Internet Software Consortium (http://www.isc.org) and are per 10,000 people.

SOURCE: World Bank. *World Development Indicators 2000.*

tions to register themselves under the Panamanian flag. In 2000, there were 4,732 ship registered under Panamanian registry, including ships from 71 different nations. Given these ships, Panama has the largest merchant fleet in the world, followed by Liberia with 1,644 ships.

The nation's telecommunications company is in the midst of a multi-million-dollar upgrade and expansion of the country's phone system. INTEL employs about 3,400 people, and the government retains 49 percent of the company's stock. Panama's telephone density is close to 200 phone lines per 1,000 people. The U.S. firm, Bell South, paid $72.6 million for the rights to offer cellular service. Both Bell South and the national telephone company have begun to offer cellular phone service, and the country has about 200,000 mobile phones in use. By 1999, Panama had 3 Internet service providers.

Electric production in the country in 1998 was 4.523 billion kilowatt hours (kWh). Electric consumption was 4.3 billion kWh. The excess production was exported. The majority of production (73.78 percent) was done by hydroelectric plants. Fossil fuel provided the majority of the rest of production (25.56 percent). That same year, Panama imported 136 million kWh of electricity and exported 13 million kWh.

ECONOMIC SECTORS

The Panamanian economy is dependent on trade. The canal provides the main source of economic activity, although efforts to diversify the economy are ongoing. The service sector is the dominant part of the Panamanian economy and continues to grow. In 1997, the service sector accounted for 67 percent of the nation's GDP, but by

2000 that percentage had grown to 80 percent. As such, the country's economy is geared toward banking, commerce, and maritime services. Services provide 67 percent of employment.

Agriculture, including forestry and fisheries, only accounts for about 7 percent of the nation's GDP. However, they provide 25 percent of the country's employment and provide the main exports. Among the country's major crops are bananas, coffee, rice, and sugar cane. Like agriculture, industry only accounts for a small percentage of the GDP when compared to the service sector. Industry provides about 25 percent of the country's GDP and 8 percent of employment. Panamanian industry includes manufacturing, construction, mining, and processed foods.

AGRICULTURE

Agriculture employs such a large number of Panamanians (in relation to its percentage of the country's GDP) because many farmers are engaged in **subsistence farming** and only produce enough for their family to consume. Concurrently, agricultural products also provide the nation's main exports. In 1998, agricultural exports were valued at US$409.3 million (out of the nation's total exports of $640 million), while imports totaled US$397.7 million. That same year bananas accounted for 33 percent of the nation's exports, shrimp 11 percent, sugar 4 percent, and coffee 2 percent. About half of the land in Panama is used for agriculture.

Several large international companies dominate Panamanian exports, especially when it comes to export

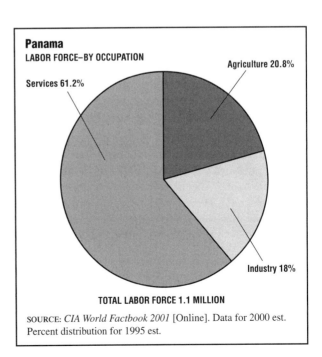

Panama
GDP–COMPOSITION BY SECTOR–1997 est.

Services 67%

Agriculture 8%

Industry 25%

SOURCE: *CIA World Factbook 2000* [Online].

Panama
LABOR FORCE–BY OCCUPATION

Services 61.2%

Agriculture 20.8%

Industry 18%

TOTAL LABOR FORCE 1.1 MILLION

SOURCE: *CIA World Factbook 2001* [Online]. Data for 2000 est. Percent distribution for 1995 est.

crops such as bananas. For instance, the U.S. company, Chiriqui Land Company, which operates under the brand name Chiquita, is one of the largest landowners in Panama, as well as the main banana exporter. Other major foreign agricultural companies include Del Monte Corporation and Dole Foods.

The primary crops are bananas, cocoa beans, coffee, coconuts, corn, potatoes, rice, soybeans, and sugar cane. Throughout the 1990s, agricultural production increased by an average of 5 percent per year, with the exception of 1998 when Hurricane Mitch caused extensive damage to crops. In 1999, sugar cane production was at 2.05 million metric tons, bananas at 650,000 metric tons, rice at 232,370 metric tons and corn at 89,806 metric tons. The main export crop was bananas with exports worth US$182 million in 2000. There has been a steady increase in tropical fruit exports which were worth US$14 million in 2000.

The main livestock products in Panama are beef, veal, chicken, and pork. Panama has the highest rate of chicken consumption per capita in Latin America. The main fishing product is shrimp, both sea-caught and farm-raised. Although the industry has suffered from the outbreak of disease, in 1999 it was worth US$69 million.

Panama has significant stocks of timber, mainly mahogany. There are also 61,000 hectares of planted forests, mainly teak and pine. However, concerns over deforestation have led to increased regulation of the timber industry. During the 1990s, Panama annually lost 2.1 percent of its forested areas to logging. However, after 1996, timber production dropped by 50 percent. There are 3 major timber companies which own 41 sawmills. Annual output is now around 60,000 cubic meters of forest products.

INDUSTRY

Industry in Panama is dominated by mining, construction, and milling. The sector's growth rate was 4.6 percent in 1999. Mining continues to expand in importance. In 1999, mining was worth US$25 million. In 1991, there were only 20 mining operations in the nation, but by 1999 there were 120 mining projects. The key mineral produced was gold. In 1997, 1,550 kilograms of gold were mined. The nation has 2 billion tons of proven copper reserves. There are 2 major copper mines set to begin operations. At Cerro Colorado, the mine is estimated to be worth US$150 million and another, at Petaquilla, is estimated at US$800 million.

CONSTRUCTION. Construction rose 12 percent in 1999 as the government initiated a series of infrastructure programs, including highway construction and expansion and the renovation and expansion of port facilities. In 2000, the total private construction market was worth

US$336 million. Clay and cement are produced for the construction industry. Production of building materials was worth US$150 million in 2000.

After the privatization of 2 of the nation's main sugar mills, production increased 13.1 percent in 1999 and is now worth US$25.5 million. However, the refining industry suffers from excess production of at least 15,000 metric tons per year. As a result, many mills are closing, and some producers have begun shipping raw sugar overseas for processing and then re-importing the refined sugar. The government has also sold an orange processing plant to private investors for US$5 million.

ENERGY. The U.S. company Texaco operates an oil refinery in Panama that has a capacity of 60,000 barrels per day. The refinery provides all of the nation's gasoline and a majority of its fuel oil. In addition, about 8,000 barrels of refined petroleum are exported from the refinery. There are plans to implement a US$400 million project to build a pipeline from Colombia which will bring substantial natural gas into Panama and reduce the nation's dependency on oil. The government is engaged in negotiations with other Central American nations to join their electrical grids which would increase the nation's electricity exports.

SERVICES

Services make up the largest share of the Panamanian economy and are the country's largest employer. The largest segments of this sector are financial services and trade services related to the Canal. Service exports amounted to US$585.3 million in 1999. The nation's retail sector caters mainly to the middle and upper classes, and it experienced a 3.4 percent decline because of the country's continuing high level of unemployment. The strongest segment of the retail sector is new car sales. While there is no local production, new car sales were worth US$74 million in 2000. Franchising of businesses is increasing dramatically and there are 50 different franchises operating in Panama. Among those franchises experiencing the greatest growth are McDonald's, Chevron, Coca-Cola, and Sherwin Williams. Franchising is expected to provide US$3 to US$6 million annually in new investment.

FINANCIAL SERVICES. In 1999, there were 82 licensed banks in Panama with assets of US$37 billion. This number included a number of foreign firms such as Citibank, Chase and Bank Boston. Panama has endeavored to establish itself as an international banking center, but instability and economic problems have impaired this effort. The total number of banks has declined from a high of 104 in the mid 1990s, and total assets declined by US$400 million in 2000. Foreign businesses may incorporate in Panama for the small sum of US$200. Doing so provides a way to escape high corporate taxes in certain countries. In 2000, there were over 400,000 companies incorporated in Panama.

TOURISM. During the 1990s, tourism experienced strong growth. However, much of the tourist trade was based on visits by relatives of U.S. military personnel to the country and concurrently, tourist trips within Panama by U.S. troops and their dependents. In 2000, the number of foreign visitors who stayed overnight had declined to 300,000 from a peak of 420,000. Nonetheless, foreign and domestic tourism is worth US$300 million annually. Each year, 276 cruise ships shop in Panama. In order to promote tourism, the government exempts all new tourist businesses from income and real **estate taxes**. The government plans to use many of the former U.S. Army facilities as tourist areas, including Fort Amador which already has extensive golf courses, boating facilities and buildings which can be converted into hotel space. The area is also home to the Smithsonian Institute for Tropical Research laboratories.

The form of tourism that is expected to experience the most dramatic growth is **ecotourism**. Panama has the most comprehensive wildlife management systems in Central America. About 29 percent of the nation's territory is protected by a series of 15 national parks, wildlife refuges and reserves. Panama has over 10,000 varieties of plants and at least 933 bird species (more than the total of Europe and North America combined).

PANAMA CANAL. On average, 50 ships per day travel the Panama Canal. In 1999, there was a total of 14,336 ship crossings of the canal. The largest commodity that is shipped through the canal is grain. However, the canal is a major shipping route for oil, the number-two commodity in volume (17 percent of total volume). Each day, approximately 600,000 barrels of oil are shipped through the canal. A large amount of coal is also transshipped. Coal accounts for 6 percent of total volume. That same year, the canal generated US$569 million in tolls and an additional US$50 million in revenues for the government. About 10,000 people work for the Panama Canal Authority, the company that oversees the operations of the canal.

A special, but distinct, part of the service sector is the Colón Free Trade Zone (CFTZ). This area was established in 1948 at the Atlantic entrance of the Panama Canal. The CFTZ is a trans-shipment area where foreign companies import products to be **re-exported** to other nations. In 1999, the CFTZ received US$4.9 billion in imports of which US$4 billion were re-exported. Most exports are sent to Latin America. The largest exports to the CFTZ were Hong Kong (27 percent), Japan (13 percent), the United States (11 percent), South Korea (10 percent), and Taiwan (8 percent). The majority of exports went to Colombia (27 percent), Ecuador (9 percent),

Panama (6 percent), and both Venezuela and the United States (5 percent each). These figures are not included in the overall trade statistics for the nation. The products that were imported to or exported from the CFTZ included electronics (22 percent), apparel (17 percent), textiles (7 percent), footwear (5 percent), and jewelry (5 percent). The Panamanian government received US$899 million in revenues from the CFTZ in 1999.

INTERNATIONAL TRADE

Because of the Panama Canal, the country's economy is heavily reliant on international trade. The entry of Panama into the WTO opened new trade opportunities. Panama now has the lowest tariff rates in Latin America. Despite these expansions, the United States remains the nation's main trade partner. In 1998, the United States provided 40 percent of the nation's imports and exports. Other major export partners are Sweden, Costa Rica, Spain, the Benelux nations (Belgium, the Netherlands, and Luxembourg) and Honduras. Besides the United States, Panama's main import partners are Japan and other nations in Central America.

As a result of entry into the WTO, the government lowered tariffs on imported goods to a maximum of 15 percent. The average tariff on goods is now 12 percent which is the lowest in the region. The higher tariff rates are maintained on agricultural products in an effort to protect the nation's farmers from foreign competition. However, negotiations continue under WTO auspices to lower the agricultural tariffs. Panama and the United States are engaged in a longstanding dispute with the EU over banana imports. The EU places high tariffs on imported bananas and the United States has led an effort to force the EU to lower these trade impediments.

Improvements and renovations in the Canal Zone and the CFTZ have expanded capacity. The nation's container handling capacity has been expanded from 250,000 containers per year in 1997 to 1 million per year in 2000. An American firm, Kansas City Southern, is building a

Trade (expressed in billions of US$): Panama		
	Exports	Imports
1975	.283	.892
1980	.358	1.449
1985	.334	1.392
1990	.340	1.539
1995	.625	2.511
1998	.786	3.350

SOURCE: International Monetary Fund. *International Financial Statistics Yearbook 1999.*

railway across the isthmus that will further expand trade by allowing shipment of goods between the coasts.

In addition to the WTO, Panama has a variety of agreements that regulate its trade. Panama also has a variety of agreements with individual countries; among the most significant are those with the United States, the United Kingdom, France, Germany, Switzerland, and Taiwan. It also has preferential trade agreements with most of the nations of Latin America. In 2000, it signed an accord with Mexico to ultimately allow complete freedom of trade. Panama has also sought to negotiate agreements with nations to establish country-specific free trade zones. The first of these was signed in 2000 and grants Taiwan an area of the former military base at Fort Davis. It has also entered into negotiations to join the Andean Pact and the Central American Market.

In 1998, direct foreign investment in Panama totaled $3.76 billion and was responsible for 13.2 percent of the nation's GDP. The United States was the largest investor with 40 percent of all investments ($1.5 billion). The United Kingdom ranked second with 23 percent of investments ($880 million), Mexico was third with 19 percent ($700 million), and Taiwan fourth with 8 percent ($300 million). Transportation and maritime services accounted for 33 percent of investment ($1.29 billion), services 31 percent ($1.15 billion), manufacturing 11 percent ($400 million), and real estate 11 percent ($400 million).

MONEY

Panama uses the U.S. dollar as its currency, calling it the balboa. Although its value fluctuates freely on world markets, the dollar has remained relatively stable. The use of the dollar as the nation's currency has provided a number of benefits for the Panamanian economy. The dollar has provided monetary stability, since the Panamanian government cannot devalue the currency or print new supplies. However, it also means that the government has no control over monetary policy and that the

nation is dependent on the U.S. economy. Many goods which are imported into Panama are more expensive than they would be in the United States. This has created local inflation that is slightly higher than that of the United States: the U.S. **inflation rate** is 3.4 percent, that of Panama can be up to 10 percent higher. Panamanian banks are overseen by the Superintendent of Banks, a government agency whose head is appointed by the president. The agency regulates mortgages, loans, and liens.

POVERTY AND WEALTH

Panama has extremes of wealth and poverty. The wealthiest 20 percent of Panamanians control more than 50 percent of the country's wealth, while the poorest 40 percent only control 12 percent. The wealthiest Panamanians live a lifestyle that is similar to that of many Americans—they have access to **consumer goods** such as cars, televisions, cellular phones, and so forth. However, the majority of the nation's people live in poverty. Government estimates in 1999, classified 48 percent of the nation as living in poverty and 9.8 percent as living in extreme poverty. The *Human Development Report 2000* by the United Nations ranked Panama number 59 out of 172 countries. This places Panama in the middle rankings of countries. The survey measures nations' GDPs, education levels, and standard of living to rate them in comparison with other countries. Many Western, industrialized countries such as the United States, Canada, Norway, and Luxembourg, usually rank among the highest in the survey, while lesser developed nations in the poorer areas of the world rank toward the bottom of the survey. Although Panama has a high GDP per capita, the reality is that most of the income in the country is concentrated among the wealthy few. For instance, in 2000, the nation's per capita GDP was US$3,513. However, most poor people earn less than the average. A worker making minimum wage in some areas of Panama would only earn US$2,080 per year. Regulations on the minimum wage, social security provisions, and working conditions are rarely enforced by the government which means that many workers are unable to earn even the minimum wage.

Exchange rates: Panama

balboas (B) per US$1

Jan 2001	1.0000
2000	1.0000
1999	1.0000
1998	1.0000
1997	1.0000
1996	1.0000

Note: Currency is fixed at 1 balboa per US$.

SOURCE: CIA *World Factbook 2001* [ONLINE].

GDP per Capita (US$)

Country	1975	1980	1985	1990	1998
Panama	2,572	2,709	2,887	2,523	3,200
United States	19,364	21,529	23,200	25,363	29,683
Mexico	3,380	4,167	4,106	4,046	4,459
Costa Rica	2,231	2,482	2,176	2,403	2,800

SOURCE: United Nations. *Human Development Report 2000; Trends in human development and per capita income.*

Distribution of Income or Consumption by Percentage Share: Panama

Lowest 10%	1.2
Lowest 20%	3.6
Second 20%	8.1
Third 20%	13.6
Fourth 20%	21.9
Highest 20%	52.8
Highest 10%	35.7

Survey year: 1997
Note: This information refers to expenditure shares by percentiles of the population and is ranked by per capita expenditure.

SOURCE: *2000 World Development Indicators* [CD-ROM].

Poverty in Panama tends to be concentrated in specific geographic regions. For instance, the nation's second largest city, Colón, has the highest rates of poverty and crime in the Panama. Unemployment among youth (ages 15 to 25) in Colón is estimated to be 50 percent. There are also high levels of drug use, and Panama is often cited as one of the main areas for the shipment of drugs from South America to the United States.

Among the poorest in Panama are the indigenous native peoples, who make up about 8 percent of the population (194,000). Native Americans suffer from malnutrition and higher levels of disease and illiteracy. This minority tends to live in the more remote areas of the nation where access to education and health care is limited. In addition, the Native Americans face discrimination in hiring and educational opportunities. Minority groups, including ethnic Chinese and Indian, also face discrimination.

WORKING CONDITIONS

A 1995 law significantly expanded the right of workers to establish unions. However, only about 10 percent of the workforce is unionized. There are over 250 active unions with approximately 80,000 members. Many employees in the **public sector**, including police and healthcare workers, are not allowed to strike. In addition, the 10,000 employees who work for the Panama Canal Authority are also not allowed to strike.

There are laws against child labor, but children between the ages of 12 and 14 may work on farms or as domestic workers. In addition, children as young as 9 are employed in occupations such as street vendors, car washers, or baggers in grocery stores. Nonetheless, the government estimates that the worst excesses of child labor occur in agriculture, especially on coffee, sugar cane, and banana plantations. Children between the ages of 14 and 16 may be employed with a 36-hour workweek. The national workweek is 48 hours with a minimum one day rest period per week. The Ministry of Labor is responsible for overseeing worker health and safety issues.

Panama has the highest minimum wage in Central America. The nation's minimum wage varies from province to province and ranges from US$0.80 percent per hour to US$1.50 per hour. The highest wage is in the capital region, the lowest is in the rural regions. The government of President Mireya Elisa Moscoso Rodriguez plans to increase the minimum wage by 40 percent by 2005. In spite of the minimum wage, most workers in the rural areas only earn between US$3 to US$6 per day. Government estimates are that as much as 39 percent of the population earns less than the minimum wage. Women earn an average of 20 percent less than men do in similar occupations. Women also face discrimination in hiring and promotion.

COUNTRY HISTORY AND ECONOMIC DEVELOPMENT

10,000–20,000 B.C. Panama is settled by Native-Americans.

1501 A.D. Rodrigo de Bastidas is the first European to explore the isthmus of Panama.

Household Consumption in PPP Terms

Country	All food	Clothing and footwear	Fuel and power[a]	Health care[b]	Education[b]	Transport & Communications	Other
Panama	22	8	18	14	4	7	27
United States	13	9	9	4	6	8	51
Mexico	30	6	4	2	7	5	46
Costa Rica	N/A	N/A	N/A	N/A	N/A	N/A	N/A

Data represent percentage of consumption in PPP terms.
[a]Excludes energy used for transport.
[b]Includes government and private expenditures.

SOURCE: World Bank. *World Development Indicators 2000.*

1510. First Spanish colony is established at Nombre de Dios.

1513. Vasco Nunez de Balboa reaches the Pacific Ocean by crossing the isthmus.

1534. Charles I of Spain orders the first survey for a potential canal through Panama.

1538–1821. Panama is the crossroads of Spanish trade in Central and South America. The region is known as the Camino Real or Royal Road since it is the point of departure for gold and silver shipments to Spain.

1821. Panama gains independence from Spain as part of the new nation of Colombia.

1846. Colombia signs treaty with the United States to allow the American construction of a railway across the isthmus.

1848. The discovery of gold in California leads thousands of Americans to travel across Panama in an effort to shorten their trip to the gold mines.

1870. U.S. President Ulysses S. Grant appoints a commission to examine the possibility of constructing a canal across Central America.

1880–1900. A French company undertakes an unsuccessful effort to build a canal across Panama. During the attempt, some 22,000 people die as a result of malaria and other tropical diseases.

1903. With U.S. support, Panama becomes independent. The United States begins work on the Panama Canal.

1905. Yellow fever is eradicated in Panama.

1906. Theodore Roosevelt becomes the first president to leave the continental United States while in office when he visits Panama to observe progress on the canal.

1914. The canal is completed at a cost to the United States of US$375 million making it the most expensive construction project in the nation's history at the time.

1921. The United States pays Colombia US$25 million in compensation for American support of the Panamanian revolution. The completed canal has 4 times the volume that was envisioned by the original French plan.

1968. The civilian government is overthrown by a military coup.

1972. A new constitution is adopted.

1977. The United States and Panama conclude the Torrijos-Carter Treaty to turn control of the canal over to Panama. Under the terms of the Treaty, the United States retains the right to defend the canal. Also under

the terms of the accord, tolls are increased by 29.3 percent.

1983. Reforms are enacted to the constitution.

1984. Manuel Noriega becomes dictator of Panama.

1987. In response to Noreiga's actions, the United States suspends aid to Panama.

1989. After invalidating legal elections, Noriega is ousted from power by a U.S. military invasion. Noriega is taken to the United States and tried for drug-smuggling. He is convicted and sentenced to 40 years in prison. The legally-elected president is restored to power.

1993. The Interoceanic Region Authority is established to promote commercial development in the Canal Zone.

1994. The military is abolished through a constitutional amendment, and additional reforms are added to the constitution to ensure democracy.

1996. Panama joins the WTO.

1999. The canal is transferred to Panamanian control.

FUTURE TRENDS

The potential economic benefits of the Panama Canal are substantial. However, in order to capitalize on this potential, the nation needs a significant amount of investment. This is problematic since the current government has announced an end to privatization programs and many foreign firms are unwilling to invest new monies into Panama until there is further privatization. The loss of income from American forces in the Canal Zone will continue to impact the economy for some years. There is also widespread domestic pressure to increase tariffs that were lowered in order to join the WTO. A rise in tariffs could significantly harm foreign trade. The wide gaps between the rich and poor in the nation may mean future political instability. The country's high unemployment rate poses the same threat. The nation's high foreign debt also continues to constrain the economy by forcing the government to pay over US$740 million per year in debt payments.

There is international support to widen the canal to allow 2-way traffic by large vessels which is expected to increase traffic by 20 percent. The government has a US$1.3 billion fund as a reserve to provide increased social spending to compensate for the loss of funds associated with the American presence in the Canal zone. In addition, the government has received loans from the Inter-American Development Band to help develop rural areas (the most significant being a US$18 million loan to improve infrastructure in the Darien province). The commitment of the government to the development of new, and the expansion of existing, free trade areas means that the nation will continue to attract new foreign investment and new businesses.

DEPENDENCIES

Panama has no territories or colonies.

BIBLIOGRAPHY

Economist Intelligence Unit. *Country Profile: Panama.* London: Economist Intelligence Unit, 2001.

Major, John. *Prize Possession: The United States and the Panama Canal, 1903–1979.* New York: Cambridge University Press, 1993.

U.S. Central Intelligence Agency. *World Factbook 2000.* <http://www.odci.gov/cia/publications/factbook/index.html>. Accessed August 2001.

U.S. Department of State. *Background Notes: Panama.* <http://www.state.gov/www/background_notes/panama_0100_bgn.html>. Accessed April 2001.

———. *FY 2001 Country Commercial Guide: Panama.* <http://www1.usatrade.gov/Website/CCG.nsf/ShowCCG?OpenForm&Country=Panama>. Accessed April 2001.

———. "Panama." *1999 Country Reports on Human Rights Practices.* <http://www.state.gov/www/global/human_rights?1999_hrp_report/panama.html>. Accessed April 2001.

Zimbalist, Andrew, and John Weeks. *Panama at the Crossroads: Economic Development and Political Change in the Twentieth Century.* Berkeley: University of California Press, 1991.

—Tom Lansford

PARAGUAY

Republic of Paraguay
República del Paraguay

CAPITAL: Asunción.

MONETARY UNIT: Guaraní (G). Coins are in denominations of G500, G100, 50, 10, and 5. Paper currency is in denominations of G100,000, G50,000, 10,000, 5,000, and 1,000.

CHIEF EXPORTS: Soybeans, feed, cotton, meat, and edible oils.

CHIEF IMPORTS: Road vehicles, consumer goods, tobacco, petroleum products, and electrical machinery.

GROSS DOMESTIC PRODUCT: US$26.2 billion (purchasing power parity, 2000 est.).

BALANCE OF TRADE: Exports: US$3.5 billion (1999 est.). **Imports:** US$3.3 billion (2000 est.).

COUNTRY OVERVIEW

LOCATION AND SIZE. Paraguay is located in the center of the southern half of South America, northeast of Argentina. It is also bordered by Bolivia to the northwest and Brazil to the east. With an area of 406,750 square kilometers (157,046 square miles), Paraguay is almost as large as the state of California. Asunción, the nation's capital, is situated on the easternmost point of the Argentine border, just south of the center of Paraguay. The nation is landlocked, which sets it apart from virtually all of Latin America, and could be seen as a detriment to the nation's economy. Major cities that provide river ports, such as Asunción, Villeta, and Encarnación (both to the south of Asunción), help to alleviate the economic consequences of the nation's lack of coastline. Ciudad del Este, a commercial center on the Parana River, is another important city to the east of the capital. Paraguay's Argentine border to the southwest measures 1,880 kilometers (1,168 miles), its Bolivian border is 750 kilometers (466 miles), and the Brazilian border is 1,290 kilometers (802 miles).

POPULATION. Recent estimates place the population of Paraguay at 5,734,139 (July 2001). Due to its Spanish colonization and heritage, at least 90 percent of the pop-

ulation is Roman Catholic and 95 percent of the population is mestizo (a racial mix of Spanish and Amerindian) This makes the population surprisingly homogenous in comparison to most of Latin America. The mestizo population has strong pride in their Guaraní (the primary indigenous group and culture of Paraguay) ancestry and traditions. Spanish was the only official language until 1992 when Guaraní also became an official language. Guaraní is spoken by approximately 90 percent of the population. Spanish is used predominantly in business and government matters, but both languages are utilized in education. At least half of the population is bilingual.

People between the ages of 0 and 14 make up 39 percent of the population, while those between the ages of 15 and 64 constitute 56 percent. At least half of this second age group is below 30 years of age, making two-thirds of the population younger than 30. The population of Paraguay grew from 2.4 million to 4.3 million between 1970 and 1990 (80 percent), and grew 30 percent from 1990 to 2000. With a yearly population growth rate of 2.6 percent as of 2001, the population is estimated to reach 6,980,000 by 2010. The average life expectancy of the population is 73.92 years (2001 est.).

Migration to the urban areas of Paraguay is common, but more than half of the nation's population still lives in rural areas, mostly in the east. Only about 5 percent of the population lives west of the Paraguay River. High rates of **emigration** from 1950 to 2000 have contributed to the large percentage (40 percent) of Paraguayans living outside their country and help to alleviate the high growth rate. Many Paraguayans have historically emigrated to Argentina, particularly during and after the Chaco War of 1936 and the Civil War of 1947, and also during the 1950s and 1970s. Paraguay has one of the world's lowest population densities. The nation's most densely populated area is Asunción and its surroundings.

The Colorado Party's clientelistic agrarian reform (giving unused land outside of Asunción to the party's supporters in exchange for political favors or funding) of the 1960s helped to alleviate overcrowding in the capital by drawing peasant labor into previously unused territory. However, the effects were not lasting and overcrowding is still a problem today.

One of the most surprising features of the Paraguayan population is its high literacy rate of more than 92 percent despite its poorly-developed education system. School is mandatory only between the ages of 7 and 13 and this requirement is not well enforced. There are in-

sufficient numbers of primary and secondary schools and severe shortages of educational resources, especially in rural areas. The shortage is worst at the secondary level. There are only 2 universities, vocational schools are concentrated in the main cities, and there is a severe shortage of teaching resources throughout the nation.

OVERVIEW OF ECONOMY

Paraguay's geographic location has had a large impact on its economic development. Being one of only two landlocked nations in all of South America, Paraguay has had to rely on its rivers for transportation and trade routes and has developed a sufficient network of roads, highways, railways, and airports to increase trade possibilities. The Paraguay and Parana Rivers provide direct routes to the Atlantic Ocean through Brazilian territory, and the U.S., Japan, Germany, Italy, and the Netherlands now use these routes for imports and exports. Paraguay has also turned to its rivers for a power source. In fact, due to its substantial hydroelectric power, the nation is on its way to becoming one of the world's largest producers of power. In addition to commerce and power production, Paraguay also relies on agriculture, but only one-fifth of the nation's land is arable and even less is actually farmed. Still, almost half of the nation's workforce is in agriculture and particularly **subsistence farming** (growing only enough to survive). The country is self-sufficient in food production, but the agricultural sector has suffered from unpredictable weather and climate conditions and changing world market prices.

Paraguay also relies heavily on Ciudad del Este, the world's third-largest **retail** center. This city is a border town on the Parana River (on the Brazilian border) and as a result is susceptible to heavy smuggling. Crime is also a serious problem there and the police force of Ciudad del Este is suspected of widespread corruption. Storeowners have hired guards to monitor their stores around the clock, and these guards outnumber police officers by more than 5 to 1. The mayor even has 4 bodyguards at all times. Theft is prevalent. Crime is a less extreme problem in Asunción.

Paraguay has strong commerce, power, agriculture, and retail sectors, but most of the economy's strengths tend to be focused in small areas. The retail sector is concentrated in Ciudad del Este, tourism is concentrated in the capital, and the power industry, trade, and transport are concentrated along the Paraguay and Parana Rivers. Despite these specific areas with strong, focused economic sectors, Paraguay is still one of South America's less-developed nations in an economic sense.

General Alfredo Stroessner, president from 1954 to 1989, encouraged private investment at both domestic and international levels, especially in commercial agriculture ventures. He emphasized cotton and soybean production through government favors in terms of land and money. Before the 1970s, public investment was low and focused mainly on the expansion of **infrastructure** and communications, but after the 1970s, several new state-owned businesses increased **public sector** spending and employment rates. During the 1970s and early 1980s, Paraguay offset its crippling **foreign debt** and **trade deficit** with international loans, but paying back these loans in the years to come weakened the national economy. The economic growth of the 1970s did not benefit the entire nation equitably, but did benefit the police and

military, as well as the upper class involved in business, agro-industry, and industry. The military and the agro-industrial elite both had ties to the Colorado Party in power. The working class was held back by low wages and limitations placed on the activities of labor unions.

Foreign investment has played a substantial role in Paraguay's economic growth, particularly in the 1970s and 1980s. **Joint ventures** with Brazil and Argentina in building hydroelectric power plants gave Paraguay a surplus of power and made it a leading power producer. Also, the government tried to attract foreign investors through low **income taxes** and tax exemptions during this time.

The years of President Andres Rodriguez (1989–93) were marked by reforms implemented to ensure transition to a market economy. He abolished the multiple **exchange rates**, low-cost **subsidies** to state enterprises, and export taxes. He also **privatized** several state enterprises and broke up state **monopolies** in telephone, water, and energy. Ecuador's airline, Cielos de America, bought 80 percent of the national Paraguayan airline; the remaining 20 percent was reserved for employees. The trade deficit caused by the international loans of the early 1980s was severely exaggerated by inaccurate figures stemming from large-scale smuggling, until Rodriguez's reforms weakened the causes of smuggling.

The 1990s were marked by substantial foreign investment in the form of **multinational corporations**. Joint ventures using foreign capital to spur domestic development include hydroelectric power plants built with Argentina and Brazil, cotton mills and spinning plants built with Italy and Brazil, and foreign oil companies searching for possible drilling sites. The late 1990s have been a time of consolidation in the transition to a market economy, but the national economy is still underdeveloped in comparison to other Latin American nations.

POLITICS, GOVERNMENT, AND TAXATION

According to the 1992 Constitution, Paraguay is a representative democracy that embraces separation of powers. The government has 3 branches: the legislative, the executive, and the judiciary. The legislative branch, called the Congress, is comprised of the Senate (with at least 45 members) and the Chamber of Deputies (with at least 80 members). Members of Congress are popularly elected from Paraguay's 17 departments (states) for 5-year terms that coincide with the president's 5-year term. The president is chief executive and Commander in Chief of both the armed forces and the police. Emergency powers to declare a state of exception (suspending the constitution) in times of war or unrest belong to both the president and Congress.

The judiciary includes a Supreme Court of 9 Supreme Court Justices, who are appointed by the president and the Senate for 5-year terms, which are renewable. Judges cannot be removed after 2 consecutive terms until they reach retirement age. The Supreme Court controls its own budget and heads a system of lower courts and magistrates.

On the local level, each of the 17 departments popularly elects a governor and a departmental board, as well as local mayors. The Electoral Code ensures that everyone over 18 years of age votes, and congressional seats are filled by a **proportional representation** system (a proportional representation system ensures that one area of the nation is not over-represented or under-represented in comparison to another in terms of population).

The Paraguayan government has played a large role in the nation's economy, most notably in the last half of the 20th century. In the 1960s, the government used incentives to encourage the settlement of undeveloped or unused rural areas, to alleviate overcrowding in the Asunción metropolis, and to stave off Brazilian territorial advance (Brazil and Paraguay have a history of border disputes) in the area. Most of the land sold during this agrarian reform was to people with connections to the ruling Colorado Party. These landowners produced large quantities of soybeans for profitable international agro-industries. Also when the Colorado Party replaced the Liberals in power in 1954, officials directed government favors and funds to soybean and cotton producers, which developed a strong system of clientelism. While the Colorado Party is responsible for the birth of heavy cotton and soybean production, which spurred growth in the agricultural sector and now account for two-thirds of all agricultural exports, it also encouraged the widespread exploitation of peasant labor. The party's clientelistic focus on the elite widened the gap between the small upper class and the poor masses. The Colorado Party, which has strong military ties, has dominated Paraguayan politics and government for the last half of the 20th century.

Beginning in the 1970s, the Stroessner government (1954–89) used low income taxes and tax exemptions to attract foreign capital and foreign investment. The government handed out state subsidies for farming as well. The Rodriguez government (1989–93) continued to encourage foreign investment while implementing market reforms, beginning in 1989. Rodriguez put an end to the multiple exchange rates, expensive subsidies for state enterprises, and export taxes. The government also privatized several important state-run companies.

The Stroessner government placed strict controls on labor unions and maintained low minimum wages. As a result of Paraguayan labor laws, the U.S. placed trade restrictions on Paraguay but continued to trade with the country as a part of its Cold War policy. Labor union activism was low in Paraguay until the very late 1980s, when unions began to garner more political influence. As several labor unions emerged, particularly the Unitary Workers Central, the United States and Paraguay reinstated the Generalized System of Preferences (GSP). The GSP is a trade incentive package making trade between developed nations and developing nations profitable for each party. The 1990s spurred the Paraguayan Workers Confederation and the National Workers Central, and these 3 unions are now strong political interest groups in Paraguay. The new Constitution of 1992 embraced workers' rights, protecting the right to strike and the freedom of association.

The 1990s have been a decade of fast political changes including: an attempted coup, President Cubas's implication in the assassination of his vice president Luis María Argaña, Senate head Luis Gonzalez Macchi stepping up to assume the presidency, and the election of liberal vice president Julio Cesar Franco. Despite this political instability, the 1990s were a decade of heavy government involvement in economics. Paraguay **liberalized** and **deregulated** much of its economy, eliminating foreign exchange controls, reducing **tariffs**, establishing tax incentives and exemptions to stimulate foreign investment, creating a stock market, and restructuring the tax system. Paraguay has South America's least burdensome tax system. There is no personal income tax, business taxes are limited, and there is a **value-added tax** (VAT) of 10 percent. Investors in their first 5 years are eligible for tax exemptions of 95 percent and the **duty-free import** of **capital goods**. Corporate taxes are 30 percent but reinvested profit is only taxed 10 percent, which also encourages long-term investment and growth.

Today, there are 2 main political parties, each of which is an alliance: the Colorado Party (formally called the National Republican Association/Colorado Party) and the Democratic Alliance, which includes the EN (Encuentro Nacional) and the PLRA (Partido Liberal Radical Auténtico), a left-wing radical party. Both the Colorado Party and the Democratic Alliance formally support social equality and oppose the exploitation of the working class. The focus on working class economic issues has been magnified in the 1990s, as labor unions and organizations have gained power.

INFRASTRUCTURE, POWER, AND COMMUNICATIONS

In economic terms, Paraguay has depended heavily on its rivers, especially in the 20th century. Waterways provide 3,100 kilometers (1,926 miles) of transport paths. Most international trade flows through the Paraguay and Parana Rivers, which connect Asunción to the Atlantic

Communications

Country	Newspapers	Radios	TV Sets[a]	Cable subscribers[a]	Mobile Phones[a]	Fax Machines[a]	Personal Computers[a]	Internet Hosts[b]	Internet Users[b]
	1996	1997	1998	1998	1998	1998	1998	1999	1999
Paraguay	43	182	101	N/A	41	N/A	9.6	2.4	20
United States	215	2,146	847	244.3	256	78.4	458.6	1,508.77	74,100
Brazil	40	444	316	16.3	47	3.1	30.1	18.45	3,500
Uruguay	293	607	241	N/A	60	N/A	91.2	38.34	300

[a]Data are from International Telecommunication Union, *World Telecommunication Development Report 1999* and are per 1,000 people.
[b]Data are from the Internet Software Consortium (http://www.isc.org) and are per 10,000 people.
SOURCE: World Bank. *World Development Indicators 2000.*

Ocean through Brazilian territory. These 2 rivers have helped alleviate the consequences of Paraguay's land-locked location. Paraguay's Flota Mercante del Estado, a merchant marine owned and operated by the state, has transported cargo on the Paraguay and Parana Rivers since 1945.

Towards the end of the 20th century, more and more freight has been carried along roads, notably to Buenos Aires, Argentina, and Santos and Paranaguá in Brazil. Paraguay has a sufficient network of roads and bridges, but about half of the roads are still unpaved. 15,000 of the 29,500 kilometers of roads were paved as of 1999. Major highways connect Asunción to Ciudad del Este, Paranaguá, and Encarnación. Another highway runs from Villa Hayes across the Chaco region to the Bolivian border.

Paraguay's railway system is limited. The railway Ferrocarril Presidente Carlos Antonio López, which stretches 441 kilometers (274 miles) from Asunción to Encarnación, makes up much of the railway system in Paraguay. Railways total 971 kilometers (603 miles), which includes privately-owned railways as well. The nation's airport network, however, is much broader. With 937 airports, Paraguay's most notable airports are the government-owned Líneas Aéreas Paraguayas, opened in 1962, and the modern international Silvio Pettirossi, established in 1980 near Asunción. Only 11 airports had paved runways as of 2000. Combined, Paraguay's network of roads, rivers, railways, and airports facilitates its strong trade and transport industry.

Paraguay has substantial economic potential in hydroelectric power, which accounted for 99.79 percent of the nation's electricity in 1999. Paraguay depended on thermoelectric power plants, located in the capital, that burned wood and oil until 1968. That year, the Acaray hydroelectric power plant was built, and there have also been large joint ventures in hydroelectricity with Argentina and Brazil. The government-owned National Power Company distributes all electricity.

The communications network in Paraguay is limited in terms of its population size. There is insufficient telephone service and poor connections outside of Asunción and its surrounding area. Still, much of the population has access to newspapers, radios, and televisions, and depends on them for news and information. The nation has 4 television stations (2001), 79 radio stations (1997), and 4 Internet service providers (1999). Foreign investment has pushed the communications technology of the nation ahead in recent years. In the mid-1990s, for example, PanAmSat signed a 15-year contract with 2 Paraguayan television stations to provide satellite service.

ECONOMIC SECTORS

In Paraguay, while agriculture contributes 28 percent of the GDP, 21 percent comes from industry and 51 percent comes from services (1999 est.). Some 45 percent of the population depends on agriculture, particularly subsistence farming. Agricultural concentrations include

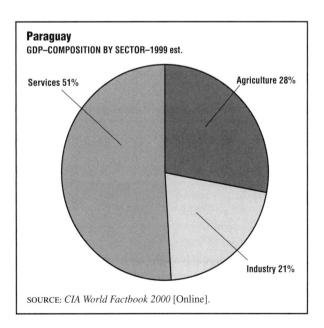

Paraguay
GDP–COMPOSITION BY SECTOR–1999 est.

Services 51%
Agriculture 28%
Industry 21%

SOURCE: *CIA World Factbook 2000* [Online].

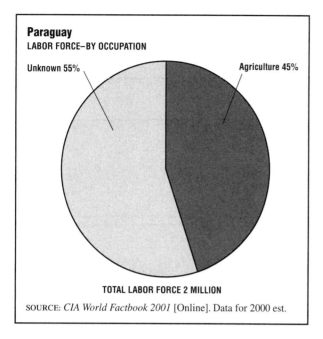

Paraguay
LABOR FORCE– BY OCCUPATION

Unknown 55%

Agriculture 45%

TOTAL LABOR FORCE 2 MILLION

SOURCE: *CIA World Factbook 2001* [Online]. Data for 2000 est.

livestock, lumber, and a variety of crops, which depend heavily on the varying climate and conditions. The industrial sector experienced a boom in hydroelectric power and construction during 1980, but since then hydroelectricity accounts for most of the industrial sector output. Trade and transport dominate the service sector, which has yet to fully realize its potential in areas such as banking and tourism. The tourist industry is developing in Asunción, but outside of the capital, tourism is virtually nonexistent.

AGRICULTURE

Agriculture provides 28 percent of Paraguay's GDP, but 45 percent of the population actually depends on agriculture and subsistence farming. This agricultural activity utilizes less than 6 percent of the nation's most arable land, concentrated in the east. Until 1970, the nation depended heavily on the production of meat, tobacco, and yerba maté (a tea). These highly-emphasized products have now been replaced by soybeans and cotton grown largely in the east.

Soybean production became important during the agrarian reform policies of the 1960s. The government sold cheap land to affiliates of the Colorado Party, which dominated the government at that time. These landowners were involved in highly profitable international agro-industrial agreements that called for large-scale production of soybeans. The government claimed that the agrarian reform would help alleviate overcrowding in the capital while developing unused land in the east. Cotton also emerged as a dominant export. The Colorado Party encouraged cotton production through government fa-

vors, but in the process encouraged the exploitation of peasant laborers as well. Nevertheless, soybeans and cotton now account for two-thirds of the nation's agricultural exports.

Cotton produced in Paraguay had generally been exported unprocessed until the 1990s. In the mid-1990s, an Italian-Paraguayan group built a US$10 million computerized cotton-spinning plant just outside of Asunción. Spinning the cotton domestically adds 140 percent profit to its export. It is exported primarily to Italy and Brazil. Brazilian investors have also built and renovated many other cotton mills in Paraguay. If the cotton industry continues to develop and farming is mechanized, many rural farmers who grow cotton may be put out of work.

Other important agricultural goods include coffee, corn, rice, wheat, citrus fruits, sugarcane, and peanuts. Paraguay produces some marijuana as well. Paraguay's productive agricultural sector makes the nation practically self-sufficient in food products.

Livestock is raised in the west, particularly in the Chaco region. Though pigs, sheep, horses, and chickens are raised, by far the most important livestock is cattle. Meat, dairy products, and hides are used both domestically and for export. Timber is another important export. Though Paraguay has utilized its rivers for transport, it has not yet developed a commercial fishing industry to tap into the abundance of fish.

INDUSTRY

Despite high industrial growth rates in the late 1970s and 1980s, manufacturing and mining have remained undeveloped. Paraguay manufactures little more than its own food products. The industrial boom climaxed in the middle of 1979 and was centered in hydroelectric power and related construction projects. Today the industry sector accounts for 21 percent of the national GDP. Of that 21 percent of GDP, more than 75 percent comes from the manufacturing of such goods as cement, sugar, textiles, beverages, and wood products. Manufacturing provides jobs for 13 percent of the **workforce**. Fully manufactured exports account for only 5 percent of all exports, but semi-processed agricultural goods make up 72 percent of all exports.

ENERGY. Paraguay's energy industry has thrived on its hydroelectric potential. Hydroelectric power replaced thermo power (power from burning wood and oil) around 1970. In 1968, Asunción's Acary hydroelectricity plant began operating, and in 1973 Paraguay and Brazil together built the US$20 billion Itaipu plant by the Parana River. This joint venture made history as Brazil bore most of the cost and Paraguayan electricity production grew 15-fold from 1970 to 1990. Initial arrangements that benefited Brazil were later modified in 1985 to ensure that Paraguay received fair compensation. Paraguay also built a dam on the Parana to create a reservoir that spans a total of 870 miles in Paraguay and Brazil. The 1990s were marked by Paraguay's joint venture with Argentina to build a hydroelectric power plant on a chain of islands in the Parana. Combined, Paraguay's ventures in hydroelectric power have ensured that the nation will become one of the world's top producers of hydroelectric power in the 21st century.

In 1999, Paraguay generated 51.554 billion kilowatt hours (bkwh) per year, but only consumed 1.915 bkwh that year. In 1999, Paraguay sold 46.03 bkwh of power for export, primarily to Brazil and Argentina, making power a large source of export earnings. Itaípu's earnings reached a record US$420 million in 1998 (equal to 15 percent of all exports) and Brazil purchased 97 percent of the plant's power. Several plans (including joint ventures with Argentina and Brazil) are being developed for expanding existing hydroelectric power plants and constructing new ones in the coming decade.

CONSTRUCTION. In the late 1970s and early 1980s, construction grew rapidly, with a drastic rise in hydroelectric dam and power plant projects, infrastructure projects, and housing development in Asunción. The construction industry's resources were primarily found locally: lime, sand, wood, and stones. Since the mid 1980s, however, construction has fluctuated dramatically as old hydroelectric power plants and infrastructure projects were completed and then new projects were begun.

In response to a growing construction industry, the nation has invested large sums of money in expanding and modernizing the production of cement, metal, and steel. The government completed a US$200 million expansion of its largest cement plant, at Vallemi, in 1986. The plant had previously used outdated production techniques and had been operating well under capacity. This expansion was financed by French banks, but ended up burdening the economy since it still operated well below capacity and was over 500 kilometers outside of Asunción, far from most industrial activity. The government also owned Acepar, the largest steel plant, in the 1980s. Acepar alone is capable of producing 5 times the amount of steel Paraguay uses each year, and there are other large steel producers in the nation as well. Unfortunately, most development in construction-related industries like cement and steel took place after most of the nation's biggest hydroelectric and infrastructure projects. However, similar projects in the late 1990s and early 2000s are capitalizing on these industries.

MANUFACTURING. Manufacturing of steel, cement, plastic, and wood products has risen since the late 1970s due to construction projects (hydroelectric power plants, infrastructure, and urban housing). Fully manufactured exports account for only 5 percent of all exports, but semi-processed agricultural goods make up 72 percent of all exports. Still, manufacturing is underdeveloped in Paraguay, and is characterized by many small- or medium-sized firms. The few larger firms are primarily foreign owned, and few companies operate at full capacity. Food, beverages, and tobacco have formed the largest manufacturing subsector; agriculture and lumber manufactures form the second-largest subsector; and textiles, clothing, leather, and shoes form the third.

MINING. Paraguay also has a small, undeveloped mining industry, concentrated along the Paraguay River where most mineral deposits have been found. Gypsum, limestone, and clays are the most heavily used minerals and are exported mostly to the building trade. Other major minerals near the river include peat, marble, salt, copper, bauxite, iron, and uranium. Other regions of the nation that have not been fully utilized show deposits of manganese, malachite, azurite, feldspar, mica, and talc. Though resources are varied and local construction mines many resources itself, the mining industry still has not been fully developed.

SERVICES

The service sector accounts for 51 percent of the nation's total GDP. The most vital component of the service sector is trade and transport. In terms of trade the nation has profited greatly from its 2 major rivers, the Paraguay and the Parana, particularly in the last half of the 20th century. Other service industries do not yet play a significant role in the national economy. The finance industry is small and state-dominated, and the nation has not yet established a profitable tourism industry. With the exception of a small but developing tourism industry in Asunción, tourism-related business is virtually nonexistent and plays an insignificant role in the economy elsewhere.

TRADE AND TRANSPORT. The Paraguay and Parana Rivers have allowed Paraguay to overcome its landlocked handicap in terms of trade and commerce. The 2 rivers join Paraguay to the Atlantic Ocean through Brazilian territory and allow for the export of such items as soybeans, cotton, meat, and timber. Aside from neighboring partners Brazil and Argentina, Paraguay's principal trading partners are in Europe: Germany, Italy, the Netherlands, and Switzerland. Paraguay also imports from Japan and the United States. All of these export and import partners utilize the Paraguay and the Parana trade routes. The nation's numerous airports, as well as its rail and highway networks, facilitate the development of this sector of the economy. Perhaps the most profitable variety of trade in Paraguay is re-export. Paraguay is widely known for its re-exporting of goods: over 50 percent of all goods imported are then re-exported for profit, with little or no change made to them. Smugglers also use this practice in the **informal economy**.

RETAIL. Paraguay has a developing retail sector in the capital, but the biggest retail center lies in Ciudad del Este, a city on the Brazilian border. Ciudad del Este grew out of a merchants' town and now has more than 6,000 shops over 20 blocks in the heart of the downtown area alone. The streets are heavily peppered with tiny shops, table vendors, and even van vendors and walking vendors. These "shops" are responsible for at least one-third of all money circulating in Paraguay, and have put, on average, US$1 billion in Paraguayan merchandise into Brazil each month during the 1990s. The richest city in the nation, Ciudad del Este is the world's third-largest commercial center, behind only Miami and Hong Kong. Ciudad del Este has a large Asian population, with Chinese who specialize in toys, house wares, and school supplies, and Koreans who specialize in electronics. The city is also responsible for a great deal of trade with Eastern Asia. The smuggling of goods into Brazil and other countries is a big problem, though. Outside of Ciudad del Este, the retail sector in Paraguay is not well developed.

FINANCE. The finance sector of Paraguay is underdeveloped. There are 2 main state banks: the Banco Central del Paraguay and the Banco Nacional de Fomento. The latter specifically handles credits and grants to agricultural ventures and entities in the manufacturing and lumber industries. Some international banks from other parts of Latin America, Europe, and the United States also have branches in Paraguay. The government encourages foreign investment and in the 1990s began developing a stock market, but there is still much more potential for growth in the finance sector.

TOURISM. Tourism in Paraguay has developed very little outside of Asunción, despite the potential of attractions such as Ciudad del Este's retail area and ruins of Jesuit missions. The nation has only 11,000 beds (more than half in Asunción), 34 percent of which are in luxury or five-star hotels, and 52 percent of which are in three- or four-star hotels. Small establishments account for the remainder. Tourism brought in US$144 million annually in the late 1990s. Just over 400,000 tourists visit Paraguay each year, 70 percent of which come from Brazil, Argentina, and Uruguay. **Ecotourism**—tourism that focuses on nature and wildlife observation—is also growing.

INTERNATIONAL TRADE

Paraguay's main trading partners are Brazil, Argentina, the United States, the Netherlands, Germany, Italy, Japan, and Switzerland. Paraguay exports soybeans, meat products, cotton, oils, and timber principally to

Trade (expressed in billions of US$): Paraguay		
	Exports	Imports
1975	.176	.206
1980	.310	.615
1985	.304	.502
1990	.959	1.352
1995	.919	3.144
1998	N/A	N/A

SOURCE: International Monetary Fund. *International Financial Statistics Yearbook 1999.*

Brazil and Argentina, as well as Germany, the Netherlands, Italy, and Sweden. Exports in 2000 totaled US$3.5 billion (not including the **black market**). Most imports come from Brazil, Argentina, the United States, and Japan, including machinery, petroleum and petroleum products, chemicals, lubricants, electronics, **consumer goods**, and cars. Local industries rely heavily on these imported goods. Imports in 2000 totaled US$3.3 billion (not including the black market). Smuggling has been prevalent in Paraguay, and in the 1980s smuggling reached new heights, severely skewing the nation's official trade figures. Computers, sound equipment, cameras, liquor, and cigarettes are among the most popular items smuggled across the Brazilian and Argentine borders. Smuggling decreased somewhat in the 1990s, but the informal economy is still estimated to be at least as large as the formal economy.

U.S./Paraguayan economic relations are strong as of the early 21st century. Each year the United States imports more than US$40 million of goods from Paraguay and exports approximately US$1billion in goods to Paraguay. The United States has more than a dozen large multinational firms with Paraguayan subsidiaries, including firms in the computer, manufacturing, agro-industrial, banking, and service industries. The U.S. also has more than 75 businesses with agents in Paraguay. The Cold War of the 1970s and 1980s actually worked in Paraguay's favor. Despite numerous human rights violations, Paraguay still received substantial aid and trade privileges from the U.S., provided that Paraguay align itself with the United States against the Soviet Union. The U.S suspended its Generalized System of Preferences—a trade agreement with Paraguay—from 1987 to 1991, due to poor labor laws and working conditions in Paraguay.

Paraguay does belong to several international trade agreements and organizations. Aside from its trade agreement with the U.S., Paraguay also belongs to Mercosur, a free trade and common market agreement between the Southern Cone nations (Paraguay, Uruguay, Argentina, and Brazil). Joining Mercosur in 1991 benefited Paraguay greatly. Trade between Mercosur members increased from US$5 billion in 1991 to US$17 billion in 1996, and the Mercosur market accounted for 5 percent of the world's total GDP in the late 1990s, making the Mercosur market very attractive to foreign investors. Paraguay is a member of the Latin American Integration Association (formerly the Latin American Free Trade Agreement) as well.

MONEY

The Paraguayan currency has been remarkably stable in comparison to most of South America. The most significant hindrance to economic stability in Paraguayan history was the War of the Triple Alliance. This war, from 1865 to 1870, killed most of the nation's male population and devastated the national economy. Soon after, in 1870, the nation began reconstruction efforts and rebuilt the economy. The economy finally found stability again in the late 1910s and early 1920s.

The 1940s and 1950s were marked by price instability, and in response the government established the Banco Central, a central bank intended to perform many tasks. Its responsibilities included regulating credit, promoting economic activity, controlling **inflation**, and issuing currency. It also regulated banks (commercial, investment, and mortgage banks), savings and loans, finance companies and institutions, and capital markets. Further, the bank administered monetary controls and price stability. The Banco Central was successful until the 1980s. The 1970s and early 1980s showed rapid growth attributed to joint hydroelectric power ventures with Argentina and Brazil, but as the power plants were completed, the rapid economic growth came to an abrupt halt. The stable prices, credit expansion, and exchange rates of the 1960s and 1970s were replaced by the increasing inflation in the mid 1980s. By 1988, inflation had risen more than 30 percent. The Central Bank successfully tamed inflation with rising interest rates during the 1990s.

The growth of the 1970s allowed Paraguay to avoid the hyperinflation and the **balance of payments** crises that plagued the rest of the Southern Cone (Brazil, Argentina, and Uruguay). Large exports of soybeans and cotton also helped maintain growth and stability in the economy during this time, with the exception of a brief period from 1981 to 1983, when GDP fell more than 15 percent because of a combination of factors. Adverse weather shrank agricultural exports, currency in neighboring Brazil and Argentina was suffering **devaluation**, and trade relations with Brazil and Argentina were unfavorable.

From 1960 to 1982, the guaraní was consistently valued at 126 guaraní to the U.S. dollar. In 1982 a new foreign exchange system was introduced using multiple **fixed exchange rates**, but the new system was unsuccessful and the government implemented a free market foreign exchange system once again in 1984. The 1984 system, still in effect, strongly favors private enterprise and foreign investors.

The 1990s were a time of mixed results in economic development. The banking system is developing but still small. In 1992, the government approved measures to develop a stock market, and in 1995 Bolsa de Valores, the Asunción Stock Exchange, was created. It showed slower growth than expected at first, but now the stock market has grown and expanded to include many foreign corporations. Countries with companies listed the United States, South Africa, and Japan.

From 1993 to 1995, the **GDP per capita** increased by 18 percent and inflation dropped from 20 percent to 15 percent. In the late 1990s, though, Paraguay suffered from the devaluation of the currencies of other Mercosur member nations, particularly Brazil in 1998 and 1999. Still, the Paraguayan economy shrank only 0.06 percent in response to Brazil's devaluation of the real (Brazilian currency). Paraguay's currency value fluctuated little in the late 1990s, though many economists expected it would, due to severe political instability. The 2000 exchange rate showed G3,502 equal to US$1.

POVERTY AND WEALTH

Paraguay has an extreme gap between the small upper class and the large lower class, and there has historically been virtually no social mobility. Paraguay has the most unequal distribution of land in the region. Less than 10 percent of the population owned and controlled over 75 percent of the nation's land in the late 1990s, leaving much of the large rural population landless and living in extreme poverty. In the mid-1990s, nearly half of the farmers in Paraguay did not own land, according to Ramón López and Alberto Valdés, writing for the World Bank. The upper 10 percent of the population accounts for 46.6 percent of income and consumption, and

Exchange rates: Paraguay	
guarani (G) US$1	
Jan 2001	3,570.0
2000	3,486.4
1999	3,119.1
1998	2,726.5
1997	2,177.9
1996	2,056.8

Note: Since early 1998, the exchange rate has operated as a managed float; prior to that, the exchange rate was determined freely in the market.

SOURCE: CIA *World Factbook 2001* [ONLINE].

GDP per Capita (US$)

Country	1975	1980	1985	1990	1998
Paraguay	1,297	1,871	1,754	1,816	1,781
United States	19,364	21,529	23,200	25,363	29,683
Brazil	3,464	4,253	4,039	4,078	4,509
Uruguay	4,092	4,962	3,964	4,611	6,029

SOURCE: United Nations. *Human Development Report 2000;
Trends in human development and per capita income.*

the upper 20 percent make up 62.4 percent of all income. The poorest 60 percent of the population earns less than 20 percent of the nation's income.

The extreme gap between the small upper class and the large lower class was widened by the clientelism of the Colorado Party during the last 50 years. During the 1960s, by selling most unused land to Colorado Party affiliates, the small elite class came to include a small, newly established agro-industrial elite class. These elites underpaid workers to maximize their own profits. Cotton and soybean producers (the elite landowners) continued to underpay peasant workers well into the 1980s, and the government kept labor unions weak and ineffective. Although the 1990s were a time of newly-developed strength for labor unions, the gap between the rich and the poor did not change significantly.

There are not enough schools or educational resources throughout the nation, but shortages are worst in poor, rural areas. Rural areas also have less effective health care available to them. Virtually all urban areas have access to safe water and good medical care, but only 15 percent of the rural population has access to safe drinking water and only 42 percent of the rural population has access to medical care. Despite these problems, it is important to note that Paraguay's government does subsidize education and health care. The government finances schools and makes teacher training courses available.

Distribution of Income or Consumption by Percentage Share: Paraguay

Lowest 10%	0.7
Lowest 20%	2.3
Second 20%	5.9
Third 20%	10.7
Fourth 20%	18.7
Highest 20%	62.4
Highest 10%	46.6

Survey year: 1995
Note: This information refers to income shares by percentiles of the population and is ranked by per capita income.

SOURCE: *2000 World Development Indicators* [CD-ROM].

Paraguay's Social Insurance Institute (SII) oversees the social security system. Some 9.5 percent of employees' own earnings, 16.5 percent of employers' earnings, and 1.5 percent of government funds go toward social security. The Institute offers pensions for old age, invalidity, maternity, sick leave, and on-the-job injury. The SII also runs its own hospitals and health clinics.

Though as a rule there is little socioeconomic mobility in Paraguay (especially in agriculture), the commercial city of Ciudad del Este is the exception. In Ciudad del Este, a man pushing handcarts can work for US$15 a day, save up enough capital to buy a small spot on the street sidewalk and a table to sell goods. Then he can save enough money to buy a van and gradually work his way up the economic ladder.

WORKING CONDITIONS

The Stroessner government placed strict controls on labor unions and maintained low minimum wages from 1960s through the 1980s. As a result, labor union activism was low in Paraguay until the very late 1980s, when unions began to garner more political influence. As several labor unions emerged around 1990, the Unitary Workers Central, the Paraguayan Workers Confederation, and the National Workers Central all became strong political interest groups in Paraguay. The Paraguayan Workers Confederation (CPT) had 60,000 official members as of 1985, but claimed to represent 90 percent of the workforce. The CPT refused to comply with workers' strikes due to government control, and the union lost its membership in the International Labor Organization (ILO). Despite this new union activism in the 1990s, labor laws have improved very little. Only a small percentage of the workforce receives benefits like pensions, pay in times of illness, and medical care. Wages have only slightly increased in the late twentieth century.

Roughly 45 percent of the labor force works in agriculture, largely in subsistence farming. Though some of these workers receive government subsidies, they have no benefits or security and suffer from the changing climate and the fluctuation of the world market. The few workers who do receive benefits work in urban areas. As of 1998, unemployment had reached 12 percent, up 4 percent from 1996. An increasingly industrialized economy continues to threaten the jobs of farmers, still a considerable portion of the workforce.

Women in the workplace earn substantially less than men do, despite equal or greater education. Women with 6 years of education or less earn only half of men's salaries in equivalent jobs, while women having 7–13 years of education earn only 60–70 percent of men's salaries for the same positions. Women outnumber men in professional and technical occupations, but women occupy only 20 percent of the nation's administration and management jobs and only 5 percent of higher-level occupations. Social security does pay women on maternity leave half of their salary for a period of 12 weeks.

COUNTRY HISTORY AND ECONOMIC DEVELOPMENT

1500s. Paraguay is inhabited by Guaraní Indians before the Spaniards arrive.

1608. Spanish Jesuits take root in Paraguay after several failed colonization attempts. The Jesuits control reducciones (centers of religious conversion for the Guaraní Indians). These settlements are also centers of labor for agricultural production, manufacturing, and trade.

1767. Spanish landowners—envious of the military, political, and economic control of the Jesuits—expel the Jesuits to regain control of the area.

1776. Establishment of Viceroyalty of Rio de la Plata by the Spanish.

1811. Paraguay revolts against Spain to become a republic.

1865–1870. War of the Triple Alliance (against Brazil, Argentina, and Uruguay) decimates Paraguay's male population.

1870. New constitution begins reconstruction after war, but dictatorial oppression continues.

1932–1935. Chaco War against Bolivia: Paraguay wins western territory.

1954. General Alfredo Stroessner becomes president and remains in power until 1989.

1968. Acary power plant begins operation and Paraguay's national power production increases 15-fold from 1970–1990.

1970s. Government encourages foreign investment through tax incentives.

1970s. Soybeans and cotton replace tannin, meat, yerba maté, and tobacco as primary agricultural exports.

1970s-1980s. Despite serious human rights violations under the Stroessner regime, the U.S. continues to provide military aid because of Cold War policy.

1973. Itaipu hydroelectric power plant construction begins (finished in 1982) with Brazilian cooperation.

1980s. Foreign loans accruing interest begin to severely burden the economy.

1987. Generalized System of Preferences (trade agreement with U.S.) suspended because of poor labor laws.

1989. General Andrés Rodríguez leads coup that overthrows the Stroessner regime. Rodríguez becomes president in a multi-candidate election and announces that democracy has come to Paraguay. He enacts sweeping reforms to implement a market economy.

EARLY 1990s. Labor unions begin to grow in numbers and in political influence.

1991. Constituent Assembly elected to draft new constitution.

1991. Paraguay, Uruguay, Argentina, and Brazil sign Mercosur (a free trade agreement among the countries of the Southern Cone). Generalized System of Preferences reinstated between Paraguay and the United States.

1992. New constitution takes effect, making Paraguay a representative democracy. Government approves laws to encourage foreign investment and establish a stock market.

1993. Juan Carlos Wasmosy of the Colorado Party is elected as president. These elections are deemed fair and democratic by the world community.

1995. The Asuncion Stock Exchange, Bolsa de Valores, is established.

1997. Banking crisis strikes due to political corruption.

1998. Raúl Cubas Grau of the Colorado Party elected president in May.

1999. Vice president Luis María Argaña is assassinated in March and President Cubas, implicated, is forced out of office. Luis Gonzalez Macchi, the head of the senate, becomes president.

2000. Julio Cesar Franco of the Liberal Party is elected vice president. This is the Liberal Party's first major victory against the Colorado Party in 50 years.

FUTURE TRENDS

The 1990s were a time of many economic and political changes in Paraguay. The nation has become arguably more democratic and has implemented a market economy system, but still Paraguay remains one of Latin America's more underdeveloped nations in many ways. The future of Paraguay is uncertain: Paraguay faces the challenges of consolidating its semi-democracy and possibly further democratizing while developing its weak economy at the same time. Trade and transport, and imports and exports, continue to carry the Paraguayan economy as development is slow in agriculture, banking, tourism, mining, and industry. Paraguay's membership in Mercosur is beneficial in terms of stability and growth prospects, but the other member nations are apprehensive as to whether or not Paraguay will successfully consolidate its recent democratic and market economy reforms. Spectrum Oil Corporation is currently exploring potential oil sites in and around the Chaco region. Foreign investment is steadily increasing due to government incentives and the size and success of the Mercosur market.

Furthermore, government incentives are designed to keep foreign investors' goods in the Paraguayan market, so foreign companies cannot exploit Paraguayan labor. Labor will not be simply performing tasks contributing to goods being shipped back out of the country to be sold elsewhere. The government also gives larger tax cuts to profits reinvested in the nation, which is conducive to sustaining long-term investment and development. The Paraguayan economy is growing at its most rapid pace since the late 1970s, but the growth rate is slower than some of its neighbors. Overall, prospects are good for economic growth and development in Paraguay's near future.

DEPENDENCIES

Paraguay has no territories or colonies.

BIBLIOGRAPHY

Embajada del Paraguay: Embassy of Paraguay. <http://www.magma.ca/~embapar/index.html>. Accessed March 2001.

Grinbaum, Ricardo. "In Paraguay, Smugglers' Paradise." *World Press Review.* Vol. 43, No. 1, January 1996.

López, Ramón, and Alberto Valdés. *Poverty in Rural Latin America.* Washington, D.C.: World Bank, 1996.

Pagan, Rafael A., Jr. "Paraguay Emerges as a Significant Southern Cone Market." *Business America.* Vol. 116, No. 8, August 1995.

Tradeport. *Paraguay.* <http://www.tradeport.org/ts/countries/paraguay/>. Accessed March 2001.

U.S. Central Intelligence Agency. *World Factbook 2000: Paraguay.* <http://www.odci.gov/cia/publications/factbook/index.html>. Accessed January 2001.

U.S. Department of State Background Notes. *Background Notes: Paraguay.* <http://www.state.gov/www/background_notes/paraguay_0799_bgn.html>. Accessed March 2001.

U.S. Energy Information Administration. *Paraguay.* <http://www.eia.doe.gov/emeu/cabs/paraguay.html>. Accessed March 2001.

U.S. Library of Congress. *Paraguay: A Country Study.* <http://lcweb2.loc.gov/frd/cs/pytoc.html>. Accessed March 2001.

Wilke, James W., editor. *Statistical Abstract of Latin America.* Volume 36. Los Angeles: UCLA Latin American Center Publications, 2000.

—David L. Childree

PERU

Republic of Peru
República del Perú

CAPITAL: Lima.

MONETARY UNIT: The Nuevo Sol (S/.). One nuevo sol equals 100 céntimos. Coins are in denominations of S/.1, 2, 5, and 5, 10, 20, as well as 50 céntimos. Paper currency comes in denominations of S/.10, 20, 50, 100, and 200.

CHIEF EXPORTS: Minerals (gold, zinc, silver, lead, and copper), petroleum and byproducts, fish (fishmeal), agriculture (coffee, asparagus), manufactured goods (textiles).

CHIEF IMPORTS: Machinery and transportation and telecommunication equipment, oil and other petroleum products, agriculture inputs (fertilizers, animal feed), medicines.

GROSS DOMESTIC PRODUCT: US$116 billion (purchasing power parity, 1999 est.).

BALANCE OF TRADE: Exports: US$5.9 billion (f.o.b., 1999 est.). **Imports:** US$8.4 billion (c.i.f., 1999 est.).

COUNTRY OVERVIEW

LOCATION AND SIZE. Peru is located on South America's central Pacific coast. The world's twentieth-largest nation, it borders Bolivia, Brazil, and Chile to the east and south, and Colombia and Ecuador to the north. Lima, the capital, is located on the central coast. Peru's 1,326,074 square kilometers (512,000 square miles) make it roughly the size of Alaska. Lima is approximately the size of Rhode Island.

Peru is divided into 3 distinct geographic regions with a narrow, arid coast, steep Andes Mountains running north to south, and the Amazon jungle in the east. The Amazon covers 57.6 percent of the nation's territory, representing 13.2 percent of the Amazon forest and 7.3 percent of the world's rainforest. The Amazon River system, the world's largest, holds 20 percent of the planet's fresh water. The coastal region represents 10.6 percent of the nation's territory and the highlands 31.8 percent.

Its distinctive geography gives it 84 of the 104 known ecosystems and 28 of the 32 known climate zones, making Peru one of the world's most ecologically diverse nations, according to the **United Nations Development Program** (UNDP).

POPULATION. The population currently stands at 27 million and is growing by 1.75 percent annually, according to estimates for 2000. The birth rate is an estimated 24.48 per 1,000, while the death rate is 5.84 per 1,000. Life expectancy in 2000 was 70 years.

The Peruvian population is extremely young, with 53.8 percent of the population below the age of 25. Only 4 percent of the population is over 65. The majority of Peruvians live in urban areas along the coast, which reflects the general migratory trend in Latin America over the past 60 years. In 1940, 65 percent of the population lived in the highlands, while only 28.3 percent lived along the coast. Today, 52.2 percent live along the coast, 35.7 percent live in the highlands, and 12.1 percent live in the jungle region. Lima is the largest city, home to nearly 8 million people. The second largest city, Arequipa in the southern highlands, is home to 700,000 people.

The largest population group is Amerindian, accounting for 45 percent of the population. The principal Amerindian groups are Quechua and Aymara highland indigenous people. Lowland indigenous groups, representing roughly 350,000 people, are divided into 52 different peoples, the largest of which is the Ashaninkas. Mestizos—mixed Amerindian and Caucasian—represent 37 percent and whites account for 15 percent. The remaining 3 percent of the population is formed principally of blacks, Chinese, and Japanese—descendants of people brought over as slaves or indentured servants. In 2000, Chinese-Peruvians celebrated the 150th anniversary of

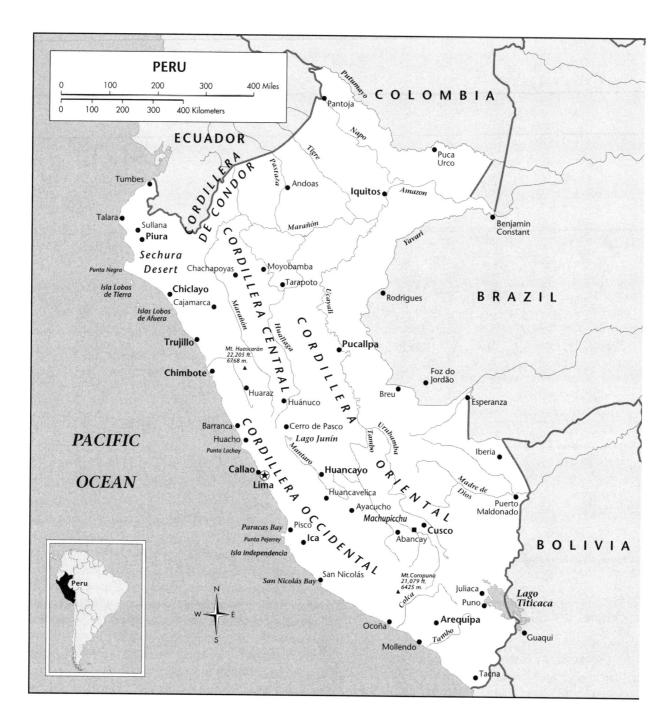

their arrival in Peru, while the Japanese community celebrated its 100th anniversary.

Peru adopted an aggressive family planning program in 1995, which former President Alberto Fujimori announced at the United Nations Women's Summit in Beijing that same year. The plan included free access to birth control and a nationwide education campaign. The Ministry of Women and Human Development was created at the same time. The plan, however, was attacked for employing forced sterilization of women and men, including 300,000 tubal ligations and 100,000 vasectomies. At least 36 deaths were blamed on the sterilization campaign.

Despite the government's efforts, the birth rate did not decline in the second half of the 1990s, remaining at 24.48 per 1,000. (In contrast, the birth rate per 1,000 in the United States is 14.2, a little more than half the Peruvian rate.) The plan came under review in early 2000, and women's rights groups are calling for a "truth commission" to investigate the forced sterilization component.

OVERVIEW OF ECONOMY

Since the Spanish conquest in 1532 and the Declaration of Independence from Spain in 1821, Peru has been a raw material exporting nation that has experienced cycles of short-term export booms and long periods of economic stagnation, the last of which began in 1997. The first major boom was gold and silver, which the Spaniards found in abundant supply in the Inca Empire. The Spaniards sent tons of gold objects home annually. Peru became the principal vice royalty of the Spanish Crown during colonization. In addition to minerals, the Spaniards also brought numerous examples of domesticated plants to Europe. Peru has supplied the world with 120 domesticated plants, the largest number of any country, according to the UNDP.

Minerals have remained the mainstay of the Peruvian export economy, with gold topping the list in the last decade. Peru exported US$1.1 billion in gold in 2000, with the Yanacocha (Cajamarca) and Pierina (Ancash) mines ranked among the top 5 most profitable and productive gold mines in the world, according to the World Gold Council. Peru is the world's eighth-largest gold producer, second in silver and copper, and ranks in the top 5 in zinc and lead.

Other export booms have included guano and rubber, but the cycles were short-lived in the late 19th and early 20th centuries. One export product that has remained important since the early decades of the 20th century is fishing, with fishmeal (used as animal feed and fertilizer) being the chief export in the sector. Peru is the world's leading fishmeal producer, supplying nearly one-third of worldwide production in 2000, according to the Paris-based Fishmeal Exporters' Organization. Fishmeal accounted for US$900 million in exports in 2000. Major agricultural export crops have included coffee, sugar, and cotton. Coffee continues to be a major export, but sugar and cotton exports have crashed, with Peru currently importing both products.

In the 1960s, Peru attempted to break its dependence on exporting raw materials with a new nationalistic approach to economic management-based **import substitution**. Under the leadership of Gen. Juan Velasco, a **socialist** military government took power in 1968, immediately **nationalizing** most industries and implementing a sweeping agrarian reform program that took over all major farmlands, either distributing land to peasant communities or forming cooperatives to run them. The government took control of most industries, including nearly all mines, public services (telephone, electricity, and water), and the media. The government adopted an aggressive import-substitution program, trying to stimulate local production and making imports difficult by applying exorbitant **tariffs**. The Velasco experiment lasted until 1975, when a more conservative military junta (an internal military revolt against a government) overthrew him. The economic model remained basically intact, however, until the late 1980s.

The final years of the statist model were disastrous. Under the leadership of former president Alán García (1985–90), the government attempted to stimulate growth by freezing prices and raising wages, and offering businesses below-market **exchange rates** for exports and imports. The result was 7,600 percent **inflation** (1990), an annual GDP decrease of 5 percent, and depleted reserves.

Peru began changing the economic model with the election of Alberto Fujimori in 1990, adopting an International Monetary Fund-designed (IMF) program that lowered or eliminated most tariffs, **privatized** nearly all state-owned industries and courted foreign investment in banking, telecommunications, and service industries. The program promoted raw material exports, specifically mining—an industry that was offered tax incentives. Along with garments (US$693.6 million in exports in 2000), Peru's principal exports are minerals (49 percent of exports in 2000) and fishmeal. A large percentage of manufactured goods are imported, with the country running a **trade deficit** for 2 decades. The economy became increasingly "dollarized" throughout the 1990s, with 80 percent of bank deposits and 85 percent of debts now in dollars. Industry grew increasingly concentrated in Lima, with approximately 80 percent of manufacturing now based in the capital.

The government is dependent on foreign assistance from multilateral institutions (IMF, World Bank, and Inter-American Development Bank) and foreign governments. The government missed the IMF-set fiscal deficit target of 1.5 percent of GDP in 1999 and 2000. The **foreign debt** (US$31 billion in 1998) represents 56 percent of GDP. Foreign debt payments for 2001 and 2002 total US$3 billion, and the government signed a standby agreement with the IMF in early 2000 that frees up US$1.5 billion to service its debt.

It is difficult to calculate the value of the **black market** in Peru, but the impact is significant. The International Intellectual Property Alliance estimates (1998) that 50 percent of motion pictures, 85 percent of recordings, and 60 percent of computer programs are pirated. Peru's 5 borders make it relatively easy for many manufactured goods to illegally enter the country. In addition, an estimated 10 percent of the country's hundreds of thousands cable television hook-ups are illegal. The largest illicit sector, however, is the drug trade. Peru is the second-most important producer of coca, used to make cocaine, and cocaine itself. Black market money from drug sales and **money laundering** are calculated to be worth between 1 and 2 percent of GDP.

Unemployment, according to the International Labor Organization, stands at 10 percent, but **underemployment** is approximately 60 percent. An estimated 54 percent of the population lives in poverty, earning the equivalent of US$1.50 a day.

POLITICS, GOVERNMENT, AND TAXATION

Peru has been politically unstable since independence was declared in 1821 and formally granted by Spain 3 years later. Since independence Peru has had 109 presidents, 18 percent of whom were democratically elected. The remaining presidents came to power through military coups (24 percent), replaced a sitting president (21 percent), were named by Congress (18 percent), were delegated (16 percent), or formed part of a commission of notables (3 percent).

Political parties have generally been tied to 1 man, representing the traditional caudillo (strongman) model that is present in many Latin American countries. When back-to-back democratic elections are held, a rarity in Peru, the ruling party has never held on to the presidency. The country's oldest party, the American Popular Revolutionary Alliance (APRA), was founded by Victor Raul de la Torre in the 1920s. It continues to have a strong presence, despite decades of political persecution and one disastrous term in power. The party's founder, Haya de la Torre, was exiled for years and never reached the presidency. He received the most votes in the 1962 election, but a military junta stepped in after the election and took power for a year. Haya de la Torre lost by a slim margin in the election held in late 1963.

Those elections were won by Fernando Belaúnde Terry who, with Haya de la Torre, is one of the most important political figures in Peru in the second half of the 20th century. Belaúnde's Popular Action party remains active and at 90 he is still the titular head of the party. Belaúnde was deposed in a left-leaning military coup in 1968 and the generals ruled Peru for 12 years, nationalizing most industries and implementing a sweeping agrarian reform program. When the military returned the country to democracy in 1980, Belaúnde was again elected president.

APRA had its first chance to govern Peru in 1985, when Alán García was elected. At 35, García was Peru's youngest president and came to power with a decidedly left-wing platform. García's populist approach and attempt to re-establish some of the programs of the military regime—he tried to nationalize the banks in 1988—worked for 2 years but began crumbling in 1987. He ended his term in 1990 with 7,600 percent inflation and a bankrupt treasury.

The experience of Popular Action and APRA in the 1980s inspired a wave of independent candidates, personified by Alberto Fujimori. An obscure math professor, Fujimori emerged from obscurity in 1990 to win the presidency. Peruvians were tired of "politics as usual" and gambled on an outsider. With no political experience or party, Fujimori turned to the armed forces and used them to consolidate power. When Congress balked at his plans for sweeping economic reforms and harsh laws to control a growing subversive threat, Fujimori and the military took complete control, closing Congress and the courts in 1992 in what is known as a "self-coup." Fujimori received the backing of the population and a year later introduced a new constitution allowing for his re-election. He ran again in 1995 and was overwhelmingly re-elected because he had tamed inflation and his government had arrested the leadership of 2 violent subversive groups.

Although he came to power as an outsider, Fujimori rapidly developed the qualities and policies of Peru's traditional caudillos, concentrating power in the executive and bypassing Congress and the judicial branch whenever necessary.

Unsatisfied with only 2 terms, Fujimori and his allies tinkered with the constitution and decided he could run for a third term in 2000. He ran and won, although the elections were labeled fraudulent by local and international observers. Pressure from opposition parties calling for democracy and evidence of widespread corruption, however, never allowed Fujimori to consolidate his third term. He resigned in November 2000 and fled to Japan, his parents' homeland.

Fujimori's rapid decline set the stage for new elections in April 2001. The elections saw the consolidation of a new party, Peru's Potential, led by Alejandro Toledo. It also marked the return of Alán García—Fujimori forced García into exile in 1992—and APRA. Toledo was elected president of Peru in a close race, narrowly defeating former president García.

The free-market economic policies in place since 1990 will not change in the coming years. The incoming government, which took office in July of 2001, will maintain strict **macroeconomic** discipline guided by a Fiscal Discipline Law that does not permit the deficit to be higher than 1.5 percent of GDP. The economic situation will be difficult, nevertheless. The Peruvian economy has been in a **recession** since 1997, partly due to poor fiscal management on the part of the former government and partly because of the Brazilian, Russian, and Asian economic troubles. The collapse of Fujimori's administration also scared off local and foreign investors, with direct foreign investment reaching only US$600 million in 2000, compared to US$2 billion a year earlier.

The incoming government promises to reduce taxes and tariffs as a way of stimulating the economy and ensuring the 6 percent GDP growth economists say is needed to begin lowering poverty rates. Toledo, who has a Ph.D. in economics from Stanford University, is a political centrist, and wants to award small-business loans to farmers, balance the budget, lure foreign investment, and create jobs. Job creation is an especially important priority, considering Peru's current under- and unemployment, and the 300,000 young people joining the labor market each year.

The government's principal source of revenue comes from taxes. Of the US$8.39 billion brought in by the government in 2000, US$7.03 billion came from taxes. The largest chunk comes from **value-added taxes**, which accounted for US$3.4 billion in revenue in 2000. The second-largest category is **income tax**, which generated US$1.6 billion. A 15 percent tax is applied to personal income and a 30 percent tax is applied to business income. Other important taxes include the excise on gasoline, liquor, tobacco, and other luxury items, which brought in US$1.1 billion. Peru has the world's third-highest tax on beer, after South Korea and Kenya, accounting for 75 percent of the price of 1 liter. Taxes on imports generated US$704 million and assorted other taxes accounted for US$714 million. Government revenue in 2000 represented 14.1 percent of GDP.

INFRASTRUCTURE, POWER, AND COMMUNICATIONS

Peru has an extensive system of roads that cross most of the mountain and coastal regions. Of the 72,887 kilometers (45,300 miles) of roads, 8,698 kilometers (5,406 miles) are paved. The government dedicated a significant number of resources to building and rebuilding the highway system throughout the 1990s. The principal roads are the Pan-American Highway, which runs the length of the country down the coast; the Central Highway, which connects the capital, Lima, to the Andean highlands; and the Marginal Highway, which penetrates deep into the northeastern jungle region. The number of automobiles and buses more than doubled in the 1990s, making major cities congested and leading to massive increases in roadway fatalities. An average of 3 people a day died in 2000 in public transportation-related accidents. The government has a liberal policy for imports, allowing for a

steady influx of older, used automobiles. The Transportation Department estimates that 75 percent of mass transportation vehicles are more than 20 years old. A light rail mass transportation system was started in Lima in the mid-1980s, but abandoned by the central government for all of the 1990s. The project is now in the hands of the city government, which hopes to have the first 8 miles of tracks operational by 2005.

The nation's rail system, which was privatized in 2000, services highland mining operations. Passenger service on the rail system is limited to certain areas, particularly serving the tourist trade between the highland states of Puno, Cusco, and Arequipa. Several highways are in the process of being privatized and the process should conclude this year. One highway, in the state of Arequipa, has already been privatized.

Peru has 234 airports, but the majority are simple airfields serving small, private planes. The principal airport is the Jorge Chavez International Airport located in Lima, with other modern airfields in the major cities. Of the total number of airports, 44 have paved runways. Jorge Chavez International Airport was privatized in February 2001 and 5 other airports, including the tourist destination Cusco are in the final stages of privatization. Peru has a series of excellent, deep-water ports. The largest port facility is in Callao, the port city adjacent to Lima. In addition to Pacific Ocean ports, the country also has 3 large river ports: Iquitos, Pucallpa, and Yurimaguas. Iquitos is located on the Amazon River, while the other 2 ports are located on major tributaries. Peru has 8,598 kilometers (5,344 miles) of navigable riverways. Lake Titicaca, located on the border with Bolivia, is the world's highest navigable lake.

A mix of private and public companies generates electricity, the bulk of which is hydroelectric (74.79 percent). The Peruvian government began privatizing electricity generation, transmission, and supply in the mid-1990s and is continuing the process. U.S. and Spanish companies are the major investors in the sector, which produces 18.28

Communications

Country	Newspapers	Radios	TV Sets[a]	Cable subscribers[a]	Mobile Phones[a]	Fax Machines[a]	Personal Computers[a]	Internet Hosts[b]	Internet Users[b]
	1996	1997	1998	1998	1998	1998	1998	1999	1999
Peru	84	273	144	14.1	30	N/A	18.1	3.09	400
United States	215	2,146	847	244.3	256	78.4	458.6	1,508.77	74,100
Brazil	40	444	316	16.3	47	3.1	30.1	18.45	3,500
Ecuador	70	419	293	11.7	25	N/A	18.5	1.42	35

[a]Data are from International Telecommunication Union, *World Telecommunication Development Report 1999* and are per 1,000 people.
[b]Data are from the Internet Software Consortium (http://www.isc.org) and are per 10,000 people.

SOURCE: World Bank. *World Development Indicators 2000.*

billion kWh per year. Major natural gas reserves, which should be available to the market by 2003–04, will help diversify dependence on water sources.

Telecommunications services have improved dramatically since the state-owned telephone service was privatized in 1993. Major players in the market include Spain's Telefonica, U.S.-based BellSouth and AT&T, and Italy's TIM. The *CIA World Factbook* reports that there are 1.5 million fixed lines, while cellular phones top 500,000 (1998 estimates). Telephone analysts predict that mobile phones will outnumber fixed lines in Peru within 3 to 5 years.

There are an estimated 3 million television sets and 13 broadcast stations. Cable television has not yet penetrated the national market, with nearly all of the subscribers concentrated in Lima. There are an estimated 6.65 million radios that can tune into 472 AM stations and 198 FM stations nationwide.

There are 15 Internet service providers and an estimated 800,000 people use the Internet, according to the Economist Intelligence Unit. Peru has a relatively low per capita number of personal computers, but the country is a pioneer in setting up public Internet booths to allow Internet access at a low cost. These public booths are both public and privately run, with the government installing thousands of Internet access centers in rural areas.

ECONOMIC SECTORS

Peru's diverse geography and climates, as well as its location along South America's central Pacific coast, give it privileges enjoyed by few nations. However, the country's natural wealth in agriculture, mining, and fishing

has not been harnessed to the benefit of the population. The country's principal problems have been, and continue to be, its reliance on raw material exports and its unstable political climate. As a result of its dependence on raw materials, Peru's economy is highly susceptible to downturns in the world economy. Natural phenomena, particularly El Niño (a warm water current that changes ocean and air patterns off the coast of Peru and provokes droughts in some parts of the world and flooding in others), periodically play havoc on fishing and agriculture, as well as destroy **infrastructure**. Because of political turbulence, Peru has had 3 presidents between November 2000 and November 2001, a disturbing trend that keeps local and foreign investors skeptical about placing their money in the country.

The administration of former president Alberto Fujimori (1990–2000) emphasized the raw material export model, offering incentives to capital-intensive investments, particularly in mining. By privatizing telecommunication services, the government opened this as a new and important sector within the economy, with investments totaling nearly US$4 billion throughout the last decade. The new government, while recognizing the importance of mining, is pledging to emphasize labor-intensive sectors, particularly manufacturing, farming, and tourism as a way to diversify the economy and create jobs.

AGRICULTURE

Peru's climate and different geographical zones make it an important agricultural nation. Of the 120 domesticated plants Peru has provided the world, the potato is the most important. There are more than 3,000 varieties of potatoes found in Peru, making it the world's genetic center for the crop. Other important crops include sugarcane, coffee, and cotton, with Peru producing 2 of the world's finest strains of cotton: Pima and Tanguis. In addition to these staples, the UNDP estimates that the Andean and jungle food baskets include important vegetables and fruits that are relatively unknown but high in vitamins and proteins. These include camu-camu, a small jungle fruit with the highest known levels of vitamin C, and quinoa, a highland grain. In addition, Peru is also a major supplier of crops such as asparagus, because of its unique climate. Peru has a window for asparagus (US$120 million in export earnings in 1999) exports between November and January, months in which almost no other country exports the product. Other "designer" products include mangos, sweet onions, and herbs.

Other important elements in the agricultural sector are domesticated Andean animals including llamas, alpacas, guanacos, and vicuñas. All 4 belong to the same family and provide varying levels of fine wool. The

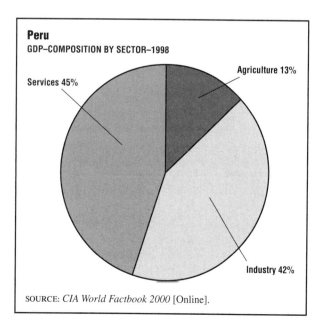

Peru
GDP–COMPOSITION BY SECTOR–1998

Services 45%

Agriculture 13%

Industry 42%

SOURCE: *CIA World Factbook 2000* [Online].

vicuña, which is not domesticated, has the world's finest wool. Vicuñas have been on the endangered species list for decades, but are rebounding, numbering close to 150,000 today. Vicuñas are protected under the CITES convention, which means their wool cannot be commercialized. The Peruvian government is lobbying to have the prohibition changed.

A potentially important source of income could come from Peru's virgin forest in the form of logging. The Peruvian government began overhauling its laws governing the timber industry in 2000, dividing up parcels and placing conditions on logging and exports of slow-growth hardwood trees such as cedar and mahogany. Together with Guyana, in northern South America, Peru is one of the few countries on the planet that has most of its forest reserves relatively untouched.

Despite its history of agriculture and immense natural wealth, agriculture has received little attention in the past few decades. The sector continues to struggle after years of government intervention in the 1960s and 1970s (when the military government undertook agrarian reform), and benign neglect throughout most of the 1980s and 1990s. For a brief period in the 1980s, during Alán García's presidency (1985–90), the government attempted to offer interest-free loans to farmers through a state-run farmers' bank. The bank was a failure, with negligible returns on loans and declining production.

Agriculture represents 13 percent of GDP but employs 30 percent of the country's population. The incoming government proposes upping the sector's percentage of GDP as well as its employment participation by focusing on **value-added** products and concentrating on **vertical integration**. Cotton production is one agricultural product that the government is attempting to increase through vertical integration. Cotton production is linked to the country's textile manufacturing. The country's textile industry exported more than US$700 million in 2000 and includes several vertically-integrated companies, such as Textiles San Cristobal, which produces for U.S. manufacturer Ralph Lauren and other high-end clothing companies. They run cotton plantations, thread and fabric factories, garment producers, and exporters of the final product.

The goal of Toledo's government is to get Peruvian textiles included in the list of products exported to the United States tariff-free under the Andean Trade Preference Act, passed in 1990. The Peruvian government is pushing for them to be included in an extension of the act, which is currently being negotiated. The Peruvian government believes that if textiles receive tariff-free status, there will be a boom throughout the textile industry, beginning in the cotton fields.

The government plans on doubling the number of acres dedicated to cotton in order to increase cloth production to feed the textile industry. Other targeted products include hard yellow corn for the poultry industry, coffee for the specialty coffee market in the United States and Europe, and sugarcane. Peru currently imports corn and sugarcane, despite its long history of development of both crops. According to the Department of Agriculture, Peru has been a net agricultural importer since 1980, with agriculture imports worth roughly US$200 million more than exports in 1999.

Hundreds of laws were passed under the previous administration to stimulate the agriculture sector. These included privatization of fallow lands and irrigation systems, as well as removing conditions on land ownership and tenure. However, the government failed to pass 2 important pieces of legislation governing community-owned lands and water rights. Without these 2 laws, large agroindustry projects will not be able to operate.

One of Peru's best-known crops is coca, which is the raw material used to make cocaine. In addition to coca, Peru also produces substantial quantities of marijuana and, in recent years, poppies used in opium production. The government, together with its U.S., European, and UN partners, has been reducing coca crops since the mid-1990s, with promising results. Coca crops have fallen from 276,000 acres in 1992 to 84,000 acres currently. Neighboring Colombia has passed Peru as the leading producer of coca.

INDUSTRY

FISHING. Peru is an international leader in fishing, producing nearly 10 percent of the world's fish catch. The cold-water Humboldt Current brings nutrient-rich cold waters that create ideal fishing grounds. Peru exported more than US$1 billion in fish products in 2000—most of it as fishmeal—and fished nearly 10 billion tons, making fishing the second-most important industry after mining. Fishing has been a mainstay in Peru for thousands of years, playing a key role in ancient societies. In modern times, fishing has boomed due to whaling in the late 19th century and demand for guano (bird dung), a byproduct of fishing found on small islands off the coast.

While always important, the full use of Peru's fishing resources did not occur until the mid-20th century with the introduction of fishmeal production. The star of the fishmeal, which is used for animal feed or fertilizer, is the Peruvian anchovy. For most of the 1960s and 1970s, Peruvian anchovies accounted for 44 percent of the world fish catch destined for non-human consumption. The fishing industry's participation in the GDP varies yearly, depending upon the catch and ocean conditions. In years when El Niño is present, such as 1998, the sector's participation falls to below 1 percent of GDP. Fishing currently accounts for roughly 3.5 percent of GDP and, because it is not a labor-intensive industry, employs approximately 80,000 people.

The government began privatizing the fisheries industry, PescaPeru, in 1994 in a process that continues today. The government has sold its participation in all processing plants and fishing fleets, and is now preparing to privatize fishing ports as a general program to privatize all the nation's ports. The Fisheries Ministry is also beginning a process of privatizing experimental and research centers as well as fish-farming installations. The industry is facing another potential downturn because of the fear created by "mad cow" disease in Europe. The European Union nations voted in early 2001 to ban all feed products made from animals, including fishmeal. The scope of the ban was later reduced, but restrictions still apply. Peru's fishmeal exports to Europe declined by 41 percent in the first quarter of 2001.

MINING. Mining has been a central element in Peru's history for thousands of years. The Andes are rich in minerals and gold, and silver pieces can be found in numerous pre-Columbian societies. Mineral exports are a key to the country's economy, representing nearly half of Peru's exports in 2000. Peru ranks eighth worldwide in gold production (first in Latin America), second in copper, and among the top 5 producers of lead and zinc. Two of Peru's gold mines, Yanacocha and Pierina, are among the most productive and profitable gold mines in the world. Peru has an estimated 21 million fine ounces of gold reserves in mines currently under operation and 42 million fine metric tons of copper reserves. An additional 100 gold mines are predicted to come on line in the next 5 years. Also looming in the near future is the massive Antamina project, a Canadian-led mining operation that will require US$2.3 billion in investments and is expected to produce copper, zinc, lead, gold, and silver for the next 30 to 40 years. Antamina is the largest mining project underway in the world.

Mining activity and exports have grown exponentially since 1991, when the government adopted a series of new rules and tax benefits for large-scale mining, streamlined the process for filing a mineral claim, and allowed companies to re-invest upward to 80 percent of profits tax free. Mining exports grew from US$1.2 billion in 1987 to US$2.7 billion in 1997. Gold witnessed the greatest increase, rising from less than US$1 million in exports in 1987 to US$500 million in 1997. Gold exports are now US$1.2 billion, according to the World Gold Council.

Like fishing, however, mining is not a labor-intensive activity, creating few jobs and demanding huge investments for each job created. Nevertheless, mining represents one of the few money-making activities in the Peru-

vian highlands, particularly in areas higher than 12,000 feet above sea level where most mining operations are located. Mining represents 10 percent of GDP, according to the U.S. State Department's Country Commercial Guide.

MANUFACTURING. Because of its long dependence on raw material exports, Peru has never developed a strong manufacturing sector. The sector represents 15 percent of GDP and is tied heavily to mining, fishing, agriculture, and textiles. Manufacturing is mainly devoted to processing a percentage of the raw materials to gain a value-added advantage. The most promising sector is textiles, with Peru exporting nearly US$700 million in garments in 2000, mainly to the United States and Europe. Textiles represent the largest non-raw material portion of the Peruvian export economy. Peruvian textiles are currently exported **duty**-free to European Union nations under an agreement to help the country fight the drug trade. The U.S. Andean Trade Preference Act (ATPA), passed in 1991, has the same goal, exempting nearly 6,000 products produced in Bolivia, Colombia, Ecuador, and Peru (all major drug-producing nations) from tariffs. Textiles, however, were left off the list. The 4 governments are lobbying for the U.S. Congress to include textiles on the trade list when ATPA is renegotiated in December 2001. Peruvian garment makers generally produce high-end products for the U.S. markets, including brand names such as Ralph Lauren, Brooks Brothers, and Bobby Jones.

SERVICES

TOURISM. Tourism has represented a new growth industry in Peru since the early 1990s, with the government and **private sector** dedicating considerable energies to boosting the country's tourist destinations both to Peruvians and foreigners. Foreign tourist arrivals have jumped from approximately 90,000 in 1990 to more than 1 million in 2001, with a corresponding upswing in investment in services. The U.S. State Department's Country Commercial Guide estimates that US$330 million will be spent on new hotels alone between 2000 and 2005. The government estimates that 1 million new jobs will be created if it reaches the goal of 2.5 million tourists by 2005.

The public and private sector are promoting the country's tourist industry in 2 specific categories: **ecotourism** and historical/cultural tourism. The main draws are the Amazon rain forest and high Andes, including the Colca Canyon, the world's deepest, and archaeological sites such as Machu Picchu, considered to be the "lost city of the Incas."

FINANCIAL SERVICES. With the exception of Banco de Credito—Peru's largest financial institution (US$8.5 billion in assets)—nearly all the financial sector has fallen into foreign hands. The financial system has been on somewhat shaky ground since 1997, with a number of bank mergers or failures. The number of banks in the system fell from 25 in 1998 to 16 in 2001. There were 2 interventions by the government to save banks in late 2000, and authorities say the system is solid although it might not be flush with cash.

RETAIL. Nearly all **retail** is concentrated in Lima and, with a few important exceptions, is controlled by foreign capital. The 2 major department store chains, Saga and Ripley, are Chilean-owned and one of the 2 supermarket chains, Santa Isabel, belongs to the Dutch conglomerate Ahold. The other supermarket, E. Wong, is Peruvian-owned and solid. Supermarket sales, however, account for less than 10 percent of overall sales nationwide. In the past 10 years, Peru has attracted international franchises from apparel to gas stations and fast-food chains, including McDonald's and Burger King. The most successful franchise in terms of profit has been Dunkin' Donuts.

INTERNATIONAL TRADE

Peru has had a trade deficit for the past few decades, with exports reaching US$6.7 billion (2000 estimate) and imports of US$7.4 billion (2000 estimate). The trade gap has narrowed since 1997, as the country has fallen deeper into recession and imports have declined. The United States is Peru's largest trading partner, absorbing 25 percent of the country's exports (1997). It is followed by China (8 percent, mainly minerals and fishmeal) and Japan (7 percent, mainly minerals). The United States is also the largest source of imports, representing 19 percent of goods. Other important sources for imports are Colombia (6 percent), Venezuela (5 percent), Chile (4 percent), and Brazil (4 percent). Major exports include fish products, minerals (gold, silver, copper, zinc, lead), agricultural products (coffee, asparagus), petroleum products, and textiles. Major imports include machinery, transportation equipment, food (wheat, corn, rice), petroleum, medical equipment, and iron and steel.

Peru is a founding member of the Andean Community of Nations, which groups together Peru, Colombia, Ecuador, Bolivia, and Venezuela. Peru has had difficulties with the group, and, under Fujimori, threatened to pull out. The Andean group has joined forces to lobby for an extension of ATPA and all nations are flirting with Brazil to test the possibility of adjunct membership in the Southern Cone Common Market (Brazil, Argentina, Uruguay, and Paraguay).

The incoming government promises to move the country away from raw material exports as a way of stimulating other industries and generating a trade surplus within 5 years. The emphasis will be on textiles, agroindustry (principally "niche" crops like asparagus where Peru has a comparative advantage because of climate), and fossil fuels. The massive Camisea natural gas fields,

Trade (expressed in billions of US$): Peru		
	Exports	Imports
1975	1.291	2.550
1980	3.898	2.499
1985	2.979	1.835
1990	3.231	3.470
1995	5.575	9.224
1998	5.723	N/A

SOURCE: International Monetary Fund. *International Financial Statistics Yearbook 1999.*

located in the south-central jungle region, should be completed within 3 years, giving Peru an energy surplus it hopes to export to Ecuador and Chile and possibly Brazil by hooking into a Bolivian natural gas pipeline already sending fuel to Brazil.

MONEY

Peru has been in a recession since 1997, which has resulted in a tight money supply and declining internal consumption. Domestic demand fell by 0.9 percent in 1998 and by 2.4 percent in 1999. Demand did not increase in 2000, and the first quarter of 2001 showed that Peruvians were still cautious about spending their money. Demand growth for 2001 was estimated to be less than 1 percent, according to the U.S.-based Institute of International Finance.

While external factors like the economic crises in Asia, Russia, and Brazil affected the economy, the most serious effects came from political turbulence within Peru. Former president Alberto Fujimori's decisions to run for a third term in late 1999 and his victory in mid-2000 (in elections widely criticized as fraudulent), kept spending down and scared off foreign investors. The political crisis, which eventually saw Fujimori abandon the presidency and flee to Japan in November 2000, has had a negative effect on tax collection, with tax receipts dropping an average of 10 percent a month between October 2000 and February 2001.

Exchange rates: Peru	
nuevo sol (S/.) per US$1	
Jan 2001	3.5230
2000	3.4900
1999	3.383
1998	2.930
1997	2.664
1996	2.453

SOURCE: CIA *World Factbook 2001* [ONLINE].

The crisis, however, has not affected the exchange rate or inflation, which have fluctuated but not taken off as in earlier times in Peru's history. Inflation has been declining annually since 1990, when it reached 7,600 percent. Inflation has been in low digits since the early 1990s and has been declining steadily since 1994, dropping from 15.4 percent to 3.7 percent in 2000. The currency has also remained stable, moving only from 3.38 nuevos soles to the U.S. dollar in 1999 to 3.5 by year-end 2000. The exchange rate in the first quarter of 2001 remained steady at 3.5 nuevos soles to the U.S. dollar.

The Peruvian government, in agreement with the International Monetary Fund, maintains a floating currency. The government has rejected any possibility of switching currency to the U.S. dollar, as has neighboring Ecuador, or pegging the rate to the dollar, as has Argentina in its "convertibility" plan.

The Lima Stock Market—re-opened in 1971—is relatively small, trading blue chips and local shares. Daily transactions average US$3.5 million.

POVERTY AND WEALTH

Despite years of promises and billions in social programs, the bulk of Peru's population (54 percent) lives in poverty, according to the *CIA World Factbook.* Of the poor, the UNDP estimates that 19 percent live in "absolute poverty," meaning they survive on less than US$1 a day.

The contrasts between rich and poor are clearly seen in Lima, the capital, which has more than doubled in size in the past 2 decades. The majority of the capital's population live in shantytowns, known as *pueblos jovenes* locally, most of which are perched on barren sand dunes near the Pacific coast or on rocky outcrops in the foothills of the Andes. The shantytowns surround upscale neighborhoods, most of which are a cross between Miami homes and Spanish villas.

Income distribution continues to be extremely skewed, with the top 10 percent of the population controlling 35.4 percent of the nation's wealth, while the bottom 10 percent controls just 1.6 percent. The gap is seen

Distribution of Income or Consumption by Percentage Share: Peru	
Lowest 10%	1.6
Lowest 20%	4.4
Second 20%	9.1
Third 20%	14.1
Fourth 20%	21.3
Highest 20%	51.2
Highest 10%	35.4

Survey year: 1996
Note: This information refers to income shares by percentiles of the population and is ranked by per capita income.

SOURCE: *2000 World Development Indicators* [CD-ROM].

in access to basic services. While the wealthy neighborhoods have had access to potable water, waste removal, paved roads, and electricity for decades, these services are newcomers to most shantytowns. In fact, only in the 1990s did most of Lima receive electricity, and water for many areas is still brought in by cistern trucks.

The literacy rate in Peru is 88.7 percent and education is universal and free. An estimated 7 million children and adolescents are of school age. Of these numbers, the U.S. State Department estimates that 6 percent of children and 17 percent of young people either never attend or drop out of school. The high school drop-out rate in rural areas is more than 50 percent. An estimated 750,000 students attend nearly 50 state and private universities.

There are 455 hospitals and 1,083 clinics in Peru, serving a population of 27 million people. There are 23,700 doctors, 7,950 dentists, and 15,000 nurses.

The government tried to offset many of its social problems with programs, but these programs were aimed more at ensuring voter support than solving the root causes of the problems. In 2000, 60 percent of rural Peruvians and 40 percent of urban residents were receiving some sort of government aid through community soup kitchens, food give-aways, or school-based breakfast, lunch, or health-care programs. The incoming government has pledged to maintain most of the programs, but says it will de-politicize them.

The World Bank and International Monetary Fund estimate that the Peruvian economy needs to grow by 6 percent annually over a sustained period of time if the country is going to adequately reduce poverty levels. Compared to neighboring Bolivia and Ecuador, Peru is not doing poorly, but it lags well behind Chile and Colombia in terms of per capita income and access to goods and services.

GDP per Capita (US$)					
Country	1975	1980	1985	1990	1998
Peru	2,835	2,777	2,452	2,012	2,611
United States	19,364	21,529	23,200	25,363	29,683
Brazil	3,464	4,253	4,039	4,078	4,509
Ecuador	1,301	1,547	1,504	1,475	1,562

SOURCE: United Nations. *Human Development Report 2000; Trends in human development and per capita income.*

Household Consumption in PPP Terms

Country	All food	Clothing and footwear	Fuel and power[a]	Health care[b]	Education[b]	Transport & Communications	Other
Peru	26	7	17	13	5	7	25
United States	13	9	9	4	6	8	51
Brazil	22	13	18	15	34	4	−6
Ecuador	26	9	15	13	10	3	24

Data represent percentage of consumption in PPP terms.

[a]Excludes energy used for transport.

[b]Includes government and private expenditures.

SOURCE: World Bank. *World Development Indicators 2000.*

WORKING CONDITIONS

Because the Peruvian population is so young—with 53.8 percent of the population under the age of 25—the working-age population is growing by 300,000 people a year. The U.S. State Department's *2001 Human Rights Report* estimates the workforce to number 8.5 million, of whom 5 percent are unionized. Official unemployment, according to the International Labor Organization, was 10 percent in 2000, but even the government admits that the statistics are misleading. An estimated 60 percent of the population is underemployed. The workforce remains largely unskilled, with many skilled laborers leaving the country to search for work abroad. An estimated 1 million Peruvians now live abroad, the majority of them in the United States or Spain.

The government raised the monthly minimum wage to the equivalent of US$117 in March 2000. The U.S. State Department estimates that more than half the workforce earns less than the minimum wage.

The government began dismantling labor laws in the early 1990s as part of the efforts to streamline the economy, open the country to foreign investment, and privatize state-run industries. As a result, labor union activity has declined substantially with the Construction Workers Union and Teachers Union the only 2 organizations retaining a nationwide profile. Strikes called in 1999 and 2000 had little national importance. Under current laws, strikes not approved by the government are illegal.

The 1992 labor law made striking and collective bargaining difficult. While collective bargaining is legal, the law says it can only be carried out if it is "in harmony with broader social objectives." Local and international labor groups also complain about provisions that allow companies to hire 30 percent of the workforce on an "internship" basis, meaning 3-month contracts without social benefits. In addition to government changes to the laws, the Maoist Shining Path guerrillas also made it a policy to infiltrate unions or create their own unions as a way of weakening companies and whole economic sectors. While the Shining Path's leadership was jailed in 1992 and the group has all but disappeared, the stigma it created for unions remains.

COUNTRY HISTORY AND ECONOMIC DEVELOPMENT

1438–1530. Height of the Inca Empire, expansion north to Panama and south to Argentina.

1532. Francisco Pizarro lands in Peru and conquers the Incas.

1821. Independence from Spain is proclaimed.

1824. Independence is granted.

1879–83. War of the Pacific with Chile. Peru loses a large chunk of its southern territory, and its economy is destroyed.

1924. APRA party is founded.

1941. War with Ecuador.

1968. Left-wing military coup led by Gen. Juan Velasco. Agrarian reform begins; industries nationalized.

1975. Right-wing military coup; dismantling of statist model begins.

1980. Return to democracy. Fernando Belaúnde is elected president.

1980. Shining Path launches first attack.

1985. Alán García is elected president. Foreign debt cap is announced.

1988. The government attempts to nationalize the banks; economy collapses.

1990. Alberto Fujimori elected. Structural adjustment program announced. Inflation reaches 7,600 percent.

1992. Shining Path leadership arrested.

1993. Telephone company privatized for US$2 billion.

1995. Fujimori is re-elected.

2000. Fujimori re-elected in fraudulent May elections. He resigns in November.

2000. Valentin Paniagua takes over as interim president in November. Alejandro Toledo is elected Peru's new president.

FUTURE TRENDS

Peru is a nation rich in natural resources and human potential, but it has been plagued by political turmoil throughout its history. The country has had 109 presidents in less than 180 years as an independent nation. In 2000–01 alone it had 3 presidents. The past administration of Alberto Fujimori is accused of stealing as much as US$1 billion—roughly 10 percent of the government's annual budget—through bribes, kickbacks, and graft. Peru must rid its public administration of corruption if it hopes to attract foreign and local investors.

The current generation of politicians and economists are correct in pointing out that Peru needs to diversify its economy and its exports, relying less on raw materials and more on value-added goods. A decision to concentrate on the agricultural sector is sensible because it takes advantage of the country's natural wealth, exploits niches in the world market, and most importantly for Peruvians, creates jobs.

The government has hard choices to make in the coming years. The **budget deficit** cannot be greater than 1.5 percent of GDP as part of the agreement with the International Monetary Fund. Peru missed the target in 1999 and 2000, and another miss will not be taken lightly. The country needs to adopt a new round of reforms, including additional privatizations and reduced government spending, which will make already tough social conditions even more difficult. The government needs to find a balance where it can satisfy creditors and keep international channels open while making sure the basic needs of the population are met.

DEPENDENCIES

Peru has no territories or colonies.

BIBLIOGRAPHY

Brack Egg, Antonio, and Cecilia Mendiola. *Ecologia del Peru* (Ecology of Peru). Lima: United Nations Development Program, 2000.

Hudson, Rex, editor. *Peru: A Country Study.* Washington: Federal Research Division, Library of Congress, 1993.

Tamariz, Domingo. *Historia del Poder: Elecciones y Golpes de Estado en el Peru* (History of Power: Elections and Coups in Peru). Lima: Jamie Campodonico Ediciones, 1995.

Turner, Barry, editor. *The Statesman's Yearbook.* New York: St. Martin's Press, 2000.

U.S. Central Intelligence Agency. *World Factbook 2000: Peru.* <http://www.cia.gov/cia/publications/factbook/geos/pe.html>. Accessed February 2001.

Webb, Richard, and Graciela Fernandez Baca. *Peru en Numeros 1999* (Peru in Numbers in 1999). Lima: Cuanto Institute, 1999.

—Lucien O. Chauvin

PUERTO RICO

Commonwealth of Puerto Rico
Estado Libre Asociado de Puerto Rico

CAPITAL: San Juan.

MONETARY UNIT: U.S. dollar ($). One dollar equals 100 cents. There are coins of 1, 5, 10, 25, and 50 cents, and 1 dollar, and bills of 1, 2, 5, 10, 20, 50, 100, 500, 1,000, 5,000, and 10,000 dollars.

CHIEF EXPORTS: Pharmaceuticals, electronics, apparel, canned tuna, rum, beverage concentrates, medical equipment.

CHIEF IMPORTS: Chemicals, machinery and equipment, apparel, food, fish, petroleum products.

GROSS DOMESTIC PRODUCT: US$38.1 billion (purchasing power parity, 1999 est.).

BALANCE OF TRADE: Exports: US$34.9 billion (f.o.b., 1999). **Imports:** US$25.3 billion (c.i.f., 1999).

COUNTRY OVERVIEW

LOCATION AND SIZE. Puerto Rico, an island situated between the Caribbean Sea and the Atlantic Ocean, lies just east of the Dominican Republic. With an area of 9,104 square kilometers (3,515 square miles), Puerto Rico is almost 3 times the size of the state of Rhode Island. As an island commonwealth with a coastline of 501 kilometers (311 miles), Puerto Rico shares no borders with other nations. San Juan, the capital, is located on the northeastern shore of the main island; there are also 3 small islands included in the Commonwealth: Vieques and Culebra to the east and Mona to the west. San Juan's location makes it one of the Caribbean Sea's most valuable ports. The Mona Passage, off Puerto Rico's west shore, is also a crucial shipping route to the Panama Canal. Major cities include Guánica, Playa de Ponce, and Guayanilla, all 3 along the southern coast, in east-to-west order. Puerto Rico's most important cities are port cities, vital to the Puerto Rican economy.

POPULATION. Puerto Rico's colonial history with Spain resulted in a racially mixed population (Spanish, African, and indigenous Taino), 85 percent of which is Roman Catholic. The population was estimated at 3,915,798 in July 2000, a growth of 10 percent between 1990 and 1999, according to the U.S. Census Bureau. People between the ages of 15 and 64 constitute two-thirds of the population, and people 14 and under make up roughly one-fourth. With an annual population growth rate of 0.56 percent as of 2000, the population is estimated to reach 4,117,633 by 2010. The average life expectancy of the population is 75.55 years.

Population growth is discouraged by the government, which supports family-planning programs and birth-control measures on the community and national levels. In the 20th century, large-scale migration to the U.S. mainland had slowed population growth and alleviated overcrowding, but since the 1990s there has been a growing movement of Puerto Ricans from the mainland returning to the island because of improved living conditions. The government also places high emphasis on education, which explains the high literacy rate on the

island (90 percent). Bilingual education measures are growing, and are the source of great debate on the island.

The population of Puerto Rico shows high concentrations in urban areas along the coastal lowlands. Several pairs of neighboring cities are virtually growing together due to urban expansion. For example, the capital and its surrounding areas have a population of more than 1.5 million. Still, almost 70 percent of the island's population remains rural.

OVERVIEW OF ECONOMY

Until about 1950, the Puerto Rican economy depended heavily upon the sugar plantations typical of Caribbean islands. By the mid-1950s, however, industry began to surpass agriculture as the base of the economy, especially in pharmaceuticals, electronics, textiles and clothing, petrochemicals, processed foods, and tourist-related businesses. By 1999, industry provided 45 percent of total GDP, and services provided 54 percent, with agriculture accounting for only 1 percent. Dairy and livestock production has replaced sugar as the leading source of agricultural income.

Puerto Rico is relatively poor in natural resources, which resulted in economic dependence on the United States. Imports include chemicals, machinery, food, textiles, and fuel, most of which come from the continental United States. Puerto Rico's ideal location, however, allows the island to profit greatly from trade and commerce, thanks to its many port cities. The island is situated on many paths between the Americas as well as paths from Europe to the Panama Canal.

Since Puerto Rico is a U.S. commonwealth, the United States has a large impact on the island's economy. Tax incentives and **duty**-free access to the island encourage the U.S. firms that have invested a great deal in Puerto Rico since the 1950s and that now dominate industry, finance, and trade on the island. An overwhelming majority of Puerto Rico's foreign trade is with the United States, but the North American Free Trade Agreement (NAFTA) also encourages Puerto Rico to trade with Canada and Mexico. Still, the economy relies heavily on the United States, and receives many forms of federal economic aid. The island's biggest government expenditures are in health, education, and welfare. As a U.S. commonwealth, Puerto Rico's **external debt** is part of the U.S. debt, but the island has a public debt approaching US$16 billion.

POLITICS, GOVERNMENT, AND TAXATION

The structure of the Puerto Rican government is similar to that of the United States, with executive, legislative, and judicial branches. The island has a governor and a resident commissioner who has a non-voting seat in the U.S. House of Representatives. The governor, 28-seat Senate, and 54-seat House of Representatives are popularly elected for 4-year terms. Members of the Supreme Court and lower courts are appointed by the governor with the consent of the Senate.

The 4 major political parties differ primarily in their views about whether Puerto Rico should change its relationship with the United States. The pro-statehood New Progressive Party emphasizes that the island is already economically dependent on the United States and believes that making the island a state would gain it representation in Washington. The Popular Democratic Party emphasizes the economic incentives that the island enjoys under its commonwealth status, including federal tax exemption and foreign-investment incentives. The 2 other major parties, the Puerto Rican Independence Party and the Puerto Rican Socialist Party, advocate independence for the island state. These latter parties are much smaller and less significant.

The Puerto Rican government is heavily involved in its economy. Fomento, the island's Economic Development Corporation, stimulates and guides economic growth. Since the 1950s, government involvement in economic affairs has included Operation Bootstrap, a plan to mix local labor and foreign investment by boosting industrialization based on exports; Fomento's efforts to promote petrochemicals and advanced technology industries in the 1960s; and high government spending in social welfare programs. In 1994, the government created the Foreign Trade Board to stimulate foreign investment and encourage exports. The board was mainly concerned with providing support to small businesses that had the potential to export goods to foreign markets. Puerto Rico's was the first economy in the world to become industrialized around a program that fully relied on exports, and Puerto Rico continues to focus its efforts on an economy for export, bolstering its image as an ideal location for tourism and business.

Since there is no official representation in the U.S. government, Puerto Rican citizens on the island do not pay federal taxes, although they do enjoy U.S. citizenship. Customs taxes and **excise taxes** on imports and exports go to the federal treasury. The island also has welfare programs similar to those in the United States. Today more than ever, the U.S. government plays a large role in Puerto Rico's economy, via tax incentives and exemptions, duty-free access, and wage and **infrastructure** incentives that encourage large U.S. firms and corporations to invest in the island's economy. As a U.S. commonwealth, Puerto Rico controls only its internal affairs; the U.S. federal government controls all interstate and international trade relations. The island has no military of its own, so, unlike the situation in most of Latin America, the military exerts no control over the economy. The

Communications

Country	Telephones[a]	Telephones, Mobile/Cellular[a]	Radio Stations[b]	Radios[a]	TV Stations[a]	Televisions[a]	Internet Service Providers[c]	Internet Users[c]
Puerto Rico	1.322 M	169,265 (1996)	AM 72; FM 17; shortwave 0	2.7 M	18	1.021 M	76	110,000
United States	194 M	69.209 M (1998)	AM 4,762; FM 5,542; shortwave 18	575 M	1,500	219 M	7,800	148 M
Jamaica	353,000 (1996)	54,640 (1996)	AM 10; FM 13; shortwave 0	1.215 M	7	460,000	21	60,000
Cuba	473,031 (2000)	2,994	AM 169; FM 55; shortwave 1	3.9 M	58	2.64 M	4 (2001)	60,000

[a]Data is for 1997 unless otherwise noted.
[b]Data is for 1998 unless otherwise noted.
[c]Data is for 2000 unless otherwise noted.

SOURCE: CIA *World Factbook 2001* [Online].

island's tax system is independent of the U.S. tax system, with the U.S. legislature deciding how tax revenues are spent.

INFRASTRUCTURE, POWER, AND COMMUNICATIONS

Except for its lack of a public railway system, Puerto Rico has a well-developed infrastructure and transportation network. The island's minimal railways are used only for hauling sugarcane. The vast majority of the island's 14,400 kilometers (8,949 miles) of roadways are paved. Some 30 international and domestic airports allow for easy access to various cities on the island and provide transportation for industry and tourism. Economically speaking, the most important form of transportation in Puerto Rico is by water. Puerto Rico's location between the Americas and en route to the Panama Canal, coupled with its valuable port cities, boosts the economy through trade and commerce. There is no Puerto Rican merchant marine; the majority of its ships are owned by the United States. The advanced infrastructure and transportation systems also make it easier to profit from the booming tourism industry.

Power is widely available on the island, with even isolated rural villages receiving electricity and running water. The island is self-sufficient in power production; it produces and consumes almost 18 billion kWh each year (1998). Puerto Rico generates 98 percent of its electric power from oil, with coal and hydroelectric power accounting for the remainder. PREPA, the Puerto Rico Electric Power Authority, is the only distributor of power on the island.

Puerto Rico's media include a free press, some of which is independent and some of which is politically aligned. Local and U.S. mainland newspapers are easily accessible. The 2 major daily papers on the island are *El Vocero de Puerto Rico* and *El Nuevo Día*. Radio and television are easily accessible, and have programs similar to those on the U.S. mainland. As of 1997 there were 18 television stations and 3 stations of the U.S. armed forces. Islanders owned more than 1 million televisions and 2.7 million radio sets. Puerto Rico has a modern telephone network, integrated with the United States. The network includes digital and cellular services, and 18 Internet service providers.

ECONOMIC SECTORS

Before the 1950s, the Puerto Rican economy was typical for a Caribbean island, relying heavily on the plantation system. Agriculture was the primary source of income, and sugar production was particularly vital. From about 1950, largely due to government involvement in the island's economy, the industry and service sectors experienced exponential growth and quickly replaced agriculture as the foundation of the economy. As of 1999, agriculture provided only 1 percent of the island's GDP

GDP per Capita (US$)

Country	1996	1997	1998	1999	2000
Puerto Rico	8,200	8,600	9,000	9,800	10,000
United States	28,600	30,200	31,500	33,900	36,200
Jamaica	3,260	N/A	3,300	3,350	3,700
Cuba	1,480	1,540	1,560	1,700	1,700

Note: Data are estimates.

SOURCE: *Handbook of the Nations*, 17th, 18th, 19th and 20th editions for 1996, 1997, 1998 and 1999 data; CIA *World Factbook 2001* [Online] for 2000 data.

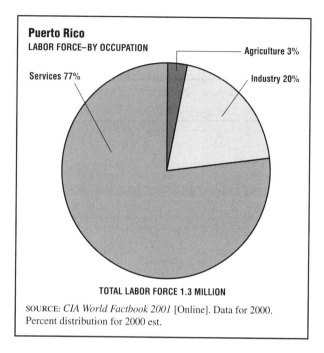

Puerto Rico
LABOR FORCE—BY OCCUPATION

Agriculture 3%

Services 77%

Industry 20%

TOTAL LABOR FORCE 1.3 MILLION

SOURCE: *CIA World Factbook 2001* [Online]. Data for 2000.
Percent distribution for 2000 est.

and provided jobs for only 3 percent of the island's **workforce**. Foreign investment incentives offered by the U.S. federal government have attracted much foreign capital, and by 1999, the industry sector produced 45 percent, and the service sector 54 percent, of total GDP. The island depends heavily on trade, commerce, and tourism, the latter of which is the most rapidly growing sector of the Puerto Rican economy currently.

AGRICULTURE

Puerto Rico lacks arable flat lands and natural resources. The only truly abundant resources on the island are clay, sand, and limestone. Despite these drawbacks, Puerto Rico depended heavily on agriculture until the mid-1950s, when industry and services showed rapid growth and development. Sugar, exported in large quantities to the United States, was the primary **cash crop**. Other major crops were coffee and tobacco. The production of these 3 crops has declined considerably since the 1950s, although sugar production is still important for the production of rum and molasses. Despite expansion in dairy products, livestock, poultry and eggs, and exotic citrus fruits, the importance of the agricultural sector has diminished. In addition, tropical and hard woods supply a very small furniture industry on the island. From an environmentalist standpoint, deforestation rates are almost nonexistent. Game fishing exists in the coastal regions, but most of the island's fish come from the U.S. fishing industry in waters closer to Africa. These U.S. fleets bring their catch to Puerto Rico to be processed and exported.

INDUSTRY

MANUFACTURING. With the government-run Operation Bootstrap, Puerto Rico began intensive industrialization efforts and strong economic development in the late 1940s and early 1950s. Investment incentives and tax exemptions also encouraged foreign investment in industry, and the island's labor force shifted from agriculture to manufacturing. The manufacturing sector also saw a rapid shift from labor-intensive industry (food, tobacco, leather, and clothing) to capital-intensive industry (pharmaceuticals, chemicals, machinery, metal products, and electronics). Industry now accounts for 45 percent of the island's GDP, while manufacturing accounts for almost three-fourths of that percentage. Many manufacturers are offshore extensions of U.S. companies, importing raw materials mainly from the United States, adding value with low-cost labor, and then exporting products back to the United States and other wealthy nations. Some 161 of the Fortune 500 companies have facilities in Puerto Rico. Major U.S. companies operating in Puerto Rico include the Pepsi-Cola Bottling Company, K-Mart, Walgreen's, Woolworth's, and Kraft General Foods.

CONSTRUCTION. The construction industry in Puerto Rico is one of the most rapidly growing components of the economy, particularly in response to heavy expansion in manufacturing and tourism. In 1994, Governor Pedro Rosello backed a US$7.5 billion construction project with aims to improve the country's image and tourist appeal. Large sums of money have been allocated to the construction of hotels, roads, and infrastructure, and the renovation of existing tourist industries. The Transportation Infrastructure Finance and Innovation Act of 1999 approved US$1.7 billion for the construction of a rail system called Tren Urbano. As with most industries, the United States backs the majority of the construction companies, and most materials and machinery parts are imported from the United States as well.

SERVICES

TOURISM. With visitors spending over US$2 billion each year, tourism has blossomed as the fastest growing industry on the "Enchanted Island" (the tourism marketing slogan). Puerto Rico's attractive beaches and tropical climate are perhaps the island's greatest natural assets. Virtually all of the major cities are coastal tourist attractions; the most popular include San Juan, Ponce, Mayaguez, Bayamón, and Caguas, which together attracted more than 4 million tourists each year during the 1990s. Puerto Rico's uniquely blended African, Spanish, and indigenous Taino traditions have produced colorful and diverse cuisine, music, and customs that appeal to the international tourist. The island has also effectively developed its transportation network to enhance the tourism industry. Some 30 airports (domestic and international) provide easy access to a variety of locales on the island. Hotels, restaurants, and **retail** stores and centers have multiplied nearby.

Tourism produces 7 percent of the island's GNP and employs more than 60,000 islanders, a figure that is rapidly increasing. Hotels provide over 12,000 rooms, operating at full occupancy. Hotels built on the island enjoy a 90 percent local tax exemption while hotels built on Vieques and Culebra receive 100 percent exemptions. These exemptions also apply to condominiums, inns, theme parks, golf courses, marinas, and land used for other tourism-related activity. Largely due to the 1993 Tourism Incentives Act, the government is repaving roads, erecting signs and billboards around cities, financing a US$30 million facelift for the island's main airport, pouring money into cruise ships, and investing large sums of money in every aspect of the industry.

FINANCIAL SERVICES. By far, the United States is the island's largest trading and financial partner. More than one-third of U.S. investment in Latin America goes to Puerto Rico. Banks, retailers, hotels, restaurants, airlines, and many other firms have capitalized on the island's economy and have taken advantage of the booming tourism sector. The U.S. monetary system and tax incentives are among many forces that attract international investment in Puerto Rican finances.

Local corporations own most commercial banks. Banco Popular is the largest one, with more than 100 branches. The government owns and operates 2 banks: the Government Development Bank (GDB) and the Economic Development Bank (EDB). There are also several foreign-owned banks and 2 U.S. banks on the island: Citibank and FirstBank. The Federal Deposit Insurance Corporation insures all banks, which are subject to U.S. banking regulations and federal controls.

INTERNATIONAL TRADE

Puerto Rico's economy is highly dependent on imports and exports, both of which doubled between 1987 and 1997. In 1999, the island imported US$25.3 billion in goods, and it exported US$34.9 billion. For a century, the United States has been by far Puerto Rico's largest trading partner, accounting for 60 percent of imports and 88 percent of exports in 1999. The remainder of the island's trade is with various nations from Europe, Asia, and the Americas. The United States has created a variety of incentives for foreign investment in Puerto Rico, including tax incentives and exemptions, the use of U.S. currency, and government-backed startup costs. The island imports chemicals, machinery and equipment, clothing, food, fish, petroleum products, and raw materials; it exports pharmaceuticals, electronics, apparel, canned tuna, rum, beverage concentrates, and medical equipment.

Exchange rates: Puerto Rico	
US$	
Jan 2001	1.0000
2000	1.0000
1999	1.0000
1998	1.0000
1997	1.0000
1996	1.0000

Note: US currency is used in Puerto Ricos.

SOURCE: CIA *World Factbook 2001* [ONLINE].

MONEY

As a commonwealth of the United States, Puerto Rico enjoys many benefits of the stable U.S. dollar, referred to as a "peso" by most local people, and the U.S. central banking structure. Economic trends tend to follow those on the mainland, and the dollar retains a relatively strong and stable monetary value. The monetary stability gives the island an advantage over many other Latin American countries. Puerto Rico's per capita income at **purchasing power parity** (an economic measure of the strength of a nation's currency) of US$9,800 (1999 est.) is one of the highest in all of Latin America, and the **inflation rate** is a relatively low 5.2 percent.

POVERTY AND WEALTH

The average family size in Puerto Rico is 3.6, and the average family income is just over US$27,000. The government has consistently focused on making education, health care, and better housing more available to the population. Some 7 percent of the island's GDP is earmarked for education. Although literacy has increased to 90 percent, and most children complete at least 8 years of school, a high drop-out rate is still a problem for Puerto Rico. The University of Puerto Rico,

GDP per Capita (US$)					
Country	1996	1997	1998	1999	2000
Puerto Rico	8,200	8,600	9,000	9,800	10,000
United States	28,600	30,200	31,500	33,900	36,200
Jamaica	3,260	N/A	3,300	3,350	3,700
Cuba	1,480	1,540	1,560	1,700	1,700

Note: Data are estimates.

SOURCE: *Handbook of the Nations*, 17th, 18th, 19th and 20th editions for 1996, 1997, 1998 and 1999 data; CIA *World Factbook 2001* [Online] for 2000 data.

the main public university, offers a wide variety of programs. There are also several private universities. Vocational schools have recently helped to combat unemployment rates.

Health conditions and standards are approaching those of the United States. The government funds urban and rural health clinics to provide basic health care on a local level. Medicare, Medicaid, and other social programs have also contributed to maintaining health standards. The Urban Renewal and Housing Corporation oversees a broad range of specialized housing programs and focuses on projects in low-income areas. Although birth control and family planning efforts have helped reduce population growth, improved conditions on the island have recently encouraged many Puerto Rican outmigrants to return from the continental United States, which puts more strains on health-care delivery and housing.

Although Puerto Rico's per capita GDP is remarkably high in comparison to the rest of the Caribbean, it is still lower than the per capita GDP of the poorest U.S. state, Mississippi. Even though the GDP is growing more rapidly than the island's population, about half of the people in Puerto Rico receive Food Stamps, a benefit available only to those whose incomes fall below a certain level.

WORKING CONDITIONS

The largest obstacles to better working conditions in Puerto Rico are overcrowding, its high unemployment rate of 12.5 percent (1999 est.), and its high drop-out rate. Since Operation Bootstrap in the 1950s, the government has consistently worked to reduce unemployment. Working conditions in Puerto Rico are better than most in Latin America, largely due to its U.S. commonwealth status. U.S. labor laws, including those regulating minimum wages and workplace safety, apply to Puerto Rico and protect workers from abuse. Four major labor unions, with 115,000 members, protect workers' interests. The largest of them is the General Confederation of Puerto Rican Workers, with 35,000 members.

COUNTRY HISTORY AND ECONOMIC DEVELOPMENT

PRE-1400s. Puerto Rico is inhabited by the Taino Indians.

1493. Christopher Columbus arrives; gold mining begins.

1508. Formal Spanish colonization begins.

1509. Repartimiento begins (a system of using the indigenous population as indentured labor).

1513. Spain brings first African slaves to the island.

1519. Spain establishes a capital at San Juan.

1530. Sugar becomes the most important agricultural product.

1570. Gold mines are depleted by the Spaniards.

1598. The British Navy conquers Spanish forces and holds the island for several months. Ginger emerges as the primary cash crop.

1810s-1820s. Liberal Party gains more political support; the island gains experience in self-government.

1897. Spain gives Puerto Rico powers of self-government.

1898. Spain cedes Puerto Rico to the United States after the Spanish-American War.

1917. United States grants Puerto Rico partial self-government powers.

1930s. Political parties organize around statehood/independence issue, a debate that continues into the 21st century.

1940. Overpopulation becomes a serious problem.

1946. The first native governor, Jesus T. Piñero, is appointed by the United States.

1952. Puerto Rico becomes a U.S. commonwealth under a constitution following the U.S. model.

1950s. Operation Bootstrap shifts economic priorities from agriculture to labor-intensive manufacturing industries.

1967. Commonwealth status is approved in a plebiscite, the first time Puerto Ricans vote for the status of their own island.

1987-97. Imports and exports double in value.

1992. North American Free Trade Agreement (NAFTA) is signed by the countries of North America, encouraging more trade between Puerto Rico and Canada and Mexico.

1993. Commonwealth status is approved by a very narrow margin over statehood in a controversial plebiscite boycotted by many voters.

1994. The Foreign Trade Board is established to promote foreign business and investment.

FUTURE TRENDS

Puerto Rico has excellent prospects for future economic growth and development. The incentives for domestic and foreign investment provided by the U.S. government are highly successful and show no signs of slowing down. The island's severe lack of natural resources has been overcome by the practice of mixing local labor with external capital to produce a booming import/export economy. Improving social and economic conditions on the island may slow economic progress as Puerto Rican outmigrants return to the island from the continental United States. It is unlikely that the small independence movement will gain enough strength to be effective, but the United States is bound to respect Puerto Rican self-determination in regular plebiscites. If Puerto Ricans were to choose independence over commonwealth status, economic stability would be a significant challenge. Realistically speaking, the Puerto Rican economy is strong and well developed, and all signs point to a future of growth and prosperity.

DEPENDENCIES

Puerto Rico has no territories or colonies.

BIBLIOGRAPHY

Braus, Patricia. "The Spending Power of Puerto Rico." *American Demographics*. Vol. 13, No. 4, April 1991.

Economist Intelligence Unit. *Country Profile: Puerto Rico*. London: Economist Intelligence Unit, 2001.

Polin, Zena. "Tourism: Puerto Rico's 'Rising Star.'" *The Washington Times*. 29 September 1999.

"Puerto Rico Fact Sheet." *Energy Information Administration*. <http://www.eia.doe.gov/emeu/cabs/prico.html>. Accessed March 2001.

U.S. Central Intelligence Agency. *World Factbook 2000*. <http://www.odci.gov/cia/publications/factbook/index.html>. Accessed August 2001.

—David L. Childree

ST. KITTS AND NEVIS

Federation of Saint Kitts and Nevis

CAPITAL: Basseterre.

MONETARY UNIT: The currency of St. Kitts and Nevis is the Eastern Caribbean dollar (EC$). One EC dollar equals 100 cents. There are coins of 10, 20 and 50 cents, and notes of 5, 10, 20, and 100.

CHIEF EXPORTS: Machinery, food, electronics, beverages, tobacco.

CHIEF IMPORTS: Machinery, manufactures, food, fuels.

GROSS DOMESTIC PRODUCT: US$274 million (purchasing power parity, 2000 est.).

BALANCE OF TRADE: Exports: US$53.2 million (2000 est.). **Imports:** US$151.5 million (2000 est.).

Most Kittitians and Nevisians are of African descent, and there are smaller communities composed of people of mixed race and European descent. There is a small community in St. Kitts descended from immigrants of Middle Eastern origin. The population is fairly evenly distributed over age groups, with 30 percent of people aged between 1 and 14.

COUNTRY OVERVIEW

LOCATION AND SIZE. St. Kitts and Nevis are islands in the Caribbean Sea, in the Leeward Island chain to the west of Antigua. The area of the twin-island state is 261 square kilometers (101 square miles), with St. Kitts occupying 168 square kilometers (65 square miles) and Nevis 93 square kilometers (36 square miles). The country is approximately 1.5 times the size of Washington, D.C., and has a coastline measuring 135 kilometers (84 miles). The capital and main settlement of St. Kitts, Basseterre, is on the island's southern coast, while Charleston, the main town of Nevis, lies on the west coast.

POPULATION. The population of St. Kitts and Nevis was estimated at 38,819 in July 2000, a fall of 0.22 percent on the previous year's figure and a decline from the mid-1998 estimate of 40,700. According to the Caribbean Development Bank (CDB), the islands' population declined by an annual average rate of 2.4 percent between 1995 and 1998. The principal reason for the falling population is **emigration**, estimated at 11.85 migrants per 1,000 population in 2000. This migration is caused by **labor mobility** and a lack of employment and other opportunities on the islands.

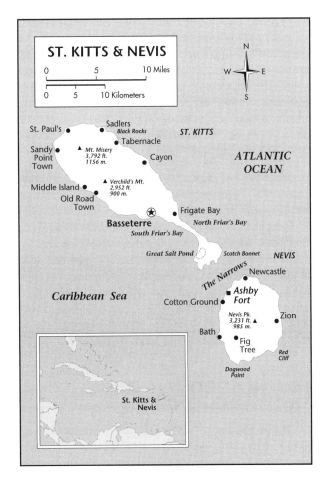

OVERVIEW OF ECONOMY

St. Kitts has been extremely dependent on sugar production, and, until the 1980s, sugar was the island's principal export and source of employment. Nevis, less fertile than St. Kitts, was a cotton-producing island. Both, however, have diversified their economies over the last 3 decades, although the sugar industry remains an important employer in St. Kitts. Currently the major industry in the islands is tourism, encouraged by government investment in cruise ship facilities and by **private-sector** investment in hotels.

In the late 1990s St. Kitts and Nevis were badly affected by recurring hurricanes. Extensive damage to agriculture and buildings occurred after Hurricane Georges in 1998 and Hurricane Lenny in 1999. In 1999 the government estimated that Hurricane Georges had caused over US$400 million of damage and was forced to turn to the International Monetary Fund (IMF) for emergency assistance with reconstruction. The devastation slowed tourist arrivals, due to damaged **infrastructure** and closed hotels, and also reduced the 1999 sugar crop. Construction, on the other hand, increased as people repaired their homes and the government rebuilt infrastructure.

The government has partly succeeded in reducing the country's dependence on sugar by encouraging other forms of agriculture, manufacturing, and financial services, as well as tourism. The light manufacturing sector includes electronic components, textiles, and packaging, for the U.S. market, while 1 industrial estate specializes in heavy operational machinery. Tourism, despite natural disasters, showed steady growth throughout the 1990s, and the government is attempting to build up an offshore financial sector. Nevis already has an international reputation as an established "**tax haven**."

St. Kitts and Nevis has a mix of small, local companies and larger, U.S.-owned corporations. The state sector is still large, despite attempts by the government to divest itself of the state-owned and anachronistic Sugar Company, which drains government resources and remains a liability rather than an asset. Despite this state of affairs and diversification, sugar continues to occupy a large place in the islands' economic and social life. One persistent cause for concern is the country's growing debt, made worse by hurricane damage and the need to borrow to pay for reconstruction projects.

POLITICS, GOVERNMENT, AND TAXATION

Since gaining its independence from the United Kingdom in 1983, the federation of St. Kitts and Nevis has experienced some turbulent political developments, particularly a concerted move by Nevisians to secede from the federation. There have also been political crises relating to disputed election results, alleged drug trafficking, and other forms of corruption.

In St. Kitts the main political party is the St. Kitts and Nevis Labour Party (SKNLP), which won elections in 1995 and 2000. Dominant in the 1960s and 1970s under self-government, in 1995 the SKNLP replaced a coalition government headed by the People's Action Movement (PAM), which remains the main opposition party. In Nevis the main party is the Concerned Citizens' Movement (CCM), which advocates secession from the federation and is opposed by the Nevis Reformation Party (NRP). A referendum on the issue of secession was held in Nevis in 1998, with 61.7 percent of the electorate voting in favor (just short of the two-thirds majority required for constitutional change). Relations between the 2 islands are sporadically tense, with Nevisians accusing St. Kitts of benefiting from their taxes without providing adequate services from central government.

Since its election in 1995, the SKNLP has made progress in modernizing the country's economy and attracting investment in manufacturing, tourism, and financial services. The party differs little from the PAM in terms of its general pro-business outlook but has attempted to put an end to the alleged corruption and drug-related activity that occurred in the early 1990s. Then in 1994 several high-profile murders occurred and British police officers were invited by the government to assist with anti-drug operations. The main issue of political difference remains between St. Kitts and Nevis, a conflict reminiscent of Anguilla's rebellion in 1969, which was based on Anguilla's desire not to be part of a state with St. Kitts and Nevis.

The government of St. Kitts and Nevis is able to exert considerable influence on economic development with its management of the state sector (which includes the money-losing St. Kitts Sugar Manufacturing Corporation), its policies on foreign investment, and taxation. About the former, it has tried to increase foreign investment by offering tax concessions and other inducements to companies and individuals willing to invest in a range of industries and sectors. Government policy on taxation has been to increase needed revenue by spreading the range of taxation over sales taxes, property taxes, fees, and other taxes paid by foreign businesses. There is no personal **income tax**, but the government raised electricity and water **tariffs** and introduced a substantial rise in petroleum prices in 2000. The revenue earned through these measures was offset by falling income from taxes on hotel-room occupancy and other forms of tourist expenditure in the wake of hurricanes.

Communications

Country	Telephones[a]	Telephones, Mobile/Cellular[a]	Radio Stations[b]	Radios[a]	TV Stations[a]	Televisions[a]	Internet Service Providers[c]	Internet Users[c]
St. Kitts & Nevis	17,000	205	AM 3; FM 1; shortwave 0	28,000	1	10,000	16	2,000
United States	194 M	69.209 M (1998)	AM 4,762; FM 5,542; shortwave 18	575 M	1,500	219 M	7,800	148 M
Jamaica	353,000 (1996)	54,640 (1996)	AM 10; FM 13; shortwave 0	1.215 M	7	460,000	21	60,000
St. Lucia	37,000	1,600	AM 2; FM 7; shortwave 0	111,000	3	32,000	15	5,000

[a]Data is for 1997 unless otherwise noted.
[b]Data is for 1998 unless otherwise noted.
[c]Data is for 2000 unless otherwise noted.

SOURCE: CIA *World Factbook 2001* [Online].

INFRASTRUCTURE, POWER, AND COMMUNICATIONS

The road infrastructure in the islands is adequate though underdeveloped, with 320 kilometers (199 miles) of roads of which 136 kilometers (84 miles) are paved. There are 58 kilometers (36 miles) of railway track on St. Kitts for transporting sugarcane only. A deep-water port was opened in Basseterre in 1981, and more recently, the government has invested in cruise ship facilities in the capital, creating the Port Zante terminal that can receive 2 cruise ships at once. Other ports and harbors are less developed, and in Nevis there is only a small jetty at Charlestown. The main airport, R.L. Bradshaw International, is near Basseterre and can handle international flights. Nevis, on the other hand, has only a small airport and receives most of its tourists through St. Kitts, another source of friction between the 2 islands. The main focus for tourist infrastructure is now St. Kitts' southeast peninsula, where there are several large resorts. Much of the island, however, is undeveloped in tourism terms, but there are several hotels and guesthouses in former plantation houses.

St. Kitts and Nevis has no natural power resources and is obliged to import fuel, mostly oil from Trinidad and Tobago, for electricity generation. According to the CIA Handbook, electricity generation in 1998 was 85 million kilowatt hours (kWh) and consumption was 79 million kWh. Telecommunications have improved in recent years, with widespread access to telephones and growing use of cellular phones and the Internet. There are no recent statistics, however, regarding telecommunications.

ECONOMIC SECTORS

Although an important employer and source of export earnings, agriculture accounted for only 5.5 percent

of the **gross domestic product** (GDP) in 1996. According to World Bank figures, by 1999 its share had decreased still further to about 3.6 percent of the GDP. This drop represents a massive fall from the 1960s when sugar was the major economic force on the island, contributing 25 percent of the GDP, and 1979 when agriculture represented 15.5 percent. Sugar remains the largest employer and source of revenue in agricultural terms.

Industry was estimated to contribute 22.5 percent of the GDP in 1996 and, according to the World Bank, 23.8 percent in 1999. Industry has always represented a high percentage of the GDP in St. Kitts and Nevis because the country has well-established, traditional manufacturing such as sugar refining.

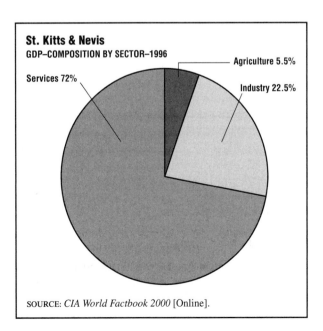

St. Kitts & Nevis
GDP–COMPOSITION BY SECTOR–1996

Services 72%
Agriculture 5.5%
Industry 22.5%

SOURCE: *CIA World Factbook 2000* [Online].

The services sector has shown sustained growth, rising from 59.6 percent of the GDP in 1979 to 72 percent in 1996. The World Bank figure for 1999 is almost unchanged at 72.6 percent. The main service sector is tourism, but financial services are becoming an increasingly important source of revenue.

AGRICULTURE

The first British colonial possession in the Caribbean, St. Kitts with, to a lesser degree, Nevis, was among the earliest plantation economies in the region. Sugar production dominated the island for 350 years. According to Eric Williams in his *From Columbus to Castro: The History of the Caribbean, 1492–1969,* in 1897, when the peak of sugar production was long past, St. Kitts still had over 15,000 sugar workers, 136 factories, and 35 plantations with over 500 acres each.

What remains is a fragment of the former industry, but the extensive plantations of the St. Kitts Sugar Manufacturing Corporation (SSMC) still employed about 10 percent of the **labor force**, or 1,500 people, in 1994. In government hands since 1975, the SSMC loses money each year, and its output is subsidized by the government through the state-owned National Bank. According to the *St. Kitts-Nevis Observer,* production costs per ton are 25 percent higher than the price received from the European Union (EU), which offers the country a guaranteed annual quota of 15,600 tons. The United States also buys a fixed annual quota of sugar from St. Kitts-Nevis at above world market prices. But despite these preferential markets, the SSMC is a loss-maker, costing the government the equivalent of 3.5 percent of the GDP annually. In his 2001 New Year speech, Prime Minister Denzil Douglas spoke of the urgent need to reduce the SSMC's losses by divesting itself of its land and other assets to avoid a "national disaster."

The situation has been worsened by recent hurricane damage. In 1999 exports fell 24.7 percent from the previous year, totaling 17,178 tons and earning only US$9.6 million. This followed a brief upsurge in 1997, when production reached 31,374 tons. Bad weather conditions caused the tonnage of cane cut per hectare also to fall from 65 in 1998 to 53.5 in 1999. There is a recurring labor shortage in the industry since few younger Kittitians want to work long and hard hours for little reward. The government has been obliged to contract seasonal cane cutters from Guyana, and there have been complaints of low wages paid to these temporary workers and of their poor conditions.

The government has been encouraged by the IMF and others to diversify the country's agricultural output and to reduce the high food imports. There has been an increase in vegetable cultivation on St. Kitts, while Nevis

produces sea-island cotton and coconuts. One successful by-product of the otherwise ailing sugar industry is cane spirit, a white rum exported to Europe or North America.

INDUSTRY

Traditional industries such as sugar refining, rum distilling, and tobacco processing are well established in St. Kitts. The island has also witnessed the steady growth of newer manufacturing interests in recent years, leading to a 23.8 percent share of the GDP in 1999. In fact, 4 industrial sites have been developed, specializing in heavy machinery, electronic components, and other manufactured goods destined for the North American market. Garment manufacturing has expanded since the mid-1990s and now accounts for a large share of export earnings. Upgrading the Port Zante harbor complex in Basseterre enables large container ships to call, further enhancing St. Kitts' attractiveness as an offshore manufacturing base. According to the World Bank, manufactured exports were valued at US$20 million in 1998 and 1999, suggesting that this sector was the least affected by hurricane damage. There is no manufacturing on Nevis. In 1997 the IMF estimated that 1,290 people worked in the manufacturing sector.

SERVICES

TOURISM. This sector was badly hit by the effects of the hurricanes in 1998 and 1999. The country had just started to rebuild after Georges in 1998 when Lenny created substantial damage in 1999. The Port Zante complex, where the pier and terminal buildings are located, suffered serious damage. In Nevis, the only large hotel was forced to close for 6 months, resulting in lay-offs of staff (although many were employed to re-landscape devastated gardens) and decreased government revenue. Overall visitor arrivals, both of those staying over and those on cruise ship calls, fell about 15 percent in 1999, with a resulting decrease in visitor expenditure from the 1998 figure of US$75.7 million.

Tourism has become important to St. Kitts and Nevis, which has created a network of often small but upmarket hotels and guesthouses in former plantation houses. Larger hotel complexes exist as well, especially in the Frigate Bay area of St. Kitts where there are golf courses, casinos, and condominiums. Cruise ships have become an important part of the tourist industry, especially since the construction of the Port Zante terminal. Tourism is vital to Nevis, where manufacturing and other economic activity is much less diversified than in St. Kitts. There is considerable concern that any slowdown in the United States or European economies could have a serious effect on the tourist industry if U.S. and European consumers should decide they cannot afford a Caribbean vacation.

FINANCIAL SERVICES. As elsewhere in the Eastern Caribbean, financial services are of growing importance. This is especially true in Nevis, which has a reputation as an efficient and discreet tax haven. Most investors are based in North America and Europe, and few are local. The banks and other businesses offer services to customers, individuals, and businesses seeking to avoid taxation in the countries in which they are based. According to the IMF, the current legal framework "provides for a high degree of confidentiality and for income tax exemption." In early 2001 the international Financial Action Task Force (FATF), supported by European and North American governments, named St. Kitts and Nevis, among other Caribbean countries, as a suspected location of financial irregularities. The government has agreed to close loopholes in its legal and regulatory structures about offshore financial transactions. There are several dozen banks and other businesses based in St. Kitts-Nevis, but they provide little local employment, as most business is conducted electronically. Details as to customer identity and the value of deposits are well-kept secrets.

INTERNATIONAL TRADE

St. Kitts and Nevis imports approximately 4 times more value than it exports (US$160 million in imports against US$42 million in exports in 1998). This trade imbalance is only partly offset by tourism and other service revenues. Most troubling is the large food import bill, much of which is due to foodstuffs imported for the tourist sector but which also suggests that the islands are dependent on imports for basic nutritional requirements. Other imports are machinery, cars, fuel, and—since the recent hurricanes—building materials.

According to 1995 figures (the most recent available), the United States was the most important export market, taking 68.5 percent of merchandise, mostly garments and electronic components. The United Kingdom took 22.3 percent of exports, primarily sugar, while

Exchange rates: St. Kitts and Nevis	
East Caribbean dollars (EC$) per US$1	
2001	2.7000
2000	2.7000
1999	2.7000
1998	2.7000
1997	2.7000
1996	2.7000
Note: The rate for St. Kitts and Nevis has been fixed since 1976.	
SOURCE: CIA *World Factbook 2001* [ONLINE].	

Caribbean Community (CARICOM) countries received the remainder of exported goods. The United States was also the main source of imports (42.4 percent), with CARICOM countries supplying 17.2 percent, primarily food and fuel.

MONEY

Hurricanes notwithstanding, St. Kitts and Nevis enjoyed average annual GDP growth rates of 5 percent in the 1990s. **Inflation** has also been low, largely because St. Kitts and Nevis is a member of regional financial institutions such as the Eastern Caribbean Central Bank (ECCB). The Eastern Caribbean dollar, a currency shared with the 7 other members of the ECCB, is stable and has been pegged at a rate of EC$2.7 to US$1 for many years. Thus St. Kitts and Nevis is not too vulnerable to fluctuating **exchange rates**, although transactions with EU countries have been affected by the low value of the euro. There are plans for ECCB member countries to participate in a regional stock exchange, further integrating the economies of the small islands. In its 2000 analysis of the St. Kitts and Nevis economy, the IMF "considered that the exchange rate system operated by the Eastern Caribbean Central Bank has served the country well in maintaining **macroeconomic** stability and low inflation."

The ECCB is headquartered in Basseterre, and there are 3 major international banks as well as the international business companies (IBCs) that operate in the financial services sector.

POVERTY AND WEALTH

St. Kitts and Nevis is not one of the poorer countries of the Eastern Caribbean. The Caribbean Development Bank estimated per capita GDP at US$7,086 in 1998, which is above the regional average. There are no statistics for the distribution of wealth, but there are distinct pockets of poverty, especially in rural areas and those communities still dependent on the sugar industry. Few

Trade (expressed in billions of US$): St. Kitts & Nevis		
	Exports	**Imports**
1975	.022	.024
1980	.024	.045
1985	.020	.051
1990	.028	.110
1995	.019	.133
1998	N/A	N/A
SOURCE: International Monetary Fund. *International Financial Statistics Yearbook 1999.*		

GDP per Capita (US$)

Country	1975	1980	1985	1990	1998
St. Kitts & Nevis	N/A	2,569	3,123	4,479	6,716
United States	19,364	21,529	23,200	25,363	29,683
Jamaica	1,819	1,458	1,353	1,651	1,559
St. Lucia	N/A	2,076	2,150	3,542	3,907

SOURCE: United Nations. *Human Development Report 2000; Trends in human development and per capita income.*

of the benefits from economic growth and diversification are to be seen in the more remote north-coast areas of St. Kitts, where living conditions and social services are still rudimentary. Although free primary education is available and there is a network of rural medical clinics, costs attached to education and medical treatment are too high for poorer families. In many cases, regular **remittances** from family members working overseas are an essential economic lifeline.

In contrast, there is a conspicuously wealthy class based in Basseterre, in the Frigate Bay area. Some of this wealth is alleged to derive from drug-trafficking and other illegal activity, while other, legal, sources of prosperity are linked to real estate, tourism development, and the growth of financial services. There is a sizable and wealthy British expatriate community, especially in Nevis, while some older people are rich after a lifetime of working and saving abroad. But neither St. Kitts nor Nevis has the facilities to cater to the really rich, and those with large **disposable incomes** shop in Miami, Caracas or, less expensively, larger Caribbean islands. Education and health facilities are also found abroad.

WORKING CONDITIONS

In 1997 unemployment was estimated at 4.5 percent. Conditions in the antiquated agricultural sector are poor, with long hours and hard labor demanded, especially during the cane-cutting season. Average day rates in the sugar industry can be as low as US$10. A part of the labor force, especially during the annual harvest, has to be imported from poorer nations such as Guyana. The sugar labor force varies according to the season, but in the cutting season from March to July there are approximately 1,500 workers employed. The St. Kitts-Nevis Labor Union, once a powerful voice for the rights of sugar workers, is now severely weakened.

In contrast, wages and conditions in manufacturing, tourism, and the financial services sector are average or above-average for the region, and trade unions are effective in monitoring compliance with labor laws. There is no **informal sector** and little evidence of child labor, while women are active in most areas of employment except the sugar industry. Basic labor rights such as sick pay are observed.

COUNTRY HISTORY AND ECONOMIC DEVELOPMENT

1493. Christopher Columbus sights and names St. Kitts and Nevis.

1623. St. Kitts becomes the site of the first British settlement in the Caribbean.

1783. St. Kitts is officially ceded to Britain after 150 years of shared Anglo-French occupation.

1816. St. Kitts, Nevis, Anguilla, and the British Virgin Islands are administered as a single colony.

1967. St. Kitts, Nevis, and Anguilla together become a "state in voluntary association with Britain" and is granted self-government.

1969. Anguilla unilaterally secedes from the tripartite grouping and is re-established as a separate British Crown Colony in 1971.

1983. St. Kitts and Nevis attains full independence as a federal state.

Household Consumption in PPP Terms

Country	All food	Clothing and footwear	Fuel and power[a]	Health care[b]	Education[b]	Transport & Communications	Other
St. Kitts & Nevis	33	4	11	5	13	18	14
United States	13	9	9	4	6	8	51
Jamaica	24	7	3	1	9	8	48
St. Lucia	40	5	11	4	17	11	11

Data represent percentage of consumption in PPP terms.
[a]Excludes energy used for transport.
[b]Includes government and private expenditures.

SOURCE: World Bank. *World Development Indicators 2000.*

1994. Political crisis occurs amid allegations of corruption and official involvement in drug trafficking.

1995. St. Kitts and Nevis Labor Party (SKNLP) returns to power.

1998. Secession referendum in Nevis narrowly votes to retain federation; Hurricane Georges causes US$400 million in damages.

2000. SKNLP wins a second term in office.

FUTURE TRENDS

Apart from the unpredictable issue of future hurricanes, economic prospects for St. Kitts and Nevis will be determined by the sugar industry and relations between the 2 islands. The government will seek to reduce its **subsidies** to the faltering state-owned sugar company, either by **privatizing** any profitable parts of its operations or by closing it altogether. The latter course of action would carry with it drastic social consequences, including wide-scale unemployment.

Much also depends on whether St. Kitts and Nevis remain within their federal relationship or whether Nevis eventually decides to go its own way. If it should do so, the island would be one of the smallest sovereign states in the world and even more vulnerable to unexpected economic shocks such as another hurricane. What is more likely is that Nevis will extract concessions from St. Kitts, especially on tax and government spending issues, and will remain within the federation, if rather reluctantly.

The broader picture for the 2 islands is also uncertain. If there is a general crackdown on offshore finan-cial centers, as advocated by the wealthy nations of the OECS, then the budding financial sector in St. Kitts and Nevis will suffer as investors move their money elsewhere. Manufacturing, too, is also vulnerable to increased competition from elsewhere in the Caribbean and Latin America as trade barriers come down and foreign companies look for the cheapest sources of labor. Tourism, despite the risks it faces from weather and a possible **recession** in the United States, looks like the safest future option for these small and vulnerable islands.

DEPENDENCIES

St. Kitts and Nevis has no territories or colonies.

BIBLIOGRAPHY

Caribbean Development Bank, *Annual Report 1999.* Barbados: 2000.

Economist Intelligence Unit. *Country Profile: OECS.* London: Economist Intelligence Unit, 2000.

International Monetary Fund. <http://www.imf.org/external/np>. Accessed February 2001.

"St. Kitts and Nevis." *South America, Central America and the Caribbean 2001.* London: Europa Publications, 2001.

St. Kitts and Nevis: Official Government Web Site. <http://www .stkittsnevis.net>. Accessed February 2001.

U.S. Central Intelligence Agency. *World Factbook 2000.* <http:// www.odci.gov/cia/publications/factbook/index.html>. Accessed August 2001.

U.S. Central Intelligence Agency. *World Factbook 2001.* <http:// www.odci.gov/cia/publications/factbook/index.html>. Accessed September 2001.

—James Ferguson

ST. LUCIA

Saint Lucia Statistics Department. The other important

CAPITAL: Castries.

MONETARY UNIT: Eastern Caribbean dollar (EC$).
There are coins of 10, 20, and 50 cents. One EC
dollar equals 100 cents. The currency is fixed to the
U.S. dollar at a rate of EC$2.70 to US$1.00.

CHIEF EXPORTS: Bananas, clothing, cocoa, vegetables, fruit, coconut oil.

CHIEF IMPORTS: Food, manufactured goods, machinery and transportation equipment, chemicals,
fuel.

GROSS DOMESTIC PRODUCT: US$656 million
(purchasing power parity, 1998 est.).

BALANCE OF TRADE: **Exports:** US$75 million
(1998). **Imports:** US$290 million (1998).

COUNTRY OVERVIEW

LOCATION AND SIZE. The island of St. Lucia is situated
between the Atlantic Ocean and the Caribbean Sea, north
of Trinidad and Tobago. Part of the Windward Island
chain, it lies between the French overseas departments of
Martinique and St. Vincent. Its total area is 620 square
kilometers (239 square miles), approximately 3.5 times the
size of Washington, D.C. Its coastline measures 158 kilometers (98 miles), and its capital and main town, Castries,
lies in a sheltered bay on the island's northwest coast.

POPULATION. St. Lucia's population was estimated at
156,260 in mid-2000, an increase of 1.21 percent on the
previous year. The island's population grew at an average annual rate of 1.5 percent between 1995 and 1998,
and if current growth rates are sustained, its population
will stand at approximately 180,000 in 2010. St. Lucia's
population has grown steadily during the 1990s despite a
high level of **emigration** (people moving away from the
country), estimated at 4.67 per 1,000 people. This, however, is a lower rate of emigration than that experienced
by the neighboring islands of Dominica and St. Vincent.

Approximately half of the population lives in or near
the capital, Castries (57,401 in 1996), according to the

Saint Lucia Statistics Department. The other important
centers of population are Vieux Fort in the south (14,512
people) and Soufrière on the southwest coast (8,478 people). Otherwise, the population is scattered in small towns
and villages, mostly near the flatter coastal regions. More
than 90 percent of the population is of African descent,
a legacy of the island's past as a plantation economy.
African slaves were brought to St. Lucia by Europeans
(mostly the French) to work on the plantations. English
is the official language, but there are strong French influences because the island was colonized by France for
much of the 17th and 18th centuries. Many St. Lucians
speak a French Creole. Catholicism is the main religion.

OVERVIEW OF ECONOMY

St. Lucia has traditionally had an agricultural economy, one geared towards exporting tropical commodities
and importing manufactured goods. Sugar was the main
crop from the 17th century until the 1920s. The end of
slavery in 1838 allowed those who had worked on the
large plantations to start their own, privately-owned
farms producing fruits and vegetables. Bananas were introduced in the 1950s and rapidly became the island's
main export, benefiting from preferential access to the
British market and, after independence from Britain in
1979, to the entire European market. The heyday of the
banana industry was during the 1980s, when exports were
consistently above 100,000 tons annually, representing as
much as 70 percent of export income.

St. Lucia's banana industry was troubled by uncertainty and crisis during the 1990s. The World Trade Organization (WTO) ruled in 1995 that the European Union
(EU) went against free trade legislation by giving preference to Caribbean banana exports. This caused concern that the St. Lucian banana industry had lost its most
profitable fruit market. As a result, many farmers abandoned banana cultivation and planted other crops. Making matters worse for the banana industry, the govern-
ment-supported St. Lucia Banana Growers' Association
(SLBGA) was bankrupted in 1994 under rumors of corruption. The SLBGA helped banana growers, but the organization was also illegally used by the government to

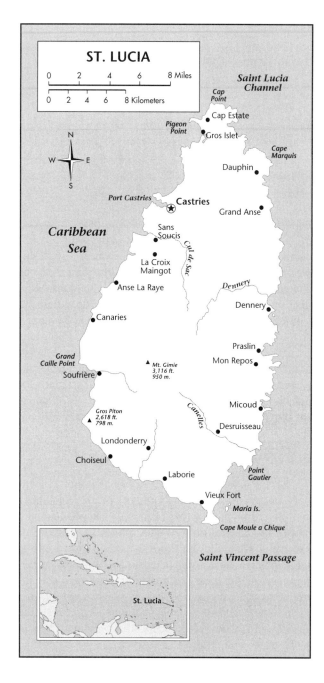

ST. LUCIA

The main areas of growth have been related to the tourism industry, in services and construction. On average, over 250,000 tourists visited the island each year during the 1990s. Government-sponsored **infrastructure** projects such as construction of new roads, ports, and several hotels have contributed to the economy's growth since the late 1990s. St. Lucia is also trying to establish itself as a center for **offshore banking**, where foreign investors and companies can avoid paying taxes in their own countries, and where the tax rates are comparatively low.

POLITICS, GOVERNMENT, AND TAXATION

St. Lucia is a multi-party parliamentary democracy, based on the British model of government. As part of the British Commonwealth, St. Lucia has the British queen serve as chief of state and is represented by a governor general. A prime minister and deputy prime minister lead the government. There is a **bicameral** parliament. The East Caribbean Supreme Court has jurisdiction over St. Lucia as well as several other Caribbean islands.

From 1964 until 1996 the island's politics were dominated by the United Workers' Party (UWP) led by John Compton. He held power during that entire period with the exception of 1979–82, when the St. Lucia Labour Party (SLP) was in office. Compton retired in 1996 under allegations of corruption, and in 1997 the SLP, headed by Kenny Anthony, won an overwhelming election victory. The SLP is generally considered to be more left-wing and sympathetic to the trade unions than the UWP, while the UWP was supported during the 1980s and early 1990s by a more prosperous sector of banana growers. Little separates the 2 parties in policy now that the banana industry has collapsed. Both are keen to diversify St. Lucia's economy away from dependence on bananas and both welcome foreign investments in all areas of the economy. The SLP government has particularly tried to promote the island as a reputable center for international finance, but as yet it has not attracted a large number of foreign financial ventures.

Until the reform of the SLBGA and the ousting of the UWP in 1996, the banana industry was primarily owned and operated by the government. The minority UWP continues to provide advice and support though the ministry of agriculture and other state bodies, but the SLP has majority power in St. Lucia's formal economic policies. The Kenny Anthony government is more active in promoting the country's industrial and financial development than in saving the banana industry. The National Development Corporation (NDC) offers incentives to potential foreign investors. Roads, ports, and industrial complexes have all been built by the government in order to attract foreign investment in manufacturing and services.

control the island's money supply. Attempts to reform the SLBGA and **restructure** the banana industry met with only partial success after the scandal was revealed.

St. Lucia has quite a large manufacturing sector, mainly geared towards supplying the U.S. market with clothes and sporting goods, and there is a factory that produces cardboard packaging for bananas and other agricultural crops. Several plants closed and many jobs were lost in 1996 due to the difficult economic situation. The new administration attempted to impose taxes on foreign operations in St. Lucia, and failed. These manufacturing operations quickly closed and left the island, rather than pay corporate taxes.

Tax concessions are offered to foreign investors and there are plans to open a **free zone** at Vieux Fort, where foreign businesses would be able to import and export goods without paying **duties**. The government raises revenue from foreign companies after a **tax holiday** has expired, but many foreign companies leave just before the tax holiday has ended. Other principal sources of government revenue are sales and property taxes as well as the various taxes charged to tourists, including hotel room taxes and airport departure taxes. In a 1999 report on the St. Lucian economy, the World Bank suggested that the government's concessions to foreign businesses were too generous and that the economy would benefit from the introduction of a uniform **value-added tax**.

INFRASTRUCTURE, POWER, AND COMMUNICATIONS

St. Lucia is a small island with a relatively underdeveloped infrastructure, although the government has invested in modernizing road and port facilities since the mid-1990s. There are 1,210 kilometers (752 miles) of roads, but only about a half of these are paved. Many rural roads, particularly in the interior, are unpaved and vulnerable to landslides and storm damage. In 2000 the government began a large-scale project to resurface and upgrade 116 kilometers (72 miles) of primary and secondary roads. There are 2 airports, of which Hewanorra, in the south near Vieux Fort, is the main international airport, while George F.L. Charles airport, near Castries, receives mostly inter-island flights. The main commercial port is at Vieux Fort, where modernized deep-water container facilities were opened in 1993. In addition to commercial ships, cruise ships call at Castries, where there is a specially constructed duty-free shopping complex at Pointe Seraphine.

St. Lucia imports oil from Trinidad and Tobago and Venezuela to meet its energy needs, and there is a large oil transshipment terminal south of Castries, used for **re-exporting** oil to other islands. In 1998 electricity production was estimated at 110 million kilowatts and consumption at 102 million kilowatts. Communications are generally good, but in early 2001 the island's dominant service provider, Cable and Wireless, was preparing to close after the government decided to end its **monopoly**. According to the World Bank, there were 268 mainline telephones per 1,000 people in 1998 and 136 personal computers per 1,000 people.

ECONOMIC SECTORS

The contribution made by agriculture to **gross domestic product** fell steadily throughout the 1990s, from 14.5 percent in 1990 to 8.1 percent in 1998. This fall reflected the crisis in the banana industry and the resulting decrease in agricultural production and exports. Attempts to diversify agricultural products (plant new kinds of crops) did not improve the agricultural sector as a whole. Despite the decline in output, agriculture was St. Lucia's second largest source of employment, providing jobs for 13,150 people in 1999 or approximately 20 percent of the workforce.

Industry's contribution to gross domestic product remained constant throughout the 1990s, rising only slightly from 18.1 percent in 1990 to 18.9 percent in 1998. The main sector of industry was manufacturing, which provided 5,160 jobs in 1999, or 8 percent of total employment. Most manufacturing work was done for the U.S. market, although there were also some industrial plants producing goods such as processed foods and beverages for the local market. Export-oriented

Communications

Country	Telephones[a]	Telephones, Mobile/Cellular[a]	Radio Stations[b]	Radios[a]	TV Stations[a]	Televisions[a]	Internet Service Providers[c]	Internet Users[c]
St. Lucia	37,000	1,600	AM 2; FM 7; shortwave 0	111,000	3	32,000	15	5,000
United States	194 M	69.209 M (1998)	AM 4,762; FM 5,542; shortwave 18	575 M	1,500	219 M	7,800	148 M
Jamaica	353,000 (1996)	54,640 (1996)	AM 10; FM 13; shortwave 0	1.215 M	7	460,000	21	60,000
Bahamas	96,000	6,152	AM 3; FM 4; shortwave 0	215,000	1	67,000	19	15,000

[a]Data is for 1997 unless otherwise noted.
[b]Data is for 1998 unless otherwise noted.
[c]Data is for 2000 unless otherwise noted.

SOURCE: CIA *World Factbook 2001* [Online].

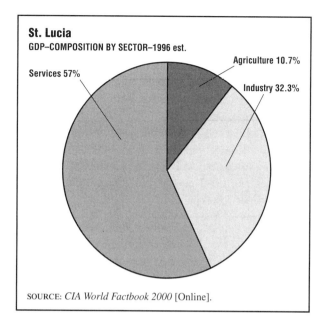

St. Lucia
GDP–COMPOSITION BY SECTOR–1996 est.

Services 57%

Agriculture 10.7%

Industry 32.3%

SOURCE: *CIA World Factbook 2000* [Online].

manufacturing declined during the 1990s, but was balanced out by a boom in construction activity.

Services grew as a percentage of gross domestic product through the 1990s, from 67.3 percent in 1990 to 72.9 percent in 1998. Tourism was the main factor in this growth, and the industry was responsible for 5,390 jobs in hotels and restaurants in 1998 (8 percent of employment). An additional 11,300 people, or 17 percent of the workforce, were employed in the **retail** sector, which had strong links with tourism. The fastest-growing economic force in St. Lucia during the 1990s was tourism, affecting not only the services and retail sectors, but the con-

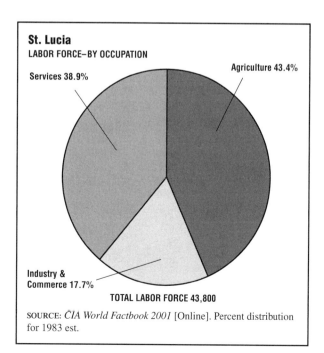

St. Lucia
LABOR FORCE–BY OCCUPATION

Services 38.9%

Agriculture 43.4%

Industry & Commerce 17.7%

TOTAL LABOR FORCE 43,800

SOURCE: *CIA World Factbook 2001* [Online]. Percent distribution for 1983 est.

struction sector as well, accounting for at least 25 percent of workforce employment.

AGRICULTURE

Since the heyday of the late 1980s, banana production in St. Lucia has faced a number of challenges and crises. The growers' association, the SLBGA, was plagued by inefficiency and corruption. After extensive reorganization, the newly elected SLP government paid off the SLBGA's debts and turned it into a private company, owned and managed by farmers. The new company, the St. Lucia Banana Corporation, was launched in 1998, but has been unable to reverse the decline within the industry. The biggest problem has been the loss of preferential access to the European market following the 1995 WTO ruling. The EU donated US$7.7 million in 1999 to support the reorganization and diversification of the agricultural industry.

Even so, bananas occupy a vital place within the island's economy, not merely in terms of employment but also as an earner of foreign exchange. During the 1980s and 1990s, St. Lucia could have been called a banana republic. In 2000, according to the Windward Islands Banana Development and Exporting Company (WIBDECO), St. Lucia exported 70,281 tons of bananas to Europe, earning slightly over US$30 million in export income. Bananas represented approximately 60 percent of the island's export income, but only a minimal amount of foreign exchange was gained when compared to the success of the tourism industry. Other agriculture in St. Lucia included dairy farming, flowers, and fisheries, but export income from these crops were still small.

INDUSTRY

Since the 1990s the government in St. Lucia has tried to build up a manufacturing sector as an alternative to the reliance on bananas and tourism. The island's population is too small to support the manufacture of goods for domestic consumption (St. Lucia's citizens cannot afford to buy expensive manufactured items), so the emphasis has been on export-oriented products such as garments, sporting goods, toys, and diving equipment. Most of the larger factories are situated in an industrial park near the container port at Vieux Fort, for the easy transportation of goods off the island. In 1996 the manufacturing sector was badly hit when 3 foreign companies closed because they were nearing the end of their 10-year tax holiday. Since then, more plants have closed and manufacturing as a whole has stagnated.

The majority of manufacturing plants in St. Lucia are owned and operated by foreign companies. They open plants on the island to take advantage of the cheap labor, low tax rates, and easy access to the U.S. market. However, because the government of St. Lucia gives tax incentives to these companies, the island community does not receive many benefits from the arrangement apart from employment gains.

In employment terms, however, manufacturing is still much less important than agriculture and tourism, and 1999 export figures show that all manufacturing, including beverages and tobacco, earned only US$21 million. Construction, on the other hand, has grown sharply since the mid-1990s with a mixture of **public-sector** investment, such as roads, and **private-sector** hotel projects. Construction of a new large Hyatt hotel in the north of the island created many jobs and gave a boost to local builders and suppliers.

SERVICES

Services account for almost three-quarters of St. Lucia's gross domestic product, supported by tourism. There were 688,460 visitors to the island in 1999, according to the Caribbean Development Bank (CDB), with 259,371 of these staying on the island and 423,114 visiting briefly aboard cruise ships. In 1998 St. Lucia earned US$291.3 million from tourism, almost 10 times the value of banana exports. Unlike other Caribbean destinations, St. Lucia has enjoyed steady growth in its tourism industry since the 1990s, with an encouraging year-on-year increase in the number of visitors who spend a week or more on the island. Much of the tourism sector, however, is concentrated in the all-inclusive category, where vacationers prepay their accommodation, food, and leisure activities in a single package. This means that small, independent hotels and restaurants receive fewer customers, and tourists are deterred from spending money outside the hotel perimeter. Some smaller businesses have reported a 75 percent drop in earnings since the construction of the 8 main all-inclusive hotels.

Tourists come for the island's natural beauty, and St. Lucia hosts special events such as the annual jazz festival and the Atlantic Rally for Cruisers. This latter event alone earns the island US$2 million annually in tourism spending. But as tourism increases, there are concerns about its impact on the island's ecosystem as well as on its social structures. Reports of crimes committed against tourists are now commonplace, and there are anxieties about the long-term future of such natural splendors as coral reefs and the world-famous Pitons, the forest-clad mountains that rise steeply out of the sea.

The government has also declared its intention to turn St. Lucia into a center for international financial services, such as banking and insurance. Like other Caribbean countries, the island hoped to attract foreign investors, both corporate and individual, who wished to avoid paying taxes in their own countries. In early 2001, however, only 1 full bank had been registered in comparison to 117 International Business Companies, companies set up mainly to provide a system for foreign tax evasion. Unfortunately, the launching of the financial services sector coincided with a crackdown on illegal **tax havens** by the international Financial Action Task Force (FATF), supported by Europe and North America, aimed at stopping **money laundering**. In 1999 only 990 St. Lucians were employed in the financial sector.

INTERNATIONAL TRADE

St. Lucia's **trade deficit**, US$215 million in 1998, was balanced out by the island's income from tourism. In terms of exports, the main buyer was the United Kingdom, which paid St. Lucia US$33.2 million for goods in 1998 (mostly bananas). The second biggest buyer of St. Lucian goods was the Caribbean Community (CARICOM), at US$10.5 million. As for the island's imports, the biggest provider was the United States, which sold US$120.7 million of goods to St. Lucia in 1998, while CARICOM countries provided US$70.5 million of imports.

MONEY

After steady growth in the 1980s and early 1990s, St. Lucia's economy slowed, partly due to the banana crisis and hurricane damage, and partly to a decline in manufacturing output. Gross domestic product growth from 1996 averaged 1.5 percent annually, the lowest rate in the Eastern Caribbean apart from volcano-devastated Montserrat. In 1998 and 1999 gross domestic product growth increased to 2.9 percent and 3.1 percent, respectively, largely because of increased tourism and associated construction. **Inflation** has been low since the early 1990s, but prices rose by 3.5 percent in 1999, due in part to higher oil prices and increases in light and fuel bills.

St. Lucia's currency, the Eastern Caribbean dollar, is shared with the 7 other members of the Eastern Caribbean

Trade (expressed in billions of US$): St. Lucia		
	Exports	Imports
1975	.017	.046
1980	.058	.124
1985	.057	.125
1990	.127	.271
1995	.109	.307
1998	N/A	N/A

SOURCE: International Monetary Fund. *International Financial Statistics Yearbook 1999.*

Exchange rates: St. Lucia

East Caribbean dollars (EC$) per US$1

2001	2.7000
2000	2.7000
1999	2.7000
1998	2.7000
1997	2.7000
1996	2.7000

Note: The rate for St. Lucia has been fixed since 1976.

SOURCE: CIA *World Factbook 2001* [ONLINE].

Distribution of Income or Consumption by Percentage Share: St. Lucia

Lowest 10%	2.0
Lowest 20%	5.2
Second 20%	9.9
Third 20%	14.8
Fourth 20%	21.8
Highest 20%	48.3
Highest 10%	32.5

Survey year: 1995
Note: This information refers to income shares by percentiles of the population and is ranked by per capita income.

SOURCE: *2000 World Development Indicators* [CD-ROM].

Central Bank (ECCB): Anguilla, Antigua and Barbuda, Commonwealth of Dominica, Grenada, Montserrat, St. Kitts and Nevis, and St. Vincent and The Grenadines. It is stable and has been fixed at a rate of EC$2.70=US$1.00. This means that St. Lucia is less vulnerable to the fluctuating **exchange rates** of other countries, although transactions with Europe are affected by the value of the euro. When the euro is worth less than the dollar, Europe is able to buy fewer bananas from St. Lucia than the United States. There are plans for ECCB member countries to participate in a regional stock exchange, further integrating the economies of the small islands.

POVERTY AND WEALTH

There is little drastic poverty in St. Lucia, but there are clear differences between a wealthy minority, a comfortable middle class, and a poor lower class. With per capita income estimated at approximately US$4,000 in 1998, the island is one of the more prosperous in the Eastern Caribbean. This is largely due to the success of the banana industry during the 1980s and the early 1990s, and continues because of the tourism industry. Many rural villages in banana-growing areas have solid housing and expensive imported vehicles, signs of the banana industry's economic impact. But there are also many smaller farmers, some with as little as an acre or two, who have not shared in the benefits of the banana boom.

GDP per Capita (US$)

Country	1975	1980	1985	1990	1998
St. Lucia	N/A	2,076	2,150	3,542	3,907
United States	19,364	21,529	23,200	25,363	29,683
Jamaica	1,819	1,458	1,353	1,651	1,559
Bahamas	8,030	12,727	13,835	13,919	N/A

SOURCE: United Nations. *Human Development Report 2000; Trends in human development and per capita income.*

In contrast, the wealthy minority in St. Lucia are situated in the plush residential developments to the north of Castries, around which many tourist resorts are to be found. Here, shopping malls, golf courses, and marinas testify to a luxurious lifestyle. Those who are richest in St. Lucia are white collar professionals such as lawyers and doctors, local managers of foreign companies, and people connected with successful tourism ventures and private sector construction. Included in this employment sector is a large number of European and American expatriates (citizens who moved from their native country to live in St. Lucia). The island's middle class is composed of urban professionals and those involved in traditional retail, while in the countryside there are many owners of large farms who have made enough money to consider themselves middle class.

Primary education is free and compulsory, but poor families often find it hard to afford uniforms and school books for their children. Medical care is available throughout the island, but doctors charge for visits and prescriptions are expensive. Housing conditions vary enormously, from the luxury villas of the island's northern tip to the ramshackle villages of the eastern coast.

WORKING CONDITIONS

The banana industry has depended on small family farms for over 150 years. Rural labor is different from many banana-producing countries in that there are few large plantations. The vast sugar plantations operating during colonial times have disappeared, replaced by small banana farms. As a result, rural working relationships tend to be based on the family or the community. Wages are generally US$5–10 per day. Manufacturing and the tourism sector offer better wages and conditions to St. Lucians, but pay is still approximately one-third of what would be paid for similar work in the United States.

Household Consumption in PPP Terms

Country	All food	Clothing and footwear	Fuel and power[a]	Health care[b]	Education[b]	Transport & Communications	Other
St. Lucia	40	5	11	4	17	11	11
United States	13	9	9	4	6	8	51
Jamaica	24	7	3	1	9	8	48
Bahamas	32	4	5	3	8	9	41

Data represent percentage of consumption in PPP terms.
[a]Excludes energy used for transport.
[b]Includes government and private expenditures.

SOURCE: World Bank. *World Development Indicators 2000.*

The St. Lucia government estimated that the total **labor force** was about 73,000 in 1999, and that the unemployed comprised about 15 percent of the workforce. There is no unemployment relief in St. Lucia and those without work quickly face extreme hardship.

Most workers, especially in the larger factories, are entitled to join trade unions and enjoy certain guaranteed rights such as sick pay. There is a national insurance scheme, which provides basic benefits for industrial injury, maternity leave for mothers, and pensions for the elderly. In most cases, however, payments are barely adequate to cover the essentials. Trade unions are influential in St. Lucia, especially those representing public sector employees. They are less active in the tourism industry, where employment is usually casual and part-time in nature. There is little overt child labor in St. Lucia, and women are well represented in all areas of work, especially in business and education.

COUNTRY HISTORY AND ECONOMIC DEVELOPMENT

1502. Alleged sighting and naming of island by Columbus on his fourth expedition.

1638. First English settlement on island lasts only 3 years before attack by Carib Indians.

1642. France claims possession of St. Lucia.

1814. St. Lucia finally becomes British Crown Colony after changing hands 14 times.

1838. Island included in colonial Windward Islands federation.

1950s. Beginning of banana industry.

1964. United Workers' Party starts 33 years of almost unbroken rule.

1967. Advent of full internal self-government.

1979. St. Lucia becomes independent from United Kingdom, but remains a member of the British Commonwealth.

1997. Sweeping election victory for St. Lucia Labour Party.

FUTURE TRENDS

St. Lucia's economic future depends to a large extent on the fate of its banana industry. If, as the pessimists fear, the EU is forced to abandon its preferential market arrangement, St. Lucia and the other Caribbean producers will be unable to compete with large-scale plantation economies in Latin America. This will spell the end of an export-oriented banana industry and may create severe hardship and increased unemployment in the countryside. It is possible that the banana industry will survive, but even so, the need for agricultural diversification remains acute. Some hope may lie in organic and fair-trade initiatives, especially in Europe, where growing numbers of consumers are prepared to pay higher prices for goods deemed to be environmentally and ethically produced.

Manufacturing does not seem to provide a working alternative to the banana industry as of yet. The greatest potential lies in continuing the growth of tourism and sustaining a program of construction works. St. Lucia's ambition to become a financial center may be realized, but that route is not without its own consequences. The construction of a financial industry on St. Lucia would leave the island open to illegal money laundering operations. The island's success story as a tourist destination offers the greatest grounds for optimism. The problem remains of how to link the tourism sector to the rest of the economy so that the benefits may be felt through all social classes on the island: farmers, tour guides, and bankers alike.

DEPENDENCIES

St. Lucia has no territories or colonies.

BIBLIOGRAPHY

Caribbean Development Bank. *Annual Report 1999*. Barbados, 2000.

Economist Intelligence Unit. *Country Profile: OECS*. London: Economist Intelligence Unit, 2000.

International Monetary Fund. <http://www.imf.org/external/np>. Accessed March 2001.

St. Lucia Central Statistics Office. <http://www.stats.gov.lc>. Accessed April 2001.

St. Lucia Government Information Service. <http://www.stlucia.gov.lc>. Accessed March 2001.

St. Lucia. *South America, Central America and the Caribbean 2001*. London: Europa Publications, 2001.

U.S. Central Intelligence Agency. *World Factbook 2000*. <http://www.odci.gov/cia/publications/factbook/index.html>. Accessed April 2001.

—*James Ferguson*

ST. VINCENT AND THE GRENADINES

CAPITAL: Kingstown.

MONETARY UNIT: Eastern Caribbean dollar (EC$). One EC dollar equals 100 cents. There are coins of 1, 2, 5, 10, 25, and 50 cents and 1 EC dollar, and notes of 5, 10, 20, 50, and 100 EC dollars.

CHIEF EXPORTS: Bananas, fruit and vegetables, arrowroot, sporting goods.

CHIEF IMPORTS: Foodstuffs, machinery and equipment, chemicals and fertilizers, minerals and fuels.

GROSS DOMESTIC PRODUCT: US$309 million (1999 est.).

BALANCE OF TRADE: Exports: US$47.8 million (1998 est.). Imports: US$180 million (1998 est.).

COUNTRY OVERVIEW

LOCATION AND SIZE. Saint Vincent and the Grenadines are islands situated between the Atlantic Ocean and Caribbean Sea, north of Trinidad and Tobago. They form part of the Windward Islands, which also include St. Lucia, Dominica, Grenada, and Martinique. The island of Saint Vincent has an area of 344 square kilometers (133 square miles) and its 32 dependent islands and cays in the Grenadine island chain have a total area of 45 square kilometers (17 square miles). The main inhabited islands of the Grenadines are Bequia, Mustique, Union Island, and Canouan. Others are privately owned. Saint Vincent is approximately twice the size of Washington, D.C., and has a coastline of 84 kilometers (52 miles). The capital and only town of any size is Kingstown, situated on the island's southwest coast.

POPULATION. The population of Saint Vincent and the Grenadines was estimated at 115,461 in mid-2000. This represented a population growth rate of 0.43 percent from the previous year, consistent with annual average increases of 0.4 percent from 1995 onwards. At this rate of growth, the population will stand at approximately 125,000 in 2010. The great majority of Vincentians live on the main island of Saint Vincent, with the population of Bequia, the largest dependency, numbering no more than 5,000.

Saint Vincent and the Grenadines' relatively low population growth rate is partly the result of family planning campaigns supported by the government and partly a consequence of marked patterns of migration. The island has traditionally depended on migration to the United Kingdom, United States, and other, larger Caribbean islands as a solution to its chronic unemployment problem, and in 2000 there were an estimated 7.75 migrants per 1,000 population. The country's population is evenly distributed among age groups, with 30 percent of Vincentians aged between 0 and 14 years, 63 percent between 15 and 64, and 7 percent 65 and older. Life expectancy on the islands is 72.3 years. Approximately 66 percent of the population is of African descent, with smaller communities of mixed-race, white, and Indian-descended Vincentians. The Anglican church is the largest in the country, attracting 47 percent of the population; 28 percent of the people are Methodists and 13 percent Roman Catholics, with the remainder adhering to other faiths. Most people live in small villages or towns, which are mostly situated around the coast.

OVERVIEW OF ECONOMY

Saint Vincent and the Grenadines' economy is largely based on agriculture, bananas in particular. It has been so for many years, but other economic activities have become more important in recent years, namely tourism, manufacturing, and financial services. Bananas have been Saint Vincent's main export and source of revenue since the 1950s, when the British colonial authorities actively encouraged the establishment of a local banana industry. The regularity of income from banana-growing lay behind the island's steady economic growth in the 1980s and early 1990s, but the crop is always vulnerable to hurricanes, drought, and disease, and suffered serious problems in 1994. The removal of preferential access into the European Union (EU) market was threatened by a 1997 ruling by the World Trade Organization (WTO). The ruling stated that the EU was unfairly favoring Caribbean producers at

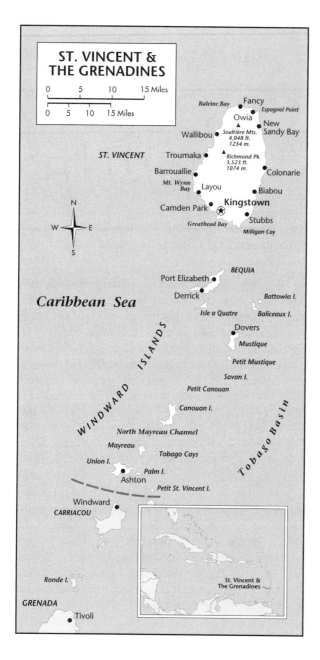

Industry is divided between manufacturing for the local and regional market and that destined for export to North America. The former includes food processing (flour and rice) and brewing, while the latter includes some garment and electronic components assembly, as well as the manufacture of sporting goods such as tennis rackets. There is a mixture of small local companies and local subsidiaries of foreign corporations.

Saint Vincent and the Grenadines has also sought to develop a range of service industries, of which tourism is the most important. Tourist facilities range from extremely exclusive, mostly privately-owned resorts and villas on islands such as Mustique and Canouan to a growing cruise ship facility in Kingstown. Yachting is also extremely popular around the beautiful Grenadine island chain. In recent years, the country has entered the financial services sector, with a large number of banks and other financial institutions present in Kingstown. This sector has attracted some controversy on account of its alleged secrecy. Saint Vincent has also been subject to criticism from the United States, both for its large-scale marijuana cultivation and for the alleged role played by the southern Grenadine islands as shipment points for cocaine en route from South America to the United States.

According to the Caribbean Development Bank (CDB), Saint Vincent and the Grenadines had a total **external debt** of $99.3 million at the beginning of 1999. The country's major economic problem, however, remains a high level of unemployment, affecting at least 22 percent of the workforce in 1999. According to the World Bank, some 30 percent of people in the English-speaking Windward Islands live in conditions of poverty.

POLITICS, GOVERNMENT, AND TAXATION

Saint Vincent and the Grenadines is an independent state within the British Commonwealth. It claims as its head of state Queen Elizabeth, who is represented on the islands by a governor general. The nation's form of government is a parliamentary democracy. The governor general selects the prime minister, usually the leader of the majority party in the **unicameral** (one-house) House of Assembly. The House of Assembly consists of 21 seats (15 representatives chosen by popular election and 6 appointed senators). The Eastern Caribbean Supreme Court, based in Saint Lucia, carries out judicial functions. One judge from the court is based in Saint Vincent.

the expense of Latin American exporters. This created a loss of confidence in the industry's long-term future. Even so, recent years have witnessed an attempt to improve the regularity and quality of banana exports through an irrigation and rehabilitation scheme initiated by the government and the Windward Islands Banana Development and Exporting Company (WIBDECO).

Recent governments have tried to encourage diversification into other agricultural exports, and Saint Vincent exports a wide range of fruits and vegetables both to the United Kingdom and to regional (that is, Caribbean) markets. The traditional cultivation of arrowroot has been expanded as an export industry, and fishing is an important sector within the economy.

Vincentian politics have been dominated by the figure of Sir James Mitchell since he and his National Democratic Party (NDP) first won elections in 1984. Elections in 1998 gave the NDP its fourth consecutive victory, but there was considerable controversy. The NDP won 8 out of 15 seats in parliament but only 45.3 percent of votes cast. The opposition Unity Labour Party (ULP) won only 7 seats but 54.6 percent of the vote. After political unrest and subsequent mediation from representatives of the Caribbean Community (CARICOM) in 2000, it was agreed that fresh elections would be brought forward by 2 years to March 2001. In those elections the ULP took 56.7 percent of the vote and occupied 12 of the 15 seats in the National Assembly; the NDP took 40.7 percent of the vote and held only 3 seats. Ralph Gonsalves was subsequently appointed as prime minister.

There is little ideological difference between the 2 main parties in Saint Vincent and the Grenadines, and both support a mixed economy in which government encourages and regulates **private-sector** growth and foreign investment. Differences tend to be as much personal as political, although the ULP puts particular emphasis on the need to reduce unemployment through the continued rehabilitation of agriculture and government spending on **infrastructure**. Governments are able to exert particular influence on the economy, in part because it is so small and in part because there is a relatively large **public sector**.

Taxation is made up of a mixture of **income tax**, indirect sales taxes, and taxes levied on companies and foreign-owned financial institutions. In an attempt to increase fiscal revenues from International Business Companies (IBCs), the government introduced legislation in 1996 ensuring almost complete secrecy concerning their financial transactions. The government has also attempted to raise revenues by acting as a flag of convenience, offering registration facilities for foreign shipping companies. Both of these measures have led to criticism not only from the political opposition but also from international bodies concerned with **money-laundering** and marine safety.

INFRASTRUCTURE, POWER, AND COMMUNICATIONS

The infrastructure of Saint Vincent and the Grenadines is not fully developed, although recent government initiatives have involved improvements in roads, port facilities, and hospitals. Of 1,040 kilometers (646 miles) of roads only 320 kilometers (199 miles) were paved in 1996. Roads in rural areas, particularly in the north of Saint Vincent, are often poor. There are no railways, and the single international airport, near Kingstown, is unable to receive wide-bodied jets. Discussions have taken place with potential foreign investors concerning the runway's extension, while opponents of this scheme favor a new airport.

Lack of infrastructure has hampered the growth of tourism, even though the government has recently invested in a cruise ship jetty (landing wharf) at Kingstown as well as an airport on Canouan. Small farmers also complain that poor roads are an obstacle to transporting fragile commodities such as bananas to dock or to inland collection points. Saint Vincent and the Grenadines also suffers from having to import most of its energy supplies, mainly petroleum, from Trinidad and Tobago. About one-third of the country's annual electricity production of 64 million kilowatt hours (kWh) is derived from hydro-electric schemes, while annual consumption is estimated at 60 million kWh.

Telecommunications, dominated by Cable & Wireless, are generally good, and there is growing use of cellular phones. There were an estimated 20,500 main line telephones in use in 1998, but Internet use is as yet relatively underdeveloped.

Communications

Country	Telephones[a]	Telephones, Mobile/Cellular[a]	Radio Stations[b]	Radios[a]	TV Stations[a]	Televisions[a]	Internet Service Providers[c]	Internet Users[c]
St. Vincent & the Grenadines	20,500 (1998)	N/A	AM 1; FM 3; shortwave 0	77,000	1	18,000	15	2,000
United States	194 M	69.209 M (1998)	AM 4,762; FM 5,542; shortwave 18	575 M	1,500	219 M	7,800	148 M
Jamaica	353,000 (1996)	54,640 (1996)	AM 10; FM 13; shortwave 0	1.215 M	7	460,000	21	60,000
St. Lucia	37,000	1,600	AM 2; FM 7; shortwave 0	111,000	3	32,000	15	5,000

[a]Data is for 1997 unless otherwise noted.
[b]Data is for 1998 unless otherwise noted.
[c]Data is for 2000 unless otherwise noted.

SOURCE: CIA *World Factbook 2001* [Online].

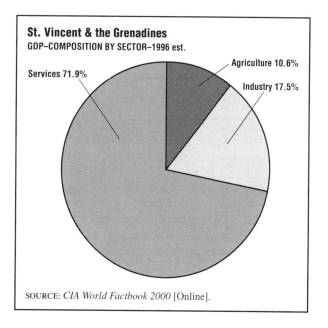

St. Vincent & the Grenadines
GDP–COMPOSITION BY SECTOR–1996 est.

Services 71.9%

Agriculture 10.6%

Industry 17.5%

SOURCE: *CIA World Factbook 2000* [Online].

ECONOMIC SECTORS

The most recent available statistics (1996) show that agriculture accounted for 10.6 percent of Saint Vincent and the Grenadines' **gross domestic product** (GDP). Farming, and banana cultivation in particular, is, however, an important source of employment and constitutes the country's main export, valued at $14.4 million in 1999. The most recent employment statistics, dating from 1991, show that approximately 22 percent of Vincentians worked in agriculture.

Industry accounted for 17.5 percent of GDP in 1996 and has grown considerably since the 1980s. Even so, it

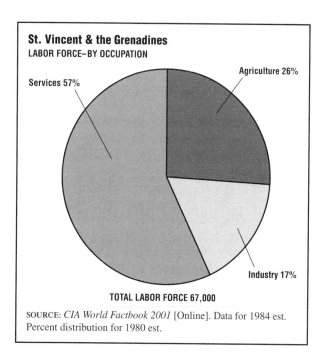

St. Vincent & the Grenadines
LABOR FORCE–BY OCCUPATION

Services 57%

Agriculture 26%

Industry 17%

TOTAL LABOR FORCE 67,000

SOURCE: *CIA World Factbook 2001* [Online]. Data for 1984 est. Percent distribution for 1980 est.

is still a relatively small sector, comprising mainly food processing for local markets and some export-oriented manufacturing. In 1991, some 9 percent of the **labor force** was employed in manufacturing, with a further 11 percent working in construction.

Services accounted for 71.9 percent of GDP in 1996. Leaving aside government services, the largest contributor to this sector was tourism, which produced approximately $74 million in visitor expenditures in 1998. Other growing segments of the service sector were those related to offshore financial transactions and related informatics (information science) or electronic data processing. In 1991, before the financial sector grew, about 5 percent of the working population were employed in hotels and restaurants, while less than 2 percent were classified as involved in "financial intermediation."

AGRICULTURE

Saint Vincent's mountainous terrain made it less suitable as a sugar-producing center than most other Caribbean islands, but the banana industry, beginning in the 1950s, was well suited to a territory mostly made up of small, family-run farms. A combination of protective quotas and stable prices guaranteed by Britain and then the European Union (EU) underpinned the steady growth of the banana industry in the 1980s and early 1990s, despite occasional hurricanes and other natural disasters. In the 1980s, bananas contributed, on average, 60 percent of export earnings and were the island's single biggest economic activity. This situation changed dramatically in 1995 when the United States complained to the WTO that the EU banana regime discriminated against Latin American producers. A series of legal rulings ensued, with the U.S. introducing trade **sanctions** against the EU, which has sought to find a compromise between the WTO ruling and its commitments to Caribbean banana producers. As a result, the late 1990s were marked by considerable uncertainty in Saint Vincent's banana industry and a drop in production from almost 80,000 tons in 1990 to 37,435 tons in 1999. According to the World Bank, the banana crisis has already caused "a decline in the central government's revenue growth, a slowdown in the pace of domestically financed investment, a rise in unemployment, and major financial difficulties for the Banana Growers' Association." Even so, recent efforts to improve banana production through irrigation schemes show a determination on the part of local farmers and their organizations to ensure the industry's survival. One possible strategy is to concentrate on the organic and "fair trade" markets in Europe.

Other important crops include coconuts, sweet potatoes, and ornamental flowers, some of which are exported to "niche markets" in the UK and U.S. The government has encouraged diversified small farming by splitting up some 7,000 acres of state-owned land into 1,500 **small-holdings**. Arrowroot, traditionally used as a food thickener, is now grown as a dressing for computer paper, and acreage of this crop has expanded in recent years, making Saint Vincent and the Grenadines the world's largest producer. Less well documented is the significant cultivation of marijuana, which is believed to be grown in the mountainous interior of Saint Vincent. In January 2000, U.S. Marines participated in a controversial crop eradication program, in which millions of plants were reportedly destroyed.

The fishing sector has benefited from extensive foreign development funding, most notably from Japan. There are now jetties and fish refrigeration facilities in Saint Vincent, Bequia, and Canouan, the large complex in Kingstown having been dubbed "Little Tokyo."

INDUSTRY

Saint Vincent and the Grenadines has a small industrial sector, but one that has grown in importance in recent years. Most manufacturing revolves around food processing, such as rice milling and flour production, for the local and regional market. The major producer is the East Caribbean Group of Companies. There is also large-scale production of chicken feed and polypropylene bags, while the local brewery, the Saint Vincent Brewery Ltd., which produces beer and soft drinks, accounts for approximately 30 percent of total industrial production. The other industrial sector is geared towards exports into the North American market and includes a handful of assembly plants producing garments and sports goods, especially tennis rackets.

Saint Vincent's industrial growth (there is no industry on the Grenadines) is hampered by several factors, including poor infrastructure, relatively high wages, and fierce competition from lower-wage areas elsewhere in the Caribbean and Latin America. Increasingly, Saint Vincent's industrial output has been directed towards other territories in the Eastern Caribbean.

SERVICES

Saint Vincent came relatively late to tourism, although its dependencies such as Bequia and Mustique had developed a reputation for exclusive luxury tourism as early as the 1960s. In recent years, the main island of Saint Vincent has tried to capitalize on its spectacular natural beauty by encouraging cruise ship companies to include it on their itineraries and by developing the yachting sector. In 1999, according to the Caribbean Development Bank, these 2 sectors showed a marked increase in visitor arrivals, bringing total arrivals to 223,125. On the other hand, stayover arrivals declined slightly by 1.5 percent from the previous year. There are few large hotels in Saint Vincent or in its dependencies, and as a result the $75 million annual tourist expenditure is more widely distributed through small hotels and retailers than in many other Caribbean countries.

The government has sought to expand tourism by opening a new cruise ship pier at Kingstown, upgrading the airport on Canouan, and improving the Leeward Highway on the west coast. Deliberations on the enlargement of the existing airport or the building of a new one continue. But Saint Vincent, which has few white sand beaches and an otherwise underdeveloped infrastructure, is not suitable for mass tourism and has wisely concentrated on attracting a small "upmarket" tourist clientele.

The other major service sector deals with overseas financial business. The 1996 legislation ensuring near total secrecy on taxation and other financial activity encouraged the arrival of many IBCs, totaling 2,698 in 1999. But there have been persistent allegations that the country's stringent secrecy provisions have served to conceal illegal financial operations such as tax evasion and drug money laundering. In early 2001, the international Financial Action Task Force (FATF), supported by European and North American governments, named Saint Vincent and the Grenadines, among other Caribbean countries, as a suspected location of financial irregularities. Related to the financial sector is a small data processing sub-sector, in which there is limited employment in computerized financial dealings.

The **retail** sector is underdeveloped, with few large stores or supermarkets. Markets, both in Kingstown and Bequia, are busy, and many rural Vincentians depend on small village corner stores. The growth of tourism and yacht chartering in particular has produced a noticeable increase in specialist retail outlets.

INTERNATIONAL TRADE

With imports of $180 million and exports of $47.8 million in 1998, Saint Vincent and the Grenadines' import bill is on average approximately 4 times that of what it earns through exports. Its main source of imports in 1998 was the United States, which contributed some 35 percent of the total. The other main suppliers of the country's imports were other CARICOM countries (22 percent) and the United Kingdom (11 percent). The main imports of foodstuffs, fuel, and machinery are distributed among those suppliers.

The main export, bananas, is directed towards the United Kingdom, which accounts for 42 percent of Vincentian exports. The other main export market is

Trade (expressed in billions of US$): St. Vincent & the Grenadines

	Exports	Imports
1975	.008	.025
1980	.015	.057
1985	.063	.079
1990	.083	.136
1995	.043	.136
1998	.050	.193

SOURCE: International Monetary Fund. *International Financial Statistics Yearbook 1999.*

Saint Vincent and the Grenadines' financial stability is in part because of its membership in regional financial institutions. The Eastern Caribbean dollar, a currency shared with the 7 other members of the Eastern Caribbean Central Bank (ECCB), is stable and has been pegged at a rate of EC$2.7: US$1 for many years. This means that Saint Vincent and the Grenadines is not particularly vulnerable to fluctuating **exchange rates**, although transactions with Europe have been affected by the low value of the euro. There are plans for ECCB member countries to participate in a regional stock exchange, further integrating the economies of the small islands, but by early 2001 little real progress had been made.

comprised of CARICOM members such as Trinidad & Tobago, which imports much of Saint Vincent's agricultural produce. Rice, flour, and other food items are also exported regionally.

The deficit in the **balance of trade** is partly offset by tourism receipts and by revenue from the financial sector. Another important source of foreign exchange is the regular **remittance** payments sent back by Vincentians working overseas.

MONEY

Saint Vincent and the Grenadines has experienced steady growth in GDP in recent years (except in 1994), averaging over 3 percent annually since the mid-1990s. In 1999, GDP growth stood at 4.5 percent, a fall from the 1998 figure of 5.7 percent. This economic progress reflects a steady increase in tourism and the revenues generated by financial services, which has partly counterbalanced problems in the banana industry. **Inflation** has been low in recent years and, in 1999, was estimated at less than 1 percent. As a result, consumer prices are relatively low, and visitors from neighboring islands such as Grenada and Barbados now come to Saint Vincent to take advantage of lower prices.

POVERTY AND WEALTH

Saint Vincent and the Grenadines is not a country of social extremes. There is a small middle class, traditionally involved in retailing and the professions, while a significant group of small farmers benefited from the "banana boom" of the 1980s, resulting in much improved housing conditions in many rural communities. Society is not prohibitively stratified, and educational opportunities exist for upward mobility. The literacy rate is high at 98 percent for both men and women.

There are no recent figures relating to income distribution in Saint Vincent and the Grenadines, but World Bank and other sources suggest that at least 30 percent of the population still lives in poverty, including the large numbers of unemployed. The most underdeveloped and marginalized area of the main island is the north, where villages such as Sandy Bay, Owia, and Fancy are still without electricity (although a project to connect them was underway in 2000). Here, the volcanic terrain limits the development of agriculture and there are few economic opportunities other than cultivating marijuana. The inhabitants of the poorest north coast settlements include the last descendants of the Black Caribs, a community descended from the island's indigenous population and slaves who escaped the sugar plantations in the 18th century and revolted against the British. On the east coast, the once thriving town of Georgetown is now almost deserted, abandoned since the government-owned sugar mill was closed

Exchange rates: St. Vincent and the Grenadines

East Caribbean dollars (EC$) per US$1

2001	2.7000
2000	2.7000
1999	2.7000
1998	2.7000
1997	2.7000
1996	2.7000

Note: The rate for St. Vincent and the Grenadines has been fixed since 1970.

SOURCE: CIA *World Factbook 2001* [ONLINE].

GDP per Capita (US$)

Country	1975	1980	1985	1990	1998
St. Vincent & the Grenadines	N/A	1,322	1,649	2,168	2,635
United States	19,364	21,529	23,200	25,363	29,683
Jamaica	1,819	1,458	1,353	1,651	1,559
St. Lucia	N/A	2,076	2,150	3,542	3,907

SOURCE: United Nations. *Human Development Report 2000; Trends in human development and per capita income.*

Household Consumption in PPP Terms

Country	All food	Clothing and footwear	Fuel and power[a]	Health care[b]	Education[b]	Transport & Communications	Other
St. Vincent & the Grenadines	27	4	8	2	13	24	22
United States	13	9	9	4	6	8	51
Jamaica	24	7	3	1	9	8	48
St. Lucia	40	5	11	4	17	11	11

Data represent percentage of consumption in PPP terms.

[a]Excludes energy used for transport.

[b]Includes government and private expenditures.

SOURCE: World Bank. *World Development Indicators 2000.*

in the 1970s. Here, as elsewhere beyond the Kingstown area, educational and medical services are basic.

In contrast, the wealthier middle-class suburbs around Kingstown have a full range of amenities and facilities. The more prosperous banana-growing villages of the fertile inland valleys are also evidence of economic success. The wealthiest sectors of the population include those involved in the tourism industry, the new financial services sector and, according to critics, those with political connections.

WORKING CONDITIONS

Figures from 1991 (the most recent available) showed a total employed workforce of 33,440, with unemployment standing at 19.8 percent. More recent statistics, from 1999, suggest that unemployment stood at 22 percent. Figures cited by the newly elected Unity Labour Party say unemployment may be as high as 45 percent (although this number may be inflated for political reasons). Pay and working conditions are average by regional standards, and workers in agriculture, manufacturing, and the large public sector enjoy the protection of well-organized growers' associations and trade unions. According to the International Labor Organization (ILO), the government observes basic working legislation. Wages, although low by North American standards, are higher than in many poorer Caribbean nations and range between $100 and $300 per week for jobs in agriculture and manufacturing. The large civil service is well represented by trade unions and is able to negotiate substantial salary increases.

Conditions are toughest in agriculture, where many small farmers work remote and usually mountainous holdings without adequate irrigation or other inputs. Much of this work is carried out by families, and women, as well as some children, are widely involved in agricultural production as well as retailing.

COUNTRY HISTORY AND ECONOMIC DEVELOPMENT

1498. Saint Vincent sighted by Columbus on his third voyage of discovery.

1627–73. Islands claimed but not settled by Great Britain.

1673–1762. Jointly administered by Great Britain and France as neutral territory.

1763. Saint Vincent ceded to British after conflict with France.

1779–83. Islands occupied by French forces.

1796. Suppression and mass deportation of the Black Caribs by General Abercrombie.

1833–1960. Islands are part of the British Windward Islands colony.

1950s. First banana exports to United Kingdom.

1979. Islands declare independence from United Kingdom and become part of the British Commonwealth.

1984. James Mitchell of the conservative New Democratic Party becomes prime minister and dominates politics until 2000.

1987. Hurricane Emily destroys 70 percent of banana crop.

2000. Mitchell resigns amidst political controversy; Ralph Gonsalves, head of the United Labour Party, is elected in 2001.

FUTURE TRENDS

Saint Vincent and the Grenadines' short-term economic prospects depend to a large extent on the fate of its banana industry. If preferential access into the EU is removed or substantially reduced, the industry will not be able to compete with large Latin American producers and will collapse, creating widespread poverty among small farmers. Attempts to diversify away from dependency on bananas have begun, but will need to be accelerated over the next decade. The country's food processing and export industry also faces potential threats from cheaper regional competitors such as the Dominican Republic, which are now involved in reciprocal free-trade agreements with CARICOM countries.

Tourism seems to have a more healthy future, and the potential of the main island and its dependencies has yet to be fully realized. The authorities will have to balance the need for increased visitor arrivals with keeping the islands' reputation as an unspoiled and exclusive destination for the wealthier tourist. More doubtful is the outlook for the financial services sector, especially if the government is forced to remove secrecy provisions through international pressure. Overall, the medium-term future for Saint Vincent and the Grenadines does not look particularly bright, and the government will face an uphill task in reducing current levels of unemployment and poverty.

The Unity Labour Party, which attained a majority in the 2001 parliamentary elections in March of 2001, has stated that its aim is to add 1,500 jobs to the economy right away, invest in infrastructure to allow for the creation of more jobs in the medium and long term, boost the information technology and tourism industries, and provide more support for the production of bananas, sugar, and arrowroot. However, it is too early to say whether these ambitious plans can be realized, especially as many of these plans rely on government expenditures which may not be possible given existing government funding.

DEPENDENCIES

St. Vincent and the Grenadines has no territories or colonies.

BIBLIOGRAPHY

Caribbean Development Bank. *Annual Report 1999.* Barbados, 2000.

Economist Intelligence Unit. *Country Profile: OECS.* London: Economist Intelligence Unit, 2000.

"The Path to Caribbean Nationhood." *Unity Labour Party.* <http://www.ulpsvg.com/manifesto/manifesto2.htm>. Accessed July 2001.

"Saint Vincent and the Grenadines." *South America, Central America and the Caribbean 2001.* London: Europa Publications, 2001.

"St. Vincent and the Grenadines and the IMF." *International Monetary Fund.* <http://www.imf.org/external/country/VCT/index.htm>. Accessed July 2001.

U.S. Central Intelligence Agency. *World Factbook 2000.* <http://www.odci.gov/cia/publications/factbook/index.html>. Accessed July 2001.

U.S. State Department. *Background Notes: St. Vincent & the Grenadines.* <http://www.state.gov/www/background_notes/stvincent_0600_bgn.html>. Accessed July 2001.

—*James Ferguson*

SURINAME

Republic of Suriname
Republiek Suriname

CAPITAL: Paramaribo.

MONETARY UNIT: Surinamese guilder (SG). One guilder equals 100 cents. There are notes of 5, 10, 25, 100, 250, 500, and 1,000 guilders and coins of 1, 5, 10, and 25 cents and 1 and 2.5 guilders.

CHIEF EXPORTS: Alumina, aluminum, crude oil, lumber, shrimp and fish, rice, bananas.

CHIEF IMPORTS: Capital equipment, petroleum, foodstuffs, cotton, consumer goods.

GROSS DOMESTIC PRODUCT: US$1.48 billion (1999 est.).

BALANCE OF TRADE: Exports: US$406.1 million (f.o.b., 1998 est.). Imports: US$461.4 million (f.o.b., 1998 est.).

COUNTRY OVERVIEW

LOCATION AND SIZE. Suriname sits on the northern shoulder of South America, facing the Atlantic Ocean between Guyana to the west, French Guiana to the east, and Brazil to the south. It shares with these 3 nations 1,707 kilometers (1,061 miles) of border and has a coastline of about 386 kilometers (240 miles). With an area of 163,270 square kilometers (63,038 square miles), Suriname is slightly larger than the state of Georgia. The capital, Paramaribo, lies on the Atlantic coast.

POPULATION. The population of Suriname was estimated at 431,303 in mid-2000. Population density is one of the lowest on earth: 6.9 people per square mile compared with 921.8 people per square mile in Aruba, another former Dutch colony in the region. The heaviest population density is on the coast, with around 45 percent of the population living in the capital district. The birthrate of 21.08 births per 1,000 people is relatively high (more than one and a half times that of Aruba's), but very high levels of **emigration**—8.92 out of every 1,000 Surinamers left in 2000—have kept the annual growth rate to a modest 0.65 percent. One-third of all Surinamers live abroad, mostly in the Netherlands, Netherlands An-

tilles, and the United States. The life expectancy is 71.36 years. About one-third of the population is younger than 15, and 6 percent is older than 65.

Suriname's ethnic composition is diverse. Slightly more than one-third of the population (37 percent) is of Indian origin, descended from 19th-century indentured laborers brought from northern India. Other large population groups are mixed black-white Creole (31 percent), Javanese (15 percent), and Maroons (10 percent), the descendants of West African slaves who were imported in the 17th and 18th centuries and escaped inland. The rest of the population is comprised of Amerindians (2 percent), Chinese (2 percent), whites (1 percent), and assorted others (2 percent). The official language is Dutch, though English is widely used, as is the Surinamese Creole, Sranang Tongo (also called Taki-Taki). Hindustani (a dialect of Hindi), and Javanese are also spoken.

OVERVIEW OF ECONOMY

Suriname is richly endowed with natural resources. With large reserves of minerals and timber and considerable opportunities for agriculture, industry, and fishing, Suriname has the makings of a prosperous nation, but years of political turbulence and military misrule have taken a heavy toll, and Suriname still struggles to turn its natural assets into national wealth.

The Surinamese economy had long been based on sugar cane, introduced by the Dutch in the 17th century. Most Surinamers are the descendants of African, Indian, and Javanese laborers imported to work on sugar plantations. Since the beginning of the 20th century, the core of the economy has been bauxite mining and processing, an industry that continues to supply over 70 percent of official export revenue. With geological surveys suggesting existing mines will be exhausted by 2006, continued

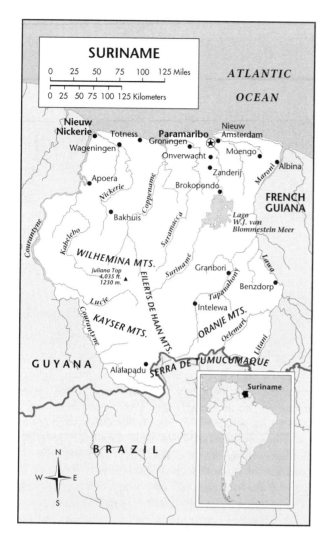

SURINAME

0 25 50 75 100 125 Miles

0 25 50 75 100 125 Kilometers

ATLANTIC OCEAN

Nieuw Nickerie
Totness
Groningen
Paramaribo
Nieuw Amsterdam
Wageningen
Onverwacht
Moengo
Zanderij
Albina
Apoera
Brokopondo
FRENCH GUIANA
Nickerie
Coppername
Lago W.J. van Blommestein Meer
Bakhuis
Saramacca
WILHEMINA MTS.
Juliana Top 4,035 ft. 1230 m.
Granbori
EILERTS DE HAAN MTS.
Suriname
Lawa
Maroni
Tapanahony
Benzdorp
Kabalebo
Lucie
Intelewa
ORANJE MTS.
Oelemari
KAYSER MTS.
Courantyne
Litani
GUYANA
Alalapadu
SERRA DE TUMUCUMAQUE
BRAZIL

N W E S

Suriname

(bringing it from 400 percent in 1994 to less than 1 percent in 1996), it failed to address the more difficult reforms, such as trimming the civil service and **privatizing** government-owned industries. In the absence of a clear and rigorous economic plan, Suriname experienced a soaring **inflation rate** in the late 1990s and its currency began to tumble.

POLITICS, GOVERNMENT, AND TAXATION

Occupied by the Dutch in 1667, Suriname (then Dutch Guiana) was ruled from the Netherlands until 1954, when it gained autonomous status under Dutch sovereignty. Full independence was achieved in 1975. Since then Suriname has had a turbulent history. The first elected government was ejected by the military in 1980, followed by a long period of political instability and deteriorating economic conditions. Although popular pressure led to elections in 1988, the military reasserted itself in another coup in 1990. Elections in 1991 and 1996 resulted in the establishment of fragile coalition governments. Growing frustration at the worsening state of the economy led to widespread strikes and demonstrations and forced the government of President Jules Wijdenbosch to resign in 2000. After new elections, a coalition led by the New Front (Nieuw Front or NF) was formed under the leadership of Ronald Venetiaan, who had been president from 1991 to 1996.

The president is both the chief of state and the head of government. The president and vice president are elected by the 51-member National Assembly or, in case of deadlock, by the larger People's Assembly, which has 869 representatives from national, local, and regional councils. Legislative power is vested in the **unicameral** National Assembly, whose members are elected to 5-year terms. Judicial power is vested in a Court of Justice, in which justices serve for life.

While the transition to multi-party democracy has been essentially peaceful, the threat of civil disorder remains ever present. The government has little control over the interior, where remnants of the Maroon Jungle Commando rebellion, officially quelled in 1992, continue to operate, along with bandits, drug traffickers, and illegally armed gold miners, making development difficult and even dangerous. Corruption and favoritism in the bureaucracy also combine to undermine government's effectiveness. In October 2000 it was discovered that 98 percent of Suriname's gold reserves had disappeared. Foreign investors are discouraged by a legal and regulatory system they consider inefficient and unreliable.

Since the 1990s, relations with the Netherlands, once an important source of foreign aid, have been strained. The United States suspects Suriname of being a trans-

bauxite production will require the exploration and development of new mines, a difficult venture in the face of Suriname's serious infrastructural shortcomings.

Most of the country's population and **infrastructure** are concentrated on the narrow coastal plain, leaving the interior largely empty, inaccessible, and outside the government's full control. Consequently, exploiting Suriname's reserves of oil, gold, kaolin, stone, and timber tends to be difficult and expensive, and the natural resource sector, for all of its potential, remains underdeveloped.

Political uncertainty and mismanagement have also been significant problems. In 1982 the Netherlands, Suriname's largest benefactor, cut off aid to the military junta, exacerbating a pattern of economic deterioration. A **structural adjustment program** initiated in 1992 aimed at economic stabilization through improved tax collection, removal of certain government **subsidies**, and the harmonization of **exchange rates**. Although the program succeeded in taming Suriname's rampant **inflation** shipment base for both South American cocaine and illegal Chinese immigrants. Suriname is also embroiled in long-standing disputes with neighboring Guyana and French Guiana over rival territorial and maritime claims.

Suriname's **tariff** regime is cumbersome and complex. Average import **duties** range from 30 to 40 percent. New legislation is being drafted to **liberalize** and streamline the system. To compensate for losses in tariff revenues, the government plans to enact more aggressive strategies for collecting taxes from the country's large **informal economy**. **Direct taxes** accounted for only a third of revenue in 1996, and the government hopes to increase this by 20 percent.

INFRASTRUCTURE, POWER, AND COMMUNICATIONS

Suriname's poor transportation deteriorated further due to neglect during the period of military rule in the 1980s. The country has 4,530 kilometers (2,814 miles) of road, about 26 percent of which are paved. Although these roads have been joined together into 1 integrated system with the construction of bridges across the Coppename and Suriname Rivers in 1999 and 2000 respectively, they are overwhelmingly concentrated in the northern coastal region. Transportation into the heavily forested and sparsely populated interior is still extremely difficult. The logging and bauxite industries use Suriname's 166 kilometers (103 miles) of railway; others must depend on the river system, whose 1,200 kilometers (746 miles) of navigable waterways are an essential means of travel and transport, and on air transport. Paramaribo, the capital, is the major seaport and handles around 500 to 600 vessels a year. There are about 46 airports throughout the country, but only 5 paved runways.

International air links are through Johan Adolf Pengel Airport outside Paramaribo.

Telecommunications are largely the preserve of the state-owned Telesur, though the **private-sector** operator ICMS is also active, and there are plans to open the industry up to full competition. Services are generally good, and infrastructural development has seen the number of telephones rise from 71 per 1,000 people in 1985 to 152 in 1998. By the late 1990s, there were 18 radio stations, 3 television stations, and 1 Internet service provider.

Suriname is largely self-sufficient in energy production. Three-quarters of its power consumption is supplied by the state-owned hydroelectric stations at Paramaribo and Nickerie and by the Suriname Aluminum Company's station on the Blommestein Meer, whose electricity is bought by the government. Oil production at the Tambaradjo oil field outside Paramaribo is 12,500 barrels per day (more than 300 percent over its 1982 levels), which is enough to meet all of Suriname's own oil needs, and leave about 40 percent for export. The government is planning to develop the industry further but needs an overseas strategic partner to help it with the cost of exploration.

ECONOMIC SECTORS

Precise data about the Surinamese economy are not always available, especially because of the large informal sector that runs from street vending and casual labor through illegal mining and drug trafficking. Mining is the predominant sector in the official economy, as it has been for most of the 20th century. Along with quarrying, it generated 14.5 percent of the GDP in 1998. Altogether, industry contributed 22 percent of the GDP, while agriculture contributed 13 percent and services 65 percent.

Communications

Country	Telephones[a]	Telephones, Mobile/Cellular[a]	Radio Stations[b]	Radios[a]	TV Stations[a]	Televisions[a]	Internet Service Providers[c]	Internet Users[c]
Suriname	64,000	4,090	AM 4; FM 13; shortwave 1	300,000	3 (2000)	63,000	2	10,000
United States	194 M	69.209 M (1998)	AM 4,762; FM 5,542; shortwave 18	575 M	1,500	219 M	7,800	148 M
Brazil	17.039 M	4.4 M	AM 1,365; FM 296; shortwave 161 (1999)	71 M	138	36.5 M	50	8.65 M
Guyana	70,000 (2000)	6,100 (2000)	AM 3; FM 3; shortwave 1	420,000	3	46,000	3	3,000

[a]Data is for 1997 unless otherwise noted.
[b]Data is for 1998 unless otherwise noted.
[c]Data is for 2000 unless otherwise noted.

SOURCE: CIA *World Factbook 2001* [Online].

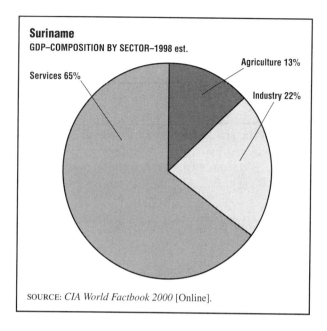

Suriname
GDP–COMPOSITION BY SECTOR–1998 est.

Agriculture 13%

Services 65%

Industry 22%

SOURCE: *CIA World Factbook 2000* [Online].

AGRICULTURE

AGRICULTURE. With only 0.4 percent of Suriname's total land area cultivable, cropping and farming play a secondary role in the economy, employing around 12 percent of the workforce. Half of the cultivable land, mostly in the alluvial coastland, is devoted to rice production, which makes up around 10 percent of Suriname's total exports. The rest is used for fruit and vegetable production, especially bananas, which account for 2.5 percent of total export revenues. As the European Union moves to scale down the special trading access it allows to developing nations, Suriname's rice and banana sales can be expected to suffer. Beef and cut-flower production are being investigated.

FORESTRY. About 90 percent of Suriname's land area is forest and woodland, but the government has tried to preserve its fragile ecology by opting against large-scale logging operations in favor of sustainable harvesting. Lumber generated about US$3 million in export receipts in 1998. A promising ancillary industry is the production of traditional homeopathic remedies from forest plants.

FISHING. Fishing, especially for shellfish, is an important sector, with wild-harvest shrimp accounting for US$29 million, or 6.7 percent of all exports in 1998, and scalefish another 0.8 percent. Fish, shrimp, and crabs are also farmed, though a major setback occurred in October 2000, when a ban was imposed on Suriname's aquaculture products because of unacceptably high levels of toxic residues.

INDUSTRY

Bauxite mining and alumina smelting are the backbone of Suriname's economy, bringing in two-thirds of

its export revenues. With 3.9 million tons produced annually, Suriname is the eighth largest producer of bauxite in the world and responsible for an estimated 3.2 percent of all bauxite production globally in 1998. The industry is entirely in the hands of 2 corporations: the Suriname Aluminum Company (Suralco), a subsidiary of the Aluminum Company of America (Alcoa); and Billiton Maatschappij Suriname (BMS). The government is looking for new partners to develop mines in the western Bakhuys Mountains in preparation for the exhaustion of existing mines, expected around 2006.

In 1998 Suriname's gold production reached an estimated 770,000 ounces, but much of the gold mining industry, which includes some 14,000 small producers, either mines illegally or evades government tax **levies**. The government tried to bring miners into the formal economy by lowering the levy rate from 3 percent to 1 percent in 1997, but with limited success. Legitimate mining operations have been further discouraged by low prices for gold on the world market.

Other resources include oil, kaolin (used in ceramic, rubber, plastic, paper, and cosmetics production), nickel, silver, and granite. Deposits of manganese, platinum, uranium, iron ore, phosphate, and diamonds have also been found. The discovery of offshore oil and gas reserves also suggests significant promise.

Manufacturing, which generated around 12 percent of the GDP in 1998, is dominated by food processing, which accounts for 60 percent of the revenues of this sector, and by the refining of bauxite into alumina and aluminum.

SERVICES

TOURISM. Suriname has hopes of capitalizing on its lush forests and enormously diverse plant life to appeal to the **ecotourist** nature-holiday market. While the potential is significant, prospects are seriously hindered by the deficiencies in Suriname's infrastructure, which has few tourist amenities, and by the inaccessibility and hazards of so much of the rain-forested interior. Most of Suriname's 500 or so hotel rooms are in Paramaribo and cater to business travelers, who made up a large proportion of its 89,000 visitor arrivals in 1997; the remaining visitors were largely emigrants making trips home.

FINANCIAL SERVICES. Financial services are rudimentary and consist of the Central Bank of Suriname, which supplies the foreign exchange market and 3 major commercial banks. Difficulties in financing are further complicated by the economy's instability, especially the parallel currency markets. The financial services industry, a valuable source of foreign exchange for many of Suriname's neighbors, is a potential growth sector for the country, and the government is preparing new legislation designed to stimulate activity.

RETAIL. Suriname's consumer tastes are fairly thoroughly Westernized, and the retail trade is consequently well developed, especially in the capital district. Complicated and expensive import procedures, however, do limit the availability of goods. Paramaribo also has a full complement of "American-style" fast-food chains such as Kentucky Fried Chicken, Pizza Hut, and McDonald's restaurants.

INTERNATIONAL TRADE

Suriname's bauxite exports and aid grants (especially from the Netherlands, Belgium, and the European Union) have tended to keep its trade account more or less balanced, and the country ran a **balance of payments** surplus until 1997. A heavy reliance on imports—especially food and **consumer goods**—combined with the fall of commodity prices for Surinamese products and the suspension of Dutch aid in 1997, pushed the account in 1998 into the red. In that year, exports were valued at US$406.1 million and imports at US$461.4 million.

In 1999 alumina and aluminum accounted for 71 percent of all exports, with the remaining 29 percent derived from rice, bananas, shrimp, and timber. Suriname's main export customers in that year were the United States (23.2 percent), Norway (19 percent), Canada (10.8 percent), and the Netherlands (9.6 percent). The main import suppliers were the United States (34.9 percent), the Netherlands (14.8 percent), and Trinidad and Tobago (12.2 percent).

Suriname joined the Caribbean Community (CARICOM) in 1995, eliminating all tariffs on CARICOM products in 1996 and with the hope that the region would one day be a pan-American free-trade area. This move has tended to shift trading relations away from Europe, Suriname's traditional source of imports, and towards the U.S. and Caribbean region.

Exchange rates: Suriname

Surinamese guilders, gulden, or florins per US$1

Dec 2001	N/A
Dec 2000	2,178.50
Dec 1999	987.50
Dec 1998	401.00
Dec 1997	401.00
Dec 1996	401.26

Note: Beginning in July 1994, the central bank midpoint exchange rate was unified and became market determined; during 1998, the exchange rate splintered into four distinct rates; in January 1999 the government floated the guilder, but subsequently fixed it when the black-market rate plunged; the government currently allows trading within a band of SRG 500 around the official rate.

SOURCE: CIA *World Factbook 2001* [ONLINE].

MONEY

The withdrawal of Dutch support in 1982 forced the government to meet its budgetary shortfall by borrowing on the domestic market, diverting credit from private investment. The strain on the money supply sent inflation into triple digits. Brought briefly under control in the 1990s, the deficit began to increase again, and in 1999 it reached an estimated US$52.6 million, or 16 percent of the GDP. Debt has also climbed as the government substantially expanded its spending on the transportation infrastructure in the late 1990s. The debt rose from US$154 million in 1996 to US$282 million in August 2000. One of the consequences has been the separation of Suriname's currency, beginning in late 1998, into parallel markets, with its bank valuation falling well below the official exchange rate. The result was a 40 percent **devaluation** in January 1999 to SG998 per U.S. dollar. With the discovery of the disappearance of the country's gold reserves in October 2000, the rate fell even further, to SG2,200 per dollar. Inflation rose rapidly, increasing by 9 percent per month through 1999, and peaking at 126.7 percent in October 1999 before dropping back to 38.1 percent in June 2000.

POVERTY AND WEALTH

Suriname ranked 67th out of 174 countries in the **United Nations Development Program**'s development index, which places it in the middle spectrum of nations. This ranking conceals the wide variety of living standards in the country, ranging from Paramaribo, with its roads, full electricity and water services, cosmopolitan shops, and affluent suburbs, to the Maroon and Amerindian villages of the interior, often accessible only by river and with little or no telephone and electricity connections. The index also does not convey quality of life, which even in Paramaribo has been increasingly undermined by

Trade (expressed in billions of US$): Suriname

	Exports	Imports
1975	.277	.262
1980	.514	.504
1985	.329	.299
1990	.472	.472
1995	N/A	N/A
1998	N/A	N/A

SOURCE: International Monetary Fund. *International Financial Statistics Yearbook 1999.*

GDP per Capita (US$)					
Country	1975	1980	1985	1990	1998
Suriname	888	930	801	787	N/A
United States	19,364	21,529	23,200	25,363	29,683
Brazil	3,464	4,253	4,039	4,078	4,509
Guyana	873	819	626	554	825

SOURCE: United Nations. *Human Development Report 2000; Trends in human development and per capita income.*

urban crimes such as household burglary and armed robbery. The interior, which has considerably less police supervision, can be even more dangerous. Crime reflects growing disparities in wealth and opportunity, not just between the employed and growing numbers of unemployed, but even within the wage and salary sector, where industry salaries run significantly higher than those in the **public sector**.

WORKING CONDITIONS

Suriname has a workforce of around 100,000, of which half either work directly for the government or for government-owned businesses. Attempts to downsize the public sector have caused considerable unrest, leading to mass street demonstrations by opposition groups and labor unions in 1999, which forced President Jules Wijdenbosch from office. **Restructuring** and the slow pace of economic development has sent the unemployment rate up to 20 percent (1997) and precipitated an exodus of manpower that in 2000 ran to 8.92 Surinamers per 1,000. Most emigrants tend to be under 30 and well-educated; the literacy rate in Suriname, despite a long-neglected education system, is high (93 percent, according to 1995 estimates), and many speak English. This drain of expertise is likely continue.

The concentration of workers in government departments and large industries has created a powerful role for trade unions in the economy. This role has been further strengthened by the government's traditional sympathy for worker issues, enshrined in the 1947 labor laws that still regulate the labor market and safeguard worker rights. Union membership is high, and unions are instrumental in determining pay scales and wage increases.

COUNTRY HISTORY AND ECONOMIC DEVELOPMENT

1667. By the Treaty of Breda, England cedes Dutch Guiana (now Suriname) to the Netherlands in exchange for New Amsterdam (later New York City); Dutch colonization and plantation settlement begins.

1799–1815. Britain controls Dutch Guiana during the Napoleonic wars.

1863. Slavery is abolished.

1954. Suriname becomes internally autonomous (with foreign affairs and defense still controlled from the Netherlands).

1975. With independence from the Netherlands, Suriname becomes a republic under a new constitution.

1980. A military coup ejects the civilian government of Henck Arron and suspends the constitution, replacing it with a government by Lieutenant-Colonel Deysi Bouterse's National Military Council.

1982. The so-called "December Bloodbath" occurs in which 15 critics of the junta are murdered. Dutch aid suspended.

1988. Elective government is restored.

1990. Deysi Bouterse stages another military coup.

1991. Elections are held, but no party carries the required two-thirds majority of seats, so parliament chooses Ronald Venetiaan, a former education minister, as president.

1992. Deysi Bourtese resigns as army chief.

1994. Bread riots occur in Paramaribo.

1996. Elections are held; again no party carries the required two-thirds majority of seats, so parliament selects Jules Wijdenbosch as president and forms a 5-party coalition.

1997. The Dutch government again suspends aid after Suriname refuses to extradite Deysi Bouterse, indicted in the Netherlands on drug charges.

2000. President Wijdenbosch resigns in face of mounting crises and mass demonstrations; new elections are called; with no party able to command a two-thirds majority, parliament selects Ronald Venetiaan as president.

FUTURE TRENDS

Military rule in the 1980s, which was marked by poor economic management, the disappearance of foreign aid, and highly disruptive guerrilla insurgencies, ushered in a period of steep economic decline for Suriname. Subsequent economic policy has been concerned with addressing this legacy and rebuilding the country's economic foundations, especially dismantling the state's overly dominant role in the economy. The process has been a slow one, and the social cost of restructuring has prevented the government from pursuing these aims with full vigor. Fundamental economic instability, with high inflation and a weak currency, continues to be a chronic problem. Positive indicators, such as an improving relationship with the Netherlands, the promise of better economic management by the Venetiaan government, and the strong state of the bauxite industry, will not be enough to stave off continued hardship and economic crisis for Suriname.

DEPENDENCIES

Suriname has no territories or colonies.

BIBLIOGRAPHY

Economist Intelligence Unit. Country Profile: Trinidad and Tobago, Guyana, Suriname. London: Economist Intelligence Unit, 2000.

Suriname General Bureau of Statistics. Suriname. <http://www.parbo.com/information/surdata.html>. Accessed March 2001.

U.S. Central Intelligence Agency. The World Factbook, 2000. <http://www.cia.gov/cia/publications/factbook>. Accessed January 2001.

U.S. Department of State. FY 2000 Country Commercial Guide: Suriname. Website: <http://www.state.gov/www/about_state/business/com_guides/index.html>. Accessed March 2001.

—Alexander Schubert

TRINIDAD AND TOBAGO

Republic of Trinidad and Tobago

CAPITAL: Port of Spain.

MONETARY UNIT: The Trinidad and Tobago dollar (TT$). One TT dollar equals 100 cents. There are coins of 1, 5, 10, 25, and 50 cents and 1 dollar, and notes of 1, 5, 10, 20, and 100 dollars.

CHIEF EXPORTS: Petroleum and petroleum products, chemicals, steel products, fertilizer, sugar, cocoa, coffee, citrus, and flowers.

CHIEF IMPORTS: Machinery, transportation equipment, manufactured goods, food, and live animals.

GROSS DOMESTIC PRODUCT: US$9.41 billion (1999).

BALANCE OF TRADE: Exports: US$2.4 billion (1998 est.). **Imports:** US$3 billion (1998 est.).

COUNTRY OVERVIEW

LOCATION AND SIZE. The 2 islands of Trinidad and Tobago are between the Atlantic Ocean and the Caribbean Sea, northeast of Venezuela. The southern tip of Trinidad lies only 11 kilometers (7 miles) from the Venezuelan mainland, while Tobago lies approximately 30 kilometers (19 miles) northeast of Trinidad. The total area of the 2-island state is 5,128 square kilometers (1,980 square miles), of which Trinidad accounts for 4,828 square kilometers (1,864 square miles) and Tobago 300 square kilometers (116 square miles). Slightly smaller than Delaware, Trinidad and Tobago has 362 kilometers (225 miles) of coastline. Its capital and main urban center, Port of Spain, is on the northwest coast of Trinidad, while Tobago's capital, Scarborough, lies on the island's southwest coast.

POPULATION. Trinidad and Tobago's population was estimated at 1,175,523 in July 2000, declining 0.49 percent from the previous year and below the mid-1996 estimate of 1,263,600. The decline can mostly be explained by a relatively high level of **emigration**, estimated at 9.92 persons per 1,000 population in 2000. Most Trinidadians emigrate to the United States or Canada in search of bet-

ter work opportunities and higher wage levels than those available at home. Because of emigration and government-sponsored birth control programs, the population is expected to decline to about 1.11 million by 2010.

Trinidad and Tobago has one of the most ethnically diverse populations in the Caribbean. According to the 1990 government census (the most recent available), 40.3 percent of the people are of "East Indian" descent. The "East Indians" are descended from indentured laborers brought to Trinidad in the second half of the 19th century to work on sugar plantations. Some 39.5 percent define themselves as of African descent, while 18.4 percent are classified as "mixed." There are significant communities of Chinese, Middle Eastern, Portuguese, and people of other European descent. The East Indian population tends to be more evenly distributed throughout rural areas, while the African-descended population is more urban in character. About one-half of the population lives in an urbanized east-west corridor stretching from Diego Martin in the west to Arima in the east.

OVERVIEW OF ECONOMY

In regional terms, Trinidad and Tobago is an economic powerhouse, endowed with extensive reserves of oil and natural gas and possessing a diversified range of manufacturing industries. Unlike other Caribbean nations, its dependence on tourism and agriculture is very limited, and tourism in Trinidad is not yet fully developed. Tobago, with much less heavy industry, is a much smaller, quieter island where tourism is an important source of employment and foreign exchange.

Trinidad's economic fortunes changed dramatically at the beginning of the 20th century when commercial petroleum extraction began. Previously, the island had been mainly a sugar producer, with large plantations established on the fertile central plains. Oil rapidly replaced

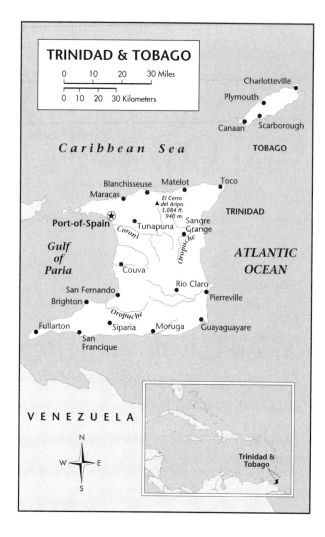

ing sector that produces food, beverages, and cement for local and regional markets.

Agriculture has been neglected since the 1970s, and the main crop remains sugar, most of which is exported to the European Union (EU). Other crops are cocoa and citrus, but these are not grown on a large scale. Tourism is also less important in Trinidad than in most other Caribbean islands, although in the 1990s the government made efforts to attract a larger number of visitors. Tobago is the main tourist destination, with more than half of the country's hotel rooms.

Although Trinidad and Tobago remains vulnerable to fluctuations in world oil prices, it has developed other areas of its economy to balance its economic risks. It has also attracted a cross-section of foreign companies, principally involved in oil and gas production, while retaining a strong element of state control. Poverty remains a serious problem despite oil-related income. The World Bank estimated in 2001 that 21 percent of the population lives in poverty and 17 percent are unemployed.

POLITICS, GOVERNMENT, AND TAXATION

Trinidad and Tobago is a parliamentary democracy, with a president elected for a 5-year term by members of Parliament. A prime minister, usually the leader of the majority party, is appointed from among the members of Parliament after elections, which happen every 5 years. The **bicameral** (2-house) Parliament consists of a 31-seat Senate appointed by the president and a 36-seat House of Representatives elected by popular vote. The Supreme Court consists of a High Court of Justice and a Court of Appeals, to which judges are appointed by the president after consultation with the prime minister.

Politics in Trinidad and Tobago has tended to be organized along ethnic lines since self-government began in the 1950s. After independence from the United Kingdom in 1962, the dominant political party was the People's National Movement (PNM), led by the influential Dr. Eric Williams, until his death in 1981. The PNM remained in power throughout the following period until 1986, when an opposition alliance won elections. Although not explicitly racialist in outlook, the PNM attracted African-descended supporters and concentrated on the urban electorate with promises of jobs and welfare programs. The PNM returned to power in 1992, but in 1995, a party dominated by East Indians, the United National Congress (UNC), led by Basdeo Panday, took power with a prime minister descended from that ethnic group for the first time. The UNC won elections again in December 2000 but amidst considerable controversy over alleged irregularities.

agriculture and by the 1950s represented almost 30 percent of **gross domestic product** (GDP). Since then, Trinidad and Tobago's economy has reflected the ups and downs of the world oil industry. During the 1970s, the country experienced a spectacular boom as international oil prices soared. During that time, the government was able to invest some of this income in **infrastructure** and state-controlled industries, especially gas production. From 1982 on, however, oil prices fell and Trinidad and Tobago underwent a long and painful **recession**, with the economy shrinking at an average annual rate of 6 percent between 1982 and 1987. Unemployment, poverty, and emigration all increased.

Since the early 1990s, the economy has recovered to a large extent, and oil and gas production income has generated steady growth, averaging 4 percent annually between 1994 and 1999. The economy grew strongly in 1999, by 6.9 percent, because of an oil price increase. Thanks to the oil boom of the 1970s, Trinidad is also a major exporter of petroleum byproducts such as methanol and ammonia. There is also a significant steel industry, powered by cheap natural gas, as well as a manufactur-

Despite marked differences in ethnic composition and allegations of racial bias, the 2 main parties are not radically different in terms of ideas and policies. The PNM was initially in favor of strong state intervention and ownership during the 1960s and 1970s, but the recession of the 1980s forced the government to accept advice from the International Monetary Fund (IMF). This advice included reducing import **tariffs**, abolishing foreign-exchange controls and generally opening up the economy to foreign investors. The UNC government has maintained these policies, encouraging foreign investment in key areas of oil and gas extraction.

Governments in Trinidad and Tobago have a strong impact on economic development, largely because the state retains a controlling interest in the management of the country's natural resources. There are state-owned corporations in oil, gas, steel, and telecommunications. The government also influences the economy to a great extent by its relationship with foreign companies, from which it derives significant income in the form of taxation and royalties on oil and gas exports. Organizations such as the World Bank are critical of Trinidad and Tobago's large state sector, claiming that it is over-staffed, bureaucratic, and obstructive to real competition in the energy industries.

Tax revenues in Trinidad and Tobago come from a variety of sources. The oil industry accounted for about 20 percent of tax revenues in 1998, while **income tax** provided 30 percent, and sales and service taxes about 20 percent. A **value-added tax** (VAT) was introduced in 1990 at the suggestion of the IMF when oil revenues had fallen significantly.

INFRASTRUCTURE, POWER, AND COMMUNICATIONS

Although a small country, Trinidad and Tobago has a developed infrastructure, revolving around its oil and gas industries and other manufacturing. There are 8,320 kilometers (5,158 miles) of roads, half of them paved, with main routes covered by 4-lane highways. Even so, traffic congestion has been a problem since the boom period of the 1970s, especially since petroleum is extremely cheap. There are extensive port facilities at the country's 6 major ports, specializing in container, cargo, and cruise shipping, with special infrastructure for oil, gas, cement, and bauxite. Tobago has a general port with cruise-ship facilities. The international airport near Port of Spain has regular connections to Europe and North and South America. The national airline, British West Indian Airways (BWIA), was **privatized** in 1996, with the government retaining a 33.5 percent share.

Trinidad and Tobago is self-sufficient in energy and a major exporter of fuels. In 1998, the country produced 4.763 billion kilowatt-hours (kWh) of electricity and consumed 4.43 billion kWh. The availability of low-cost fuels has been instrumental in building up the country's industrial infrastructure. In terms of tourism, the infrastructure is less developed than elsewhere in the region. Telecommunications are still dominated by the government-owned Telecommunications Services of Trinidad and Tobago (TSTT), and competition is restricted. Independent Internet providers are obliged to use TSTT lines, and cellular phones are also monopolized by the state sector. Radio and television ownership is widespread, and there were 4 national TV stations in 1997, with satellite service widely available.

ECONOMIC SECTORS

Once the mainstay of Trinidad's colonial economy, agriculture accounted for only 2 percent of GDP in 1998, as opposed to 6.9 percent in 1972. The sector is still an important source of employment, however, employing 8.1 percent of the workforce, or 40,000 people, in 1999. Sugar is the main commercial crop, with most production geared towards the guaranteed European Union market.

Communications

Country	Newspapers	Radios	TV Sets[a]	Cable subscribers[a]	Mobile Phones[a]	Fax Machines[a]	Personal Computers[a]	Internet Hosts[b]	Internet Users[b]
	1996	1997	1998	1998	1998	1998	1998	1999	1999
Trinidad & Tobago	123	534	334	N/A	20	3.9	46.8	28.20	30
United States	215	2,146	847	244.3	256	78.4	458.6	1,508.77	74,100
Venezuela	206	468	185	25.8	87	3.0	43.0	3.98	525
Uruguay	293	607	241	N/A	60	N/A	91.2	38.34	300

[a]Data are from International Telecommunication Union, *World Telecommunication Development Report 1999* and are per 1,000 people.
[b]Data are from the Internet Software Consortium (http://www.isc.org) and are per 10,000 people.
SOURCE: World Bank. *World Development Indicators 2000.*

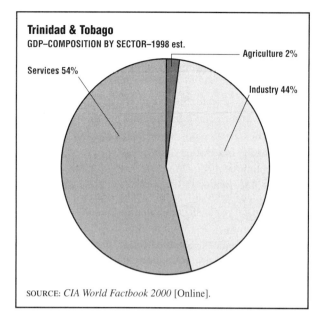

Trinidad & Tobago
GDP–COMPOSITION BY SECTOR–1998 est.

Agriculture 2%
Services 54%
Industry 44%

SOURCE: *CIA World Factbook 2000* [Online].

Industry is the dominant sector within Trinidad and Tobago's economy. The oil and gas industries are the most important, contributing 25 percent of GDP in 1999 and accounting for 73.1 percent of total exports. The petroleum sector is not, however, a major employer, providing jobs for only 3.2 percent of the workforce, or 14,000 people. Other manufacturing employs many more workers (11 percent of the workforce or 60,000 people) and contributed 8.1 percent of GDP in 1999. In 1998, industry's overall share of GDP stood at 44 percent.

Services accounted for 54 percent of GDP in 1998, encompassing transport, **retail**, government services, and

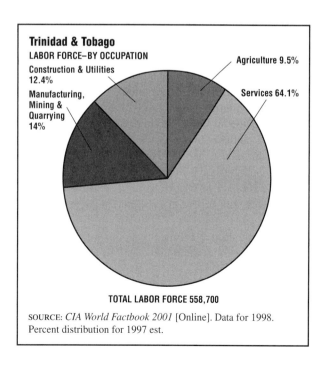

Trinidad & Tobago
LABOR FORCE–BY OCCUPATION
Construction & Utilities 12.4%
Manufacturing, Mining & Quarrying 14%
Agriculture 9.5%
Services 64.1%

TOTAL LABOR FORCE 558,700

SOURCE: *CIA World Factbook 2001* [Online]. Data for 1998. Percent distribution for 1997 est.

tourism. Of these, personal services and retail were the most significant employers, providing jobs for 28 percent and 16 percent of the workforce, respectively. Tourism is a minor source of revenue and employment in Trinidad, with Tobago earning more in this sector.

AGRICULTURE

Agriculture experienced a sharp decline during the oil-boom decade of the 1970s, when food imports increased and wage levels in agricultural jobs were low in comparison to other sectors. Sugar remains the main export crop and the main employer, especially during the cane-cutting season. Sugar production reached 227,400 tons in 1965 but fell dramatically to 48,300 tons by 1982. In 1999, 112,100 tons were produced, falling short of the government's target of 130,000. Most production is carried out by the state-owned Caroni Ltd., which has 2 sugar factories, but smaller, independent farmers were responsible for growing 56 percent of cane in 1999. Most sugar exports go to Europe at preferential and guaranteed prices negotiated with the European Union, for which Trinidad and Tobago exports an annual quota of 43,751 tons. In 1998, sugar earned an estimated US$32 million. Despite this guaranteed market access, the sugar industry is highly unprofitable, with the government obliged to subsidize Caroni by $25 million in 1998. There have been repeated calls for the government to sell its sugar operations or to gradually abandon the industry altogether, but this would cause widespread unemployment. Cocoa and coffee have also declined in importance, with only 1,160 tons of cocoa and 343 tons of coffee produced in 1999. Some exotic flowers are exported to the United States, and a wide range of fruits and vegetables are grown for local consumption.

INDUSTRY

OIL AND GAS. Petroleum has dominated the economy since the 1950s, when offshore production began. In 1999, there were 18 international companies involved in oil and gas exploration and production, while the state-owned Petroleum Company of Trinidad and Tobago (Petrotrin) was involved in extraction and refining at its refinery at Pointe-à-Pierre. The oil and gas sectors are divided between foreign and national companies, the former paying the government a royalty on all oil and gas produced. In the 1990s, production of refined petroleum averaged 125,000 barrels per day. This increased in 1999–2000 when world crude oil prices rose from US$11.64 per barrel in early 1999 to US$17.37 6 months later. In 1998, total oil-related exports, including crude oil, refined petrol, and gas, earned just over $1 billion, but this was expected to rise from 1999 onwards.

Trinidad and Tobago's oil and gas industry appears to have many years ahead of it, with proven reserves of oil standing at 605 million barrels in 1999 (with possible reserves estimated at 2.6 billion barrels) and gas reserves standing at 22.9 billion cubic feet, enough to last 51 years at current rates of extraction. Recent findings have suggested that there may be even greater reserves of gas and oil off the shores of Trinidad. A relatively small amount of Trinidad's gas is exported, and most is used in other sectors of industry.

MANUFACTURING. Trinidad and Tobago's manufacturing sector is very different from that of other Caribbean countries in that it does not depend on cheap labor or the export of garments and electronics into the United States. Instead, the emphasis is on heavy industry and petrochemicals, all related to bountiful natural resources. Unlike other smaller Caribbean countries, Trinidad and Tobago is home to several large local companies, producing a wide range of **consumer goods** for national and regional markets. Manufacturing depends to a large degree on the availability of cheap fuel. In 1999, about 65 percent of the gas produced by the National Gas Company went towards producing ammonia and methanol, which in 1998 earned US$248 million and US$148 million, respectively. In 2000, Trinidad and Tobago became the world's largest exporter of methanol, a liquid used as a solvent or fuel, while it was also the world's leading exporter of ammonia, a gas used in industry. Locally produced gas also fuels the steel and cement industries; in 1998, Trinidad and Tobago earned US$206 million from steel exports. Cement, glass, and food and drink processing also benefit from cheap energy supplies.

SERVICES

TOURISM. Tobago has a significant tourism industry, with more than half of the country's 4,200 hotel rooms situated on the smaller island. But in energy-rich Trinidad, tourism has not been considered a priority, and most visitors come as business travelers or to visit relatives. The exception is the annual Carnival in February, when many thousands of tourists arrive to witness the famous calypso and steel band music and the colorful marches. In 1998, receipts from tourism amounted to US$201 million, with an estimated one-third of tourists arriving from the United States. Since the 1990s, the government has shown greater interest in tourism's potential and has invested in a cruise-ship terminal at Port of Spain and more international marketing. In 1999, cruise-ship arrivals rose significantly, reaching over 65,000.

RETAIL SERVICES. Retail is well developed in Trinidad and Tobago, with several large distributors, wholesalers, and supermarket chains. There are also many small local stores, especially in the countryside.

Trade (expressed in billions of US$): Trinidad & Tobago		
	Exports	Imports
1975	1.757	1.471
1980	3.955	3.161
1985	2.196	1.586
1990	1.718	1.121
1995	2.455	1.714
1998	N/A	N/A

SOURCE: International Monetary Fund. *International Financial Statistics Yearbook 1999.*

INTERNATIONAL TRADE

Unlike most other Caribbean nations, Trinidad and Tobago does not suffer from a permanent **trade deficit** and frequently exports more than it imports. The main exports are oil and petroleum products. The deficit of US$600 million in 1998 was largely due to unusually high imports of machinery and other expensive goods for investment in heavy manufacturing. In 1999, the trade balance showed a surplus of US$63.6 million. In 1998, the United States was the main trading partner, accounting for 36.9 percent of exports. Caribbean Community (Caricom) countries took 29.4 percent of exports, mostly petroleum, while the European Union took 6.3 percent.

In terms of imports, the United States was again the major partner, supplying Trinidad and Tobago with 44.7 percent of its imports, including machinery, vehicles, and manufactured goods. Latin America was a major supplier of foods (18.9 percent of imports), and the European Union accounted for 13.7 percent.

Although the United Kingdom was its most important trading partner until the 1960s, Trinidad and Tobago is now increasingly diversified in its access to North and South American markets as well as being a major supplier of fuel and chemicals throughout the Caribbean.

MONEY

After the boom years of the 1970s, the recession of the 1980s came as a rude awakening. The government was forced to adopt a more cautious attitude towards spending and taxation. After enjoying an average annual GDP growth of 5.5 percent between 1974 and 1981, Trinidad and Tobago saw its GDP shrink by an average of 6.1 percent between 1982 and 1987, forcing the government to cut its spending, slash **public-sector** workers' salaries, and restrict imports with high taxes. Following the advice of the International Monetary Fund (IMF), the government raised taxes through the introduction of a value-added tax (VAT) and devalued the currency. Since the mid-1990s, the economic situation has been much

Exchange rates: Trinidad and Tobago

Trinidad and Tobago dollars (TT$) per US$1

Jan 2001	6.2688
2000	6.2998
1999	6.2989
1998	6.2983
1997	6.2517
1996	6.0051

SOURCE: CIA *World Factbook 2001* [ONLINE].

Distribution of Income or Consumption by Percentage Share: Trinidad and Tobago

Lowest 10%	2.1
Lowest 20%	5.5
Second 20%	10.3
Third 20%	15.5
Fourth 20%	22.7
Highest 20%	45.9
Highest 10%	29.9

Survey year: 1992
Note: This information refers to income shares by percentiles of the population and is ranked by per capita income.

SOURCE: *2000 World Development Indicators* [CD-ROM].

more stable. There has been steady growth and relatively low levels of **inflation**, averaging 4 percent annually. The TT dollar stood at 6.26 to the U.S. dollar in 2001, representing a fall in value from 4.25 in 1993, when it was allowed to float freely against the U.S. dollar.

Trinidad and Tobago has a strong domestic banking sector, with 2 of the 5 principal banks under local, **private-sector** control. The country is also a regional center for financial services, with Trinidadian banks holding interests in subsidiaries elsewhere in the Caribbean. The Central Bank of Trinidad and Tobago acts as the country's central bank, controlling the flow of currency and setting interest rates. The Trinidad and Tobago Stock Exchange, which opened in October of 1981, listed 23 local companies and 4 companies from Barbados and Jamaica in 1999.

POVERTY AND WEALTH

Distribution of wealth has always been uneven in Trinidad and Tobago. Although there is a large middle class, there are also extremes of wealth and poverty. The wealthy minority is made up of those with interests in private-sector manufacturing and, it is widely rumored, with good contacts in politics and the state corporations. There is a small elite descended from the traditional plantation owners, often light-skinned and educated abroad, but there is also a larger group of entrepreneurs, many of whom owe their fortunes to the boom years of the 1970s when land prices rocketed and money flowed freely. Another wealthy group is comprised of business people of

East Indian origin who have set up lucrative operations in the retail and import-export sectors. The richest citizens of Trinidad are to be seen in the hillside suburbs of Port of Spain, where large villas boast satellite dishes and swimming pools. Trinidad and Tobago's rich tend to live a transnational lifestyle, with assets and interests in the United States. Shopping trips to Miami or Caracas are commonplace, and some upper-class families prefer to send their children abroad for education rather than to the local University of the West Indies.

The other extreme is to be found in deprived inner-city ghettos such as Laventille, where the poorest members of society live. It is here, in areas of ramshackle shacks and self-built cinder-block houses, that the worst problems of poverty, unemployment, and crime grow unabated. Unemployment is worst among the 15–19 age group, of whom an estimated 43 percent are out of work. This has contributed to an alarming rise in violent crime, much of it connected with drugs and gang warfare. The other areas of greatest deprivation are small villages, often inhabited by agricultural laborers of Indian descent, around the central sugar belt.

Trinidadian society is not hugely stratified on color lines, although there is often considerable tension between the African- and Indian-descended sectors of the community. Social mobility is possible, but there is often little opportunity for poor families to improve their economic outlook other than through migration.

Despite areas of poverty, health care and education are generally of a high standard in Trinidad and Tobago, especially in the urban areas. Primary education is free and compulsory, and there is a high level of literacy, estimated by the Pan-American Health Organization at 95 percent. Secondary school enrollment, beginning at 12, is also free, but only 69 percent of eligible children were enrolled in 1999. Social security is extremely basic, and much of the care of the old and sick is entrusted to family networks or charitable agencies.

GDP per Capita (US$)

Country	1975	1980	1985	1990	1998
Trinidad & Tobago	3,302	4,615	4,731	4,095	4,618
United States	19,364	21,529	23,200	25,363	29,683
Venezuela	4,195	3,995	3,357	3,353	3,499
St. Lucia	N/A	2,076	2,150	3,542	3,907

SOURCE: United Nations. *Human Development Report 2000; Trends in human development and per capita income.*

Household Consumption in PPP Terms

Country	All food	Clothing and footwear	Fuel and power[a]	Health care[b]	Education[b]	Transport & Communications	Other
Trinidad & Tobagao	20	10	23	5	13	7	22
United States	13	9	9	4	6	8	51
Venezuela	30	6	17	16	13	7	12
St. Lucia	40	5	11	4	17	11	11

Data represent percentage of consumption in PPP terms.
[a]Excludes energy used for transport.
[b]Includes government and private expenditures.

SOURCE: World Bank. *World Development Indicators 2000.*

WORKING CONDITIONS

Trinidad and Tobago has an established tradition of strong trade unions, especially in the key oil sector. The Oilfield Workers' Trade Union is part of the National Trade Union Centre, an umbrella grouping of unions that protects its members' interests as regards pay and working conditions. Labor legislation, as a result, is generally observed in Trinidad and Tobago, and working conditions are often good. Although workers receive on average only a third of what similar workers in the United States would earn, they are better paid than in many other low-wage economies. Statutory sick pay and other benefits are widespread, while job security, particularly in the heavy industries, is good.

There is little child labor, and women are well represented in most areas of work, except heavy industry and sugar production. Agriculture tends to offer the worst in terms of pay and conditions, and for this reason few younger Trinidadians are attracted to such work.

COUNTRY HISTORY AND ECONOMIC DEVELOPMENT

1498. Trinidad sighted and named by Christopher Columbus.

1592. Large-scale Spanish settlement begins in Trinidad.

1797. Trinidad becomes British colony.

1814. British take control of Tobago from French.

1838. End of slavery creates labor shortages on plantations.

1845. First arrival of indentured Indian laborers.

1857. First oil well drilled.

1888. Trinidad and Tobago are formally combined as political entity.

1917. End of indentureship system.

1956. Self-government begins.

1962. Independence from Great Britain, but the country remains a member of the British Commonwealth. Eric Williams of the People's National Movement (PNM) becomes first prime minister, a position he holds until his death in 1981.

1976. Trinidad and Tobago declare independence as a republic, creating the office of president to take the place of the British monarch as chief of state.

1970S. Economic boom as world oil prices rise sharply.

1982. Collapse of oil prices leads to a 10-year recession.

1995. Indian-dominated United National Congress (UNC) wins elections.

2000. UNC wins second term in office amidst contested elections.

FUTURE TRENDS

Trinidad and Tobago's future, like its past, is inextricably linked to the international oil market and the price of petroleum. When world oil prices are high, the country prospers; when they fall, it suffers. Although not a member of the Organization of Petroleum Exporting Countries (OPEC), Trinidad and Tobago's economic well-being is largely decided by OPEC's manipulation of international oil prices. The advent of gas production and the policy of developing other industries has reduced Trinidad and Tobago's long-term dependence on oil, a direction that will be followed by the government in the future. At the heart of this industrial diversification will be the expansion of heavy industries and a growing capacity for manufactured exports.

Tourism will also be encouraged as the government contemplates the possibility of falling oil prices and even the eventual exhaustion of oil reserves. This sector has barely been explored and has enormous potential, especially with the country's proximity to South America. At the same time, the government will seek to rid itself of the loss-making and old-fashioned sugar industry. It remains to be seen whether it also seeks to reduce the role of the state in the strategic oil and gas industries as well as telecommunications.

DEPENDENCIES

Trinidad and Tobago has no territories or colonies.

BIBLIOGRAPHY

Caribbean Development Bank. *Annual Report 1999.* Barbados, 2000.

Central Bank of Trinidad and Tobago. <http://www.central-bank.org.tt>. Accessed July 2001.

Government of the Republic of Trinidad & Tobago. <http://www.gov.tt/ttgov/default.asp>. Accessed July 2001.

"Trinidad and Tobago and the IMF." *International Monetary Fund.* <http://www.imf.org/external/country/tto/index.htm>. Accessed May 2001.

The Trinidad & Tobago Stock Exchange Limited. <http://www.stockex.co.tt>. Accessed July 2001.

U.S. Central Intelligence Agency. *The World Factbook, 2000.* <http://www.cia.gov/cia/publications/factbook>. Accessed May 2001.

U.S. Department of State. *FY 2000 Country Commercial Guide: Trinidad & Tobago.* <http://www.state.gov/www/about_state/business/com_guides/index.html>. Accessed May 2001.

—*James Ferguson*

UNITED STATES OF AMERICA

CAPITAL: Washington, D.C. (District of Columbia).

MONETARY UNIT: United States dollar ($). One U.S. dollar equals 100 cents. There are coins of 1, 5, 10, 25, 50 cents and 1 dollar. There are notes of 1, 2, 5, 10, 20, 50, 100, 1,000, and 10,000 dollars.

CHIEF EXPORTS: Capital goods, automobiles, industrial supplies and raw materials, consumer goods, and agricultural products.

CHIEF IMPORTS: Crude oil and refined petroleum products, machinery, automobiles, consumer goods, industrial raw materials, and food and beverages.

GROSS DOMESTIC PRODUCT: $9.963 trillion (2000 est.).

BALANCE OF TRADE: Exports: $776 billion (2000 est.). **Imports:** $1.223 trillion (2000 est.).

COUNTRY OVERVIEW

LOCATION AND SIZE. The 48 states that make up the continental United States are located in North America between Mexico and Canada. The state of Hawaii is located in the Pacific Ocean, midway between North America and Asia, and the state of Alaska is located on the extreme northwest corner of North America. The United States also controls a number of small islands in the Caribbean and the Pacific. The nation is the third-largest country in the world in area behind Russia and Canada. It has a total area of 9,629,091 square kilometers (3,717,792 square miles). This total includes the 50 states and the District of Columbia, but not the nation's territories and dependencies. Of this territory, 9,158,960 square kilometers (3,536,274 square miles) are land, while there are 470,131 square kilometers (181,517 square miles) of water. The United States is about one-half the size of Russia, and slightly larger than either Brazil or China. It shares long borders with both Canada (8,893 kilometers or 5,526 miles) and Mexico (3,326 kilometers or 2,066 miles). The nation's total borders are 12,248 kilometers (7,610 miles) long. The Eastern United States borders the Atlantic Ocean and the Caribbean Sea,

while the West Coast borders the Pacific Ocean. Areas of Alaska border the Arctic Ocean. In all, the country has 19,924 kilometers (12,380 miles) of coastline. The nation's capital is Washington, D.C., which is located on the East Coast, almost midway between Maine and Florida. The capital has a population of 519,000, but America's largest cities are New York, with a population of 7,428,162, followed by Los Angeles with 3,633,591 people, and Chicago with 2,799,050.

POPULATION. The population of the United States was estimated to be 275,562,673 in July 2000. Females slightly outnumbered males and there were 0.96 males for every female in the population. This phenomenon is most pronounced among the elderly and is partially the result of longer life spans for women. In the United States, the life expectancy for males is 74.24 years, but 79.9 for females. The elderly are the fastest growing segment of the population and thus have contributed to the "greying" (aging) of the American population. In 2000, those aged 65 and older accounted for 12.64 percent of the population. Meanwhile, those Americans age 14 and younger accounted for 21.25 percent of the population. The most significant factor causing the greying of the population is the aging of the baby-boomers (those people born in the aftermath of World War II when there was rapid population growth or a "boom" period of births). Over the next decade, many of the baby-boomers will reach retirement age, creating new pressures on the health-care and retirement systems. By 2030, the elderly population in the United States will have doubled.

After periods of dramatic population growth early in the 20th century, the American population is now growing at a slow rate of 0.91 percent per year. By 2010, the population is expected to be 297,976,000. The birth rate is 14.2 births per 1,000 people, and the mortality rate is 8.7 deaths per 1,000. The fertility rate is 2.06 children born per woman. Fertility rates have thus stabilized at replacement levels (a point at which there are just enough births to replace the children's parents). Much of the increase in the population is not the result of the birth rate, but rather because of **immigration**. There are about 3.5 new immigrants to the United States for every

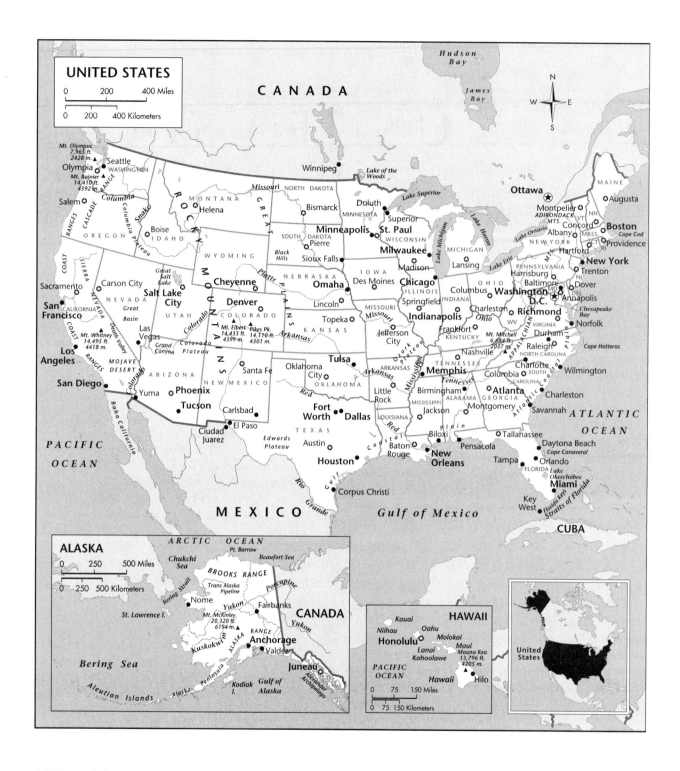

1,000 people in the country. In 1998, there were 660,477 legal immigrants admitted to the United States. In addition, there were an estimated 500,000 to 1 million illegal immigrants.

The American population is one of the most diverse in the world and is constantly changing because of immigration and differences in birth rates. In 1970, non-white minority groups accounted for 16 percent of the population, but by 1998 these groups accounted for 27 percent of the population and estimates are that by 2050, minorities will account for more than 50 percent of the population. Currently, whites make up 72.2 percent of the population. African Americans are the largest minority group at 12.6 percent of the population, followed by Hispanics at 10.6 percent, Asians at 3.7 percent, and Native Americans at 0.8 percent. However, between 2005 and 2010, Hispanics are expected to overtake African Americans to become the largest minority group. The largest ethnic group in the United States is the Germans

(42.9 percent), followed by the Irish (28.6 percent), Africans (12.6 percent), and the Italians (10.8 percent).

For most of its history the United States was a rural nation, but through the 20th century there was increasing urbanization. In 2000, 76 percent of the American population lived in urban areas and 53 percent lived in or near the nation's 20 largest cities. There are now 9 cities in the United States that have populations of more than 1 million people. In order of size, they are New York, Los Angeles, Chicago, Houston, Philadelphia, San Diego, Phoenix, San Antonio, and Dallas. In addition, there are a number of cities, including Detroit and San Jose, with populations near 1 million.

Despite the nation's size, the population density of the United States is relatively low. There are 28.4 people per square kilometer (73.5 people per square mile) in the United States. However, this density is uneven. For instance, the population density of New York City is 8,880 per square kilometer (23,000 per square mile). The state with the highest population density is New Jersey (386 people per square kilometer, or 1,000 per square mile). Alaska has the lowest density with less than 1 person per square kilometer (at about 1 person per square mile). The United States also has one of the most mobile populations in the world. Although 84 percent of the population lives in the same residence as they have for the past 5 years, the average American will move 6 times during his or her lifetime.

OVERVIEW OF ECONOMY

The United States has the largest, most technologically-advanced, and most diverse economy in the world. While the United States accounts for only about 4 percent of the world's population, its GDP is 26 percent of the world's total economic output. The American economy is a free-market, private enterprise system that has only limited government intervention in areas such as health care, transportation, and retirement. American companies are among the most productive and competitive in the world. In 1998, 9 of the 10 most profitable companies in the world were American (even the non-U.S. exception, Germany's Daimler-Chrysler, has a substantial part of its operations in the United States). Unlike their Japanese or Western European counterparts, American corporations have considerable freedom of operation and little government control over issues of product development, plant openings or closures, and employment. The United States also has a clear edge over the rest of the world in many high-tech industries, including computers, medical care, aerospace, and military equipment.

In the 1990s, the American economy experienced the second-longest period of growth in the nation's history. The economy grew at an average rate of 3–4 percent per year and unemployment fell below 5 percent. In addition, there were dramatic gains in the stock market and many of the nation's largest companies had record profits. Finally, a record number of Americans owned their own homes. This long period of growth ended in 2001, when the economy slowed dramatically following a crash in the high-technology sector.

The United States has considerable natural resources. These resources include coal, copper, lead, phosphates, uranium, bauxite, gold, iron, mercury, nickel, silver, tungsten, zinc, petroleum, natural gas, and timber. It also has highly productive agricultural resources and is the world's largest food producer. The economy is bolstered by an excellent, though aging, **infrastructure** which makes the transport of goods relatively easy.

Despite its impressive advantages, the American economy faces a number of problems. Most of the products and services of the nation are consumed internally, but the economy cannot produce enough goods to keep up with consumer demand. As a result, for several decades the United States has imported far more products than it exports. This **trade deficit** exists entirely in manufactured goods. The United States actually has trade surpluses in agriculture and services. When adjusted for the surpluses, the U.S. trade deficit in 2000 amounted to a record $447 billion. The United States has been able to sustain trade deficits year after year because foreign individuals and companies remain willing to invest in the United States. In 2000, there was $270 billion in new foreign investment in American companies and businesses.

Another major problem for the American economy is growth of a 2-tier economy, with some Americans enjoying very high income levels while others remain in poverty. As the workplace becomes more technologically sophisticated, unskilled workers find themselves trapped in minimum wage or menial jobs. In 1999, despite the strong economic growth of the 1990s, 12.7 percent of Americans lived below the poverty line. There are other wage problems in the United States. Although the economy has grown substantially, most of the gains in income have gone to the top 20 percent of households. The top 10 percent of households earned 28.5 percent of the nation's wealth, while the bottom 10 percent accounted for only 1.5 percent. There is also a growing number of Americans who are not covered by medical insurance.

Although there is great diversity in the American economy, services dominate economic activity. Together, services account for approximately 80 percent of the country's GDP. Manufacturing accounts for only 18 percent, while agriculture accounts for 2 percent. Financial services, health care, and information technology are among the fastest growing areas of the service sector. Although industry has declined steeply from its height in the 1950s, the American manufacturing sector remains strong. Two of the largest American corporations, General Electric and General Motors, have manufacturing and production as their base, although they have both diversified into the service sector as well. Meanwhile, despite continuing declines, agriculture remains strong in the United States. One of the main trends in the agricultural sector has been the erosion of the family farm and its replacement by the large corporate farm. This has made the sector more productive, although there has also been a decrease in the number of farmers and farm workers.

Since the middle of the 20th century, the United States has aggressively pursued free and open trade. It helped found a number of international organizations whose purpose is to promote free trade, including the General Agreement on Tariffs and Trade (GATT), now known as the World Trade Organization (WTO). It has also engaged in free trade agreements with particular nations. The North American Free Trade Agreement (NAFTA) between the United States, Canada, and Mexico is an example of this. One continuing problem for American companies engaged in foreign trade is that the United States is much more open to trade than many other nations. As a result, it is easy for foreign companies to sell their goods and services in the United States, but American firms often find it difficult to export their products to other countries.

The nation is a net provider of economic aid. It provides $6.9 billion in direct aid to nations. In addition, the United States funds many international organizations. It provides 25 percent of the operating budget of the United Nations and almost 50 percent of the budget for day-to-day NATO operations. (The North Atlantic Treaty Organization is a military alliance of 19 countries in Europe and North America.) Nonetheless, this aid has only a small impact on the U.S. budget. All spending on international affairs, including the costs of maintaining embassies overseas, foreign aid, and support for international organizations, amounted to $19.5 billion in 1999. That was only 0.01 percent of the federal budget. In comparison, in 1999 the United States spent $26.7 billion to fund the Central Intelligence Agency (CIA).

POLITICS, GOVERNMENT, AND TAXATION

The United States is a democratic, federal republic. It is one of the oldest functioning democracies in the world. Government in the United States is divided into 3 levels: federal, state, and local. In addition to the national government, there are 50 state governments, and over 80,000 local governments, including counties, towns, and cities.

The chief executive and head of state is a president who is elected for a 4-year term, and who may not be elected more than twice. The nation's legislature is known as the Congress and is **bicameral** (it has 2 chambers). The upper chamber is the Senate. There are 2 senators from each state, and they are elected for 6-year terms. The lower house is the House of Representatives, which has 435 members who serve 2-year terms. The number of representatives a state has depends on its population. For example California has 52 representatives, while states such as North Dakota, South Dakota, and Wyoming only have 1 representative because of their small populations.

Both federal and state governments have only limited impact on the economy. There are laws that establish worker safety conditions and the minimum wage as well as restrictions on hazardous products and the manner in which companies do business. Most economic policies and laws are designed to protect consumers and workers and to promote economic development. The main impact of the government, besides taxation, is the operation of such agencies as the Post Office and regulatory agencies that oversee various aspects of the economy, including the Federal Trade Commission, the Securities and Exchange Commission, and the Nuclear Regulatory Commission.

In the United States, Congress and the president control **fiscal policy** while a semi-independent body, the Federal Reserve Board, controls **monetary policy**. The members of the Federal Reserve Board are appointed by the president and confirmed by the Senate, but once in office they have almost complete freedom of action to set interest rates and take action to control the amount of money in circulation.

There are 2 main political parties in the United States. The Democratic Party is liberal and generally supports government action to address economic or social problems. The Republican Party is conservative and advocates limited government and a strong national defense. Both parties support the **free market system**, but Republicans tend to be more supportive of free trade at the international level. Meanwhile the Democrats tend to emphasize workers' rights and increased social spending. Republicans controlled the presidency and the House of Representatives after the 2000 elections (in which George W. Bush was elected president) while the Democrats had a slim majority in the Senate.

The United States has an independent judiciary and a dual court system in which there are both federal and state courts. The highest court is the federal Supreme Court, whose 9 judges are appointed for life by the president. Each state also has a supreme court for state matters. The American court system is often the final arbiter for economic disputes. Consumers use the court system to get compensation for faulty products or service and to stop unfair business practices. Businesses and governments use the courts to settle disputes and enforce laws. For instance, the courts have been used to break up **monopolies**.

The nation's tax rate is low when compared with other industrialized nations. However, there are wide variations in taxation since the individual states also tax citizens. For instance, Arkansas, Florida, New Hampshire, South Dakota, Washington, and Wyoming do not have state **income taxes**, while other states, such as Ohio or California, have income taxes as high as 10 percent of earnings.

In 2000, the federal government's revenues were about $1.9 trillion and it spent about $1.75 trillion. The result was a $115 billion **budget surplus**. In the same year, state governments collected $500 billion in revenues and spent $800 billion (most of the $300 billion in excess spending was provided by the federal government). On the federal level, 47.8 percent of revenues came from individual income taxes. The tax rates ranged from 15 percent to 39.6 percent of income. Other sources of revenue were corporate taxes at 10.1 percent, **social security taxes** at 33.8 percent, and **excise taxes** (in the United States, these are taxes on goods such as gasoline and cigarettes) at 3.7 percent. There were also small amounts from gift and **estate taxes** and customs **duties**. The main government expenditures were social security ($408.6 billion), welfare programs ($274.6 billion), national defense ($274.1 billion), Medicare ($216.6 billion), and interest on the **national debt** ($215.2 billion). In 2000, the national debt was $5.7 trillion, or 67 percent of GDP. This is higher than the average for industrialized nations and payments on the large debt take an enormous amount of money out of the economy.

The American military influences the economy in an indirect way. The size of the nation's military and its needs for equipment and supplies have created a military-industrial complex (a series of deep relationships between the military and companies that provide services and equipment for national defense). This military-industrial complex has resulted in a number of multi-billion dollar companies that develop and sell expensive equipment to the military including naval ships and submarines, fighter aircraft, missiles, tanks, and other equipment. In 1999 alone, the federal government spent $48.9 billion to acquire new weapons.

INFRASTRUCTURE, POWER, AND COMMUNICATIONS

In general, the United States has an excellent infrastructure. Some areas of the country have aging or overburdened roadways and utility systems, but the nationwide infrastructure is capable of supporting the needs of the economy. Roadways connect all 50 states and 90 percent of all major cities and towns are serviced by expressways. The sheer size of the United States necessitates a vast highway network so that goods can be transported throughout the country. The nation has 6,348,277 kilometers (3,944,819 miles) of roadways, including 3,732,757 kilometers (2,319,535 miles) of paved roads. Of this total, 1 percent or 74,071 kilometers (46,036 miles) are interstate highways and a total of 180,959 kilometers (112,467 miles) are part of the national highway system. These roads are needed to accommodate the country's 208 million vehicles, including 199 million private cars and trucks, 7 million commercial trucks, and 697,000 buses.

The country's railway system is privately owned and includes 240,000 kilometers (149,136 miles) of mainline rail. There are 116,000 people in the United States who are employed by railways. Amtrak, the national passenger carrier, is government-owned, but there is ongoing discussion in Congress over whether the system should be **privatized**. Amtrak has 38,616 kilometers (24,000 miles) of track and services 500 stations across the country. The importance of transportation to the American economy is exemplified by the fact that in 1996, $847 billion, or 11 percent of the nation's GDP, was spent on transportation.

Communications

Country	Newspapers	Radios	TV Sets[a]	Cable subscribers[a]	Mobile Phones[a]	Fax Machines[a]	Personal Computers[a]	Internet Hosts[b]	Internet Users[b]
	1996	1997	1998	1998	1998	1998	1998	1999	1999
United States	215	2,146	847	244.3	256	78.4	458.6	1,508.77	74,100
Canada	159	1,077	715	263.8	176	33.3	330.0	422.97	11,000
Japan	578	955	707	114.8	374	126.8	237.2	163.75	27,060
Germany	311	948	580	214.5	170	73.1	304.7	173.96	14,400

[a]Data are from International Telecommunication Union, *World Telecommunication Development Report 1999* and are per 1,000 people.

[b]Data are from the Internet Software Consortium (http://www.isc.org) and are per 10,000 people.

SOURCE: World Bank. *World Development Indicators 2000.*

Not counting the massive Great Lakes, there are 41,009 kilometers (25,483 miles) of navigable waterways in the United States. During the 19th century, a massive system of canals was constructed around the nation and many remain in use. The Mississippi River is one of the busiest waterways in the world and the main north-south shipping route. The United States is serviced by a number of ports. Among the busiest ports are Baltimore, Boston, Charleston, Chicago, Hampton Roads, Los Angeles, New Orleans, New York, Philadelphia, San Francisco, Savannah, Seattle, and Tampa. The nation's merchant marine has 386 ships with gross tonnages of more than 1,000 tons each. The total weight of the fleet is 11,634,608 gross tons. This does not include thousands of barges, tugboats, and smaller craft. In order to supply the nation's energy needs there is an extensive network of pipelines.

The United States also has an excellent telecommunications system. Telephone service is widespread and easily available. Many cities and states have large and state-of-the-art fiber-optic cable systems. There are also microwave radio relay stations and extensive coaxial cable networks. The nation has a well-developed and expanding cellular system which includes thousands of relay towers. There are an estimated 70 million mobile phones in use in the country. For international communications, there are 24 ocean cable systems to carry transoceanic communications. The telecommunications system is enhanced by a broad network of satellites. The United States has 70 satellite earth stations to relay transmissions. In 1999, there were 7,600 Internet service providers in the United States.

There are 14,572 airports in the United States, although only 5,174 have paved runways. There are also 118 heliports. Some 241,000 people were employed by the air transport companies as of early 2001, although after the terrorist attack on the World Trade Center in September of that year, the airlines began massive layoffs of employees. All American airlines are privately owned. The largest airlines in the country are American Airlines, United, Continental, Northwest, and Delta. The nation's busiest airports are Hartford International in Atlanta and O'Hare International in Chicago. The United States also has the world's largest space program. The National Aeronautics and Space Administration's (NASA) budget in 2000 was $13.7 billion. Of this total, $9.8 billion was spent on contractors. The largest payments were to Boeing, United Space Alliance, and Lockheed Martin. The space program is an example of government cooperation with private industry since NASA conducts many space launches for private companies (mainly satellite launches).

In 1998, the nation consumed 3.36 trillion kilowatt hours (kWh) of power. It imported 39.51 billion kWh (mainly from Canada) and exported 12.77 billion kWh.

Domestic electricity production was 3.62 trillion kWh. The majority of electricity was produced by fossil fuels (70.34 percent). Atomic power supplied the second-largest share of electricity (18.61), followed by hydroelectric power (8.96 percent), and a variety of renewable energy sources including wind and solar power (2.09 percent).

ECONOMIC SECTORS

The United States has a highly diversified economy with a mix of large and small companies and a variety of industries and services. Although relatively small when compared with the other sectors of the economy, American agriculture is highly diverse and well developed. The differences in climate, soil, and rainfall across the country allow for a great assortment of crops to be cultivated. Citrus products grow well in Florida and areas of California, while the Midwest is suited to raising wheat and corn, and areas of the Southeast produce the majority of the nation's tobacco and cotton. In overall terms, the main crops are wheat and other grains, corn, fruits, vegetables, and cotton. The main livestock products are beef, pork, poultry, dairy products, turkey, and fish. There is also a significant industry based on forest products such as timber. Most crops and livestock grown in the United States are used for domestic consumption, but the country also exports a considerable amount of products. Agriculture accounts for about 2.4 percent of total employment.

The United States remains the world's dominant industrial power. Like other economic sectors, industry in the United States is technologically sophisticated and includes a wide variety of different manufacturers and products. While industry has declined in relation to other

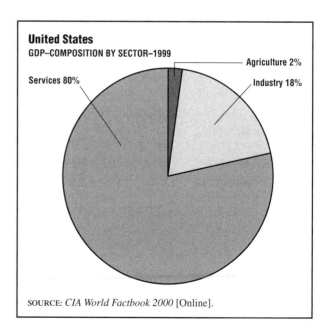

SOURCE: *CIA World Factbook 2000* [Online].

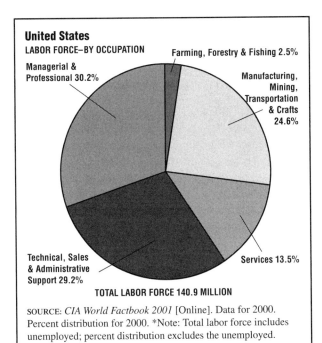

United States
LABOR FORCE–BY OCCUPATION

Managerial & Professional 30.2%

Farming, Forestry & Fishing 2.5%

Manufacturing, Mining, Transportation & Crafts 24.6%

Technical, Sales & Administrative Support 29.2%

Services 13.5%

TOTAL LABOR FORCE 140.9 MILLION

SOURCE: *CIA World Factbook 2001* [Online]. Data for 2000. Percent distribution for 2000. *Note: Total labor force includes unemployed; percent distribution excludes the unemployed.

information products and services. By 1999, one-third of all new investments in the United States were in IT-based companies. The nation's **retail** sector is also strong. Consumer spending on products and services has helped drive the economic growth of the past decade. Major American retailers such as Wal-Mart, K-Mart, and Target have developed new methods of marketing and sales that have revolutionized the retail market. Services employ 77 percent of American workers.

AGRICULTURE

American agriculture is marked by several trends. The first is the continuing decline of small family farms. Since 1979, 300,000 small farms have disappeared in the United States, and since 1946 the number of people employed in agriculture has been cut in half. Increasingly, large companies such as Archer-Daniels Midland (ADM) have come to dominate American agriculture. In 2000, ADM had worldwide sales of $12.9 billion. In the beef industry, 4 firms control 80 percent of the U.S. market. Almost 91 percent of U.S. farms are considered to be small (less than 1,000 acres). Large farms (more than 1,000 acres) made up just 9 percent of farms but received 51 percent of total agricultural revenues in 2000. The second trend is the increasing productivity of the sector. Agricultural production in the United States has increased by an average of 5 percent each year since 1990. In addition, the output of each agricultural worker has grown by an average of 0.84 percent each year. On average, one American farmer produces enough food for 96 people. This improvement is partially as a result of the consolidation of farms and partially a result of new technologies and farming methods. The third trend is the growth in both exports and imports. In 1998 total agricultural exports were $60.5 billion. That same year, total imports were $48.9 billion. The fourth and final trend is the loss of agricultural **subsidies**. Some of these subsidies are in the form of outright payments in exchange for farmers not growing certain crops and are provided to keep the price of crops high. Since the early 1990s, Congress has gradually reduced these subsidies. However, support and aid for certain types of farmers, including tobacco farmers, continues. After declining to a low point of $9 billion in 1997, government spending on agriculture increased to $23 billion in 1999 and $38.4 billion in 2000. The increases mainly came from emergency aid to farmers because of natural disasters during these 2 years.

About 40 percent of the land in the United States is used for agriculture of some form, including livestock grazing. This includes 431.1 million acres of cropland, 396.9 million acres of pasture, and 71.5 million acres of forests. In 1998, the total crop output of the United States was 489,976,030 metric tons with a value of $102.14 billion. The largest single crop was corn, which accounted

sectors, it has experienced steady growth. In 1999, industry grew by 2.4 percent. The leading industries are petroleum, steel, motor vehicles, aerospace, telecommunications, chemicals, electronics, food processing, **consumer goods**, lumber, and mining. Industry employs 24.5 percent of the American workforce. One ongoing trend in industry is the increasing consolidation and diversification of companies. Larger corporations have absorbed other companies both in an effort to reduce competition and also to branch into new markets. In 1997, there were a total of 11,128 business mergers or acquisitions in the United States, with a total value of $906 billion. American firms were involved in 9 out of the world's 10 largest mergers from 1989 to 1999. Mergers were particularly common in industries such as oil and natural gas processing, consumer goods, and medical equipment. American industry has also branched out into new areas. For instance, companies such as General Electric or General Motors no longer concentrate solely on manufacturing, but engage in a variety of economic endeavors including media broadcasting, financial services and telecommunications. Among the world's largest industrial companies are the American firms General Electric, Exxon, IBM, Ford Motor Company, General Motors, and Philip Morris.

The service sector is the largest component of the American economy. The United States has established itself as a world leader in telecommunications, financial services, and information technology or IT (computer-based information systems and communications). The growth of IT has propelled the "new economy" of the United States, based less on manufacturing and more on for more than half of the nation's crop output with 247,882,000 metric tons. The second largest crop was soybeans with 74,598,000 metric tons. Wheat is third with 69,327,000 metric tons. Other major crops include sugar cane, sugar beets, potatoes, bananas, and coffee. Tobacco also provides substantial cash returns, although yields are small when compared with many other crops. Total animal output in 1998 was $94.19 billion while forestry products, including timber, totaled $24.68 billion. Of the total American livestock, there were 101.2 million head of cattle, 56.2 million pigs, 8.3 million sheep, 6.15 million horses and 1.5 billion chicken. The remaining livestock includes a variety of species such as bison, turkeys, and geese.

Commercial fishing has declined significantly in the United States over the past 30 years. The majority of U.S. fish cultivation is used domestically, and about half is for human consumption. There is a wide variety of species caught, including cod, haddock, pollock, tuna, and salmon. Various shellfish such as lobster, shrimp, or crab account for about 20 percent of the annual harvest, but provide about one-half of the total revenues. Commercial fish farms are increasingly common and used for species such as salmon, catfish, and shrimp. Total fish harvests amounted to $3.7 billion in 1998, of which shellfish totals were $1.6 billion.

There have been dramatic improvements in agricultural technology in the United States. Improvements include increased use of computers, scientific soil and crop analysis, and more sophisticated machinery. Genetic engineering of seeds has also increased crop yields but created controversy over the safety of genetically altered products. There has subsequently been a decrease in soil erosion caused by over-farming and an overall decline in the use of pesticides and fertilizers. However, the pesticides used are much more powerful and lethal than earlier chemicals. About two-thirds of the states have had deep reductions in agriculture. Agriculture has declined most significantly in the New England states and New Jersey. In the West and southern plains, some states have had minor declines, while others have had small increases. The only regions of the nation that have seen major expansion of agriculture have been the middle-Atlantic area and the Pacific Northwest. The states with the largest increases in output were Arkansas, Washington, Delaware, Florida, and Georgia.

Progress in technology and crop yields has made the United States among the most productive agricultural producers in the world. The United States produces about half of the world's corn and 10 percent of its wheat. It also accounts for 20 percent of the globe's beef, pork, and lamb. With such progress in increasing output and the efficiency of agriculture, food prices for American consumers have had little increase over the past 20 years.

Americans spend less on food, as a proportion of their income, than any other nation in the world. U.S. consumers spent 10.9 percent of their income on food. In comparison, the average British consumer spent 11.2 percent, the French 14.8 percent, the Japanese 17.6 percent, and Indians spent 51.3 percent.

The United States is the world's largest producer of timber. About 70 percent of the nation's forests are privately owned, but there is also limited logging allowed in federally-owned or managed forests. Almost 80 percent of timber harvested is soft woods such as pine or Douglas Fir. Hardwoods such as oak account for the remaining 20 percent.

INDUSTRY

Although American industry has declined as a percentage of the nation's GDP, it remains an integral part of the economy and has experienced some growth in certain areas. Since the 1960s, manufacturing has been in an overall decline, but specific American-made products have increased their sales and become more productive by using new technology and manufacturing methods. For instance, the automotive industry has increased production and produced 1.2 percent of the GDP although there have been cutbacks and shifts in employment. Many automotive workers now work for smaller independent manufacturers instead of the large companies such as Ford and General Motors. One of the main trends in U.S. industry is the increasing consolidation of small and medium companies into larger firms.

In 1999, there were 390,000 manufacturing companies in the United States with 18.5 million employees. There were also 27,000 mining companies with 627,000 workers, and 634,000 construction companies with 5 million employees (this includes individual contractors involved in construction such as plumbers and electricians). The largest industrial companies in the United States in 2000 were General Motors with 392,000 employees, Ford Motor Company with 364,600 employees, General Electric with 316,500, and Boeing with 211,000 employees. Many companies that once concentrated in manufacturing now are engaged in a variety of economic activities. For instance, General Electric is one of the largest industrial companies, but only about half of its employees work in manufacturing. The rest are employed in such activities as media operations (General Electric owns the television network NBC), sales, and marketing.

MANUFACTURING AND CONSTRUCTION. The strong economy of the 1990s produced record profits for many American manufacturing firms. Sales of manufactured goods totaled $354.9 billion in 1999. One result of this has been increased investment in new factories and equipment and in research and development of new products.

Profits in industry have also been aided by the increased productivity of workers. New investment by industry increased by 9 percent since 1995.

In the manufacturing sector, durable goods (products that are designed to last 5 years or more) accounted for 9.5 percent of the nation's GDP while non-durable goods, such as food or clothing, accounted for 6.9 percent of GDP. In 2000, the main durable goods were electronic products, motor vehicles, industrial machinery, fabricated metal products, lumber and wood products, and other transportation goods (including airplanes and aerospace equipment). In 1999, there were 11.1 million people employed in the manufacture of durable goods. The main non-durable goods sectors were food and foodstuffs, printing and publishing, chemicals and pharmaceuticals, rubber and plastics, textiles and clothing, and tobacco. In 1999, there were 7.44 million Americans working in the non-durable goods production sector of the economy.

Because of increased production, many American workers in the manufacturing sector worked more than 40 hours a week in order to keep up with demand. In 1999, the average manufacturing employee worked 4.6 hours of overtime per week. Average earnings in the manufacturing sector were $13.24 per hour. This marked a 3.3 percent increase in earnings from the previous year. American manufacturing companies were operating at about 82 percent of total capacity in 1999. In comparison, throughout the 1980s and early 1990s these companies were operating at an average of only 76 percent of capacity. The greatest gains in productivity in the manufacturing sector were in electronics, industrial machinery, and automobile production.

In 1999, 6.4 million Americans worked in the construction industry. The total value of new construction that same year was $764 billion. This included $172.1 billion worth of construction by local, state, and national governments. There were 1.66 million new houses built and 299,700 business structures completed.

ENERGY AND MINING. The United States produces 74 percent of its energy needs. The nation has significant reserves of coal, natural gas, and hydroelectric power. The United States has the sixth-largest reserves of natural gas and is one of the world's largest producers of gas. The United States is also the third-largest exporter of coal. The nation has the twelfth-largest reserves of oil, but it is one of the world's largest importers of oil. About 57 percent of the oil consumed in the United States is imported. The majority of the nation's oil production is concentrated in Alaska, Texas, Louisiana, and California. Although profits for U.S. energy companies have doubled since 1990, many companies have shifted their efforts to develop new oil fields overseas. The 15 largest U.S. energy companies now have operations in such diverse places as Asia, Africa, and South America. There

has been increased consolidation in the energy field. In 1999, Exxon and Mobil merged to form the largest private energy company in the world, worth $81 billion. This was followed in 2000 by a merger announcement between Chevron and Texaco. Rising oil prices in the United States contributed to the economic slowdown that began in 2000.

Non-fuel mineral production in the United States in 1997 amounted to $39.6 billion. The major minerals included zinc, lead, gold, iron ore, phosphates, and platinum. Eleven states accounted for 56 percent of total production. There were also $26.7 billion worth of mineral commodities produced. The main commodities were crushed stone, cement, copper, sand, lime and clays. Many of these products were used in the construction industry. In 1999, mining employed about 535,000 people.

SERVICES

While there has been a trade deficit in manufactured items between the United States and the rest of the world, the nation has built a trade surplus in services. In 1998, services accounted for 28 percent of total U.S. exports, but only 16.5 percent of imports. Since 1995, services have grown by an average of 6 percent per year. Leading segments of the service sector include telecommunications, financial services, and IT. The main export markets for American services are the European Union, which spent $85 billion on American services in 1999, Japan at $30 billion, and Canada at $21 billion. Among developing nations, Mexico was the number-one source for the export of U.S. services, and in 1999, it spent $13 billion.

FINANCIAL SERVICES. The financial sector is composed of banking, insurance, and real estate operations. Financial firms provide a range of services. Commercial banks provide loans to consumers and businesses, including revolving loans in the form of credit cards. They also offer a variety of safe investment opportunities, such as savings accounts. Most savings and checking accounts in U.S. banks are insured by the Federal Deposit Insurance Corporation for up to $100,000. Other financial firms concentrate on investment opportunities such as stocks and bonds, and manage long-term retirement plans. Still others provide a range of insurance needs including life, car, and home insurance. Financial service firms account for about 8.5 percent of all companies and just 5.8 percent of U.S. workers. Because of the high level of education and training required for employment in this sector, workers in financial services are among the highest-paid in the United States. In 1999, their average hourly wage was $14.61 compared with the national hourly average of $13.24. They also have a lower unemployment rate. Unemployment among financial service workers was just 2.3 percent in 1999, while the national unemployment rate was 4.3 percent. The largest financial service firms are Citigroup with 173,500 workers, Bank of America with 163,400, Wells Fargo with 90,400, and Chase Manhattan with 73,800.

INFORMATION TECHNOLOGY. One of the fastest growing areas of the U.S. economy is IT. This includes the development of computer software and computer applications for business and government, as well as new methods of communication. The IT sector also covers systems that integrate new technologies. For instance, IT includes systems that link Internet access and mobile phones. Although IT accounts for only a small part of the U.S. GDP (8.3 percent in 2000), it is responsible for one-third of new output. In addition, spending on IT software and services accounted for 11 percent of the 14 percent increase in business spending on **procurement** in 2000. IT was also responsible for a 30 percent growth in personal income. Most of the technology involved in this sector of the economy was invented before 1990, including the personal computer, fax machine, cellular phone and Internet. It has only been since 1995 that systems have been developed that integrate these new technologies.

RETAIL. Retail and wholesale trade has posted substantial growth since 1993. By 2000, retail and wholesale trade employed 25 percent of all workers in the **private sector** and accounted for 19.3 percent of all businesses. Strong sales in these sectors have been bolstered by increases in productivity. Average worker productivity has increased by about 5 percent per year since 1995. Wages in the retail sector are far lower than the national average. In 1999, the average wage for retail workers was $9.08 per hour, while the national average wage was $13.24 per hour. In addition, retail workers usually work less than 40 hours per week (on average just 29 hours) and often do not have benefits such as health insurance and retirement.

Increases in sales and productivity have meant dramatic profits for many retailers. However, many companies have not been able to compete with the mega-retail firms such as Wal-Mart, K-Mart, and Target. By 2001, many of the country's oldest and most respected firms—including Montgomery Ward and Bradlees—were bankrupt. Wal-Mart is the nation's number-one retail store, and in 2000, it came in second place only to General Electric in overall sales among all American companies (including such firms as Ford, Microsoft, and Exxon Mobil). The number-two retail firm was Home Depot. Along with this trend has been the slow demise of the mom-and-pop stores (small, independent, often family-owned businesses that are usually involved in retail ventures such as service stations and neighborhood grocery stores). One of the fastest growing segments of the retail sector is **e-commerce** (business that is conducted through the Internet). The United States currently leads the world in e-commerce. In 2000, e-commerce was worth $35 billion in the United States as 11 million consumers purchased products via the Internet. However, initial estimates of wild growth in the sector have not come true and many online companies have struggled to become profitable. Official government estimates were that e-commerce would be worth $800 billion by 2005, but new estimates place that figure at only $230 billion.

TOURISM. The United States is the world leader in tourism. This is true of both tourists coming to the United States and Americans visiting overseas. In 2000, foreign visitors spent $75 billion in the United States, while American tourists spent $50 billion abroad. In 1998, some 45 million people visited the United States. The majority of these tourists were from Canada (14 million), followed by Mexico (9.8 million) and Europe (9 million). About 50 million Americans traveled abroad, mainly to Mexico and Canada.

INTERNATIONAL TRADE

Because of the massive size of the American economy, the country has a significant impact on global trade. When the American economy is expanding, it can prompt growth in other nations. However, when the U.S. economy contracts, it usually initiates parallel declines in other countries. Imports of foreign goods have helped keep prices low and meet consumer demand in the United States. The volume of these imports has resulted in a record $447 billion trade deficit, but foreign investment in the country has underwritten this deficit and provided new capital for the economy to expand. Exports in 2000 stood at $776 billion, while imports stood at $1.223 trillion.

In 2000, the country's main export partners were Canada at 23 percent of trade, Mexico at 14 percent, Japan at 8 percent, the United Kingdom at 5 percent, Germany at 4 percent and both France and the Netherlands at 3 percent each. The nation's main import partners are Canada at 19 percent, Japan at 11 percent, Mexico at 11 percent, China at 8 percent, Germany at 5 percent, and both the United Kingdom and Taiwan at 4 percent each. During the 1990s, trade with Canada and Mexico expanded as a result of trade agreements. Meanwhile, consumer demand for electronic products and automobiles led to increases in Japanese imports. At the same time, trade with Europe grew more slowly and even declined in certain markets.

The country's closest trade relationship is with Canada. On average, $1 billion worth of goods and services cross the border between the United States and Canada each day. Trade with Canada exceeds the volume of trade between the United States and all of South America or the European Union (EU). The volume of trade that moves between Michigan and the Canadian

Trade (expressed in billions of US$): United States		
	Exports	Imports
1975	108.856	105.880
1980	225.566	256.984
1985	218.815	352.463
1990	393.592	516.987
1995	584.743	770.852
1998	682.497	944.353

SOURCE: International Monetary Fund. *International Financial Statistics Yearbook 1999.*

province of Ontario is itself equal to the country's trade with Japan. While close trade relations have existed for 2 centuries, this interdependence began to be formalized in 1965 with the Auto Pact between the 2 nations, which removed restrictions on the automobile trade. In 1964, the 2-way trade in automobiles was $715 million, but with the Auto Pact it increased to $104.1 billion in 1999. This accord was followed in 1989 by the Free Trade Agreement (FTA) which removed trade restrictions on most goods and services. As a result, trade increased by 50 percent between the 2 countries. These open trade patterns between Canada and the United States were expanded to include Mexico in 1994, through the North American Free Trade Agreement (NAFTA). NAFTA established the largest free-trade area in the world with more than 380 million consumers.

American exports of services have doubled since 1989, rising from $118 billion that year to $255 billion in 1999. The United States is one of the world's leading suppliers of financial services. In 1997, U.S. firms had foreign insurance sales of $47.2 billion. Meanwhile, U.S. banking and financial service companies had $13.9 billion in direct sales and American-owned firms based in foreign nations had sales of $13 billion. The success of American service products in foreign markets has helped stimulate the export of other U.S. products to support these companies. For instance, U.S. firms that set up offices overseas usually select American telecommunications equipment and computers. This helps get these products into overseas markets.

The United States has signed a number of foreign trade agreements. In 1934, the nation signed its first reciprocal trade accord, which lowered **tariffs** on goods and services. Since then, the country has consistently promoted free and open trade. This includes efforts to establish trade relationships with individual countries and attempts to develop international trade organizations. In the 1990s, the United States signed more than 300 trade agreements with both specific countries and international groups. Individual trade agreements between the United States and individual countries in the Caribbean and

South America are coordinated through the Caribbean Basin Economic Recovery Act (CEBRA) and the Andean Trade Preferences Act (ATPA).

On a global level, the United States has been responsible for much of the growth in free trade. In 1944, the United States sponsored the foundation of the Bretton Woods economic system. This global system created 3 institutions. The first was the World Bank, to provide loans to countries to rebuild or establish their economies and industry. The second was the International Monetary Fund (IMF), which helped regulate currency and aid countries with financial crises. The third was the General Agreement on Tariffs and Trade (GATT), which promotes free trade by establishing rules for its member states. The United States still provides about 25 percent of the funding for the World Bank and the IMF. In 1994, the World Trade Organization (WTO) replaced the GATT. The United States has used the WTO to its advantage to open trade with nations and to settle trade disputes. The United States is the most frequent user of the WTO Dispute Settlement system and used this to resolve 48 economic disputes between 1996 and 1998.

The WTO forms the main international trade agreement of the United States. The nation is also pursuing the establishment of regional trade agreements such as NAFTA. It is currently a member of the Asia-Pacific Economic Cooperation Forum (APEC) and has proposed the creation of a Free Trade of the Americas Agreement (FTAA), which would include all of North and South America, not just the NAFTA nations. The United States has also proposed the establishment of a Transatlantic Economic Partnership (TEP) which would open trade between the United States and the EU.

MONEY

The American dollar is the main currency used for trade throughout the world. A number of countries around the world have tied their currency to the dollar on a one-for-one basis, including Argentina and the Bahamas. Although the value of the dollar fluctuates freely on world markets, it has remained relatively stable. In late 2001, 0.67 British pounds equaled 1 U.S. dollar; 1.56 Canadian dollars equaled 1 U.S. dollar; 1.09 EU euros equaled 1 U.S. dollar; and 120.63 Japanese yen equaled 1 U.S. dollar.

The banking system of the United States is overseen by the Federal Reserve System, which is made up of 12 regional Reserve banks. These banks control the nation's money and credit supply. The Federal Reserve (commonly referred to as "the Fed") can raise or lower the discount rate that it charges banks to borrow money, thereby raising or lowering national interest rates. It can also control the amount of money in circulation by altering the

Exchange rates: United States

	British pounds per US$1	Canadian dollars (Can$) per US$1	yen per US$1
Jan 2001	0.6764	1.5032	117.10
2000	0.6596	1.4851	107.77
1999	0.6180	1.4857	113.91
1998	0.6037	1.4835	130.91
1997	0.6106	1.3846	120.99
1996	0.6403	1.3635	108.78

SOURCE: CIA *World Factbook 2001* [ONLINE].

banks' **reserve ratios**. The Fed also buys and sells government bonds.

Traditionally, the nation had a number of laws that made it difficult to establish branches of banks in other states. Although many of these laws have been rescinded, their impact has led to the establishment of thousands of individual commercial banks. Only recently have large mega-banks begun to establish multiple branches across the country. The nation is also served by thousands of small non-profit credit unions and savings and loan organizations. About 40 percent of all commercial banks in the United States belong to the Federal Reserve System. These banks account for almost 75 percent of total deposits. All banks that are incorporated under national charters must belong to the system, which imposes various requirements on its members, including the maintenance of specific reserve funds.

The 2 largest stock exchanges in the country are both based in New York City. They are the New York Stock Exchange and the American Stock Exchange. Other major stock exchanges include the Boston Exchange, Cincinnati Exchange, Pacific Exchange, and the Philadelphia Exchange. The main commodity exchange is the Chicago Board of Trade and the main currency market is the Chicago Mercantile Exchange. There are also a number of smaller stock markets across the country. The NASDAQ, which is part of the American Stock Exchange, was created in 1971 as the world's first electronic stock trading index (a listing of a predetermined group of stocks within an exchange). The NASDAQ contains many of the nation's high-tech companies and is the fastest growing of the indexes. Other major indexes include the Dow Jones Industrial Average (which lists the 30 largest industrial companies in the United States) and the Standard and Poor 500 (which lists 500 medium-sized companies).

From 1995 to 1998, the nation's stocks experienced one of their most dramatic periods of growth in U.S. history. However, beginning in 1998 the major stock markets underwent a series of corrections that lowered their overall value and contributed to an eventual economic slowdown. The total value of U.S. stock markets declined from $6.88 trillion in 1997 to $5.58 trillion in 1998. At the end of 1998, the value of the major U.S. stock markets were: New York, $4.695 trillion; American Exchange, $207.6 billion; Boston, $79.9 billion; Cincinnati, $58.6 billion; Pacific, $113.4 billion; and Philadelphia, $63.9 billion. In addition, the value of the Chicago Board of Trade was $131.2 billion, while the value of the Chicago Mercantile Exchange was $212.9 billion. Reevaluations of the value of technology stocks and an economic slowdown that began in 2000 have led to dramatic declines in the U.S. stock market. By March of 2001 the NASDAQ had fallen to its lowest level since November of 1998, while the Dow Jones declined by 8 percent to its lowest level since 1999. With declines of more than 20 percent in the major American stock exchanges, by early 2001 the United States was precariously close to slipping into a **bear market** as well as a **recession**.

POVERTY AND WEALTH

Income distribution in the United States has remained relatively constant since World War II, but by the 1990s the wealthiest groups had gained a larger share of the nation's wealth. In 1950, the richest 20 percent of Americans controlled 42.8 percent of wealth, the middle 20 percent controlled 17.4 percent, and the poorest controlled just 4.5 percent. By 1980, the wealthiest group controlled 41.6 percent, the middle group 17.5 percent, and the poorest 5.1 percent. However, by 1998, the poor and middle groups had lost some ground to the wealthy. The richest group controlled 49.2 percent of wealth, the middle group just 15 percent, and the poor just 3.6 percent. That same year the richest 5 percent of the population controlled 21.4 percent of wealth. The trend toward the greater concentration of wealth by the rich has accelerated throughout the 1990s. While the relative income of the poorest families in the United States declined by 11.6 percent since 1980, the income of the richest group increased by 17.7 percent.

The United States has a high standard of living and ranks number 3 in the world in human development ac-

GDP per Capita (US$)

Country	1975	1980	1985	1990	1998
United States	19,364	21,529	23,200	25,363	29,683
Canada	14,535	16,423	17,850	19,160	20,458
Japan	23,296	27,672	31,588	38,713	42,081
Germany	N/A	N/A	N/A	N/A	31,141

SOURCE: United Nations. *Human Development Report 2000; Trends in human development and per capita income.*

Distribution of Income or Consumption by Percentage Share: United States

Lowest 10%	1.8
Lowest 20%	5.2
Second 20%	10.5
Third 20%	15.6
Fourth 20%	22.4
Highest 20%	46.4
Highest 10%	30.5

Survey year: 1997
Note: This information refers to income shares by percentiles of the population and is ranked by per capita income.

SOURCE: *2000 World Development Indicators* [CD-ROM].

cording to the *Human Development Report 2000* published by the United Nations (Canada ranks number 1, while Norway ranks 2). The average American workweek is 39.2 hours and the per capita income is $29,683. The average household in the United States had 2.6 people in it, but 25 percent of all homes had only 1 person. Only 10.4 percent of households had 5 or more people.

Almost 100 percent of households in the country have access to electricity and 99.4 percent have access to safe drinking water. In addition, 93.9 percent of homes had telephones while 98.3 percent had televisions and 99 percent had radios. The nation's sewage system is highly developed and 77 percent of dwellings are serviced by public sewage systems, and most of the remainder by septic tanks (22.8 percent). The mobility of the population is reflected in the high level of car ownership (84.9 percent of the people own an automobile). The average American spends 22.4 minutes commuting to and from work each day. Almost 80 percent of people who drive to work commute alone, while 14.7 percent car pool and 5.3 percent use public transportation.

In spite of the high overall standard of living, many groups in the United States are excluded from the prosperity of the mainstream. For instance, the unemployment rate for African Americans and Hispanics is almost twice as high as that of Asians and whites. Among workers, average wages for white males was $600 per week, $450 per week for African American males, and $390 per week for Hispanic males. Wages for women mirror the trends among male workers, with the major exception that females on average earn about 70 percent of what males earn.

In 1997, the poverty level in the United States was $16,036 for a family of 4. As with income differences, the poverty rate varies greatly among ethnic groups. In 1997, the poverty rate for whites was 11 percent. For Asians it was 15 percent, while for African Americans it was 28 percent, and 29 percent for Hispanics. Differences in poverty and income have a major impact on health. African Americans and Hispanics are twice as likely as whites not to have health insurance. One result of this disparity in health care is that whites have longer life expectancies. In 1997, the average life expectancy for white women was 80 years, but for African American women it was 74 years. Meanwhile the life expectancy for white males was 75 years, but for African American males it was 66 years.

WORKING CONDITIONS

The American workforce numbers 139.4 million. This includes those working or actively seeking employment in the United States. In 2001 unemployment in the United States reached a 30-year low of 4.2 percent. In 1970, it was 3.9 percent, by 1980 it had risen to 7.5 percent, and it was 5.7 percent in 1990. Unemployment is higher among youths (age 18–24) than among the general population. In 2000, the youth unemployment rate was 8 percent. Unemployment is also higher among females with an average rate of 6 percent.

One long-term problem for the American workforce is the greying of the population. As more workers age and then retire, the financial burdens for the remaining workers will increase. In 1950, there were 12 workers for

Household Consumption in PPP Terms

Country	All food	Clothing and footwear	Fuel and power[a]	Health care[b]	Education[b]	Transport & Communications	Other
United States	13	9	9	4	6	8	51
Canada	14	5	10	4	21	9	38
Japan	12	7	7	2	22	13	37
Germany	14	6	7	2	10	7	53

Data represent percentage of consumption in PPP terms.
[a]Excludes energy used for transport.
[b]Includes government and private expenditures.

SOURCE: World Bank. *World Development Indicators 2000.*

every 1 retiree, but currently there are only 3 and this ratio will continue to shrink. This means workers will have to pay higher taxes to support programs such as social security and Medicare (the government-funded healthcare program for the elderly). At current projections, social security is predicted to go bankrupt in 2038 while Medicare will run out of money in 2035.

American workers have various legal protections that allow them to organize and join unions. However, the United States has one of the lowest rates of unionization among the major industrialized nations. Of those Americans who belong to unions, almost 75 percent are affiliated in some form with the American Federation of Labor-Congress of Industrial Organizations (AFL-CIO). The major trend in organized labor in the United States has been the continuing decline in union membership. During the 1950s, about 40 percent of American workers belonged to unions, but by 1981, that proportion had fallen to 20.1 percent. In 2000, only 13.5 percent of American workers (16.3 million people) belonged to a union. However, there are widespread regional differences. Union membership is greatest in the Northeast and the industrial states of the Midwest. New York, New Jersey, and Michigan had union membership rates of more than 20 percent. On the other hand, all Southern states had union membership below 15 percent and 2 states, North Carolina and South Carolina, had rates below 5 percent. Among the different sectors of the economy, government employees at the local, state, and national level had the highest union rates (on average 37 percent). Unionization was lowest in the sales sector (3.5 percent).

Working conditions are governed by both state and federal law. There are national provisions against child labor, but states are free to enact supplemental legislation. For instance, many states set the minimum age for employment at 16, while others allow children as young as 14 to be employed with parental consent and impose other restrictions on the amount of hours worked. There are also both national and state laws that govern the number of breaks employees are entitled to and issues of worker safety. Enforcement of labor laws is the province of a variety of state and federal agencies. On the federal level, the Department of Labor, the Equal Employment Opportunity Commission of the Justice Department, and the Occupational Health and Safety Administration (OSHA) are the primary agencies which enforce labor and safety laws. Most state governments have similar agencies that mirror the federal organizations.

In 2001, the national minimum wage was $5.15 per hour, but many states have minimum wages that exceed that amount. The standard workweek is 40 hours, although many salaried positions (held by workers who are paid weekly or monthly, not by the hour) entail standard workweeks in excess of 40 hours. For hourly employees who work more than 40 hours, overtime pay equal to one and one-half times regular salary is standard. In addition to a number of national holidays, most American workers receive 2 weeks vacation per year and 2 weeks sick leave.

As with many other aspects of the economy, there are wide gaps in income depending on race, gender, and geography. Income levels for whites tend to be higher than minority groups, and average salaries for women are only about 75 percent of the pay of their male counterparts. Discrimination also continues to exist in hiring and promotion practices, so that many women and minorities have difficulty in obtaining jobs and promotions. There are also great regional differences in pay and cost of living, with the Northeast having the highest income levels and cost of living, while areas of the South have the lowest rates.

When compared with Europe's industrialized nations, American workers tend to be paid less and have to work longer hours. They also have less vacation time. Despite this, American workers are among the most productive in the world and produce more goods or services per hour than most of their European counterparts. On the other hand, Americans have significantly lower taxes and the cost of living in many regions of the nation is far lower than in other industrialized nations. As a result, the level of **disposable income** of the average American worker is among the highest in the world. One result of these factors has been continued immigration to the United States as people seek economic opportunity.

COUNTRY HISTORY AND ECONOMIC DEVELOPMENT

1492. Spanish explorer Christopher Columbus lands in the Caribbean and initiates the era of European colonization.

1565. The first permanent European settlement was established at St. Augustine, Florida, by the Spanish.

1607. The British establish their first permanent settlement at Jamestown in present-day Virginia.

1611. First tobacco harvests in Virginia.

1619. First Thanksgiving is celebrated. The first slaves arrive in Jamestown.

1775–1783. Revolutionary War. The United States becomes independent from Great Britain.

1787. The Constitution is adopted and the present system of government put in place.

1789. George Washington becomes the first president of the United States.

1790. Samuel Slater establishes the first textile factory in Pawtucket, Rhode Island.

1794. The Post Office is established. Eli Whitney invents the cotton gin which spurs the expansion of the cotton industry.

1797. Eli Whitney develops interchangeable parts. This dramatically speeds up production and makes it easier to replace parts.

1803. The United States purchases the Louisiana Territory for $15 million, tripling the size of the nation.

1817. Work on the Erie Canal is begun. When it is completed the canal stretches 363 miles and joins the Hudson River to Lake Eire.

1846–1848. The United States fights the Mexican-American War and gains the territory that will become Arizona, California, Nevada, New Mexico, Utah, and parts of Colorado and Wyoming.

1849. Gold is discovered at Sutter's Mill in California, initiating a gold rush and mass migration to the West.

1859. The oil well is used for the first time and an oil boom is initiated in Pennsylvania.

1861–1865. American Civil War. In 1862, President Abraham Lincoln issues the Emancipation Proclamation which frees the slaves in the Confederate states.

1867. Barbed wire is invented. This makes it easier for Americans to settle the West. The United States purchases Alaska from Russia for $7.2 million.

1869. The transcontinental railroad is completed.

1898. The Spanish-American War ends with a U.S. victory and the nation acquires the Philippines, Guam, and Puerto Rico.

1901. The Open Door Policy is established to guarantee American companies the right to trade in China.

1913. The Sixteenth Amendment establishes the income tax.

1917–1918. The United States becomes involved in World War I.

1919. In separate constitutional amendments, women are given the right to vote and prohibition is established, making alcohol illegal in the United States.

1929. The New York Stock Exchange crashes and falls to its lowest level. The Great Depression begins.

1941–1945. The United States fights in World War II. The war ends when the United States drops the first atomic bombs on Hiroshima and Nagasaki, Japan. The United States helps establish the United Nations. The

Cold War begins between the United States and its allies and the Soviet Union and its allies.

1951. The first commercial computer, UNIVAC, is sold to the U.S. Census Bureau.

1963–1973. American forces fight in Vietnam.

1965. The United States and Canada sign the Auto Pact.

1970s. The United States undergoes its worst economic recession since the Great Depression, partially as the result of oil crises in 1972 and 1979.

1989. US-Canada Free Trade Agreement goes into effect.

1992. The Cold War is officially declared to be over. The nation begins the second-longest period of economic expansion in its history.

1994. The United States, Canada, and Mexico establish the North American Free Trade Agreement (NAFTA).

2001. Terrorist attacks on New York's World Trade Center and the Pentagon on September 11 draw the United States into a military conflict with Taliban forces in Afghanistan.

FUTURE TRENDS

The fundamental structure of the American economy is very strong. All of the major sectors of the economy experienced growth through the 1990s. After declining for many years, agriculture and manufacturing have stabilized and undergone significant transformations that have made them more successful. Throughout the economy, company consolidation as a result of mergers and acquisitions continues. Large firms are increasingly common, but small companies still make up the majority of American businesses. These big American firms have also sought to acquire companies in foreign countries in order to broaden their business and to enter new markets. In 1996, some 364 foreign companies were acquired by U.S. firms, either through mergers or outright sales. The value of these acquisitions was $59 billion. As a result, American firms have become increasingly global, and this trend will continue. By expanding into other markets and countries, American companies have reduced their economic risks by diversifying and spreading their assets.

The main strengths of the U.S. economy are its adaptability and the workforce productivity. During the 1970s, the country underwent a traumatic transformation away from industry toward a service-oriented economy. By the mid-1980s, the main elements for the dramatic growth of the 1990s were in place. Increases in productivity and the development of new technologies, goods, and services combined with increased consumer demand to spur the growth of the 1990s. The United States leads the world in the development of IT and other high-tech goods and services. This area of the economy has been one of the main sources of new growth and it will continue. These factors will remain in place for the near future so that the economy should remain strong for the next decade.

The nation has a low tax burden, which attracts foreign investment and provides workers with more income for purchasing products. Recent government surpluses have fueled the incentives for tax reduction. A number of states have already reduced taxes, and in 2001, the Congress passed the president's massive tax rebate. Increased free trade arrangements have resulted in lower-cost imports and reduced both the cost of production for U.S. companies and the cost of many goods and services for U.S. consumers. Lower taxes and production costs for U.S. companies will continue to spur the economy.

There are several main weaknesses of the U.S. economy that will affect future growth. The nation's dependency on energy imports makes it vulnerable to increases in oil prices. Since the majority of oil imports come from the Middle East, an area of political instability, actions that affect the region also have an impact on the United States. Another major problem in the American economy is the growing gap between rich and poor. The resultant 2-tier economy may mean that a segment of the American population will untouched by future economic growth.

The aging of the American population is another of the most significant potential problems. This problem exists on 2 levels. First, as more Americans retire over the next 20 years, there will be fewer employees in the workforce to provide goods and services. Second, fewer workers mean that there will be less money going into the national retirement system, Social Security. Social Security is expected to begin having financial problems in 2035 as it has to pay more money out to retirees while it receives less money in revenues.

DEPENDENCIES

GUAM. As part of the Treaty of Paris, which ended the Spanish-America War in 1898, Guam became part of the United States. The island is currently a dependency of the nation, but many on Guam seek commonwealth status, like Puerto Rico, which would give the territory increased autonomy and control over its government and economy. The territory has an elected governor and assembly and sends 1 non-voting representative to the U.S. House of Representatives.

Guam is located in the Pacific Ocean and has an area of 541 square kilometers (211 square miles). Its population is 150,000. The territory's GDP is $4.6 billion and its **GDP per capita** is $24,000. Guam uses the American dollar as its currency. There is a substantial U.S. military presence in Guam, with 23,000 troops and their dependents. The main products and industries of Guam's economy include petroleum products, tourism, retail sales, construction materials, and fish. Its main trading partners are the United States and Japan.

In 1997, Guam had a total of 2,707 businesses, which ranged from construction companies to retail stores and included hotels and a variety of service companies. Total employment on Guam in 1997 was 42,477 (this does not include the military and those engaged in **subsistence farming** and fishing). Tourism plays a strong part in the territory's economy and hotels and motels had $460 million in revenues in 1997, while tourist shops and souvenir businesses had $415.9 million in sales. Total sales for the retail sector were $1.8 billion. Total employees numbered 15,334. Two factors have helped maintain the growth of the retail industry. The first is sales to military families. The second is sales to foreign tourists. Guam allows tourists to buy goods without paying a sales tax. Since U.S. products are cheaper on Guam than in Japan, this tax-break further lowers the cost and has made the island a popular stop for Japanese tourists to shop. The island is also home to the world's largest K-Mart store.

Behind retail and tourism, all other service industries including, legal, medical, maintenance and transportation services had combined total revenues of $1.18 billion and employed 15,336 people. Manufacturing and construction made up only a small part of the economy. In 1997, manufacturing employed 1,320 people and had revenues of $164 million. Construction employed 7,094 people and had revenues of $505 million.

During the 1990s, the economy of Guam expanded significantly. Although construction was down by 29 percent during the decade, most other segments of the economy have posted impressive gains. Retail sales were up by 65 percent while wholesale revenues have increased by 120 percent. Service revenues have increased by 81 percent and manufacturing by 49 percent. This growth has led to a higher **inflation rate** than the American average, 4 percent compared with 1.7 percent. The economy will likely continue to grow in the near future. The island's dependency on food imports and tourism makes it vulnerable to price increases and economic slowdowns by its major trade partners.

THE VIRGIN ISLANDS. The territory of the U.S. Virgin Islands consists of 3 islands and small cays (low island or reef) in the Caribbean. The 3 main islands are St. Croix, St. Thomas, and St. John. Combined, these islands have a total area of 350 square kilometers (135 square miles). The total population of the territory is 125,000. The majority of the population lives on St. Croix and St. Thomas (only about 4,500 people live on St. John).

In 1997, the GDP of the Virgin Islands was $2.3 billion and its per capita GDP was $17,000. The economy of the Virgin Islands employs about 41,800 people. There are a further number of seasonal jobs that are dependent on tourism, and a percentage of the population works outside of regular businesses in subsistence farming and fishing. The dominant industry is tourism. There is also a significant retail sector in the islands and some minor oil refining. The territory's main trade partners are the United States and Puerto Rico. The majority of the citizens of the islands are of African descent (75 percent), but there is also a significant community of whites who moved to the islands from the United States (13 percent) as well as Puerto Ricans (5 percent).

Because of their strategic importance as naval ports, the United States purchased what is now the U.S. Virgin Islands from Denmark at the outbreak of World War I in 1914 for $25 million. The islands were granted home rule in 1970 and remain unincorporated American territories.

Tourism dominates the economy of the Virgin Islands. Not only does it provide income for people who directly work in tourist-related activities, but it also drives the retail and service sectors of the economy. The islands are serviced by most major American airlines and many of the world's major cruise lines. About 2 million tourists visit the islands each year. Services, including tourism and retail sales, produced $1.8 billion in revenues in 1997. This represented a 20 percent increase since 1990. Retailers and wholesalers employed about 9,000 people, while other services—including lodging, transportation and personal services—employed 10,600 people.

Industry, mainly oil production and construction, employed 3,500 workers and had a total output of $200 million. A small number of financial institutions have established themselves on the islands. Financial services, including banking, insurance and real estate, employ about 1,900 people.

The economy of the Virgin Islands was stable throughout the 1990s, but the tourist industry experienced a period of slow—and in some years, negative—growth. Crime and high costs prompted many tourists to go elsewhere in the Caribbean. As a result, several major airlines cut service to the territory. A reform program that cut the number of government workers from 12,000 to 10,200 employees caused a slight increase in unemployment. These factors will continue to constrain the economy and limit the potential for future growth.

BIBLIOGRAPHY

Carson, Thomas, editor. *Gale Encyclopedia of U.S. Economic History.* Detroit: Gale Group, 1999.

Collins, Robert M. *More: The Politics of Economic Growth in Postwar America.* Oxford and New York: Oxford University Press, 2000.

Dahms, Harry F., editor. *Transformations of Capitalism: Economy, Society, and the State in Modern Times.* New York: New York University Press, 2000.

Economist Intelligence Unit. *Country Profile: United States of America.* London: Economist Intelligence Unit, 2001.

"Fiscal Year 2002 Budget." *Office of Managment and Budget, Executive Office of the President of the United States.* <http://w3.access.gpo.gov/usbudget/index.html>. Accessed October 2001.

Stein, Herbert, and Murray Foss, with Matthew Clement. *The Illustrated Guide to the American Economy.* Washington, D.C.: AEI Press, 1999.

U.S. Central Intelligence Agency. *World Factbook 2001.* <http://www.odci.gov/cia/publications/factbook/index.html>. Accessed September 2001.

U.S. Council of Economic Advisers. *Changing America: Indicators of Social and Economic Well-Being by Race and Hispanic Origin.* <http://w3.access.gpo.gov/eop/ca/index.html>. Accessed February 2001.

The U.S. Economy. Lexington, MA: Standard & Poor's DRI, 1999.

Weis, Linda and John M. Hobson. *States and Economic Development: A Comparative Historical Analysis.* Cambridge, USA: Polity Press, 1995.

World Trade Organization. *Trade Policy Review: United States, July 1999.* <http://www.wto.org/english/tratop_e/tpr_e/tp108_e.htm#Government%20report>. Accessed October 2001.

Wurman, Richard Saul. *Understanding.* Newport, RI: TED Conferences, 2000.

Zupnick, Elliot. *Visions and Revisions: The United States in the Global Economy.* Boulder, CO: Westview Press, 1999.

—Tom Lansford

URUGUAY

Oriental Republic of Uruguay
República Oriental del Uruguay

CAPITAL: Montevideo.

MONETARY UNIT: Uruguayan peso (UP). One peso equals 100 centésimos. There are notes of 50, 100, 500, 1,000, 5,000, and 10,000 pesos and coins of 1, 2, 5, and 10 pesos.

CHIEF EXPORTS: Meat, rice, leather products, vehicles, dairy products, wool, and electricity.

CHIEF IMPORTS: Road vehicles, electrical machinery, metal products, heavy industrial machinery, and crude petroleum.

GROSS DOMESTIC PRODUCT: US$28 billion (1999 est.).

BALANCE OF TRADE: Exports: US$2.1 billion (1999 est.). **Imports:** US$3.4 billion (1999 est.).

COUNTRY OVERVIEW

LOCATION AND SIZE. Uruguay is located in the southern region of South America. It is bordered by Argentina on the west and Brazil on the north and east. Its southern coastline of 660 kilometers (410 miles) is formed by the Rio de la Plata, which separates Uruguay from Argentina and opens into the Atlantic Ocean. The nation's total area is 176,220 square kilometers (68,038 square miles), including 2,600 square kilometers (1,004 square miles) of water. The country is slightly smaller than the state of Washington. The nation's capital, Montevideo, is located on the southern coast, where the Rio de la Plata meets the Atlantic Ocean. The capital is also the nation's largest city, with a population of 1.4 million.

POPULATION. The population of Uruguay was estimated at 3,334,074 in July 2000. The country has a very stable population, with a low growth rate of 0.77 percent. By 2010, the population is expected to be 3.6 million. Uruguay's birth rate is 17.42 per 1,000 people; its fertility rate is 2.37 births per woman. The infant mortality rate is 15.14 deaths per 1,000 live births. This rate is high when compared with nations such as Canada (which has a rate of 5.08 deaths per 1,000 live births), but is aver-

age when compared with most Latin American countries. The nation's overall mortality rate is 17.42 deaths per 1,000. Uruguay loses a small portion of its population to **emigration** (0.63 emigrants for every 1,000 people). Since 1980, about 500,000 Uruguayans, mostly younger people, have emigrated, mainly to Argentina and Brazil. The life expectancy is 71.9 years for males and 78.75 years for females. The elderly population is small, with only 13 percent of Uruguayans over the age of 65. This segment of the population is growing rapidly and is expected to increase by 40 percent by 2010.

The majority of the Uruguayan population is urban. Almost 80 percent live in towns or cities. About half of the population lives in the greater Montevideo urban area and the rest of the urban population is concentrated in about 20 towns. Population density is 19 people per square kilometer, one of the lowest rates in the Western Hemisphere. (By comparison, U.S. density is 29 per square kilometer and Mexico's is 50.) However, the high urban concentration makes the figure misleading, since density in major urban areas is 55 per square kilometer.

Uruguayans are generally well-educated, and the nation's literacy rate is 97.3 percent. While Spanish is the official language, a mixture of Portuguese and Spanish known as Portunol or Brazilero, is commonly spoken in the border regions between Uruguay and Brazil. Some 88 percent of the population is white and of Spanish or other European descent. Mestizos (people of mixed ethnic backgrounds, mainly Spanish and Native American) make up 8 percent of the population, and blacks make up 4 percent. During the colonial period, the Native American population was nearly eradicated. Although 66 percent of the nation professes to be Roman Catholic, only about half the population attends church. About 2 percent of Uruguayans are Protestant, and another 2 percent are Jewish. About 30 percent have no religious affiliation.

cant in Uruguay. In 1999, after 8 years of positive growth, the Uruguayan economy declined by 3.4 percent. In 2000, the economy continued its stagnation with a decline in GDP of 0.5 percent. This decline is significant because it marked the end of the longest, sustained period of economic growth since the 1970s. In 1999, exports declined by 20 percent and imports dropped by 12 percent. The economic slowdown led to an increase in unemployment, from 10.1 percent in 1998 to 11.2 percent in 1999. In August of 2000, it reached its highest level in 15 years, a peak of 12.4 percent.

During the 1970s, the nation underwent a period of dramatic economic reform. In response to a deep **recession** and declining economic performance, the government began to **restructure** the economy by reducing **inflation** and decreasing government's role in business. However, after the peso declined in value against the U.S. dollar by 140 percent, the nation's GDP fell by 16 percent. This led to another recession in 1982–83. Although there was positive economic growth for the rest of the 1980s, inflation continued to be a problem. By lifting **price controls** and **privatizing** government-controlled companies, Uruguay was eventually able to reduce inflation from 130 percent in 1990 to 44.1 percent in 1995 and to 4 percent in 1999.

By 1995, the government had privatized numerous companies and sectors, including the national airline, the national gas company, all seaport services, the insurance industry, and home-mortgage services. At the same time, the size of the civil service was drastically reduced, as was government spending. Even so, the government still plays a major role in the economy and continues to operate the nation's telecommunications services, electric-power industry, and railway freight services.

Uruguay has a prosperous and developed economy that includes agriculture, industry, and a diversified service sector. While agriculture accounts for only 7 percent of the country's GDP, it continues to dominate the economy in several ways. Agriculture is responsible for more than half of exports, and many of the country's industries and services are related to or dependent on the agricultural sector. The main industries include meat processing, leather production (including footwear, accessories, and apparel), and textiles. Services are a growing part of the nation's economy, but efforts to improve the financial-services sector have yet to succeed since foreign investment remains low.

In an effort to attract more foreign companies and investment, successive governments have established a number of **free-trade zones** in the country. In these areas, foreign firms are offered tax incentives and reduced tariffs in exchange for locating new factories and businesses there and employing a workforce that is at least 75 percent Uruguayan. The nation benefits from **foreign**

OVERVIEW OF ECONOMY

Uruguay has a strong domestic economy which provides a high standard of living and moderately high **GDP per capita** of US$8,500. The country is small, with limited markets, and geographical and historical factors have made Uruguay dependent on trade with its larger neighbors, Argentina and Brazil. These trade linkages were formalized in 1991 through the creation of the MERCOSUR free-trade area that links Uruguay, Argentina, Brazil, and Paraguay (Chile and Bolivia are associate members). Montevideo is the administrative capital of MERCOSUR.

While MERCOSUR has lowered **tariffs** and increased trade, it has also furthered the dependence of Uruguay on its trade partners. Almost half of the nation's imports and exports are with other members of the group. Hence, when Argentina and Brazil underwent economic downturns in 1998 (including the **devaluation** of the Brazilian currency), the impact was signifi-

direct investments totaling US$5.4 billion. The United States is the single largest investor, contributing 32 percent (US$1.72 billion) of the total.

Despite recent economic problems, the Uruguayan economy is recognized as one of the most solid in Latin America. Uruguay is the only nation in MERCOSUR and one of only two countries in all of Latin America to have investment-grade status. This means that major international financial registries, such as Standard & Poor's or Moody's, recommend the country's government bonds to financiers. Following a slight decline in 2000, GDP growth is expected to resume in 2001.

Uruguay's economic stability is based in part on the high usage of the U.S. dollar in financial transactions. More than 90 percent of private savings in Uruguay is dollar-denominated, as is more than 81 percent of credit granted to the **private sector**. Many consumers use dollars for their purchases of expensive products.

Beginning in 1988, successive governments worked to lower the nation's debt as a percentage of GDP. The economic downturn in 1998 reversed this trend, and the debt-to-GDP ratio increased by 5 percent to 15 percent of GDP, or US$3.1 billion for the year. About 90 percent of the total debt ($8 billion in U.S. dollars) is owned by private investors. Uruguay receives no formal foreign aid, although the European Union (EU) and the United States do help underwrite specific economic projects. In 1996, the EU provided 6.68 million euros for vocational-training centers and 147,000 euros for the development of tourist programs. In 1997, the United States provided US$8 million in aid to train the military for peacekeeping missions and purchase equipment for such missions.

POLITICS, GOVERNMENT, AND TAXATION

Uruguay become independent from Spain after a revolt that began in 1811, but the nation then joined a federation with Argentina. In 1821, Brazil annexed Uruguay, but the country achieved full independence in 1828 after an Argentine-backed revolt. In the early 20th century, President José Batlle Y Ordonez led the creation of the first **welfare state** in Latin America, with broad government participation in the economy and the social system. This tradition continues to influence Uruguay.

Political turmoil led to a new constitution in 1967, and in 1973, the military took control of the government, remaining in power until 1984, when Maria Sanguinetti was elected president. Under the Sanguinetti administration, the government carried out reforms that stabilized the economy and reinforced democracy. Luis Alberto Lacalle succeeded Sanguinetti in 1989. It was he who negotiated inclusion of Uruguay in MERCOSUR and began

efforts to curb inflation and cut government involvement in the economy. His economic reform efforts were curtailed in 1992, when voters rejected a plan to privatize ANTEL, the national telephone company. Sanguinetti was reelected in 1994 and oversaw constitutional changes in 1996. In 1999, Jorge Batlle was elected president on a platform that promised to increase international trade and expand economic reforms, including reducing the size and scope of government.

Uruguay is a constitutional democracy with a political system similar to that of the United States. Elected for a 5-year term, the president is the head of state and chief of the government. If no presidential candidate receives an absolute majority of 51 percent of the vote, there is a runoff election in which only the top 2 candidates compete. The president chooses the cabinet and generally sets government policy, subject to oversight from the nation's legislature. The legislative branch of government is the **bicameral** (2-chamber) General Assembly. The upper house, the Chamber of Senators, has 30 members who serve 5-year terms. The lower house, the Chamber of Representatives, has 99 members who also serve 5-year terms. The judicial branch of government is headed by a national Supreme Court. The country is organized into 19 regional departments or states, each headed by an elected governor.

All of Uruguay's major political parties support economic reforms and free trade. There are 3 main political parties. The Colorado Party, which traditionally represented the urban areas and the working class, is led by President Batlle and ex-President Sanguinetti. In the 1990s, this party increased its support for smaller government and less state control. The National Party, or Blanco, is the main party of rural voters, and is generally regarded as the most conservative of the nation's parties and a staunch supporter of free enterprise. Ex-President Lacalle belonged to Blanco. Encuentro Progresista-Frente Amplio (EP-FA) is a leftist coalition that supports limited free trade and private enterprise, but favors the implementation of an **income tax** as a means to redistribute wealth and increase social spending.

In 1998, the government's budget amounted to US$4.6 billion, while its revenues were US$4.4 billion. Because of the economic downturn in 1999, government revenues fell and the nation's deficit increased 4-fold to 3.9 percent of GDP. The government projects a reduction of the deficit to 1 percent by the end of 2001. Uruguay has made commitments to the International Monetary Fund (IMF) not to raise taxes in its effort to reduce the deficit and to pay down the debt in exchange for a short-term credit line of US$200 million to be used in fighting inflation. Uruguay has one of the proportionally lowest defense budgets of all of the Latin American nations, spending just US$172 million, or 0.9 percent of GDP, on defense.

Since the late 1980s, successive administrations have tried to reduce the role of government in the economy by privatizing government-owned businesses, such as PLUNA, the national airline, Montevideo Gas Company, and most port services. Government-owned enterprises account for 18 percent of GDP and the same percentage of total employment. The government continues to own a variety of businesses, including those engaged in insurance, water supply, telecommunications, electricity, railways, banking, and petroleum refining. The nation's social security system, which prior to 1996 had a deficit equal to 6 percent of GDP, was successfully privatized. By allowing individuals to join private pension plans, privatization has reduced the social security deficit to 1 percent of GDP. Nationwide, 550,000 people, one-third of the workforce, have opted for the private plans that now manage $700 million.

INFRASTRUCTURE, POWER, AND COMMUNICATIONS

Uruguay is situated in the middle of a corridor that connects the Atlantic and Pacific oceans and is the gateway to the Panama-Paraguay River transportation system. The corridor is inhabited by 40 million people and covers an area of 3.1 million square kilometers (1.2 million square miles). To take full advantage of its geographic position, Uruguay needs to make significant improvement to its transportation **infrastructure**. This would reduce Uruguay's freight costs, which are among the highest in South America.

The nation has 8,983 kilometers (5,582 miles) of roads, almost all paved. There are plans to build a combination passenger railway and underground subway system for Montevideo and its suburbs. Uruguay and Argentina are constructing a 35-kilometer (22-mile) bridge between Buenos Aires, Argentina, and Colonia, Uruguay.

This bridge, the longest of its kind in the world, will greatly expand direct trade between the 2 nations. Uruguay has 2,073 kilometers (1,288 miles) of railways and 1,600 kilometers (994 miles) of navigable waterways, many of which are used to transport small quantities of goods. Uruguay, Paraguay, Argentina, Bolivia, and Brazil have announced plans to develop the 4,022 kilometer (2,500 miles) Panama-Paraguay-Uruguay rivers in order to transport goods to ports on the Atlantic Ocean. The plans call for a combination of construction, dredging, and port development that will ultimately cost US$935 million. Uruguay's main port is Montevideo; other ports include Fray Bentos, Nueva Palmira, Paysandu, Punta del Este, Colonia, and Piriapolis. The nation's merchant marine consists of only 1 ship, a petroleum tanker.

Uruguay has 65 airports, but only 15 have paved runways, served by 10 international airlines and the national carrier, PLUNA. Carrasco International Airport in Montevideo is the nation's main international airport. It is undergoing a $60 million renovation that will significantly expand capacity. The nation is also building a $40 million airport at the resort town of Punta del Este.

There are 27 telephones per 100 people in Uruguay. Plans to privatize the telecommunications industry may dramatically lower costs and expand service, especially in the mobile phone market. In 1998, there were 100,000 mobile phones in the country, and 5 Internet service providers for the 12 percent of the population with access.

Uruguay has no fossil-fuel resources. More than 50 percent of its energy needs are met through imported oil (an average of 38,000 barrels per day). While natural gas currently does not contribute to the nation's energy needs, an $8 million, 19-kilometer (12-mile) pipeline was constructed in 1998 to provide natural gas from Argentina. A more substantial 213-kilometer (133-mile) pipeline is being constructed by British Gas and Pan American Energy (a **joint venture** between BP, Amoco, and ANCAP). These pipelines will eventually supply natural gas to over 70 Uruguayan towns and cities. In 1998, the nation's

Communications

Country	Newspapers	Radios	TV Sets[a]	Cable subscribers[a]	Mobile Phones[a]	Fax Machines[a]	Personal Computers[a]	Internet Hosts[b]	Internet Users[b]
	1996	1997	1998	1998	1998	1998	1998	1999	1999
Uruguay	293	607	241	N/A	60	N/A	91.2	38.34	300
United States	215	2,146	847	244.3	256	78.4	458.6	1,508.77	74,100
Brazil	40	444	316	16.3	47	3.1	30.1	18.45	3,500
Paraguay	43	182	101	N/A	41	N/A	9.6	2.43	20

[a]Data are from International Telecommunication Union, *World Telecommunication Development Report 1999* and are per 1,000 people.
[b]Data are from the Internet Software Consortium (http://www.isc.org) and are per 10,000 people.

SOURCE: World Bank. *World Development Indicators 2000.*

power plants produced 9.474 billion kilowatt-hours (kWh) of electricity, 95.62 percent of which was provided by water power. In 1998, electricity consumption in Uruguay was 6.526 billion kWh. The nation has one of the highest rates of electrification, 96 percent, in the Western Hemisphere.

ECONOMIC SECTORS

While agriculture accounted for only 4 percent of the nation's workforce, it provided 10 percent of Uruguay's GDP and more than half of the country's exports. More significantly, agricultural products provided the main raw materials for the nation's largest industries. Among the main agricultural products are beef, wool, grains, fruits, and vegetables. Agriculture is also one of the few areas of the economy in which there is little government interference. A late 1990s devaluation of the Brazilian currency hurt Uruguayan agriculture by making Brazilian products cheaper and Uruguayan goods more expensive. As a result, agricultural output declined by 8 percent in 1999. For the 3-year period prior to 1999, agriculture experienced little or no growth.

Industry accounts for 28 percent of the nation's GDP and 30 percent of the workforce. The nation's main industries include food processing, construction, and leather production. In the late 1990s, Uruguayan industry has had mixed performance. In 1999, manufacturing fell by 8.4 percent, but construction grew by 6 percent.

Services make up the largest segment of the Uruguayan economy, accounting for 62 percent of GDP (1999) and 66 percent of the workforce. While much of the Uruguayan economy declined in 1999, services experienced 2 percent growth (even though general commerce, including the **retail** trade, declined by 3 percent). The major elements of the service sector include banking and financial services, tourism, and commerce.

AGRICULTURE

The geography of Uruguay makes the nation well-suited to pastoral agriculture, including raising cattle and sheep. As a result, much of the countryside (90 percent) is used for such agriculture. After experiencing a period of substantial growth in the 1990s, Uruguay's agricultural sector experienced a period of stagnation in the late 1990s. In 1996, the last year of significant growth, agricultural production grew by 8.6 percent. In 1997, agricultural production declined by 1.3 percent, and continued to decline, by 1 percent in 1998 and 8 percent in 1999. These declines resulted from increased competition in foreign markets and contractions in the economies of Uruguay's main trade partners, Argentina and Brazil. In 1998, the total value of agricultural exports was $1.49 billion, but the nation also imported $458.2 million in agricultural goods. Employment in agriculture has remained relatively constant since the mid-1990s, at approximately 50,000.

While the overall agricultural sector has been stagnant, crop production has increased. After 2 years of decline, in 1999 crop harvests grew by 10.5 percent and total output was 2.4 million tons. The main food crops are rice, wheat, corn, potatoes, barley, sugarcane, and soybeans. Production of rice in 1999 was 1.3 million tons, wheat 377,200 tons, and corn 242,500 tons. Barley harvests dropped significantly as a result of reduced demand, falling from 340,000 tons in 1996 to 111,000 in 1999.

Total livestock exports were worth US$1 billion in 2000. The primary livestock products are beef, veal, horse, chicken, duck, goose, lamb, pork, and turkey. There were 10.5 million head of cattle in Uruguay in 1999, and 14.4 million sheep. An outbreak of foot-and-mouth disease in 1999 led several nations to ban the import of Uruguayan beef and lamb, but efforts to eradicate the disease were successful and in 2000 there were record exports. Beef, the main livestock export, accounted for 58.6 percent of exports in 2000, followed by lamb (4.12 percent) and horsemeat (1.4 percent). Mixed meat by-products accounted for 30.8 percent of exports. Israel was the number-one market for Uruguayan beef, taking 25.09 percent of exports, although the North American Free Trade Agreement (NAFTA) countries—the United States, Canada and Mexico—were the main overall market with 33.4 percent of exports. MERCOSUR accounted for 16 percent of livestock exports and the EU 10.8 percent.

The fishing sector employs about 12,000 people. Uruguay has substantial stocks of a variety of fish species, but fishing accounts for only 0.1 percent of GDP. Pollu-

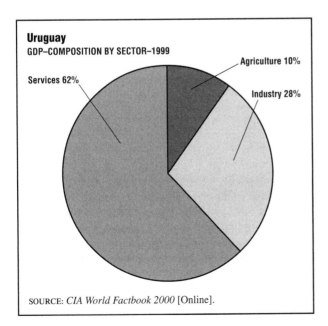

Uruguay
GDP–COMPOSITION BY SECTOR–1999

Services 62%

Agriculture 10%

Industry 28%

SOURCE: *CIA World Factbook 2000* [Online].

tion from Uruguayan ports, such as the 1997 oil spill by the Argentine ship San Jorge off the coastal resort of Punta del Este, has significantly impacted fish stocks. This spill affected 20 miles of Uruguayan coastline and did significant damage to a variety of species ranging from sea lions to croaker. Currently, hake accounts for about 70 percent of catches, followed by croaker (14 percent) and striped weakfish (5 percent). There are increasing efforts to develop the industry to catch deep-water species such as swordfish, squid, and anchovy. In 1998, swordfish catches surpassed 930 tons and the nation exceeded its quota under international fishing regulations. The United States is the major destination for fish exports.

INDUSTRY

Manufacturing and refining employ some 250,000 people in Uruguay. Much of the country's industrial sector is linked to agriculture. About half of all industrial production is based on food processing or the refining of agricultural products such as leather. Food and beverage production are the largest single manufacturing sectors, with food processing accounting for 25 percent of production and beverages accounting for 11 percent. Exports of processed foods were valued at US$1.06 billion in 1997, or 40 percent of all exports. Prepared rice, chocolate, meat, cookies, and pasta were the main exports, although frozen foods have been growing steadily in value. This sector of industry has been the recipient of almost 50 percent of all new foreign investment in Uruguay. The main markets for processed foods and beverages are Uruguay's MERCOSUR partners. The nation's principal food processing plants are concentrated in the towns of Fray Bentos and Paysanduu.

Since 1997, most other industries in Uruguay have experienced declines in production and value. Industries such as textiles, clothing, chemicals, and metallic products have suffered the largest declines, with mining and oil refining the main exceptions. After 3 years with annual growth of more than 6.5 percent, mining grew by 2.6 percent in 1999. It still accounted for only 0.2 percent of GDP and employed about 2,000 people. Gold is the major mineral produced by the mining sector; in 1998, 2000 kilograms were mined from the nation's proven gold reserves of 5.06 metric tons. Marble, stone, granite, and bauxite are also produced. The nation's crude-oil imports are refined at the La Teja refinery in Montevideo. The refinery is owned by the state-owned oil company, ANCAP, and has a capacity of 37,000 barrels per day.

The construction industry, which employs about 80,000 people, has also continued to grow, although the growth rate has slowed, especially in private construction. The average growth rate for the sector has been 4.6 percent since 1996. Government infrastructure programs and the construction of tourist-related facilities have been leading segments in the construction industry.

SERVICES

Services in Uruguay account for the highest level of GDP and the greatest employment, with almost 80,000 Uruguayans working in some segment of the service sector. Financial services and tourism are among the best performing sectors of the economy, and services also account for a significant proportion of foreign investment.

FINANCIAL SERVICES AND BANKING. The financial sector employs about 60,000 Uruguayans. The country's private banking sector has 21 banks, 9 financial institutions, and 10 savings and loan organizations. There are also 11 **offshore banks**. These banks and institutions account for about 50 percent of the financial sector. Major foreign-owned banks include American Express Bank, Citibank, Bankboston, and Republic National Bank. The rest of the financial sector is controlled by 3 government-owned banks, including the Central Bank. The largest bank is the government-owned Banco de la Republica Oriental del Uruguay, which has 30 percent of the nation's total savings. Total banking assets in Uruguay were US$7.1 billion in 1999 (including US$600 million from foreign sources). In 1996, the government **deregulated** the insurance and mortgage sectors and opened them to private investment. The government-owned Banco Hipotecario del Uruguay (BHU) remains the largest mortgage lender. The nation has 2 small stock markets, but both are undervalued. U.S. investment in Uruguayan financial services totals US$37 million.

COMMERCE AND TRADE. Hotels, restaurants, retail, and wholesale trade employ 200,000 Uruguayans. The franchising of stores and restaurants has produced dramatic growth in many areas of Latin America, but in Uruguay there are only a limited number of food, hotel, car-rental, and some clothing outlets. This is mainly the result of the small size of Uruguay's domestic market. Increased Internet use and the potential deregulation of the telecommunications industry have fueled growth in the sale of electronic equipment, though most of these products have to be imported.

TOURISM. Tourism has become the main source of foreign currency earnings for Uruguay and the third-largest component of GDP. It provides an average of $800 million per year to the economy. Since 1998, the number of foreign visitors has declined by 5 percent because of contractions in the Brazilian and Argentine economies that have reduced the number of tourists from these countries. Since 1997, the average number of tourists has been 2.3 million per year. Argentina is the number-one source of foreign visitors (78 percent in 1998). American hotel chains, such as Sheraton, Radisson, Holiday Inn, and

Trade (expressed in billions of US$): Uruguay		
	Exports	Imports
1975	.384	.556
1980	1.059	1.680
1985	.909	.708
1990	1.693	1.343
1995	2.106	2.867
1998	2.769	3.808

SOURCE: International Monetary Fund. *International Financial Statistics Yearbook 1999.*

Exchange rates: Uruguay	
Uruguayan pesos per US$1	
Jan 2001	12.5610
2000	12.0996
1999	11.3393
1998	10.4719
1997	9.4418
1996	7.9718

SOURCE: CIA *World Factbook 2001* [ONLINE].

Days Inn, have a presence in Uruguay. The main tourist destination is the coastal resort area of Punta del Este.

INTERNATIONAL TRADE

Uruguay is a member of a variety of international organizations that promote free trade. In addition to membership in MERCOSUR, Uruguay also belongs to the World Trade Organization (WTO) and the Latin American Integration Association (ALADI). Membership in these organizations has dramatically lowered the tariffs Uruguay places on imported goods. Tariffs on raw materials have been reduced to 2–6 percent of the value of the imports and now average 8–10 percent on all goods. MERCOSUR rules still allow for tariff rates as high as 23 percent on certain goods, and tariffs of 20 percent are common on some **consumer goods**.

Uruguay has also sought to develop bilateral (one-on-one) free trade agreements, such as the one signed with Mexico in 1999, with major European and Asian nations. Uruguay does not have such a treaty with the United States, although the United States is a major trading partner and the largest foreign investor in Uruguay (with 32 percent of all foreign investment).

The government actively seeks to attract foreign companies to Uruguay. In 1999, there were 756 foreign companies operating in Uruguay. Foreign investment in Uruguay was US$5.6 billion in 1999. There are no restrictions on foreign ownership of businesses, and the government offers certain tax breaks and other incentives to foreign companies that relocate to Uruguay. In the government-sponsored free-trade zones, companies may be exempt from all taxes except **social-security taxes**. Goods can be shipped to and from these zones without any tariffs or export **duties**.

In 2000, Uruguay imported US$3.4 billion in goods and services and exported US$2.1 billion. Uruguay's main export markets are its MERCOSUR partners (45 percent of exports), the EU (20 percent) and the United States (7 percent). The main import providers are the MERCOSUR nations (43 percent), the EU (20 percent), and the United States (11 percent).

MONEY

The Uruguayan peso has declined in value since the 1990s, mainly due to inflation. In 1994, 5.0439 pesos equaled US$1; by 1999 the peso had declined to 11.3393 per dollar. In an effort to maintain the value of the peso, the Uruguayan Central Bank uses its reserves to purchase dollars.

Monetary policy is overseen by the nation's Central Bank, which also issues currency. The Central Bank is not independent, but is subject to control and influence by the government. Almost 90 percent of bank deposits and transactions in Uruguay are done in U.S. dollars. Uruguay's financial reserves declined in 1999 by US$13 million as a result of the government's deficit. In 2000, the reserves totaled US$2.4 billion, or enough to service the nation's debt for at least 2 years.

POVERTY AND WEALTH

Uruguay has one of the most equal distributions of income and wealth in the world. Since 1986, taxation and social services have been used to redistribute income from the nation's wealthiest 10 percent to the less affluent members of society. The wealthiest 10 percent of Uruguay's population controls about 25 percent of the nation's

GDP per Capita (US$)					
Country	1975	1980	1985	1990	1998
Uruguay	4,092	4,962	3,964	4,611	6,029
United States	19,364	21,529	23,200	25,363	29,683
Brazil	3,464	4,253	4,039	4,078	4,509
Paraguay	1,297	1,871	1,754	1,816	1,781

SOURCE: United Nations. *Human Development Report 2000; Trends in human development and per capita income.*

Distribution of Income or Consumption by Percentage Share: Uruguay

Lowest 10%	2.1
Lowest 20%	5.4
Second 20%	10.0
Third 20%	14.8
Fourth 20%	21.5
Highest 20%	48.3
Highest 10%	32.7

Survey year: 1989
Note: This information refers to income shares by percentiles of the population and is ranked by per capita income.

SOURCE: *2000 World Development Indicators* [CD-ROM].

wealth, which is still low by regional standards: comparable figures for the amount of wealth controlled by the richest 10 percent are 41.9 percent in Brazil, 39 percent in the United States, and 34.3 percent in Argentina.

In 2000, 8 percent of the population of Uruguay was considered to be living in poverty, not having enough income to pay for basic needs, including food, housing, and health care. In an effort to reduce poverty further, the government is engaged in a long-term program to improve education. Since the mid-1990s, it has spent an additional 0.1 percent of GDP on improvements to the educational system, including classroom renovations, teacher training, and programs to keep youths in school. The main impetus for these programs is the fact that 40 percent of all Uruguayan children under the age of 5 live in the poorest 20 percent of households.

WORKING CONDITIONS

The Uruguayan workforce is highly skilled and educated. The nation's literacy rate, 97 percent, is the highest in Latin America and comparable to that of the United States. There is some evidence of racial and gender disparity. The nation's blacks have an unemployment rate 1.5 times higher than that of the general population, and

their average pay is 20 percent lower than their white counterparts in the same occupations. While women have full equality under the law, they face discrimination in hiring, promotion, and wages. A government study in 1999 found that women receive only 65 percent of the pay men receive in similar occupations.

There is little legislation concerning unions in Uruguay, although workers have the right to strike and to collective bargaining. About 15 percent of the workforce is unionized, mainly those employed in construction, industry, and banking. Union membership in the **public sector** is almost 80 percent, but the rate for private companies is 5 percent. All employees, including those who work for the government, may join unions. The government has the legal power to end a strike if it poses a threat to public welfare. Although workers may organize in the nation's free-trade zones, there are no unions in these areas. Foreign workers have the same rights and legal protections as Uruguayans.

The nation's minimum wage is equivalent to US$93 per month, not enough to support a family, though the overwhelming majority of workers earn more than the minimum. Uruguay's standard work week is 48 hours in industry and 44 hours in commerce. In both sectors, workers must have a minimum 36-hour rest period per week and they receive overtime pay for excess hours worked. All workers are entitled to a minimum of 20 days paid vacation per year. The national retirement age is 60. Because of the country's extensive social security system, employers must pay taxes that equal 50 percent of each worker's pay.

The government forbids forced labor and child labor under the age of 14. Children 16 and older may work if they have completed 9 years of compulsory education. Some children drop out of school and work illegally on the streets as vendors or beggars. The nation has started a program to pay parents $83 a month in exchange for taking these children off the streets and returning them to school. In order to encourage employers to hire more youths, the government provides tax reductions of 12–18

Household Consumption in PPP Terms

Country	All food	Clothing and footwear	Fuel and power[a]	Health care[b]	Education[b]	Transport & Communications	Other
Uruguay	22	7	14	11	30	12	3
United States	13	9	9	4	6	8	51
Brazil	22	13	18	15	34	4	−6
Paraguay	N/A	N/A	N/A	N/A	N/A	N/A	N/A

Data represent percentage of consumption in PPP terms.
[a]Excludes energy used for transport.
[b]Includes government and private expenditures.

SOURCE: World Bank. *World Development Indicators 2000.*

percent on social security taxes for these employees. Unemployment in 2000 was 12 percent and about 0.5 to 2 percent higher in Montevideo and other urban areas. GDP per capita in Uruguay is equivalent to US$8,500.

COUNTRY HISTORY AND ECONOMIC DEVELOPMENT

10,000–20,000 B.C. Uruguay is settled by Native Americans.

1516. An indigenous tribe, the Charrua, kill the Spanish explorer Juan Diaz de Solis and members of his party as they explore the coast of Uruguay.

1600s. The Charrua develop trade relations with the Spanish.

1680. The Portuguese establish a settlement at Colonia on the Rio de la Plata in order to counterbalance the Spanish colony of Buenos Aires.

1811. Jose Gervasio Artigas launches a revolution against Spain that ultimately results in independence and a regional federation with Argentina.

1821. Uruguay is annexed to Brazil by Portugal.

1825. Rebels initiate an independence movement against Brazil.

1828. Uruguay becomes independent.

1830. The nation's first constitution is adopted.

1838–51. Supporters of a federal union with Argentina conduct a war against nationalist forces. The 2 groups ultimately form Uruguay's main political factions, the liberal Colorados and the conservative Blancos.

1903. Jose Batlle y Ordonez is elected president; during his 2 terms (1903–07 and 1911–15), he initiates a series of reforms that give Uruguay one of the most advanced **social welfare systems** in the hemisphere.

1960s. The nation's prosperity declines as state-owned companies become inefficient and corrupt and the nation's industries cannot compete on the world market.

1967. An urban guerrilla movement, the Tupamaros, initiates an armed struggle against the government. A new constitution is put in place.

1971. Because of the armed insurrection, the military is invited to join the government. As a result, the Tupamaros are effectively destroyed.

1973. Congress is suspended by the military.

1978. In an effort to control inflation, the government initiates a program of currency devaluation.

1982–84. Uruguay experiences a severe economic recession.

1984. After national elections, the military relinquishes power to a new civilian government.

1985. After a lengthy period of economic stagnation, Uruguay begin a modest period of recovery.

1991. Uruguay joins MERCOSUR.

1992. Voters reject a government proposal to privatize ANTEL, the nation's telecommunications company.

1999. Uruguay undergoes a significant recession.

FUTURE TRENDS

Continuing economic problems in Argentina and Brazil will limit the Uruguayan economy since the majority of the nation's trade is with these countries. The country's continuing recession has made it less attractive to foreign investment. The inability of the government to enact further privatizations also reduces the attractiveness of the nation to foreign investors and prevents competition in certain sectors. The high level of unemployment has caused increased government spending that has itself led to increases in the government's operating deficit and the nation's total debt.

The nation's high standard of living and the high level of education and skill continue to make it attractive to foreign businesses. This is especially true as the Uruguayan government expands its system of free-trade areas. While the economic downturns in Argentina and Brazil have harmed Uruguayan trade, these conditions have also increased the flow of investments from these nations into Uruguay as investors have sought to protect their money. Uruguayan membership in international trade organizations will continue to expand trade as tariffs are reduced. As such, Uruguay has been a strong supporter of the establishment of a Free Trade Area of the Americas.

Uruguay's plans to continue economic **liberalization** will help the economy become more efficient and productive. The main goals of the government in the economic sphere are directed toward reductions in unemployment, inflation, and deficit spending. Programs to improve the nation's infrastructure, including renovations to airports and transport systems, are also designed to enhance the economic base. The government plans to continue privatization of state-owned industries and to reduce the size of government and the government's share of the nation's GDP.

DEPENDENCIES

Uruguay has no territories or colonies.

BIBLIOGRAPHY

República Oriental del Uruguay. <http://www.presidencia .gub.uy>. Accessed July 2001.

Uruguay, The Uruguayan Economy. <http://www.embassy.org/ uruguay/econ/economy.htm>. Accessed March 2001.

U.S. Central Intelligence Agency. *The World Factbook, 2000.* <http://www.cia.gov/cia/publications/factbook>. Accessed January 2001.

U.S. Department of State. *FY 2001 Country Commercial Guide: Uruguay.* <http://www.state.gov/www/about_state/business/ com_guides/index.html>. Accessed March 2001.

U.S. Department of State. *1998 Country Report on Economic Policy and Trade Practices: Uruguay.* <http://www.tradeport .org/ts/countries/uruguay/ecopol.html>. Accessed July 2001.

World Bank. *Uruguay: The Private Sector.* Washington, D.C.: World Bank, 1994.

—Tom Lansford

VENEZUELA

Republic of Venezuela
República de Venezuela

CAPITAL: Caracas.

MONETARY UNIT: Bolívar (B). One bolívar (B) equals 100 céntimos. There are coins of 5, 10, 25, and 50 céntimos and 1, 2, and 5 bolívars. There are notes of 5, 10, 20, 50, 100, 500, and 1,000 bolívars.

CHIEF EXPORTS: Petroleum, bauxite and aluminum, steel, chemicals, and agricultural products.

CHIEF IMPORTS: Raw materials, machinery and equipment, transport equipment, and construction materials.

GROSS DOMESTIC PRODUCT: US$146.2 billion (2000 est.).

BALANCE OF TRADE: Exports: US$32.8 billion (2000 est.). Imports: US$14.7 billion (2000 est.).

COUNTRY OVERVIEW

LOCATION AND SIZE. Venezuela, located on the northern coast of South America, has an area of 912,050 square kilometers (352,143 square miles), with a total coastline of 2,800 kilometers (1,740 miles). It is bordered by Colombia to the west, Guyana to the east, and Brazil to the south. Venezuela is a little more than twice the size of California. Caracas, the capital, is located on its northern coast.

POPULATION. As of July 2000, the population of Venezuela was estimated to be 23,542,649, an increase of 21.8 percent over the population in 1990. In 2000, the birth rate was 21.09 per 1,000, and the death rate 4.94 per 1,000. Based on a projected annual growth rate of 1.6 percent, the population is expected to number 27.3 million by 2010. Until 1990, Venezuela had one of the highest population growth rates in the world (3.4 percent annually from 1950–86), despite an educated populace and the wide availability of contraceptives. This high population growth rate is credited to improved sanitary and health conditions from the 1950s onward that resulted in a high birth rate and a low death rate.

People of mixed race (pardo) or Indian/Spanish heritage (mestizo) are estimated to account for two-thirds of the population of Venezuela. The term *pardo* refers to people who are the product of any racial mixture while the term *mestizo* refers specifically to people who are of Indian/Spanish heritage. Caucasians represent 21 percent of the population, Africans about 10 percent, and Indians about 2 percent of the population. This is a relatively young population: only 4 percent of Venezuelans are over the age of 65 while 33 percent are under the age of 14. It has been estimated that 60 to 70 percent of the population is under the age of 30. Some 88.8 percent of the population live in urban areas, while 11.2 percent live in rural areas. Almost all of the population growth since 1940 has occurred in urban areas, a consequence of the modernization that has resulted from Venezuela's development of its oil industry.

It has been estimated that 75 to 85 percent of the population lives on just 20 percent of the country's land mass, while 4 or 5 percent of the population lives on 50 percent of the land. The most densely populated region is the upper northwest, where Venezuela's 3 largest cities are located. The most sparsely populated portion is the southern and eastern portions of the country, even though the government has tried to relocate industry there. The 2 regions are separated by the Orinoco river.

OVERVIEW OF ECONOMY

Venezuela is very much a country built by oil. Among Latin American countries, it has the highest GDP and the fifth highest **GDP per capita**. Oil was first pumped from the bed of Lake Maracaibo, in upper northwest Venezuela, in 1917. Some 75 percent of Venezuela's oil continues to be pumped from the area in and around Lake Maracaibo. Before 1917, cocoa and coffee were

Venezuela's main exported products, but oil has been its chief export since 1926. In 1960, Venezuela was a founding member of the Oil Producing and Exporting Countries (OPEC), a cartel (a group of countries that work together to control the buying and selling price of a product) that has enormous influence in world oil prices. Until 1970, Venezuela was the world's largest exporter of oil; it has since fallen to third place.

The extent to which the country relies of oil production can be seen in the numbers: in 1999, oil production contributed 27.9 percent to the Venezuelan GDP, 60 percent of the government's revenues, and 78 percent of the country's export earnings. As a result of this dependence on oil production, when oil prices have gone up on the world's market, the country's economy benefits. After OPEC increased world oil prices by 400 percent in 1973 Venezuela enjoyed a large windfall; in the 5 years from

1974 to 1979, the government earned—and spent—more money than it had in the preceding 144 years put together. In 1999, the Venezuelan economy shrank as a result of falling oil prices. The economy then experienced a **recession** (a fall in GDP for 2 consecutive quarters) with GDP falling by 7.2 percent in comparison to the GDP of the previous year. With oil prices rising again in 2000, the economy rebounded with annual growth of 3.2 percent.

Despite these fluctuations, the average annual growth of the GDP from 1979 to 1999 was only 0.9 percent. During that time, the population grew by 2.5 percent every year, causing per capita income to fall. Consumer prices rose an average of 54 percent per year from 1995 through 1999, a period when 12 percent of the **labor force** was unemployed. Dependence on oil also means that the government must borrow money when oil revenues are not available. Venezuela's **external debt** in 1998 was one-third of that year's GDP, and one-third of the government's oil revenues had to be used to pay the interest on the debt. Dependence on oil means that the Venezuelan economy cannot devote the resources to produce the food that its people consume, as it was able to do before 1920. Since the 1980s, Venezuela has had to import even the most basic foodstuffs, such as sugar and potatoes.

Despite periods of dictatorship and official corruption and patronage over the years, the general economic and political trajectory for Venezuela in the 20th century has been a positive one, and, since 1958, it has devoted much of its public funds to building a physical and social **infrastructure** for its people. Since that time, the government has practiced more or less free-market policies, allowing others to participate in the economy as it has seen fit. For example, **multinational corporations** were forced to sell their rights to pump oil to the government in 1976, but they were allowed back into the country in 1996.

POLITICS, GOVERNMENT, AND TAXATION

Under its present constitution, approved in 1999, Venezuela is a federal republic with 1 federal district, 2 federal territories, 23 states, and 72 federal (island) dependencies. The president is elected to a 6-year term and can be reelected. The president selects a cabinet that is called the Council of Ministers. Legislative power is vested in a National Assembly of 165 members elected to 5-year terms. Upon receiving nominations from various civilian groups, the legislature selects the 18 judges of the Supreme Justice Tribunal for 12-year terms. The Supreme Justice Tribunal is the highest court in Venezuela; its 18 judges appoint lower-court judges and magistrates. Local government officials are chosen in local elections.

The political history and the economic history of Venezuela are inseparably intertwined. This is because since 1936, the government has pursued a policy of "sowing the oil," or using the government revenues from the tax on the sale of oil to promote the economic growth of the country. That policy has been pursued in earnest since the time of Venezuela's first democratically elected president, Rómulo Betancourt, in 1958. From the time of its independence from Spain in 1811 until 1958, Venezuela was ruled by a series of military dictators. From 1936 to 1958, although some public projects were constructed by the government, much of the government's oil revenues ended up in the pockets of the dictators and various government officials. From 1958 until the present, Venezuela has enjoyed uninterrupted democratic rule.

Two political parties dominated Venezuelan politics from 1958 to 1993: the liberal Democratic Action or Acción Democrática (AD) party, and the conservative Partido Social Cristiano, known as COPEI. The policies of these 2 parties did not differ from one another because of an agreement called the Pact of Punto Fijo signed by party political leaders in 1958. Under that pact, political leaders decided on a policy agenda before the election and agreed to divide cabinet and other government offices among the major parties after the election regardless of which candidate won in the vote count. The agreement ultimately broke down because political appointments were increasingly being made on the basis of patronage and because neither political party had succeeded in controlling excessive government spending. Dissatisfaction with the policies of the major political parties manifested itself in riots in 1989 that left hundreds dead, and in 2 unsuccessful military coups in 1992. In 1993, Rafael Caldera won the presidency under a 19-party alliance called the Convergencia Nacional (CN). It was the first time since 1958 that the presidency was held by a candidate from a party other than the AD or the COPEI.

Caldera faced a banking crisis in 1994, a fall in world oil prices (with decreasing government revenues) in 1997, and was ultimately forced to adopt unpopular budget cuts. His successor, Hugo Chávez Frias, elected in 1998, had been one of the military officers involved in the attempted coups of 1992. He campaigned on promises of changing the constitution to fight corruption and patronage, and also promised to move the economy away from its dependence on oil. A new constitution was adopted in 1999, and Chávez was reelected president. His party, the Movimiento Quinta República (MVR) has formed a governing alliance with the **socialist** party, the Movimiento al Socialismo (MAS).

Moving the economy of Venezuela away from its dependence on oil will be a difficult task. This is because government spending based on oil revenues has been the engine of economic growth for so long. The increased tax revenues that resulted from the higher oil prices after 1973 were used by the government to **nationalize** the entire oil industry. The government also established hundreds of new state-owned industries, as in steel, mining, and hydroelectricity. The Chávez government has continued the effort of the Caldera government to **privatize** a number of these industries.

If Venezuela is to move away from its dependence on oil, its government will have to increase the tax revenues it gets from other sources. Venezuela has an **income tax** on all economic activity by individuals and businesses, but tax evasion by individuals remains a significant problem. In 1996, the government was taxing the profits of private oil companies at the very high rate of 67.7 percent. It is not clear that the taxing of other entities within Venezuela will provide sufficient revenues to the government.

Communications

Country	Newspapers	Radios	TV Sets[a]	Cable subscribers[a]	Mobile Phones[a]	Fax Machines[a]	Personal Computers[a]	Internet Hosts[b]	Internet Users[b]
	1996	1997	1998	1998	1998	1998	1998	1999	1999
Venezuela	206	468	185	25.8	87	3.0	43.0	3.98	525
United States	215	2,146	847	244.3	256	78.4	458.6	1,508.77	74,100
Brazil	40	444	316	16.3	47	3.1	30.1	18.45	3,500
Colombia	46	581	217	16.7	49	4.8	27.9	7.51	664

[a]Data are from International Telecommunication Union, *World Telecommunication Development Report 1999* and are per 1,000 people.
[b]Data are from the Internet Software Consortium (http://www.isc.org) and are per 10,000 people.

SOURCE: World Bank. *World Development Indicators 2000.*

INFRASTRUCTURE, POWER, AND COMMUNICATIONS

Venezuela has the distinction of having the most paved highways of any country in Latin America, 60 percent of its 94,929 kilometers (58,989 miles) of roads. Most of these highways are located in the northern part of the country, where population density is greatest. The southern half of the country is more heavily dependent on aircraft or river travel for transport. Almost 98 percent of goods are moved by trucks over the nation's highways. Although the capital city of Caracas has a subway system, the rest of the country is served by a very small railway system of 584 kilometers (363 miles). The railway system is used to transport freight, and the government is seeking ways to expand this system.

Venezuela has 11 international and 36 domestic airports, with the major one in Caracas processing 90 percent of international flights, 84 percent of air cargo, and 40 percent of domestic passengers. Many of the country's airports are not high quality facilities. Venezuela has 13 ports and harbors, but 80 percent of bulk cargo is handled by 3 ports on the Caribbean Sea: Maracaibo, La Guaira, and Puerto Cabello. The facilities at La Guaira were significantly damaged by the December 1999 mudslides.

Venezuela produced 70.39 billion kilowatt-hours (kWh) of electricity in 1998, of which 65.463 billion were consumed internally, giving the country one of the highest electricity consumption levels in South America. Some 90 percent of households have electricity. Three-fourths of Venezuela's power comes from hydroelectric plants on its rivers. With reserves of 143 trillion cubic feet, Venezuela is believed to have the fifth largest reserves of natural gas in the world, 11 percent of which is consumed daily to generate power. Since 1998, the government has been privatizing its power-production system.

After the oil industry, the telecommunications industry is the fastest growing industry in Venezuela. The government recently ended its **monopoly** on fixed-line telephone service. CANTV, the national telephone company, has 2.5 million customers, compared with 3.5 million in the cellular telephone market. Venezuela had 11 Internet service providers in 1999, servicing 650,000 users, a number that is expected to double in 2000. In 1997, there were 10.75 million radios and 4.1 million televisions in Venezuela.

ECONOMIC SECTORS

The single most important sector in the Venezuelan economy is mining, which includes the large oil industry. In 1999, 24 percent of Venezuela's GDP was accounted for by industry (80 percent of which came from the oil industry), 71 percent by services, and just 5 percent by agriculture. Various government administrations have attempted to diversify the Venezuelan economy away from its dependence on oil, but, as indicated by the figures above, oil production continues to increase as a

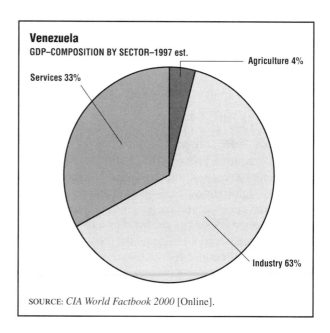

Venezuela
GDP–COMPOSITION BY SECTOR–1997 est.

Agriculture 4%
Services 33%
Industry 63%

SOURCE: *CIA World Factbook 2000* [Online].

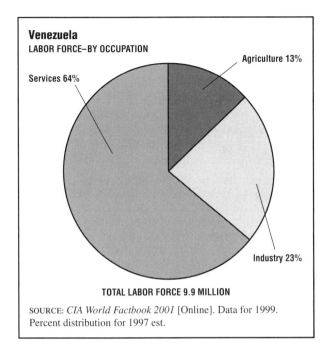

Venezuela
LABOR FORCE–BY OCCUPATION

Agriculture 13%

Services 64%

Industry 23%

TOTAL LABOR FORCE 9.9 MILLION

SOURCE: *CIA World Factbook 2001* [Online]. Data for 1999.
Percent distribution for 1997 est.

percentage of GDP. Other minerals that can be found in abundance in Venezuela are iron, bauxite, and natural gas.

In 1995, the manufacturing sector accounted for 16.6 percent of GDP, dropping to 14.2 percent by 1999. The services sector, another source that could help reduce Venezuela's dependence on oil, has not reflected consistent growth in its contributions to the Venezuelan GDP. One exception to that is the transport and communications industry, which has shown a consistent annual growth from 1995 to 1999 (4.9 to 6.0 percent of GDP).

AGRICULTURE

For centuries prior to the beginnings of the oil industry in 1917, agriculture served as the engine of the Venezuelan economy. As recently as the 1930s, agriculture employed 60 percent of the labor force and accounted for 21 percent of GDP. Today, agriculture is one of Venezuela's weakest sectors: as of 1999, it employed 13 percent of the labor force and accounted for 5 percent of GDP. Major crops include sugar cane (56 percent of total production in 1999), bananas (9 percent), maize (7 percent), and rice (5 percent). Crops are grown in the northern mountains of Venezuela and their foothills. In 1998, of the country's 15.367 million heads of livestock, 61 percent were cattle and 19 percent were pigs. Cattle grazing takes place in the plains (Llanos) area of Venezuela. This is an area about 800 miles wide that lies between the Mérida mountain range in the east of the country and the Orinoco River in the middle. Of its 2.708 million tons of livestock product in 1998, 56 percent came from cow's

milk, 18 percent from poultry meat, and 13 percent from beef and veal.

Subsidization (government payments to farmers to grow or not grow their crops) of agriculture is a tool that has been consistently used by various administrations to assist Venezuela's ailing agricultural sector. The right of farmers to receive government **subsidies** was made a part of the new 1999 Venezuelan Constitution. This policy has given rise to a powerful farmers' lobby that is dedicated to maintaining the subsidies, often criticized for maintaining inefficient and obsolete production techniques and ineffective management strategies. Since the 1980s, however, subsidies have resulted in an increase in the country's agricultural output.

Another approach used by the Venezuelan government to bolster the agricultural sector has been the redistribution of land that can be used for planting and grazing. These land giveaways have had the added benefit of addressing the problem of land concentrated in the hands of a few owners. Today, only 3 percent of landowners hold 70 percent of the agricultural land in Venezuela. In 1999, after 12,350 acres of land were forcibly occupied by squatters, the government responded by promising that it would redistribute 6.175 million acres of government land, create 504,000 farming jobs, and give significant tax breaks to farmers. The government had been pursuing such policies since 1958, when it created its National Agrarian Institute. Although at least 10 percent of the country's land has been redistributed, these redistribution policies have had limited success because the dropout rates for participants has been as high as 33 percent. The government has also tried to protect Venezuelan farmers from international competition by limiting the number of competing crops that can be imported into the country.

Despite all of these difficulties, the Venezuelan agricultural industry has remarkable promise. In the 1990s, only 4 percent of the country's land area was being used for agriculture, but it has been estimated that 30 percent of the total is suitable for such purposes. Some 50 percent of the agriculture industry's revenues came from cattle ranching in 1999, though production of such basic food crops like rice and maize has been declining.

INDUSTRY

OIL. The country ranks sixth in the world in proven oil reserves. In 1999, Venezuela had 74.1 billion barrels of proven reserves of crude oil, another 270 billion barrels of heavy oil has been found in the belt in and around the Orinoco River, and more has been found in the eastern Venezuela basin. From 1929 to 1970, Venezuela exported more oil than any other country, and, since 1990, has ranked third, behind Saudi Arabia and Iran. In 1989, production and sale of oil accounted for 13 percent of

GDP, 51 percent of government revenues, and 81 percent of exports. By 1999, oil accounted for 27.9 percent of GDP, 46 percent of government revenues, and 75 percent of exports. In 1999, the country's national oil company, Petróleos de Venezuela, S.A. (PDVSA), exported 90 percent of its oil and paid 70 percent of its profits to the government. More than 60 percent of oil exports were to the United States.

Although the PDVSA was not formally established until later, it was in 1935 that the government began its policy of "sowing the oil" or using oil wealth to develop the Venezuelan infrastructure. The policy was pursued in earnest in 1958, with the administration of Rómulo Betancourt, Venezuela's first democratically elected civilian president. In 1960, the government established the predecessor of the PDVSA, the Venezuelan Petroleum Corporation, for the purpose of overseeing the oil industry. In 1975, it nationalized the oil industry and, in 1977, the PDVSA was formed, and 14 foreign oil companies were compensated for their assets. This was helped by the fact that the Venezuelan government was flush with capital because the OPEC oil **embargo** of 1973 had increased oil prices by 400 percent.

From 1975 to 1995, decreases in the price of oil made it clear that Venezuela could not rely completely on itself for the production of its oil. Especially after 1981, the PDVSA began to face financial difficulties. Complete nationalization of the oil industry was proving to be a costly idea. For example, in 1981, decreasing oil prices resulted in decreased government revenues, causing the government to borrow capital and thereby increase the country's **foreign debt**. In 1982, the Central Bank of Venezuela responded to this crisis by simply seizing US$6 billion of PDVSA's profits to pay off some of the country's foreign debt. In 1995, private companies were once again allowed to explore and mine Venezuela's oil fields. While PDVSA remains a viable entity that has expanded into the oil-refining business, the idea of complete and exclusive nationalization has given way to an arrangement in which the PDVSA coexists with private companies. However, the government has not succeeded in its goal of reducing the country's dependence on the oil industry.

IRON. After oil, iron is the second most-mined mineral in Venezuela. It is estimated that Venezuela has 1.8 billion tons of high-grade iron ore reserves. In the 1950s, the Venezuelan government gave mining rights to 2 American companies, Bethlehem Steel and the United States Steel Corporation. In 1960, the government formed a corporation, the Venezuelan Corporation of Guayana, that was given mining rights to several iron-ore mines and an interest in the country's only steel complex, Siderórgica del Orinoco (Sidor), that had been built in 1955 by the American companies. In 1975, the govern-

ment nationalized Sidor and in effect purchased the foreign interest in iron and steel production. The transition was smooth and the American companies were compensated. Because of government mismanagement and the large capital outlay involved, Sidor did not show its first profit until 1986, fully 11 years after the government had acquired it. In 1998, Sidor was privatized once again. In 1999, steel production fell to its lowest point in 7 years because of low prices on the world market, though it rebounded in 2000. In 1998, 35 percent of Venezuela's iron and steel exports went to the United States, its largest trading partner.

ALUMINUM. In the 1980s, Venezuela enjoyed a reputation as one of the most efficient aluminum producers in the world. During that time, Venezuela exported 60 percent of its aluminum which, after oil, brought in the most foreign dollars. As of 1990, Venezuela's proven reserves of bauxite (aluminum ore) stood at 500 million tons, with 5 billion more tons in probable reserves. As a result of mismanagement the government's aluminum production facilities have debts amounting to US$1.25 billion. The government has consistently refused to sell its interests in its aluminum subsidiaries and is seeking private entities to partner with. Production of aluminum has declined from 627 thousand tons in 1995 to 570 thousand tons in 1999.

OTHER MINERALS. Venezuela's coal reserves total 10.2 billion tons of coal. The country's largest coal field, Carbozulia, is located in the state of Zulia and is controlled by a subsidiary of PDVSA. In 1999, the government announced that the coal field would close because it had consistently operated at a loss. Venezuela also has estimated gold reserves of 10,000 tons. Exploitation of one of the country's main gold mines, Las Cristinas, has been placed in limbo because of a legal dispute between 2 Canadian companies. In early 2000, a Chinese company announced its intention of reopening the Sosa Méndez gold mine that had been closed for 30 years.

MANUFACTURING. In 1998, the latest year for which data is available, 13.9 percent of the Venezuelan labor force worked within the manufacturing sector, which accounted for 16 percent of GDP in that year. As measured by the value of their output, the two most important industries were the food products industry with 17.8 percent, and the refined petroleum industry with 10.9 percent. The remaining 71 percent of the manufacturing sector's output was accounted for by industrial chemicals, iron and steel, transportation, and tobacco. From 1980 to 1990, the GDP produced by the manufacturing sector increased by an average of 4.3 percent per year, a figure that fell to 1.8 percent per year from 1990 to 1997.

As of 1988, slightly more than half of Venezuela's manufacturing firms were categorized as basic industries like food processing and wood products, 75 percent of which were small, family-owned businesses. Another 18 percent of firms were categorized as intermediate, like paper or plastics manufacturers. Some 19 percent of firms produced **capital goods** (goods used to make other products), and 9 percent made miscellaneous goods. Despite the existence of many small firms, as of 1988, a few large firms employed 64 percent of the manufacturing-sector labor force and produced 78 percent of its output.

Venezuela's manufacturing sector benefited and grew as a result of government policies pursued in the 1950s and especially in the 1970s, when the country's oil wealth was abundant. The government's ownership interest in manufacturing grew from 4 percent in the early 1970s to 42 percent by the late 1980s. The fall in the price of oil in the 1990s and loss of oil wealth has caused the government to scale back its subsidization of the manufacturing sector. The result has been a dramatic fluctuation in the sector's output. For example, manufacturing output grew 6.8 percent in 1995, contracted 5.2 percent in 1996, grew 4.4 percent in 1997, and shrank again in 1998.

SERVICES

In 1999, services accounted for roughly 71 percent of Venezuela's GDP and in 1997, employed 64 percent of its labor force. According to estimates by the World Bank, the GDP attributable to the services sector grew by an average of 0.5 percent every year from 1980 to 1998. In 1997, the largest part of the services sector was the 15.4 percent generated by the **retail**, restaurants, and hotels sector. Another 12.4 percent of GDP was generated by finance, insurance, real estate, and business services. Transport, storage, and communication accounted for 8.4 percent, followed by other services (7.2 percent), construction (5.1 percent), government services (4.8 percent), and electricity and water (1.5 percent).

RETAIL. Retail operations in Venezuela do not look very different from those in the United States. Although there are few department stores, there are numerous malls, and price haggling is uncommon. In 1995, 69.5 percent of the national income (GDP) was spent on private consumption, a figure that fell to 63.2 percent in 1996, rose to 65.8 percent in 1997, to 72.1 percent in 1998, and fell again to 70.2 percent in 1999. The year 2000 saw an increase in sales by clothing and food stores, sellers of telecommunication equipment, electrical appliances, and lottery tickets. Decreased sales were experienced by sellers of cars, pharmaceutical products, and hardware items. Venezuela has a well-developed professional services sector (physicians, attorneys, accountants, engineers and architects), with prestige attached to being a member of one of these professions.

TOURISM. Tourism has improved considerably in Venezuela since the late 1990s, and the industry con-

tributes roughly 6 percent of GDP. In 1999, Venezuela received about 1 million tourists, 3 times greater than 1993 numbers. The government has targeted tourism as one of its priority areas, and intends to partner with the **private sector** to expand the country's tourist attractions. As of 1994, the latest year for which data are available, a large number of tourists visited from Europe and North America, attracted to Venezuela's beaches, the Andes Mountains, and Angel Falls, the world's highest waterfall.

FINANCIAL SERVICES. Since the 1950s, and especially in the 1970s, this industry grew rapidly thanks to profits from the oil industry. By 1989, Venezuela had an extensive array of specialized financial institutions, including 41 commercial banks (9 of them **public-sector** banks) with hundreds of branch offices, 23 development finance institutions owned by the government, and 29 finance companies. In 1994, a banking crisis forced the closure of a number of the nation's 41 commercial banks, while some others were taken over by the government. By 1999, 41 percent of Venezuela's banks were partially foreign-owned.

Commercial banks remain at the heart of this industry, and they are estimated to hold 70 percent of financial assets. Another 20 percent of those assets are held by finance companies that provide consumer loans and short-term and medium-term loans to industry. Mortgage banks and savings-and-loan institutions hold the remaining financial assets within the economy. In 1999, Venezuelan banks continued to charge an interest rate high enough to allow them to earn a profit given the high cost of money. In that year, when the **inflation rate** was 20 percent, the banks charged at least 31.89 percent on loans.

CONSTRUCTION. Perhaps more so than any other sector, the construction sector has been affected by fluctuations in government spending. The industry thrived from the 1970s through the 1980s when the Venezuelan government used its oil revenues to improve and expand the country's infrastructure. In the 1980s and the late 1990s, with a decrease in government spending, the impact on the construction sector was disproportionately negative. Although the Venezuelan economy suffered a recession of 7.2 percent in 1999, the construction industry experienced a contraction of 20.4 percent, with an unemployment rate of 40 percent. The industry is expected to benefit from construction projects in the state of Verges, which experienced significant destruction from mud slides in 1999, and from a government program to build 63,000 new homes.

INTERNATIONAL TRADE

Venezuela's imports increased 3-fold between 1975 and 2000. The increased importance of oil to the nation's economy has caused Venezuela to import more

Trade (expressed in billions of US$): Venezuela		
	Exports	Imports
1975	8.800	6.000
1980	19.221	11.827
1985	14.438	8.106
1990	17.497	7.335
1995	18.457	12.650
1998	17.161	N/A

SOURCE: International Monetary Fund. *International Financial Statistics Yearbook 1999.*

machinery, equipment, and food because enough resources cannot be devoted to producing those items at home. Imports have also increased because the availability of foreign currency resulting from the sale of oil has increased the demand for foreign goods in Venezuela. A large portion of Venezuela's imports and exports has traditionally been provided by the United States. In 1998, Venezuela exported US$9.157 billion of goods (52 percent of its exports) to the United States, with oil accounting for 57.6 percent of the total. Other exported goods included chemicals, iron and steel, and aluminum. The next most important export-trading partner for Venezuela was Colombia, which received 8.3 percent of Venezuela's exports, followed by Suriname, the Netherlands Antilles, and Brazil. Oil accounted for 45.6 percent of the total value of Venezuela's exports overall.

In 1998, Venezuela imported US$6.520 billion (44 percent of its imports) from the United States. The next most important import-trading partner was Colombia, from which it received 6.4 percent of its imports, followed by Japan, Italy, Germany, and Brazil. Machinery and transport equipment accounted for 53 percent of Venezuela's imports from the United States in 1998.

Because of fluctuations in the world market price of oil, the value of Venezuela's exports can vary significantly from year to year. In 1997, for example, when world oil prices fell by 33 percent, the value of Venezuela's exports declined from US$23.707 billion in 1997 to $17.564 billion in 1998, a fall of 25.9 percent. With oil prices rebounding in 2000, the value of exports rebounded to US$32.8 billion in 2000. Venezuela has also been running a negative **balance of trade** in services, as when Venezuelans take money out of the country by traveling abroad, or when they purchase foreign products, like automobiles, thereby subsidizing both the foreign manufacturer and the shipping companies that deliver the vehicle to them. In 1998, Venezuelans imported US$5.054 billion in services while exporting only US$1.457 billion. However, Venezuela's overall trade

balance is positive. In 2000, that trade surplus reached US$18.1 billion, on imports of US$14.7 billion.

Venezuela has amassed foreign debt as a result of the government borrowing money abroad and individual Venezuelans investing their money overseas because of fears of political and economic instability. It has been estimated that Venezuelans have invested US$50 billion abroad. In 1990, the country's foreign debt was estimated at US$38 billion, which the government has tried to reduce by **restructuring** (changing the terms of the loan and reducing the interest rate it owes).

MONEY

Since 1985, Venezuela's currency, the bolívar, has become worth much less in terms of the U.S. dollar. In 1985, US$1 could buy 7.5 bolívars, but by 1999, it could buy 648.25 bolívars. **Inflation**, resulting from government spending in excess of revenues, is primarily responsible for this phenomenon. Since 1996, Venezuela has used a "**crawling peg" exchange rate** system, which attempts to slow down the process by which the bolívar loses value against the dollar. The annual rate of inflation has gradually declined since 1996, to a rate of 23.6 percent in 1999 and 13 percent in 2000. One reason for this is because demand for goods and services in Venezuela has declined. It is not clear if more economic reforms will be implemented in 2001, because the government of President Chávez has made it clear that its first priority is political, not economic, reform.

There are 3 small stock exchanges in Venezuela. The most active of these is the Caracas Stock Exchange, where the shares of only 91 companies are listed and only 12 are actively traded. The dollar value of the shares traded fell by 46.6 percent in 1999, partly as a result of the 7.2 percent recession that the economy experienced that year.

POVERTY AND WEALTH

The oil wealth that has, within the past 50 years, transformed the Venezuelan economy from an agrarian,

Exchange rates: Venezuela	
bolivares (B) per US$1	
Jan 2001	699.700
2000	679.960
1999	605.717
1998	547.556
1997	488.635
1996	417.333

SOURCE: CIA *World Factbook 2001* [ONLINE].

GDP per Capita (US$)

Country	1975	1980	1985	1990	1998
Venezuela	4,195	3,995	3,357	3,353	3,499
United States	19,364	21,529	23,200	25,363	29,683
Brazil	3,464	4,253	4,039	4,078	4,509
Colombia	1,612	1,868	1,875	2,119	2,392

SOURCE: United Nations. *Human Development Report 2000; Trends in human development and per capita income.*

Distribution of Income or Consumption by Percentage Share: Venezuela

Lowest 10%	1.3
Lowest 20%	3.7
Second 20%	8.4
Third 20%	13.6
Fourth 20%	21.2
Highest 20%	53.1
Highest 10%	37.0

Survey year: 1996
Note: This information refers to income shares by percentiles of the population and is ranked by per capita income.

SOURCE: *2000 World Development Indicators* [CD-ROM].

rural economy to a modern, urban one, has also significantly transformed Venezuelan society. Venezuelans today are more literate (91.1 percent in 1995 as opposed to 30 percent in the 1920s) and have a longer life expectancy (73.07 years in 2000 as opposed to 43 years in 1940). Still, in 1997, 67 percent of the population lived below the poverty line, and poverty appears to be increasing due to inflation and the 70 percent decrease in **real wages** since the 1980s. Venezuela has made great strides in meeting the basic needs of its citizens since the 1950s, but economic problems since the 1980s have eroded these early successes.

Education is compulsory in Venezuela up to the age of 14, and 75 percent of the country's students are enrolled in its public primary and secondary schools, though there are high rates of absenteeism attributed to poverty. Since the 1980s, educational spending has fallen below the average in South America. In 1983, Venezuela spent 7.4 percent of its GDP on education, but only 3.8 percent in 1998, and low pay has led to teacher shortages.

There are 99 public and private colleges and universities in Venezuela. The public university system in Venezuela has fared better than the lower education system. Venezuela boasts a number of national universities in various states that offer degrees through to the graduate and professional level. There are 2 national universities in Caracas alone. Tuition is free. Promising students are often given scholarships to study at foreign universities. The ministry of education has also begun to emphasize the importance of technical and vocational education in secondary schools. A system of adult-education has been developed to teach literacy and job skills to Venezuelans.

Venezuela enjoys some of the highest health standards in South America in terms of infant mortality (26.4 per 1,000 population) and longevity (73.07 life expectancy). Much of this was made possible by government intervention. Much of the population gets its medical care from facilities and hospitals operated by the Venezuelan Social Security Institute. Treatment at the country's clinics is free, though there is a small charge for prescription drugs. At the public hospitals, the poor receive treatment for free, and a small fee is charged to those who can afford to pay it. There is also a public welfare program that provides survivor and old-age pensions, maternity benefits, and payment for work-related accidents and illnesses. The institute finances its activities by a mandatory payment of 12 percent of the salaries of all Venezuelan workers. The government has had great success in implementing programs of prenatal care and children's immunization, improving water and sanitary conditions, and eliminating diseases.

Household Consumption in PPP Terms

Country	All food	Clothing and footwear	Fuel and power[a]	Health care[b]	Education[b]	Transport & Communications	Other
Venezuela	30	6	17	16	13	7	12
United States	13	9	9	4	6	8	51
Brazil	22	13	18	15	34	4	−6
Colombia	N/A	N/A	N/A	N/A	N/A	N/A	N/A

Data represent percentage of consumption in PPP terms.
[a]Excludes energy used for transport.
[b]Includes government and private expenditures.

SOURCE: World Bank. *World Development Indicators 2000.*

The 1999 constitution guarantees to Venezuela's citizens a health-care system that is funded by the government. In 1979, 14 percent of the government's budget was targeted to providing health services, but by 1999, that percentage had fallen to 6 percent of the national budget. A fall in the salaries of health care providers has been accompanied by a decrease in the quantity and quality of services provided. One response to this problem has been for the central government to allow the states to make more decisions about how to spend the country's health care budget. This approach has had some success in improving the delivery of health care in some areas. Another approach, rejected by the Chávez government, called for the privatization of the Venezuelan Social Security Institute.

The urbanization of Venezuelan society since the 1950s has created its own class structures by leaving behind many rural workers, many of whom are poor, illiterate, and undocumented. Some of them live in public housing, others live rent-free in the barrios (slums) of Venezuela's cities, of which there are more than 1,000 in Caracas alone.

WORKING CONDITIONS

In 1999, some 10.225 million Venezuelans were part of the formal labor force (accounted for in official statistics), but it is possible that another 4 million workers may be part of the informal labor force (workers, mostly in menial jobs, who lack legal protections and benefits). Working conditions in Venezuela appear to vary according to the degree of urbanization that the worker enjoys, with more workers in cities represented by a union. Many of the work benefits made available by the Venezuelan Social Security Institute (such as maternity benefits or payment for work-related illnesses) are less available to rural workers than to their urban counterparts. Although only 25 percent of workers in the formal labor force are organized, the unions have been able to exert an influence over politics that is far greater than the number of workers they represent. For example, unions were instrumental in getting a 10 percent increase in the minimum wage in 1999 and a 20 percent increase in 2000. The Constitution of 1999 includes progressive provisions that regulate working hours and conditions.

Urbanization has also encouraged the increased participation and empowerment of women in the Venezuelan workforce. In 1987, women constituted 31 percent of the labor force. Still, women continue to receive lower salaries than men for comparable work, and are more likely to be members of the informal labor sector.

Venezuelans with a university degree are more likely to hold the prestigious jobs in business and the professions, and they are generally more philanthropic and active in their communities than their counterparts in other South American countries.

COUNTRY HISTORY AND ECONOMIC DEVELOPMENT

1498. Christopher Columbus arrives in Venezuela.

1527. The city of Coro is founded.

1567. Caracas is founded after Spanish defeat Caracas and Teque Indians.

1728. Merchants from the Basque region of Spain are given a monopoly by the Spanish king over imports and export of cocoa in Venezuela. African slaves are imported and the economy prospers.

1811. On July 5, Venezuela declares independence from Spain. Francisco Miranda becomes the dictator of the First Republic. Spanish royalists retake Caracas and other cities in Venezuela within the year.

1813. Simón Bolívar invades Venezuela, liberates Caracas, and establishes the Second Republic, of which he is dictator. The Second Republic is destroyed by royalists by 1814, but Bolívar retakes the country and forms the Third Republic by 1817.

1818. Republic of Gran Colombia (Colombia, Venezuela, Ecuador) is proclaimed.

1829. Venezuela breaks away peacefully from Gran Colombia, led by José Páez.

1830. First Venezuelan Constitution is adopted.

1858–72. Civil wars and political disputes between liberals and conservatives disrupt the country. By 1872, the liberals gain control, introduce a new constitution, and institute economic reforms.

1899. The rule of the Andinos (5 military rulers from the Andean state of Táchira) begins with the military takeover of Caracas by General Cipriano Castro. The rule of the Andinos continues until 1958 (with exception of 1945–48).

1908–35. Dictatorial General Juan Vicent Gómez assumes power and rules until 1935.

1945. First revolution by a political party with popular support (Acción Democrática party). Liberal junta rules, headed by Rómulo Betancourt. Schools, hospitals and public housing are built.

1947. In the first free election in Venezuelan history, Rómulo Gallegos is elected president, but is deposed by the military after 9 months in office.

1951. Major Marcoz Pérez Jiménez assumes power, outlawing all political activity.

1958. A military coup against the Pérez government returns civilian rule and Rómulo Betancourt is re-elected as president.

1969. First peaceful transition of power from Betancourt's AD to COPEI.

MID-1970s. Booming oil prices lead to increased government spending.

1979. Decrease in oil revenues leads to increasing inflation, unemployment, and **capital flight**.

1985. An austerity plan is put in place by President Lusinchi. The austerity measures lead to massive riots in which hundreds are killed in 1989.

1992. Junior military officers, including Hugo Chávez, make 2 unsuccessful coup attempts.

1993. Rafael Caldera is elected president.

1998. Hugo Chávez Frias is elected president; a new constitution is approved by the people. Venezuela experiences the worst natural disaster in its history, with floods and mudslides in the northern state of Vargas.

2000. Chávez reelected president under the new constitution.

FUTURE TRENDS

The single most important issue that faces the Venezuelan economy today is its dependence on oil. Fluctuations in oil revenue have led to a predictable cycle of deficit spending, currency **devaluation**, inflation, recession, and unemployment. Venezuela is rich in natural resources and has a concerned citizenry, which can bolster the government's efforts to promote economic stability through privatization and the discipline of the marketplace. Though there is promise for Venezuela, the road ahead is fraught with difficulties.

The adoption of a new constitution in 1998 and the nationwide federal and local elections held in 2000 have ensured the legitimacy of the government. Now that government must continue to encourage growth in non-oil related industries. Telecommunications and power generation hold great promise for growth in the coming years, as do petroleum-related industries. Should the economy remain fairly strong, construction should also gain strength. Venezuela's future looks bright if it can spur similar growth in other, export-oriented industries, while maintaining its strengths in oil production.

DEPENDENCIES

Venezuela has no territories or colonies.

BIBLIOGRAPHY

Economist Intelligence Unit. *Country Profile: Venezuela.* London: Economist Intelligence Unit, 2001.

Embassy of the Bolivarian Republic of Venezuela in the United States of America. <http://www.embavenez-us.org>. Accessed September 2001.

Enright, Michael J., Antonio Francés, and Edith Scott Saavedra. *Venezuela: The Challenge of Competitiveness.* New York: St. Martin's Press, 1996.

Hagerty, Richard A., editor. *Venezuela: A Country Study.* Washington, D.C.: Federal Research Division, Library of Congress, 1990.

U.S. Central Intelligence Agency. *World Factbook 2001.* <http://www.odci.gov/cia/publications/factbook/index.html>. Accessed September 2001.

U.S. Department of State. *FY 2001 Country Commercial Guide: Venezuela.* <http://www.state.gov/www/about_state/business/com_guides/2001/wha/index.html>. Accessed September 2001.

"Venezuela." *International Financial Statistics Yearbook.* Washington, D.C.: International Monetary Fund, 2000.

—Linz Audain

GLOSSARY

Advance Tax: A percentage of the previous year's tax bill which is paid at the beginning of the new fiscal year and later credited back at its end.

Agribusiness: Agricultural and livestock production on a large scale, often engaged in by large, multinational companies; also used to refer to the companies themselves.

Arrear: Usually plural, **arrears**. Unpaid, overdue debt.

Bad Loan: An unrecoverable loan; the amount cannot be reclaimed by the lender.

Balance of Payments: The measure of all the money coming into a country and all the money leaving the country in a given period, usually a year. The balance of payments includes merchandise exports and imports, the measure of which is called the **balance of trade**, as well as several other factors.

Balance of Trade: A measure of the value of exports and imports, not including services. When imports exceed exports, there is a trade deficit. When exports exceed imports, there is a trade surplus.

Bank of Issue: The bank that is given the right to issue and circulate currency in a country.

Barter System: An exchange of goods and/or services for other goods and/or services, rather than for money.

Bear Market: A sustained period of negative growth in the stock market.

Bicameral: A legislative body consisting of two houses or chambers.

Black Market: An informal market in which buyers and sellers can negotiate and exchange prohibited or illegal goods (such as exchanging local money for foreign currency). Black markets often exist to avoid government controls. *See also* **Informal Sector.**

Budget Deficit: A government budget deficit occurs when a government spends more money on government programs than it generates in revenues. Governments must borrow money or print currency to pay for this excess spending, thus creating potential financial difficulties. *See also* **Budget Surplus.**

Budget Surplus: A government budget surplus occurs when a government generates more revenues than it spends on government programs. Governments can adjust to surpluses by lowering tax rates, paying down the national debt, or stockpiling the money. *See also* **Budget Deficit.**

Cadre: A group of important and influential members of political parties who direct the actions of that party.

Capital Adequacy: The state of a bank having enough capital to maintain its loans and operating costs.

Capital Flight; also called **Capital Outflow:** Money sent abroad because investors fear that economic conditions within a country are too risky.

Capital Good: A manufactured good used in the production of other goods. For example, factories or machinery used to produce goods are considered capital goods.

Capitalism: An economic system based on the private ownership of the means of production and on an open system of competitive markets. It is assumed that producers in a capitalist system can use their skills and capital in the pursuit of profit.

Capital Outflow: *See* **Capital Flight.**

Cash Crop: An agricultural good produced for direct sale on the market.

Centrally-planned Economy: An economy in which the government exerts a great deal of control over economic planning, including the control of production, the allocation of goods, distribution, and prices. Common in **socialist** countries.

c.i.f.: Abbreviation of **cost, insurance, and freight**; a method of determining the value of imports or exports that includes cost, insurance, and freight in determining the total amount.

Commonwealth of Independent States (CIS): A loose union of 12 of the former republics of the Soviet Union, excluding Estonia, Latvia, and Lithuania.

Communism: An economic system in which the means of production and distribution are held in common by all members of the society, and in which the rewards are distributed based on need. In actual communist countries, the state usually controls all the capital and land, and the economy is centrally planned. *See also* **Centrally-planned Economy.**

Consumer Good: A product sold directly to the end user, or consumer, such as food and clothing.

Crawling Peg: A fixed **exchange rate** between two currencies which is adjusted incrementally based on the movement of an economic indicator such as inflation.

Currency Board: An arrangement whereby a currency's value is fixed in some proportion to a strong foreign currency and such an exchange rate is guaranteed by the country's foreign exchange reserves.

Current Account Balance: The portion of the **balance of payments** that includes merchandise imports and exports (known as the **balance of trade**) plus imports and exports of services.

Debt Relief: Partial or full forgiveness of debts, offered to impoverished countries by lenders, usually after it becomes clear that continued payment on such debt is likely to ruin the country's economy.

Debt Service: Payment of interest on a loan or other debt. Debt servicing can be very expensive and debilitating for developing countries.

Deflation: Falling prices across an economy, expressed as a percentage per year. *See also* **Inflation.**

Dependency Ratio: The ratio of **pensioners** to the number of people employed.

Deregulation: A lessening of government restrictions on the economy.

Desertification: The progressive drying of the land.

Devaluation: An act by the government or central bank which decreases the official price of a nation's currency. When a currency is devalued, it can result in the country's exports becoming cheaper and more attractive.

Direct Tax: A tax levied directly on individuals or companies, such as income and property taxes. *See also* **Indirect Tax.**

Disposable Income: Those parts of a household income not needed for essentials such as food, healthcare, or housing costs. Disposable income may be saved, invested, or spent on non-essential goods.

Duty: A tax imposed on imported goods. *See also* **Indirect Tax.**

E-commerce: Economic activity conducted on the Internet.

Ecotourism: Tourism to natural and cultural areas which tries to minimize environmental impacts.

Embargo: A prohibition by a government against some or all trade with a foreign nation. *See also* **Sanctions.**

Emerging Market: A country with still evolving economic, social, and political structures that shows evidence of moving toward an open market system.

Emigration: To leave one's country to live elsewhere.

Enterprise Entry: The creation of new, predominantly small and medium size enterprises.

Enterprise Exit: The removal of businesses from an economy, either through bankruptcy or downsizing.

Equity: The value of all the shares in a company.

Estate Tax: A tax on inherited property and wealth.

Exchange Rate: The rate at which one country's currency is exchanged for that of another country.

Exchange Rate Mechanism (ERM): A mechanism set up in 1978 to handle fluctuations in the **exchange rates** of various European currencies. Each currency in the ERM may fluctuate only within agreed limits against any other currency.

Exchange Rate Regime: The mode of determining the **exchange rate** between the national currency and other major foreign currencies. In a fixed exchange rate regime, a currency is fixed or "pegged" to the currency of another, usually very stable currency, such as that of the United States. In a **floating** or flexible exchange rate regime, governments allow the value of their currency to be determined by supply and demand in the foreign exchange market.

Excise Tax: A tax on the sale or use of certain products or transactions, sometimes luxury or non-essential items.

Exclusive Economic Zone (EEZ): The area extending from a country's coastline over which that country has exclusive control of its resources.

External Debt: The total amount of money in a country's economy owed to enterprises and financial institutions outside the country.

Fiduciary: Related to a trust or trusteeship.

Fiscal Policy: The programs of a national government relating to spending on goods, services, **transfer payments**, and the tax system.

Fiscal Year: Any period of 12 consecutive months for which a company or a government calculates earnings, profits, and losses.

Fixed Exchange Rate: *See* **Exchange Rate Regime.**

Floating Exchange Rate: *See* **Exchange Rate Regime.**

Floor Price: The minimum price for a good or service which normally cannot be further reduced due to political, economic, or trade considerations.

f.o.b.: Abbreviation of **Free on board**; a method of determining the value of exports or imports that considers the value of goods excluding the cost of insurance and freight charges.

Foreign Debt: *See* **External Debt.**

Foreign Direct Investment (FDI): The total value of investment by foreign entities in a country, usually expressed on an annual or cumulative basis.

Foreign Exchange Reserves: The amount of money a country has in its treasury consisting of currency from foreign countries.

Free Market System: An economic system based on little government intervention and the freedom of private association and control of goods. *See also* **Capitalism.**

Free Trade Zone: Also called **Free Zone.** An industrial area where foreign companies may import, store, and sometimes export goods without paying taxes.

Full Employment: The level of employment at which a minimal amount of involuntary unemployment exists. It is considered the maximum level of employment in an economy.

Fully Convertible Currency: A currency that can be freely traded in international foreign exchanges for units of another currency.

GDP per Capita: Gross domestic product divided by the number of people in a country. GDP per capita is a convenient way to measure comparative international wealth.

Gini Index: An index used to measure the extent to which the distribution of income within an economy deviates from perfectly equal distribution. A score of 0 would mean perfect equality (with everyone having the same level of wealth) and 100 would signify perfect inequality (with a few extraordinarily wealthy people and the large majority living in dire poverty).

Glut: An excess of goods in a particular market, which typically causes the price of that good to fall.

Grey Economy: Economic activity that takes place in both the formal and **informal economy,** meaning that some but not all economic activity is reported to authorities such as tax collectors.

Gross Domestic Product (GDP): The total market value of all goods and services produced inside a country in a given year, which excludes money made by citizens or companies working abroad.

Gross National Product (GNP): The total market value of all goods and services produced in a year by a nation, including those goods produced by citizens or companies working abroad.

Guarantor: An institution or individual that guarantees to pay the debts of another institution or individual in the case of bankruptcy.

Guest Worker: Persons from a foreign country who are allowed to live in a host country so long as they are employed. Many guest workers send **remittances** to their native country.

Hard Currency: Money that can be exchanged on the foreign market and is stable enough to purchase goods from other countries.

Hawking: Selling wares, often pirated goods, in the **informal sector.**

Holding Company: A company that owns or controls several other companies.

Immigration: To move into a country that is not one's native country.

Import Substitution: A policy which calls for the local production of goods that have traditionally been imported. The goal of import substitution is to lessen a country's dependence on foreign suppliers.

Income Tax: A **direct tax** on an individual's earned income.

Indirect Tax: A tax which is not paid directly, but is passed on as part of the cost of an item or service. For instance, **tariffs** and **value-added taxes** are passed on to the consumer and included in the final price of the product. *See also* **Direct Tax.**

Inflation: A persistent increase in the average price of goods in an economy, usually accompanied by declining purchasing power of the national currency.

Inflation Rate: The rate at which prices rise from one period to the next.

Informal Sector: Also called **Informal Economy.** The part of an economy that lies outside government regulations and tax systems. It usually consists of small-scale and usually labor-intensive activities; it often includes illegal activities. *See also* **Black Market.**

Infrastructure: The system of public facilities, services, and resources in a country, including roads, railways, airports, power generation, and communication systems.

Intermediate Good: A good used as an ingredient or component in the production of other goods. For instance, wood pulp is used to produce paper.

Internally Displaced Person: A person fleeing danger (such as war or persecution) who has not crossed international boundaries. Those who relocate to another country are called "refugees."

Joint Sector: An economic sector in which private enterprise and the government invest jointly.

Joint Venture: A special economic initiative or company formed by a foreign firm and a domestic company, usually in a developing state. The domestic partner often holds a majority interest, thus allowing the host country to control the amount and kind of foreign economic activity. Can also be a simple joint operation by two or more companies.

Labor Force: Also called **Workforce.** The total number of people employed in a country plus the number of people unemployed and looking for a job.

Labor Mobility: The ability and readiness of workers to move to regions or sectors of higher growth within a country or economy.

Levy: A tax based on the assessed value of personal property and/or income.

Liberal Economy: An economy in which markets operate with minimal government interference and in which individual choice and private ownership are the guiding forces.

Liberalization: The opening of an economy to free competition and a self-regulating market, with minimal government-imposed regulations or limitations.

Liquidity: Generally, the amount of money on hand. When related to government, it refers to the amount of money in circulation.

Macroeconomics: Economic issues large enough to impact the nation as a whole.

Market Capitalization: The total market value of a company, expressed by multiplying the value of a company's outstanding shares by the current price of the stock.

Marxism: A set of economic and political theories based on the work of 19th century theorists Karl Marx and Friedrich Engels that holds that human history is a struggle between classes, especially those who own property and those who do not (the workers). Marxism provided the theoretical basis for the economic systems of modern **communism** and **socialism.**

Microcredit: The lending of small amounts of startup capital to the very poor as a way of helping them out of poverty. The World Bank and other aid agencies often make mircrocredit loans to small-scale entrepreneurs in the developing world.

Monetary Policy: A government policy designed to regulate the money supply and interest rates in an economy. These policies are usually determined by the central bank or treasury in order to react to or to anticipate inflationary trends and other factors that affect an economy. They are said to be "tight" when interest rates are raised and other measures are implemented in an effort to control inflation and stabilize currency values.

Monetized Economy: An economy based on money as opposed to barter.

Money Laundering: A method used by criminal organizations to hide income gained from illicit activities, such as drug smuggling, by manipulating banks to provide a legitimate explanation for the source of money.

Monopoly: A company or corporation that has exclusive control over the distribution and availability of a product or service.

Multinational Corporation (MNC): A corporation which has economic ties to or operations in two or more countries.

National Debt: The amount of money owed to lenders by a government. The debt occurs when a government spends more each year than it has raised through taxes. Thus, to spend more than it has, the government must borrow money from banks or through the issuance of bonds.

Nationalization: The movement of privately-owned (and usually foreign-owned) companies into government ownership. Companies have often been nationalized by the developing countries whose government argued that the foreign firms involved did not pay their fair share of the profits to the host country and unfairly exploited it in other ways.

Nomenklatura: The elite members of the Communist Party in communist nations, who were often given privileges not extended to ordinary citizens.

Nomenklatura Privatization: A system of **privatization** in communist nations that openly or covertly transferred ownership of state assets to the **nomenklatura.**

Non-performing Loan: A delinquent loan or one in danger of going into default.

Offshore Banking: Banking operations that offer financial services to people and companies from other countries, usually with associated tax benefits. Offshore banking operations are often suspected as a cover for **money laundering** or other illegal financial activities.

Overheated Economy: An economy that is growing at a very high annual rate, which leads to low interest rates, a high borrowing rate, and an abundance of money in the economy—all of which can lead to **inflation.**

Parastatal: A partly or wholly government-owned enterprise.

Participation Rate: The ratio between the labor force and the total population, which indicates how many people are either working or actively seeking work.

Pensioner: A retired person who lives off a government pension.

Price Control: Artificial limitation on the prices of goods set by the government, usually in a **centrally-planned economy.**

Price Index: An index that shows how the average price of a commodity or bundle of goods has changed over a period of time, usually by comparing their value in constant dollars.

Primary Commodity: A commodity, such as a particular crop or mineral, which is a natural rather than manufactured resource.

Private Sector: The part of an economy that is not directly controlled by the government, including businesses and households.

Privatization: The transition of a company or companies from state ownership or control to private ownership. Privatization often takes place in societies that are making a transition from a **socialist** or mixed-socialist economy to a **capitalist** economy.

Procurement: The purchase of goods or services by the government.

Progressive Taxation: An income taxation system in which tax rates rise in accordance with income levels. Thus, a person making a large salary will be taxed at a higher rate than someone who makes less money.

Proportional Representation: An electoral system whereby the number of legislative seats allocated to a particular political party is decided in proportion to the number of votes that party won in an election.

Protectionist Policy: A government policy used to protect local producers from competition from imported foreign goods. Countries may erect various trade barriers such as **tariffs** or quotas in an effort to protect domestic firms or products.

Public Sector: The part of the economy that is owned and operated by the government.

Purchasing Power Parity (PPP): The purchasing power parity method attempts to determine that relative purchasing power of different currencies over equivalent goods and services. For example, if it costs someone in the United States US$300 to buy a month's worth of groceries, but it costs someone in Ghana only US$100 to buy the same amount of groceries, then the person in Ghana can purchase three times as much for the same amount of money. This means that though the average citizen of Ghana may earn less money than the average citizen of the United States, that money buys more because goods and services cost less in Ghana. The PPP calculation attempts to account for these differences in prices and is used to calculate **GDP** and **GDP per capita** figures that are comparable across nations. Note: GDP

figured at purchasing power parity may be three or more times as large as GDP figured at **exchange rate** parity.

Pyramid Scheme: Fraudulent investment strategy involving a series of buying and selling transactions that generate a paper profit, which, in turn, is used to buy more stocks. They were prevalent in Eastern Europe following the fall of the Soviet Union, and preyed on the average citizen's lack of understanding of **free-market** investment transactions.

Real GDP: The **gross domestic product** of a country expressed in constant prices which are determined by a baseline year. Real GDP thus ignores the effects of inflation and deflation and allows for comparisons over time.

Real Wage: Income measured in constant dollars, and thus corrected to account for the effects of inflation.

Recession: A period of negative growth in an economy, usually defined as two consecutive quarters of negative **GDP** growth. A recession is characterized by factors such as low consumer spending, low output, and high unemployment.

Re-export: An imported good that does not undergo any changes (e.g., not turned into a new product) before being exported.

Relative Income Poverty: This is a measure of the overall equality in income among employed workers. Relative income poverty is high when a high percentage of the sum of total income is concentrated in the hands of a small percentage of the working population, and it is low when income is more equally spread among all workers.

Remittance: Money that is sent back to people, usually relatives, living in the home country of a national working abroad.

Repatriation: Taking money out of a foreign country in which it had been invested and reinvesting it in the country where it originated.

Reserve Ratio: The percentage of a bank's assets in reserve against the possibility of customers withdrawing their deposited funds. Some governments impose a minimum percentage, usually enforced by a central bank in proportion to the total amount of currency in circulation.

Restructuring: A catch-all phrase for turning around a company, involving cutting costs, restoring finances, and improving products.

Retail: The sale of goods and services to individuals in small amounts.

Sanction: A penalty, often in the form of a trade restriction, placed on one country by one or several other countries as a penalty for an action by the country under sanctions. Sanctions are designed to force the country experiencing them to change a policy, such as its human rights practices.

Shadow Economy: Economic interactions that are invisible to standard accounting and taxing procedures. See **Informal Economy.**

Sharecropper: A farmer who works someone else's land in exchange for a share of the crops they produce.

Smallholder: A farmer who has only a very small farm or plot of land.

Social Security Tax: A **direct tax** levied partly on the worker and partly on the employer in order to provide funds for a nation's **social welfare system.**

Social Welfare System: A set of government programs that provides for the needs of the unemployed, aged, disabled, or other groups deemed in need of government assistance.

Socialism: An economic system in which means of production and distribution are owned by the community, and profits are shared among the community. Countries with socialist economies put a premium on centralized control over an economy rather than allowing market forces to operate, and tend to have a relatively equal distribution of income.

Solvency: Financial stability.

Statist Economic Policy: A policy in **capitalist** or quasi-capitalist countries that favor state control or guidance of companies or sectors of the economy that are thought to be vital.

Strategic Industry: An industry considered extremely important to the well being of a country.

Structural Adjustment Program (SAP): A set of economic programs and policies aimed at stabilizing the overall structure of a troubled economy. Structural adjustment programs are often required by international lending agencies such as the World Bank and the International Monetary Fund. These programs often involve devaluing the currency, reducing government spending, and increasing exports.

Structural Unemployment: Unemployment caused by a mismatch between the needs of employers and the skills and training of the labor force.

Subsidy: A payment made by a government to an individual or company that produces a specific good or commodity. Some countries subsidize the production of certain agricultural crops, while others may subsidize mass transit or public art.

Subsistence Farming: Farming which generates only enough produce to feed the farmer's family, with little or nothing left over to sell.

Tariff: An **indirect tax** that is applied to an imported product or class of products.

Tax Haven: A place where investors shield their money from the national taxes of their own country. *See also* **Offshore Banking.**

Tax Holiday: A period of time in which businesses or investors enjoy exemptions from paying taxes. Tax holidays are offered as a lure to investment or business development.

Technocrat: Government official who is expert in specialized—usually technological—areas.

Trade Deficit: *See* **Balance of Trade.**

Trade Surplus: *See* **Balance of Trade.**

Transfer Payment: Cash paid directly to individuals by a government, usually as part of a **social welfare system.**

Transfer Pricing: A method used by foreign firms to overprice their overseas costs and thereby reduce their local tax liabilities.

Treasury Bill: Also called a **T-bill**. A guaranteed government investment bond sold to the public. They usually reach maturity after short periods, for example, three months or six months.

Trickle Down: An economic theory that contends that tax relief and other governmental incentives should be given primarily to the highest income earners in a society, on the assumption that their increased economic investment and other activity will provide benefits that "trickle down" to the lower- and middle-income wage-earners.

Turnover: The measure of trade activity in terms of the aggregated prices of all goods and services sold in the country during a year.

Two-tier Economy: An economy where skilled or educated workers enjoy a high standard of living, but unskilled workers are trapped in poverty.

Underemployment: A situation in which people are not reaching their economic potential because they are employed in low-paying or part-time jobs. For example, an engineer who is working in a fast food restaurant would be said to be experiencing underemployment.

Underground Economy: Economic transactions that are not reported to government, and therefore not taxable. **Informal sectors** and **black markets** are examples of underground economic activity.

Unicameral: A legislative body consisting of a single house or chamber.

United Nations Development Program (UNDP): The United Nations' principal provider of development advice, advocacy, and grant support.

Value Added: The increase in the value of a good at each stage in the production process. When a company adds value to its products it is able to gain a higher price for them, but it may be liable for a **value-added tax.**

Value-added Tax (VAT): A tax levied on the amount of **value added** to a total product at each stage of its manufacture.

Vertical Integration: Control over all stages of the production and distribution of a certain product. For example, if one company owns the mines, the steel plant, the transportation network, the factories, and the dealerships involved in making and selling automobiles, it is vertically integrated.

Voucher Privatization: A system for selling off state-owned companies in which citizens are given "vouchers" which they may invest in such companies. This system was devised to allow all citizens the opportunity to invest in formerly state-owned businesses; however, in practice many citizens invest their vouchers in voucher funds, which are professionally managed investment groups who amass vouchers in order to exert control over the direction of companies.

Welfare State: A government that assumes the responsibility for the well-being of its citizens by providing institutions and organizations that contribute to their care. *See also* **Social Welfare System.**

Workforce: *See* **Labor Force.**

INDEX

Page numbers appearing in bold-face indicate major treatment of entries. A page number accompanied by an italicized "t" indicates that there is a table on that page, while a page number accompanied by an italicized "f" indicates there is a figure on that page.

A

Abacha, Sani, **I:**352
Aboriginal lands, Australia, **III:**17
Abubakar, Abdulsalami, **I:**352–353
Acquired Immune Deficiency Syndrome (AIDS). *See* AIDS and HIV
Advertising industry, Lebanon, **III:**331
Affirmative action, South Africa, **I:**427–428
Afghani (money), **III:**8
Afghanistan, **III:1–10**
African National Congress (South Africa), **I:**420
African Party for the Independence of Cape Verde, **I:**69
"Agenda 2000," Spain, **IV:**439–440
Aging populations
  Japan, **III:**239
  Romania, **IV:**375
  United Kingdom, **IV:**501
  United States, **II:**375–376
Agriculture
  Afghanistan, **III:**5–6
  Albania, **IV:**4
  Algeria, **I:**6–7
  Andorra, **IV:**12–13
  Angola, **I:**17
  Antigua and Barbuda, **II:**4–5
  Argentina, **II:**14, 15–16
  Armenia, **IV:**20
  Australia, **III:**16
  Austria, **IV:**31, 36
  Azerbaijan, **III:**28
  The Bahamas, **II:**28

Bahrain, **III:**35
Bangladesh, **III:**47–48
Barbados, **II:**36–37
Belarus, **IV:**40–41
Belgium, **IV:**53–54
Belize, **II:**44–45
Benin, **I:**24–25
Bhutan, **III:**61
Bolivia, **II:**54–55
Bosnia and Herzegovina, **IV:**66
Botswana, **I:**32
Brazil, **II:**67–69
Brunei Darussalam, **III:**68
Bulgaria, **IV:**75–76
Burkina Faso, **I:**41–42
Burma, **III:**78–79
Burundi, **I:**50
Cambodia, **III:**89
Cameroon, **I:**60–61
Canada, **II:**83–84
Cape Verde, **I:**70
Central African Republic, **I:**78–79
Chad, **I:**87
Chile, **II:**98–99
China, **III:**101
Colombia, **II:**113–114
Comoros, **I:**94
Congo, Democratic Republic of the, **I:**103–104
Congo, Republic of the, **I:**112
Costa Rica, **II:**125–126
Côte d'Ivoire, **I:**122
Croatia, **IV:**88
Cuba, **II:**137–138
Cyprus, **III:**120
Czech Republic, **IV:**99
Denmark, **IV:**111
Djibouti, **I:**130–131
Dominica, **II:**146–147
Dominican Republic, **II:**155
Ecuador, **II:**164–165
Egypt, **I:**141
El Salvador, **II:**175
Equatorial Guinea, **I:**154–155
Eritrea, **I:**162–163

Estonia, **IV:**121–122
Ethiopia, **I:**172–173
Fiji, **III:**130–131
Finland, **IV:**132–133
France, **IV:**143, 147–148
French Antilles and French Guiana, **II:**185–186
French Polynesia, **III:**138
Gabon, **I:**182–183
The Gambia, **I:**190
Georgia, **IV:**159
Germany, **IV:**171
Ghana, **I:**199–200
Greece, **IV:**184–185
Grenada, **II:**194–195
Guatemala, **II:**203
Guinea, **I:**209
Guinea-Bissau, **I:**219
Guyana, **II:**213
Haiti, **II:**221
Honduras, **II:**229
Hong Kong, **III:**149
Hungary, **IV:**199–200
Iceland, **IV:**209
India, **III:**165
Indonesia, **III:**178–179
Iran, **III:**194–195
Iraq, **III:**207–208
Ireland, **IV:**219–220
Israel, **III:**217–218
Italy, **IV:**235–236
Jamaica, **II:**239
Japan, **III:**231
Jordan, **III:**244–245
Kazakhstan, **III:**256–257
Kenya, **I:**228
Kiribati, **III:**268
Korea, North, **III:**276
Korea, South, **III:**287
Kuwait, **III:**299–300
Kyrgyzstan, **III:**309
Laos, **III:**319
Latvia, **IV:**249
Lebanon, **III:**330
Lesotho, **I:**238–239

Sierra Leone, **I:**401, 408
Singapore, **III:**507–508, 515–516
Slovakia, **IV:**411, 419
Slovenia, **IV:**421, 428–429
Solomon Islands, **III:**519, 524–525
Somalia, **I:**409–410, 415–416
South Africa, **I:**417–418, 428–429
Spain, **IV:**431–432, 444–445
Sri Lanka, **III:**527–528, 537
Sudan, **I:**431, 439–440
Suriname, **II:**347, 352
Swaziland, **I:**441, 446–447
Sweden, **IV:**447–448, 456–457
Switzerland, **IV:**459–460, 471–472
Syria, **III:**539, 548–549
Taiwan, **III:**551–552, 564–565
Tajikistan, **III:**567, 574
Tanzania, **I:**449–451, 459–460
Thailand, **III:**577, 591–592
Togo, **I:**463, 470
Tonga, **III:**595, 600
Trinidad and Tobago, **II:**355, 361
Tunisia, **I:**473, 480
Turkey, **III:**603, 617–618
Turkmenistan, **III:**621, 628–629
Tuvalu, **III:**631–632, 636
Uganda, **I:**483–484, 492–493
Ukraine, **IV:**475, 484–485
United Arab Emirates, **III:**636, 645
United Kingdom, **IV:**487–489, 499–501
United States, **II:**363–365, 376–377
Uruguay, **II:**381, 389
Uzbekistan, **III:**647, 655–656
Vanuatu, **III:**657, 663
Vatican City, **IV:**505, 509
Venezuela, **II:**391, 400–401
Vietnam, **III:**665, 673–674
Yemen, **III:**677, 683
Yugoslavia, **IV:**511, 517–518
Zambia, **I:**495, 503
Zimbabwe, **I:**505–506, 513–514
Croatia, **IV:83–94**
Crop production. *See* Agriculture; *specific crops*
Crude oil. *See* Oil and gas industry
Cuba, **II:133–142**
Curaçao. *See* Netherlands Antilles and Aruba
Currency. *See* Money
Customs and duties. *See* International trade
Cyprus, **III:115–125**
Czech Republic, **IV:95–103**

D

Dairy production
Belgium, **IV:**54

Brazil, **II:**68–69
Netherlands, **IV:**321–322
New Zealand, **III:**413
Poland, **IV:**349
Dalasi (money), **I:**191
Data processing and telemarketing
Barbados, **II:**37
Grenada, **II:**195
Date production, Algeria, **I:**6
Debt
Algeria, **I:**3
Angola, **I:**15
Antigua and Barbuda, **II:**2
Argentina, **II:**11
Armenia, **IV:**18
Australia, **III:**13
Bangladesh, **III:**43
Barbados, **II:**34
Belgium, **IV:**50
Benin, **I:**26
Bhutan, **III:**58
Brazil, **II:**65
Bulgaria, **IV:**73
Burundi, **I:**48
Cameroon, **I:**57
Comoros, **I:**93
Congo, Republic of the, **I:**115
Croatia, **IV:**85
Cuba, **II:**135
Denmark, **IV:**107
Egypt, **I:**138
Finland, **IV:**129
Guyana, **II:**210
Jordan, **III:**242–243
Korea, South, **III:**283
Lithuania, **IV:**270
Malta, **IV:**294
Mexico, **II:**247, 254
Netherlands Antilles and Aruba, **II:**263, 268
Nicaragua, **II:**273
Nigeria, **I:**350
Pakistan, **III:**431, 441
Portugal, **IV:**363, 367
Spain, **IV:**434
Syria, **III:**541
Thailand, **III:**579
Uganda, **I:**485
Ukraine, **IV:**478
Uruguay, **II:**383
Venezuela, **II:**398
Vietnam, **III:**672
Zambia, **I:**497
See also Economic overviews and trends
Defense spending. *See* Politics and government

Deforestation and desertification
Burkina Faso, **I:**42
Burma, **III:**78
Central African Republic, **I:**91
Comoros, **I:**94
Côte d'Ivoire, **I:**122
Ethiopia, **I:**172–173
Laos, **III:**320
Malaysia, **III:**349–350
Nepal, **III:**402
Panama, **II:**284
Poland, **IV:**349
Senegal, **I:**385
Thailand, **III:**584
Democratic Labour Party (Barbados), **II:**34
Democratic Party (United States), **II:**366
Democratic Progressive Party (Taiwan), **III:**554–555
Democratic Republic of the Congo. *See* Congo, Democratic Republic of the
Denar (money), **IV:**290
Denmark, **IV:105–118**
Dependencies
Denmark, **IV:**117–118
Israel, **III:**223
United Kingdom, **IV:**501–503
United States, **II:**378–379
Depression. *See* Economic overviews and trends
Deregulation. *See* Economic overviews and trends
Derg regime (Ethiopia), **I:**169, 175–176
Desalinization plants, United Arab Emirates, **III:**640
Devaluation of currency. *See* Money; *specific currencies*
Diamond mining
Angola, **I:**17
Botswana, **I:**30–31, 34
Central African Republic, **I:**78, 79
Congo, Democratic Republic of the, **I:**104
Ghana, **I:**200
Guinea, **I:**210
Lesotho, **I:**239
Liberia, **I:**247
Sierra Leone, **I:**404
Diamond processing and trading
Belgium, **IV:**54
Israel, **III:**218
Dinar (money)
Algeria, **I:**32
Bahrain, **III:**37
Iraq, **III:**210

Nicaragua, **II:**275
Niger, **I:**342
Nigeria, **I:**358
Norway, **IV:**337
Oman, **III:**424
Pakistan, **III:**439
Palau, **III:**448
Panama, **II:**284–285
Paraguay, **II:**298
Peru, **II:**310–311
Philippines, **III:**469
Poland, **IV:**351–352
Portugal, **IV:**366–367
Puerto Rico, **II:**319
Qatar, **III:**479
Romania, **IV:**381
Russia, **IV:**396–397
Rwanda, **I:**368–369
St. Kitts and Nevis, **II:**327
St. Lucia, **II:**335
St. Vincent and the Grenadines,
  II:343
Samoa, **III:**487
San Marino, **IV:**408–409
São Tomé and Príncipe, **I:**377
Saudi Arabia, **III:**501
Senegal, **I:**386–387
Seychelles, **I:**397
Sierra Leone, **I:**405
Singapore, **III:**512–513
Slovakia, **IV:**416
Slovenia, **IV:**425
Solomon Islands, **III:**523
Somalia, **I:**414
South Africa, **I:**425
Spain, **IV:**440–441
Sri Lanka, **III:**534
Suriname, **II:**350–351
Sweden, **IV:**452–453
Switzerland, **IV:**466
Syria, **III:**546
Taiwan, **III:**560
Tajikistan, **III:**571–572
Tanzania, **I:**456
Thailand, **III:**586
Togo, **I:**468
Tonga, **III:**598
Trinidad and Tobago, **II:**360
Tunisia, **I:**477
Turkey, **III:**612–613
Turkmenistan, **III:**626
Uganda, **I:**490
Ukraine, **IV:**481–482
United Arab Emirates, **III:**642
United Kingdom, **IV:**496
United States, **II:**371–372, 373
Uruguay, **II:**386

Uzbekistan, **III:**653
Venezuela, **II:**397
Vietnam, **III:**670
Yemen, **III:**681
Yugoslavia, **IV:**515
Zambia, **I:**501
Zimbabwe, **I:**510
See also Money
Fine Gael Party (Ireland), **IV:**217
Finland, **IV:127–140**
First era, Sri Lanka economy,
  III:529
First Republic, Zambia, **I:**497
Fishing and aquaculture
  Algeria, **I:**7
  Angola, **I:**17
  Antigua and Barbuda, **II:**5
  Argentina, **II:**15–16
  Austria, **IV:**32
  The Bahamas, **II:**28
  Bahrain, **III:**36
  Bangladesh, **III:**48
  Belgium, **IV:**54
  Brunei Darussalam, **III:**68
  Burkina Faso, **I:**42
  Burma, **III:**79
  Cambodia, **III:**89
  Canada, **II:**84
  Cape Verde, **I:**70
  Chile, **II:**99
  China, **III:**102
  Comoros, **I:**94
  Côte d'Ivoire, **I:**122
  Croatia, **IV:**88
  Cyprus, **III:**120
  Denmark, **IV:**111
  Djibouti, **I:**131
  Dominica, **II:**147
  Dominican Republic, **II:**155
  Equatorial Guinea, **I:**154–155
  Eritrea, **I:**163
  Fiji, **III:**131
  France, **IV:**143, 148
  French Antilles and French Guiana,
    II:185–186
  The Gambia, **I:**190
  Greece, **IV:**184
  Guinea, **I:**209
  Guinea-Bissau, **I:**219
  Honduras, **II:**229
  Hong Kong, **III:**149–150
  Iceland, **IV:**209
  Indonesia, **III:**179
  Iran, **III:**195
  Ireland, **IV:**220
  Jamaica, **II:**239
  Japan, **III:**232

Kiribati, **III:**268, 270
Korea, North, **III:**276
Korea, South, **III:**288
Kuwait, **III:**300
Libya, **I:**255
Madagascar, **I:**265
Maldives, **III:**363
Mali, **I:**281
Marshall Islands, **III:**370
Micronesia, **III:**376, 381–382
Morocco, **I:**307–308
Namibia, **I:**331
Netherlands, **IV:**322
New Zealand, **III:**414
Nicaragua, **II:**274
Oman, **III:**423
Pakistan, **III:**437
Palau, **III:**448
Peru, **II:**309–310
Philippines, **III:**466
St. Vincent and the Grenadines,
  II:343
Samoa, **III:**486
São Tomé and Príncipe, **I:**376
Senegal, **I:**386
Seychelles, **I:**396
Solomon Islands, **III:**522–523
Somalia, **I:**413–414
Spain, **IV:**440
Sri Lanka, **III:**533
Sudan, **I:**436
Suriname, **II:**350
Taiwan, **III:**558, 559
Thailand, **III:**584
Tonga, **III:**598
Tunisia, **I:**476
Tuvalu, **III:**634
United Arab Emirates, **III:**641
United Kingdom, **IV:**494
United States, **II:**370
Uruguay, **II:**385–386
Vanuatu, **III:**660–661
Vietnam, **III:**669
Yemen, **III:**680–681
Five year plans, Saudi Arabia,
  III:493
"Flag of convenience"
  Liberia, **I:**248
  Panama, **II:**282–283
  Vanuatu, **III:**659
"Flatted factories," Hong Kong,
  III:150
Flemish-Walloon disputes, **IV:**48
Flexible work schedules, United
  Kingdom, **IV:**499
Flotas, **II:**53
Folketing, **IV:**107

Vietnam, **III:**670
Yugoslavia, **IV:**515
Zambia, **I:**500
Zimbabwe, **I:**510
See also Oil and gas industry;
specific types of mining
Moldova, **IV:301–308**
Monaco, **IV:309–314**
Moncloa Pacts, **IV:**433
Money
Afghanistan, **III:**8, 8*t*
Albania, **IV:**5–6, 6*t*
Algeria, **I:**8, 8*t*
Andorra, **IV:**13–14, 13*t*
Angola, **I:**18–19, 18*t*
Antigua and Barbuda, **II:**6, 6*t*
Argentina, **II:**19, 19*t*
Armenia, **IV:**22, 22*t*
Australia, **III:**20, 20*t*
Austria, **IV:**34, 34*t*
Azerbaijan, **III:**29–30, 30*t*
The Bahamas, **II:**30, 30*t*
Bahrain, **III:**37, 37*t*
Bangladesh, **III:**50–51, 50*t*
Barbados, **II:**38, 38*t*
Belarus, **IV:**43, 43*t*
Belgium, **IV:**57–58, 57*t*
Belize, **II:**46, 46*t*
Benin, **I:**26, 26*t*
Bhutan, **III:**62, 62*t*
Bolivia, **II:**57, 57*t*
Bosnia and Herzegovina, **IV:**67–68, 68*t*
Botswana, **I:**33, 33*t*
Brazil, **II:**71–72, 72*t*
Brunei Darussalam, **III:**70, 70*t*
Bulgaria, **IV:**78, 78*t*
Burkina Faso, **I:**43, 43*t*
Burma, **III:**81, 81*t*
Burundi, **I:**51–52, 51*t*
Cambodia, **III:**90–91, 90*t*
Cameroon, **I:**63, 63*t*
Canada, **II:**87–88, 87*t*
Cape Verde, **I:**71–72, 71*t*
Central African Republic, **I:**80, 80*t*
Chad, **I:**89, 89*t*
Chile, **II:**103, 103*t*
China, **III:**105–107, 105*t*
Colombia, **II:**116, 116*t*
Comoros, **I:**95, 95*t*
Congo, Democratic Republic of the, **I:**101, 105, 105*t*
Congo, Republic of the, **I:**113, 113*t*
Costa Rica, **II:**128–129, 128*t*
Côte d'Ivoire, **I:**124, 124*t*
Croatia, **IV:**90, 90*t*
Cuba, **II:**139, 139*t*

Cyprus, **III:**122–123, 123*t*
Czech Republic, **IV:**101, 101*t*
Denmark, **IV:**109, 114, 114*t*
Djibouti, **I:**132–133, 132*t*
Dominica, **II:**148, 148*t*
Dominican Republic, **II:**157, 157*t*
Ecuador, **II:**166–167, 166*t*
Egypt, **I:**145, 145*t*
El Salvador, **II:**177, 177*t*
Equatorial Guinea, **I:**155–156, 156*t*
Eritrea, **I:**164, 164*t*
Estonia, **IV:**123, 123*t*
Ethiopia, **I:**175, 175*t*
Fiji, **III:**132, 132*t*
Finland, **IV:**136, 136*t*
France, **IV:**151–152, 151*t*
French Antilles and French Guiana, **II:**188, 188*t*
French Polynesia, **III:**139–140, 140*t*
Gabon, **I:**184, 184*t*
The Gambia, **I:**191, 191*t*
Georgia, **IV:**160–161, 160*t*
Germany, **IV:**175, 175*t*
Ghana, **I:**201, 201*t*
Greece, **IV:**188, 188*t*
Grenada, **II:**196, 196*t*
Guatemala, **II:**204–205, 205*t*
Guinea, **I:**211, 211*t*
Guinea-Bissau, **I:**220, 220*t*
Guyana, **II:**214, 214*t*
Haiti, **II:**222, 222*t*
Honduras, **II:**231–232, 231*t*
Hong Kong, **III:**153–154, 153*t*
Hungary, **IV:**201, 201*t*
Iceland, **IV:**211, 211*t*
India, **III:**167–168, 167*t*
Indonesia, **III:**181–182, 181*t*
Iran, **III:**199, 199*t*
Iraq, **III:**210, 210*t*
Ireland, **IV:**223, 223*t*
Israel, **III:**220, 220*t*
Italy, **IV:**239, 239*t*
Jamaica, **II:**241*t*, 242
Japan, **III:**235–236, 236*t*
Jordan, **III:**247, 247*t*
Kazakhstan, **III:**259–260, 259*t*
Kenya, **I:**231, 231*t*
Kiribati, **III:**269, 269*t*
Korea, North, **III:**278, 278*t*
Korea, South, **III:**291, 291*t*
Kuwait, **III:**301, 301*t*
Kyrgyzstan, **III:**310–311, 311*t*
Laos, **III:**322, 322*t*
Latvia, **IV:**251, 251*t*
Lebanon, **III:**332, 332*t*
Lesotho, **I:**240, 240*t*
Liberia, **I:**248–249, 248*t*

Libya, **I:**257, 257*t*
Liechtenstein, **IV:**260, 260*t*
Lithuania, **IV:**270–271, 270*t*
Luxembourg, **IV:**282, 282*t*
Macau, **III:**339–340, 340*t*
Macedonia, **IV:**289–290, 289*t*
Madagascar, **I:**266, 266*t*
Malawi, **I:**274, 274*t*
Malaysia, **III:**353–354, 353*t*
Maldives, **III:**364, 364*t*
Mali, **I:**282, 282*t*
Malta, **IV:**297, 297*t*
Marshall Islands, **III:**371, 371*t*
Mauritania, **I:**290, 290*t*
Mauritius, **I:**298–299, 298*t*
Mexico, **II:**253–255, 254*t*
Micronesia, **III:**380, 380*t*
Moldova, **IV:**305–306, 306*t*
Monaco, **IV:**313, 313*t*
Mongolia, **III:**388, 388*t*
Morocco, **I:**310, 310*t*
Mozambique, **I:**321–322, 321*t*
Namibia, **I:**333, 333*t*
Nauru, **III:**394, 394*t*
Nepal, **III:**404, 404*t*
Netherlands, **IV:**325, 325*t*
Netherlands Antilles and Aruba, **II:**269, 269*t*
New Zealand, **III:**416, 416*t*
Nicaragua, **II:**276, 276*t*
Niger, **I:**343, 343*t*
Nigeria, **I:**359, 359*t*
Norway, **IV:**338, 338*t*
Oman, **III:**425, 425*t*
Pakistan, **III:**440–441, 441*t*
Palau, **III:**448–449, 449*t*
Panama, **II:**286, 286*t*
Papua New Guinea, **III:**457–458, 457*t*
Paraguay, **II:**299, 299*t*
Peru, **II:**311–312, 311*t*
Philippines, **III:**468–469, 468*t*
Poland, **IV:**353–354, 353*t*
Portugal, **IV:**368–369, 368*t*
Puerto Rico, **II:**319, 319*t*
Qatar, **III:**480, 480*t*
Romania, **IV:**382, 382*t*
Russia, **IV:**397–399, 398*t*
Rwanda, **I:**369, 369*t*
St. Kitts and Nevis, **II:**327, 327*t*
St. Lucia, **II:**335–336, 336*t*
St. Vincent and the Grenadines, **II:**344, 344*t*
Samoa, **III:**487, 487*t*
San Marino, **IV:**409, 409*t*
São Tomé and Príncipe, **I:**377, 377*t*
Saudi Arabia, **III:**502, 502*t*

Money (*continued*)

Senegal, **I:**388, 388*t*

Seychelles, **I:**397, 397*t*

Sierra Leone, **I:**406, 406*t*

Singapore, **III:**513–514, 514*t*

Slovakia, **IV:**417, 417*t*

Slovenia, **IV:**426–427, 426*t*

Solomon Islands, **III:**524, 524*t*

Somalia, **I:**414–415, 414*t*

South Africa, **I:**426–427, 426*t*

Spain, **IV:**441–442, 442*t*

Sri Lanka, **III:**535, 535*t*

Sudan, **I:**438, 438*t*

Suriname, **II:**351, 351*t*

Swaziland, **I:**445, 445*t*

Sweden, **IV:**454–455, 455*t*

Switzerland, **IV:**468–470, 468*t*

Syria, **III:**547, 547*t*

Taiwan, **III:**561–562, 562*t*

Tajikistan, **III:**572, 572*t*

Tanzania, **I:**457, 457*t*

Thailand, **III:**587, 587*t*

Togo, **I:**469, 469*t*

Tonga, **III:**599, 599*t*

Trinidad and Tobago, **II:**359–360, 360*t*

Tunisia, **I:**478, 478*t*

Turkey, **III:**614–615, 614*t*

Turkmenistan, **III:**627, 627*t*

Tuvalu, **III:**635, 635*t*

Uganda, **I:**491, 491*t*

Ukraine, **IV:**482, 482*t*

United Arab Emirates, **III:**643–644, 643*t*

United Kingdom, **IV:**491, 497–498, 498*t*

United States, **II:**373–374, 374*t*

Uruguay, **II:**387, 387*t*

Uzbekistan, **III:**654, 654*t*

Vanuatu, **III:**662, 662*t*

Venezuela, **II:**398, 398*t*

Vietnam, **III:**672, 672*t*

Yemen, **III:**682, 682*t*

Yugoslavia, **IV:**516, 516*t*

Zambia, **I:**502, 502*t*

Zimbabwe, **I:**511, 511*t*

Money laundering

Antigua and Barbuda, **II:**5

El Salvador, **II:**172–173

Liechtenstein, **IV:**257, 259, 260

Nauru, **III:**394

Netherlands Antilles and Aruba, **II:**267

St. Vincent and the Grenadines, **II:**343

Switzerland, **IV:**469

Mongolia, III:383–390

Mongolian People's Revolutionary Party, **III:**385

Montenegro. *See* Yugoslavia

Morales, Ramon, **II:**227

Morocco, I:303–312

Moshavim (Israeli settlements), **III:**217

Motherland Party (Turkey), **III:**606

Movement for a Democratic Slovakia, **IV:**413

Movement for Democracy (Cape Verde), **I:**69

Movement for the Liberation of São Tomé and Príncipe, **I:**374–375

Movement of the National Revolution Party (Bolivia), **II:**52

Mozambique, I:313–325

Mubarak, Hosni, **I:**138

Multi-Fibre Agreement, **I:**298

Musharraf, Pervez, **III:**433

The Muslim Brotherhood. *See* Ikhwan al-Muslimin

Musveni, Yoweri, **I:**486

Mutawaa'in, **III:**496

Myanmar. *See* Burma

N

NAFTA. *See* North American Free Trade Agreement (NAFTA)

al-Nahyan, Shaykh Zayid, **III:**639

Naira (money), **I:**359

Nakfa (money), **I:**164

Namibia, I:327–335

Nasser, Gamal Abdel, **I:**137–138

National Agricultural Information Service, **III:**558

National banks. *See* Money

National Confederation of Senegalese Workers, **I:**389–390

National debt. *See* Debt

National Liberation Front (Algeria), **I:**3–4, 9

National Resistance Movement (Uganda), **I:**486

National Union for the Total Independence of Angola, **I:**13–14, 15

Nationalism, Bhutan, **III:**59

Nationalist Movement Party (Turkey), **III:**606

Nationalist Party (Taiwan), **III:**554

Nationalrat, Austria, **IV:**28

Native peoples. *See* Country overviews

Natural gas. *See* Oil and gas industry

Nauru, III:391–396

Nepal, III:397–408

Nepali Congress Party, **III:**399

Netherlands, IV:315–329

Netherlands Antilles and Aruba, II:261–270

Netpin, **IV:**367

Neutrality, Switzerland, **IV:**462

Nevis. *See* St. Kitts and Nevis

New Democratic Party (Egypt), **I:**138

New Economic Policy (Malaysia), **III:**346, 354

New National Party (Grenada), **II:**193

"New Order," Indonesia, **III:**176, 177

New Party (Taiwan), **III:**555

New Zealand, III:409–418

Newspapers. *See* Publishing

Nguema, Francisco Macias, **I:**153

Nicaragua, II:271–278

Nickel mining, Cuba, **II:**138

Niger, I:337–345

Nigeria, I:347–363

Nike, Inc., **III:**673

al-Nimairi, Jaafar, **I:**433

Nokia, **IV:**133–134

North American Free Trade Agreement (NAFTA)

Canada, **II:**83, 87

El Salvador, **II:**176, 177

Honduras, **II:**230

Mexico, **II:**247, 254

United States, **II:**373

North Korea. *See* Korea, North

Northern Ireland, **IV:**501

Northern League Party (Italy), **IV:**231

Norway, IV:331–341

Nova kwanza (money), **I:**18

Nuclear power

China, **III:**99–100

South Africa, **I:**424

Ukraine, **IV:**479

Nut production, Turkey, **III:**610

Nutmeg production, Grenada, **II:**195

O

Obote, Milton, **I:**485

ODP-MT Party (Burkina Faso), **I:**39

"Offsets" program, United Arab Emirates, **III:**642

Offshore banking. *See* Financial services

Oil and gas industry

Afghanistan, **III:**6–7

Algeria, **I:**2, 5–6, 7

Angola, **I:**14, 17–18

Sierra Leone, **I:**402–403
Singapore, **III:**509
Slovakia, **IV:**413
Slovenia, **IV:**423
Solomon Islands, **III:**520–521
Somalia, **I:**411–412
South Africa, **I:**419–420
Spain, **IV:**435–436
Sri Lanka, **III:**529–530
Sudan, **I:**433–434
Suriname, **II:**348–349
Swaziland, **I:**442–443
Sweden, **IV:**449–450
Switzerland, **IV:**461–462
Syria, **III:**541
Taiwan, **III:**553–554
Tajikistan, **III:**568
Tanzania, **I:**451–452
Thailand, **III:**579–580
Togo, **I:**465–466
Tonga, **III:**596
Trinidad and Tobago, **II:**356–357
Tunisia, **I:**474–475
Turkey, **III:**605–606
Turkmenistan, **III:**622–623
Tuvalu, **III:**632–633
Uganda, **I:**485–486
Ukraine, **IV:**477–478
United Arab Emirates, **III:**639
United Kingdom, **IV:**490–492
United States, **II:**366–367
Uruguay, **II:**383–384
Uzbekistan, **III:**649–650
Vanuatu, **III:**658
Vatican City, **IV:**507
Venezuela, **II:**393
Vietnam, **III:**667–668
Yemen, **III:**679
Zambia, **I:**497–498
Zimbabwe, **I:**507–508
Pope, status of, **IV:**507
Popular Movement for the
  Liberation of Angola, **I:**13, 15
Popular Party (Spain), **IV:**435–436
Population control policies
  Bangladesh, **III:**41–42
  China, **III:**95–96
  Egypt, **I:**135–136
  India, **III:**159–161
  Indonesia, **III:**174
  Jamaica, **II:**235
  Nepal, **III:**397
  Peru, **II:**304
  Solomon Islands, **III:**519
  Tunisia, **I:**473
Population demographics. *See*
  Country overviews; Poverty and
  wealth

Portillo, Alfonso, **II:**201
Ports and waterways
  Argentina, **II:**13
  Australia, **III:**15
  Azerbaijan, **III:**27
  The Bahamas, **II:**27
  Bangladesh, **III:**46
  Belgium, **IV:**52
  Benin, **I:**23
  Bolivia, **II:**53
  Burma, **III:**76
  Cameroon, **I:**59, 62
  Canada, **II:**82
  Cape Verde, **I:**69
  Central African Republic, **I:**77
  Chile, **II:**97
  China, **III:**99
  Côte d'Ivoire, **I:**120–121
  Cuba, **II:**136
  Djibouti, **I:**130, 132
  Ecuador, **II:**164
  French Antilles and French Guiana,
    II:184
  Gabon, **I:**181
  The Gambia, **I:**189
  Germany, **IV:**169
  Ghana, **I:**198
  Honduras, **II:**228
  Hong Kong, **III:**148
  Indonesia, **III:**177
  Iran, **III:**193
  Italy, **IV:**233
  Jamaica, **II:**238
  Japan, **III:**230
  Kenya, **I:**226–227
  Kiribati, **III:**268
  Korea, South, **III:**286
  Latvia, **IV:**248
  Liberia, **I:**246
  Malaysia, **III:**348
  Mauritania, **I:**288
  Mauritius, **I:**295
  Micronesia, **III:**377–378
  Morocco, **I:**306
  Mozambique, **I:**317
  Namibia, **I:**330
  Netherlands, **IV:**319–320
  Netherlands Antilles and Aruba,
    II:264–265
  Nigeria, **I:**355
  Norway, **IV:**335
  Pakistan, **III:**434
  Panama, **II:**282–283
  Paraguay, **II:**292–293, 294–295
  Peru, **II:**307
  Philippines, **III:**464
  Poland, **IV:**347

Russia, **IV:**393
São Tomé and Príncipe, **I:**375
Saudi Arabia, **III:**497
Sierra Leone, **I:**404
Singapore, **III:**508, 510
Somalia, **I:**413
Spain, **IV:**437
Sri Lanka, **III:**531
Sudan, **I:**435
Taiwan, **III:**556
Thailand, **III:**581–582
Togo, **I:**466
Turkey, **III:**607
Tuvalu, **III:**633–634
Uganda, **I:**487
Ukraine, **IV:**478
United Kingdom, **IV:**492
United States, **II:**368
Vanuatu, **III:**659
Portugal, **IV:359–373**
"Positive non-intervention," Hong
  Kong, **III:**146
Postage stamp sales, Vatican City,
  IV:507
Postal Savings System of Taiwan,
  III:562
Postal service, Poland, **IV:**348
Poultry production, Brazil, **II:**69
Pound (money)
  Cyprus, **III:**122
  Egypt, **I:**145
  Lebanon, **III:**332
  United Kingdom, **IV:**497
Poverty and wealth
  Afghanistan, **III:**8–9
  Albania, **IV:**6
  Algeria, **I:**9
  Andorra, **IV:**14
  Angola, **I:**19
  Antigua and Barbuda, **II:**6–7
  Argentina, **II:**19–20
  Armenia, **IV:**22
  Australia, **III:**20–22
  Austria, **IV:**34
  Azerbaijan, **III:**30–31
  The Bahamas, **II:**30
  Bahrain, **III:**37–38
  Bangladesh, **III:**51–52
  Barbados, **II:**38
  Belarus, **IV:**43
  Belgium, **IV:**58
  Belize, **II:**46–47
  Benin, **I:**26
  Bhutan, **III:**62–63
  Bolivia, **II:**57–58
  Bosnia and Herzegovina, **IV:**68
  Botswana, **I:**33–34

Somalia, **I:**412
Spain, **IV:**436–437
Sri Lanka, **III:**531
Sudan, **I:**434–435
Tajikistan, **III:**569
Tanzania, **I:**452
Thailand, **III:**581
Togo, **I:**466
Tunisia, **I:**475
Turkey, **III:**607
Turkmenistan, **III:**624
Uganda, **I:**486–487
United States, **II:**367
Vietnam, **III:**668
Yemen, **III:**679
Romania, **IV:375–386**
Rubber production
Cameroon, **I:**61
Côte d'Ivoire, **I:**122
Liberia, **I:**247
Sri Lanka, **III:**533
Ruble (money)
Belarus, **IV:**43
Russia, **IV:**398
Tajikistan, **III:**572
Rupee (money)
Mauritius, **I:**298
Nepal, **III:**404
Seychelles, **I:**397
Russia, **IV:387–403**
Russian financial crisis of 1998, **IV:**389–390, 400
Rwanda, **I:365–371**

S

Sadat, Anwar, **I:**138
St. Kitts and Nevis, **II:323–329**
St. Kitts and Nevis Labour Party, **II:**324
St. Lucia, **II:331–338**
St. Lucia Labour Party, **II:**332
St. Vincent and the Grenadines, **II:339–346**
Sales taxes. *See* Taxation
Salt mining, Cape Verde, **I:**71
Samoa, **III:483–489**
San Marino, **IV:405–410**
Sanitation. *See* Poverty and wealth
Sankara, Thomas, **I:**39
São Tomé and Príncipe, **I:373–379**
Sasso-Nguesso, Denis, **I:**111
Al Saud family, **III:**494–495
Saudi Arabia, **III:491–505**
Schilling (money), **IV:**34
Scotland. *See* United Kingdom
Second era, Sri Lanka economy, **III:**529

Second Republic, Zambia, **I:**497–498
Seko, Mobutu Sese, **I:**100–101
Senegal, **I:381–391**
Serbia. *See* Yugoslavia
Service industries. *See* Financial services; Retail, wholesale, and food services; Tourism
Seychelles, **I:393–399**
Sheep production, New Zealand, **III:**413
Shell corporations, Bahamas, **II:**29
Shilling (money)
Kenya, **I:**231
Somalia, **I:**414
Tanzania, **I:**457
Uganda, **I:**491
Shipbuilding
Finland, **IV:**133
Netherlands, **IV:**322
Norway, **IV:**337
Shipping industry
Greece, **IV:**186–187
Malta, **IV:**296
Norway, **IV:**335
"Shock therapy" economic policy
Poland, **IV:**345
Russia, **IV:**397–398
Shrimp farming, Ecuador, **II:**165
Sierra Leone, **I:401–408**
Silver mining
Bolivia, **II:**51
Mexico, **II:**251
Singapore, **III:507–517**
Sino-British Joint Declaration, **III:**144
Sint Eustatius. *See* Netherlands Antilles and Aruba
Sint Maarten. *See* Netherlands Antilles and Aruba
Slovak Nationalist Party, **IV:**413
Slovakia, **IV:411–420**
Slovenia, **IV:421–430**
Soap production, Dominica, **II:**147
SOCATEL (company), **I:**77, 79
Social class and status. *See* Caste systems; Discrimination; Poverty and wealth
Social Democratic Party
Austria, **IV:**27–28
Finland, **IV:**129
Ukraine, **IV:**477
Social partnership, Austria, **IV:**28–29
Social welfare. *See* Health and social welfare programs; Poverty and wealth; Working conditions

Soglo, Nicephore, **I:**23
Solomon Islands, **III:519–525**
Som (money), **III:**310–311
Somalia, **I:409–416**
Somaliland, **I:**411–412, 417
Somoni (money), **III:**572
South Africa, **I:417–430**
South African Customs Union, **I:**33
South African Development Community, **I:**321, 426
South Korea. *See* Korea, South
Southeastern Anatolian Project, **III:**610
Soviet Union
dissolution of, **IV:**391
economic system, **IV:**389
relations with Cuba, **II:**134
relations with Finland, **IV:**128–129, 135
relations with Latvia, **IV:**246–247
relations with Lithuania, **IV:**264
Soybean production
Brazil, **II:**68
Paraguay, **II:**294, 296
Spain, **IV:431–446**
Spanish Socialist Workers Party, **IV:**433–434, 435
Spice production, Comoros, **I:**94
Squash production
Tonga, **III:**598
Vanuatu, **III:**660
Sri Lanka, **III:527–538**
Standard of living. *See* Poverty and wealth
State Law and Order Restoration Council (Burma), **III:**75
State-owned enterprises
China, **III:**105–106
Finland, **IV:**130
Steel. *See* Iron and steel production
Stock exchanges
Antigua and Barbuda, **II:**6
Argentina, **II:**19
Armenia, **IV:**22
Australia, **III:**20
Bahrain, **III:**37
Bangladesh, **III:**51
Belgium, **IV:**57
Benin, **I:**25
Bolivia, **II:**57
Botswana, **I:**33
Brazil, **II:**72
Burkina Faso, **I:**43
Canada, **II:**88
China, **III:**106–107
Congo, Republic of the, **I:**113
Costa Rica, **II:**127